Paradise and Hell in Islamic Traditions

The Muslim afterworld, with its imagery rich in sensual promises, has shaped Western perceptions of Islam for centuries. However, to date, no single study has done justice to the full spectrum of traditions of thinking about the topic in Islamic history. The Muslim hell, in particular, remains a little-studied subject. This book, which is based on a wide array of carefully selected Arabic and Persian texts, covers not only the theological and exegetical but also the philosophical, mystical, topographical, architectural, and ritual aspects of the Muslim belief in paradise and hell, in both the Sunni and the Shiʿi world. By examining a broad range of sources related to the afterlife, Christian Lange shows that Muslim religious literature, against transcendentalist assumptions to the contrary, often pictures the boundary between this world and the otherworld as being remarkably thin, or even permeable.

Christian Lange is Professor of Arabic and Islamic Studies at Utrecht University. He is the author of *Justice, Punishment and the Medieval Muslim Imagination* (2008) and the editor of several scholarly volumes, including *Locating Hell in Islamic Traditions* (2015). From 2011 to 2015, he was Principal Investigator of the European Research Council project, "The Here and the Hereafter in Islamic Traditions." He is a member of the Young Academy of the Dutch Royal Academy of Sciences.

Paradise and Hell in Islamic Traditions

CHRISTIAN LANGE
Utrecht University

CAMBRIDGE
UNIVERSITY PRESS

CAMBRIDGE
UNIVERSITY PRESS

32 Avenue of the Americas, New York, NY 10013-2473, USA

Cambridge University Press is part of the University of Cambridge.

It furthers the University's mission by disseminating knowledge in the pursuit of education, learning, and research at the highest international levels of excellence.

www.cambridge.org
Information on this title: www.cambridge.org/9780521738156

First published 2016

Printed in the United States of America

A catalog record for this publication is available from the British Library.

Library of Congress Cataloging in Publication Data
Lange, Christian Robert, 1975–
Paradise and hell in Islamic traditions / Christian Lange.
pages cm
Includes bibliographical references and index.
ISBN 978-0-521-50637-3 (hardback) – ISBN 978-0-521-73815-6 (paperback)
1. Islamic eschatology. 2. Paradise – Islam 3. Future punishment – Islam. I. Title.
BP166.8.L36 2015
297.2′3–dc23 2015021998

ISBN 978-0-521-50637-3 Hardback
ISBN 978-0-521-73815-6 Paperback

Für A. und M.,

قرة عيني

Contents

Figures

Table and Charts

Table

Charts

Acknowledgements

The research for, and writing of, this book was carried out in the framework of the research project "The here and the hereafter in Islamic traditions" (HHIT), which I had the good fortune to oversee, as Principal Investigator, at the University of Utrecht from March 2011 to April 2015 (http://hhit.wp.hum.uu.nl/). I want to acknowledge the European Research Council for funding this project (ERC Starting Grant, project no. 263308) as well as thank my co-investigators Pieter Coppens, Eric van Lit, Simon O'Meara, and Yunus Yaldiz for going the distance with me. Our joint journey through the vast horizons of Islamic eschatology, whether in our weekly Arabic and Persian reading workshops or in three memorable *heidesessies* in Eckwarden (2012), Frankfurt (2013), and Doetinchem Castle (2014), has shaped, in profound ways, the structure and argument of this study. I owe a particularly great deal to Simon O'Meara, who, at the eleventh hour, selflessly read the entire manuscript and saved me from many blunders and infelicities.

Next to the members of HHIT, I should also like to thank Ghassan El Masri, Bill Graham, Ahmet Karamustafa, Christopher Melchert, Harald Motzki, Mohammed Rustom, Tommaso Tesei, Jamel Velji, and my much admired teacher, Josef van Ess, for reading parts of this book and providing helpful suggestions for improvement. Scholars with whom I had the pleasure of discussing specific points include Frederick Colby, Michael Ebstein, Maribel Fierro, Christiane Gruber, Sebastian Günther, Carole Hillenbrand, Robert Hillenbrand, Jon Hoover, Remke Kruk, Herman Landolt, Pierre Lory, Kevin Reinhart, Nicolai Sinai, Daniel de Smet, Wheeler Thackston, Roberto Tottoli, and Wim Raven. The two anonymous reviewers of the original proposal steered my thinking in important directions, and I'm deeply grateful to both. Colleagues in Utrecht and other Dutch universities have likewise enriched the process of researching and writing this book in significant ways, among them Bob Becking, Nico Landman, Birgit Meyer,

Eric Ottenheijm, Marcel Poorthuis, Arjan Post, Bernd Radtke, Amr Ryad, and Joost Vanderlijn. It goes without saying that I don't mention these learned friends and teachers in order to claim their credentials; I merely wish to express my gratitude for their support and readiness to provide advice. I alone remain responsible for any shortcomings there may be in this book.

I also want to salute a number of people who provided logistical and editorial support. Kobi Gal, in unfailing friendship, regaled me with PDFs that I could only get through him. My department's librarian, Joost van Gemert, tirelessly tried to cater to my research needs. At Cambridge University Press, Marigold Acland and Patricia Crone launched me on this book, which would never have come about without their initial support and inspiration. Because it grew out of size, the book could not be published in Patricia's series *Themes in Islamic History*, for which it had been originally commissioned. I am grateful to the Cambridge University Press for allowing me to publish it as a stand-alone title. Kate Gavino, Will Hammell, and Maria Marsh saw the manuscript through press, while Nishanthini Vetrivel and Christine Dunn guided me patiently through the painstaking process of copy editing the final version.

Abbreviations

ANT	*The apocryphal New Testament: A collection of apocryphal Christian literature in an English translation based on M. R. James*. Edited and translated by J. K. Elliot. Oxford: Oxford University Press, 1993
BSOAS	*Bulletin of the School of Oriental and African Studies*
BT	*Babylonian Talmud*. Translated under the general editorship of I. Epstein. 36 vols. London: Soncino Press, 1935–52
CMR	*Christian-Muslim relations: A bibliographical history*. Edited by David Thomas and Barbara Roggema. Leiden and Boston: Brill, 2009–. Online publication
CTM	Wensinck, Arent Jan, et al. *Concordance et indices de la tradition musulmane: Les six livres, le Musnad d'Al-Dārimī, le Muwaṭṭaʾ de Mālik, le Musnad de Aḥmad ibn Ḥanbal*. 2nd ed. 8 parts in 4 vols. Leiden and New York: Brill, 1992
ECḤ	Juynboll, G. H. A. *Encyclopedia of canonical ḥadīth*. Leiden and Boston: Brill, 2007
EI1	*The encyclopaedia of Islam*. Edited by T. Houtsma et al. 5 vols. Leiden: Brill, 1913–34
EI2	*The encyclopaedia of Islam: New edition*. Edited by H. A. R. Gibb et al. 12 vols. Leiden: Brill, 1954–2004
EI3	*The encyclopaedia of Islam: THREE*. Edited by Kate Fleet, Gudrun Krämer, Denis Matringe, and Everett Rowson. Leiden: Brill, 2007–. Online publication
EIr	*Encyclopaedia Iranica*. Edited by Ehsan Yarshater et al. Bibliotheca Persica Press, 1985–. Online publication
EQ	*The encyclopedia of the Qurʾān*. Edited by Jane Dammen McAuliffe et al. Leiden: Brill, 2001–6

GAL	Brockelmann, Carl. *Geschichte der arabischen Litteratur.* First published 1898. Leiden: Brill, 1943–9
GAS	Sezgin, Fuat. *Geschichte des arabischen Schrifttums.* Leiden: Brill, 1967–
IOS	*Israel Oriental Studies*
JAOS	*Journal of the American Oriental Society*
JIS	*Journal of Islamic Studies*
JQS	*Journal of Qurʾānic Studies*
JRAS	*Journal of the Royal Asiatic Society*
JSAI	*Jerusalem Studies in Arabic and Islam*
JT	*Jerusalem Talmud.* French translation by Moïse Schwab. *Le Talmud de Jérusalem.* 6 vols. Paris: Éditions G.-P. Maisonneuve et Larose, 1972
MIDEO	*Mélanges de l'Institut Dominicain d'Études Orientales du Caire*
MW	*Muslim World*
OTP	*The Old Testament pseudoepigrapha.* Edited by James H. Charlesworth. 2 vols. First published 1982. Peabody, MA: Hendrickson Publishers, 2011
REI	*Revue des Études Islamiques*
SI	*Studia Islamica*
TG	van Ess, Josef. *Theologie und Gesellschaft im 2. und 3. Jahrhundert Hidschra: Eine Geschichte des religiösen Denkens im frühen Islam.* Berlin and New York: de Gruyter, 1991–7
ZDMG	*Zeitschrift der Deutschen Morgenländischen Gesellschaft*

Note on Dates, Citation, Translations, and Transliteration

In the text, Islamic dates for the premodern era are given both according to the Islamic hijri calendar and the Julian/Gregorian calendar. For convenience, in this book I have used the term *Late Medieval* to refer to the post-Mongol period of Islamic history up to the nineteenth century CE. In the bibliography, books issuing from Iran are occasionally listed according to their year of publication in the Iranian solar calendar, and accordingly marked with "sh." Throughout this book, footnotes only show the short title of books and articles; full information is given in the bibliography at the end. Abbreviations that appear in the footnotes, including the less frequently used ones, are explained in the List of Abbreviations. Entries from the *Encyclopaedia of Islam*, the *Encyclopaedia of the Qur'ān*, and the *Encyclopaedia Iranica* do not feature in the bibliography; they only appear in the footnotes. Hadiths from the Six Books are quoted following the convention established in Arent Jan Wensinck's *Concordance et indices de la tradition musulmane*, that is, by the name of the *kitāb* and number of the *bāb*. To facilitate use of my references, I have also provided the title of the *bāb* (if applicable) and page numbers referring to the printed editions that I have consulted.

All translations into English from the Arabic, Persian, and European languages are mine unless otherwise indicated. As for translations from the Qur'ān, I have mostly relied on Alan Jones's rendering, although I have in places diverted from it if the argument seemed to call for it. The transliteration of foreign words in this book follows the rules applied in the third edition of *The Encyclopaedia of Islam*. However, I have chosen to use a simplified transliteration of Persian words in which vowels are reduced to the three long and short vowels (*ā/a*, *ī/i*, *ū/u*) of the Arabic alphabet and labiodental *v* becomes *w* (as in *Mathnawī*, instead of *Mathnavī*). No transliteration has been used for place names and for anglicized words such as hadith, houri, and Kaaba.

Introduction

According to legend, after the caliph ʿUmar b. al-Khaṭṭāb's (r. 13–23/634–44) conquest of Jerusalem in the year 16/637, one of his soldiers, a man named Shurayk b. Khabāsha al-Numayrī, went to fetch water from a well on the Temple Mount. As al-Wāsiṭī (d. *ca.* 360/970), a preacher in the al-Aqṣā mosque, relates in his hagiography of Jerusalem, *The Virtues of the Holy City* (*Faḍā'il Bayt al-Muqaddas*),

suddenly the bucket fell from [Shurayk's] hands, and so he descended [into the well] to search for it. A man appeared to him in the well and told him to follow him, taking him by the hand and ushering him into the Garden. Shurayk took leaves [from a tree in the Garden]. Then the man led him back, and [Shurayk] exited [the well]. He went to his companions and told them about it. His story was brought before ʿUmar b. al-Khaṭṭāb, who said: "Shall a man from this community enter the Garden while he is alive among you? Look at the leaves! If they have withered, they are not from the Garden. If they haven't withered, they are." ... And indeed, the leaves had not withered.[1]

Shurayk is said to have kept the leaves he brought from his subterranean visit to paradise, guarding them in his personal copy of the Qur'ān until his death, and to have been buried with them, placed delicately between his chest and the burial shroud covering his corpse, when he was laid to rest in the Syrian village of al-Salamiyya.[2] Some thirteen centuries later, between 1938 and 1942, archaeologists excavated what appeared to be the remains of the well inside the al-Aqṣā mosque.[3] To this day, one can see, to the left of the entrance to the mosque, the stairway leading down into the vast system

[1] Wāsiṭī, *Faḍā'il*, 93–4 (#154: *Ḥadīth al-waraqāt*). The story also appears in Maqdisī, *Muthīr al-gharām*, 58; Nuwayrī, *Nihāyat al-arab*, I, 339; Suyūṭī, *Durr*, I, 136. For the little biographical information that is available for al-Wāsiṭī, see ʿUlaymī, *Uns*, II, 482.

[2] Wāsiṭī, *Faḍā'il*, 94 (#155); Maqdisī, *Muthīr al-gharām*, 46.

[3] See Hamilton, *The structural history*, 63–4.

of tunnels below the Temple Mount, a mysterious subterranean maze in which, according to Muslim tradition, flow the rivers of paradise.[4]

The "Story of the Leaves" (*ḥadīth al-waraqāt*), as it is known, encapsulates a tension that underpins conceptualisations of the otherworld across a wide spectrum of Islamic religious discourses. The idea that the boundary between this world (*al-dunyā*) and the hereafter (*al-ākhira*) cannot be traversed, except after death, is etched deeply into Muslim thought. ʿUmar's reticence is a case in point. Though seemingly aware of the ancient prophecy that "a man shall enter the Garden alive, walking on his two feet,"[5] he remains sceptical. In fact, according to one version of the story, when ʿUmar first hears about Shurayk's miraculous journey,[6] he consults his advisor Kaʿb al-Aḥbār, a Jewish convert to Islam and an authority on the Bible. Kaʿb confirms the correctness of Shurayk's claim. Still, ʿUmar insists on further proof.

After all, does not the Qur'ān state that behind the dead, "there is a barrier (*barzakh*) until the day that they shall be raised up" (23:100), sealing off the otherworld from this world? In fact, according to a notion that circulated widely in Islamic literature, not even the imagination, that most transgressive of human faculties, is capable of crossing this barrier. In the collections of sayings (hadiths) traced to the prophet Muḥammad, from the early centuries of Islam onwards, it is affirmed time and again that God prepares for His servants in paradise "that which no eye has seen, no ear has heard, no mind has conceived."[7] This is an apophatic statement that is also found in the Gospel, as well as in Talmudic and Christian Syriac literature.[8] Muslims

[4] Cf. the cover image. For the rivers of paradise underneath the Temple Mount, see Wāsiṭī, *Faḍā'il*, 67 (#108), 68 (#110); Ibn al-Murajjā, *Faḍā'il*, 268, 6–8 (#407). See further Shalem, "Bi'r al-waraqa," 58; Kaplony, *The Ḥaram*, 359, 512. Cf. Psalm 46:5; Ezekiel 47:1–12.

[5] Yāqūt, *Buldān*, s.v. al-Qalt, IV, 386b, reports from Kaʿb al-Aḥbār (d. between 32/652 and 35/655) that the prophecy is already found in the scriptures of the Jews. There is no such prophecy in the Hebrew Bible, although Ezekiel 47:1–12 is vaguely reminiscent. Most authors appear to attribute the prophecy directly to the prophet Muḥammad. See, e.g., Shams al-Dīn al-Suyūṭī (writing around 875/1470), *Ithāf al-akhissā'*, quoted in Le Strange, *Palestine under the Muslims*, 198.

[6] Cf. this and other versions of the story in the translation of Le Strange, "Description of the Noble Sanctuary," 270–2; Shalem, "Bi'r al-waraqa," 50–61.

[7] Hammām, *Ṣaḥīfa*, 25 (#31); Ibn al-Mubārak, *Musnad*, 73 (#121); Bukhārī, *Ṣaḥīḥ*, *k. bad' al-khalq* 8 (*b. mā jā'a fī ṣifat al-janna*), II, 324; Muslim, *Ṣaḥīḥ*, *k. al-janna* 2, IV, 2174; Tirmidhī, *Jāmiʿ*, *k. al-janna* 15 (*b. mā jā'a fī sūq al-janna*), IV, 685; Hannād b. Sarī, *Zuhd*, I, 47 (#1); Abū Nuʿaym, *Ṣifat al-janna*, 36–7 (#8), 41–2 (#16), 135–48 (##109–24); Ibn al-Kharrāṭ, *ʿĀqiba*, 313; Qurṭubī, *Tadhkira*, II, 165–6; Suyūṭī, *Budūr*, 488; Lamaṭī, *Ibrīz* (tr. O'Kane/Radtke), 901; Ashqar, *Yawm*, III, 117. Cf. *CTM*, s.v. kh-ṭ-r, II, 48a; Graham, *Divine word*, 117–19. G. H. A. Juynboll (*ECḤ*, 57), pinpoints the Kufan *mawlā* and traditionist Abū Muʿāwiya Muḥammad b. Khāzim (d. 194–5/810–11) as an important launch pad for the tradition in Muslim circles, even though the hadith is likely to have circulated earlier, as is suggested by the examples of Hammām (d. 131/749 or 132/750) and Ibn al-Mubārak (d. 181/797).

[8] While in Paul (*1 Corinthians* 2:9), the eschatological content of the adage is only alluded to, the Babylonian Talmud (*Sanhedrin* 99a, XXIV, 671) refers it explicitly to Eden and the

of the early centuries of Islam sought to anchor the adage in their own scripture and in the exemplary lives of the Prophet and his Companions. Thus, the Companion ʿAbdallāh b. Masʿūd (d. 32/652–3?) reportedly taught that "in the Torah it is written: 'God has prepared for those who draw their sides away from the couches that which no eye has seen, no ear has heard and no human mind has conceived, that which no angel or messenger knows about.'" The expression "those who draw their sides away from the couches" (*alladhīna tatajāfā junūbuhum ʿan al-maḍājiʿ*) refers to the pious who perform nightly vigils instead of sleeping. An addendum to the adage in its original form, the phrase is taken *verbatim* from the Qurʾān (32:16) and from there projected into Jewish scripture. As ʿAbdallāh b. Masʿūd continues, after reading this verse, "we would recite: 'No soul knows what joy (*qurrat aʿyun*) is hidden away for them' (Q 32:17)."[9]

It is undeniable, however, that the Qurʾān pictures paradise and hell in intimately concrete and worldly terms.[10] In a canonical hadith, one reads that "the Garden is closer to you than the strap of your sandal, and so is the Fire."[11] This remarkable tradition echoes the Qurʾānic verse that declares God to be closer to man than his jugular vein (50:16), but raises the notion to a cosmological level. While the "jugular vein" verse emphasises the bond that connects God with individual believers, the "sandal" hadith extends this relationship of intimacy more generally speaking to the relationship between the otherworld and this world, between the "world of the hidden" (*ʿālam al-ghayb*) and "the world of witnessing" (*ʿālam al-shahāda*, cf. Q 6:73). The otherworld, in this view, cuts through earthly reality in the way in which the strap of the sandal penetrates the cavity between the toes of the foot. The image is vivid and palpable. It suggests that this world and the otherworld are intertwined, that there is a measure of immanence of the divine in creation.[12]

In al-Wāsiṭī's account of the "Story of the Leaves," the caliph ʿUmar b. al-Khaṭṭāb, though inclining towards the transcendentalist view that this world and the next are two fundamentally different realms of existence, is proven wrong. The leaves Shurayk brings back from his tour of paradise,

world to come, as does the Syrian Church Father Aphrahat (d. *ca.* 345) in one of his homilies. See Aphrahat, *Homilies*, 357–8. For further references in Christian literature, see Wilk, "Jesajanische Prophetie." On the question of "material eschatology" in Talmudic literature, see Costa, *L'au-delà*, 287–94.

[9] Ibn Abī Shayba, *Muṣannaf*, IX, 137; Muslim, *Ṣaḥīḥ*, *k. al-janna* 5, IV, 2175.

[10] See Q 13:35, where the Qurʾān speaks of the "picture of paradise" (*mathal al-janna*). Certain exegetes understood *mathal* as "likeness," not as "picture," thus "making the concrete descriptions of Paradise the representation of an inexpressible reality." See *EI2*, "Dj̲anna," II, 447a–452a, at 448a (L. Gardet); Poonawala, "Ismāʿīlī *taʾwīl*," 212.

[11] Bukhārī, *Ṣaḥīḥ*, *k. al-riqāq* 29 (*b. al-janna aqrabu ilā aḥadikum*), IV, 194; Ibn Ḥanbal, *Musnad*, I, 287, 413, 442. See *CTM*, s.v. *sh-r-k*, III, 117a.

[12] Unsurprisingly, Sufi authors were particularly fond of the "sandal" hadith. E.g., Farīd al-Dīn ʿAṭṭār (d. 627/1230) quotes it in his *Asrārnāmeh*. See Ritter, *Meer*, 187.

"looking like the leaves of the Syrian peach tree, as big as the palm of a hand and with a pointed head,"[13] do not wither. They partake of eternal life, thus demonstrating beyond doubt that Shurayk really has crossed the boundary between the here and the hereafter, and that humans, "while they are alive among you," can reach out beyond the imperfections of this world and connect with an otherworld in which humankind's spiritual and material potentialities are realised and lived to the full. As I argue in this book, the story of Shurayk's traversing the divide between *dunyā* and *ākhira* is not as exceptional as it may seem at first sight. Rather, it is indicative of a much broader theme, a nostalgia for immanence and a sense of realised eschatology that has its point of departure in the Qur'ān and from there runs through an impressive range of Islamic religious discourses and practices.

Reconceptualising the *Dunyā/Ākhira* Divide

Islam shares with Christianity the story of Adam's and Eve's eating from the forbidden tree in paradise, the primordial sin resulting in the Fall of humankind and banishment from the garden of Eden. Paradise, accordingly, is lost and will be regained only at the end of time by those whom God chooses or by those who deserve to be saved on account of their beliefs and actions. Those whom God does not elect, or those who fail to accumulate enough merit in the time that elapses between the Fall and Judgement, conversely, go to hell. Historical time begins with the Fall from the primordial garden; it is followed by three major successive eras of world history: the pre-Islamic period, a time of ignorance (*jāhiliyya*) that is sporadically illuminated by the appearance of prophets; the Islamic period, in which God's revelation is available, though not to all of humanity; and the apocalypse (the "history of the future," in Franz Rosenthal's phrase[14]), which ushers in the end of the world, and the end of history. At Judgement, history is abolished; eternity begins; *al-ākhira* replaces *al-dunyā*. This sequence is what may be called the diachronic mode of conceptualising the relationship between *al-dunyā* and *al-ākhira* (see Chart 1).

Augustine of Hippo's (d. 430) doctrine of original sin was a dominant idea in the history of Christian thought.[15] In Islam, the notion had far less purchase. No Muslim scholar would have absolved Adam and Eve from blame, but there was a clear tendency among exegetes to make light of Adam's sin.[16] Evil in Islam, as Gustav von Grunebaum suggested, is "accidental"

[13] Wāsiṭī, *Faḍā'il*, 94 (#155); Maqdisī, *Muthīr al-gharām*, 46.

[14] Rosenthal, *History*, 23.

[15] Segal, *Life after death*, 584–5; Benjamins, "Paradisiacal life." However, writing a century after Augustine, the Eastern Church Father Jacob of Serugh (d. 521) could still maintain that "Adam sinned, but God did not curse him, for He loved him and did not hate him." See Jacob of Serugh, *Quatre homélies*, 12.

[16] Kister, "Adam," 149. Cf. Anawati, "La notion de 'péché originel'," 31.

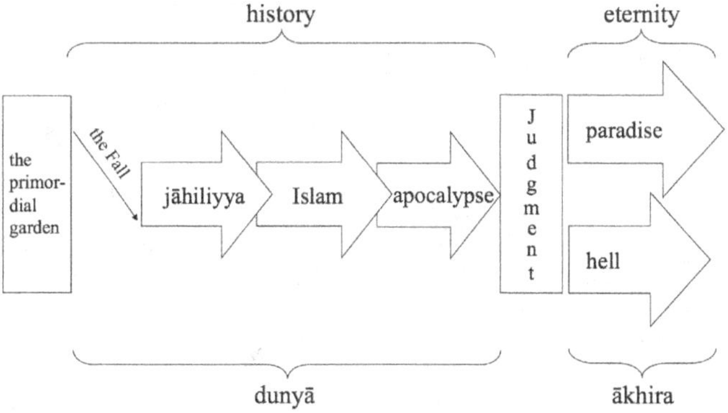

CHART 1. The *dunyā/ākhira* relationship: The diachronic view.

rather than a "structural" given of human nature.[17] Adam's and Eve's departure from paradise was frequently painted by Muslim artists, especially in the later centuries, but depictions of Eve handing the fatal fruit to Adam remain to be found.[18] A Persian painting from around 700/1300 shows the primordial couple first and foremost as victims of the devil's cunning, and thus minimises their guilt.

Arguably, this is a perspective rooted in the Qurʾān. Whatever the degree of their own responsibility, Adam and Eve are said to have received God's forgiveness immediately after their expulsion (20:122–3). They did not pass on any essential, inherited human depravity to their descendants. As the Qurʾān affirms, "every soul only bears its own burden" (6:164). In Islam, therefore, the fall, or rather the descent, from paradise does not signify an ontological shift from a state of grace to one of sin and damnation but rather, a momentary loss of divine favour. Humankind's connection with the otherworld may require repair, but it is not severed completely. The door between this world and the otherworld remains ajar.

Similarly, the world that humankind inhabits is not a place of corruption. In the Qurʾān, "the earthly manifestation of creation is not a cursed place of punishment and suffering; rather, it shows a clear affinity with paradise."[19] What is more, this optimism is not restricted to the Qurʾān. There are numerous traditions of Islamic religious thought that lean in the direction of an accessible paradise. They speak of objects, substances, or beings that move to and fro between this world and the otherworld. One category of such go-betweens is select individuals who travel to the otherworld and back.

[17] Von Grunebaum, "Observations," 119. See also Anawati, "La notion de 'péché originel'," 37.
[18] Milstein, "Paradise as a parable," 147.
[19] Neuwirth, *Koran*, 439, 744–8.

FIGURE 1. The devil tempts Adam and Eve to eat the fruit of the forbidden tree. From al-Birūnī, *al-Āthār al-bāqiya* (*The Chronology of Ancient Nations*). Tabriz/Persia, 707/1307–8. Edinburgh University Library, Centre for Research Collections, MS Edinburgh Or. 161, fol. 48v.

This concerns, most famously, the prophet Muḥammad during his Ascension (*miʿrāj*), but there are others, too. In the popular genre of *Qiṣaṣ al-anbiyāʾ* (*Tales of the Prophets*), the prophet Idrīs, the Islamic Enoch, is said to have toured paradise and hell. The same goes for Bulūqiya, a figure that harkens back to the Babylonian Gilgamesh.[20] A number of visionaries and mystics in the history of Islam claimed to have emulated the Prophet's heavenly journey (and less frequently, his *descensus ad inferos*).[21] There are also examples of ordinary human beings going on otherworldly journeys. Shurayk, the hero of the "Story of the Leaves," is one of them. In the *Arabian Nights* one occasionally comes across narratives about the exploits of heroes who reach paradise or hell, or earthly utopias and dystopias that resemble them closely.[22] In one of the *Nights*' most famous tales, "The

[20] Dalley, "Gilgamesh." On these narratives of otherworldly journeys, see the following text, pp. 112–9.

[21] See the following text, pp. 227–8.

[22] For paradise in the *Arabian Nights*, see Ott, "Paradies"; eadem, "Paradise, Alexander, and the *Arabian nights*." For travels to the underworld, see Fudge, "Underworlds."

FIGURE 2. The prophet Muḥammad approaching the gate of heaven during his ascension. From Rashīd al-Dīn, *Jāmiʿ al-tawārīkh* (*The Comprehensive History*). Tabriz/Persia, *ca.* 705/[1306] or 714/[1314–15]. Edinburgh University Library, Centre for Research Collections, MS Edinburgh Or. 20, fol. 55r.

Second Qalandar's Tale," the hero stumbles upon the entry to a subterranean paradisiacal cave, complete with a heavenly maid, cushioned couches, and wine.[23] Lastly in this category, dream visions allowed for an easy way to travel to the otherworld and back again. The Islamic literature on dreaming is vast, and frequently features visions of, and conversations with, the dead in paradise and hell.[24]

Other types of go-betweens include liquids, winds, sounds, smells, and material objects that move between the otherworld and this world, or flow from one to the other. The Nile, Euphrates, and the two eastern Turkish rivers Sayḥān and Jayḥān, for example, are said to spring from the al-Kawthar well in paradise.[25] Pleasant fragrances are wafted into this world from paradise; in fact, all perfume originates in Eden.[26] The sweet scent of babies (*rīḥ al-walad*) comes from paradise.[27] Salutary plants are likewise thought to

[23] *The Arabian nights*, I, 73–5.

[24] See Kinberg, "Interaction," 295–301; Schimmel, *Die Träume des Kalifen*, 198–200; Katz, "Dreams," 190; Sirriyeh, *Sufi visionary*, 57–67. On al-Ghazālī's view of the "reality" of dreams, see Moosa, *Al-Ghazālī*, 74–5. A modern, ironic take on this theme is Zahāwī, *Thawra*. Cf. the following text, pp. 279–80.

[25] Qurṭubī, *Tadhkira*, II, 167–8; Majlisī, *Biḥār*, VIII, 352; Nābulusī, *Ahl al-janna*, 49–50.

[26] See Wheeler, *Mecca and Eden*, 65, and the references given there. On the scent of paradise entering the world through the tombs of saints, see Diem and Schöller, *The living and the dead*, II, 90–6. The most prominent example is, of course, the tomb of the Prophet in Medina. See, e.g., Būṣīrī, *Burda*, 13 (v. 58).

[27] Nābulusī, *Ahl al-janna*, 51.

derive from the heavenly realms.[28] Adam is said to have taken seeds from the Garden with him and to have planted them in India, thus bringing nutmeg (*shajar al-ṭīb*) into the world.[29] According to another tradition, the date-palm, the first plant to have grown on the face of the earth, came to this world from heaven.[30] Every pomegranate contains at least one seed that is from paradise.[31] In Shīʿism, one finds the notion that Abū Ṭālib, the father of the first Imam ʿAlī (d. 40/661), used to eat pomegranates, "and from it ʿAlī was born"[32] – who then passed on this heavenly seed to his progeny, the Imams.

As for sounds, it is true that revelation, according to standard doctrine, has come to an end with Muḥammad, the "seal of the prophets" (*khātam al-anbiyāʾ*). However, acoustically, Arabs, and with them all Muslims, continue to be connected to the otherworld. Arabic, after all, is the language Adam and Eve spoke in paradise, and brought with them to earth.[33] According to the Egyptian polygraph, al-Suyūṭī (d. 911/1505), the famous exegete of early Islam, Ibn ʿAbbās (d. *ca.* 68/687–8), taught that Adam's language in paradise was Arabic. "However, when Adam disobeyed his Lord, God deprived him of Arabic, and he came to speak Syriac. Then, however, God restored Adam to His grace and gave Arabic back to him."[34] Muslims are made particularly aware of this primordial linguistic bond with God when listening to the Qurʾān, the "recitation" (Arab. *qurʾān*) of the divine text located on the "preserved tablet" (*lawḥ maḥfūẓ*, Q 85:21) in heaven, an act first performed by the prophet Muḥammad and by his Muslim followers ever since. In this perpetual global concert of simultaneous voices, a piece of the otherworld is present all the time among Muslim audiences, the "recitation" functioning rather like a ceaseless radio transmission that people can tune into at their leisure.[35] "God Himself," affirms the Ḥanbalī theologian Ibn al-Farrāʾ (d. 458/1065), "recites through the tongue of every Qurʾān reader," so that "when one listens to the Qurʾān recitation of a reader, one hears it from God."[36] In Islam perhaps more than any other tradition, to

[28] In addition to the examples provided in the following text, see ibid., 52 (truffle and honeydew).
[29] Fākihī, *Akhbār Makka*, I, 90 (#23).
[30] Baḥrānī, *Nuzhat*, 294. Cf. Nābulusī, *Ahl al-janna*, 52, according to which pressed dates (*ʿajwa*) are "the fruit of paradise."
[31] Ṭabarānī, *al-Muʿjam al-kabīr*, X, 263.
[32] Baḥrānī, *Nuzhat*, 98.
[33] Cf. Goldziher, *History of grammar*, 44–5; Loucel, "L'origine du language," 167–8.
[34] Suyūṭī, *Muzhir*, I, 30 (tr. Czapkiewicz, *Views*, 66). Similarly in Ibn Ḥabīb (d. 239/853), *Taʾrīkh*, 27–8; Thaʿlabī, *Kashf*, IX, 177 (*ad* Q 55:4), from an anonymous source.
[35] On the concept of a Qurʾānic *lingua sacra*, which is closely related to the doctrine of the inimitability (*iʿjāz*) of the Qurʾān, see Wansbrough, *Qurʾanic studies*, 85–118. According to the early exegete Muqātil b. Sulayman (d. 150/767), those Muslims who are not native speakers of Arabic are washed in two rivers situated at the entry to the eternal garden. One purifies their bodies, the other purifies their heart, so that they emerge with bodies as beautiful as that of the prophet Joseph, with hearts like that of the prophet Job, and speaking Arabic like Muḥammad. See Muqātil, *Tafsīr*, IV, 532 (*ad* Q 76:21).
[36] Ibn al-Farrāʾ, *Muʿtamad*, 186, quoted in Böwering, *Mystical vision*, 95.

borrow Michel de Certeau's phrase, "the sacred text is a voice."[37] By this voice, practitioners gain access to paradise. "Every verse of the Qur'ān," writes al-Ghazālī (d. 505/1111) in his celebrated *opus magnum*, the *Revivification of the Religious Sciences* (*Iḥyā' ʿulūm al-dīn*), "is a degree (*daraja*) in paradise and a light in your houses."[38]

The point is not, however, that the world of the here-and-now, in Islam, is in all respects paradisiacal. No such reductionist notion is proffered here. In this book, rather, traditions that resolutely place the primordial and eschatological paradise in the distant past and future are given equally full attention.[39] Further, it would be fallacious to underestimate the important place that hell occupies in the Muslim religious imagination.[40] In fact, hell, as the "sandal" hadith tells us, is as closely intertwined with this world as paradise. To illustrate this point with just one example, according to the Qur'ān, there grows at the bottom of hell the poisonous tree of Zaqqum, which sprouts fruits "like the heads of devils" (*ka-ru'ūs al-shayāṭīn*, 37:65). Some Muslim exegetes understood this expression figuratively, or simply accepted the existence of such a tree in hell without further inquiring into the matter.[41] Others, however, argued that "head of devils" was the name of a disgustingly bitter tree growing in the Tihāma region in Yemen.[42] There was some debate about this, but according to the fifth/eleventh-century exegete al-Thaʿlabī, the most well-known answer to the question was the latter, that is, that Zaqqūm is a hellish plant simultaneously found in this world and the other.[43] Hell and the world inhabited by human beings, in other words, overlap.

Certain animals, in particular snakes and scorpions, were believed to shuttle back and forth between the earth and the hellish netherworlds.[44] Hellish sounds, such as the crashing noise of a stone hitting hell's floor, were heard by the Prophet and his Companions.[45] Suggesting an analogy to the four rivers of paradise, the Prophet allegedly held the view that hell-water

[37] De Certeau, *The practice of everyday life*, 137. In Qur'ānic studies, the phenomenon of the divine immanence in and during the recitation of the text is analysed by Neuwirth, *Koran*, 166–72, 178–81. See also Graham, *Beyond the written word*, 81, 87, 103–4; idem, "*Qur'ān* as spoken word"; Kermani, *Gott ist schön*, 212–32.

[38] Ghazālī, *Iḥyā'*, I, 450.

[39] An intriguing typology of three paradises in medieval Christianity is sketched by Christoph Auffarth, who writes that "[i]n addition to the primordial paradise on the one hand and the eschatological paradise on the other, there is yet another paradise type in the Middle Ages, one which is neither closed off, nor in a distant future of uncertain reality." See Auffarth, "Paradise now," 169.

[40] See Lange, "Introducing hell in Islamic Studies."

[41] Samarqandī, *Tafsīr*, III, 135.

[42] Ibn al-Jawzī, *Zād al-masīr*, VII, 62.

[43] Thaʿlabī, *Kashf*, VIII, 146. Cf. Hamadhānī, *Maqāmāt*, 218 (*al-Maqāma al-Dīnāriyya*).

[44] For an example, see Wellhausen, *Reste*, 153. See also Jīlī, *Insan*, 246.

[45] Muslim, *Ṣaḥīḥ*, *k. al-janna* 31 (*b. fī shiddat ḥarr nār jahannam*), IV, 2184–5; Suyūṭī, *Budūr*, 424. See *CTM*, s.v. w-j-b, VII, 140a.

leaks into the world, warning against bathing in hot mountain springs, "for they flow from hell."[46] The most extreme heat in summer is no other than the heat of hell, which has escaped to the surface of the earth, while the most extreme cold in winter is breathed into the world from the reservoir of extreme cold in hell.[47] In more abstract terms, a hadith asserts that "fever flows from hell (*al-ḥummā min fayḥ jahannam*)."[48] The list could be continued, but a more thorough discussion of these and other examples is reserved for the chapters to follow. Here, I use these instances to highlight what I see as a key theme of Islamic eschatological literature, a theme that runs like a thread through this book: the disappearing boundary between this world and the otherworld. By this formulation I mean the perceived proximity, spatial, temporal, and conceptual, of *al-dunyā* and *al-ākhira*, as well as the openness of Islamic traditions towards the idea of "realised eschatology" in the full, utopian *and* dystopian sense, not just in that of the optimistic feeling of "paradise now."

At this point, let us pause and note that important objections can be raised against approaching the history of Islamic eschatology along such lines. Arguably, the boundary between *al-dunyā* and *al-ākhira* is far from passable, the opposite of what I claim in many places in this book. In fact, the radical difference between *al-dunyā* and *al-ākhira*, it might be countered, is a fundamental a priori of the Islamic tradition. One scholar, for example, has suggested that the rigorous distinction between *al-dunyā* and *al-ākhira* is as constitutive for Islam as the mind/body dyad is for the intellectual history of the West (the mind/body distinction, supposedly, played a lesser role in Islam).[49] Islam tends to be characterised, not least by Muslim thinkers, as the most antimythological of the Abrahamic faiths, as *that* tradition which has most efficiently wedded the concept of the sacred with that of transcendence, thereby banishing the magical and mythical from this world. Statements to this effect abound. The Arab Muslim conquerors, writes Patricia Crone, "disseminated a religion that drained the world of divinity to concentrate it in a single transcendental God."[50] In the words of Josef van Ess, "Islam does not know the idea of a mediating instance.... All bridges are torn down: there are no sacraments, no images to be worshipped, no church music. God is transcendent."[51]

[46] Majlisī, *Biḥār*, VIII, 486.

[47] Tottoli, "The Qur'an," 144. The Prophet is said to have allowed the delay of the *ẓuhr* prayer in the case of great afternoon heat, "for the severity of the heat flows from hell (*shiddat al-ḥarr fayḥ min jahannam*)." Cf. Bukhārī, *Ṣaḥīḥ*, *k. mawāqīt al-ṣalāt* 9 (*b. al-ibrād bi-l-ẓuhr*), I, 173, and passim in Bukhārī and other canonical collections. See *CTM*, s.v. f-y-ḥ, V, 214a.

[48] Daylamī, *Firdaws*, II, 156; Nābulusī, *Ahl al-janna*, 75–7.

[49] Winter, "Islamic attitudes," 37.

[50] Crone, *Nativist prophets*, 276.

[51] Van Ess, *Christentum und Weltreligionen*, 110.

It is undoubtedly the case that mainstream Islamic theology, in order to safeguard God's unique alterity, shows a strong concern to preserve the ontological gap that separates Creator from creation. The scholastic theologians of Islam, the *mutakallimūn*, consistently stress the impossibility of crossing the divide between *al-dunyā* and *al-ākhira*; they deny that transcendence within the boundaries of this world can be achieved; and they generally reject theories of divine indwelling in creation (*ḥulūl*) or any other kinds of immanentist or anthropomorphist thought. However, as I suggest in this book, this attitude is undermined from within the Islamic tradition by a rich storehouse of currents of thought, images, and practices that make the boundary between *al-dunyā* and *al-ākhira* appear rather thin and permeable.

This book argues that the idea of an utterly removed otherworld in the Islamic tradition deserves to be nuanced and qualified in important respects. To quote van Ess again, "it only sounds *to us* as if God [in Islam] is remote or impersonal." For Muslims, van Ess maintains, God is "the one towards whom everything is directed and who takes care of everything; He is the Lord and the All-Merciful."[52] It is relevant in this context that the Muslim literature on the otherworld often stresses that God does not reside *in* paradise, but *above* it. Thus, even if Muslim religious authors generally hold that there can be no direct access to God, and certainly none in this life, many of them allow for multiple ways of exploring God's two antechambers: paradise and hell. As Crone observes, faced with the idea of an utterly transcendent, unfathomable God, "believers direct[ed] their attention to lesser emanations of manifestations of God, who function[ed] as intermediaries between the divine and the human worlds; it is thanks to these intermediaries that there can be communication between the two otherwise incompatible networks."[53]

As noted previously, a plethora of Muslim traditions conceive of the two otherworldly abodes as being proximate both in a spatial and a temporal sense. Paradise and hell, according to a certain (and as I argue, widespread) view in Islam, cannot be fixed in time; they are everywhen.[54] I further submit that in many instances of Islamic eschatological thought, this world and the otherworld do not simply coexist in time. Instead, there is a continuum between the two, a relationship of synchronicity, in the Jungian sense of a meaningful coincidence.[55] As will become clear in the course of this book,

52 Ibid., 110–11.

53 Crone, *Nativist prophets*, 453. To my mind, Crone distinguishes somewhat too neatly between Iranian immanentism and Muslim transcendentalism, but on the whole her nuanced discussion of the struggle of the two concepts in the history of Islam is a monumental achievement. See esp. ibid., 453–72.

54 I borrow this expression from anthropologist W. E. H. Stanner. See Stanner, "The Dreaming," 58.

55 Cf. Jung, "On synchronicity," 206. Cf. Fritz Stolz's suggestion to conceive of the various "paradises" of religious history as "counterworlds" (*Gegenwelten*). See Stolz, "Paradiese und Gegenwelten," esp. 21. For pertinent comments on the tangible immediacy of counterworlds

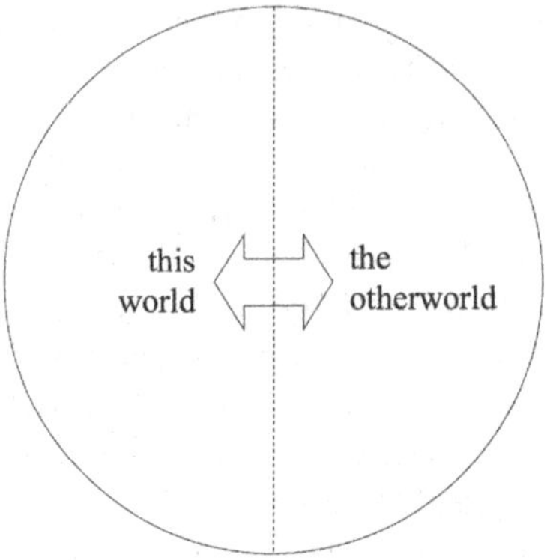

CHART 2. The *dunyā/ākhira* relationship: The synchronic view.

it is therefore often misleading to speak about the Islamic otherworld in terms of a "here*after*," an "*after*life," an "*after*world," or a "world to come." Notions about what happens *after* death and resurrection of course do exist in Islam, but equally strong, perhaps even stronger, is a sense that the otherworld is in a continuous and intimate conversation with the world of the here-and-now (see Chart 2).

Propinquity, then, not distance, is the baseline of this book on the Muslim paradise and hell. In this, I take inspiration from recent theorising in comparative religion. As Thomas Tweed observes, "[religions] draw on tropes, artifacts, and rituals to produce teleographies, representations of the ultimate horizon and the means of crossing it."[56] Tweed's notion of teleography applies well to this book, given that much of the discursive, material, and practical traditions that I survey in the chapters that follow do just that: they point out ways of, and impediments to, traversing the perceived divide between ordinary and ultimate reality. Considered within these parameters, eschatology is concerned not with "the last things," the literal meaning of its etymological origin, the Greek *τὰ ἔσχατα*, but with "the ultimate things" and how to reach them; not with what is over there far away, but with that which is (almost) here, that which most matters *now*. Religions, ventures Tweed, "do not deal with *the beyond*, as most interpreters suggest"; rather, "[*t*]*he near* is religion's domain."[57] Tweed here picks up on an idea of Bruno Latour, who writes that "religious talk" is not about "the far away, the above, the supernatural, the infinite, the distant, the transcendent, the mysterious, the misty, the sublime, the eternal," but about a

in the context of ancient Egypt, but taking a broad view of religious history in general, see Assmann, *Tod und Jenseits*, 1–25, at 21–2.

[56] Tweed, *Crossing and dwelling*, 151.

[57] Ibid., 157.

"transform[ation of] the listeners in being close and present."[58] Tweed develops this insight further by stressing the importance of "crossing," that is, to-and-fro movement between here and there. "Religions," he writes, "move between what is imagined as the most distant horizon and what is imagined as the most intimate domain ... they travel vertically back and forth between transcendence and immanence. They bring the gods to earth and transport the faithful to the heavens."[59]

Conceiving of the Islamic otherworld as that which is most close, in other words, fits in with recent theorising about the dynamic, boundary-crossing propensity inherent to religious cosmographies. Islamic eschatology, I argue in this book, speaks to a wide and variegated array of the most intimate and immediate human fears, hopes, and desires. What is more, interpretations of the otherworld along these lines are not limited to peripheral areas and periods in Islamic religious history, such as late medieval monism, nor can such interpretations easily be reserved to messianic movements, Sufism, gnosticism, Neoplatonism, or Illuminationism, Islamic currents of thought that affirm, potentially at least, the immanence of the divine in the world. The examples presented in the preceding text, for example, are taken from widely available traditional Sunni and Shiʿi sources. As we survey the various teleographies in Islam in the course of this book, more evidence to this effect will come to the fore.

The Muslim Eschatological Imagination

The Muslim paradise and hell, as the various chapters in this book illustrate, have manifold functions. They put words and images to fears of misery and hopes of happiness; they serve to inculcate a catechism of sins and virtues, offering taxonomies of the morally good and bad; they provide allegories for intellectual and spiritual fulfilment and failure; they are structured reflections of earthly utopias and dystopias, as well as blueprints for the creation of various paradises and hells on earth. First and foremost, however, they are theatres of and for the imagination. Herewith a second major theme of this book, in addition to the synchronicity of *dunyā* and *ākhira*, is announced.

The stuff of the imagination, in Jacques Le Goff's phrasing, is "created rather than reproduced from external objects."[60] In this sense the imagination neither produces mere copy-images of worldly phenomena, nor is it equal to free-floating fancy. Rather, by a process of *bricolage*, the imagination combines elements of "external objects" into novel, often marvellous images. The Muslim paradise and hell are filled with a plethora

[58] Latour, "Thou shall not freeze-frame," 32.
[59] Tweed, *Crossing and dwelling*, 158.
[60] Le Goff, "Introduction," 1.

of such images.[61] Literal translations of the Islamic term *al-janna* as "the Garden" and *al-nār* as "the Fire," the way I see it, fail to capture this versatile, image-making capacity of the Muslim eschatological imagination.[62] *Al-janna* is much more than a garden: there are large rivers in it, walls and buildings made of precious stones, and tall dunes of musk, but also fabulous tents, pavilions, and palaces, not to mention the extravagant luxury items enjoyed by its inhabitants, including embroidered couches and cushions, multicoloured brocaded garments, translucent cups of silver and gold, and so forth. There is no *nudisme eschatologique* in the Muslim paradise.[63] Likewise, *al-nār* is much more than a fire: its craggy landscape is filled to the brim with unwholesome plants, monstrous animals, and infernal architecture. Fire is not, as has been asserted, the "source of all suffering" in *al-nār*.[64] In fact, fire is no more than the most basic element in an arsenal of tortures and punishments perpetrated upon the damned. In sum, to translate *al-janna* as "paradise" and *al-nār* as "hell," as I choose to do in most instances, appears justified, as both terms sketch out a much broader horizon than that captured by their literal meaning, "the Garden" and "the Fire."[65]

The concept of the imagination has a checkered history in Western thought,[66] and herein lies another potential objection to the agenda of this book, or at the very least, to certain chapters of it. Why bother with the imagination? The imagination, writes anthropologist Amira Mittermaier, "was eyed with suspicion throughout the history of Western philosophy because it … could … play with sense impressions, creating images of non-existent things – a danger that could be circumvented only by reason's firm grip on the imagination."[67] Hobbes, for example, considered the imagination to decay sense.[68] Western scholars have viewed traditional Islamic eschatology, one of the most fertile areas for the imagination in Islamic religious

[61] The pages devoted to eschatology in Chebel, *L'imaginaire arabo-musulman*, 157–65, only give a faint impression. Also the various contributions in Arkoun, Le Goff, Fahd, and Rodinson, *L'étrange et le merveilleux*, do not address the (post-Qur'ānic) eschatological imagination in Islam. This may have to do with the fact that scholarship on the marvellous in Islam has largely focused on *'Ajā'ib al-makhlūqāt* (*The Marvels of Creation*), a genre that tends to bypass paradise and hell. It should be noted, however, that the *'Ajā'ib al-makhlūqāt* tradition is not merely a "literature of the marvellous." See von Hees, "The astonishing." It is also not entirely inimical to religious cosmography. See Saleh, "Paradise in an Islamic *'ajā'ib* work."

[62] This, notwithstanding the title of her work, is also noted by Rustomji, *The Garden and the Fire*, 63.

[63] Cf. Eliade, "Les Américains en Océanie et le nudisme eschatologique."

[64] El-Saleh, *Vie future*, 51.

[65] For Arab. *firdaws*, usually described in the literature as a layer, or compartment *within* paradise, I prefer to use the proper name "Firdaws" in translation.

[66] See Mainusch and Warning, "Imagination"; Iser, *Das Fiktive*, esp. 292–411.

[67] Mittermayer, *Dreams that matter*, 16.

[68] Hobbes, *Leviathan*, 23, quoted in Mittermayer, *Dreams*, 16. Cf. Iser, *Das Fiktive*, 296–7.

thought, with similar suspicion. "The whole basic view of ultimate origins and the hereafter," wrote Fritz Meier, "is hidden in Islamic literature behind a decorative structure of baroque traditions."[69] At the end of the nineteenth century, the Orientalist aristocrat, the Baron Carra de Vaux, wondered at the "bizarre marvels" and "puerile legends" of Islamic eschatology. While acknowledging that there are expressions of the marvellous (*merveilleux*) also in the Christian tradition, Carra de Vaux concluded that "we have come to realize to what degree the marvellous [of Islamic eschatology] lacks in spontaneity, life and richness.... The superiority of the Christian marvellous (*le merveilleux chrétien*) is overwhelming."[70]

At the same time, from the eighteenth century onwards, and prominently in the Age of Romanticism, the imagination has been framed not as dangerous and decadent, but as a positive, creative faculty; according to Samuel Coleridge (d. 1834), it is even the hallmark of poetic genius.[71] There have been few willing or daring enough to suggest that the Islamic eschatological imagination bears the traces of such poetic genius. Thomas Carlyle (1840), taking his inspiration from Goethe, was a harbinger of this view,[72] but his ideas have found few followers. Perhaps it takes an outsider to the field of Islamic studies like John Casey, an Oxford scholar of literature, to grant Islamic eschatology an "extraordinary ... capacity to find arresting visual images for scarcely graspable ideas."[73] One of the few strong voices emerging from within Islamic Studies is that of Aziz al-Azmeh, who detects in the Muslim traditionist literature on paradise "a canon which imagines the unimaginable, delights in beholding it, and glories in the possibility of possessing it and of endlessly repeating its possession and enjoyment...."[74] As for hell, it is no exaggeration to say that it is pictured equally sumptuously, a gigantic, intricate mechanism of endless punishment and pain.

To what an extent such characterisations are accurate or indeed appropriate, readers must decide for themselves. Let us add the significant point here that Muslims of all colours and persuasions have, throughout Islamic history, characterised the otherworld as that which is truly and fully real (*ḥaqq*).[75] The Qurʾān provides an important anchor for this idea, poetically

[69] Meier, "The ultimate origin," 103. Cf. the similar comments of Gardet, *Dieu*, 314, 325; Smith and Haddad, *The Islamic understanding*, 86n71.

[70] Carra de Vaux, "Fragments," 5, 25–6.

[71] Iser, *Das Fiktive*, 292–331.

[72] Carlyle attests the Islamic paradise and hell a "bursting earnestness" and "fierce savage sincerity." See Carlyle, "The hero as prophet," 86. Cf. Goethe's *Buch des Paradieses* in his *West-östlicher Divan*, I, 127–36.

[73] Casey, *After lives*, 144.

[74] Al-Azmeh, "Rhetoric for the senses," 218. See also Sebastian Günther's more recent comments on the "richness of symbolic imagery, metaphors and colors so distinctive to [Muslim] eschatological texts." See Günther, "God disdains not to strike a simile (Q 2:26)."

[75] Cf. Arkoun, "Peut-on parler," 1–2.

announcing that "this lower life (*al-ḥayāt al-dunyā*) is but sport and play, but the other abode: that is truly life (*la-hiya l-ḥayawān*)" (29:64). Thus, to borrow again from Le Goff, what is perceived by the Islamic eschatological imagination is "the whisper of a world more real than this one, a world of eternal truths."[76]

While there was a broad consensus among the scholars of Islam that the otherworld is real, the modality of this realness was the subject of much debate. It is striking that, from the time of Avicenna in the fourth/tenth century onwards, the imaginative faculty (*al-quwwa al-wahmiyya*) slowly but inexorably comes to play a central role in Muslim understandings of the otherworld. For the exegete al-Zamakhsharī (d. 538/1144), imagining (*takhyīl*) is a mode of revelatory speech aimed at capturing fathomless realities, it is the "visualisation of an abstract notion such as God's majesty and omnipotence in a comprehensive picture." In the words of a rhetorician of a later century, *takhyīl* is the "depicting [of] the essence of something, so that it might be assumed that it has a form that can be seen with the eyes."[77] For the followers of the "Shaykh of Illumination" (*shaykh al-ishrāq*), al-Suhrawardī of Aleppo (d. 587/1191), the imagination (*khayāl*) becomes the favoured organ for giving the individual access to the hereafter, providing insight into the "realities" of the otherworld.[78]

Readers are referred to later chapters, particularly Chapters 5 and 6, for a fuller discussion of the intricate relationships between the imagination, epistemology, ontology, and eschatology in Islam. Here, let me note that in the academic study of religion, the imagination has long been divested of the stigma of pertaining to "popular" or "irrational" religion. Not only is there a tendency to see the imagination not as an irrational but rather, as a kind of a pararational faculty.[79] Also the distinction between high and popular religion has increasingly come under criticism, a criticism that in recent decades has also had a tangible impact on Islamic studies.[80] To study the variegated eschatological imaginaries in Islam is therefore not so much an exercise in rewriting the history of Islamic religion from the bottom up but rather, of

[76] Le Goff, "Introduction," 6. The continuity of this notion into contemporary Muslim religious thought and practice has recently been highlighted by Amira Mittermaier. See Mittermaier, *Dreams that matter*, 19.

[77] See Heinrichs, "*Takhyīl*," 13–4, referring to Zamakhsharī, *Kashhāf*, IV, 137–8 (*ad* Q 39:67: "On the Day of Resurrection, the earth in its entirety will be His handful, and the heavens will be rolled up in His right hand"); Ibn al-Zamlakānī, *Tibyān*, 178.

[78] On the history of the imagination in Islam, as well as its multiple permutations, primarily in Arabic poetics, see van Gelder and Hammond (eds.), "Takhyīl."

[79] Cognitive philosophers sometimes assert that mental images represent objects in a manner not much different from linguistic descriptions, and vice versa. See Tye, "Imagery," 704a. Mohamed Arkoun comments that "one must not oppose the notion of reason with that of the marvellous (*merveilleux*) or the imagination but try to see how they function in parallel (*d'une façon corrélative*)." See Arkoun, "Peut-on parler," 53.

[80] See, e.g., Berkey, *Popular preaching*, 9–12; Karamustafa, *God's unruly friends*, 9–11; Shoshan, "High culture and popular culture."

paying proper attention to the history of the Muslim imagination, a concept that transcends the dichotomies of high/low and rational/irrational religion. Al-Ghazālī, a wildly imaginative writer if ever there was one in Islam,[81] may be invoked here as a prime example of an author combining an interest in imaginary worlds with "rational" thought, and doing so prominently in the area of eschatology.[82]

As others have suggested,[83] it is not implausible that the drive to create graphic images of the otherworld was channelled in Islam into a great mosaic of literary traditions, for the reason that the figurative arts were not an available medium of expression. The least one can say is that it would be wrong to dismiss the Muslim eschatological imagination and the kind of literature it produced as "nursery-tales for the lower-classes,"[84] the result of "geriatric libidinousness,"[85] or of a proclivity, tinged by a sadistic fascination with violence, towards the "bizarre."[86] "The imagination nourishes man and causes him to act," writes Le Goff, "[i]t is a collective, social, and historical phenomenon ... [a] history without the imagination is a mutilated, disembodied history."[87] The imagination may occasionally give birth to monsters, but then, monsters are worth studying, given that "perhaps what makes monsters horrifically *unheimlich* is that we see ourselves in them."[88] Paradise and hell, in this perspective, may not be such foreign places after all. And, to quote Jonathan Z. Smith, "if we do not persist in the quest for intelligibility, there can be no human sciences, let alone, any place for the study of religion within them."[89]

Premodern Views of the Islamic Otherworld among Non-Muslims

There is also a history of the Christian and the Western imagination of the Muslim paradise and hell, and this history deserves to be surveyed in the

[81] Cf. Moosa, *Al-Ghazālī*, 69. According to Moosa, al-Ghazāli "push[ed] reason into a conversation with the poetic imagination." See Moosa, *Al-Ghazālī*, 186.

[82] See the following text, pp. 186–9.

[83] Nwyia, *Exégèse*, 102; Wild, "Lost in philology?," 643. Cf. al-Azmeh, "Preamble," 30: "[F]igural representation reigned supreme in classical Arabic culture in the form of literary and linguistic representation but was not confined to this. It displayed itself equally in ... verbal accounts of dreams and visions."

[84] Carra de Vaux voices doubts that heavyweight scholars like al-Ghazālī and al-Suyūṭī really believed in the traditions about the physical aspects of the *barzakh*. See Carra de Vaux, "Fragments," 6. Eklund, however, rightly comments that "[i]t would be to misjudge orthodox Islam if we were to ascribe to it a European view of life after death as a nursery-tale for the lower classes." See Eklund, *Life between death and resurrection*, 28.

[85] I borrow this term from al-Azmeh, "Rhetoric," 224, who is likewise critical of the idea.

[86] Cf. Meier, "The ultimate origin," 104; Carra de Vaux, "Fragments," 5.

[87] Le Goff, "Introduction," 5.

[88] Beal, *Religion and its monsters*, 196.

[89] Smith, "The devil in Mr. Jones," 120.

introduction to this book, even though for reasons of space, we must do so in giant steps. It is no exaggeration to say that the Islamic otherworld, from the earliest times of Christian-Muslim relations, was a favoured battlefield for polemics. "It was the Islamic paradise," writes Norman Daniel, "which, more than any other theme, summed up the Christian notion of Islam. It was always thought to prove the contention that this was no spiritual religion."[90] Christian criticism focused on three aspects of Islamic eschatology in particular: the carnality of the Islamic paradise, which was seen contrary to the pure, spiritual afterlife preached in Christian doctrine; Islamic salvific optimism, which was interpreted to facilitate a permissive attitude of moral laxity; and the treatment of women in the hereafter (although this particular criticism appears to have come about only from early modern times onwards).

One should note at the beginning that Christian theologians of Late Antiquity, sometimes also of later periods, were not completely opposed to the idea that there were sensual pleasures in the afterlife. Irenaeus of Lyon (*fl. ca.* 140–200), for example, described a paradise full of them. In Ephrem's (d. 373) *Hymns of Paradise*, which, as I show in Chapter 1, display important intertextual parallels with the Qurʾān, the blessed enjoy food and drink. Also in the paradise of Renaissance theologians there are corporal delights. Later, Swedenborg (d. 1772) even imagined the angels praising conjugal intercourse in heaven.[91] The asceticism of Christian monasticism, combined with Augustine's doctrine of original sin, however, led to a broad repudiation of bodily pleasure and sexuality in this life as well as the next; paradise, in mainstream Christian thought, was declared to be above it, and thus, devoid of it.[92]

Christian theologians living under Islamic rule, such as Job of Edessa (d. 708), John of Damascus (d. 749), and Theodor Abū Qurra (d. 823), as well as the Byzantine theologians who read their works, mocked and criticised the somaticity of the Muslim paradise.[93] Already in the alleged correspondence between the Armenian king Leo III (r. 717–41) and the caliph ʿUmar II (r. 99–101/717–20), parts of which go back to the early second/eighth century, Leo rebukes ʿUmar "for saying that the inhabitants of paradise eat, drink, wear clothes and get married."[94] A Christian school teacher in Basra

[90] Daniel, *Islam and the West*, 172–6, at 172. For a study of this view in Victorian England, see Almond, *Heretic and hero*, 44–9.

[91] MacDannell and Lang, *Heaven*, 47–68, 124–44, 219–20.

[92] There is, of course, an enormous body of literature on this topic. See, e.g., Brown, "Late antiquity," 235–312, esp. 297ff.; Le Goff, "The repudiation of pleasure"; Ciulianu, "The body reexamined."

[93] *TG*, IV, 556; Hoyland, *Seeing Islam*, 487–8; Lamoreaux, "Abū Qurra."

[94] The correspondence is contained in chapters 13 and 14 of the eighth- or ninth-century Armenian chronicle of Łewond. See Łewond, *History*, 70–1. Cf. Hoyland, *Seeing Islam*, 495; Greenwood, "Correspondence."

is reported to have provoked the Muslim judge of the city, Iyās b. Muʿāwiya (d. 122/740), with the statement that if the inhabitants of paradise eat, they must also defecate. Iyās responded that, like fetuses in their mother's womb, bodies in paradise have the ability to ingest everything, without the need to excrete.[95] This is an argument that left traces in some of the earliest hadith collections. In a tradition preserved in the *Scroll* (*ṣaḥīfa*) of Hammām b. Munabbih (Egypt, d. 131/749 or 132/750) one learns that the inhabitants of paradise do not spit, blow their nose, or defecate.[96] Later elaborations of this theme add that digestion in paradise is by way of a light sweat.[97]

In the west of the Islamic world, in early third/ninth-century al-Andalus, the abbot Speraindeo of Cordoba and his student Paulus Alvarus wrote biting polemics against Islam in which they defamed the Islamic paradise as a brothel (*lupanar*) and claimed that Muḥammad had "promised as a gift for those who believe in him harlots for the taking, scattered about in the paradise of his god."[98] Meanwhile, in the east, a contemporary of Alvarus, the Iranian convert ʿAlī b. Rabbān al-Ṭabarī (d. *ca.* 240/855) defended the Muslim paradise by pointing out that the wine of paradise is also mentioned in Matthew 26:29: "I will not drink of the fruit of the vine until I drink it again with you in the kingdom of heaven."[99] The Muslim theologian Ḥumayd b. Bakhtiyār (Iraq, *fl.* middle of third/ninth c.) wrote a defence against Christian attacks entitled *Against the Christians on Felicity and Eating and Drinking in the Hereafter, and against Whoever Teaches in Opposition to This.*[100] The Baghdadi littérateur al-Tawḥīdī (d. 414/1023) reports that when a Christian pontificated that in his paradise, there was no drink, food, or sex, a Muslim theologian laconically commented: "What a sad affair!"[101]

Christian writers of the time of the crusades eagerly picked up on the theme of the sensuality of the Islamic paradise, fanning the Crusaders' "obsession with Muslim concupiscence."[102] From the widely read polemicist Petrus Alfonsi (d. after 1116) to the abbot of Cluny, Peter of Cluny (d. 1156), the bishop of Paris, William of Auvergne (d. 1249), and the Majorcan

95 See Wakīʿ, *Akhbār al-quḍāt*, I, 373, quoted in *TG*, II, 130. See also Aguadé, "*Inna llaḏī yaʾkulu.*"

96 Hammām, *Ṣaḥīfa*, 35 (#86).

97 Qurṭubī, *Tadhkira*, II, 197; Suyūṭī, *Budūr*, 536, 554, 590; Majlisī, *Biḥār*, VIII, 332, 347, 356, 365; Baḥrānī, *Maʿālim*, III, 121, 135.

98 See Hoyland, *Seeing Islam*, 229; Tolan, *Saracens*, 86; Coffey, "Contesting the eschaton in medieval Iberia," 99, 102; Wolf, "Muhammad as antichrist," 11.

99 See Ibn Rabbān, *K. al-Dīn wa-l-dawla*, 201, quoted in Hoyland, *Seeing Islam*, 499. The technique of using biblical quotations to prove the correctness of Islamic paradise notions is already used in (Pseudo-)ʿUmar II's letter to Leo II. See Roggema, "Letter of ʿUmar."

100 Thomas, "Ḥumayd." Cf. *TG*, IV, 132–3. Ḥumayd's text is lost.

101 See Tawḥīdī, *Imtāʿ*, III, 192, quoted in *TG*, IV, 557.

102 Housley, "The crusades and Islam," 202.

missionary Ramon Llull (d. *ca.* 1315), influential Christian theologians of the high Middle Ages penned refutations of Islam in which the Muslim afterlife was a favourite target of criticism.[103] The bull *Quia maior* of Pope Innocent III (d. 1216), which launched the Fifth Crusade, proclaimed that "the false prophet Muhammad ... seduced many men from the truth by worldly enticements and the pleasures of the flesh."[104] A century later, still writing under the impression of the failure of the crusades, the Dominican monk and missionary from Florence, Riccoldo da Monte Croce (d. 1320), belittled Islam as the "easy and wide road" (*lata et spatiosa via*) towards salvation, invoking Matthew 7:13–14: "The gate is wide and the way is easy that leads to destruction, and those who enter by it are many, for the gate is narrow and the way is hard that leads to life, and those who find it are few."[105] In the Renaissance, following the fall of Constantinople, attacks continued unabated. Pope Pius II (d. 1464), in a letter to the Ottoman sultan, Mehmet II (d. 1481), scoffed that the Muslim paradise was "the paradise of an ox or an ass, not of a man."[106] Little, in fact, had changed since the days of Petrus Alfonsi, with the alleged cupidity of the prophet Muḥammad still serving as the explanation for the promise of carnal pleasure in the Islamic paradise.[107] Martin Luther (d. 1546) fumed: "How drowned is this Mahmet in woman's flesh, in all his thoughts, words, works. On account of his lust, he can neither speak nor act due to his lust, everything has to be flesh, flesh, flesh."[108] Despite the fact that European scholars of the centuries following Luther became increasingly aware of the spiritual, immaterial dimensions of Islamic eschatology, "in the West, the image of a Paradise intended to satisfy male sensuality predominated."[109]

The first truly informed scholarly attempt to come to terms with Muslim eschatology is found in chapter 7 of the *Notae miscellaneae* of Edward Pococke (d. 1691), the first Laudian Chair of Arabic at Oxford. Pococke appended the *Notae* to his annotated edition-*cum*-translation of a part of Maimonides's Mishnah commentary, the *Porta Mosis* (1655).[110] Unlike

[103] On the works of Peter of Cluny, *Contra sectam Saracenorum*; William of Auvergne (d. 1249), *De fide et legibus* (ch. 19); and Llull, *Libre del gentil i dels tres savis*, see *CMR*, s.v.v. Peter of Cluny; William of Auvergne; Ramon Llull. See also Daniel, *Islam and the West*, 172–6.

[104] See Phillips, *Holy warriors*, 216.

[105] On *lata et spatiosa via*, see Daniel, *Islam and the West*, 177–80. On Riccoldo and other Dominican missions, see Tolan, *Saracens*, 233–55. This, one might add, came not so long after the preacher Jacques de Vitry (d. 1240) had promised that Christians would be able to buy paradise "cheaply," by signing up to carry the cross. See Tolan, "Sermons."

[106] Pius II, *Epistola ad Mahomatem II*, 61. Cf. Bisaha, *Creating East and West*, 150. Ironically, part of Pius II's fame rested on the fact that he had authored an erotic novel (*The tale of the two lovers*, 1444) when still a layman.

[107] Tolan, *Petrus Alfonsi*, 31.

[108] Quoted in Bobzin, *Koran*, 143n285; Wild, "Lost in philology?," 631.

[109] Almond, *Heretic and hero*, 45.

[110] Pococke, *Notae*, 223–301.

previous descriptions of the Muslim paradise and hell, which were based on a selective reading of the Qur'ān or simply regurgitated the received polemical tradition, Pococke availed himself of numerous Arabic manuscripts, many of which he had collected during his years of travel in Turkey and the Near East. In the *Notae*, he refers, among other works, to the Ashʿarite theological summa, the *K. al-Mawāqif* of al-Ījī (d. 756/1355), to the Qur'ān commentaries of al-Bayḍāwī (d. 674/1275?) and al-Jalālayn (Jalāl al-Dīn al-Maḥallī [d. 864/1459] and Jalāl al-Dīn al-Suyūṭī), to the writings of al-Ghazālī and Fakhr al-Dīn al-Rāzī (d. 606/1210), but also to texts from the Islamic sceptical and philosophical tradition, such al-Maʿarrī's (d. 449/1058) *Epistle of Forgiveness* (*Risālat al-ghufrān*) and various treatises of Avicenna (d. 428/1037), including his *Book of Origin and Return* (*K. al-Mabda' wa-l-maʿād*).

Pococke begins his account with a nod to the Islamic philosophical tradition, referring to Avicenna's *Book of Healing* (*K. al-Shifā'*), in which it is stated that the wise (*al-ḥukamā'*) desire intellectual felicity, not corporeal bliss, "nay, they ignore the latter, and if it is given to them, they belittle it."[111] Pococke then sets out to describe what he sees as the "orthodox" Muslim view, discussing, first, Muslim notions of the interrogation and torture in the grave (he suspects a Jewish influence); secondly, resurrection (he rehearses al-Ghazālī's argument that God can resurrect even the bodies of those who were eaten by wild animals); thirdly, the question of where souls reside between death and resurrection (in various localities: al-ʿIlliyyīn in heaven, the well of Zamzam in Mecca, Sijjīn below the earth, or the valley of "Borhut" in Hadramawt); fourthly, the apocalypse (he mentions Gog and Magog, the Mahdī, and so forth); fifthly, judgement (he notes that animals are judged, too); and, finally, hell and paradise. The Islamic hell, Pococke relates, is divided into seven layers, of which the top layer is home to the *jahannamiyyūn* ("Gehennales" in his phrase), the only group of sinners for whom punishment is not eternal.[112] In paradise, however, there is the tree of Ṭūbā, from which spring the rivers Salsabīl and Tasnīm. The heavenly maidens ("candidas megalo[y]talmys" in Pococke's learned translation of the term *ḥūr ʿīn*, "white ones, with big eyes") give pleasure to the believers, next to their earthly wives. The blessed drink wine, which does not inebriate.[113]

After listing many more such particulars of the Islamic paradise and hell, Pococke concludes his account by highlighting that "the greatest pleasure in paradise," according to Islam, is the heavenly concert (*samāʿ*) of the believers in God's palace. He states that Muslims agree that the ultimate pleasure

[111] Ibid., 225. The notion that the "wise men" of Islam, such as Avicenna, had turned their backs on their religion because of the sensuality of the Islamic afterlife was a *topos* of Christian polemics. See Daniel, *Islam and the West*, 173; Tolan, *Saracens*, 240.

[112] Pococke, *Notae*, 278–9.

[113] Ibid., 281–2, 288.

in paradise is "what no eye has seen and no ear has heard, and no mind has conceived."[114] Pococke also draws attention to the fact that in a certain reading of Avicenna, the corporeal delights and torments of the Islamic afterlife are no more than the imaginings of the soul in its postmortem state. However, this philosophical interpretation, Pococke assures his readers, is considered "heretical" by orthodox Islam. In the end, Muslims are left to believe "what even mad Orestes himself would swear were the words of a madman."[115] Islamic views of the afterlife, in Pococke's final assessment, are "as different as can be from what the Christians believe"; they are "plainly ridiculous, nay, absurd."[116]

Despite their polemical conclusion, Pococke's *Notae* are unprecedented in the wealth of detail and insight they offer, and as such continued to form the basis of the Western knowledge of Islamic eschatology for almost two centuries. For example, the substantial section on eschatology in George Sale's (d. 1736) introduction to his English translation of the Qurʾān (1735) is largely based on Pococke.[117] Echoing Pococke, Sale writes that the Christian doctrine of the afterlife exhibits "none of those puerile imaginations which reign throughout that of Mohammed, much less any of the most distant intimation of sensual delights, which he was so fond of," quoting Matthew 22:34 to the effect that Christians "in the resurrection neither marry nor are given in marriage, but will be as angels of God in heaven."[118]

While Sale's understanding of the Muslim hereafter is largely modelled on that of Pococke, there is, next to Pococke's, another groundbreaking early modern contribution to the Western understanding of Islamic eschatology, that of the Dutchman Adriaan Reland (d. 1718). A professor of Oriental languages at Utrecht University,[119] Reland is the author of *De religione Mohammedica* (1705), a watershed work on Islamic beliefs and practices that was translated in the eighteenth century into French, German, English, and Spanish, earning a place on the index of forbidden books of the Catholic Church. In *De religione Mohammedica*, Reland reacts against the work of Gisbertus Voetius (d. 1676), professor of theology at Utrecht and nemesis of René Descartes.[120] Voetius, who to his credit had initiated the study of Arabic at Utrecht, translated and recommended for study polemical works written against Islam, such as the *Confusio sectae Mahometanae* of the Spanish

114 Ibid., 291.

115 Ibid., 293: *quod ipse non sani esse hominis non sanus juret Orestes*, a quote from the *Third Satire* (v. 118) of the Latin satirist Persius (d. 62). See Persius, *Satires*, 112.

116 Pococke, *Notae*, 299.

117 Sale, "Preliminary discourse," 98–111.

118 Ibid., 109.

119 On Reland and his work, see van Amersfoort and van Asselt, *Liever Turks dan Paaps?*, 23–8; Vrolijk and van Leeuwen, *Arabic Studies*, 65–72.

120 On Voetius's view of Islam, see van Amersfoort and van Asselt, *Liever Turks dan Paaps?*, 19–23.

convert Juan Andrés/Johannes Maurus (Valencia, *fl. ca.* 1487–1515), "a theological polemic which emphasized the differences between Islam and Christianity, such as ... the 'sensual' Islamic idea of the afterlife."[121]

The second part of Reland's *De religione Mohammedica* is devoted entirely to a refutation of false charges against Islam.[122] Based on a careful reading of Arabic primary sources, Reland shows that Islam is not the *via lata et spatiosa* of which Riccoldo wrote. He demonstrates that Muslims *do* reckon with punishment of Muslim sinners in hell (§ 9); that it is erroneous to believe that corporeal pleasures are viewed as the "highest pleasure" of the Islamic paradise – Reland stresses the importance of the beatific vision in Islam and draws attention to Muslim metaphorical interpretations of the paradisiacal delights (§ 17); and that the view that women do not enter the Islamic paradise cannot be upheld (§ 18).[123]

Reland's remarkable impartiality becomes vividly evident when one compares his deliberations with those of certain French *philosophes* writing a couple of decades later. For instance, in his *Lettres persanes* (1721), Montesquieu (d. 1755) has his fictional hero, a prince from Isfahan, muse that "women are of an inferior nature to ours, and given that our prophets tell us that they do not enter paradise, why should they bother reading a book [i.e., the Qur'ān] whose sole purpose is to learn what the path to paradise is?"[124] Diderot, in an article of the *Encyclopédie* published in 1765, affirms that "for those [women] they [Muslim men] gather in their serails, paradise is closed," reproducing a pernicious prejudice found in the sixteenth-to-eighteenth-century French literature on Islam, as well as in some later European imaginings of the Islamic heaven.[125] Elsewhere in the *Encyclopédie*, it is stated that "Mahomet had to do with a people strongly given to sensual pleasures; therefore he deemed it necessary to limit eternal felicity to an unlimited ability to satisfy their desires in this regard."[126]

In sum, as concerns Western understandings of the Islamic paradise and hell, the Enlightenment was a two-edged sword: on the one hand, scholars with access to the primary sources written in Arabic and other Oriental languages began to reconsider long-held polemical assumptions; on the other,

[121] See Vrolijk and van Leeuwen, *Arabic Studies*, 64, who note that Voetius's *Disputatio de Mohammedanismo* (1648) cites the *Confusio* many times.

[122] Reland, *De religione Mohammedica*, 125–272 (*Lib. II agens de nonnulis, quae falso Mohammedanis tribuuntur*).

[123] Ibid., 174 (§ 9), 199–205 (§ 17), 205–8 (§ 18).

[124] Montesquieu, *Lettres persanes*, 92 (Lettre XXIV).

[125] *Encyclopédie*, s.v. Houris, (*Hist. mod.*), VIII, 327 (Diderot). See Smith, "Old French travel accounts," 230–2. Also Byron, in the *Bride of Abydos* (1813), writes of a Muslim paradise forbidden to women. See Reeves, *Muhammad in Europe*, 219. At the end of the nineteenth century, according to Pautz, *Muhammeds Lehre*, 212n3, the question was still "on occasion raised."

[126] *Encyclopédie*, s.v. Alcoran ou Al-Coran, (*Theol.*), I, 250 (unknown author [1751]).

the enlightened critique of religion resulted in an entrenchment of common perceptions of the Islamic otherworld as exceedingly sensual, permissive, and misogynist. As we will have occasion to show, the discursive polarity between the spiritual eschatology of Christianity and the carnal eschatology of Islam, which is embedded in larger imaginary distinctions between the rational West and the sensual East, lingers to this day.

Modern and Contemporary Scholarship on Paradise and Hell in Islam

Modern Western scholarship on Islamic eschatology begins with the edition of two popular medieval Arabic manuals of eschatology. In 1872, Prussian-born Moritz Wolff, a rabbi in Sweden, edited and translated (into German) the anonymous *Daqāʾiq al-akhbār fī dhikr al-janna wa-l-nār* (*Subtle Traditions about the Garden and the Fire*),[127] while in 1878, the Swiss professor of Hebrew at Lausanne, Lucien Gautier (d. 1924), published, accompanied by a translation, *al-Durra al-fākhira* (*The Precious Pearl*), a text commonly attributed to al-Ghazālī.[128] The text edited by Wolff, in particular, exerted a considerable influence on Western Islamic studies, seeing numerous re-editions and translations into a variety of languages.[129] J. B. Rüling, in his *Beiträge zur islamischen Eschatologie* (1895), originally a doctoral dissertation defended at Leipzig University, attempted a thematic overview of "Qurʾānic, dogmatic-Sunnaic and philosophical-apologetic" eschatological thought in Islam, noting that in Pococke's classic account, these three dimensions tend to get mixed up.[130] Rüling's study, though not without merit, is marred by the narrow textual basis on which it rests, as well as by its author's sanctimonious attitude. He judges, for example, that to trace the minutiae of Muslim theological eschatology is "without meaning or interest" and suggests that Muḥammad, "while borrowing much from Christianity did not understand its deep moral view (*sittliche Auffassung*)."[131] Baron Carra de Vaux, in a study published in the same year as Rüling's, could also not do without such judgemental posturing. Though offering valuable insights, he feels compelled to dismiss the eschatological imagery

[127] This was originally Wolff's PhD dissertation. Wolff published the text under a different title, *Aḥwāl al-qiyāma*. Cf. idem, "Bemerkungen zu der Schrift Aḥwāl al-ḳiyâme." *ZDMG* 52 (1898), 418–24. For other editions of this text, under a variety of titles, see *Daqāʾiq al-akhbār*. Wolff's choice of title is misleading, as the work should not be confused with the Ottoman *Aḥwāl-i qiyāmat*, of which there are a number of spectacularly illustrated manuscripts. See, e.g., Ms. StaBi Or. Oct. 1596. Cf. the study by Yıldız, *Aḥwāl-i ḳiyāmet*. There is also an Ottoman eschatological poem with the same title. See Flügel, *Handschriften*, III, 140, referring to ms. Vienna KK Hofbibliothek 1700, fols. 31v–48r.

[128] Ghazālī, *Durra*. See the following text, pp. 107–8.

[129] Cf. Tottoli, "Muslim eschatological literature." See also the following text, pp. 108–12.

[130] See Rüling, *Beiträge*, 2.

[131] Ibid., 3.

of Islam as profoundly "inferior" to the Christian one, lacking as it does in spontaneity and the capacity to devise original images.[132]

Rudolf Leszynsky, in his 1909 Heidelberg dissertation on the *Book of Renunciation* (*K. al-Zuhd*) of the third/ninth-century Egyptian traditionist, Asad b. Mūsā, is appropriately critical of the attitudes shown by the likes of Rüling and Carra de Vaux. The task of the scholar of Islamic eschatology, Leszynsky declares, is to develop a historical understanding of the genealogy and gradual unfolding of Muslim ideas about the afterlife. This, in his view, depends crucially on the comparison with the eschatological ideas of other religious traditions, particularly Judaism and Christianity. For example, the notion, or what Leszynsky refers to as the "dogma of our day," that Muḥammad's views of paradise and hell result from his "fiery (*überschäumende*) phantasy," loses much of its plausibility as soon as one considers Judeo-Christian precedents, which are no less phantastical.[133] In the 1920s, the scholarly search for the origins of Islamic eschatology seems to have manifested itself primarily in studies of the Judeo-Christian background of Qur'ānic eschatology, such as those of the Swedish historian of religion, Tor Andræ (1923–5), and, particularly, of the Jewish German Orientalist, Josef Horovitz (1923), who combined the search for precedents with a processual reading of the Qur'ān as reflecting four phases in the development of Muḥammad's predication.[134] However, despite some exceptions,[135] this line of research had few followers in twentieth-century scholarship. A number of reasons account for this, but one cannot help wonder whether the lack of interest in Qur'ānic eschatology had to do with a twentieth-century scholarly aversion against seeing Muḥammad as the fervently eschatological prophet he was, a "warner" (*nadhīr*) who preached the imminent end of the world, preferring instead to portray him, in line with much of the Islamic tradition, as a social and ethical reformer who laid the lasting bases for Islamic civilisation. Only in recent decades has this trend been challenged anew and, in some instances, reversed.[136]

More continuous attention has been given to Islamic eschatology understood as a discipline of dialectic theology, or *kalām*, an area of Muslim

[132] Carra de Vaux, "Fragments," 6, 26. Also Ataa Denkha, in a recent study, concludes that "Christianity possesses a way of thinking about this topic that is more open and flexible." See Denkha, *L'imaginaire du paradis*, 340.

[133] Lesyzynski, *Mohammedanische Traditionen*, 4. Leszynsky's edition of Asad's *K. al-Zuhd* is superseded by the 1976 edition of the same text by Raif Georges Khoury.

[134] Andræ, *Ursprung*; Horovitz, "Das islamische Paradies."

[135] See, e.g., the thorough though somewhat mechanical studies of O'Shaughnessy, "The seven names"; idem, *Eschatological themes*.

[136] On this point, see the excellent discussion by Shoemaker, *The death of a prophet*, 14–15, 120–36. See now also Lawson, "The music of apocalypse." The forthcoming study of Carlos Segovia on *The Quranic Noah and the making of the Islamic Prophet* also appears to contribute to this line of inquiry, but I have not been able to see it in time.

thought that involves discussions of soteriology (doctrines of virtues and sins, repentance, intercession of the saints, and God's salvation and damnation) as well as of the ontology of the afterworld, that is, its mode of reality. The standard reference work in the field is *Dieu et la destinée de l'homme* (1967) of the Catholic French priest, Louis Gardet, a study that is based on late-medieval Sunni theological *summae* in which centuries of eschatological thought in Islam are conveniently synthesised.[137] Only a couple of years after the appearance of Gardet's classic study, his student in Paris, Soubhi El-Saleh, published *La vie future selon le Coran* (1971). El-Saleh, a graduate of Azhar University who in later years became a professor at the Lebanese University in Beirut and a prominent contributor to Muslim-Christian dialogue, does not provide the detail and depth of analysis shown by Gardet; nonetheless his work remains the most useful survey of Islamic eschatology to date.[138] Focusing on traditionist-literal, rational, and mystical exegesis of Qur'ānic eschatology, El-Saleh introduces readers to a broad range of traditions of afterlife thought in Islam, surpassing Pococke's and Rüling's earlier attempts at a comprehensive treatment of the topic. The standard textbook on Islamic eschatology in English, Jane Smith's and Yvonne Haddad's *The Islamic Understanding of Death and Resurrection* (1981, republished 2002), by contrast, presents a less varied picture, focusing primarily on traditionist (i.e., hadith based) and *kalām* discussions, and conflating Ashʿarī, Māturīdī, Salafī, and popular doctrines. What is novel and valuable in Smith and Haddad's account is that it includes important typological observations about the modern permutations of Muslim eschatological thought.[139]

As well-balanced and thoroughly researched as the work of Smith and Haddad is, it also showcases a number of blind spots of twentieth-century Western scholarship on the Islamic hereafter. First of all, there is a tacit assumption that Islam, at least in its "orthodox" Sunni form, offers its adherents a supreme degree of salvation certainty. Already Ignaz Goldziher, in 1920, wrote about the "pure optimism" of Muslim soteriology.[140] According to Gustav von Grunebaum's classic formulation (1969), Islam does away with the idea of original sin and reduces salvation to obedience to an all-powerful God, thus making salvation "a door that is easily unlocked."[141] According to Smith and Haddad, not just the *kalām* tradition but also "popular belief chose

[137] Gardet, *Dieu et la destinée de l'homme*. Gardet's volume should be read alongside *TG*, which contains a wealth of information particularly on the early centuries. Other useful surveys of eschatology in Sunni *kalām* include Stieglecker, *Glaubenslehren*, 730–98; Martin, *La vie future*.

[138] El-Saleh was murdered in 1986, a victim of the Lebanese civil war.

[139] Smith and Haddad, *The Islamic understanding*, 127–46.

[140] Goldziher, *Richtungen*, 160.

[141] Von Grunebaum, "Ausbreitungs- und Anpassungsfähigkeit," 15.

to see that all but the most sinful will be saved by Muḥammad's intercession and God's mercy at the final time."[142] Paradise, in consequence, is assigned a far more central role in Islamic eschatology than hell. While the precise degree to which the certainty of salvation characterises the Islamic tradition remains a subject worthy of study, despite all generalisations to the contrary, the fact is that hell has fallen almost completely through the grid of Western scholarship on Islam.[143] The only book-length study of the Muslim hell, a 1901 Basel dissertation by Jonas Meyer (*Die Hölle im Islam*), is largely a paraphrase of certain sections in a medieval eschatological manual, *al-Takhwīf min al-nār (Causing Fear of the Fire)* of Ibn Rajab al-Ḥanbalī (d. 795/1393). As such, it offers little analysis. On the whole, the study of Islam has tended to privilege notions of spiritual ascent over the descent into the nether regions of the otherworld. Perhaps this is because the notion that the god of Islam is essentially merciful has proven more palatable to liberal scholars of religion than the terrifying spectre of a punisher deity. The Muslim hell is a messy, sometimes shockingly violent place, an interpretive challenge that few have been interested in meeting head-on. It is telling that the entry on paradise (1965) in the second edition of the *Encyclopaedia of Islam* (1954–2005) counts eleven columns in the printed edition, while hell (written in the same year) is awarded less than one column.[144]

Secondly, much of the scholarly literature on Islamic eschatology suffers from a lack of historical argument, or takes too narrow a view of what is historically relevant. For El-Saleh, for example, Muslim eschatological thought ends more or less with Ibn al-ʿArabī (d. 638/1240); after him, there is only "total decadence" (*décadence totale*).[145] Smith and Haddad divide the entire history of Islamic eschatology into "classical" and "modern." This rather dramatically overstates the break between "classical" and "modern" Islamic thought, while failing to see the important continuities that connect the precolonial and postcolonial periods. It also makes "classical" Islam into one homogenous, static block, only shaken into movement by the encounter with (Western) modernity, a view that seems increasingly vulnerable to criticism.

142 Smith and Haddad, *The Islamic understanding*, 81.

143 Exceptions include Lange, "Islamische Höllenvorstellungen"; idem, *Justice, punishment*, 101–75; idem, "Where on earth is hell?"; Thomassen, "Islamic hell." Some further studies dealing with aspects of hell in the Quran are discussed in Chapter 1 of this book. See also Hamza, "To hell and back," which deals specifically with the emergence of the doctrine of the temporary punishment in hell of Muslim sinners.

144 *EI2*, s.v. D̲janna (L. Gardet); s.v. D̲jahannam (L. Gardet). The entry on "al-Nār" (1995) deals exclusively with fire as one of the four elements. The more recent *Encyclopaedia of the Qurʾān* (2001–6) shows a more balanced approach, but still favours paradise (sixteen columns) over hell (twelve columns). See *EQ*, s.v. Paradise, 12a-20a (L. Kinberg); ibid., s.v. Hell and Hellfire, II, 414a-420a (R. W. Gwynne).

145 El-Saleh, *Vie future*, 120.

Thirdly and finally, there is a tendency to privilege Sunni traditionism and *kalām* over mystical, philosophical, and literary expressions of Muslim eschatology, including those of a non-Sunni provenance. To be fair, Smith and Haddad explicitly acknowledge that their study is limited to the Sunni tradition, due to "the wealth of material ... and in the interests of feasibility"; and they encourage "other scholars" to study "Shiʿi thought as well as philosophical and mystical interpretation[s]" of the Islamic afterlife.[146] Such methodological restraint deserves applause; nonetheless, the title of Smith's and Haddad's work misleadingly promises its readers that they will learn about "*the* Islamic understanding of death and resurrection." Be that as it may, as things stand, there are to date no synthetic, book-length studies in any Western language of either Shiʿi eschatology, or philosophical and mystical conceptions of paradise and hell in Islam.[147]

Scholarly explorations of the literary aspects of the Islamic paradise and hell have fared somewhat better. This is primarily due to the 1919 landmark study of the Spanish Jesuit, Miguel Asín Palacios, *La escatologia musulmana en la Divina comedia*, quite possibly the most erudite contribution to the study of Islamic eschatology in the twentieth century.[148] Asín uses the tools and methods of literary criticism to bring to the surface the striking structural similarities that exist between accounts of otherworldly journeys in Islam and Dante's *Divine Comedy*. Famously, Asín concludes that Dante must have known the Islamic sources, and used them. While containing much valuable information gleaned from an impressive range of primary sources, Asín is interested, first and foremost, in the comparison with Dante's work, and with the genre of otherworldly journeys in particular. This largely restricts his attention, as far as Islamic traditions are concerned, to the various versions of the Ascension (*miʿrāj*) of the prophet Muḥammad. Since the days of Asín, a comparatively large body of scholarship on the *miʿrāj* has accumulated, although few scholars have focused on the paradise and hell sections of the narrative; recent studies, however, have begun to redress this situation.[149]

146 Smith and Haddad, *The Islamic understanding*, xii.

147 There are, of course, important articles devoted to aspects of these fields. Readers are invited to turn to the first paragraphs of the relevant chapters of this book for references.

148 Asín, *Escatologia*. A partial English translation appeared in 1926. One should consult Asín's work in conjunction with Enrico Cerulli's two follow-up volumes (1949, 1972), in which Cerulli builds up an impressive amount of evidence in support of Asín's suggestion. For a history of the controversy following the first publication of Asín's book, see the appendix to the revised edition ("Historia y crítica de una polémica"). See also Kennedy, "Muslim sources of Dante?"; Kremer, "Islamische Einflüsse"; Strohmaier, "Die angeblichen und die wirklichen orientalischen Quellen"; and the recent discussion by Attar, "An Islamic *paradiso*?"

149 See, in particular, Colby, "Fire in the upper heavens"; Tottoli, "Muslim eschatology"; idem, "Tours of hell"; Vuckovic, *Heavenly journeys*.

As for scholarly engagements with Muslim narrative eschatology in the form of hadith,[150] two studies deserve special mention. Franz Rosenthal, in "Reflections on Love in Paradise" (1987), unabashedly and soberly discusses the preponderance of somatic and sexual imagery in Muslim eschatology, noting "the extreme delicacy with which rationalists ... had to approach metaphysical problems" and providing a *sangfroid* assessment of the gender imbalances in the Muslim hereafter.[151] While Rosenthal should be given credit for laying to rest a long tradition of high-brow dismissal of, and moral indignation over, Muslim narrative eschatology,[152] Aziz al-Azmeh, in "Rhetoric for the Senses: A Consideration of Muslim Paradise Narratives" (1995), goes a step further, celebrating the "cognizance of desire" in Islamic paradise narratives, while also emphasising that "the pleasures of Paradise are polymorphous and engage *all* the senses, although genital carnality is a pronounced element."[153] Al-Azmeh, who writes from the perspective of Lacan-inspired literary studies, focuses his attention on the aspect of the "spectacular" of Muslim paradise narratives, but he also lists a whole range of additional ways of studying the "aesthetics of reception of these narratives." Among the topics deserving scholarly attention, he not only names the "insertion [of these narratives] in social and temporal instances of pietistic practice and belief, in preachers' art, their relative weight and location in the imaginary life of various times, places, and socio-cultural locations, their relation to non-canonical materials," but also "the metaphorical use of Paradise to articulate mundane matters" and "the ironical and irreverent pronouncements on the descriptions of Paradise." Finally, he flags up the importance of studying "the literary genres in which paradisiacal narratives are inserted," the "structural study of these narratives as myths [and] in terms of psychoanalytical categories," as well as "motifemic analysis and cross-cultural comparison."[154]

150 On fictional narrativity and the imagination as a characteristic of hadith literature, see Günther, "Fictional narration." For a literary analysis of select aspects of Qur'ānic and hadith-based eschatology, see idem, "God disdains not to strike a simile (Q 2:26)."

151 Rosenthal, "Reflections on love," 249, 252.

152 Continuing earlier dismissals into the nineteenth and early twentieth centuries, Berthels wrote that "the houris [in Islam] are a sensual reification (*Versinnlichung*) of Zoroastrian spiritual beings ... degraded (*herabgedrückt*) to accord with a primitive people of the desert.... In the orthodox commentaries and popular traditions, the sensual details increase, such that the image becomes almost repugnant to European taste. The heavenly bride eventually becomes a kind of eternal young prostitute." See Berthels, "Die paradiesischen Jungfraun," 268. Max Weber called the Islamic paradise "a soldier's sensual paradise." See Turner, *Weber and Islam*, 139.

153 Al-Azmeh, "Rhetoric of the senses," 215, 217 (emphasis is mine). Also written in the Lacanian tradition is Ibrāhīm Maḥmūd's *Jughrāfiyyat al-maladhdhāt: al-jins fī l-janna* ('The geography of pleasures: Sex in paradise') from 1998, a veritable encyclopaedia of the pleasures of the senses in paradise, a sprawling, garrulous meditation on Muslim traditionist literature.

154 Al-Azmeh, "Rhetoric of the senses," 219–20.

Al-Azmeh's list is a mouthful. In recent years, a number of studies have begun to fill in the slots in the analytical grid sketched out by al-Azmeh. Thomas Bauer, for example, has traced the genealogy of the genre of the Islamic "Books of the Dead" (2002); Brooke Olson Vuckovic has proposed a reading of *miʿrāj* narratives about the otherworld in the light of the social divisions and hierarchies of medieval Islamic society (2005); Brannon Wheeler, in a remarkable monograph, has studied the ideological underpinnings of the paradise myth centred on the sanctuary in Mecca (2006); Zoltán Szombathy has analysed metaphorical usage of paradise and hell in classical Arabic poetry and belles-lettres (2008).[155] In various publications, I have examined eschatological narratives through the lens of the structuralist analysis of myth, the psychology of religion, as well as the study of ritual (2008, 2009, 2011, forthcoming).[156] Nerina Rustomji's *The Garden and the Fire* (2009) explores overlaps between the materiality of the Sunni "canonical" or "mainstream"[157] afterlife and Islamic material culture on earth, a theme that I also pursue in this book, particularly in Chapters 5 and 8. Recently, Ataa Denkha, in *L'imaginaire du paradise et de l'au-delà dans le christianisme et l'islam*, has attempted the kind of "cross-cultural comparison" al-Azmeh calls for.[158]

Shortly after this book went to press, two edited volumes devoted to the Islamic paradise and the Islamic hell saw the light of the day.[159] In as much as the manifold contributions to these two collections were available to me, and with the kind permission of authors, I have referred to them in this book as forthcoming. However, I have not been able to incorporate every single chapter. In sum, although the small body of scholarship on Islamic eschatology has substantially increased in the last decade or so, much remains to be done. As Alan S. Segal rightly remarks in his recent magisterial history

[155] Bauer, "Islamische Totenbücher"; Vuckovic, *Heavenly journeys*; Wheeler, *Mecca and Eden*; Szombathy, "Come hell or high water."

[156] Lange, *Justice*, 101–75; idem, "Where on earth is hell?"; idem, "Sitting by the ruler's throne"; idem, "The 'eight gates of paradise'-tradition."

[157] Rustomji, *The Garden and the Fire*, xvi.

[158] Denkha, *L'imaginaire du paradis*. As in the case with Rustomji, Denkha's grasp of the primary and secondary sources is patchy. E.g., Denkha fails to mention Rosenthal's and al-Azmeh's fundamental studies, nor does she seem to have consulted Ebrahim Moosa's *Ghazālī and the poetics of imagination* or Christiane Gruber's various publications on the illustrated *miʿrāj* manuscripts, despite the fact that both the concept of the imagination and the figurative depictions of paradise and hell in Islamic art are central concerns of her work. Rustomji misses references to Bauer's "Islamische Totenbücher," Gardet's *Dieu et la destinée de l'homme*, Horovitz's "Das islamische Paradies," and most of the German scholarship, including Andræ's *Ursprung*. As for primary sources, the bibliographies and notes show that only a fraction of the available material has been considered.

[159] Günther and Lawson (eds.), *Roads to paradise*; Lange (ed.), *Locating hell*. Another recent collection of papers on the Islamic paradise and hell (though mostly on the former) is Dévényi and Fodor (eds.), *Proceedings* (2008, 2012).

of the afterlife in Western religions, "Islamic views of the afterlife are just as rich and manifold as in Judaism or Christianity, but ... different in some important ways." This leads Segal to conclude that the study of "the whole tradition" is an important desideratum of scholarship.[160] Taking Segal by the word, this book aims to provide as full an account of the history of the Islamic paradise and hell as is presently possible on the basis of the published and unpublished primary sources, as well as the scholarship produced on the topic in the major modern research languages. Of course, there are limits to this undertaking. I am sure to have missed some books, particularly when written in languages to which I have only restricted access (such as Russian or Turkish). In other cases, I also decided against including some sources. On the whole, however, I am confident that what I offer here is the most complete overview of Islamic eschatology hitherto available in the literature.

Overview of Chapters and Note on Illustrations

I recommend general readers start their journey through this book not at the beginning, in Chapter 1, but plunge instead into the middle, that is, Chapter 4, where stock is taken of the vast reservoir of images and ideas about paradise and hell in late-medieval Muslim hadith literature. Similar surveys, more or less systematic and concise, exist in the scholarly literature, but none is based on the four authoritative sources that I put under the magnifying glass here, and none offers an integrated discussion of both Sunni and Shiʿi traditions. I present the material gleaned from these four Sunni and Shiʿi eschatological compendia under five main headings: paradise and hell between death and resurrection; time and space in the Muslim otherworld; animals and nonhuman beings in paradise and hell; the bodies of the human inhabitants of the otherworld; and sins and virtues of the blessed and the damned. This serves, I hope, to lay bare the core concerns that structure these texts.

Chapters 1 to 3, which may be read next, trace the genealogy of Islamic narrative eschatology, the pretexts, so to speak, to the panoptic vision of paradise and hell that I sketch in Chapter 4. Chapter 1 looks at the discourse of paradise and hell in the Qurʾān. First, it outlines the phenomenology of paradise and hell in the Qurʾān, treating the text as if it were an analogously related, internally consistent unity, in order to take stock of the repertoire of images and ideas about the otherworld that the Qurʾān has in store. In a second step, I advance hypotheses regarding the gradual inner-Qurʾānic development of eschatological themes. This serves to complicate the assumption of the analogous consistency of the text, be it eschatological or otherwise. Thirdly and finally, I trace the Qurʾān's intertextual relations with the literatures of the Late Antique Near East. This allows me, at the end the chapter, to draw some fresh conclusions about what I see as a salient characteristic

160 Segal, *Life after death*, 639.

of Qur'ānic eschatology, namely, its propensity to conceive of this world and the otherworld as a synchronic whole, a *merismos*. In my view, the Qur'an thus facilitated, rather than hampered,[161] the development of immanentist eschatological thought in Islam.

Chapters 2 and 3, which should be read in tandem, tell the history of several literary genres of narrative eschatology in Islam. There is, on the one hand, the traditionist, hadith-based literature on paradise and hell, a genre that developed its own formal and qualitative standards and whose long-term continuity through the centuries deserves notice (Chapter 2). As I show, it is possible to distinguish between three different phases of expansion and contraction of this genre, marked by shifting views about what kind of hadiths could legitimately be included and what not. On the other hand, we are faced with copious amounts of eschatological texts written in a hortatory and popular vein (Chapter 3). While the former, hortatory type uses narratives about paradise and hell primarily in order to cultivate a proper pious mixture of hope and fear and to inculcate correct moral conduct in the believers, the latter, popular tradition is concerned with the awe-inspiring and the marvellous of the Islamic otherworld. Often, it is quite simply a question of telling a good story. It is in this chapter that I deal with the well-known eschatological manuals such as the *Subtle Traditions about the Garden and the Fire* or *The Precious Pearl*, first edited by Moritz Wolff and Lucien Gautier (see preceding text); also the various ascension tales in Islam, as well as a number of other often-told stories about the otherworld, are discussed here. On the whole, Chapters 1 through 4, which together form Part I of this book, trace the gradual growth of the increasingly differentiated Muslim narrative literature of the otherworld.

Part II examines the various theological, mystical, and philosophical accounts of paradise and hell, as well as the innerworldly, material manifestations of the Muslim otherworld. In the course of the chapters in Part II, a diverse spectrum of alternative visions of the otherworld gradually comes into relief. This serves to demonstrate that there is no single Islamic understanding of paradise and hell, a fact that on occasion troubled Muslim scholars. Some even felt propelled to insist that all deviations from their normative view of the otherworld amounted to a distortion of the faith. Clad in the form of an apocalyptic hadith, it was averred that the antichrist (*dajjāl*) appearing at the end of time "will bring a paradise and a hell, and his hell is paradise, and his paradise is hell."[162] Chapters 5 and 6 deal with theological and philosophical teleographies in Sunni and Shi'i traditions. Chapter 5

[161] Crone, *Nativist prophets*, 462.

[162] Muslim, *Ṣaḥīḥ*, *k. al-fitan* 104 (*b. dhikr al-dajjāl*), IV, 2249; Ibn Māja, *Sunan*, *k. al-fitan* 33 (*b. fitnat al-dajjāl*), III, 448; Ibn Ḥanbal, *Musnad*, V, 383, 397. See *CTM*, s.v. *j-f-l*, I, 351a.

critically revisits three common characterisations of Sunni theological eschatology: first, that it stresses the utter transcendence of the otherworld in both space and time; secondly, that it is supremely optimistic, promising easy salvation for believers; and thirdly, that its conception of the otherworld is unfailingly materialistic. I end this chapter with a consideration of the gradual rise of the idea of an "imaginable" (*khayālī*) otherworld, excavating its roots in the thought of Avicenna in the fourth/tenth century and passing through al-Ghazālī in the fifth/eleventh and al-Suhrawardī in the sixth/twelfth century. Chapter 6 pursues this theme of a "World of Image" (*ʿālam al-mithāl*) into late-medieval Shiʿi eschatology, but then moves back in time to tell the history of Twelver-Shiʿi traditionist and systematic, *kalām*-style literature on the otherworld. I also devote some space to the flowering of eschatological hadith in eleventh/seventeenth-century Akhbārī Shiʿism, concluding this chapter with a survey of the philosophical eschatology of the Ismaʿilis.

Chapter 7 presents a sevenfold typology of Muslim renunciant and mystical interpretations of the otherworld. The only previous attempt to do something similar that I am aware of, a chapter in El-Saleh's *La vie future selon le Coran*, remains fundamental, but I feel that a recalibration of El-Saleh's findings is overdue. It is true, as El-Saleh asserts, that the mystics of Islam never explicitly deny the corporeality of the afterlife, but more relevant and indeed more interesting, I believe, is the question of the *relative* importance they attribute (or do not attribute) to this physicality. Furthermore, I disagree with El-Saleh when he states that the Sufis' intense preoccupation with the otherworld results in a diminution, in their eyes, of the status of the world of the here-and-now. Sufis of various periods speak eloquently of the ways in which this world and the otherworld are intertwined, or mirror each other. In addition, it deserves our attention that ethical and interiorising eschatologies flourished in Sufi milieus, and not only in the centuries up until Ibn al-ʿArabī, but also in later times, in which the concept of the imagination played an ever more important role. On both accounts, it seems to me, El-Saleh is hostage to a modern reflex, that is, to see Sufi-inspired eschatology, particularly in its late-medieval manifestations, as inimical to the fundamental principles and values of modernity.

The concluding Chapter 8 is an exploration of the manifold innerworldly manifestations of paradise and hell in Islamic topography, architecture, and ritual. As I argue, paradise and hell were not only models of, but also served as models for, human society on earth. I discuss a number of places, buildings, and rituals that were assimilated, and sometimes equated, with places, buildings, and rituals in paradise and hell, and thereby provided with otherworldly layers of meaning. It is perhaps in this area of concrete cultural production that the theme of "eschatology now," the slippage between this world and the otherworld, which runs like a baseline through the chapters of this book, becomes most tangible. At the same time, the observations and conclusions drawn in this chapter are the most tentative and speculative of this study; for eschatological interpretations of the kind presented here never impose, only suggest themselves. It should also be noted that the question of *cui bono* is notoriously difficult to decide in all cases. In certain instances, it is possible that multiple parties stood to benefit from the presence of paradise and hell on earth.

Finally, in the Epilogue I review some of the major transformations of the traditional Muslim picture of paradise and hell in the modern and contemporary period. I have kept this section deliberately short. This is because, on the one hand, I tend to see more continuities than discontinuities in the modern and contemporary Muslim discourse on paradise and hell. On the other hand, a full discussion of eschatology in Islamic (post-)modernity would have required me to delve into a vast sea of additional texts and traditions. This would inevitably have led to a further swelling of the manuscript, which has already become worryingly more voluminous than what I intended in the beginning. This is not to say that it would not be worthwhile to write a study of modern and contemporary Islamic eschatology, examining its various types, concerns, and sensibilities; but this is a project for another time. In the Conclusion, therefore, I only highlight some salient contributions to the Muslim discourse on paradise and hell in the last two hundred years or so, and end by offering some synthetic reflections.

To conclude this Introduction, a note on illustrations. The tradition of depicting paradise and hell in Islamic figurative arts is not particularly rich, certainly not when compared to the European history of painting the otherworld. As suggested previously, more creative energy was poured into linguistic representations of the two otherworldly abodes. Nonetheless, there is an unbroken tradition of such depictions from at least the eighth/fourteenth century onwards, including diagrammatic and topographical representations of paradise and hell. I have thought it appropriate to include a number of examples, some of which are well known, others less so. These examples are derived from illustrated manuscripts of the prophet Muḥammad's Ascension (*miʿrāj*), of the popular genre known under the title of *The Stories of the Prophets* (*Qiṣaṣ al-anbiyāʾ*), of the so-called *Books of Omen* (*Fālnama*s), of the *Marvels of Creation* (*ʿAjāʾib al-makhlūqāt*), and of hajj guidebooks (*Ḥajjnāma*s).[163] I should like to note that I have not chosen these images for their artistic merits, which, not being an art historian, I am ill positioned to judge anyway. While these images doubtlessly deserve a proper art historical analysis, a comprehensive study of paradise and hell in Islamic figurative art remains to be written.

[163] Interested readers should further refer to the following works, in which most of the known images are published: And, *Minyatür*; idem, *Minyatürlerle*; Blair and Bloom, *Images of paradise*; Farhad, *Falnama*; Milstein, Rührdanz, and Schmitz, *Stories of the prophets*; Séguy, *The miraculous journey*. For a recent overview, see also Gruber, "Signs of the Hour."

PART I

TEXTUAL FOUNDATIONS: NARRATING THE OTHERWORLD

I

The Otherworld Revealed: Paradise and Hell in the Qur'ān

Even a cursory reading shows that the Qur'ān is a text that is deeply concerned with the relationship between this world (*al-dunyā*) and the otherworld (*al-ākhira*).[1] The Qur'ān states that, next to the belief in God, His angels, scriptures, and prophets, the belief in the "last day" (*al-yawm al-ākhir*) is one of the five essential tenets of faith (4:136); this contrasts with the view of those who deny the message brought by Muḥammad, "who say: 'There is none but our worldly life, and we shall not be resurrected' " (Q 6:29). In virtually every sura one finds verses, often long passages amounting to colourful *tableaux*, that relate to the events surrounding resurrection, judgement, paradise, and hell. Roughly a tenth of the Qur'ān, perhaps more, deals with matters eschatological. The terms *al-dunyā* and *al-ākhira*, in their cosmological sense, each appear in 108 verses of the Qur'ān. In half of these instances, that is, in fifty-four verses, *al-dunyā* and *al-ākhira* are paired. In the other instances, *al-dunyā* is found in combination with synonyms of *al-ākhira*, or is accompanied by references to the Day of Judgement or the rewards in paradise (e.g., 3:14, 10:7–10; 11:15–16; 33:28–29). Meanwhile, *al-ākhira* occurs several times in tandem with *al-ūlā* ("the first [abode]," e.g., 28:70). In sum, *al-dunyā* and *al-ākhira* are wedded closely in the Qur'ān.

What catches the eye is that *al-dunyā* ("the nearer [abode]") is a spatial concept (cf. 37:6, 67:5), while *al-ākhira* ("the last [abode]") denotes a temporal relationship. The Arabic adjective *ākhir* ("last"), however, oscillates into the semantic range of *ākhar* ("other"), both deriving from the same

[1] This has repeatedly been noted in the scholarly literature. See, e.g., Goldziher, *Introduction*, 7; Stytkevych, *Muḥammad*, 10–11; Reynolds, *The Qur'ān and its biblical subtext*, 251; Sinai, *Die heilige Schrift*, 78; Shoemaker, *The death of a prophet*, 120, and the references provided there (n6). Recently, Raymond Farrin has argued that eschatology is central to the Qur'ān not just in quantitative, but also in structural and compositional terms. See Farrin, *Structure and Qur'anic interpretation*, xvi, 5–69. On the "marginalization of eschatology" in mainstream Qur'ānic studies, see Shoemaker, *The death of a prophet*, 120–36, and the discussion that follows, n159.

consonantal root (*ʾ-kh-r*).[2] *Al-ākhira*, therefore, also indicates a spatially "distant" or simply, an "other abode."[3] As such, it also occurs as the antonym of "the earth" (*al-arḍ*, 28:83). The superiority of this "other abode" over the "nearer abode" is stressed throughout the Qurʾān. *Al-ākhira* is "better" (93:4, 12:109, 16:30, passim); the "enjoyment" of *al-dunyā* is trivial compared to that of *al-ākhira* (9:38); people are urged to "sell" their life on earth for life in *al-ākhira* (4:74); and so forth. Only *al-ākhira* offers a sense of structured security – it is "the abode of stability" (*dār al-qarār*, 40:39). The world of the here and now, by contrast, is "the fleeting one" (*al-ʿājila*, 17:18, 75:20, 76:23), a "place of temporary lodging" (2:35–6). As one verse puts it succinctly, "this lower life (*al-ḥayāt al-dunyā*) is but sport and play, but the other abode: that is truly life" (29:64). The term *al-ākhira*, in this perspective, also refers to "the ultimate abode." In consequence, one may question common renderings of the Qurʾānic *al-ākhira* as "the afterworld." As is argued in this chapter and indeed in many other places of this book, rather than restricting the term to its diachronic, temporal meaning, we should consider a broader translation of *al-ākhira* as "the otherworld."

How much room does the Qurʾān give to paradise and hell, respectively? How optimistic or pessimistic, judging on this basis, is it in regard to humankind's prospects of salvation? Counting the number of Qurʾānic verses in which paradise and hell figure is less straightforward than one might think. Both have multiple synonyms in the Qurʾān: paradise is usually referred to as "the Garden" (*al-janna*, used more than eighty times), but one also encounters its plural, *jannāt* (more than forty occurrences), often in compounds such as *jannāt ʿadn* ("the gardens of Eden," eleven occurrences), *jannat/jannāt al-naʿīm* ("the garden/s of delight," five occurrences), *jannat/jannāt al-maʾwā* ("the garden/s of refuge," 32:19, 53:15), or *jannāt al-firdaws* ("the gardens of paradise," 18:107). In addition, expressions such as *ʿilliyyūn* ("the highest," 83:18–21) and *dār al-salām* ("the abode of peace," 6:127, 10:25), while also allowing for other interpretations, are usually understood by exegetes and scholars to figure among the names of paradise.[4] Hell is most commonly designated as "the Fire" (*al-nār*, some 125 occurrences), its proper name being *jahannam* ("Gehenna," some seventy-seven occurrences). In addition, one finds *al-jaḥīm* ("the furnace," twenty-six occurrences), *al-saʿīr* ("the blaze," eighteen occurrences), *saqar* ("extreme heat" [?], four occurrences), *ḥuṭama* ("the insatiable," 104:4,

[2] A relatively common synonym in classical Arabic for *al-ākhira* is *al-ukhrā*, "the other[world]." See Lane, *Arabic-English lexicon*, s.v. ʾ-kh-r. Cf. Zamitt, *A comparative lexical study*, 70.

[3] Cf. Bravmann, *Spiritual background*, 32–7. On *al-ākhira* and cognates in pre-Islamic poetry, see now El Masri, "*Min al-baʿd ilá l-āḫira*."

[4] On the names of paradise in the Qurʾān, see Horovitz, "Das islamische Paradies," esp. 59–61; *EQ*, s.v. Paradise, IV, 12a-20a, at 12b-15a (L. Kinberg).

5), *laẓā* ("blazing fire," 70:15), and *hāwiya* ("pit, abyss" [?], 101:9),[5] among others.

Further complicating the attempt to quantify the appearance of paradise and hell in the Qur'ān is the fact that the text is replete with metonymical expressions that conjure up, in one image, the bounties and the miseries of the otherworld. Thus, in multiple verses the believers are promised as future reward a "rich provision" (e.g., 34:4), while the unbelievers and sinners are laconically threatened with a "painful chastisement" (e.g., 34:5). Somewhat more elaborate are brief, evocative vignettes of paradise and hell, stereotyped phrases such as the promise of "gardens under which rivers flow, in which they will remain forever" (5:85 and passim in some fifty places). Not counting the metonymical expressions, but adding up all verses, including the vignettes, in which the two otherworldly realms are named and described at some length, it results that about 320 Qur'ānic verses relate to paradise and about 400 to hell. Different counts remain possible, but it is hardly the case that paradise occupies "significantly more space" in the Qur'ān than hell, as has been claimed.[6] If anything, the opposite is true.[7]

Time and Space in the Qur'ānic Otherworld

No doubt the concept of a final reckoning of souls on the Day of Resurrection is a dominant theme in Qur'ānic eschatology. In several passages (10:45, 20:103–4, 23:112–3, 36:52), the Qur'ān suggests that the souls of the dead fall into sleep until the Day of Judgement, so that the intermittent time span seems of no consequence to them when they wake up at the end of time.[8] On

[5] On these names, see O'Shaughnessy, "The seven names." On *jahannam*, see also *EI2*, s.v. Djahannam, II, 381b-382a (L. Gardet); Jeffery, *Foreign vocabulary*, 105–6. On *saqar*, see Bell and Watt, *Introduction*, 161 (stating that the meaning is unknown); *EI2*, s.v. Saḳar, VIII, 881a (D. Gimaret). On *ḥuṭama*, see Neuwirth, *Koran*, 709; eadem, *Handkommentar*, 149, 151–3 (*ad* Q 104:4); Jeffery, *Materials*, 112. On *hāwiya*, see Bellamy, "*Fa-ummuhū hāwiyah*"; *EQ*, s.v. Pit, IV, 100a-104a (D. Stewart); Paret, *Kommentar*, 518–9 (*ad* Q 101:6–11).

[6] Neuwirth, *Koran*, 439. Tellingly, the index of Neuwirth's study has an entry for "paradise," but not for "hell." Similar statements can be found in Andræ, *Mohammed: The man and his faith*, 56; Neuwirth, "Reclaiming paradise lost," 333; Madigan, "Themes and topics," 91; Sviri, "Between fear and hope," 323 (stressing Q 7:156: "He said, I smite with my punishment those whom I wish, but My mercy embraces everything."); Andræ, *Ursprung*, 234. Andræ adds that paradise is not as central in the Qur'ān as certain Christian polemicists made it to be. Meanwhile, Sells, *Approaching the Qur'ān*, 23, contends that it is a "standard stereotype about ... the Qur'ān ... that Islam is a religion of fear." Less focused on potential polemic uses of the argument is Rosenthal, "*Sweeter than hope*," 79, who prefers to leave the question open (stressing Q 17:57, according to which the believers "will hope for God's mercy and fear His punishment.")

[7] Geiger, *Was hat Mohammed*, 67–8; Bell, *The origins*, 103n1. Jones, "Paradise and hell," 110, counts ninety-two "significant passages" about hell and sixty-two about paradise.

[8] Several scholars stress the dependence of this idea on the eschatology of Syriac Christian writers. See Andræ, *Origines*, 165–7; idem, *Ursprung*, 153–63; idem, *Mohammed*, 89–90; O'Shaughnessy, *Muhammad's Thoughts*, 69–70. See now also Tesei, "*Barzakh*."

multiple occasions, however, the Qur'ān also refers to the simultaneity of life on earth and in the otherworld.[9] In 3:169, the Qur'ān declares that the believers must not think that those who are killed "in God's way" are dead; rather, they are "alive with their Lord and provided for." Presumably, this indicates that paradise is *now*, at least for some, namely, the martyrs.[10] However, the Qur'ān does not reserve immediate postmortem retribution to martyrs alone. In a story told in Q 36:13–26, a man from a mythical past age is told: "enter the Garden!" This is after he has come to the defence of three prophets sent by God. How he dies, or indeed whether he is dead, is not said, although it seems reasonable to assume that he is martyred. Others, such as the wives of Noah and Lot (66:10), pass into hell without delay. The Qur'ān states that "the family of Pharaoh" are "fuel for the Fire" and that God "seized" them on account of their sins (3:10–11). One passage makes an explicit connection between the moment of death and the punishment that immediately follows it: "When the wrong-doers are in the floods of death ... the angels are stretching out their hands [saying]: 'Give up your souls. Today you are recompensed with the torment of humiliation'. . ." (6:93).

It might be countered that the Qur'ān regularly employs preterite verb forms, as it does when God is said to "have made" certain people "fuel for the Fire," to describe a future event (e.g., 7:44, 11:98, 14:21, 18:99, 77:37–8).[11] This is no doubt true. However, the Qur'ān in general is "lacking a notion of time as divided into past, present and future."[12] The line between the time of the mythical past, the time of the here and now, and the time of the otherworld is oftentimes blurred.[13] Let us recall that the Qur'ān challenges the fatalistic conception, common among pre-Islamic Arabs, of time (*dahr*) as an irreversible, linear process to which all humans must yield. In contrast, the Qur'ān disempowers time and subjects it to God's sovereignty.[14]

9 This suggests a difference with the Gospel, in which "[t]here are only very few instances ... that refer to a paradise existing in the present time, immediately accessible ... Jesus's words of consolation for the thief hanging on the cross beside him, 'Today you will be with me in Paradise', are not representative of biblical theology...." See Auffarth, "Paradise now," 169.

10 Cf. Q 2:154. See on this point, Reynolds, *The Qur'ān and its biblical subtext*, 156–67. Cf. Revelation 2:10; 19:16; 20:4, where martyrs are singled out as inhabitants of paradise. Cf. Lang, *Himmel und Hölle*, 30–1; Segal, *Life after death*, 481. On the Church Fathers, who usually restrict direct access to paradise to martyrs, see Andræ, *Origines*, 168. For Jewish examples, see Volz, *Jüdische Eschatologie*, 377.

11 The perfect and the imperfect verb forms in the Qur'ān indicate an action's *aspect*, that is, whether it is concluded or still-to-be concluded, rather than its taking place in the past, present, or future. See Reuschel, *Aspekt und Tempus*, 211–17, 289. The Qur'ān's use of the perfect to indicate the eschatological future is mentioned neither in Reckendorf's *Syntaktische Verhältnisse* (1895) nor in Wright's *Grammar* (1896, 3rd ed.), but see Ewald, *Grammatica*, II, 347. I owe this reference to Holger Gzella.

12 *EQ*, s.v. Chronology of the Qur'ān, I, 316a-335a, at 318b (G. Böwering).

13 Cf. Dayeh, "Al-ḥawāmīm," 461–98, at 489.

14 I borrow this phrase from Tamer, *Zeit und Gott*, 187–214. Tamer speaks of the "disempowerment of time" in the Qur'ān (197–205) while also noting that "eschatology is the lance

Consequently, the *dunyā/ākhira* relationship in the Qurʾān should really not be understood in temporal terms alone. Indeed, what gives the Qurʾān its "depth, psychological subtlety, texture, and tone" is the overlap of earthly and otherworldly time, "the way the future is collapsed into the present."[15] Again, this suggests that equations of the Qurʾānic *al-ākhira* with the "*after*-life," "*after*world," or "the end"[16] should be revisited, for such renderings imply a linear conception of time that is alien to Qurʾānic eschatology.[17] The difference between *al-dunyā* and *al-ākhira* in the Qurʾān is, rather, one of space.

Or is it? It is true, the Qurʾān pictures paradise as a remote heavenly realm, accessed vertically through the "gates of heaven" (7:40). One ascends towards these gates over ladders (*maʿārij*, 70:3) or sky-ropes (*asbāb*, 40:36–7) that hold the edifice of the cosmos in place.[18] These "courses high above" offer an escape through the roof (*saqf*, 21:32) of the world, towards the other side of the firmament – but only to select beings such as prophets and angels. The outcast Iblīs (Satan) as well as demons who try to breach these gates and eavesdrop on the Heavenly Council (*al-malaʾ al-aʿlā*) are repelled by star-hurling angels (37:6–10).[19] Paradise, "a great kingdom" (76:20), stretches out over the entire width of the cosmic roof: it is "a garden whose breadth (*ʿaraḍ*) is like that of heaven and earth" (57:21). Paradise, in other words, sits on top of the heavenly dome, which stretches out like a tent fixed to the earth by tent pegs (78:6–7).

However, the Qurʾān also suggests in several places that the garden of Eden is located somewhere in the high regions *of the earth*: God tells Adam and Eve to "go down [from it]" (*ihbiṭū*, 2:36, 7:24, passim), as if from a mountain. This can be compared to a Qurʾānic verse in which Moses tells the Israelites to "go down to Egypt" (*ihbiṭū Miṣr*, 2:61), as in general the verb *habaṭa*, in the Qurʾān, tends to signify a horizontal or diagonal movement rather than a vertical one.[20] The image of a stratified paradise mountain, which finds further elaboration in the Qurʾān (see the following text),

directed in the Qurʾān against the pagans" (198). See also Neuwirth, "Qurʾanic readings," 775; Stowasser, *The day begins at sunset*, 31. Michael Morony notes similar arguments by early seventh-century Christian theologians (in particular Babai the Great, d. 628 CE) against "the belief in fate at the end of the Sasanian period." See Morony, *Iraq after the Muslim conquest*, 427.

[15] Sells, *Approaching the Qurʾān*, 24. Sells argues with regard to the early revelations in particular, but his points seems applicable to the entire Qurʾān.

[16] Rahman, *Major Themes*, 106.

[17] Cf. Brown, "The apocalypse of Islam," 372–3.

[18] Van Bladel, "Heavenly cords," 231.

[19] On the "outcast" (*rajīm*) Iblīs and other repelled angels, see Reynolds, *The Qurʾān and its biblical subtext*, 54–64. On the many possible meanings of Qurʾānic *rajīm*, see Silverstein, "On the original meaning."

[20] Cf. Q 2:24, 2:36, 2:38, 2:61, 7:13, 7:24, 11:48, 20:123. In Q 2:74, the stones on earth "prostrate themselves in awe of God" (*yahbiṭu min khashiyat Allāh*), but they do not "fall down."

suggests a physical connection between paradise and earth. It also bears mentioning that *janna*, in the Qur'ān, is the word for both otherworldly and earthly gardens (for the latter usage, see 26:57, 44:25–6, and passim) – only in later times was a distinction made in Arabic between *janna* as the eschatological garden, and *ḥadīqa* or *bustān* as its earthly counterpart.[21] We shall come back to this tension between a vertical and a horizontal conception of paradise in due course; suffice it here to note that paradise, in the Qur'ān, is not neatly separated from the earth.

There are fewer clues about the cosmological and structural coordinates of hell in the Qur'ān. According to Q 6:35, there are two ways to cross over into the otherworld: either one ascends into the heavens, or one "seeks a hole in the earth" and goes down into it – one presumes into the subterranean hell-pit. There are "seven gates" of hell, each of which leads into a separate compartment inhabited by a different class of the damned (15:44). Hell is likened to a trench (85:4)[22] and to a structure with a brink (*shafā*, 9:109). On Judgement Day, all people will be made to "kneel around hell" to look into the abyss; only the god-fearing will be picked out and lifted into paradise (19:68–72).[23] In another verse, hell is said to have a "lowest level" (*al-dark al-asfal*, 4:145), which indicates that it is a terraced funnel or a building with storeys, supported by columns (104:8–9).[24] The Qur'ān suggests that the sun, whose heat is known to cause havoc on earth (18:90), derives its fire from hellfire: it is said to set in the west in a "fetid [boiling?] spring" (*'ayn ḥami'a*, 18:86). One infers from this that during the night it traverses the netherworld, where it takes in a supply of fire before at dawn it rises in the east.[25]

When creation is undone during the apocalypse, paradise and hell do not perish together with "whosoever is on the earth" (55:26), then to be recreated anew; instead, as the Qur'ān puts it, they are "brought near" (26:90–1) to the place where the resurrected are gathered. There they are shown to those who are waiting to be judged.[26] It is as if the pegs on which the cosmic tent rests are knocked out, so that the roof collapses onto the tent's foundation. Paradise and hell are now so close that their inhabitants can see each other and talk (57:13–5); only a "partition" (*ḥijāb*, 7:46) or "wall" (*sūr*, 57:13) separates them.

In sum, while the Qur'ān is unequivocal about the difference in *value* of *al-dunyā* and *al-ākhira*, it does not make a neat temporal distinction between the two. Neither is the spatial divide between them clear-cut. Paradise and

[21] See Hämeen-Anttila, "Paradise and nature in the Quran."
[22] On the interpretation of this verse as a reference to hell, see the following text, pp. 61–2.
[23] See Andræ, *Ursprung*, 232–4, who also notes other possible interpretations of this passage.
[24] Cf. Rüling, *Beiträge*, 28.
[25] See *EQ*, s.v. Fire, II, 210a-213a, at 212a (H. Toelle).
[26] The image resembles that sketched in 4 *Ezra* 7:36 rather closely.

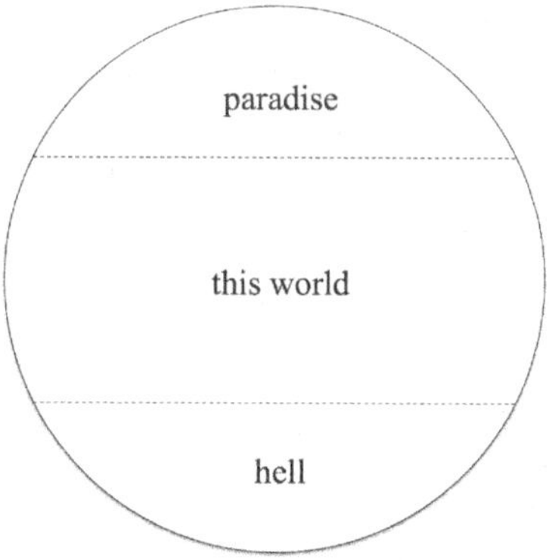

CHART 3. *Al-dunyā* and *al-ākhira* as *merismos.*

hell are contiguous with the earth, to the extent that to-and-fro movement remains possible, at least potentially. Paradise and hell exercise a certain apocalyptic pressure on the earth. Hell, as one verse has it, is an "ambush" (78:21). The otherworld threatens to invade this world on that momentous day, near at hand, "when the sky is stripped, when hell is set ablaze, and when the Garden is brought near" (81:11–13). The world that humankind inhabits is thus squeezed in between heaven and hell, while all three realms form an integrated whole, reality *in toto* (see Chart 3).[27]

The Joys and Torments of the Qur'ānic Paradise and Hell

In the Qur'ānic paradise there is "neither [excessive] sun nor cold" (76:13) but rather the refreshing comfort of a landscape characterised by lush green and shaded cool (77:41). Abundant water is found in springs and rivers that flow through this landscape (16:31). In one place the Qur'ān specifies that there are rivers of water, milk, wine, and honey (47:15). Vegetation consists in meadows (*rawḍa*, 30:15), palms and pomegranate trees (55:68), vineyards (78:32), acacias (*ṭalḥ*, 56:29), and a version of the evergreen Jujube tree (*sidr*, 56:28).

The Qur'ān differentiates between two categories of inhabitants of paradise (56:7–10).[28] There are "those who precede [others in faith or status]" (*al-sābiqūn*), a group also referred to as "those who are brought near [to God]" (*al-muqarrabūn*, 56:11), comprising both humans and angels (cf. 4:172). A marginally lower rank seems occupied by the "companions of the

[27] *EQ*, s.v. Spatial relations, V, 104a–108b, at 105a (A. Neuwirth).

[28] See also Q 4:95–6: "Those who strive, in preference to those who sit still, are promised degrees of rank from Him."

right" (*aṣḥāb al-maymana*, 90:18).[29] Sura 55, in fact, speaks of two separate gardens sitting on top of each other (55:46–58 and 55:62–76); this may in fact refer to the division between the two classes.[30] A special status in paradise is also reserved for the inhabitants of the "lofty chambers" (*ghuraf/ghurufāt*, 29:58, 34:37), a kind of *belétage* with further "chambers built over them" (39:20). Such stratificatory concepts possibly reflect the idea of gardens built on terraces on the slope of a hill or mountain (cf. 69:22, 88:10), a notion that might explain the Qur'ānic phrase that rivers flow "beneath" these gardens and chambers (*min taḥtihā*, 2:25, 39:20), that is, in the depressions running between the hills.[31]

The blessed will experience no fatigue (15:48) and their faces will be "radiant" from the joy of seeing God (75:22–3; cf. 83:24, 88:8).[32] It is also stated that the wives of the believers are "purified" (*muṭahhara*, 2:25, 3:15, 4:57) when they join their husbands in paradise.[33] Otherwise, the bodies of the blessed are largely the same that they possessed on earth, with the exception that they are lavishly adorned with clothes and jewellery: the inhabitants of paradise are clad in "green garments made of silk and brocade" (18:31, cf. 76:21, 22:23), and they wear bracelets of silver and gold (76:21, 22:23).

The material culture of the Qur'ānic paradise is rich: people dwell in palaces (25:10) and luxurious tents (55:72), lounging on "raised couches" (56:34) that are arranged in rows (52:20) and bedecked with carpets and cushions (88:15–6). Of physical pleasures there are plenty. Delicious fruit, dates, grapes, and pomegranates are readily available (55:68). Fruit clusters lower themselves into reach over the heads of the happy couch sitters (76:14). Meat (52:22) and fowl (56:21) are likewise served, as is a wine "whose seal is musk" (83:26) and that is variously mixed with the water of fountains called *tasnīm* (83:26–7) and *salsabīl* (76:18), or with camphor (76:5) and ginger (76:17). "Immortal youths" (76:19, cf. 52:24) present drinks in cups of silver and glass (76:15–6) on trays of gold (43:71). Although the connection is not explicitly made, the houris, "doe-eyed women" (*ḥūr ʿīn*, 44:54),[34] also belong into this context of a paradisiacal banquet. The inhabitants are

[29] On the "companions of the right" and the "companions on the left," cf. Matthew 25:34 and 25:41.

[30] Cf. Horovitz, "Das koranische Paradies," 55–6.

[31] Paret, *Kommentar*, 14–5 (*ad* Q 2:25). For an alternative and, in my view, more cogent explanation, see the following text, p. 58.

[32] That the vision of God's face is the greatest joy of the inhabitants of paradise is not stated as clearly in the Qur'ān as in the later exegetical literature. Cf. Grimme, *Mohammed*, II, 161.

[33] Note also that God "purifies" (*yuzakkī*) the blessed on the Day of Resurrection (2:174), but II *z-k-y* denotes moral rather than physical cleansing, while II *ṭ-h-r* is both.

[34] On the meaning of *aḥwar* (fem. *ḥawrāʾ*, pl. *ḥūr*) as "doe-eyed," or "having eyes in which the white is clearly distinguished from the black," see Fischer, *Farb- und Formbezeichnungen*, 57, 62.

wedded to these virginal "high-bosomed" maidens (52:20, 56:36–8, 78:31) as a "recompense for what they have done" (56:24). However, in comparison with the culinary pleasures and the extravagant material riches enjoyed by the blessed, sexuality in the Qurʾānic paradise is a rather subdued affair: the houris are "of modest gaze" (*qāṣirāt al-ṭarf*, 37:48–9; 38:52; 55:56); they are "restrained in tents" (55:72) "like hidden pearls" (56:23).[35] The houris, in other words, comply with what the Qurʾān enjoins upon pious men and women on earth, namely to "lower the gaze" (*ghaḍḍ al-abṣār*) and safeguard chastity (24:30–1). As for the married couples who enter paradise together, the Qurʾān delicately intimates congress by noting that "they recline on couches in the shade" (36:56).

The blessed enjoy the company of their family (52:21), including their forefathers, spouses, and children (13:23), although the Qurʾān is also very clear that fathers and sons cannot intercede for each other on the Day of Judgement (3:10, 3:116, 31:33, 60:3, 80:34–6), as in general intercession seems categorically denied (see, e.g., 2:48, 2:123). By contrast, some verses aver that intercession is possible "by His [God's] permission" (2:255; 10:3; passim). Angels may intercede (40:7), and the Prophet is encouraged to "seek forgiveness for your sin, and for the believers, men and women" (47:19), although this probably only indicates that he should pray for God's mercy. This is a tension that remains unresolved.[36]

One point that is stressed repeatedly is the absence of "idle chatter" or "imputations" in paradise (52:23; cf. 78:35, 88:11). Instead, the inhabitants of paradise greet each other with the word "Peace!" (19:62), a salutation that is also directed to them by the angels (13:24) and by God (36:58). The blessed are free from rancour (7:43). The serenity of their minds is perfectly undisturbed, as they are relieved of any anxiety about hell (21:103). In fact, as one verse has it, "they will not hear the slightest sound from it" (21:102). However, one also finds the notion that the blessed witness the torments in hell, talk to the damned (7:44, 7:50–1, 74:40–7),[37] and even laugh at them (83:34). In one particularly striking scene (37:50–7), two of the blessed muse about their lives on earth. "I had a comrade," says one, "who used to say: 'Are you [really] one of those who believe [the message]?' " "Will you look down?" suggests the other, and there he spots his former comrade "in the midst of hell." "By God," mutters the first to himself and to his acquaintance of old, "you almost destroyed me [by tempting me to disbelieve] ... I would have been one of those brought into hell."

[35] As Angelika Neuwirth notes, "[i]n spite of the prominence of the maidens' virginity (vv. 56.74), no erotic dynamics is perceivable between them and the blessed, who remain as unmoved as the maidens themselves, fixed to their luxurious seats." See Neuwirth, "Qur'anic readings," 762.

[36] For an overview, see *EQ*, s.v. Intercession, II, 551a-555b (V. Hoffman).

[37] Cf. 40:32, where the Day of Judgement is called *yawm al-tanādī*, the "Day of Mutual Calling."

The Qur'ānic landscape of hell is more developed and detailed than that of paradise.[38] In one place, it is said that the damned "go back and forth between" *jahannam* and "boiling hot water" (*ḥamīm*, 55:44), which appears to suggest that *jahannam* is a separate territorial unit within hell, adjacent to some kind of well or other body of water. There is also a spring with scalding hot water (88:5). Inside hell, there is a "searing wind" (56:42), and the damned are showered with "water like molten copper" (18:29). They live under a thick cloud of "black smoke" (56:43) and "coverings (*ghawāsh*) [of fire]" (7:41), as if under a canopy (*surādiq*, 18:29). This canopy, however, provides no more than the "shadow of three branches that gives no shade and is of no avail against the flame" (77:30–1, cf. 77:41), like a dry desert shrub that does not provide any coolness or comfort for the desperate who seek protection underneath it. While hell is in most cases pictured as a dystopian landscape, or a furnace (2:24), there are also a few instances in the Qur'ān in which *jahannam* is personified: it dialogues with God (50:30), roars and sighs (25:12),[39] and "almost bursts asunder with rage" (67:7–8). Also hell's appellation as *al-ḥuṭama* (104:4), "the Insatiable" or "the Crusher," suggests that it is conceived as a persona, or monster.

Presiding over hell are "harsh, severe angels who do not disobey God in what He commands them" (66:6), that is, to seize the damned "by the feet and forelocks" (55:41), beat them (8:50), and drag them back with "hooked iron rods" should they try to escape (22:21–2). There are nineteen of these angels (74:30). The Qur'ān also speaks of the "guardians" (*khazana*) of *jahannam* (39:71, 67:8). Finally, there are the enigmatic *zabāniya*, whom God calls forward on the Day of Judgement as a strike force to fight the unbelievers (96:18).

The inhabitants of hell are called the "companions of the left" (*aṣḥāb al-shimāl*, 56:41, cf. 56:9). They include both humans and jinn (11:119), as well as the fallen angel Iblīs (Satan) and his followers (7:18, 26:95). All these unlucky creatures are "heaped up on top of each other" and thrown into hell (8:37), where they are "flung into a narrow place" (25:13) and bound together with chains and fetters (69:30, 73:12, 76:4). The Qur'ān is a good deal more interested in the bodies of the damned than in those of the blessed in paradise. On the Day of Judgement, the damned are struck blind, deaf, and dumb (17:97), because they were blind to the truth in their earthly lives (17:72) and deaf to the message of the Qur'ān (41:4), during the recitation of which they used to encourage others to chat idly (41:26). Next to eyes, ears, and mouths, the face (*wajh*) as the seat of identity is targeted for punishment. While the believers, as the phrase has it, "surrendered their face" (*aslamū wajhahum*) to God (3:20), the unbelievers did not, and their faces

[38] This is also noted by Jones, "Paradise and hell," 107.

[39] The infinitives *zafīr* (25:12) and *shahīq* (in 67:7) denote the exhalation and inhalation of an ass. See Paret, *Kommentar*, 244 (*ad* Q 11:106). The donkey is said to have first produced its characteristic braying sound when seeing a demon. See Meier, *Bemerkungen*, I, 97.

are therefore burned in hell (21:39, 23:104) or blackened by dust (3:106, 80:40) "as though they were covered with pieces of night" (10:27). Hell's angels beat the damned on their faces (8:50) and drag them over the floor on them (17:97, 54:48).

The inhabitants of hell are clothed in rags of fire (22:19), boiling copper or pitch (14:50),[40] whereby their entire bodies are burned. To assure continuity of punishment, skins are renewed after each burning (4:56). In addition to their faces, their back side (*ẓahr*) is singled out for roasting (9:35, 21:39). This is a punishment that befits those who "turned their back" to God (17:46, 70:17), or those who cowardly "turned their backs" in battle (8:16). The general principle is that punishments of the damned are in "grades according to what they have done" (46:19). Bodies in hell are mutilated and fragmented, thus losing their power to bestow identity on the individual. When the damned are interrogated during the judgement, their hands, feet, and skins all acquire the ability to speak and "testify against them" (24:24, 41:20). The astonishment and horror these revolting body parts cause is calmly countered by their observation that "we have been given speech by God, who can give speech to everything" (41:21).

The annihilation of individuality is also effected through the bestialisation of the damned: as one of their punishments they drink scalding water "like camels desperate with thirst" (56:55);[41] they are driven like cattle "to the watering-place of the Fire" (11:98, cf. 19:86); in short, they are "like animals – nay, they are even further astray [from salvation]" (7:179). Next to the dragging on faces, beating, and burning, the damned are forced to imbibe pus (78:25), to drink "boiling water that tears apart their bowels" (47:15), and to eat thorny shrubs (*ḍarīʿ*, 88:6)[42] as well as the fruit of Zaqqūm (56:52). Zaqqūm, the Qur'ān tells us, is "a tree that comes out of the root of hell [and whose] spathes are like the heads of devils" (37:64–5). When the sinners eat from it, it boils in their bellies "like molten metal" (44:45). In one instance, branding of "foreheads, sides and backs" with molten gold and silver is also mentioned (9:35).

The psychological strain imposed on the damned is immense and no less prominent than spiritual joy is in paradise.[43] Paramount in the degradation

[40] Depending on whether one reads *qiṭrin ānin* ("boiling copper") or *qaṭirān* ("pitch").

[41] On the expression *fa-shāribūna shurba l-hīm* ("they are desperate of thirst, like camels"), see Bauer, "Relevance," 719–20.

[42] According to Heidi Toelle, this thorn shrub, called *ḍarīʿ*, is "a well known dry bush that also grows in the Najd and Tihāma (sometimes mentioned in ancient poetry as *the* exemplary bad pasture since it dries the she-camel's udders)." See *EQ*, s.v. Fire, II, 210a-214a, at 211a (H. Toelle).

[43] *Pace EQ*, s.v. Eschatology, II, 44a-54a, at 50b (J. I. Smith), where it is stated that the Qur'ān portrays the torments in hell "in physical rather than spiritual or psychological terms," while suggesting that the Qur'ānic paradise offers above all "a kind of joy that exceeds the pleasures of the flesh" (ibid., II, 51a).

of sinners is the loss of honour and bodily integrity, particularly the disgrace of losing face and the power to control limbs, but also that of being in chains and locked up like in a prison. Time and again the Qur'ān stresses that the sinners in hell are reviled and humiliated (6:124, 17:18, 25:69, 40:60). They are "exposed" (42:45). As if in a shaming ritual, sinners are resurrected with a sign of their sin "hung around their necks" (3:180). In their misery, the damned voice bitter regret over their past behaviour (26:102), cry out to God to "take us out [of hell]" (35:37), and eventually, proclaim their wish to be annihilated (43:77). By a final twist of cruelty, they constantly quarrel among themselves (26:96), wishing an equally or more severe punishment on those who misled them into unbelief (38:61).

The Development of Qur'ānic Eschatology

The preceding sketch, which makes no claim to originality,[44] has served us to take stock of the reservoir of Qur'ānic images of paradise and hell and to point out some of its salient features. This approach is vulnerable to criticism inasmuch as it coincides rather too neatly with conventional, synchronic understandings of Qur'ānic eschatology as they developed in Muslim exegesis (*tafsīr*), the earliest surviving examples of which date to more than a hundred years after the proclamation of the Qur'ān. Indeed, such a conventional reading of Qur'ānic eschatology misses a crucial aspect: the historical, processual dimension of the Qur'ān, that is, the gradual development of its eschatological imagery over the course of its gestation as a text and redaction in a codex (*muṣḥaf*).

The problem is, famously, that the Qur'ān is not ordered chronologically, and whether the actual chronological sequence of suras and verses can be reconstructed is a matter of controversy among scholars. Were such a chronology available, it might help our understanding of Qur'ānic eschatology in important respects: the rise of certain images and ideas could then be linked to the sociopolitical environment to which they respond; later eschatological passages could be shown to clarify or reinterpret earlier ones; and certain inconsistencies, a number of which have already been alluded to, might be resolved in historical perspective. For example, it can be argued that the Qur'ānic doctrine of intercession (*shafāʿa*) develops towards a more rigorously conceived monotheism, the notion that God alone decides the otherworldly destiny of humankind, and that not even the prophets and angels may intercede on behalf of others.[45]

44 Similar synchronic overviews include Grimme, *Mohammed*, II, 154–65; Pautz, *Muhammeds Lehre*, 201–20 (§ 9. Eschatologie), especially 212ff. (with Christian and Jewish parallels); El-Saleh, *Vie future*, 15–22; Toelle, *Le Coran revisité*, 23–69. See also *EQ*, s.v. Paradise, 12a-20a (L. Kinberg); ibid., s.v. Hell and Hellfire, II, 414a-420a (R. W. Gwynne).

45 Huitema, *De voorspraak*, 13–4. Cf. Wensinck, *Muslim creed*, 180–1; *EQ*, s.v. Intercession, II, 551a-555b (V. Hoffman).

The traditional narrative in both Muslim and Western scholarship is that around the year 610 CE, Muḥammad first began reciting the *qur'ān* (cf. Syr. *qeryānā*, "lectionary"), the text units that he claimed had been revealed to him, and that he continued in this vein, more or less without interruption, until his death in 632 CE. Many scholars will also agree that this process of proclamation of the Qur'ān should be measured against the biography (*sīra*) of the Prophet, the basic outlines of which are (1) that Muḥammad started out in his hometown Mecca, a cultic centre linked into the larger Late Antique religious context of Greater Syria and Arabia, as a charismatic preacher and warner (*nadhīr*) of an impending hell and bringer of good tidings (*bashīr*) of a coming paradise; (2) that he and his followers were ostracised by the Meccan community, which precipitated their migration (*hijra*) to Yathrib (some 350 kilometres north of Mecca); and (3) that in Yathrib, an oasis known in later times as Medina that was marked by the presence of both Arab and Jewish tribes, Muḥammad's fortunes changed and that he became the influential leader of a movement of "believers" (*mu'minūn*).

Assuming these basic parameters, it makes sense to approach the Qur'ān not as an internally consistent text but to see in it the gradual evolution of ideas and images that respond to shifting moral and sectarian contexts, "the drama of a controversy with others, marked by trial and error."[46] On this view, the style and the content of the Qur'ān would have changed according to the periods of its proclamation. The periods established by the German scholars Theodor Nöldeke und Gustav Weil in 1860 and 1944 – a chronological paradigm that continues to be used, although with modifications, by many scholars today – adhere to the following four divisions: (1) early Meccan (*ca.* 610–14); (2) middle Meccan (*ca.* 614–7); (3) late Meccan (*ca.* 617–22); and (4) Medinan (*ca.* 622–32). While some will go so far as to propose, with Nöldeke, a precise sequence of suras within each period,[47] others see this kind of endeavour as marred by "pseudo-preciseness" and prefer to forego exact chronological ordering, contenting themselves with clustering suras into four main periods.[48] At any rate, to postulate that in the Qur'ān a development of ideas takes place that coincides with the history of the nascent community of Muḥammad's followers remains, as also the critics of this approach concede, "a feasible ... method of interpreting the Quranic data," even though it is "hardly the only" one.[49]

[46] Neuwirth, *Koran*, 136.

[47] For the early Meccan suras, see Sinai, "The Qur'an as process." Sinai suggests that an exact chronological ordering of suras is also possible for the other three periods.

[48] Jones, "Introduction," 11. Jones clusters the suras as follows. Early Meccan suras: 1, 51–3, 55–6, 68–70, 73–5, 77–97, 99–109, 111–14 (forty-eight suras); middle Meccan: 15, 17–21, 23, 25–7, 36–8, 43–4, 50, 54, 67, 71–2, 76 (twenty-one suras); late Meccan: 6–7, 10–14, 16, 28–32, 34–5, 39–42, 45–6 (twenty-one suras); Medinan: 2–5, 8–9, 22, 24, 33, 47–9, 57–66, 98, 110 (twenty-four suras).

[49] Wansbrough, *Quranic studies*, 2. Also Reynolds, "Le problème," 501, grants that a chronological reading of the Qur'ān remains one "plausible" approach among others. Whatever

It is the aim of this section to examine how well a Nöldekian chronological framework can account for Qur'ānic eschatology. Two broad dynamics seem to emerge from such a Nöldekian reading. There is, firstly, a tendency to displace certain pagan elements in a process of aligning the eschatological imagery of the Qur'ān more closely with biblical traditions. Secondly, propelled by the changing fortunes of the nascent community of believers, the Qur'ān appears to develop a fuller soteriology and cosmology, in line with an evolving and increasingly radical monotheism.

Previous scholarship has sought to trace certain Nöldekian patterns in regard to the names given to paradise and hell. For example, in the early Meccan period, *naʿīm* ("delight") is the word that is associated with *janna* most frequently.[50] It has been suggested that the expression *jannat/jannāt al-naʿīm* ("garden/s of delight") was known in the early Meccan period as the usual Arabic rendering of the Hebrew *gan ʿeden*.[51] However, the Qur'ānic *jannāt ʿadn*, a literal translation of *gan ʿeden*, makes the link with the biblical phrase more palpable. The expression comes to be used interchangeably with *jannat/jannāt al-naʿīm* from the middle Meccan period onwards[52] and is commonest in late passages.[53]

The late Meccan period is, according to the traditional biography of the Prophet, a time of trial and suffering for Muḥammad, marked by the death of his first wife Khadīja, by the failed attempt to gain support for his movement in the neighbouring city of al-Ṭā'if, and by intensified persecution at the hands of the Meccan Quraysh. These difficult circumstances may have led some of Muḥammad's supporters to abandon his cause, and this appears to find an echo in late Meccan passages. Q 40:47 assigns some of "the weak" to hellfire because of their sin of having followed "the proud" (cf. 14:12, 34:31–3). As names of paradise that stress the aspect of salvation and safety in paradise, *dār al-qarār* ("the abode of security," 40:39) and *dār al-salām* ("the abode of peace," 6:127, 10:25) are now mentioned for the first time,[54] as in general the greatest variety of names of paradise is found in the middle

one's preferences in this matter, the statement that a comparison between Meccan and Medinan paradise descriptions is "superfluous" seems gratuitous. See *EQ*, s.v. Paradise, IV, 12a-20a, at 19a (L. Kinberg).

[50] O'Shaughnessy, *Eschatological themes*, 90.

[51] Obermann, "Islamic origins," 107.

[52] Horovitz, "Das koranische Paradies," 60–1.

[53] Jeffery, *Foreign vocabulary*, 212. Horovitz points out that *gan ʿeden* was the common name for the heavenly paradise in postbiblical Jewish but not in Christian Syriac literature (where the term is mostly used to refer to the protological garden, as in the Hebrew Bible); hence *jannāt ʿadn* appears to be a borrowing from Jewish tradition. See Horovitz, "Das koranische Paradies," 61. The term *ʿilliyyūn* (83:18–9), most likely a calque on Hebr. *ʿelyōn* ("high, most high"), and the expression *jannat al-ma'wā* ("garden of refuge") also belong to the first Meccan period, while in the middle Meccan period *firdaws* ("Paradise," 23:11) and *jannat al-khuld* ("garden of eternity," 25:15) are introduced, in addition to *jannāt ʿadn*.

[54] O'Shaughnessy, *Eschatological themes*, 100.

and late Meccan periods. In the Medinan vignettes of paradise, by contrast, it is the stereotypical plural form *jannāt* ("gardens") that is used.

Jahannam, the name most often used for hell in the Qur'ān (seventy-seven occurrences), appears throughout all four periods,[55] but *jaḥīm*, the second most frequent term (twenty-six occurrences), seems to have been abandoned some time during the middle Meccan period (even though it reappears once in the late Meccan period, and six times in the Medinan period).[56] A possible explanation for this phenomenon is that the name *jahannam* evokes in a more direct manner the biblical "valley of Hinnom" (Hebr. *gē-hinnōm*, Joshua 15:8, Jeremiah 7:31, 32:35), which the Talmudists and Late Antique Syriac authors equated with hell.[57] *Jaḥīm* is farther away from this meaning and overall more obscure.[58] Like the gradual transition from *jannat/jannāt al-na'īm* to *jannāt 'adn*, this shift in emphasis appears to illustrate a certain biblicisation of Qur'ānic eschatology that set in during the middle Meccan period.

The same tendency towards biblicisation can also be observed with regard to the topography of paradise and hell. For example, in four early and in six middle Meccan suras we read of the springs in paradise.[59] In late Meccan and in Medinan suras these springs become rivers, which are mentioned more than forty times.[60] Springs and wells are the dominant bodies of water in the Arabian Peninsula; the introduction of rivers into the Qur'ānic paradise appears to have been a gradual move away from Arabian imagery, culminating in the transposition of the four rivers of Genesis 2:10[61] to the Islamic paradise in sura 47, a sura considered by many to be among the last of the Medinan period (47:15).

If one entertains the chronology proposed by scholars working in the tradition of Nöldeke, it also results that the second Meccan period sees the gradual disappearance of the houris, who are last mentioned in Q 44:54. At the same time, from the second Meccan period, the earthly wives of believers are explicitly included among the inhabitants of paradise (43:70). In the Medinan period, they become "purified spouses" (*azwāj muṭahhara*,

55 It should be noted, however, that some Western scholars, in particular Bell and Blachère, regard all five early Meccan occurrences of *jahannam* as later insertions. See the references given in O'Shaughnessy, "The seven names," 457n5.

56 Ibid., 451–5.

57 Jeffery, *Foreign vocabulary*, 105; Braun, "Beiträge," 303; Geiger, *Was hat Muhammed*, 48–9.

58 O'Shaughnessy suggests that *jaḥīm* is a syncopated form of Eth. *gahannam*. See O'Shaughnessy, "The seven names," 452–3. However, cf. Zamitt, *A comparative lexical study*, 595.

59 15:45 (middle Meccan), 26:57, 26:134, 26:147 (middle Meccan), 36:34 (middle Meccan), 37:45 (middle Meccan), 44:25, 44:52 (middle Meccan), 51:15 (early Meccan), 55:50, 55:66 (early Meccan), 76:6, 76:18 (middle Meccan), 77:41 (early Meccan), 83:28 (early Meccan), 88:5 (a spring in hell), 88:12 (early Meccan).

60 Cf. *EQ*, s.v. Water of paradise, 466a-467a (A. El-Zein).

61 Also in the *Apocalypse of Paul*, Paul sees four rivers in paradise. See *Apocalypse of Paul*, 23.

2:25, 3:15, 4:57). Agreeably, the expression "purified spouses" cannot refer to the houris who, as heavenly beings that are separately "produced" (cf. 56:35), are not in need of ritual cleansing.[62] In the third Meccan period (13:23, 40:8), the "righteous" fathers and the children of the believers are brought in to complement the promise that families will enter paradise intact.[63] The family oriented picture that emerges corresponds to the fact that after the middle Meccan period the Qurʾān offers no more descriptions of wine banquets in paradise.[64] Along similar lines, it has been suggested that the Medinan suras develop a more spiritual conception of the pleasures of paradise.[65] While the descriptions of the Garden, as has been noted in the preceding text, become increasingly formulaic and abstract, the term *riḍwān* ("divine favour") appears among the rewards in the heavenly abode. As it is put in a sura that is considered to be among the late Medinan ones, "God has promised the believers ... good dwellings in the Garden of Eden; but [to receive] divine favour is greater (*wa-riḍwān min Allāh akbar*)" (9:72).

The *zabāniya*, hell's counterparts of the heavenly houris, also seem to have undergone a crisis of identity in the second and third Meccan periods, although they reappear triumphantly in the Medinan period, albeit under changed guise. Sura 96, the very first sura of the Qurʾān according to Nöldeke's chronology, takes aim at those who oppose Muḥammad's message and who will "call their hosts" (96:17) to support them. "Let them," the Qurʾān dramatically retorts, "for we shall call on the *zabāniya*" (96:18). The "hosts" (*nādiya*) of Muḥammad opponents appear to be supernatural beings or pagan deities (whose existence the Qurʾān thus implicitly acknowledges) of the Meccan polytheists. As for the *zabāniya*, these appear to be lesser divine beings[66] forming the strike force of the god of Muḥammad – they will seize his opponents "by the forelock" (96:15, cf. 55:41), a gesture expressing humiliation and unrestricted power over life and death.[67] Tantalisingly, it has been suggested that the cryptic name *zabāniya* refers

[62] *Pace* Bell and Watt, *Introduction*, 162, who state that "it is not clear whether these [the purified spouses] are the houris or the actual believing wives."

[63] Horovitz, "Das koranische Paradies," 57. Already Q 52:21 promises that believers will be joined with their "off-spring." Sura 52 is held to be early Meccan, but verse 21, given its unusual length, is identfied by Nöldeke as a later insertion. See Nöldeke, *Geschichte*, I, 105.

[64] Horovitz, "Das koranische Paradies," 58.

[65] El-Saleh, *Vie future*, 11.

[66] Bell and Watt also comment on the existence of a number of "lesser divine beings" in the Qurʾān, before the turn towards a purer form of monotheism. See Bell and Watt, *Introduction*, 117, 149.

[67] According to Q 7:150 and 20:93, Moses drags Aaron by his "head" (*ra's*, 7:150) [i.e. his hair] and beard (*liḥya*, 20:93), accusing him of having instigated the worshipping of the calf. Angelika Neuwirth states that 96:15 is "perhaps a meristic expression with intensifying intent." See Neuwirth, "Qurʾanic readings," 760. Cf. eadem, *Handkommentar*, 272 (*ad* Q 96:15–6).

to a class of Arabian demons.[68] The verse that "nineteen [*zabāniya*?] are set over it [hell]" (74:30), another early Meccan verse, does little to clarify the identity of these enigmatic creatures.[69] The other early Meccan verses dealing with the personnel of hell present them either as torturers (69:30–32; cf. 44:47–50 [middle Meccan]) or, in an ironic reversal of the role played by the houris as attendants at the heavenly banquet, as hosts of the infernal meal of boiling water and Zaqqūm (56:51–6, 88:5).

In the suras of the middle Meccan period, the notion of hell as an eschatological monster, which is adumbrated by the (early Meccan) name *ḥuṭama* ("glutton [?]"), is further developed (25:12, 50:30), and the *zabāniya* acquire another function: they become the "keepers" (*khazana*) of this beast (67:7–8; cf. 39:71 [late Meccan]). Q 43:77 introduces a figure addressed by the tortured in hell as *mālik* ("master"), whom they beg to intercede with God to grant them death and an end to their sufferings. Commentators and translators generally see in *mālik* a proper name, and an angel named Mālik thus becomes the chief of hell's angels.[70] This meaning, however, is not evident from the Qur'ān. In fact, the early codices (*maṣāḥif*) of the Qur'ān, purported to go back to the first two centuries of Islam, offer various alternative spellings and vocalisations,[71] which suggests that the earliest authorities for the transmission of the Qur'ān were unsure about the meaning of the word. While it is better to err on the side of caution, in this case one wonders whether the correct reading of the skeletal form (*rasm*) of the word in question (*m-l-k*) is not simply *malak*, or "angel." This reading would not only have the virtue of being considerably less complicated than what is found in tradition. Additionally, it is a reading that makes particularly good sense if we imagine a situation in which the realisation that the punishers in hell are angels, not some other class of demonic beings, had just begun to dawn on the audience of the Qur'ān.[72]

In the late Meccan period, the notion that the torturers in hell are angels is not yet spelt out fully, even if an "angel of death" (*malak al-mawt*) is introduced who "will gather you; then to your Lord you will be returned" (32:11). It is only in the Medinan period that angels are explicitly said to form the troops of hell (4:97; 8:50; 66:6). A Medinan explanatory gloss is inserted into the early Meccan sura 74 to drive the point home and to clarify the meaning of the number nineteen in Q 74:30. The vagueness of

[68] Grimme, *Mohammed*, I, 19. Cf. Paret, *Kommentar*, 516 (*ad* 96:9–19). See now, also in support of this derivation, Lange, "Revisiting hell's angels," 79–83.

[69] On the nineteen, see the following text, p. 63–4.

[70] Thus, e.g., Paret (tr.), *Koran*, 347; Abdel Haleem (tr.), *Qur'ān*, 496, Berque (tr.), *Coran*, 533; Leemhuis (tr.), *Koran*, 337.

[71] Variant readings for *mālik* include *māli* (attributed to Ibn Masʿūd, ʿAlī, Ibn Yaʿmar, al-Rabīʿ b. Khuthaym), *maliku* (attributed to Ibn Masʿūd, ʿAlī, al-Aʿmash), and *mālu* (attributed to Ibn Masʿūd, ʿAlī, Ibn Waththāb). See Jeffery, *Materials*, 88, 190, 303, 325.

[72] For a fuller articulation of this argument, see Lange, "Revisiting hell's angels," 89–91.

this verse, it appears, had triggered a polemical reaction from Muḥammad's opponents. "We have appointed only angels to be the masters of the Fire (*aṣḥāb al-nār*)," proclaims the interpolated verse, "and We have appointed their number simply as an affliction for the unbelievers.... No one knows the troops of your Lord but He" (74:31).[73] In sum, the Qur'ān appears to move from picturing a group of violent, possibly demonic mercenaries of God towards suggesting a more subsidiary and subservient role of these creatures as the nurses of *jahannam* and, finally, towards asserting their angelic nature while stressing God's omniscience and omnipotence.[74]

The processes of biblicisation hitherto discussed go hand in hand with a number of adjustments in Qur'ānic theology, pointing in the direction of a more radically conceived monotheism and moralism. For example, the notion of God's omnipotence includes His ability to mete out reward and punishment eternally. Early Meccan descriptions of paradise and hell do not mention everlasting reward and perpetual punishment; to the contrary, in the only early Meccan verse that deals with the duration of life in the otherworld, the damned are threatened that they will linger in hell "for ages" (*aḥqāb^an*, 78:23) – but not forever. Middle Meccan verses, however, state in several instances that the inhabitants of paradise "do not taste death, except the first death [on earth]" (44:56)[75] and that the damned in hell "remain in it forever" (21:99, 23:103, 43:74, 72:23). This formula continues to be used throughout the late Meccan and the Medinan period (e.g., 10:26, 33:65). Perhaps, in addition to the wish to stress God's encompassing power, the less lenient view imposed itself as a result of the gradual decline in Muḥammad's relationship with the faith communities that rejected his mission. The Jews, notably, are accused in the Qur'ān of proclaiming that punishment in hell was "only for a limited number of days" (2:80).[76]

The emphasis on perpetual reward and punishment may have stimulated a more thorough reflection upon the conditions for salvation and divine forgiveness. An important Medinan update of an early Meccan passage occurs in sura 95. The categorical prediction of a debasing punishment for "man" (*al-insān*, 95:4–5) is relativised by the Medinan interpolation of the formula that "those who believe and do righteous deeds are excepted" (95:6).[77] Not only does this interpolation circumscribe the threat of universal damnation, which so worryingly appears to underlie Q 94:5–6, but it also achieves the aim of introducing into an early sura the mature Qur'ānic view of salvation,

[73] Cf. Nagel, *Medinensische Einschübe*, 89.

[74] See Lange, "Revisiting hell's angels."

[75] Cf. Horovitz, "Das koranische Paradies," 56. See also Q 23:11, 25:16, 25:76.

[76] See Volz, *Jüdische Eschatologie*, 288; Raphael, *Jewish Views*, 144–5; Crone, "Quranic *mushrikūn* [part I]," 446. On this particular "eschatological counter discourse" in the Qur'ān, see now also Azaiez, "Les contre-discours," 114.

[77] See Nöldeke, *Geschichte*, I, 97, 104. Nöldeke suggests that the phrase *alladhīna āmanū wa-'amilū l-ṣāliḥāt* is typical of late Meccan suras.

which stresses the need for both belief *and* works. As others have noted, God's proper name *al-raḥmān* ("the All-Merciful") is abandoned in the late Meccan period and subsumed under the more universal designation *Allāh*;[78] in Medinan paradise passages, the correlating noun *raḥma* ("mercy") is likewise abandoned and replaced with *maghfira* and *takfīr*, terms whose semantic range indicates that forgiveness is conditioned on the performance of good deeds.[79] This would correspond to the situation of Muḥammad's community in Medina, where the need for social organisation shifted emphasis to the ritual and legal sphere.[80] While Meccan suras often stress belief and fear of God (the *taqwā* of the "God-fearing," *muttaqūn*), the Medinan suras stereotypically enjoin the believers to "obey God and His messenger" and to "perform the ritual prayer and give alms." Eschatological imagery increasingly appears in tandem with the notion of human ethical accountability on earth, such that both become inextricably linked in the Qur'ān.[81]

Finally, on the level of cosmology, a number of developments also appear to occur. The first observation that can be made is that in the suras commonly considered to be early and middle Meccan, the terms *al-dunyā* and *al-ākhira* tend to be used not as nouns but as adjectives. This is particularly evident when the two terms are paired with *al-ḥayāt* ("life"), as in the expression *al-ḥayāt al-dunyā*, "the lower life." Even when *al-dunyā* and *al-ākhira* appear in isolation they seem to refer back closely to *al-ḥayāt*. However, in late Meccan and Medinan suras, the two terms emerge fully as independent nouns, and are now often paired with each other by way of a *merismos*, a figure of speech that denotes a whole defined by its two extremes (cf. Chart 3).[82] This process of reification corresponds to the tendency in late Meccan and in Medinan suras to use eschatological metonyms and vignettes rather than to reproduce the more detailed images of paradise and hell one encounters in early and middle Meccan suras. The Qur'ān appears to show some awareness of this phenomenon. A late Meccan sura speaks of the "picture (*mathal*) of the Garden," which it then sketches with three quick strokes of the brush: "rivers flow through it; its food is perpetual; and [so] is its shade" (13:35; cf. 47:15). The term *mathal* here seems to sum up the late Meccan and Medinan Qur'ānic use of the Garden and the Fire as icons rather than as fully painted *tableaux*.

This ossification of the concepts of *al-dunyā* and *al-ākhira* does not imply, however, that the Qur'ān in its later stages of gestation becomes less concerned with the otherworld, or that the charismatic excitement of the early

78 See Kiltz, "The relationship," 38–9.

79 *EQ*, s.v. God and His attributes, II, 316b-331b, at 317b-318a (G. Böwering). On the meaning of *al-raḥmān* in the Qur'ān see further Jomier, "Le nom divin."

80 O'Shaughnessy, *Eschatological themes*, 107.

81 Sinai, *Die heilige Schrift*, 78–87. Cf. *EQ*, s.v. Eschatology, II, 44a-54a, at 44b (J. I. Smith).

82 *EQ*, s.v. Spatial relations, V, 104a-108b, at 106a (A. Neuwirth).

days of the Qur'ān's proclamation makes way for the routinisation of eschatological sentiment.[83] Rather, it is a case of "enough said": the picture is already set, and thus the metonyms and vignettes suffice to conjure up the full spectre of eschatological bliss and torment; the audience's imagination, schooled on previous revelations, does the rest. When in the late Meccan and Medinan suras the Qur'ān *does* delve into a description of the otherworld, this happens with as much urgency as before. For example, the hell verses in sura 9 (vv. 34–5, 63, 68, 95–6, 109–10), a sura that is commonly thought to be very late, are as vivid as the hell passage in sura 74, held to be one of the earliest suras of all.[84]

As noted previously, in addition to the pair of *al-dunyā/al-ākhira*, the Qur'ān also uses the expression *al-ūlā wa-l-ākhira* ("the first [life/abode] and the last [life/abode]). All of the five suras in which this expression occurs (28:70, 53:25, 79:25, 92:13, 93:4) are commonly counted among the early Meccan suras, with the exception of sura 28, which is considered late Meccan. One may infer that the dichotomy of *al-ūlā/al-ākhira* gradually went out of fashion. It may be that the diachronic sequence of "now" and "then" that *al-ūlā/al-ākhira* implies was gradually enriched, perhaps even superseded by the pair *al-dunyā/al-ākhira* ("the nearest/furthest [world]"), because a shift occurred from a temporal to a more spatially conceived, synchronic understanding of the relationship between this world and the otherworld.

Qur'ānic Eschatology in Its Late Antique Context

In the preceding section, I have sought to trace a number of developments in the eschatological thought of the Qur'ān. I have suggested that one can observe a shift in two major respects. Firstly, Qur'ānic eschatology appears to become more aligned with biblical traditions. This can be seen in the changes that occur on the level of the names given to paradise and hell, the descriptions of the topography of the otherworld, and the gradual disappearance of seemingly pagan elements, such as the houris (who are replaced by the resurrected wives of the believers) and the demonic *zabāniya* (who become angels). Secondly, the Qur'ān appears to move towards a fuller and more elaborate doctrine of the otherworld, one that countenances retribution for belief *and* actions, corporal *and* spiritual pleasures, a more rigorous insistence on the eternality of punishment, and a vision of the *dunyā/ākhira* relationship as a *merismos*.

[83] One example among many, O'Shaughnessy, *Eschatological themes*, 108, speaks of "a weakening vigor of imagination and a dimning of the poetic fire of the early Meccan days." See also Donner, *Muhammad*, 80.

[84] Jones, "Paradise and hell," 110.

However, the usefulness and indeed the possibility of establishing a chronology of suras and verses is often doubted, sometimes flatly denied, by scholars of the Qur'ān.[85] It is suggested, instead, that the different discourses contained in the Qur'ān simply represent different layers compiled into one text. It is true that Nöldeke's model, on which the project of a processual reading of the Qur'ān rests, is undermined by other methods of dating Qur'ānic passages, not least in the area of eschatological thought. For example, a significant chunk of sura 18 has been shown, rather plausibly, to originate after the year 629 CE,[86] while Nöldeke places it, together with the entire sura, in the middle Meccan period, that is, in the years 616–8 CE.[87] As it happens, sura 18 includes important verses dealing with resurrection, paradise and hell. In fact, it is a prime witness for Qur'ānic eschatology in general.[88]

One is therefore well advised to complement, nuance, and, where appropriate, revise the intratextual study of Qur'ānic eschatology by an analysis of the Qur'ān's intertextual connections with the literatures of the Late Antique Near East and Arabia, in particular with the contemporary Arabic sources and the vast Judeo-Christian corpus of writings of the period. These two approaches do not preclude each other, although it might be argued that the more sharply the theological and ideological boundaries of the different Qur'ānic discourses are drawn, the less likely the assumption of a single authorship of the Qur'ān becomes – an assumption usually taken for granted by scholars who espouse Nöldeke's paradigm. What critical scholars across the board agree on, regardless, is that the Qur'ān ought to be understood as a text that presupposes familiarity with a range of other literary traditions, including biblical literature, Christian and Jewish exegetical and parenetic works, as well as Arabic poetry. Seen in this light, certain eschatological images and ideas in the Qur'ān move into sharper focus. In the following pages, a number of suggestive examples will be introduced to illustrate this point. A comprehensive study of the Late Antique context of Qur'ānic eschatology, a topic that deserves a separate, book-length investigation, is beyond the scope of this chapter.

We have noted that in the Qur'ān one finds both a horizontal and a vertical conception of the relationship between paradise and earth. Both

[85] See, e.g., Gabriel Reynolds, "Le problème."

[86] Van Bladel, "The Alexander Legend." Van Bladel bases his analysis on the Syriac *Alexander Legend*, a text composed between 628 and 630 CE that he argues is the direct source of Qur'ān 18:83–102. Cf. Dye, "Le Coran et son contexte," 257–9; Tesei, "The prophecy of Ḏū l-Qarnayn."

[87] Nöldeke, *Geschichte*, I, 140–3. Nöldeke voices some doubt whether the Dhū l-Qarnayn episode was really composed together with the other parts of the sura (ibid., 141), but he ends up defending the idea on the grounds of the shared end rhyme (ibid., 143).

[88] Massignon, *Opera minora*, I, 107–25, 142–61, II, 606–12, III, 104–18; idem, "Les 'sept dormants'"; Brown, "The apocalypse of Islam."

conceptions have deep roots in biblical and indeed prebiblical literature, and a careful reading of this literature occasionally produces fresh insights into the Qur'ān. In Late Antique Christian sources, there are many references to the idea that paradise, which these sources locate on the far margin of the earth, is connected to the inhabited world through subterranean water courses running underneath the saltwater ocean.[89] Through these courses, sweet water reaches this world. Assuming that the same cosmology underlies the Qur'ān, the recurring Qur'ānic phrase that there are rivers running "underneath" (*min taḥt*) the gardens of paradise (2:25, 39:20) suddenly makes a great deal of sense.[90] At the same time, passages in the Qur'ān that speak of a paradise in heaven also have suggestive parallels in Near Eastern Judeo-Christian tradition. For example, the text known as the *Slavonic Apocalypse of Enoch* (or simply as 2 *Enoch*), probably written in the first century CE and translated from the Greek into an array of languages including Hebrew and Aramaic,[91] places paradise in the "third heaven" (8:1). The third heaven is also where the apostle Paul, according to his own testimony, was "caught up to paradise" (2 Cor. 12:3–4). The presence of paradisiacal sweet water on earth is explained, in this model, by the phenomenon of rain. In several verses, the Qur'ān seems to entertain the biblical notion of a celestial sweet-water ocean, separated from the earthly saltwater ocean by the firmament (25:53, 35:12; cf. Gen 1:6–10).[92] God sends down water that is "blessed" and "pure" (25:48, 50:9; cf. 7:96, 8:11), and this heavenly water makes the terrestrial gardens flourish, which are described in ways reminiscent of the otherworldly garden (23:19; 50:9–11).[93]

In Late Antiquity, one also finds attempts to harmonise the two notions of a terrestrial and a heavenly, transcendental paradise. Already 2 *Enoch* states that the paradise of Eden is in the east,[94] and that it "is open as far as

[89] Ephrem, *Commentary on Genesis*, 101 (§ 2,6). Cf. idem, *Hymns of paradise* 2:6. See also Narsai, *Homélies*, I, 395–6. For further references, see Tesei, "Some cosmological notions," 21–5; Minov, "Regarder la montagne sacrée," 257.

[90] Tesei, "Some cosmological notions," 25. Cf. the suggestion by David Waines and Patricia Crone that the "rivers running underneath" correspond to Arabian underground irrigation channels. See *EQ*, s.v. Agriculture and vegetation, I, 41 (D. Waines); Crone, "How did the Quranic pagans," 391. To assert that "there is not a single river in all of Arabia," as does Rustomji, *The Garden and the Fire*, 65, seems not quite accurate.

[91] Cf. *EQ*, s.v. Idrīs, II, 484a-486a (Y. Erder), where it is suggested that Muḥammad was conversant with the Jewish Enoch tradition. Cf. Q19:56–7, 21:85.

[92] See Toelle, *Le Coran revisité*, 124–6; *EQ*, s.v. Springs and fountains, V, 121b-128b, at 126a-126b (M. Radscheit). Ps 104: 1–5, 13f., 19–23 also speaks of the cosmic "tent." On the ancient Near Eastern context of this image see Lumpe and Bietenhard, "Himmel." According to the early exegete Muqātil, the heavens are prevented from pouring out over the earth by the mountains, which serve as pegs (*awtād*) to keep the firmament in place. See Muqātil, *Tafsīr*, III, 736 (*ad* Q 41:10). Cf. Fahd, "La naissance du monde."

[93] See *EQ*, s.v. Springs and fountains, V, 121b-128b, at 126b (M. Radscheit).

[94] For other instances of the eastern paradise in ancient Judaism, see Bockmuehl, "Locating paradise," 196–8.

the third heaven," even though it is "closed off from this world" (42:3).[95] The most famous of the Late Antique Christian authors writing in Syriac, Ephrem of Nisibis (d. 373), in his *Hymns of Paradise*, embraces various cosmological models, among which is the conception of paradise as a "vertical corridor" *in between* this world and the otherworld.[96] The Syriac *Cave of Treasures* (prob. sixth c. CE) describes paradise as sitting on top of mountains so high that their height cannot be measured by earthly measurements, but only by the "measurements of the Holy Spirit" (3:15).[97] Such traditions seek to combine a horizontal and a vertical conception of paradise, to place paradise, paradoxically, on earth *as well as* in heaven. Paradise, on this view, remains "a land contiguous with ours," such that "[t]he seemingly utopian in fact undergirds and verifies the world we inhabit."[98] While no unified cosmology emerges from the Qur'ān, it is arguably this sense of paradise as the nexus of the corruptible and the incorruptible that leaves the most lasting impression.

Also in regard to the interior of paradise, there are things to be learned from a look at Late Antique literature. Take Q 7:46–50 as an example. This is the well known Qur'anic passage about the people who, on the Day of Judgement, are said to be on a place called *al-aʿrāf*, a term of uncertain meaning.[99] These people, the Qur'ān tells us, have a good view of both the inhabitants of paradise and of hell, unimpeded by the partition (*ḥijāb*) that separates the two abodes. They call out to the denizens of paradise to reassure them that the sinners "have not entered it [paradise], even though they desire [it]," while they tease the damned by pointing out the happiness of the blessed, "the ones you swore God would not reach with his mercy." As for the damned, they beg the blessed to pour water on them.[100] The majority of Muslim commentators argue that the "people on *al-aʿrāf*" are those Muslims whose good and evil works are equipoised and who therefore reside on top of a wall that separates paradise from hell.[101] In no other place, however, does the Qur'ān discuss or even allude to the possibility of such a limbo, a concept of enough theological weight to warrant the assumption

[95] This seems at odds with the passage cited earlier (8:2), which places paradise in the third heaven. That there are seven heavens above the earth (as is also stated in Q 78:12) is a universal notion in classic rabbinic literature. See *3 Enoch* 17:1–3 and 18:1–2, and the references provided by the translator, P. Alexander, in the introduction to the text (p. 329).

[96] See Séd, "Les hymnes," 458–9. Cf. Minov, "Regarder la montagne sacrée," 250–1.

[97] *Meʿarrat gazze*, I, 25 (tr. II, 11). See on this passage, Ri, *Commentaire*, 159–60.

[98] Bockmuehl, "Locating paradise," 209.

[99] See *EQ*, s.v. People of the Heights, IV, 46b-48b (W. Brinner). Bellamy proposes an emendation of *al-aʿrāf* to *al-ajrāf*, "banks of a wadi," which fits the context of the verse rather neatly. See Bellamy, "Some proposed emendations," 571.

[100] According to Bell and Watt, this shows a clear Christian influence. See Bell and Watt, *Introduction*, 161.

[101] Cf. *EQ*, "People of the Heights," IV, 46b-48b (W. Brinner); Paret, *Kommentar*, 160 (*ad* Q 7:46).

that, had it been around when the Qur'ān was redacted, it would have been more fully explained.

Let us recall, once again, that the Qur'ān pictures a paradise that is stretched out over the slopes of a mountain. This is an ancient motif in Judeo-Christian eschatology, where it is often coupled with the idea of a stratification according to ranks.[102] Ephrem divides the mountain of paradise into three levels, "the foothills to the most lowly, the slopes to those in between and the heights to the exalted."[103] Ephrem further states that those "who dwell on the heights of paradise beyond the abyss espy the rich man,"[104] a reprise of the famous passage in the Gospel of Luke (Lk 16:19–31) in which Abraham and Lazarus, from their perch in paradise, observe the rich man in Hades, who calls out to them in agony to dip their finger in water and "cool my tongue" (Lk 16:24). If one is ready to allow a close intertextual relationship between the Qur'ān and the writings of Ephrem, as many scholars do,[105] it appears likely that *al-aʿrāf* refers to a privileged position *within* paradise, an elevated place on the paradise mountain from which a view over the barrier and into hell is possible, a view that is denied to the inhabitants of the lower slopes who therefore have to be told by those occupying a higher vantage. Whether the "people of *al-aʿrāf*" are identical with the privileged few "who are brought near" (*al-muqarrabūn*) and who inhabit the "lofty chambers," as has been suggested,[106] cannot be decided with certainty; but that they do not constitute a separate, third group of people caught in betwixt paradise and hell seems clear enough.

Turning to the various intertexts of hell in the Qur'ān, the various conceptualisations of hell as a monster gifted with speech that devours sinners, as a subterranean continent, as a deep ravine, and as a fiery pit or furnace all appear in different shapes and guises in Late Antique Near Eastern eschatology.[107] In *1 Enoch*, a text written around the turn of the millennium, hell is said to have a mouth with which it swallows the sinners (56:8), while in the text known as 3 Baruch (first–third c. CE), hell is the belly of a dragon (4:5; 5:3). Judeo-Christian sources mention the moaning and groaning of hell.[108] In Christian homilies and hymns of the fourth to the sixth centuries, the theme of hell as an insatiable monster is further developed. For example,

[102] See, e.g., *1 Enoch* 24:1–6. Cf. Volz, *Eschatologie*, 375; Costa, *L'au-delà*, 361; Anderson, "The cosmic mountain."

[103] Ephrem, *Hymns of paradise*, 2:10. Cf. the diagram in Buck, "Sapiential theosis," 115.

[104] Ephrem, *Hymns of paradise*, 1:12.

[105] For a list of the correspondences between Ephrem's *Hymns of paradise* and the Qur'ān, and a critical discussion of earlier scholarship, cf. Witztum, "Syriac milieu," 38–43. See now also Griffith, "St. Ephraem the Syrian."

[106] Andræ, *Ursprung*, 231–2.

[107] Cf. Volz, *Jüdische Eschatologie*, 289–90; Costa, *L'au-delà*, 359–408.

[108] According to *2 Enoch*, hell "weeps" (40:12). In a hymn of Ephrem, hell "groans" over the sinners. See Ephrem, *Nisibene Hymns*, 61:26. Elsewhere, Ephrem relates that one hears the sound of weeping and gnashing of teeth (cf. Matthew 22:13–14) of the damned from outside

Ephrem, in his *Nisibene Hymns*, repeatedly makes reference to the great appetite of both Death and Sheol/Hades, who complain about Jesus for denying them food and making them fast.[109] In one particularly graphic sermon of Ephrem, Jesus rips open the "voracious stomach of Hades" to save mankind from perdition.[110]

There is an abundance of descriptions of hell as a valley, ravine, abyss, or pit in the pre-Islamic Judeo-Christian eschatological tradition.[111] Sometimes, these intertexts provide clues for a better understanding of the Qur'ānic hell passages. For example, a text from Qumran refers to unbelievers as "the people of the pit" (*aneshe hash-shaḥat*, cf. Job 17:14, Ezekiel 28:8, Isaiah 51:14). It has been suggested that this is a remote forerunner of the Qur'ānic phrase *aṣḥāb al-ukhdūd* ("people of the pit," 85:4).[112] The word *ukhdūd* occurs only once in the Qur'ān and is uncommon in early Islamic literature, too. Most Muslim exegetes opt for a historical rather than an eschatological interpretation of the expression. The commonest etiology proposes that the "people of the pit" were a group of Christian martyrs, residents of the large oasis of Najran, burned in a ditch in 523 by the Jewish king of Yemen, Dhū l-Nuwās.[113] Many Western interpreters and translators, with some notable exceptions,[114] follow this interpretation. It is worth dwelling on this example, for the reason that it can illustrate some of the problems inherent in translating the Qur'ān with reference to Muslim exegetes who, as many have noted, have a tendency to introduce random stories into their commentaries in order to shed light on difficult passages whose original meaning is lost on them. Here is a representative translation of the passage in question:

(85:4) Slain were (*qutila*) the Men of the Pit, (85:5) the fire abounding in fuel, (85:6) when they were seated over it (85:7) and were themselves witnesses of what they did with the believers. (85:8) They took revenge on them only because they believed in the All-mighty....[115]

of hell. See Ephrem, "Letter to Publius," 340. Cf. Ephrem, "Eine Rede der Zurechtweisung," 2:93, 2:97.

109 Ephrem, *Nisibene Hymns*, 35:6, 36:2, 36:7–11, 39:7, 41:13, 52:22, 62:6.

110 Ephrem, "Sermo," 249.

111 See, e.g., *1 Enoch* 18:11–19:1, 27:1–2, 53:1, 90:24; *Apocalypse of Abraham* 21:3; *4 Ezra* 7:36; *Revelation* 9:1–4; Ephrem, *Nisibene hymns* 52:22; Aphrahat, *Homilies*, 358.

112 Philonenko, "Une expression qoumranienne," 555. On the link between the Qumran literature and the Qur'ān see Chaim Rabin, "Islam and the Qumran sect." Rabin does not discuss Qur'ān 85:4, however.

113 Nöldeke, *Geschichte*, I, 97; Nebes, "The martyrs of Najrān." Cf. *EQ*, s.v. People of the ditch, IV, 43b-44b (R. Tottoli). On pre-Islamic Najrān, see Robin, "Nagrān vers l'époque du massacre."

114 See Grimme, *Mohammed*, II, 77n4; Horovitz, *Koranische Untersuchungen*, 12, 92; Speyer, *Erzählungen*, 424; *EI2*, s.v. Aṣḥāb al-ukhdūd, I, 692b (R. Paret). Cf. Paret, *Kommentar*, 505–6 (*ad* Q 85:4–7). For a recent summary and a more radical statement of the argument, see Kropp, "Koranische Texte."

115 Arberry (tr.), *The Koran interpreted*, 332.

One notes, to begin, that the translator's choice to capitalise the "Men of the Pit" establishes that the verse addresses a specific, historically defined party of men, rather than a generic group of miscreants. Further, a number of incongruences catch the eye: Fire does not usually "slay" (*qatala*) people, rather, it burns them (both in English and Arabic); it is odd that the "Men of the Pit" should be "slain," presumably by the fire *in* the pit, while sitting *over* it; the translation of verse 85:7 implies that the "Men of the Pit," in the past, did to the believers what they are now experiencing. Overall, the impression that arises is decidedly muddled. Now compare this to the following translation:

(85:4) The people of the hell-pit shall perish!, (85:5) [the people] of the Fire with its [inexhaustible reservoir of] fuel, (85:6) when they will sit on [the brim of] it [i.e., the hell-pit] (85:7) and when they [are made to] testify to what they did with the believers. (85:8) They were angry with them [i.e., the believers] only because they believed in God.[116]

Parallels to the curse pronounced in Q 85:4 ("they shall perish," *qutila*) are found elsewhere in the Qur'ān (51:10, 74:19, 80:17). The mention of hellfire's "fuel" in 85:5 has Qur'ānic (2:24, 3:10, 66:6) as well as Judeo-Christian precedents.[117] Note, also, that this translation of Q 85:6 can lean on Q 19:68, which details how the sinners kneel around the hell-pit on the Day of Judgement. Finally, Q 85:7–8 fits in easily with other Qur'ānic threats against unbelievers and sinners that on the Day of Judgement they will have to testify, willingly or not, to their former disbelief and misbehaviour. Add to this the two verses Q 85:2 and Q 85:10 that, as if to frame Q 85:4–8, invoke the Day of Judgement, and the suggestion that the expression "people of the pit" refers to the damned in hell, and perhaps gestures back to Judeo-Christian precedents, becomes rather plausible.

As noted, the Qur'ānic hell is not just a fiery abyss, but also the reservoir of boiling hot liquids (18:29, 55:4, 88:5). This idea resonates with the old Near Eastern notion that there are masses of boiling water below the surface of the earth, heated up by the sun during its nocturnal descent to the underworld.[118] According to the Babylonian Talmud, the waters of the flood were hot,[119] and the Qur'ān picks up on this theme when it refers to the deluge as the moment "when the oven boiled" (*fāra l-tannūr*, 11:40, 23:27).[120]

[116] This translation follows, in broad strokes, the German translation by Rudi Paret. Cf. the translation proposed by Kropp, "Koranische Texte," 491.

[117] See the first/second-century *Apocalypse of Abraham*, 31:3; Ephrem, "Poem about the Judgment," 78 (stanza 16), 80 (stanza 33).

[118] See Segal, *Life after death*, 96–7, referring to the Mesopotamian sun-god Shamash. The notion, it seems, also occurs in *BT*, *Nezikin* 3, *Baba Bathra* 84a (XXI, 342–3).

[119] *BT*, *Zebaḥim* 113b (XXVII, 559–60).

[120] Cf. the Qur'ānic notion of hell as a furnace (37:97, 81:12), which is also found in Jewish apocalyptic and rabbinic literature. See O'Shaughnessy, "The seven names," 452–3.

In Q 55:44, the idea of a large subterranean body of hot water is combined with the more conventional notion of hell as a valley or abyss. This is the verse in which the sinners in hell are said to go back and forth between "boiling hot water" (*ḥamīm ānin*) and *jahannam*. Here, as in the case of the juxtaposition of a horizontal and vertical paradise, we are witness to the Qur'ānic tendency to combine various Late Antique cosmologies.

Moving to the inside of hell, the Qur'ān, though including a number of gruesome details, hardly reaches the level of gory violence of some of the Jewish and Christian Late Antique texts. Whereas in the Qur'ān, the sinners in hell imbibe boiling water and the bitter fruit of Zaqqūm, Ephrem depicts them as madmen who practice cannibalism – mothers eat their children, fathers eat their sons – and there are also instances of autosarcophagy.[121] Many of the punishments of the Qur'ānic hell are similar to those in the *Apocalypse of Paul* (mid-third c. CE): for example, the *Apocalypse of Paul* mentions that the angels in hell use "iron instruments with three hooks" to torture the sinners (cf. Q 22:21), the sinners are flung into "very narrow" torture chambers in hell (cf. Q 25:13), they are bound in "chains of fire" (cf. Q 76:4), and dressed in "rags of pitch" (cf. Q 14:50).[122] By contrast, the Qur'ān does not expound on the theme of mirror punishments as much as the *Apocalypse of Paul* does,[123] nor does the Qur'ān indulge as much in descriptions of hanging punishments, a recurrent motif in the *Apocalypse of Peter*, the *Acts of Thomas* (third c. CE?) and other related texts.[124] And if an image in the Qur'ān seems particularly shocking, chances are it is not new: the horrible vision of the fragmented bodies of sinners whose limbs one by one testify against their owners is also found in rabbinic literature, where it is projected into the Hebrew Bible.[125]

Hell's angels in the Qur'ān look back to a long and complex career in Late Antique eschatology. The seer of 2 *Enoch* claims secret knowledge of things seen in heaven, including the "armies of heaven" and their number and names.[126] When Q 74:30 confidently states that there are nineteen angels

[121] Ephrem, "Eine Rede der Zurechtweisung," II, 169, 177.

[122] Cf. *Apocalypse of Paul* 36.

[123] Ibid., 39.

[124] See *Apocalypse of Peter* 7 (Ethiopic) = §§ 21–25 (Akhmim); *Acts of Thomas* 56; *Ethiopic Apocalypse of Baruch*, 71–3.

[125] Cf. *BT*, *Ḥagiga* 16a (X, 104) and *Ta'anith* 11a (IX, 49): "A man's own limbs testify against him, as it is said: You are my witnesses, says the Lord" (Isaiah 43:10). A noncanonical tractate of the Babylonian Talmud warns people to "not let your mouth repeat calumny, because it is the first to be summoned for judgment ... because all your limbs will testify against you." See *Derek ereẓ zuṭa*, 4:6 (fol. 58b, tr. 579). Cf. Volz, *Jüdische Eschatologie*, 266. In Romans 7:23, Paul writes that the members (*melos*) of his body are "at war" with his mind. In the *Apocalypse of Peter*, specific body parts are singled out for punishment, that is, tongues, genitals, legs, and hair. See *Apocalypse of Peter* 7 (Ethiopic) = 22–24 (Akhmim). Cf. Czachesz, "Why body matters," 402–4.

[126] 2 *Enoch* 40:1–4.

set over hell, and that this number is so obscure that it is "an affliction (*fitna*) for the unbelievers" (74:31), such special knowledge seems likewise claimed. Where exactly the number nineteen originates, however, is difficult or perhaps even impossible to determine.[127] Relatively little comparative material from the pre-Islamic Near East is available. Until now, the best suggestion seems to be that the number represents the sum of seven and twelve, respectively the seven planets and the twelve signs of the zodiac, astral phenomena that were worshipped in a number of ancient Near Eastern cults, including Mazdakism and Sabianism.[128] In Mandaean literature, these nineteen celestial bodies are sometimes called *malak̲ê* (a cognate of the Arabic *malak* and other Semitic words meaning "angel") and are considered the administrators of the world, which is seen as dark and evil, as well as of nineteen purgatories in which the souls of sinners are tortured.[129]

The *Apocalypse of Paul* speaks of an angel who casts souls into darkness and is "set over the punishments."[130] In another scene, the tortured in hell cry out, "Lord have mercy upon us!," whereupon the archangel Michael descends from heaven and berates the sinners that they have "consumed in vanity the time in which you ought to have repented ... weep, and I will weep with you."[131] These two traditions seem to have become fused in Q 43:77,[132] even though the *m-l-k* addressed in this verse is somewhat less sympathetic to the plight of the sinners than Michael is in the *Apocalypse of Paul*. His troops, hell's angels of punishment, appear in a number of pre-Islamic texts.[133] The origin of the name *zabāniya*, however, is as obscure as that of the number nineteen. It has been suggested that the word *zabāniya* derives from Syriac *shabbāyā*, the name used by Ephrem for the angels who conduct the soul away after death.[134] In the ascetic milieu of Egyptian desert monasticism, particularly in the centuries before the rise of Islam, these angels were vividly pictured as repulsive and frightening demons,[135] which would seem to fit the Qur'ānic use rather well. However, linguistically, it is a long shot from *shabbāyā* to *zabāniya*. Other explanations have

[127] Cf. Eichler, *Die Dschinn*, 111–12; Ahrens, *Muhammad*, 30–1; Henninger, *Spuren*, 63–4n61; Rosenthal, "Nineteen."

[128] See Halm, "Die Sieben und die Zwölf"; Bell, *Commentary*, II, 453.

[129] The first to point to a possible Mandean background of Q 74:30 seems to have been Ahrens, *Muhammed*, 30–1. Rosenthal, "Nineteen," 304–18, cautiously accepts Ahrens's theory, as does Paret, *Kommentar*, 494 (*ad* Q 74:30). However, Bell (*Commentary*, II, 453) states that "the examples cited [by Ahrens] do not quite correspond to this." Alan Jones opines that "initially the meaning of 'nineteen' would have been vague." See Jones (tr.), *Qur'ān*, 545n3.

[130] *Apocalypse of Paul*, 16.

[131] Ibid., 43.

[132] See the preceding text, p. 53.

[133] *1 Enoch* 62:11, 90:21; *2 Enoch* 10:3; *Sybilline Oracles* 2:286–90; *Apocalypse of Peter* 23 (Akhmim); *Apocalyse of Paul* 34–40. Cf. Daley, *Hope*, 170.

[134] Andræ, *Ursprung*, 59–60.

[135] See Daley, "At the Hour of Our Death," 76–7.

been proffered,[136] including the elegant but radical suggestion that the word should be read as *rabbāniyya* instead of *zabāniya*, by replacing the initial "z" with an "r," which in the Arabic script simply requires the removal of a diacritical dot. Given that these dots were added to the Qur'ānic text only several generations after Muḥammad, the idea is not entirely far-fetched. The term *rabbāniyya* would then simply refer to the Lord's (Arabic *rabb*) angels in the heavenly council.[137] The problem with this explanation is that it is difficult to explain why and how a relatively common word such as *rabbāniyya* was changed, without traces of its earlier form, into *zabāniya*. In the case of the *zabāniya*, then, it seems best to stick to an explanation of their origin in Arabian demonology, as suggested in the preceding text.

Equally radical, and likewise rejected by a majority of scholars,[138] is the suggestion that the Qur'ān does not actually speak of houris but of grapes. The phrase translated as "We will wed them to the doe-eyed ones" (44:54), ought to be rendered, according to this theory, as "We will put them at ease under chrystal-white grapes."[139] As in the case of *rabbāniyya* > *zabāniya*, the argument builds on the removal of a number of diacritical dots ("We will wed them with" [*zawwajnāhum*] thus becomes "We will put them at ease under" [*rawwaḥnāhum*]). The argument also assumes that the passage in question, as indeed the entire Qur'ān, is best understood by deriving the meaning of its words from their cognates in the lexicon of Syriac Christianity (thus the "doe-eyed ones" become "chrystal-white grapes").

The "white grapes" hypothesis resonates with the fact that the Qur'ānic otherworld is in many ways indebted to the work of Ephrem. Ephrem has a great deal to say about the vines and grapes offered to the blessed in paradise, and he never mentions maidens.[140] However, one needs to cast a wider net. It is true, when the Qur'ān develops the image of a banquet in paradise, there are unmistakable echos from the Judeo-Christian tradition. Ephrem describes a "banquet" in heaven "with fruit of every savor," where "each type of fruit in due sequence approaches."[141] The Midrash promises "a feast for the righteous in the Garden of Eden," where there will be "no need either of balsam or of choice spices, for the north wind and the south

[136] Cf. Jeffery, *Foreign vocabulary*, 148. Eilers, "Iranisches Lehngut," 220, favours an Iranian etymology, from Middle Pers. *zen(dān)bān* "warder, keeper of a prison" (Pers. *zindānbān*). Cf. *EI2*, s.v. al-Zabāniyya. XI, 369a (ed.).

[137] Lüling, *A challenge to Islam*, 73–5. Cf. Reynolds, "Introduction," 10–11.

[138] See, among many, Stefan Wild, "Lost in philology?"; van Reeth, "Le vignoble du Paradis," 511–24; Nabielek, "Weintrauben statt Jungfrauen"; Witztum, "Syriac milieu," 52–7.

[139] Luxenberg, *Die syro-aramäische Lesart*, 256–75 (tr. 247–83). Cf. *EQ*, s.v. Readings of the Qur'ān, IV, 353b-363b, at 354b (F. Leemhuis).

[140] See Ephrem, *Hymns of paradise* 7:18. Andræ sees in this passage a hidden allusion to the maidens of paradise. See Andræ, *Mohammed*, 69–70. However, this is refuted by Beck, "Eine christliche Parallele"; idem, "Les houris du Coran," 405–8.

[141] Ephrem, *Hymns of paradise* 9:4.

wind will sweep through and sprinkle about all the perfumes of the Garden of Eden."[142] Overall, a paradise that gratifies the senses, a paradise in which also eros has a place, is not alien to Late Antique Christianity and Judaism, and the Qur'ān may thus be said simply to continue this tradition.[143] Still, numerous elements of the Qur'ānic banquet scene, including not only the female and male attendants but also the jugs and goblets of wine and other luxury items, as well as the detailed descriptions of how wine is mixed with fresh water (*mizāj*) and flavoured with ginger, camphor, and musk, seem proper to the Qur'ān's larger Arab context. As it turns out, they can be shown with some probability to be inspired by pre-Islamic Arabic poetry.[144]

In poems exalting the joys experienced in the travelling canteens that pitched their tents on the great fairs of pagan Arabia, one reads about visitors to the taverns "reclining on carpets over which are spread embroidered rugs most sumptuous" who are served "wine cooled by mixing with water" in "full flagons overflowing with foam atop" by "a boy, girt up, with two pearls in his ears" and by "white ones, with beautiful eyes" who "who carry around great cups filled full with wine."[145] The heavenly banquet in the Qur'ān is intertextually connected to another poetic genre, that of the ancient Arabic ode, or *qaṣīda*. The *qaṣīda* follows a typical pattern: it usually begins with a prologue (*naṣīb*) "in which the poet sheds some tears over what was once the camping place of his beloved now far off."[146] All traces of civilisation, of tents and material objects such as textiles, all memories of the bliss of social interaction with friends and lovers have been reduced to traces in the sand; man is left behind feeling consumed by the twin forces of brute nature and irreversible time. As has been suggested, "this perception of nature as overwhelming man and his culture ... the Qur'ān has come to

[142] *Numbers Rabbah* 13:2 (tr. VI, 500). A midrash on *Song of Songs* 4:16, some parts of *Numbers Rabbah* were composed in the third/ninth century or earlier, others as late as the sixth/twelfth century. See Strack and Stemberger, *Introduction*, 311. In the Babylonian Talmud, the inhabitants of the world to come are promised large quantities of wine. See *BT, Kethuboth* 111b (tr. XIV, 721–2). Cf. Segal, *Life after death*, 626; Hasan-Rokem, "Erotic Eden," 156–65.

[143] E.g., Irenaeus of Lyon (*fl. ca.* 140–200) describes a paradise full of sensual pleasures. See McDannell and Lang, *Heaven: A history*, 47–68; Segal, *Life after death*, 565.

[144] The first to have noticed this seems to have been Jacob, *Altarabisches Beduinenleben*, 107. Since then, a growing body of evidence has built up in support of this view. See Horovitz, "Das koranische Paradies," 64–73; Wendell, "The denizens of paradise"; Neuwirth, *Koran*, 221–2, 429–32; Lohlker and Nowak, "Das koranische Paradies," 204–6. One should also note the important role played in this context by the Arab Lakhmids and their capital al-Ḥīra, which entertained close relationships with the Persian Sassanians and with Palmyra. On al-Ḥīra, see now Tora-Niehoff, *Al-Ḥīra*, at 3–5, 73–4 and passim. Van Ess, "Zum Geleit," suggests that also Late Antique paintings and reliefs of postmortem banquets, e.g., in the tomb towers of Palmyra, may have served as a source of inspiration, referring to Henning, *Turmgräber*, 69ff.

[145] The examples are taken from Wendell, "The denizens of paradise," 35, 43.

[146] *EI2*, s.v. Ḳaṣīda. I. In Arabic, IV, 713b-714a, at 713b (F. Krenkow and G. Lecomte).

refute." The Qur'ānic heavenly banquet subverts the "emptiness of space and ... loss of communication"[147] of the *naṣīb* and converts it into its opposite, an otherworld, where there is perpetual fulfilment and unencumbered participation in nature, eros, and civilisation.

The Originality of the Qur'ānic Vision of Paradise and Hell

As we have seen, much of Qur'ānic eschatology[148] is indebted to the eschatological imagery of Late Antique Christian and Jewish literature. Where then, the reader may wonder, lies the originality, if any, of the Qur'ān's vision of paradise and hell? Among the properly novel images and ideas, details stand out. For example, water runs in one of four rivers of paradise instead of oil or balm, as in the Judeo-Christian tradition,[149] and some of the delights of the heavenly banquet as well as the food of the sinners in hell have a distinctly Arabian flavour. However, this does not mean that Qur'ānic eschatology is epigonic.[150] One should not content oneself with looking at themes and motifs in isolation in order to trace them back to their perceived original sources. More relevant, and more difficult to deal with, is the question how these sources are used, and to what degree they are reworked and combined into something new.

Let us recapitulate. The centrality of the otherworld, of paradise and hell in the Qur'ān, unequalled in other scriptures,[151] is remarkable in and of itself. The fact that sura 12 has more than one hundred verses yet makes no mention of either paradise or hell was thought to be so atypical that the Egyptian al-Zarkashī (d. 794/1392) included it in his list of astonishing curiosities in the Qur'ān.[152] The otherworld is presented as a diptych[153] in which paradise and hell are in constant dialogue.[154] To a large extent, they mirror each other closely (space vs. narrowness; houris vs. hell's angels; water vs. fire;

147 Neuwirth, "Qur'ānic readings of the psalms," 773–4. Cf. eadem, "Zeit und Ewigkeit"; eadem, *Koran*, 44, 220–3, 427–32.

148 Bell surely exaggerates when stating that "all this material is borrowed directly." See Bell, *The origin of Islam*, 103.

149 2 *Enoch* 8:5; *Sibylline Oracles* 2:317; Ephrem, *Hymns of paradise* 10:6.

150 A representative of this view is Leszynski, *Mohammedanische Traditionen*, 4–5.

151 See Murata and Chittick, *The vision of Islam*, 211: "No scripture devotes as much attention as the Koran to describing the torments of hell and the delights of paradise." See also Chittick, "Muslim eschatology," 132; idem, "Eschatology in Islamic thought," 233.

152 Zarkashī, *Burhān*, I, 253–5.

153 Neuwirth, *Studien*, 180, 186; *EQ*, s.v. Form and structure, II, 245b-266a, at 258a-258b (A. Neuwirth).

154 Islam Dayeh rightly stresses "the *dialogical* nature" of Qur'ānic eschatology, particularly in the so-called *ḥawāmīm* suras 50–6, which produces a "cinematographic effect of a grand and continuous drama." See Dayeh, "Al-ḥawāmīm," 484, 486.

Jujube vs. Zaqqūm; purification vs. defilement; and so forth),[155] while there are also a few structural asymmetries (two or four groups of the blessed vs. one group, or seven groups, of the damned). Elements of Christian and Jewish eschatology, which one can trace to influential texts such as, among others, the Jewish Enoch literature, *The Apocalypse of Paul* and the works of Ephrem are freely combined. Echoes of pagan Arabian, perhaps also of astral religions are likewise found, even if a process of biblicisation appears to take place in the successive stages of the proclamation of the Qurʾān, as also the soteriological and cosmological underpinnings of Qurʾānic eschatology gradually move into sharper focus. Overall, it is no exaggeration to say that the earlier traditions are pulverised into its constitutive elements, then shuffled around and recombined into two fully fledged otherworldly spaces. All this is done in such a way as to create a powerful and original vision of time and space: a new world.

The salient characteristic of this new world, besides the radical moralism that undergirds it, is that it is conceived as a *merismos*, a "simultaneous totality"[156] embracing both *al-dunyā* and *al-ākhira*, the here and the hereafter, this world and the otherworld. The Qurʾān makes no distinction between the paradise inhabited by Adam and Eve, the paradise that exists in the present and the paradise that will be the abode of the blessed in the world to come. All three are the same and on earth, or rather, paradise straddles the boundary between this world and the otherworld, branching out into both realms. A temporal distinction between the present life and the hereafter is, though undeniably present, not a paramount concern in the Qurʾān. *Al-dunyā* and *al-ākhira* are seen primarily as spatial units. As has been noted, this is contrary to "the likely rabbinical model for the idea of the two worlds ..., the Hebrew notion of *ha-ʿōlām ha-zeh* vs. *ha-ʿōlām ha-bā*, this world vs. the coming world, [which] does presuppose a temporal sequence, *ʿōlām* being a temporal term in both Hebrew and Aramaic (*ʿalmā*)."[157] In those instances, however, in which the otherworld *is* described in temporal terms, the Qurʾān emphasises the sense of immediacy, in some cases even that of synchronicity. In the Qurʾān, the otherworld is near at hand. Paradise and hell are ready, right now, to receive the deceased. For the world at large, the apocalypse is imminent. In fact, according to some verses of the Qurʾān, its portents are already upon us (47:18, 54:1).[158] However, the Qurʾān does not stop there. The apocalyptic urgency of the Qurʾān, which has recently

[155] Heidi Toelle provides a comprehensive inventory of such structural binaries. See Toelle, *Le Coran revisité*, 23–69.

[156] Brown, "Apocalypse of Islam," 374.

[157] *EQ*, s.v. Spatial relations, V, 104a-108b, at 105a (A. Neuwirth). According to Klein, *Comprehensive etymological dictionary* (s.v. *ʿōlām*), Hebr. *ʿōlām* "never has the meaning 'world'" in the Bible. Such apodictic assessments, however, should be nuanced in the light of José Costa's comprehensive study of Rabbinic eschatology, *L'au-delà*.

[158] Cf. Qurʾān 47:18: "Are they waiting for anything but the Hour that will come to them suddenly? For its portents have already come ..."; 54:1: "The Hour has drawn nigh, the moon

kindled the renewed interest of a number of scholars, is complemented, or fulfilled, by the notion that the present world is *already* in many ways entangled with the otherworld, and interlocked in a constant mutual embrace.[159] The Qur'ān thus seems to conceive of the otherworld in terms of an "eternal now," a kind of ever-present "dreamtime" that is "everywhen."[160]

As has been pointed out, the eschatological imagery of the Qur'ān "resounds within a vocabulary of worldly life."[161] This is particularly obvious in the Qur'ān's use of commercial terminology: every soul "will be paid in full for what it has done" (16:111); "God has bought from the believers their lives and their possessions for the price that the Garden will be theirs" (9:111); and so forth. This already indicates that the Qur'ān projects a vision of the otherworld that is congruous with the present world, but also of an earthly transhistorical society that partakes in the divine. By virtue of this "divine/immanent overlap" past, present, and future become "blended."[162] Salvation is not imagined to occur on the level of historical time, as is generally the case in orthodox Jewish and Christian traditions.[163] Instead, the most important function that the "time-less mythic world"[164] of *al-ākhira*

is split in two!." Cf. Shoemaker, *Death*, 119, 158–71; idem, "Muḥammad and the Qur'ān," 1094–5.

[159] Fred Donner suggests that the early believers were convinced that by establishing the *umma* in Medina they had already ushered in the beginning of the end of times. See Donner, *Muhammad and the believers*, 80–1. See also ibid., 246, where Donner highlights the simultaneous existence of "apocalyptic eschatology and realized eschatology" in the Qur'ān, referring, by way of comparison, to Aune, *The cultic setting*. Cf. Shoemaker, *Death*, 121; idem, "Muḥammad and the Qur'ān," 1090–91. Shoemaker refers back to Christiaan Snouck Hurgronje as the first Western scholar to have emphasised that "imminent eschatology" represents the core of Muḥammad's message. See Snouck Hurgronje, "Der Mahdi," 26. This idea is fully developed by Paul Casanova's classic study *Mohammed et la fin du monde*. Shoemaker argues – and the gist of the argument presented here supports his view – that the essentially eschatological character of the Qur'ān was "marginalised" by the dominant school of Western Qur'ān scholarship in the twentieth century, which instead preferred to stress that Muḥammad was a moral and practical, not an eschatological prophet, and that this dominant scholarly discourse continues to this day. See Shoemaker, *Death*, 134; idem, "Muḥammad and the Qur'ān," 1093.

[160] On the "eternal now" in the writings of Ephrem, see Brock, *The Luminous Eye*, 29–30; Buck, "Sapiential theosis." On "dreamtime" and the idea of "everywhen" in Aboriginal religion, see Stanner, "The dreaming," 58. Cf. Duerr, *Dreamtime*, 118.

[161] Rippin, "The commerce of eschatology," 126.

[162] Ibid., 132. Also Angelika Neuwirth opines that "the Qur'ān projects an eschatological discourse whose emphasis lies on the continuation of the present life in the hereafter." See Neuwirth, *Koran*, 438. A nuanced meditation on the apocalyptic nearness and eschatological intensity of the Qur'ān is offered in Lawson, "The music of apocalypse."

[163] One should note, however, that the early Church Fathers before Augustine, such as Irenaeus, Tertullian, and Methodius, often seem to suggest that a paradisiacal life is accessible even before death. See Benjamins, "Paradisiacal life."

[164] Neuwirth, "Qur'anic readings of the psalms," 770. Cf. eadem, "Reclaiming paradise lost," 351.

fulfils in the Qur'ān is to serve as an interpretive, meaning-bestowing matrix for the fleeting and contingent world of the here and now.

It has been affirmed that "[t]he Koran backs off from that linear organisation of time, revelation, and history which became the backbone of orthodox Christianity," or even that Islam "is wholly eschatological," a tradition in which "eschatology can break out at any moment."[165] While it would seem wise to eschew such grand generalisations, whether about the Qur'ān or Islam – as if only one reading of the Qur'ān were possible, and as if Islam as a whole necessarily resulted from that one reading – the statement provides an insight into a dimension of the Qur'ān that was to have a significant influence on all later Muslim conceptualisations of paradise and hell: it allows its audience to conceive of the boundary separating *al-dunyā* from *al-ākhira* as permeable and fluid, and hence of paradise and hell as very close indeed. How Muslim traditions have negotiated this potential, how immanent conceptions have vied with transcendentalist ones, is the topic of the following chapters.

[165] Brown, "The apocalypse of Islam," 372. Brown echos Nwyia, *Exégèse*, 74, who states that "schooled on the Koran, Muslim consciousness is spontaneously ahistorical, that is to say mythical." Similarly, Mohamed Arkoun speaks of the "eschatological consciousness"of the Qur'ān, which he opposes to ways of reading the Qur'ān with an "historical consciousness." See Arkoun, "Peut-on parler," 22.

2

The Growth of the Islamic Otherworld: A History of Muslim Traditionist Eschatology

As rich as the Qur'ān is in eschatological ideas and images, it only provides the skeleton for the variegated body of texts that form the Islamic tradition of imagining paradise and hell. This chapter and the next trace the growth of this literature from the early centuries of Islam to the eve of modernity. Our concern will not be with the theological, philosophical, mystical, or esthetic responses to the evolving picture of paradise and hell, each of which will receive separate treatment in Part 2 of this book. The aim of this and of the following chapter is, rather, to survey the development of Muslim *narrative* literature devoted to the otherworld, particularly as it took the form of collections of sayings (hadiths) attributed to the prophet Muḥammad and other early authorities. Of course, these collections cannot be defined by their narrativity alone, because they often pursue theological, philosophical, mystical, or esthetic agendas, too. Yet taken as a whole, these texts may well be said to constitute a distinct cluster of religious literature in Islam, and because the history of this body of literature has largely been ignored by scholars of Islam,[1] it is worth describing it, noting its most important types, contributors, periods, and areas of flourishing.

The Formative Period (*ca.* First–Third/ Seventh–Ninth Century)

The oldest stand-alone works devoted to collecting stories and hadiths about the otherworld date from the turn of the second to the third century of the Islamic era. Among the first specimen is that of the Baghdad littérateur, ʿAlī b. ʿUbayda al-Rayḥānī (d. *ca.* 219/834), a secretary to the ʿAbbāsid caliph al-Maʾmūn (r. 198–218/813–33). The title of al-Rayḥānī's work is

[1] A notable exception is Bauer, "Islamische Totenbücher." On works with the title *Ṣifat al-janna* as a literary genre, see now Ahmed, "The characteristics of paradise." Cf. also *EI3*, s.v. Afterlife (R. Tottoli).

What Paradise is like (*Ṣifat al-janna*).[2] Scholars of the first two centuries of Islamic history, however, preceded al-Rayḥānī in gathering materials that expanded on the Qur'ānic picture of the otherworld, often adding significant new information. A keen interest in eschatological traditions is attributed to the Jewish convert and intimate of the caliph ʿUmar b. al-Khaṭṭāb (r. 13–23/634–44), Kaʿb al-Aḥbār (d. between 32/652 and 35/655), well known in later tradition for his knowledge of biblical literature.[3] On more than one occasion, ʿUmar b. al-Khaṭṭāb would have asked Kaʿb to "make us afraid" (*khawwifnā*), a request to which Kaʿb responded by delivering graphic descriptions of hell to multitudes of enthralled listeners.[4] Students of Kaʿb, such as Abū Hurayra (d. *ca.* 58/678) and Ibn ʿAbbās (d. *ca.* 68/687–8), are likewise credited in the later literature with transmitting a plethora of narratives about the otherworld.[5] Under Kaʿb's and his students' names biblical and other Near Eastern materials were seamlessly merged into the growing storehouse of Islamic eschatological imagery.[6]

Paradise and hell play a significant role in some of the earliest collections of hadith that have come down to us, the so-called *Scrolls* (*ṣuḥuf*), short hadith lists compiled by scholars such as the Yemeni Hammām b. Munabbih (d. 131/749 or 132/750) and the Egyptian traditionist and judge, Ibn Lahīʿa (d. 174/790). One must acknowledge that the historicity of Hammām's collection has been disputed, some declaring it to be the work of the famous Yemeni collector ʿAbd al-Razzāq al-Ṣanʿānī (d. 211/827).[7] There

[2] See Ibn al-Nadīm, *Fihrist*, I, 119. Al-Rayḥānī, known for his collections of proverbs (*amthāl*) and philosophical adages (*ḥikam*), is said to have developed a penchant for *zuhd* in his late years, which may explain why he also compiled treatises on *contemptus mundi*, death, and the afterlife. See Zakeri, *Persian wisdom*, I, 250–4.

[3] On Kaʿb's role as a transmitter of biblical traditions, see Wolfensohn, "Kaʾb al-Aḥbār," esp. 36–72; Rubin, *Between Bible and Qur'ān*; Tottoli, *Biblical prophets*, 89–92; *EI2*, s.v. Kaʿb al-Aḥbār, II, 317b-318a (M. Schmitz); *GAS*, I, 303. *Pace* Rustomji, *The Garden and the Fire*, 98, who suggests that "[t]he first manual about the afterlife was probably Kaʿb al-Aḥbār's *Kitab al-akhira* [*sic*]," there is no reason to assume that Kaʿb actually left any written work of this title.

[4] Ibn Abī Shayba, *Muṣannaf, k. dhikr al-nār*, IX, 179 (#12), 189 (#46); Abū Nuʿaym, *Ḥilya*, V, 368–71; Ibn Rajab, *Takhwīf*, 87; Suyūṭī, *Budūr*, 150. Kaʿb is quoted more than fifteen times in the sections on paradise and hell in Ibn Abī Shayba's *Muṣannaf* (*k. al-janna* ##10, 30, 32, 45, 56, 81, 86, 113, 158, 163; *k. dhikr al-nār* ##2, 12, 23, 46, 56, 60). See also Abū Nuʿaym, *Ḥilya*, VI, 10–12 (the "Story of the Skull"); ibid. VI, 37–42 (the "Colloquy of Moses with God"). On these two popular stories, see following text, pp. 116–8.

[5] Cf. Wolfensohn, "Kaʿb al-Ahbār," 58.

[6] In Paul Cobb's phrase, Kaʿb is a "ghost in the *isnād* of the conversion of non-Muslim lore into Islamic tradition." See Cobb, "Virtual sacrality," 45.

[7] *ECḤ*, 29–30. Juynboll problematises the relatively polished character of the traditions in Hammām's scroll, but the discussion mainly revolves around the transmission of the scroll from Hammām b. Munabbih (d. 131/749 or 132/750) > Maʿmar b. Rāshid (d. around 153/770) > ʿAbd al-Razzāq (d. 211/827). As Juynboll points out, even if one grants the (uncertain) fact that Hammām's death date is 131/749, one is required to assume that he reached an excessively old age to be able to serve as a link between Maʿmar and the

are reasonable arguments, however, indicating that the traditions cited in Hammām's compilation provide a window into the world of ideas of early second/eighth-century Islam, perhaps even of the earlier period.[8] By my count, of the 138 hadiths included in Hammām's *Scroll*, eight dwell on paradise and eight on hell, while a further eleven deal with the apocalypse and Day of Judgement. In other words, roughly 15 percent of Hammām's material can be classified as eschatological. The material Hammām presents is heterogeneous. On the one hand, one encounters the divine saying – which henceforth I shall refer to as the unfathomability tradition – that God has prepared for his servants in paradise "that which no eye has seen, no ear has heard, no heart has conceived."[9] On the other hand, Hammām's collection includes items that display the tendency, which later exegetes and collectors sometimes sought to domesticate,[10] to give the imagination free rein in picturing the two otherworldly abodes. Hammām's elder brother, as one should note, was Wahb b. Munabbih (d. 114/732), a judge in Sanaa and a celebrated authority on biblical traditions, whose knowledge of Judeo-Christian eschatology Hammām is likely to have shared.[11] According to a tradition in Hammām's *Scroll* that picks up on a Talmudic theme, there is a tree in paradise that is so large that a horseman cannot pass underneath its shadow in a hundred years.[12] A woman finds herself in hell because in her earthly life she mistreated her cat "until it died of emaciation."[13] In a particularly dramatic,

Companion Abū Hurayra (d. between 57/677 and 59/679), from whom Hammām is said to have related his material. Cf. on this point, de Prémare, "Wahb b. Munabbih," 536, suggesting that Hammām's death occurred earlier than 131/749, but that Maʿmar could have learned his hadith from written records, rather than through oral transmission. Ibn Saʿd states that Hammām died around 101/720, and that he transmitted hadith abundantly from Abū Hurayra. See Ibn Saʿd, *Ṭabaqāt*, V, 544.

[8] See Motzki, "Review of G.A.H. Juynboll," 546–8. Motzki thinks the early death date for Hammām in Ibn Saʿd's *Ṭabaqāt* is "a copying or editing error." Ibid., 547.

[9] Hammām, *Ṣaḥīfa*, 25 (#31). On the unfathomability tradition, see further in the preceding text, pp. 2–3.

[10] Cf. the unwillingness of the exegete al-Māturīdī (d. 333/944) to interpret the word *al-kawthar* (Q 108:1) as the name of a river in paradise. Al-Māturīdī, to back up his view, refers to the unfathomability tradition. See Māturīdī, *Taʾwīlāt*, XVII, 345–6. Cf. Gilliot, "L'embarras d'un exégète," 52.

[11] On Wahb, Cf. *EI2*, "Wahb b. Munabbih," XI, 34a-36a (G. Khoury); *EI2*, "Isrāʾīliyyāt," IV, 211b-212b (G. Vajda). Two recent studies, the first critical of Wahb's alleged contribution to first- and second-century Islamic literature, the other less so, are Pregill, "Isrāʾīliyyāt"; de Prémare, "Wahb b. Munabbih."

[12] Hammām, *Ṣaḥīfa*, 21 (#5). Cf. Ibn al-Mubārak, *Musnad*, 73 (#120). According to the Jerusalem Talmud and *Genesis Rabba*, it takes five hundred years to journey around the tree of life in paradise. See *JT*, *Berakoth*, I, 7; *Genesis rabba*, 15:6 (tr. I, 122). Ibn Abī Shayba relates a commentary of Kaʿb al-Aḥbār on this report. See Ibn Abī Shayba, *Muṣannaf*, *k. al-janna*, IX, 132 (#30).

[13] Hammām, *Ṣaḥīfa*, 36 (#89). This canonical hadith (cf. *ECḤ*, 179) is related on the authority of the Companion Abū Hurayra, known for his great love of cats (whence his name, "father of a kitten").

anthropomorphist tradition, paradise and hell argue about which of them has been given precedence, until God intervenes, reassuring them that both will have their fill. God then puts His foot on hell so that it shrinks to size and cries out: "Enough, enough!"[14]

The *Scroll* of Ibn Lahīʿa, whose family hailed from Hadramawt in the Yemen, is an eclectic mix of history, asceticism, piety, and eschatology. Much of Ibn Lahīʿa's material comes to him from South Arabian sources, in particular through his teacher, Yazīd b. Abī Ḥabīb (d. 128/745), a Nubian convert known for his interest in eschatology. For example, Yazīd related a hadith according to which the Prophet was given an apple in paradise from which sprang a houri who declared she was the reward for the martyred caliph ʿUthmān.[15] The circle of traditionists forming around Yazīd and Ibn Lahīʿa in the Egyptian capital Fusṭāṭ has been characterised as a veritable school of hadith, whose members were proud to flaunt the ancient wisdom of South Arabia.[16] Ibn Lahīʿa reports, for example, that a certain Abū Qabīl, a member of the prominent South Arabian al-Maʿāfirī family in Fusṭāṭ, taught that both paradise and hell are located in the fifth and sixth heaven, a notion that does not resonate with the Qurʾān as much as with the Jewish Enoch literature and the Gnostic *Apocalypse of Paul*.[17] The dozen relevant traditions in Ibn Lahīʿa's *Scroll* (out of a total of some two hundred) do not provide a full picture of paradise and hell by any means, but they do give an impression of the kind of milieu in which such traditions flourished in the formative period of hadith.

The hadith work of another early Egyptian hadith scholar, ʿAbdallāh Ibn Wahb (d. 197/813), is primarily concerned with legal hadith, as befits a student of the celebrated Meccan jurist Mālik b. Anas (d. 179/795). Yet ʿAbdallāh is said to have spent his nights thinking about the terrors of the

[14] Hammām, *Ṣaḥīfa*, 28–9 (#52); Muslim, *Ṣaḥīḥ*, *k. al-janna* 36–7 (*b. al-nār yadkhuluhā l-jabbārūn*), IV, 2187. The motif of hell groaning is found in the popular fifth/sixth-century Gospel of Nicodemus, in which Christ descends to hell to rescue humankind. This makes hell exclaim that Christ "drew [the damned] up forcibly from my entrails ... my belly is in pain.... We are defeated, woe to us!" See *Gospel of Nicodemus*, 187–8. Juynboll (*ECḤ*, 33) attributes the tradition to ʿAbd al-Razzāq al-Ṣanʿānī. The Meccan scholar Muḥammad al-Barzanjī (d. 1103/1691) wrote a separate commentary on this hadith, called *al-Qawl al-mukhtār fī taḥājat al-janna wa-l-nār* (*The Exquisite Discussion of [the Hadith] "Paradise and hell disputed [their respective status]"*). See Baghdādī, *Hadiyat al-ʿārifīn*, II, column 303.

[15] See Suyūṭī, *La'ālī*, I, 312, 314, quoted in *TG*, II, 719.

[16] Vadet, "L'acculturation," 10.

[17] Ibn Lahīʿa, *Ṣaḥīfa*, 290–1 (lines 313–16 of the papyrus). According to 2 *Enoch* 18:1–5, the fifth heaven is the place of punishment for fallen angels, the so-called Watchers, while the sixth heaven is the place from which the angels control the world and keep records of people's actions. See Collins, "Afterlife," 132–3. In the Gnostic *Apocalypse of Paul*, Paul sees (disembodied) souls punished by angels in the fourth and fifth heavens, while the righteous live in the tenth heaven. See Wright, *Early history*, 163–4. On the transfer of hell/Hades to heaven in post-Platonic Greek literature, see Nilsson, *Geschichte*, I, 240–1.

Judgement Day and the world to come, to the point that when a group of traditionists (*aṣḥāb al-ḥadīth*) read to him a description of paradise and hell, he lost consciousness and died a couple of days later.[18] ʿAbdallāh's *Comprehensive Collection* (*al-Jāmiʿ*) provides a blatant illustration of how the interest in eschatology combined with South Arabian parochialism. The very first hadith in this collection has it that "most of the tribes in paradise are from Madhḥij."[19] The Madhḥij were a large tribal confederation of the Yemen whose members had contributed to the Muslim conquest of Egypt and settled in Fusṭāṭ.[20] Fusṭāṭ at the end of the Umayyad period was an important centre of South Arabian learning, next to Hims in Syria (the place where Kaʿb al-Aḥbār spent his last days). After the Islamic conquest, both communities had become home to numerous South Arabian tribes, and both shared an interest in predictions about the end of time.[21] When Nuʿaym b. Ḥammād (d. 229/844), the most important early collector of apocalyptic hadith, much of which he gleaned from Himsian sources, settled in Egypt, he was well received by the locals, probably because they had always liked the type of eschatological materials he brought with him.[22]

Later critics thought the transmitters belonging to this milieu to be unreliable, not least Ibn Lahīʿa.[23] This, however, did not prevent scholars who issued from his circle in Fuṣṭāṭ from becoming significant contributors to the emerging genre of works devoted to paradise and hell. Ibn Ḥabīb (d. 238/853), an author known for his espousal of "fabulous material" originating in Egypt,[24] gathered numerous traditions from Ibn Lahīʿa's student Asad b. Mūsā (d. 212/827) in Fusṭāṭ, before returning to his native Spain and

[18] Abū Nuʿaym, *Ḥilya*, VIII, 324; al-Qāḍī ʿIyād, *Tartīb al-madārik*, III, 240–1. ʿAbdallāh also spread the story that has the Prophet, in a vision, reaching out for the grapes of paradise. See *ECḤ*, 17–18.

[19] Ibn Wahb, *Jāmiʿ*, first hadith of the entire corpus. On Ibn Wahb, see *EI2*, s.v. Ibn Wahb, III, 963a (J. David-Weill); *ECḤ*, 11–20. The hadith made it into al-Nasāʾī's *Sunan*, albeit with a different *isnād*, because al-Nasāʾī thought that Ibn Wahb's informant ʿUtba b. Abī Ḥakīm (d. 147/764) was a weak (*ḍaʿīf*) traditionist. See Nasāʾī, *Sunan*, *k. manāqib aṣḥāb rasūl Allāh* 69 (*b. Madhḥij*), V, 92. An extended version can be found in Ibn Ḥanbal, *Musnad*, IV, 387 (where Maʾkūl are added to Madhḥij). On ʿUtba, see Mizzī, *Tahdhīb*, XIX, 300. ʿUtba belonged to the South Arabian tribe of Hamdān, one of the Yemeni tribes who settled in Fusṭāṭ. He was also one of the teachers of Ibn Lahīʿa. See Ibn ʿAsākir, *Taʾrīkh*, XXXVIII, 229. On the Hamdān, see *TG*, II, 702.

[20] Kaḥḥāla, *Muʿjam qabāʾil al-ʿarab*, III, 1062.

[21] See Madelung, "Apocalyptic prophecies," 143 and passim. Another centre of South Arabian tribes was Kufa. The Madhḥij shared quarters there with the Hamdān; both were pro-ʿAlid. See *EI2*, s.v. Madhḥij, V, 953b-954b (G. R. Smith and C. E. Bosworth).

[22] *TG*, II, 724.

[23] Dhahabī, *Mīzān*, II, 47583, III, 322, 419. Cf. *EI2*, s.v. Ibn Lahīʿa, III, 853b-854a (F. Rosenthal); Motzki, "The Prophet and the debtors," 153–6. Ibn Ḥanbal reports a hadith with an *isnād* going through Ibn Lahīʿa that "tax-collectors are in hell" (*inna ṣāḥib al-maks fī l-nār*). See Ibn Ḥanbal, *Musnad*, IV, 109.

[24] *EI2*, s.v. Ibn Ḥabīb (A. Huici Miranda), III, 775a.

compiling what appears to be the oldest extant work of hadiths dedicated to the Muslim paradise.[25] In the east of the expanding Islamic empire, a pivotal role was played by another student of Ibn Lahīʿa, the merchant, traditionist, and warrior-renunciant Ibn al-Mubārak (d. 181/797). Originally from Merv in Turkmenistan, Ibn al-Mubārak travelled widely to collect hadiths, including to Yemen and to Egypt, where he met Ibn Lahīʿa. Later sources make of him a larger-than-life figure. It is said that he possessed a massive library of *Scrolls*, gave generously to charity, and, above all, fought zealously in the jihad on the Arab-Byzantine frontier.[26] His works include a compilation of hadiths and stories dealing with the topic of jihad as well as a *Book of Renunciation and Exhortations that Stir the Hearts of Their Audience* (*K. al-Zuhd wa-l-raqāʾiq*). Ibn al-Mubārak's traditions, according to a recent study, "are his, only occasionally showing up in much later sources ... and on the whole only sparingly in one or a few of the canonical collections."[27]

Ibn al-Mubārak's *Book of Renunciation*, in the version assembled by his student Nuʿaym b. Ḥammād, features a chapter on paradise (with sixty-three items) and a chapter on hell (with fifty-nine items).[28] Only about a quarter of the hadiths contained in these two chapters are traced back to the prophet Muḥammad. Following common usage in the late second/eighth century, Ibn al-Mubārak freely juxtaposes Prophetic hadiths with traditions from the Companions or even later authorities. One salient type of tradition, constituting about a quarter of Ibn al-Mubārak's material, is narrative glosses on the Qurʾān, quoted from authorities such as the Companion ʿAbdallāh Ibn Masʿūd (d. 32/652–3?), the Meccan Mujāhid b. Jabr (d. 103/721 or 104/722?), or al-Ḍaḥḥāk b. Muzāḥim (d. 102/720 or 105/723?), a commentator known for his midrashic style who hailed from the frontier city of Balkh in Khorasan and who is believed, like his fellow exegete and countryman Muqātil b. Sulaymān (d. 150/767), to have actively participated in jihad.[29] Mujāhid, for example, relates that the "purified spouses" in paradise

[25] Ibn Ḥabīb takes more than two-thirds of his 317 hadiths from Egyptian informants: 142 hadiths from Asad b. Mūsā (from whose *K. al-Zuhd* he also borrows the topical arrangement of eschatological traditions), 33 from Ibn ʿAbd al-Ḥakam (d. 214/829), 30 from ʿAlī b. Maʿbad (d. 218/833), and some more from other Egyptian traditionists. Ibn Lahīʿa appears in the *isnād* of twenty-one hadiths in Ibn Ḥabīb's work. See Ibn Ḥabīb, *Waṣf al-firdaws*. Cf. the study by Juan Pedro Monferrer Sala, *Kitāb waṣf al-firdaws*, 31–2. Monfarrer Sala suggests that the original work of Ibn Ḥabīb also contained sections on death, judgement, and hell. See ibid., 30.

[26] For his biography, see Bonner, *Aristocratic violence*, 119–25; *TG*, II, 551–5; *EIr*, s.v. ʿAbdallāh b. Mobārak (P. Nwyia); *ECḤ*, 8–9.

[27] *ECḤ*, 8.

[28] A short cluster of paradise and hell traditions also appears in Ibn al-Mubārak, *Musnad*, 69–80 (##112–34).

[29] On these three exegetes, see *TG*, II, 508–9, 640–4, and passim. Other recent studies include Gilliot, "A schoolmaster" (al-Ḍaḥḥāk); idem, "Muqātil"; Sinai, *Fortschreibung und Auslegung* (Muqātil and al-Mujāhid).

FIGURE 3. An angel in the form of a heavenly horse. Adapted from al-Qazwīnī, *ʿAjāʾib al-makhlūqāt* (*The Marvels of Creation*). Baghdad/Iraq, eighth/fourteenth century. MS St Petersburg, Institute for Oriental Studies, ar. E.7.

(Q 2:25) are thus called because they do not menstruate, defecate, or urinate, and abstain from blowing their noses, expectorating, or spitting.[30] Ibn Masʿūd, commenting on the Qurʾānic verse that the sinners in hell grimace out of pain (23:104), explains that this is because the fire shrivels their lips, thus baring their teeth.[31]

Ibn al-Mubārak's portrayal of the otherworld evokes not only the raw physicality and chivalrous bravery, but also the blood-soaked gloom of a soldier's life on the frontier of Islamdom.[32] There is a fascination with horses and women. According to the *Book of Renunciation*, among the pleasures of paradise is that its inhabitants will be given noble steeds on which they visit each other every Friday. On the way, in anticipation of their rendezvous, they are met by a miraculous cloud to which they say: "Rain upon us!," whereupon riders and beasts are promptly cleansed. Then God sends a wind that scatters scented dust from a dune of musk over the forelock of the horse and over the side locks of the rider. Thus prepared, the inhabitants of paradise meet their rejuvenated wives.[33]

30 Ibn al-Mubārak, *Zuhd*, 486 (#243); idem, *Musnad*, 69–70 (#113).

31 Idem, *Zuhd*, 496 (#291); idem, *Musnad*, 76 (#126).

32 This is so regardless of the question whether or not Ibn al-Mubārak was an active frontier warrior. For a sceptical position in this regard, cf. Melchert, "Ibn al-Mubārak's *K. al-jihād*."

33 Ibn al-Mubārak, *K. al-Zuhd*, 475 (#239). Other traditions in which horses appear can be found ibid., 484, 489–91 (##231, 265–7, 271).

As for hell, several traditions reported by Ibn al-Mubārak detail that the bodies of the damned are bloated to an impossible size, while one of the commonest forms of torture consists in having one's entrails ripped out or dissolved by boiling drinks that one is forced to imbibe.[34] Ibn al-Mubārak adds warnings that Muslims, out of their certitude of faith, must not feel safe from these horrors. "Weep," he quotes the Prophet, "for the damned in hell weep tears of blood!"[35] What kind of effect such traditions had on Ibn al-Mubārak is captured by a sombre anecdote. His companions, it is related, once carried a candle into the tent they shared with him, to discover that his beard dripped with tears, for the pitch-black darkness of the open country at night reminded him of hell.[36] As his student Nuʿaym b. Ḥammād reports, when reading from his *Book of Renunciation*, Ibn al-Mubārak would "wail like a cow being slaughtered" – one presumes this was because the thought of death and judgement caused him visceral distress.[37]

Other *Books of Renunciation* include important sections on paradise and hell, notably the works of the aforementioned Asad b. Mūsā[38] and of the Iraqi Hannād b. al-Sarī (Kufa, d. 243/857), a teacher of al-Ṭabarī (d. 310/923). Hannād relates 179 items on paradise and 101 items on hell, together about a fifth of his entire work, which otherwise deals with typical renunciant topics such as the virtues of silence, fasting, and showing proper contrition for sins.[39] However, as others have noted, renunciant literature does not dwell on descriptions of the two otherworldly abodes as much as one might expect. While some collectors of renunciant materials, particularly Hannād, seem to attribute great importance to the topic, most "thought about [it] as often as about anything else."[40]

At any rate, the comprehensive collections of hadiths from the first half of the third/ninth century are no less encompassing when it comes to

[34] Ibid., 496–8 (##292–3, 298, 303–5): bloated bodies; ibid., 499, 502–3, 505 (##313–4, 327–8, 339): entrails ripped out or molten.

[35] Ibid., 496 (#295). On weeping in hell, cf. idem, *Musnad*, 75 (#125).

[36] Ibn al-Jawzī, *Ṣifat al-ṣafwa*, IV, 145, quoted in Bonner, *Aristocratic violence*, 120. According to al-Ghazālī, Ibn al-Mubārak once said to his companions: "Yesterday I behaved in an insolent way vis-à-vis God: I asked him for paradise." Cf. Ghazālī, *Iḥyāʾ*, tr. Gramlich, *Stufen*, 386.

[37] Ibn al-Jawzī, *Ṣifat al-ṣafwa*, IV, 137–8; al-Khaṭīb al-Baghdādī, *Taʾrīk Baghdād*, X, 167. Cf. Bonner, *Aristocratic violence*, 119; Melchert, "Ibn al-Mubārak's *K. al-jihād*."

[38] Rudolf Leszynski's 1905 edition, based on a unicum, has been superseded by the 1976 edition of Raif Georges Khoury, on which see the review by G. H. A. Juynboll, *Bibliotheca Orientalis* 36 (1979), 242b-244b. Asad, a grandson of the Umayyad caliph Ibrāhīm b. al-Walīd (r. 126–7/744), took refuge in Egypt after the ʿAbbāsid revolution. His *K. al-Zuhd* focuses almost exclusively on hell (thirty-eight items) and the horrors of the Judgement (sixty-one items), but there is reason to think that the work as we know it is incomplete, and that its original title is lost. Cf. *TG*, II, 726–7; Melchert, "Locating hell," 104–5.

[39] Hannād, *Zuhd*, I, 47–136 (##1–180, paradise), 157–94 (##212–313, hell).

[40] Melchert, "Locating hell," 114.

traditions about paradise and hell than their *zuhd* counterparts. While the *K. al-Muṣannaf* of the Yemeni ʿAbd al-Razzāq al-Ṣanʿānī (d. 211/827) offers a relatively modest twenty-five traditions in its chapter on paradise and eighteen traditions in its chapters on hell,[41] a generation later the *K. al-Musnad* of Aḥmad b. Ḥanbal (d. 241/855) includes numerous traditions, providing an "almost complete description"[42] of paradise and hell, such as one finds in specialised hadith collections dedicated to the otherworld compiled in later times. In the *K. al-Muṣannaf* of Ibn Ḥanbal's contemporary and fellow citizen of Baghdad Ibn Abī Shayba (d. 235/849), the chapter on paradise boasts 163 items while there are eighty-two items in the chapter on hell.[43]

The formative period of eschatological hadith is capped by the pious Baghdad littérateur Ibn Abī l-Dunyā (d. 281/894), whose work brings the first period of expansion of the Sunni corpus of eschatological traditions to an end. A tutor of two ʿAbbāsid caliphs in their youth, Ibn Abī l-Dunyā is remembered for his particular prolificacy in the twin areas of renunciation (*zuhd*) and "exhortations that stir the hearts of their audience" (*raqāʾiq*). Of the more than sixty works that are attributed to him,[44] a dozen or more deal directly with eschatological topics, including the two works entitled *What Paradise is like* (*Ṣifat al-janna*, with some 350 items) and *What Hell is like* (*Ṣifat al-nār*, with some 260 items).[45] The traditions Ibn Abī l-Dunyā reports represent a veritable storehouse of traditional eschatological imagery as it grew in the first three centuries of Islam, still largely unhampered by the more rigorous criteria of later hadith criticism. Later authors appreciated Ibn Abī l-Dunyā's erudition, but as a transmitter of hadiths he was merely considered to be "sincere" (*ṣadūq*),[46] a technical term that tended to be used as a euphemism for otherwise praiseworthy scholars thought to have circulated hadiths of less than perfect authenticity.[47]

The works of the third/ninth century up to Ibn Abī l-Dunyā, many of which were compiled in Iraq, the hub of the Islamic empire, consolidate rather than increase the body of traditions that concern us here. The formative milieu for the emerging Islamic picture of paradise and hell is to be sought in earlier times and elsewhere, among the South Arabian tribes whose acquaintance with Judeo-Christian lore was tinged by a sense of near-expectancy of the end of the world, in the circles of early exegetes

[41] ʿAbd al-Razzāq, *Muṣannaf*, *b. al-janna wa-ṣifatihā*, XI, 413–21 (##20866–90), *b. man yakhruju min al-nār*, XI, 407–13 (##20856–65), *b. ṣifat ahl al-nār*, XI, 421–3 (##20891–8).

[42] El-Saleh, *La vie future*, 26. Ibn Ḥanbal also compiled a *K. al-Zuhd*, on which cf. Melchert, "Aḥmad b. Ḥanbal's *Book of Renunciation*."

[43] Ibn Abī Shayba, *Muṣannaf*, IX, 124–74 (*k. al-janna*), 175–203 (*k. dhikr al-nār*).

[44] Cf. Weipert and Weninger, "Die erhaltenen Werke"; Weipert, "Fortsetzung und Schluss."

[45] Ibn Abī l-Dunyā, *Ṣifat al-janna*; idem, *Ṣifat al-nār*.

[46] Dhahabī, *Tadhkirat al-ḥuffāẓ*, II, 181.

[47] Juynboll, *Muslim tradition*, 158. On Ibn Abī l-Dunyā's reputation as a *ḥadith* transmitter, see also the comments made by Librande, "Ibn Abī l-Dunyā'," 12.

TABLE 1. *Occurrence of the terms* al-janna *("the Garden") and* al-nār *("the Fire") in some traditionist works of the third/ninth and later centuries*

	al-jannā/al-nār	percentage
ʿAbd al-Razzāq (d. 211/827), *Muṣannaf*	211/226 [total: 437]	48.3%/51.7%
Ibn Abī Shayba (d. 235/849), *Muṣannaf*	414/385 [total: 799]	51,8%/48,3%
Ibn Ḥanbal (d. 241/855), *Musnad*	1317/976 [total: 2293]	57,4%/42,6%
al-Bukhārī (d. 256/870), *Ṣaḥīḥ*	322/244 [total: 566]	56,9%/43,1%
Muslim (d. 261/875), *Ṣaḥīḥ*	170/152 [total: 322]	52,8%/47,2%
al-Tirmidhī (d. 279/892), *Jāmiʿ*	271/154 [total: 425]	63,8%/36,2%
al-Ṭabarānī (d. 360/971), *al-Muʿjam al-kabīr*	1663/1209 [total: 2872]	57,9%/42,1%
al-Muttaqī al-Hindī (d. 975/1567), *Kanz al-ʿummāl*	2918/1833 [total: 4751]	61,4%/38,6%

Note: This comparative table is based on keyword searches in the digital collection *al-Maktaba al-shāmila*.

who felt a need to clarify and elaborate on the Qurʾānic imagery of the otherworld, and among the frontier communities residing at the margin of empire, in regions such as the Yemen, Egypt and North Africa, Northern Syria, and Khorasan, places where interaction with the eschatological thought of other religious communities may have been more open-ended, while the frontier situation made war, death, and the afterlife a daily preoccupation.[48] It is noteworthy that in third/ninth-century collections, hell is gradually given shorter shrift (see Table 1). This may indicate a general development away from the fear-driven devotion of the second/eighth century to the more optimistic piety of later centuries, an observation that resonates with the view that there was a shift in the prevailing mood in pious circles of the Islamic third/ninth century, away from a "deliberate cultivation of anxious fear" towards an affirmation of "confidence in the salvation of all Muslims."[49]

48 Claude Gilliot suggests that the view of the Khorasanian exegete Muqātil b. Sulaymān (d. 150/767) that the inhabitants of paradise will see God with their own eyes (*muʿāyanatan*, see *Tafsīr*, IV, 513) is influenced by "concrete representations of paradise that were widespread ... in the milieu of the combatants of *jihād*." See Gilliot, "La vision de Dieu," 249. Cf. idem, "L'embarras d'un exégète," 47–8; *TG*, II, 530.

49 See Melchert, "Exaggerated fear," 300. *Pace* Rustomji, *The Garden and the Fire*, 64, who maintains that the "predominance of the Garden in early texts is in marked contrast to later

The Second Period of Expansion (*ca.* Fourth–Sixth/ Tenth–Twelfth Century)

The so-called *Six Books* of hadiths, compiled in Iraq and Persia around the turn of the third/ninth and fourth/tenth century, achieved their canonical status no earlier than the sixth/twelfth century.[50] They privilege Prophetic hadiths to the exclusion of other material. By contrast, a generation earlier, Ibn Abī Shayba, like Ibn al-Mubārak before him, traces only a quarter of his paradise and hell traditions in the *K. al-Muṣannaf* back to the Prophet. The proportion of Prophetic traditions in Ibn Abī l-Dunyā's *What Paradise is like* is somewhat higher at circa 35 percent; however, only a third of these Prophetic traditions were considered trustworthy enough by later scholars to end up in one of the *Six Books*.[51] As for the remaining circa 65 percent, they are stories and traditions quoted on the authority of the early generation of Muslims, the *salaf*.

In the canonical collections, by contrast, one encounters a reduced picture of the otherworld. The three of the *Six Books* in which paradise and hell receive the greatest attention are *The Books of Sound Traditions* (*Ṣaḥīḥ*s) of al-Bukhārī (d. 256/870) and Muslim (d. 261/875), as well as the *Comprehensive Collection* (*al-Jāmiʿ*) of al-Tirmidhī (d. 279/892). Al-Bukhārī, the most famous of the lot, does not dedicate separate chapters to either paradise or hell, but instead includes eschatological traditions in his chapters on "The Beginnings of Creation" (*K. Badʾ al-khalq*, some sixty traditions, including thirty-five Qurʾānic glosses), "Exhortations that Stir the Hearts of Their Audience" (*K. al-Riqāq*, some twenty-five traditions), and "Qurʾānic Exegesis" (*K. al-Tafsīr*, some thirty traditions), in addition to some others (e.g., the chapter on jihad, with seven paradise traditions).[52] Muslim's collection has rather less to offer. His chapter on resurrection and the afterworld, which includes many doublettes, features some twenty-three traditions on paradise, twelve on hell, and another nine combined traditions.[53] Fairly illustrative of Muslim's general distrust of eschatological traditions is an anecdote he relates about the Companion, ʿAbdallāh Ibn Masʿūd. While ʿAbdallāh leisurely rests in his house in Kufa, chatting with friends, news are brought that a popular preacher (*qāṣṣ*) at one of Kufa's city gates is telling

texts where the Fire is of greater concern," a claim that rests on the erroneous assumption that the anonymous text known as *Daqāʾiq al-akhbār* is different from, and of later provenance than, the *K. al-Ḥaqāʾiq wa-l-daqāʾiq*, commonly (mis-)attributed to Abū l-Layth al-Samarqandī. Cf. ibid., 110, and the discussion in the following text, pp. 108–12.

50 Brown, *Canonization*, 9.

51 There are forty-eight canonical traditions among the hadiths in Ibn Abī l-Dunyā's *Ṣifat al-nār*, which are found, often simultaneously, in al-Tirmidhī (17x), followed by al-Bukhārī (15x), Muslim (11x), Ibn Māja (3x), and Abū Dāwūd (2x).

52 El-Saleh, *Vie future*, 150–1.

53 Muslim, *Ṣaḥīḥ, k. al-janna* 1–53, IV, 2174–93. Some more eschatological traditions can be found scattered over Muslim's collection. Cf. El-Saleh, *Vie future*, 151.

strange stories about the end of time. Suddenly angered, ʿAbdallāh sits up on his couch and exclaims: "O people! Those who know something, let them say it! But those who don't should say: 'God knows better'!" ʿAbdallāh then provides a 'correct' piece of eschatology, traced back to the Prophet.[54]

The canonical collector who is most interested in eschatological traditions is al-Tirmidhī. His chapters on paradise and hell feature forty-nine and thirty-two items, respectively.[55] In each case, al-Tirmidhī notes the degree of authenticity that a hadith can claim. It is noteworthy that more than half of al-Tirmidhī's paradise and hell traditions suffer from a lack of corroboration in this respect; they are classified by al-Tirmidhī as *gharīb*, or "rare." This contrasts sharply with the criteria of admissibility al-Tirmidhī applies in other chapters of his work, for example, those that concern ritual and legal rules. From the traditions he cites on the topic of fasting, for example, he declares only 17 percent to be *gharīb*; from those concerning inheritance rules, only 7 percent. One sees here a greater willingness to accept hadiths with a less convincing pedigree in the area of eschatology than in that of ritual and law. Perhaps this should not surprise us, given that third/ninth-century traditionists generally seem to have been more interested in legal hadith than in other fields of knowledge. Besides, a "rare" tradition is not by definition an invented tradition. Regardless, from the mid-third/ninth century onwards, a "near consensus" emerged among scholars of hadiths that "authenticity requirements for topics such as … exhortatory (*targhīb*) and dissuasive (*tarhīb*) homiletics [as well as] descriptions of what sort of reward or punishment awaited certain deeds in the Afterlife" should be relaxed, as long as these hadiths were useful for educating the masses.[56] On the one hand, the genre of hadith collections about paradise and hell benefitted from this attitude, as it facilitated the genre's growth.[57] On the other, the subsequent history of this kind of literature is marked by regular bitter disagreements over what kind of hadiths could legitimately be included and what could not.

Around the middle of the third/ninth century, the hadith literature on paradise and hell splits up into two different strands, a traditionist and a

[54] Ibid., *k. al-munāfiqīn* 39, 40 (*b. al-dukhān*), IV, 2155–7. The *qāṣṣ* claims that the "visible smoke" that will appear in the sky on the Day of Resurrection (Qurʾān 44:10) is the combined exhalation of the unbelievers, and that the believers will catch cold by inhaling it.

[55] Tirmidhī, *Jāmiʿ*, *k. ṣifat al-janna*, IV, 670–701 (in twenty-seven *bābs*), *k. ṣifat jahannam*, IV, 701–17 (in thirteen *bābs*).

[56] Jonathan Brown cites the Basran ʿAbd al-Raḥmān b. Mahdī (d. 198/814) and Ibn Ḥanbal as early examples of this attitude. See Brown, "Even if it's not true," 7–9. On this topic, see already the remarks of Goldziher, *Muslim studies*, II, 145–7; now also Ahmed, "The characteristics of paradise"; Brown, *Misquoting Muhammad*, 220–60.

[57] As an example, one might refer to the Basran ʿAbd al-ʿAzīz b. ʿAbd al-Ṣamad (d. *ca.* 190/805), a contemporary ʿAbd al-Raḥmān b. Mahdī (cf. the previous footnote), and the likely originator of two highly imaginative paradise traditions. See *ECḤ*, 20.

parenetic one. While proponents of the first were primarily concerned with the activity of collecting, with different collectors embracing different standards of admissibility of weak or "rare" traditions, the primary aim of contributors to the second was to use this material towards moralising and hortatory ends. Particularly when it oscillates towards a broad, "popular" rather than a literate audience, this parenetic body of literature shows little concern for the correctness of the chains of transmission (*isnād*s) of hadiths, and instead stresses storytelling and the spectacular aspects of paradise and hell. Doubtlessly, these two genres of narrative eschatology were not sealed off from one another, but rather existed cheek by jowl. People could choose to participate in both of them simultaneously, if they so wished. The distinction is useful, however, if one wishes to stake out the rough contours of the history of Islamic narrative literature on paradise and hell in its mature phases, a task to which we now turn.

Traditionists living in the centuries that witnessed the gradual emergence of the *Six Books* as canon continued to compile their own substantial hadith collections, and the corpus of eschatological hadiths entered into a second period of expansion. For example, al-Ṭabarānī (d. 360/971), a scholar who spent his later life in Isfahan, authored a gargantuan hadith work, the *Great Dictionary* (*al-Muʿjam al-kabīr*), which easily surpasses Ibn Abī Shayba's or Ibn Ḥanbal's collections in regard to its eschatological material. Al-Ṭabarānī took pride "in gathering rare *ḥadīth*s found nowhere else," while authenticity "was not one of his concerns."[58] His student, Abū Nuʿaym al-Iṣfahānī (d. 430/1038), was the author of a hadith work entitled *What Paradise is like* (*Ṣifat al-janna*). The offspring of an old Iranian family of scholars, Abū Nuʿaym is known, first and foremost, for his vast compilation of biographies of the pious exemplars of the early Islamic centuries, *The Adornment of the Friends of God* (*Ḥilyat al-awliyāʾ*), a major source for the history of *zuhd* and early Sufism, that quotes freely from Ibn al-Mubārak's *Book of Renunciation* and also includes much eschatological material.[59]

What Paradise is like sets a new standard of exhaustiveness. Abū Nuʿaym collects some 450 traditions about paradise, of which roughly a third are non-Prophetic, with many exegetical glosses among them. The work, which repeatedly invokes the unfathomability tradition,[60] is ordered thematically. However, there is no visible progress of topics. For example, the vision of God is dealt with in the last third of the work,[61] but then, anticlimactically, follow traditions about, for example, the horses, trees, and tents in paradise.

[58] Brown, *Canonization*, 61. Cf. *GAS*, S I, 279.

[59] Khoury, "Importance," 84–94. As Khoury notes, Abū Nuʿaym was also familiar with the hadiths of Asad b. Mūsā. See ibid., 95. On Asad, see preceding text, pp. 75, 78.

[60] Abū Nuʿaym, *Ṣifat al-janna*, 36–7 (#8), 41–2 (#16), 135–48 (##109–24).

[61] Ibid., 225–30 (##394–7).

Abū Nuʿaym is said to have disapproved of the exaggerated anthropomorphism of Ḥanbalite theology, and his arrangement of paradise traditions, in which the vision of God occurs as if in passing, perhaps reflects this predilection. In turn, the Ḥanbalites of Iṣfahān, who dominated the hadith sessions in the city's congregational mosque, found Abū Nuʿaym's teachings suspicious and boycotted him. He later retaliated by accusing Ibn Manda (d. 395/1005), the leader of the local Ḥanbalite traditionists, of confusing hadiths in his old age.[62]

Like his contemporary al-Bayhaqī (d. 459/1066), author of several substantial collections of eschatological hadiths,[63] Abū Nuʿaym was guided by the notion that hadiths exhorting paradise as the reward for virtue and threatening hell as the punishment for sin did not require strict *isnād* criticism. This maxim had been openly embraced by al-Bayhaqī's and Abū Nuʿaym's teacher, the famous traditionist al-Ḥākim al-Naysābūrī (d. 405/1014),[64] and a century earlier, though a little less sweepingly, by Ibn Abī Ḥātim (d. 327/938) of Rayy.[65] However, there were also those who objected to this point, notably the Ḥanbalites, even if their eponym Aḥmad b. Ḥanbal was known to have been lax with regard to the *isnād*s of nonlegal hadiths.[66] One of the most vociferous medieval critics of laxity in the transmission of eschatological hadiths is the Ḥanbalī preacher and polymath of Baghdad, Ibn al-Jawzī (d. 597/1201).[67] He criticises Abū Nuʿaym for including in his works spurious (*bāṭila*) and forged (*mawḍūʿa*) hadiths. However, what really disqualifies Abū Nuʿaym, according to Ibn al-Jawzī, is that he does not make it clear to his readers when the trustworthiness of a tradition

62 *EIr*, s.v. Abū Noʿaym al-Eṣfahānī (W. Madelung); *TG*, II, 629–30.

63 Bayhaqī, *al-Baʿth wa-l-nushūr*; idem, *Ithbāt ʿadhāb al-qabr*. Also al-Bayhaqī's *Great Book of Renunciation* (*K. al-Zuhd al-kabīr*) deserves mention in this context. On his stance on the legitimacy of weak hadiths in the area of exhortatory preaching, see idem, *Dalāʾil*, I, 33–4.

64 Al-Ḥākim al-Naysābūrī, *Mustadrak*, I, 490–1 (from ʿAbd al-Raḥmān b. Mahdī [d. 198/814]).

65 Ibn Abī Ḥātim, *Taqdima*, 6. Ibn Abī Ḥātim states that transmitters of the *raqāʾiq* and exhortatory preachings must merely be known to be sincere (*ṣadūq*). Another important, though later, witness to this position is the Damascene Shāfiʿite Ibn al-Ṣalāḥ (d. 643/1245), director of the local hadith academy (*dār al-ḥadīth*). Ibn al-Ṣalāḥ explicitly acknowledges that it is not even necessary to draw attention to the weakness of *isnād*s in eschatological traditions. See Ibn al-Ṣalāḥ, *ʿUlūm al-ḥadīth*, 103, quoted in Ahmed, "The characteristics of paradise."

66 See Brown, *Misquoting Muhammad*, 231. Ibn Ḥanbal is reported to have said that knowledge about Qurʾānic exegesis, the campaigns of the Prophet (*maghāzī*) and the apocalypse (*malāḥim*) lacks proper foundations (*uṣūl*). See Ibn ʿAdī al-Qaṭṭān, *Kāmil*, I, 212; Ibn Taymiyya, *Majmūʿ fatāwā shaykh al-Islām*, XIII, 346; Ibn Rajab, *Sharḥ ʿilal al-Tirmidhī*, I, 74. Melchert, however, does not see higher standards of admissibility for legal hadith at play in Ibn Ḥanbal's *Musnad*. See Melchert, "The *Musnad* of Aḥmad," 45–7.

67 Cf. Brown, *Misquoting Muhammad*, 253–4. Later proponents of this criticism include Ibn Qayyim al-Jawziyya (d. 751/1350) and Ibn Kathīr (d. 774/1373). For references, see Ahmed, "The characteristics of paradise."

is in doubt.[68] Ibn al-Jawzī compares traditionists who proceed in this way to counterfeiters who put false money into circulation.[69]

The Third Period of Expansion (*ca.* Seventh–Ninth/Thirteenth–Fifteenth Century)

With Ibn al-Jawzī, the second period of expansion of eschatological hadiths comes to an end, to be followed by a period of contraction and careful revision of the material. So much is true, at any rate, for the Ḥanbalī contributions to the genre. In the centuries after Ibn al-Jawzī, the Ḥanbalites, whose centre of activity shifted from Baghdad to Damascus,[70] produced a continuous stream of hadith works on the afterlife; in fact this genre became a kind of Damascene speciality. At the beginning of this line of Ḥanbalite works stand two scions of the al-Maqdisī family, a scholarly dynasty that flourished from the sixth/twelfth century onwards in the Damascus suburb of al-Ṣāliḥiyya. Known for their charity and asceticism (*zuhd*), the Maqdisīs, by their "combination of charismatic and literalist elements blended by individual effort," facilitated the rise of a certain kind of traditionist "orthodox religiosity."[71] ʿAbd al-Ghanī al-Maqdisī (d. 600/1203), who spent years of his youth studying hadiths in Iraq and Iran – on one occasion, he was driven out of Isfahan for his criticism of Abū Nuʿaym[72] – compiled a collection of hell traditions that includes 114 items in its modern edition.[73] His student Ḍiyāʾ al-Dīn Muḥammad al-Maqdisī (d. 643/1245), who also travelled to Baghdad to hear hadiths and study with Ibn al-Jawzī, penned a work entitled *What Paradise is like* (with 212 items), echoing the title of Abū Nuʿaym's collection.[74] Like al-Tirmidhī did before them, ʿAbd al-Ghanī and Ḍiyāʾ al-Dīn do their due diligence, noting whether a tradition can be considered sound (*ṣaḥīḥ*). Most of the hadiths they relate do fulfill this criterion. They convey material from noncanonical authors such as Ibn Abī l-Dunyā and al-Ṭabarānī only occasionally.

About a century later, the historian and Qurʾān commentator Ibn Kathīr (d. 774/1373) finished his massive world chronicle, *The Beginning and the End* (*al-Bidāya wa-l-nihāya*), with a section dealing with the apocalypse and the afterworld. Though a Shāfiʿī of legal persuasion, Ibn Kathīr was closely

[68] Ibn al-Jawzī, *Ṣifat al-ṣafwa*, I, 24–5.

[69] Idem, *Taḥqīq*, I, 464.

[70] Goldziher, "Zur Geschichte der hanbalitischen Bewegungen," 21–2; Makdisi, "L'Islam hanbalisant," 211–44.

[71] Leder, "The Ḥanbalī Maqdisīs," 303.

[72] See ibid., 297–301; Leiser, "Ḥanbalism in Egypt," 171–2. Cf. *GAL*, I, 437–8, S I, 605–7; *Encyclopaedia Islamica*, s.v. ʿAbd al-Ghanī al-Maqdisī (A. Pakatchi).

[73] Maqdisī, *Dhikr al-nār*. On ʿAbd al-Ghanī, see Leiser, "Ḥanbalism in Egypt," 171–3.

[74] Maqdisī, *Ṣifat al-janna*. On Muḥammad, see *GAL*, I, 398–9; S I, 690.

aligned with Damascene Ḥanbalism, and with the famous Ibn Taymiyya (d. 728/1328) in particular.[75] Ibn Kathīr's teacher, the traditionist and historian al-Dhahabī (d. 748/1348), condemned the use of weak hadiths in the area of "[eschatological] exhortations";[76] he was also lukewarm in his appreciation of Abū Nuʿaym,[77] whose name figures hardly at all in Ibn Kathīr's work. Published separately in two volumes,[78] Ibn Kathīr's treatment showcases the "rigorist Sunni traditionalism"[79] that had become the hallmark of hadith scholarship in Mamluk Syria and that had made Damascus, in Ibn Kathīr's own words, the "citadel of the Sunna." Ibn Kathīr treats, first, verses of the Qurʾān, and then he quotes hadiths and their variants from the canonical collections, providing full *isnād*s. In some instances, he also includes traditions from other collections and relates the opinions of earlier scholars (including, e.g., al-Tirmidhī and Ḍiyāʾ al-Dīn al-Maqdisī) as to the degree of soundness that certain hadiths can claim.

Another Damascene traditionist of the eighth/fourteenth century, Ibn Rajab (d. 795/1393), authored a flood of works dedicated to eschatology, including one entitled *What Hell and Paradise are like* (*K. Ṣifat al-nār wa-ṣifat al-janna*).[80] The title of Ibn Rajab's work reprises that of Ibn Abī l-Dunyā's verbatim, and this does not seem happenstance: Ibn Rajab, in another of his books on eschatology, *The Terrors of the Graves* (*K. Ahwāl al-qubūr*), quotes stories and *salaf* traditions from Ibn Abī l-Dunyā liberally, and he has been held responsible for a veritable "Ibn Abī l-Dunyā renaissance."[81] Ibn Rajab, perhaps even more so than Ibn Kathīr, includes rather than banishes less reliable materials, each time carefully identifying them as such. This approach may be said to be the characteristicum of yet another period of expansion of traditionist eschatology in Sunni Islam.

Parallel to this renewed Ḥanbalī interest in eschatological hadiths in Syria, traditionists in the western parts of the Islamic world also produced works in the genre. In Muslim Spain, where the *K. al-Muṣannaf* of Ibn Abī Shayba was considered one of ten canonical collections of hadiths,[82] Ibn Ḥabīb's *What Paradise is like* was followed by several specialised hadith collections about

[75] See *EI2*, s.v. Ibn Kathīr (H. Laoust), III, 817b-818b; Ohlander, "Ibn Kathīr."

[76] Dhahabī, *Tadhkirat al-ḥuffāẓ*, I, 15–6.

[77] Idem, *Mīzān*, I, 111.

[78] Ibn Kathīr, *Nihāyat al-bidāya*. Curiously, *Nihāyat al-bidāya* was not published as part of the standard Cairo edition (1932–9) of *al-Bidāya wa-l-nihāya*. See Laoust, "Ibn Kaṯīr historien," 64n1. It is likewise missing from more recent editions, such as the one produced in Cairo by Dār al-Manār in 1321/2001.

[79] Ohlander, "Ibn Kathīr," 158.

[80] This work, which seems lost, is mentioned in Ibn al-Mibrad, *Jawhar*, 51, quoted in Bauer, "Totenbücher," 427n5. Bauer refers to Ibn Rajab's efforts as the "apogee of ḥadīth criticism" in traditionist eschatology. See ibid., 428.

[81] Ibid.

[82] *EI2*, s.v. Ibn Abī l-Shayba, III, 692b (Ch. Pellat).

the afterlife.[83] The most well known of these is al-Qurṭubī's (d. 621/1273) *Memoir about the Conditions of the Dead [in the Grave] and the Last Things* (*al-Tadhkira fī aḥwāl al-mawtā wa-umūr al-ākhira*). Al-Qurṭubī, who spent the final decades of his life in Egypt, witnessed two traumatic political upheavals during his lifetime, the conquest of his native Cordoba by Castilian forces in 633/1236 and the sack of Baghdad by the Mongols in 656/1258, events that may have strengthened his interest in things apocalyptic and eschatological.[84] It is curious that the apocalyptic portion of his *Memoir* comes *after* the parts that treat of the believers' lives in the grave, resurrection, and paradise and hell, in opposition to Ibn Kathīr's work. The great success enjoyed by al-Qurṭubī's *Memoir* may have been propelled by his declared intention to write a comprehensive yet "concise book" (*kitāb wajīz*)[85] of hadiths, divided into numerous chapters (*abwāb*) to which are appended, in as much as the material invites it, explanatory sections (*fuṣūl*) that enrich the Qur'ānic and hadith material with lexicographic and interpretive commentary.

In the centuries after al-Qurṭubī, the *Memoir* was abridged and imitated several times.[86] The *Book of Precious Knowledge in the Contemplation of Eschatology* (*K. al-ʿUlūm al-fākhira fī l-naẓar fī umūr al-ākhira*) of the Algerian Sufi scholar ʿAbd al-Raḥmān b. Muḥammad al-Thaʿālibī (d. 875/1470) relies extensively on al-Qurṭubī's work, but also invokes a plethora of other authorities, among them Ibn al-Mubārak and Abū Nuʿaym, as well as renunciant and mystical authors such as al-Muḥāsibī (d. 243/857), al-Ghazālī (d. 505/1111), Ibn al-Kharrāṭ (d. 581/1185), and Ibn al-ʿArabī (d. 638/1240).[87] Al-Thaʿālibī states that he compiled his work, at the ripe age of sixty-three, for his own contemplative use.[88] Another well-known Sufi author, the Egyptian ʿAbd al-Wahhāb al-Shaʿrānī (d. 973/1565), produced what is probably the most well-known abridgement (*mukhtaṣar*) of

83 A useful overview is provided by Lucini Baquerizo, "Aproximación," 119–21. In addition to the works discussed in the preceding text, one should mention the two works of Abū Bakr b. al-ʿArabī (d. 543/1148), *Aḥkām al-ākhira wa-l-kashf ʿan asrārihā al-bāhira*; idem (attr.), *K. al-Dhākhira fī ʿilm al-dār al-ākhira*. See ibid.

84 See Filiu, *L'apocalypse*, 64.

85 Qurṭubī, *Tadhkira*, I, 9.

86 Ḥājjī Khalīfa notes this, but provides no titles. See Ḥājjī Khalīfa, *Kashf*, II, 266. In addition to the works discussed in the text, reworkings of al-Qurṭubī's work include that by Aḥmad b. Muḥammad al-Suḥaymī, (d. 1178/1764–5), and the abridgement of Muḥammad b. ʿUthmān al-Luʾluʾī (d. 867/1463), a Shāfiʿī scholar from Damascus, under the title *al-Nujūm al-muzhira fī ikhtiṣār al-Tadhkira*. Al-Luʾluʾī also wrote his own eschatological handbook, the *Hādī l-qulūb al-ṭāhira ilā dār al-ākhira*. See Kaḥḥāla, *Muʿjam*, III, 480. Also the *Sharḥ al-ṣudūr* of al-Suyūṭī, a work on the *barzakh* (see following text, pp. 122–8), follows al-Qurṭubī's *Memoir*. On al-Qurṭubī's work and reception history, see the unpublished study by Mayor, "La *Taḏkira*." I would like to thank Rafael Mayor for sharing his piece with me.

87 Thaʿālibī, *K. al-ʿulūm al-fākhira*. On al-Thaʿālibī, see Kaḥḥāla, *Muʿjam*, II, 122; Brockelmann, *GAL*, S II, 351. On the renunciant and mystical authors used by al-Thaʿālibī, see chs. 3 and 7.

88 Thaʿālibī, *K. al-ʿulūm al-fākhira*, I, 2.

al-Qurṭubī's *Memoir*. The goal of his abridgement, explains al-Shaʿrānī in the introduction, is to free al-Qurṭubī's work from all superfluous commentary, particularly in the area of lexicography and grammar, which otherwise might distract the reader from the essence of the work, that is, the cultivation of the thought of death and its terrors.[89] Al-Thaʿālibī's and al-Shaʿrānī's works bear witness to the fact that in late-medieval times, Sufism and traditionism went hand in hand.

Arguably the most successful continuation of al-Qurṭubī's work, however, is that of the Egyptian polymath al-Suyūṭī (d. 911/1505).[90] Al-Suyūṭī, like Ibn Rajab before him, distributes a bevy of eschatological hadiths over several separate compilations, devoting one of them, entitled *The Shining Full Moons of Eschatology* (*al-Budūr al-sāfira fī ʿulūm al-ākhira*), to the events of the Resurrection and of hell and paradise.[91] While al-Suyūṭī lacks the rigour of Ibn Rajab and the Damascene hadith critics,[92] he does not simply amass everything about the topic that appears relevant to him. His work is in fact slightly shorter than that of al-Qurṭubī. Yet at the same, he cites traditions freely on the authority of virtually all the authorities of earlier times, including, notably, Ibn Abī l-Dunyā, al-Ṭabarānī, and Abū Nuʿaym. Though to a lesser extent than al-Thaʿālibī, al-Suyūṭī, a member of the Shādhiliyya order, also incorporates Sufi elements into his work. For example, he cites the early Sufi al-Basṭāmī, and he relates a tradition that accords a special place of privilege in paradise to "those who love each other in God" (*al-mutaḥābbūna fī l-lāh*).[93] In comparison with al-Qurṭubī's somewhat talkative style and meandering sequence of topics, al-Suyūṭī offers less commentary, his treatment being more concise and target oriented. He moves systematically and seamlessly from cosmological to topographical,

[89] Shaʿrānī, *Mukhtaṣar*, 2.

[90] Al-Suyūṭī's work, for reasons that ought to be studied, seems to have eclipsed that of the Cairene traditionist Ibn Ḥajar al-ʿAsqalānī (d. 852/1449), who wrote a generation or two earlier. Three manuscripts of the latter's *Brilliant Pearls in the Explanation of the Conditions of the Otherworld* (*al-Durar al-zāhira fī bayān aḥwāl ahl al-ākhira*) seem to be known, in Bankipore, Cairo, and Gotha (fragm.). See *GAL* II, 83; S II, 74 (#32); Lucini Baquerizo, "Aproximación," 115. To mention one example, *al-Budūr al-sāfira* is the standard text referenced in the chapters on paradise and hell in the work of the widely known Sufi-scholar from Fez, al-Lamaṭī (d. 1156/1743), *Ibrīz* (tr. O'Kane and Radtke), 894–924.

[91] Al-Suyūṭī, *al-Budūr al-sāfira*. A popularising eschatology ascribed to al-Suyūṭī is called *al-Durar al-ḥusān*. This work is an uneven composition, dealing with death and how one is to encounter it, and with the pleasures of paradise. Hadiths lack *isnād*s, in the style typical of late-medieval parenetic and popular literature, which makes the attribution to al-Suyūṭī doubtful.

[92] Bauer, "Totenbücher," 429.

[93] Suyūṭī, *Budūr*, 516, 615. Al-Suyūṭī's allegiance to an "orthodox" form of Sufism is demonstrated by his *Taʾyīd al-ḥaqīqa*, a work in which he defends the Shādhilī tradition against accusations of immanentism levelled at it by the likes of Ibn Taymiyya. I owe this reference to Arjan Post.

botanical, culinary, and somatic aspects of both eternal abodes. His section on hell, after reviewing different kinds of punishment, ends with the prediction of eternal damnation for the unbelievers, and then introduces various modalities of rescue from the fire for Muslim sinners. The section on paradise, after presenting a panoply of physical and spiritual pleasures, ends with the visit of the blessed to the prophets in the higher gardens, and culminates in the vision of God.

Like Ibn al-Kathīr, al-Suyūṭī generally prefaces his chapters with a topical selection of Qurʾānic verses, an approach that is characteristic of many late-medieval collections of eschatological hadith. A salient feature of al-Suyūṭī's work, which may have contributed to its popularity, are sections interspersed among the more descriptive parts that offer information on what kind of actions (*aʿmāl*) on earth will be punished in a certain way in hell or rewarded in paradise. For example, al-Suyūṭī relates that one of the punishments in hell consists in being dragged over the ground on one's face. This, one learns as one reads on, is the punishment for those seeking martyrdom merely in order to achieve fame, vainglorious scholars and Qurʾān readers, and rich people who show off their generosity.[94] Likewise, following the chapters on the rejuvenated wives and houris in paradise, readers are told in a number of hadiths that these celestial beings are reserved for those who control their earthly angers and desires, pardon their murderers, clean mosques, fast in Ramadan, perform the duty to command right and forbid wrong, pronounce supererogatory pious formulas, and in general show complete obedience to God.[95] In addition to applying structural principles of earlier traditionist works to the full arsenal of eschatological hadiths, al-Suyūṭī's *Shining Full Moons* thus doubles as an ethical work: a practical guide to paradise and hell.

Late-Medieval Developments (*ca.* Tenth–Thirteenth/ Sixteenth–Nineteenth Century)

Al-Suyūṭī's *Shining Full Moons* brought the development of hadith handbooks about paradise and hell to a certain conclusion, towering over all further attempts to contribute to the genre. There is a relative dearth of comprehensive collections written about the topic in the centuries that follow al-Suyūṭī, although there may be manuscripts still awaiting discovery and study. A number of works certainly deserve mention. For example, Muḥammad al-Saffārīnī (d. 1189/1774), a Ḥanbalī scholar from rural Palestine, compiled a collection whose title, *The Swelling Oceans of Eschatology* (*al-Buḥūr al-zākhira fī ʿulūm al-ākhira*), echoes that of al-Suyūṭī.[96] Al-Saffārīnī's work is roughly twice as long as that of al-Suyūṭī,

[94] Suyūṭī, *Budūr*, 463.

[95] Ibid., 564–6.

[96] Saffārīnī, *Buḥūr*. On al-Saffārīnī, see Al-Najdī, *Suḥub*, II, 836–46.

not only because he cites a greater number of hadiths, in each case noting the degree of their reliability, but also because he devotes more attention to commentary and discussion of seemingly contradictory or difficult hadiths. Occasionally, he proposes new solutions. For example, when discussing the notion that there are more women in hell than men – a view that relies on a hadith found in al-Bukhārī's *Book of Sound Traditions* – al-Saffārīnī states that "it seems to me ... that [this is because] there are more women than men in *this* world."[97] He defends this idea by adducing a number of Prophetic hadiths and by a line of reasoning based on the legitimacy of polygamy in Islamic law. "God's actions," he argues, "are tied to wisdom (*maqrūna bi-l-ḥikma*), and it wouldn't be wise to join [one of] the many with a group of the few. Wisdom requires, to the contrary, that the many should be distributed [in equal parts] to the few." In a self-congratulatory manner, al-Saffārīnī concludes by saying, "I know nobody to have preceded me in this an argument and line of reasoning."[98] Although it has not been made the object of a separate study, al-Saffārīnī's *Swelling Oceans* deserves recognition as a significant eighteenth-century specimen of Sunni traditionist eschatology. A one-time student in Medina of Muḥammad Ḥayāt al-Sindī (d. 1163/1750), who was also a teacher of the two famous reformers Shāh Walī Allāh (d. 1206/1762) and Muḥammad Ibn ʿAbd al-Wahhāb (d. 1176/1792), al-Saffarīnī figures importantly in the revival of hadith scholarship in the eleventh/seventeenth and twelfth/eighteenth centuries.[99]

Also in this tradition belongs *The Vigilance of the Considerate* (*Yaqaẓat ūlī l-iʿtibār*) of Ṣiddīq Ḥasan Khān (d. 1307/1890), Nabob of Bhopal and second husband of the Sultan Shahjahan Begum (r. 1868–1901). Though not a work of great originality, it helped to spread a neo-orthodox literalism in the understanding of eschatological particulars, particularly on the Indian subcontinent. It is a compilation that deserves notice also because it exerts a palpable influence on modern-day eschatologists all over the Islamic world.[100] In the 1860s, Ṣiddīq Ḥasan Khān travelled to the Yemen and to

97 This inference had been drawn earlier by the Cordovan judge al-Qāḍī ʿIyāḍ (d. 544/1149) in his *Ikmāl al-muʿlim*, VIII, 366, quoted in Brown, *Misquoting Muhammad*, 245.

98 Saffārīnī, *Buḥūr*, 1039–40.

99 See, among others, Dallal, "The origins and objectives," 342; Nafi, "A teacher of Ibn ʿ "A al-Wahhāb," 220–2; Voll, "Hadith scholars," 264–7. Ḥayāt al-Sindī is attributed a work on eschatology, a commentary (*sharḥ*) on *al-Targhīb wa-l-tarhīb* of al-Mundhirī (d. 656/1258), in two volumes. See Nafi, "A teacher of Ibn ʿAbd al-Wahhāb," 217. The well-known work of another member of the Ḥaramayn circle, Muḥammad b. ʿAbd al-Rasūl al-Barzanjī (d. 1103/1691), *Al-Ishāʿa li-ashrāṭ al-sāʿa* (*The Spreading of the Signs of the Hour*), belongs to the apocalyptic genre, but al-Barzanjī is also the author of a work entitled *al-Qawl al-mukhtār fī taḥājat al-janna wa-l-nār* (*The Exquisite Discussion of [the Hadith] "Paradise and hell disputed [their respective status]"*). For a list of al-Barzanjī's works, see Baghdādī, *Hadiyat al-ʿārifīn*, II, columns 302–3.

100 Ṣiddīq Ḥasan Khān, *Yaqaẓat ūlī l-iʿtibār.* The work published under the title *Jahannam aḥwāluhā wa-ahluhā* is an abridged version of the *Yaqaẓat ūlī l-iʿtibār*.

Mecca, a journey that strengthened his aversion to nonliteralist approaches to traditionist literature. In India, he was affiliated with the so-called Ahl-i Ḥadīth, a nativistic movement characterised by an affinity to Wahhābī and Salafī thought, which sought to restore the alleged simplicity and purity of original Islam. Ṣiddīq Ḥasan Khān's works on eschatology, including *The Vigilance of the Considerate*, offer a simplified version of traditionist teachings, usually affirming the view that the reality of the things in the afterlife is beyond human comprehension and must not be made the object of speculation.[101]

What catches the eye in the centuries after al-Suyūṭī, however, is the emergence of smaller epistles (*rasā'il*) that deal with specific aspects of paradise and hell. As has been suggested, not only did these epistles make for less strenuous reading than al-Suyūṭī's massive compilation, but they responded to the reappearance of the plague in the Near East. Short and easy to consume, they provided consolation in times of crisis.[102] Prominent among this type of literature are treatises dealing with the death and afterlife of children.[103] Other short works of this kind give the impression that compilers turned to recondite topics deliberately, in order to produce something novel. For example, one of al-Saffārīnī's teachers, ʿAbd al-Ghanī al-Nābulusī (d. 1143/1731), penned a short treatise in which he collected all the hadiths in which appear the names of individual people and animals in paradise or hell.[104] Scholars in Damascus and Cairo wrote learned epistles about the question of whether men will have beards in paradise,[105] and whether only men will enjoy the vision of God's face or whether women will be granted this privilege, too.[106] Other epistles of this period discuss whether

[101] See Saeedullah, *The life and works*, 160, 164. On Ṣiddīq Ḥasan Khān, see EI2, s.v. Nawwāb Sayyid Ṣiddīḳ Ḥasan Khān, VII, 1048b-1049b (Z. Khan); van Ess, *Der Eine*, II, 1149–50. On his relationship to Ḥanbalī literature, see now Preckel, "Screening Ṣiddīq Ḥasan Khān's library."

[102] Bauer, "Totenbücher," 432. The plague hit Egypt in 748/1348. On the theological literature produced in response to this catastrophic event, see also van Ess, *Fehltritt*, 354–9.

[103] Examples include: Ibn Abī Ḥajala al-Tilimsānī (d. 776/1374–5), *Salwat al-ḥazīn fī mawt al-banīn*; al-Suyūṭī (d. 911/1505), *Faḍl al-jalad fī faqd al-walad*; Muḥammad b. Yūsuf al-Ṣāliḥī (d. 942/1535–6), *al-Faḍl al-mubīn fī l-ṣabr ʿinda faqd al-banāt wa-l-banīn* (in *GAL*, II, 305); al-Shahīd al-Thānī (d. 966/1557–8), *Musakkin al-fu'ād ʿinda faqd al-aḥibba wa-l-awlād*. For the latter, see *EI2*, s.v. al-Shahīd al-Thānī, IX, 209a-210a, at 209b (E. Kohlberg); *GAS*, S II 449. Cf. Giladi, *Children of Islam*, chs. 6 and 7.

[104] Nābulusī, *Ahl al-janna*. The work also includes references to objects and natural phenomena that simultaneously exist in this world and the otherworld. See ibid., 44–55, 74–7. On al-Nābulusī's mysticism, see Sirriyeh, *Sufi visionary*.

[105] Nājī (Damascus, d. 900/1494), *Ḥuṣūl*. Cf. Ahlwardt, *Handschriften-Verzeichnisse*, II, 649 (#2698). See also the lost (?) work of Shams al-Dīn Muḥammad b. ʿAlī Ibn Ṭūlūn (Cairo, d. 953/1546), *al-Durar al-fākhira fī dhikr man lahu liḥya fī l-ākhira*, mentioned in Ḥājjī Khalīfa, *Kashf*, III, 217.

[106] Suyūṭī, *Isbāl al-kisā'*.

children who are born out of wedlock (*walad al-zinā*) can enter paradise[107] or whether the Prophet's parents are in hell, seeing that they were unbelievers, having died before the advent of Islam.[108] There were also short works, for example, the one by the Meccan polygraph ʿAlī al-Qārī al-Harawī (d. 1014/1605), collecting traditions that stress the need to "fear the end" (*khawf al-khātima*).[109]

To conclude, this chapter has described three successive periods of expansion and contraction of eschatological hadiths in Sunni literature, leading up to the centuries after al-Suyūṭi, a time in which the material proliferates (giving rise to new comprehensive collections especially in the eleventh/seventeenth and twelfth/eighteenth centuries[110]) and splits up into smaller units. As a segue into the next chapter, one might add that the point of the small-scale works of later times was often no longer simply to collect eschatological hadiths, but to use hadiths towards the aim of exhortation, consolation, and entertainment. This prompts us to take a step back to the third/ninth century, and trace the history of the second major strand of Sunni narrative eschatology, the parenetic and popular one.

107 Baḥrānī (d. 1120/1708?), *Fī walad al-zinā*. Cf. Ahlwardt, *Handschriften-Verzeichnisse*, II, 652 (#2708). The topic seems to have attracted the interest of Shiʿi authors in particular, including early authorities such as al-Sharīf al-Murtaḍā (d. 436/1044), who devoted a separate treatise to it. See Kohlberg, "The position of the *walad zinā*," 259–64. On the hadith that the *walad al-zinā* does not enter paradise, see Munāwī, *Fayḍ al-qadīr*, IV, 415, and the references in Kohlberg, "The position of the *walad zinā*," 238n11.

108 E.g., Suyūṭī, *Masālik al-ḥunafāʾ*. Cf. *GAL* II, 185; Ahlwardt, *Handschriften-Verzeichnisse*, II, 651b-652b, and the list of further works in this genre in idem, II, 656a. For studies of the debate, which seems to have peaked between the tenth/sixteenth and twelfth/eighteenth centuries, see Franke, "Propheteneltern-Problem" (with a list of eight tractates in addition to the five authored by al-Suyūṭī); Dreher, *Maṭāliʿ al-nūr*.

109 Qārī, *Muqaddima*.

110 This is a development seemingly paralleled by the flowering of Shiʿi Akhbārī eschatology, for which see Chapter 6.

3

Hope, Fear, and Entertainment: Parenetic and Popular Muslim Literature on the Otherworld

Next to the extensive traditionist literature devoted to paradise and hell there is an important parenetic strand in the learned Muslim literature on the afterlife, as was suggested in the previous chapter. Although the boundary between these two branches is not always clear-cut, one may say that the latter is characterised by the selection of hadiths based primarily on their moralising content, at times also by the addition of significant hortatory comment to hadiths, and by a diminished interest in *isnād*s.

The roots of this parenetic tradition, like that of traditionist eschatology, reach back into the early centuries of Islam. At its beginning stand the preachers (*quṣṣāṣ*, sg. *qāṣṣ*) of early Islam, a class of religious experts who specialised in narrative exegesis of the Qur'ān and in moralising accounts of otherworldly bliss and torment.[1] Analysis of the chains of transmitters of biblical stories (*isrā'īliyyāt*) circulating in learned Muslim circles in the third/ninth century has brought to light a high percentage of non-Arab "clients" (*mawālī*, sg. *mawlā*) among the *quṣṣāṣ* of the first/seventh and second/eighth centuries, men who used their familiarity with biblical literature to carve out a place of honour and respect for themselves in the nascent Muslim community.[2] The *quṣṣāṣ* preached the pleasures of paradise to those fighting in the early civil wars of Islam,[3] but many of them were also known to practice a renunciant lifestyle (*zuhd*).[4] This fits with the observation made in the previous chapter that collectors of *zuhd* traditions active in the second/eighth and third/ninth centuries often showed an interest in eschatological traditions.

[1] ʿAthamina, "Al-Qaṣaṣ," 64. Cf. Juynboll, *Muslim tradition*, 11–12, 17 and passim; Wansbrough, *Quranic studies*, 147–8.

[2] See Newby, "Development," who gleans his examples from al-Ṭabarī's (d. 310/923) Qur'ān commentary.

[3] See Meier, *Bemerkungen*, I, 133, quoting Ṭabarī, *Annales*, ed. de Goeje, II, 559 (s.a. 65/684).

[4] ʿAthamina, "Al-Qasas," 64–5; *TG*, I, 160, 164, II, 42, 68, 91, 97–8, 329–30, 510–16, 704.

The *quṣṣāṣ* were particularly successful in Egypt, one of the most fertile grounds for the growing imagery of the Muslim otherworld. Here they remained influential longer than in other areas.[5] Around the year 81/700, they also thrived in Hims in Syria, where their representatives included famous men like Kaʿb al-Aḥbār (d. between 32/652 and 35/655) and Abū Umāma al-Bāhilī (d. 82/701 or 86/706).[6] Under the Umayyad caliphs, they even came to function as a salaried "rudimentary clerus."[7] Their association with the Umayyads, however, precipitated their downfall. Having come under the suspicion of forging hadiths and of spreading Umayyad propaganda, they lost much of their formerly glossy reputation, so that in the third/ninth century, their profession was no longer regarded highly and no longer received government patronage.[8] In later centuries, too, they were viewed critically. A Syrian scholar and preacher of the eighth/sixteenth century, for example, castigated the *quṣṣāṣ* for telling popular audiences that even murderers could enter paradise, provided they showed proper repentance.[9] In his opinion, such dangerous ideas undermined the delicate equilibrium between hope and fear,[10] two noble sentiments that result from proper parenetic instruction, the kind of preaching style known as "stimulation and intimidation" (*al-targhīb wa-l-tarhīb*). Those who preach about the afterlife, it was widely held, should at all times strive to uphold this balance.[11]

Parenetic Works up to al-Ghazālī

The most extraordinary vision of the afterlife written in the third/ninth century of Islam is that of al-Muḥāsibī (d. 243/857), a pious moralist and theologian who passed the greater part of his life in Baghdad. More well known for the scrupulous moral psychology contained in his *Book on the Observance of the Rights of God* (*K. al-Riʿāya li-ḥuqūq Allāh*), al-Muḥāsibī is the author of a *Book of Envisioning* (*K. al-Tawahhum*), a complex and strikingly personal narrative of the passage into the otherworld that

5 Pedersen, "The Islamic preacher," 233–4.

6 Van Ess, *Fehltritt*, 326.

7 *TG*, I, 12, 14, IV, 721.

8 *TG*, IV, 732; van Ess, *Fehltritt*, 323–9.

9 Cf. the hadith according to which a man kills one hundred men, repents, and is granted paradise. See Nawawī, *Riyāḍ al-ṣāliḥīn*, 16 (#20). Ibn Ḥazm, *Risālat al-talkhīṣ*, 274, rejects the applicability of the hadith with the argument that it refers to pre-Islamic times.

10 On hope and fear in Islamic thought, see Meier, *Abū Saʿīd*, 148–84; Rosenthal, "*Sweeter than hope*," 141–7; Sviri, "Between fear and hope."

11 Shaykh ʿAlwān (d. 936/1530), *Nasamāt al-asḥār*, fols. 189a–190a, quoted in Geoffroy, *Le soufisme*, 161. *Al-Targhīb wa-l-tarhīb* is the title of many hortatory works on the afterlife. See Brown, "Even if it's not true," 51–2, for a list of works in this genre, which flourished from the early third/ninth century onwards. For hadiths establishing an analogy between the pairs *khawf/rajā* and *rahba/raghba*, see Wensinck, *CTM*, II, 276. For Sufi variations, see Chapter 7.

culminates in a description of the vision of God in paradise. At this point, God addresses the blessed with these words: "I relieve you of the burden to serve me.... You have tired out your bodies [by serving Me] and abased yourselves [before Me] long enough! Now ... ask Me for whatever you desire!"[12] It is a long journey, however, before the individual reaches this final, consuming moment of apotheosis, and the dangers and fears experienced along the way occupy at least as much space in al-Muḥāsibī's thought as the joys encountered beyond the gates of paradise.

The *Book of Envisioning* relates the progress of believers from their graves to humankind's assembly before God's throne, judgement, passage over the Bridge (*ṣirāṭ*) spanning the hell funnel, and, finally, arrival in paradise. Al-Muḥāsibī recounts all this from a bird-eye's perspective, which provides an impression of the grandeur of the events at the end of time. At regular intervals, however, he zooms in and imagines that he sees himself (or a person whom he addresses in the second person) among the damned or the blessed. For example, after painting in vivid colours the perils of the Bridge, he exclaims: "Conjure up a vision of yourself (*tawwaham nafsaka*) ... falling off the Bridge!"[13] And having described the burned and mutilated bodies of the sighing and weeping inhabitants of hell, he abruptly interjects: "Now what if you were looking at *yourself*? What if you were one of them, all hope having vanished from your heart, and only desperation having remained?"[14] The sense of impending disaster, at least in the first half of the *Book of Envisioning*, looms large. It serves al-Muḥāsibī to drive home the necessity of repentance and constant wariness of sins, thus bringing the warnings against conceit, pride, vanity, and self-delusion that one finds in his *Book on the Observance of the Rights of God* to their (eschato)logical conclusion.

The *Book of Envisioning* has been described as "a *Dies Irae* which ends up in an *In Paradisum*."[15] Al-Muḥāsibī pictures the joys in paradise in unabashedly sensual terms. Because of the surplus of pleasure that the inhabitants of paradise experience, corporal boundaries become blurred, and bodies are quite literally fulfilled: the sweet water the blessed are given to drink "flows down from your mouth to your stomach" providing "cool freshness to your chest"; the perfume of paradise "caresses your face and your entire body ... it enters your nose, brain and heart until it transpires from all your limbs"; and when the men in paradise embrace their wives, these turn out to be so translucent and delicate that "your body almost penetrates her body because it is so soft and sweet."[16] Moving on from

[12] Muḥāsibī, *Tawahhum*, § 218 (tr. 75).
[13] Ibid., § 97 (tr. 55).
[14] Ibid., § 106 (tr. 57).
[15] *EI2*, s.v. al-Muḥāsibī, VII, 467b (R. Arnaldez).
[16] Muḥāsibī, *Tawahhum*, § 123 (tr. 60), § 125 (tr. 60), § 152 (tr. 64).

FIGURE 4. Judgement scene and passage over the Bridge. From the Khalili Falnameh. Golconda/India, *ca.* 1018–39/[1610–30]. The Nasser D. Khalili Collection of Islamic Art. MS 979, fol. 10v.

such sensual highlights, al-Muḥāsibī directs the reader's attention, "gently and imperceptibly,"[17] to the procession of the blessed towards the banquet and audience in God's palace in paradise. The *Book of Envisioning* ends by celebrating the supreme happiness experienced in the vision of God, "a joy the inhabitants of paradise have not felt before, whether on earth or in paradise."[18]

In comparison to al-Muḥāsibī, the respected theologian and preacher Abū l-Layth al-Samarqandī (d. 373/983), in the chapters on the afterlife of his *Admonition to the Neglectful* (*Tanbīh al-ghāfilīn*), sticks more closely to the picture of paradise and hell that one finds in the hadith. At the same time, he does not hesitate to use traditions of doubtful authenticity,[19] takes some liberty in adding his own reflections and admonitions, digresses freely in his lengthy retelling of the prophet Muḥammad's vision of hell and paradise, and combines hadiths with sayings from unnamed "wise men" and renunciants (*zuhhād*). This puts his work into the proximity of Persian wisdom (*andarz*) literature.[20] Al-Samarqandī also includes hortatory poems in his narrative. Thus, in the chapter on hell, he inserts a poem that warns old men against lusting after youths, comparing the fire on the rosy cheek of a youthful beloved to the fire that burns in hell. The lesson al-Samarqandī wants to convey is that one must guard oneself against temptation even if this occasions a feeling of loss and discomfort. "God's garden spans the width of the heavens," he rhymes, rephrasing a well-known hadith of the Prophet, "but it is surrounded by [i.e., can only be entered by passing through] hardships (*ḥuffat bi-l-makārih*)."[21] The *Admonition of the Neglectful* was a bestseller by medieval standards, with translations in languages such as Persian and Aljamiado (Spanish in Arabic script) exercising a lasting influence in both the east and west of the Islamic world.

The two crowning works of medieval Muslim parenetic literature on paradise and hell are the chapters on the afterlife in al-Ghazālī's (d. 505/1111) *Revivification of the Religious Sciences* (*Iḥyāʾ ʿulūm al-dīn*) and the *Book of the End* (*K. al-ʿĀqiba*) of Ibn al-Kharrāṭ of Seville (d. 581/1185). Al-Ghazālī, celebrated for his efforts to reconcile the philosophical, theological, legal, and mystical traditions of Islam into one system of thought, structures his *opus magnum* in four parts, the last of which is devoted, as its title indicates, to *Things That Ensure Salvation* (*al-munjiyāt*). While the preoccupation with death informs much of al-Ghazālī's intellectual project

17 Massignon, *Essay*, 253.

18 Muḥāsibī, *Tawahhum*, § 213 (tr. 74).

19 Goldziher, *Muslim studies*, II, 146.

20 *EIr*, s.v. Abū l-Layth al-Samarqandī (J. van Ess); *GAS*, I, 445–50. One imagines that al-Rayḥānī's text may have struck a similar tone.

21 Samarqandī, *Tanbīh*, 35. See Muslim, *Ṣaḥīḥ, k. al-janna* 1, IV, 2174. Cf. *CTM*, VI, 7a (Bukhārī, Abū Dāwūd, Tirmidhī, Nasāʾī, Dārimī, and Malik).

in the *Revivification* in general, the fortieth and last section of the work, entitled *The Remembrance of Death and the Afterlife* (*K. Dhikr al-mawt wa-mā baʿdahu*),[22] concludes both the *Things That Ensure Salvation* and the work as a whole, thus forming "an elegiac climax, when the voice of the Afterlife, which has run throughout the work as a cantus firmus, finally sounds alone."[23]

The first half of the *Remembrance of Death* deals with the events that occur at one's death, during the life in the grave and up to the "blast of the trumpet" at the end of time; the second half unfolds a panorama of the final judgement of humankind, passage over the Bridge and residence in hell or paradise. Al-Ghazālī prefaces each subsection with a direct address to the reader, issuing personal warnings and admonitions. This recalls the intimate style of al-Muḥāsibī, whose works al-Ghazālī read and appreciated.[24] "O you who are beguiled by the preoccupations of this world," he begins his description of hell, "turn your minds to thoughts of your final destination!"[25] At first, it appears that al-Ghazālī strikes a rather pessimistic tone. "Your coming unto it [hell] is certain," he thunders, "while your salvation therefrom is no more than conjecture. Fill up your heart, therefore, with the dread of that destination...."[26] Al-Ghazālī then runs his readers through a number of Qurʾānic verses and hadiths that detail the horrors and punishments of hell, in each instance interweaving them skilfully with his own commentary. Thus, after relating that the lightest punishment in hell is to wear sandals of fire, "the heat of which will cause their [the damned's] brains to boil,"[27] he reminds the reader that the intensity of hellfire cannot be compared to that of the fire on earth: "Bring your finger near to a flame and draw a comparison from that [but] know that your comparison is mistaken, for there is no correspondence between the fire of this world and that of hell; it is only because the pain produced by the fire is the greatest in the world that the pain of hell is described in terms thereof."[28]

However, al-Ghazālī's section on hell, in comparison to his descriptions of paradise and its joys, is noticeably short.[29] After all, as noted in the preceding

[22] Ghazālī, *Iḥyāʾ*, V, 49–183.

[23] Winter, "Introduction," xviii.

[24] Smith, "Forerunner," 65. However, T. J. Winter opines there is "no more than a modest correspondence" between al-Muḥaṣibī's *Book of Envisioning* and al-Ghazālī's *Remembrance of Death*. See Winter, "Introduction," xxixn62.

[25] Ghazālī, *Iḥyāʾ*, V, 156 (tr. Winter, 219). Here and in what follows I reproduce the translation of the *Book of Remembrance* by T. J. Winter, with minor adjustments.

[26] Ibid., V, 156 (tr. Winter, 220).

[27] Bukhārī, *Ṣaḥīḥ*, *k. al-riqāq* 51 (*b. ṣifat al-janna wa-l-nār*), IV, 209; Muslim, *Ṣaḥīḥ*, *k. al-īmān* 364 (*b. ahwanu ahl al-nār ʿadhāban*), I, 196.

[28] Ghazālī, *Iḥyāʾ*, V, 158 (tr. Winter, 223).

[29] At the same time, let us note, with Rosenthal, that al-Ghazālī's chapter on hope (*rajāʾ*) is shorter than that on fear (*khawf*). See Rosenthal, "*Sweeter than hope*," 145.

text, the overarching theme of the fourth part of the *Revivification* is the "things that ensure salvation." Thus, while al-Ghazālī encourages his readers to "goad your soul onwards with the whip of fear," he also urges them to "lead your soul by the reins of hope ... thus you shall win a mighty kingdom and be secure from the painful chastisement [of hell]."[30] Like al-Muḥāsibī, he does not hesitate to enumerate the manifold corporal pleasures experienced by the blessed, but like his predecessor he is also keen to stress that the vision of God "is the greatest of all delights and shall cause one to be quite oblivious of the [other] pleasures of the people of paradise."[31] In fact, as he puts it in a phrase that is characteristic of his imaginative style of writing, "man's other joys in paradise are no more than those of a beast let loose in a pasture."[32] Al-Ghazālī ends his narrative with an invocation of the wide compass of God's mercy, "for optimism's sake (*'alā sabīl al-tafā'ul*)," quoting numerous traditions about the sinners in hell whom God lifts up into paradise. For, as al-Ghazālī reminds his readers, it is written on the throne of God that "My mercy outstrips my wrath, I am the most merciful of all those who show mercy."[33]

Cultivating Hope and Fear after al-Ghazālī

The *Book of the End* of Ibn al-Kharrāṭ continues the work of al-Ghazālī but also diverts from it in intriguing ways. The first couple of sentences in the *Book of the End*, written in rhymed prose, are an almost verbatim quotation of the opening lines of the *Remembrance of Death*,[34] thus announcing to the reader that Ibn al-Kharrāṭ conceives of his work as an elaboration of the latter. Both al-Ghazālī and Ibn al-Kharrāṭ rely relatively little on Prophetic hadith, which makes for 17 percent and 16 percent of their material (as opposed to, e.g., 40 percent and 42 percent in the traditionist works of al-Qurṭubī and al-Suyūṭī discussed in the previous chapter). Both add significant commentary of their own (28 percent and 25 percent, respectively).[35]

The *Book of the End*, however, unlike the *Remembrance of Death*, is not part of a larger work, but stands on its own, in fact it is the first independent example of its kind in Islam: a learned treatise that weds hadiths on death and the afterlife with commentary and exhortation, offering an encompassing vision of both individual and cosmic eschatology. Also noteworthy is Ibn al-Kharrāṭ's predilection for poetry (15 percent as opposed to a mere 1 percent in the *Remembrance of Death*). Taking poetry to constitute

30 Ghazālī, *Iḥyā'*, V, 164 (tr. Winter, 232).

31 Ibid., V, 176 (tr. Winter, 250). Cf. ibid., IV, 4.

32 Ibid., V, 177 (tr. Winter, 251).

33 Ibid., V, 178 (tr. Winter, 253). Cf. the analysis of Sviri, "Between fear and hope," 333–4. On Sufi uses of this dictum, see the following text, p. 239.

34 Ibn al-Kharrāṭ, *'Āqiba*, 20; Ghazālī, *Iḥyā'*, V, 39.

35 See Bauer, "Islamische Totenbücher," 424.

commentary, this increases the overall amount of commentary in his work significantly (from 25 percent to 40 percent), in addition to giving the *Book of the End* a distinctly literary flavour.

A strong undercurrent of renunciant piety (*zuhd*) runs through the work of Ibn al-Kharrāṭ, who indeed is remembered by his biographers as a renunciant (*zāhid*), as well as a scholar of hadith and a devoted student of poetry.[36] "Death," Ibn al-Kharrāṭ notes near the beginning of his book, "wipes out the happiness of those who seek joys [in this life], so seek a blissful state [in the afterlife] in which there is no death!"[37] To exemplify this adage, and as a warning to his readers, Ibn al-Kharrāṭ tells several cautionary tales. For example, the obsession with a slave girl, he relates, caused the demise of the Umayyad caliph Yazīd II b. ʿAbd al-Malik (r. 101–5/720–24). As the story goes, the caliph was so enamoured that he locked himself up in the private rooms of his palace to enjoy his lover's company, refusing to do any state business, angrily answering his critics that he would continue to do so "even if it means losing my kingdom." On one such occasion, the love-drunk Yazīd fed his mistress a pomegranate seed, whereupon the girl choked and quickly and unexpectedly passed away in his arms. Grief-stricken, the caliph refused all attempts to bury her, "until she began to rot and stink." A month after the girl was finally laid to rest, Yazīd had her disinterred, "and he began to hug and kiss her." Eventually, the elders of the caliph's family felt compelled to intervene, reminding Yazīd that his necrophilia might well cost him the respect and obedience of his subjects, and therefore, his throne. Yazīd acquiesced but, having lost all appetite for life, died shortly thereafter.[38]

Next to those who behave like the caliph Yazīd, "who cling to their worldly passions ... as if they never heard God's revelation that 'every soul must taste death' [Qurʾān 21:35],"[39] Ibn al-Kharrāṭ identifies a second group of people whom he charges with an improper attitude to death and the afterlife: those who fool themselves with easy hopes of salvation, those who "fill their hearts with misleading hadiths, vain promises of safety and harmful whisperings that they take ... for faith and certain knowledge." Ibn al-Kharrāṭ continues:

It is possible that such people, when their life on earth nears its end and their anxiety about this life increases because their goals have been thwarted and because they have accomplished so little of them, will wish for death so that they may find respite. However, this results from their ignorance of death and what comes after it. Those who tell others that death is easy, and likewise those who make merry about it, [let

[36] Dhahabī, *Tadhkirat al-ḥuffāẓ*, IV, 97; Kaḥḥāla, *Muʿjam*, II, 58; *GAL* I, 371.

[37] Ibn al-Kharrāṭ, *ʿĀqiba*, 22.

[38] Ibid., 48–9. The story of Yazīd II's ill-fated love of his favourite slave girl Ḥabāba is often told in Arabic literature. See Paret, *Frühislamische Liebesgeschichten*, #149; Gruendler, "That you be brought near," 12, 14, 21.

[39] Ibn al-Kharrāṭ, *ʿĀqiba*, 22–3.

them be told:] true joy comes only after the [crossing of the] Bridge, and true ease only follows divine forgiveness.[40]

Ibn al-Kharrāṭ here takes a markedly less optimistic view of death than al-Ghazālī before him. In the opening pages of the *Book of the End* he relates many hadiths that enjoin the readers to abstain from desiring death, a feature of his work that was to become standard in later compilations as well. Sins *will* be judged, he assures his readers, and although for some, death may be a "cup easy to drink," for most it is difficult. "To which of these two groups do you belong?" he asks, "to those for which it is made easy or to those for which it is difficult? What gives you certainty ... ?"[41] Much depends, therefore, on proper preparation for the final moments of this life and the first of the next, and in fact the bulk of the *Book of the End*, as is also the case in other *zuhd* works on the afterlife, is devoted to the events surrounding death and judgement, not what comes after it, that is, paradise or hell.

It is only on the last pages of the *Book of the End* that Ibn al-Kharrāṭ addresses paradise and hell proper. It is characteristic, and again in stark contrast to al-Ghazālī's *Remembrance of Death*, that Ibn al-Kharrāṭ chooses to describe first paradise and *then* hell, thus ending his treatise on a sombre note.[42] He largely refrains from commentary, simply summarising, it appears, the well-known Qur'ānic traditions and hadiths on the topic. It is as if paradise and hell cannot be explained, but only experienced directly.

The repertoire of paradise images that Ibn al-Kharrāṭ rehearses is limited, though he provides a reasonably complete picture.[43] His portrayal of paradise concludes with a brief section on the vision of God, the "lifting of the Veil," and finally, with a hadith about the market (*sūq*) in paradise, to which the blessed are sent by God so that their every desire be fulfilled.[44] In order to bridge the gap from paradise to hell, Ibn al-Kharrāṭ now inserts a poem, written in the Arabic metre called "the exuberant" (*al-wāfir*). And indeed, the poem begins exuberantly enough:

> For whom are those palaces, raised high and adorned,
> though not made of plaster?
> Palaces over palaces! Palaces showing
> the wonders of the Exalted Ruler![45]

[40] Ibid., 24.

[41] Ibid., 59.

[42] Most traditionist works first deal with hell and then with paradise. Another exception to this pattern is the work of the Ḥanbalī al-Saffārīnī, discussed in Chapter 2, see pp. 89–90. Also in the *Bahjat al-nāẓirīn wa-āyāt al-mustadillīn* (*The Delight of Onlookers and the Signs for Investigators*) of the Egyptian Ḥanbalī Marʿī ibn Yūsuf al-Karmī (d. 1033/1624), the paradise section precedes the hell section. See Saleh, "Paradise in an Islamic *ʿajāʾib* work." One suspects a Ḥanbalī convention.

[43] Ibn al-Kharrāṭ, *ʿĀqiba*, 311–25.

[44] Ibid., 325–7.

[45] Ibid., 328.2–3.

The sense of exultation quickly gives way, however, to a darker mood. Ibn al-Kharrāṭ states that by reaping worldly gains – "attaining the world's watering holes," as he puts it – he feels he has been corrupted and thus has entered the "boiling waters" of hell. Only heartfelt contrition and repentance (*tawba*) can save him:

> Repentance shall bring him to pure watering places;
> *there* he shall consume cold sweet water.
> If not, he shall be cast into a deep chasm, and he shall be
> tossed from the summit of a towering mountain.[46]

This brings Ibn al-Kharrāṭ to his summary picture of hell.[47] The final hadith in this section, taken from al-Tirmidhī's *Comprehensive Collection*, affirms the eternity of hell's punishments, and the last lines of the poem that concludes Ibn al-Kharrāṭ's account, written in the metre called "the outspread" (*al-basīṭ*), likewise strike a tone that is far from optimistic:

> Have mercy, Lord, on my weakness and lowliness!
> You have not given me the ability to endure fire,
> nor the heat of the sun, when I come close to it.
> How then, o Master, could I endure the Fire?
> If divine forgiveness wipes out my sins, I shall have hope
> for you others, too – but if not, then I'm hell's fodder![48]

Ibn al-Kharrāṭ hailed from Seville but had settled, around the middle of the sixth/twelfth century, in Béjaïa (Algeria), where he took on the office of local preacher. Béjaïa had seen its Golden Age in the first half of the sixth/twelfth century, when it was the rich capital of the Ḥammādid dynasty (r. 405–547/1015–1152) and an important centre of scholarship.[49] Although Ibn al-Kharrāṭ enjoyed the respect of his peers, receiving as his guests and students many travelling scholars from the West,[50] in his time Béjaïa was decidedly on the decline. Having become a provincial backwater under its new rulers, the Moroccan Almohads (r. 524–668/1130–1269), Béjaïa may have reminded Ibn al-Kharrāṭ of the ephemerality of worldly happiness. In fact it is tempting to see the city as the backdrop to the composition of the *Book of the End*. As it happened, Ibn al-Kharrāṭ perished in, or shortly after, an anti-Almohad uprising.[51]

Al-Ghazālī, though alienated from government in the later phases of his life, still wrote from the confident perspective of imperial Islam. Ibn al-Kharrāṭ is not the only scholar of later centuries who appears to have felt

[46] Ibid., 328.22–3.
[47] Ibid., 329–36.
[48] Ibid., 346.18–20.
[49] *EI2*, s.v.v. Bidjāya, I, 1204b-1206a (G. Marçais); Ghāniya, II, 1007a-1008b (G. Marçais).
[50] Several students of hadith who went to Béjaïa to study hadith with Ibn al-Kharrāṭ are mentioned in al-Marākushī (d. 703/1303), *Dhayl*, I, 124, 161, 257, 314–5, 417, II, 462, 467, 631.
[51] Dhahabī, *Tadhkirat al-ḥuffāẓ*, IV, 97.

rubbed the wrong way by his illustrious predecessor's optimism. For example, the Baghdad preacher and scholar, Ibn al-Jawzī (d. 597/1201), voices sharp discontent with al-Ghazālī, holding him responsible for the perpetuation of untrustworthy hadiths, which were dangerous because of their power to undermine popular morals. Ibn al-Jawzī claims that al-Ghazālī wrote the *Revivification of the Religious Sciences* for people who do not respect the law (*al-ibāḥiyya*), "in the style of the commoners," and that it is filled with untrustworthy hadiths, the provenance of which is unknown to al-Ghazālī.[52] Particularly those hadiths, spread among the masses by both irresponsible scholars and popular preachers (*quṣṣāṣ*), that promise forgiveness of sins and future salvation are the object of Ibn al-Jawzī's critique.[53] "The audience goes away," he complains, "without having been censored for their sins ... instead the popular preachers comfort [their listeners] by telling them that God's mercy is encompassing, while they fail to mention that He punishes harshly."[54] To remedy this situation, Ibn al-Jawzī wrote a programmatic treatise entitled *That Which Causes Unrest* (*al-Muqliq*). In the introduction, he notes: "I've come to realize that causing fear (*al-takhwīf*) has a healing effect [on souls] ... so in this book I have collected hadiths that inspire fear, warnings against sins, descriptions of the punishments [in hell], and upsetting stories that will cause unrest to those who feel safe."[55]

Preaching to inspire fear boasted an illustrious pedigree. Although not a widely accepted idea, the Prophet himself had devoted his last sermon to painting "in Dantesque detail" the punishment of sinners in hell.[56] As noted in the previous chapter, in one pious story, ʿUmar b. al-Khaṭṭāb instructs Kaʿb al-Aḥbār, who is preaching to people in the mosque of Medina, to "frighten us (*khawwifnā*)!" Kaʿb immediately unleashes a vision of hell that causes his listeners to walk away in distress and makes ʿUmar exclaim: "By God! This is crass (*al-amr la-shadīd*)!"[57]

[52] See Ibn al-Jawzī, *Talbīs*, 236.

[53] See Ibn al-Jawzī, *Mawḍūʿāt*, I, 98. Ibn al-Jawzī also rails against popular preachers who teach the masses prayers that they promise will nullify sins. See idem, *Quṣṣāṣ*, 103. Elsewhere, he castigates the Murjiʾa for overemphasising the prospect of salvation for Muslim believers. See Ibn al-Jawzī, *Talbīs*, 125.

[54] Ibn al-Jawzī, *Muqliq*, 28. The criticism seems not entirely fair, given that al-Ghazālī regularly reminds his readers that God is "as kind as He is harsh in punishment" (*shadīd al-ʿiqāb*)." See Ghazālī, *Iḥyāʾ*, III, 571 (*bayān dhamm al-ghurūr*). Cf. Lange, "Sitting by the ruler's throne," 142–6.

[55] Ibn al-Jawzī, *Muqliq*, 28.

[56] See *TG* II, 121. A certain Dāwūd b. al-Muḥabbar (d. 206/821), a Basran Qadarite, is remembered for relating this "last sermon" of the Prophet on the authority of Maysara b. ʿAbd Rabbih (Persian, *fl.* beginning of third/ninth century), one of the transmitters of a famous *miʿrāj* narrative attributed to Ibn ʿAbbās. The text is preserved in Suyūṭī, *Laʾālī*, II, 361–73. See also Baḥrānī, *Maʿālim*, III, 422–39, where it is related from Ibn Bābūya.

[57] Ibn Abī Shayba, *Muṣannaf*, *k. dhikr al-nār*, IX, 179 (#12); Ibn Rajab, *Takhwīf*, 87. Elsewhere, Kaʿb is also quoted as saying that "ʿUmar blocks one of the gates of hell" (*inna ʿUmar ... ʿalā*

The most celebrated of all preachers of the Islamic Middle Period, the Iraqi Ibn Nubāta (d. 374/984), is said to have died following a sermon about death and the afterlife delivered on the cemetery of his hometown al-Mayyafariqin. As the legend goes, the Prophet, impressed by Ibn Nubāta's peroration, appeared to him and spat in his mouth in a gesture of approval. Eighteen days later, Ibn Nubāta was dead. Afraid to lose the sweet scent of musk on his palate, which foreshadowed the culinary pleasures that awaited him in paradise, he had refused all food and drink.[58]

Such sombre lessons appear to have inspired Ibn al-Jawzī and those who followed in his footsteps. Prominent among the latter is the Baghdad-born Ibn Rajab (d. 795/1393), a preacher and madrasa teacher in Damascus.[59] In addition to Ibn Rajab's numerous collections of eschatological hadiths, discussed in the previous chapter, he is also the author of a compilation entitled *Causing Fear of Hell* (*al-Takhwīf min al-nār*), a work whose great popularity has ensured it several modern editions. Although this is a text of the traditionist kind, it contains many parenetic stories, in particular because it cites traditions not only from the Prophet but from the early pious exemplars as well. For instance, Mālik b. Dīnār (d. *ca.* 130/747–8) is quoted as saying that "if I found enough people to assist me, I would distribute them over the minarets of this world [and tell them to shout]: 'O people! The Fire, the Fire!"[60] Ibn Rajab, his biographers tell us, thought about the afterlife often. When he approached death, he chose a place on the Bāb al-Ṣaghīr cemetery in Damascus and had a grave dug for him. When the hole was deep enough, one of his biographers tells us, he descended into it and laid down. "He liked it and said: 'It is good.'"[61]

Popular Manuals

In Muslim societies of the premodern period, a different kind of hortatory eschatological literature flourished, next to that produced by scholars like

bāb min abwāb al-nār), and "when he dies, it will be opened." See Abū Nuʿaym, *Ḥilya*, VI, 23. Cf. Wolfensohn, "Kaʿb al-Aḥbār," 28–9.

[58] See Ibn Khallikān, III, 156–7; T. Fahd, *La divination*, 302. For a selection of Ibn Nubāta's sermons, including on death and the afterlife, see MS Staatsbibliothek Berlin 3944 Lbg. 371 (a collection of his sermons made around 629/1223). Cf. Ahlwardt, *Handschriften-Verzeichnisse*, III, 437. Spitting into the mouth of another person, a Prophetic *sunna* (cf. *CTM*, s.v. t-f-l, I, 273b), is an initiatory ritual that, in certain contexts, conveys eloquence. The *qāṣṣ* Ibn ʿAmmār al-Sulamī, a popular *zuhd* preacher active at the court of Hārūn al-Rashīd, likewise claimed the Prophet had spat into his mouth in a dream. See *TG*, III, 102–3, with further references to the practice.

[59] *GAL* II, 107, S I, 129–30.

[60] Ibn Rajab, *Takhwīf*, 14.

[61] Ibn al-Mibrad, *Jawhar*, 51. The Ḥanbalī Sufi, ʿAbdallāh al-Anṣārī (d. 481/1088–89), in his *Risāla-yi Qalandarnāma*, writes about the necessity of abandoning society by, *inter alia*, frequenting cemeteries. See Anṣārī, *Risāla*, 92–9, quoted in Karamustafa, *God's unruly friends*, 33. Cf. ibid., 21, 110n20. Dwelling in cemeteries was relatively common among

Ibn al-Kharrāṭ, Ibn al-Jawzī, or Ibn Rajab. This was a literature less bound by the criteria of scholarly accuracy and restraint, and more strongly committed to the wondrous and fantastic, in addition to the moralising elements of the Muslim otherworld. In these works, the effort to authenticate knowledge about paradise and hell by buttressing it with chains of transmitters recedes almost completely into the background. Traditions tend to be attributed offhand directly to the Prophet or one of his Companions, particularly figures such as the previously mentioned Kaʿb al-Aḥbār, Ibn ʿAbbās, or Ibn Masʿūd. What is more, it is a characteristic of works in this genre that their author-compilers are generally unknown. The various texts circulating in this area of literary production were ascribed, in later times, to a number of scholarly authorities (such as Abū l-Layth al-Samarqandī, al-Ghazālī, Fakhr al-Dīn al-Rāzī, or al-Suyūṭī), in an obvious attempt to claim their credentials. As we will see, however, none of the originators of these popular manuals can be determined with certainty.

Such is the case with the text known as *What Refreshes the Eyes and Gladdens the Sad Heart* (*Qurrat al-ʿuyūn wa-mufriḥ al-qalb al-maḥzūn*). The title of this treatise invokes the Qurʾānic verse that "no soul knows what refreshment of the eyes is hidden away for them as a reward for what they have been doing" (32:17), a passage that early commentators, as we saw previously, connected with the unfathomability tradition. *What Refreshes the Eyes* is commonly held to be the work of Abū l-Layth al-Samarqandī, the fourth/tenth-century preacher and moralist from Central Asia.[62] Indeed, some of the traditions in *What Refreshes the Eyes* also appear in al-Samarqandī's *Admonition of the Neglectful*. However, these traditions are invariably provided with a doctored chain of transmission, that is, what al-Samarqandī reports on the authority of the Companions, or simply introduces with the formula "it is said that," tends to become a Prophetic hadith in *What Refreshes the Eyes*.[63] In one case, a curse on usurers uttered by the Prophet even turns into God's own locution.[64]

Despite its promising title, *What Refreshes the Eyes* does not dwell much on the heartening prospects of a happy afterlife, but is much more interested in sins and their punishments in hell. In fact, the vision of paradise with which the text ends appears like a rather awkward tag-on.[65] The text thus serves as a moral catechism that impresses on the minds of its audience

Late Medieval Sufis. Ibn al-ʿArabī, e.g., is known to have practiced retreats in cemeteries. See Chodkiewicz, *Le sceau des saints*, 16.

[62] *GAL*, I, 196, 6. (#11); El-Saleh, *Vie future*, 158. However, Fuat Sezgin (*GAS*, I, 450 [#12]) has voiced doubt about the ascription to al-Samarqandī.

[63] Cf., e.g., the reports in Samarqandī, *Tanbīh*, 77, 174, 175, 176, with *Qurrat al-ʿuyūn*, 18, 30, 46, 48, respectively.

[64] Samarqandī, *Tanbīh*, 176. Cf. *Qurrat al-ʿuyūn*, 46.

[65] See ibid., 122–75. The paradise section in *Qurrat al-ʿuyūn* includes a lengthy description of the audience of the blessed in God's palace in paradise, culminating in the beatific vision.

the gravity of ten sins, each of which is dealt with in one chapter of the work. These ten grave sins are the abandonment of prayer, consumption of alcoholic drinks, unlawful sexual intercourse, sodomy, usury, wailing for the dead, holding back the *zakāt* tax, murder, disobedience towards one's parents, and enjoyment of music. The punishments predicted for each of these sins are painted in visceral and, at times, in vicious detail. Suffice it here to relate the punishment of a woman culpable of excessive mourning for a member of her family. When she comes to face the final judgement, the angels of hell throw the corpse of the male relative over whom she has wailed before her feet and order her to repeat her lament. She refuses, admitting that she feels ashamed to do so in the presence of God. The angels now proceed to torture her, first beating her, then breaking her foot and hand. The revivified corpse of her relative is also subjected to gruesome punishment because, as the angels tell him, "before you died, you did not prohibit your people from wailing over you." They beat him so savagely that "his body parts do not remain affixed to one another, but rather fly off from his body, and every time he receives a blow he lets out a cry of pain that makes all of creation weep, while he's cut to pieces seven times." The woman is then dressed in fire, mocked by the angels, and dragged on her face into hell.[66]

Condemnation of the practice of wailing for the dead was a hallmark of Ḥanafism,[67] a school of law that, in the centuries after al-Samarqandī, was particularly strong in Central Asia. Also in terms of its theological content, *What Refreshes the Eyes* fits into a Central Asian context. While al-Samarqandī is known to have held that God may forgive believing murderers after a purgatory sojourn in hell,[68] *What Refreshes the Eyes* likens murderers to unbelievers and stresses that they will be punished eternally.[69] As will be discussed in Chapter 5, this uncompromising stance, and in general the stress on the dogmatic necessity of otherworldly punishment for grave sins, became a characteristic feature of Central Asian Ḥanafī-Māturīdī theology from the sixth/twelfth century onwards. In sum, it appears that the compiler of *What Refreshes the Eyes* was a Central Asian like al-Samarqandī, but that he did not write before the sixth/twelfth century. He knew al-Samarqandī's work and used it freely, doctoring its chains of

See ibid., 163–74. A similarly detailed rendition of this audience can be found in another popular manual, *al-Durar al-ḥisān*, a work commonly attributed to al-Suyūṭī that awaits further study. See *Durar*, 35–41. Tottoli, "Muslim eschatological literature," 459n25, suggests that *al-Durar al-ḥisān* is "quite similar and most probably an excerpt from the *Daqā'iq al-akhbār*," but this appears unlikely, given that the *Daqā'iq al-akhbār* lacks any mention of the vision of God. See the following text, p. 111.

[66] *Qurrāt al-'uyūn*, 59–61.

[67] Halevi, *Muhammad's grave*, 114–42.

[68] Daiber, *Islamic concept of belief*, 8.

[69] *Qurrat al-'uyūn*, 91.

transmitters, but he also added a substantial number of popular narratives of his own in an apparent attempt to bring his work closer in line with the emerging local Ḥanafī-Māturīdī orthodoxy.

In contrast to *What Refreshes the Eyes*, the text known as *The Precious Pearl* (*al-Durra al-fākhira*), the authorship of which is commonly credited to al-Ghazālī, stresses not so much the dogmatic necessity of punishment for sins but rather God's absolute lordship over paradise and hell. *The Precious Pearl* does not appear to have been the title of the work when it was first put into circulation. In the seventh/thirteenth century, al-Qurṭubī refers to the text simply as *The Unveiling of Eschatology* (*Kashf ʿulūm al-ākhira*),[70] as do many other Muslim authors of the later Middle Period. A manuscript of the text in Istanbul likewise notes that this is the title, while adding that "it is also called *The Precious Pearl*."[71] As the story goes, al-Ghazālī improvised a poem immediately before giving himself up to death, exhorting his friends not to mourn over his corpse. "I am a pearl," he is said to have mused, "which has left its shell deserted; it was my prison, where I spent my time in grief."[72] Although al-Ghazāli is unlikely to have uttered these final words, the comparison of the human soul with a pearl that shines brightly when plucked from its shell resonates with his view of death; this may explain why the title, though seemingly a later addition, stuck.

In one particularly striking story in *The Precious Pearl*, a pious renunciant (*zāhid*) is brought before God on the Day of Judgement. He boasts that, while living on a desert island for five hundred years, he continually served his Lord by means of fasting, prayer, and acts of devotion. Surely, he affirms, God will reward him. God answers that the renunciant's good actions count but little in comparison with the blessings God has bestowed: He has gifted the renunciant birth and existence, provided him subsistence on his desert island, and lent him an ear whenever he prayed. The renunciant, God concludes, has no claims on Him whatsoever, and to punish his presumptuousness, He sends him to hell. However, the story has a twist. Just as the renunciant is about to disappear into oblivion, God calls him back "with a smile," and says: "Enter paradise by My mercy; you have been a good servant."[73] This story portrays God as an utterly removed and autonomous, though ultimately benign judge, an arbiter who is capable, as is affirmed on the last pages of *The Precious Pearl*, to select "70,000 who enter paradise without reckoning."[74]

70 Qurṭubī, *Tadhkira*, II, 96.

71 Bouyges, *Essai*, 79n1, referring to MS Köprülü 140.

72 See Smith, *Ghazālī*, 36–7. Elsewhere, in his *Jawāhir al-Qurʾān* (*Jewels of the Qurʾān*), al-Ghazālī refers to a hierarchy of precious stones, corresponding to certain categories of Qurʾānic verses. The "shining pearls" are those verses pertaining to knowledge of the mystical path. See Sands, *Sufi commentaries*, 7.

73 Ghazālī, *Durra*, 92–3 (tr. 77–8).

74 Ibid., 106 (tr. 86).

Although the attribution of *The Precious Pearl* to al-Ghazālī is in doubt, the gist of the story fits his understanding of divine justice and forgiveness rather well. In another work, he writes that "if God Exalted commands [His] servants to obey Him, and if they obey Him, He is not obliged to reward [them] but rather, if He so desires, He rewards them, and if not, He punishes them," concluding that this would "not contradict any of the attributes of [His] divinity."[75] *The Precious Pearl* overlaps with al-Ghazālī's work in other respects, too. For example, not only does *The Precious Pearl* reproduce verbatim several passages from the *Remembrance of Death*,[76] it also shares with this latter work the tripartite division of the cosmos into the realms of *mulk*, *jabarūt*, and *malakūt*, which correspond to three progressive levels of spiritual insight.[77] Similar to the *Remembrance of Death*, *The Precious Pearl* affirms that many of the otherworldly phenomena described in the traditionist literature, such as the Balance or the appearance of the Qur'ān as a person, are located in the intermediate of these three levels, in betwixt the material and the spiritual domain.[78] It should also be noted that *The Precious Pearl* quotes *The Book of Awakening and Resurrection* (*K. al-Ba'th wa-l-nushūr*) of al-Muḥāsibī, in the same way in which al-Ghazālī's *Remembrance of Death* is indebted to al-Muḥāsibī's *Book of Envisioning*.[79] Such parallel lines of transmission seem hardly fortuitous. In sum, against the opinion of a good number of scholars,[80] it is not implausible to attribute *The Precious Pearl* to al-Ghazālī. As noted, this was also the view of later Muslim eschatologists such as al-Qurṭubī.[81] At the very least, we seem to be dealing with an author who knew al-Ghazālī's work well and who was keen to translate his thought into a popular idiom.

Completing the triad of premodern handbooks on death, life in the grave, resurrection, final judgement, paradise, and hell in Islamic popular religious

75 Ghazālī, *Iqtiṣād*, 185.

76 Bouyges, *Essai*, 79–80.

77 The sequence of the three realms in *The Precious Pearl* is *mulk-malakūt-jabarūt*, while in al-Ghazālī's *Revivification*, it is *mulk-jabarūt-malakūt*. This is sometimes taken as an argument against al-Ghazālī's authorship of *The Precious Pearl*. However, Jane Idleman Smith suggests, convincingly I think, that this variation is not significant, noting that al-Fārābī and Ibn Sīna, by whom al-Ghazālī was influenced, likewise interchanged the terms on occasion. See Smith, "Introduction," 7. Cf. Wensinck, "On the relation," 8. As Wensinck (ibid., 191–2) points out, Abū Ṭālib al-Makkī, in his *Nourishment of the Hearts* (*Qūt al-qulūb*), follows the sequence *mulk-malakūt-jabarūt*. This was the standard also after al-Ghazālī. See, e.g., Ibn 'Ajība (d. 1224/1809), *Mi'rāj*, 36–7 (tr. 48–9).

78 See the discussion of this concept in Chapter 5, pp. 187–8.

79 *GAS*, I, 641 (#16); Smith, "The forerunner," 5.

80 Asín, *Espiritualidad*, IV, 385; Watt, "Authenticity," 32; Bauer, "Islamische Totenbücher," 422n1. Cautiously accepting the attribution to al-Ghazālī are Goldziher, *Richtungen*, 200; Bouyges, *Essai*, 79–80; now also Günther, "God disdains not to strike a simile (Q 2:26)," at n36.

81 Qurṭubī, *Tadhkira*, II, 25 and passim. See also Tha'ālibī, *al-'Ulūm al-fākhira*, 37.

literature is the anonymous text entitled *Subtle Traditions about Paradise and Hell (Daqāʾiq al-akhbār fī dhikr al-janna wa-l-nār)*. Of all medieval Muslim texts on the afterlife, this appears to be the one that circulated most widely and had the biggest readership. Almost two hundred attestations of the text in manuscript form have been identified,[82] making it far more widespread than, for example, al-Qurṭubī's *Memoir* (some eighty manuscript attestations) or al-Ghazālī's *The Precious Pearl* (some twenty-five attestations). Modern editions and translations of this text abound.

One is dealing here not with a fixed text, but with a corpus that splits up into three major clusters, a Western, Eastern, and Middle Eastern one. In North Africa and Spain, the text was known as *The Tree of Certainty* (*Shajarat al-yaqīn*) and attributed to one Abū l-Ḥasan al-Ashʿarī (*fl.* sixth/twelfth c. [?]).[83] In India and further east, the text was known under the title *[Eschatological] Realities and Subtleties* (*al-Ḥaqāʾiq wa-l-daqāʾiq*) and attributed to al-Samarqandī (sometimes also to al-Ghazālī and Fakhr al-Dīn al-Rāzī). It was also translated into a number of eastern languages, such as Persian, Urdu, Javanese, and Malay.[84] At some early point in the text's gradual spread eastwards, by accident rather than by design, a large section on hell was lost. In consequence, manuscripts in this cluster lack the sections on the passage over the Bridge, the heat and other properties of hell, the animals and angels in hell, and, finally, hell's inhabitants and their punishments; all in all about a fourth of the entire text.[85] Finally, in the Middle East and the Ottoman Empire, where the title appears regularly as *Subtle Traditions*, the work came to be connected with the name of an otherwise unknown scholar, a certain ʿAbd al-Raḥīm b. Aḥmad.

The Ottoman bibliographer Ḥājjī Khalīfa (d. 1067/1657) notes that this ʿAbd al-Raḥīm b. Aḥmad, whose date of death he does not provide, "translated" (*tarjama*) the text, and that he was "one of the judges (*min al-quḍāt*)."[86] However, that *tarjama* should mean that ʿAbd al-Raḥīm b. Aḥmad "translated" the text into Arabic (from Persian or another language) is unlikely. A different entry in Ḥājjī Khalīfa's work provides a clue. Ḥājjī Khalīfa notes

[82] Tottoli, "Muslim eschatological literature," 466.

[83] On Abū l-Ḥasan Aḥmad b. Muḥammad b. Ibrāhīm al-Ashʿarī, not to be confused with the celebrated theologian Abū l-Ḥasan ʿAlī b. Ismāʿīl al-Ashʿarī (d. 324/936), and on the attribution of the *Shajarat al-yaqīn* to this Aḥmad b. Muḥammad al-Ashʿarī, see Castillo, *Kitāb Šaŷarat al-Yaqīn*, 17–18. Cf. Tottoli, "Muslim eschatological literature," 474.

[84] Ibid., 461–2.

[85] See, e.g., Voorhoeve, *Handlist*, 57, mentioning three manuscripts from Java. Also *al-Ḥaqāʾiq wa-l-daqāʾiq* (MS Leeds 264, dated 1062/[1652]), on which John MacDonald based his series of articles on Islamic eschatology from the 1960s, falls in this group. The accidental loss of the hell section in *al-Ḥaqāʾiq wa-l-daqāʾiq* is lost on Rustomji, *The Garden and the Fire*, 108, who states that "al-Samarqandi's account … does not describe or develop the Fire," and who seems oblivious to the fact that *al-Ḥaqāʾiq wa-l-daqāʾiq* and *Daqāʾiq al-akhbār* are the same text, and that neither is attributable to al-Samarqandī or "al-Qāḍī." See ibid., 109–10.

[86] Ḥājjī Khalīfa, *Kashf*, III, 232 (#5107).

that an author took notes for his book from his illiterate (*ummī*) shaykh and then "translated (*tarjama*) his words into the common language of scholars."[87] This makes it plausible to see in the *Subtle Traditions* a popularising recension of an older, orally transmitted work.[88] At any rate, Ḥājjī Khalīfa never uses the verb *tarjama* in the sense of "to author." Nonetheless, in several manuscripts (as well as modern editions, translations, and studies) ʿAbd al-Raḥīm b. Aḥmad "al-Qāḍī" ("the judge") is mistakenly identified as the person who wrote or compiled the *Subtle Traditions*.[89]

There can be no doubt that the *Subtle Traditions* is heavily indebted to al-Samarqandī's *Admonition to the Neglectful.* Almost a third of the reports (*akhbār*) about paradise and hell in the *Subtle Traditions* are taken from al-Samarqandī, who is also mentioned by name.[90] The *Subtle Traditions*, however, reduces the *isnād*s with which al-Samarqandī prefaces these traditions to a bare minimum. At the same time, *isnād*s are doctored: about half of all reports in the *Subtle Traditions* are attributed to the Prophet directly, while al-Samarqandī does this with only a fourth of his traditions. Unlike in the *Admonition to the Neglectful*, one finds no poetry or parenetic commentary in the *Subtle Traditions*.

There is a marked imbalance, again in contrast to the *Admonition to the Neglectful*, in how much attention is devoted in the *Subtle Traditions* to hell, which is dealt with in thirty-eight reports, in comparison to eighteen reports about paradise. In this respect, one notices a certain proximity to *What Refreshes the Eyes*, a text with which the *Subtle Traditions* shares a number of elements, for example, a long description of the gruesome punishment of wine drinkers.[91] One might also observe that the sense of drama is intense throughout, fostered by the repeated use of dialogue and exclamations, both of joy and terror. There are also numerous fantastic details.[92] All of this suggests that the text was compiled with the aim not only to educate, but also to entertain. In one scene, which harkens back to the dialogue between God and hell in the Qurʾān (50:30), a monster called Ḥarīsh, "born from

[87] The work in question is that of the Egyptian Sufi author al-Shaʿrānī (d. 973/1565), *al-Jawāhir wa-l-durar*. See Ḥājjī Khalīfa, *Kashf*, II, 650–1 (#4313): *tarjamahu ʿanhu bi-l-ʿibāra al-maʾlūfa bayna l-ʿulamāʾ*. On the concept of the *ummī* shaykh in Sufism during the Mamluk period, cf. Geoffroy, *Le soufisme*, 301–7.

[88] Also Gacek, *Arabic manuscripts*, 79, suggests that *tarjama*s should on occasion be understood as "paraphrases."

[89] Tottoli, "Muslim eschatological literature," 473–4, notes that the Gazi Husrev-Begova manuscript collection in Sarajevo holds around thirty copies of *Daqāʾiq al-akhbār*, in many of which the compiler of the text is called ʿAbd al-Raḥīm b. Aḥmad al-Qāḍī.

[90] *Daqāʾiq*, 13:9 / *Aḥwāl*, 16:1 (tr. 24) / *Shajarat al-yaqīn*, 16:6 (tr. 44) / *Ḥaqāʾiq* 509:13 (tr. 493).

[91] Cf. *Daqāʾiq*, 71:3–26; *Qurrat al-ʿuyūn*, 22–5.

[92] This leads Eklund to declare that the *Subtle Traditions* is not an "orthodox" text. See Eklund, *Life*, 29.

scorpions," raises its neck from the fire on the Day of Resurrection and demands to be fed with five types of sinners: those who did not pray, did not give alms, drank wine, practiced usury, and spoke about worldly things in the mosque.[93]

The section about paradise that concludes the *Subtle Traditions* begins with a tradition about the houris, as if seeking immediately to capture the attention of the audience. Then the topography and the flora of the celestial garden are described, but the narrative quickly returns to the maidens of paradise. The blessed, who are embellished with dark green moustaches, enjoy the company of houris called playthings (*luʿba*). The bodies of these colourful beings (they are variously white, green, yellow, or red) are formed of a mixture of clay and the water of life, and they smell of musk, camphor, amber, and saffron. There is vigourous and extended intercourse between the men, who are a hundred times more potent than during their life on earth, and the houris, whose virginity is restored after each time that the men deflower them.[94] The picture of paradise is rounded off by a brief description of the banquet of the blessed, where all kinds of delicious fruit and fowl are consumed. Tellingly, there is no mention of the presence, let alone the vision of God during these festivities.[95]

The Middle Eastern textual cluster of the *Subtle Traditions*, that is, the one "transcribed" by ʿAbd al-Raḥīm b. Aḥmad, adds some flourishes that the other two clusters lack. For example, after invoking the aeons (*ḥiqab*) of intercourse between men and houris, ʿAbd al-Raḥīm appears to have added the observation that "there is no male or female ejaculation" during this otherworldly sexathon.[96] Likewise, he details that the dark green moustaches of the male inhabitants of paradise are "neatly bifurcated" (*fulj bulj*).[97] At times, ʿAbd al-Raḥīm also attempts to smoothen out contradictions in the text. For example, in the eastern tradition, the text quotes a report according to which paradise has eight gates. This is followed by another report that speaks of a mere seven gardens in paradise, seemingly oblivious to the implied incoherence. The Western textual cluster adds the information that one of the seven gardens has two gates, in an attempt, it appears, to make up

[93] *Daqāʾiq*, 70:16–23 / *Aḥwāl*, 97:16–98:5 (tr. 174) / *Shajarat al-yaqīn*, 83:8–14 (tr. 87). The manuscripts from Leipzig and Dresden that Wolff consulted offer different spellings of the name: *jarīs*, *jarlīs*, and *jarshīd*. See *Aḥwāl*, tr. Wolff, 174n338.

[94] *Daqāʾiq*, 80 (*al-ʿaynāʾ* instead of *luʿba*), 82 / *Aḥwāl*, 111, 114 (tr. 200, 204–5) / *Shajarat al-yaqīn*, 93, 95 (tr. 94, 95) / *Ḥaqāʾiq*, 371, 374 (tr. 353, 355, 357). The *Shajarat al-yaqīn* lacks the reference to green moustaches.

[95] *Daqāʾiq*, 82:13–83:5 / *Aḥwāl*, 114:19–115:19 (tr. 205–7) / *Shajarat al-yaqīn* 96:1–12 (tr. 96) / *Ḥaqāʾiq*, 375:1–376:3 (tr. 359–60).

[96] *Daqāʾiq*, 82:11–12 / *Aḥwāl*, 114:17–18 (tr. 204–5) / *Shajarat al-yaqīn*, 95:21–2 (tr. 95) / *Ḥaqāʾiq*, 374:17–8 (tr. 358).

[97] *Daqāʾiq*, 82:2–4 / *Aḥwāl*, 114:7–8 (tr. 204) / *Shajarat al-yaqīn*, 95:15 (tr. 95) / *Ḥaqāʾiq*, 374:9–11 (tr. 357).

for the one missing garden. ʿAbd al-Raḥīm b. Aḥmad overcorrects this: not only does he mention that one garden has two gates, but for good measure he adds an eighth garden to the list of seven.[98] In sum, while the Eastern version appears to represent the simplest and therefore oldest layer of the *Subtle Traditions*, the Middle Eastern one, that is, the "recension" (*tarjama*) of ʿAbd al-Raḥīm b. Aḥmad, is likely the youngest version.

The Prophet's Ascension and Other Prophetic Tours of the Otherworld

Sharing with the popular manuals an interest in the wondrous and marvellous, the group of texts known collectively under the title of the Night Journey (*isrāʾ*) and Ascension (*miʿrāj*) of the prophet Muḥammad figures large in the history of paradise and hell in Islam. Stories about the Prophet's otherworldly journey, which accumulated over the centuries into thick layers of legendary narrative, took their cue from two Qurʾānic passages. In Qurʾān 17:1, God is said to have "made His servant go by night from the Sacred Mosque to the Furthest Mosque ... to show him some of Our signs," while Qurʾān 53:1–18 speaks of two visions experienced by the Prophet, one that is of a figure "standing on the highest horizon," another of a certain "Jujube tree of the boundary (*sidrat al-muntahā*)" as well as a "garden of refuge (*jannat al-maʾwā*)." From these rudimentary elements sprang the most celebrated of all Prophetic stories in Islam, describing how Muḥammad is taken by the angel Gabriel from Mecca to Jerusalem on a winged mount called Burāq. From there, he climbs up through the seven heavens where God receives him in an audience, confirming him as His prophet and commanding him to teach his community how to pray.[99]

A vision of paradise and hell appears to have been part of the Ascension narrative from early on, but at first the nature and location of both realms remained vague. In a version preserved in al-Ṭabarī's (d. 310/923) Qurʾān commentary, quoted on the authority of the Companion Abū Hurayra but regarded as spurious by later critics, Muḥammad is shown paradise and hell while travelling from Mecca to Jerusalem, which suggests that he sees both below him on earth.[100] Indeed, the two visions reported in Qurʾān 53:1–18 seem to imply a terrestrial encounter with the otherworld, as they speak of the "descent" of a heavenly figure towards Muḥammad (53:13), rather than of

98 *Daqāʾiq*, 76:5–76:10 / *Aḥwāl*, 105:18–106:3 (tr. 189–91) / *Shajarat al-yaqīn*, 89:18–90:3 (tr. 91–2) / *Ḥaqāʾiq*, 366:15 (tr. 344).

99 Among the recent studies of the history of this genre are Buckley, *Night journey*; Colby, *Narrating*; Günther, "Gepriesen sei der, der seinen Diener." See also the volumes edited by Amir-Moezzi, *Le voyage initiatique*; and Gruber and Colby, *The Prophet's ascension*.

100 Ṭabarī, *Jāmiʿ*, XV, 11–16 (*ad* Q 17:1); Bayhaqī, *Dalāʾil*, II, 397–8. On this hadith, cf. Colby, "Constructing," 196–203; Tottoli, "Tours of hell," 12–13.

Muḥammad rising into the heaven. In fact, it may be that the Abū Hurayra hadith reflects a stage of development in which the night journey of Muḥammad was not yet an ascension but merely a horizontal (though still a miraculous) flight to Jerusalem.[101] In contrast, in a version that may have been put into circulation by the Khorasanian exegete Ḍaḥḥāk b. Muzāḥim (d. 105/723),[102] Muḥammad meets Mālik, the Guardian of Hell, in the first of seven heavens. Mālik briefly opens the door of hell for Muḥammad, who catches a glimpse of the horrors behind the door and as a result, nearly loses consciousness. Then, after his audience with God, Muḥammad inspects paradise, which is located above the seven heavens, and returns to earth.[103] In yet another version, that which appears in *The Life of the Prophet* (*Sīrat al-nabī*) of Ibn Hishām (d. 218/833), Muḥammad visits paradise in the seventh heaven *before* meeting God; as for hell, he sees groups of the punished in the first heaven, where he also encounters Mālik.[104]

Around the sixth/twelfth and seventh/thirteenth centuries Muḥammad's tour of paradise and hell begins to occupy more and more space in Ascension narratives.[105] One of the most elaborate descriptions of paradise and hell of any Ascension narrative is included in the anonymous *Liber scalae Machometi*. The Arabic original of this text, which is lost, was translated in 1264 into Castilian by a Jewish convert at the court of Alfonso X of Castile (r. 1252–84), followed shortly thereafter by a French and Latin translation from the Castilian, a fact that attests to the great prominence the text enjoyed.[106] The sixth/twelfth century is also the time around which a version of the Ascension was compiled that gives the impression, in the words of its foremost Western interpreter, of combining earlier narratives into a "fantastic novella."[107] Elements of this new narrative are thought to go back to the Basran (?) popular preacher (*qāṣṣ*) Abū l-Ḥasan al-Bakrī (*fl.* third/ninth c. [?]), a figure whose biography is shrouded in mystery but who is known to have specialised in "fantastic and wondrous details."[108] In these "al-Bakrī" versions of the Ascension, as well as in most Late Medieval versions, hell

101 Van Ess, *Flowering*, 45–77, at 54. Cf. *TG*, I, 389, 395.

102 *TG*, II, 509; Colby, "Constructing," 29–49.

103 Suyūṭī, *La'ālī*, I, 63–81. See the translation in Colby, "Constructing," 175–93.

104 Ibn Hishām, *Sīrat al-nabī*, I, 263–6, (tr. 184–7). Thus also in the *K. al-Mi'rāj* of Abū l-Ḥakam al-Jawālīqī, a student of the two Shī'ī Imams Ja'far al-Ṣādiq (d. 148/765) and his son Mūsā al-Kāẓim (d. 183/799). Al-Jawālīqī's *mi'rāj* is transmitted in al-Qummī's (alive in 307/913) *Tafsīr*, II, 3–12, and translated by Buckley, *Night journey*, 6–18. See Modarressi, *Tradition*, I, 269; *TG*, I, 345, V, 69.

105 Colby, *Narrating*, 145.

106 See Cerulli, *Il "Libro della scala,"* 24–225, for the French and Latin version of the text (the Castilian version, like the Arabic original, is lost). Cf. Buckley, *Night journey*, 193–5.

107 Colby, *Narrating*, 274n2. For a dating of this version, see ibid., 127.

108 Ibid., 128. Al-Bakrī's name figures in the collections of the *Qiṣaṣ al-anbiyā'*. Shoshan, therefore, places him in the milieu of early Islam's storytellers (*quṣṣāṣ*). See Shoshan, *Popular culture*, 35–8.

is pushed higher up into heaven, to the fifth[109] or seventh heaven,[110] occasionally also to the sixth heaven.[111] This happens for reasons that remain unclear. One aspect is perhaps that ascension stories were meant for oral performance. Placing paradise and hell at the end of the narrative is esthetically more convenient and arguably heightens the dramatic effect.

In comparison to the wealth of details that one finds in the collections of eschatological hadiths and the popular handbooks discussed earlier in this chapter, the image of paradise and hell that emerges from the standard Ascension narratives is rather cursory, even though on occasion, as in the *Liber scalae Machometi*, the treatment can go to considerable length. Particulars stand out. For example, in some of the earliest versions of the *miʿrāj*, Muḥammad meets a houri in the seventh heaven who introduces herself to him as the future bride of Zayd b. Ḥāritha, Muḥammad's adopted son.[112] One also sees a growing tendency of Ascension narratives to dwell on the description of classes and sinners and their punishments in hell, particularly those of female sinners.[113] In an early Ascension narrative, Muḥammad sees a sequence of people who are forced to eat bricks of fire, have massively swollen bellies, practice autosarcophagy, eat rotten flesh, as well as women suspended from their feet and breasts. As Gabriel explains to Muḥammad, these unfortunate creatures are, respectively, those who squandered the wealth of orphans that were entrusted to them, usurers, slanderers (lit. "those who ate the flesh of others"), adulterers ("those who forsake the women whom God permitted"), and adulteresses ("those who fathered bastards on their husbands").[114]

109 Thus in a Persian *Miʿrājnāma* dated 685/1286. See Īlkhānid *Miʿrājnāma*, 131 (tr. 52).

110 *Liber scalae Machometi*, 100–44 (paradise in the seventh heaven, inspected before the audience with God), 154–212 (hell in the seventh heaven, inspected after the audience with God). In other versions, paradise and hell are inspected *after* the audience with God in the highest heaven. See Uighur *Miʿrājnāmeh*, 68–80 (tr. 102–14); Ghayṭī, *Miʿrāj*, 633. Cf. Colby, "Fire in the upper heavens."

111 See the anonymous Persian *miʿrāj* (sixth/twelfth c. [?]) contained in the text known as *Majlis dar Qiṣṣa-yi Rasūl*, 307. Also in the "Bakrī version" of the *miʿrāj*, the vision of hell occurs in the sixth heaven. See Bakrī, *Ḥadīth al-miʿrāj*, fol. 81r.

112 Ibn Hishām, *Sīra*, I, 270 (tr. 186); al-Qummī, *Tafsīr*, II, 11 (tr. 16). Zayd, killed in the expedition to Mu'ta in 8/629, had married Muḥammad's cousin Zaynab bt. Jahsh and later divorced her, whereupon she married Muḥammad, an incident referred to in Qur'ān 33:37. In the Uighur *Miʿrājnāma*, Muḥammad sees a pavilion in paradise that is destined for ʿUmar b. al-Khaṭṭāb and, among the houris, meets Ghumayṣā', a Companion who is credited with converting her husband Abū Ṭalḥa from pagan polytheism to Islam. See Uighur *Miʿrājnāma*, 72 (tr. 107).

113 See Tottoli, "Tours of hell."

114 One first comes across this report, which is attributed to the Companion Abū Saʿīd al-Khudrī (d. *ca.* 63/682), in ʿAbd al-Razzāq's *Tafsīr* and in Ibn Hishām's *Sīra*, I, 269–70 (tr. 185–6). See Tottoli, "Tours of hell," 13. In Shiʿi tradition, a long *miʿrāj* narrative about the punishment of women in hell is traced back to ʿAlī b. Abī Ṭālib. See *Mawsūʿat al-Imām al-Ṣādiq*, XI, 307–9. Cf. Majlisī, *Biḥār*, VIII, 481–2.

The punishment of suspension by the breasts for adulteresses has a close parallel in the otherworldly journey of the Zoroastrian priest Vīrāf, related in the Pahlavi text known as *The Book of the Righteous Vīrāf* (Phlv. *Ardāvīrāfnāmak*).[115] This has led several scholars to posit a dependence of (parts of) Muḥammad's Ascension on Persian precedents.[116] It should be noted, however, that *miʿrāj* narratives also echo the paradise and hell visions of Jewish and Christian apocalyptic literature.[117] When Muḥammad, reflecting on his vision of God in paradise, says that it is forbidden to him "to describe to you what I saw of this grandeur,"[118] one is reminded of the Christian *Apocalypse of Paul.* In 2 Cor 12:4, Paul famously states that he was "caught up into paradise and heard things that are not to be told, that no mortal is permitted to repeat." The third-century *Apocalypse of Paul* relates that Paul, upon entering paradise, was instructed by the angels to "tell no one on earth" about what he had witnessed.[119] There are other parallels. The *Apocalypse of Paul*, for example, describes a group of the damned whose lips and tongues are cut "with a great fiery razor," who it identifies as "the readers [of scripture] who read to the people but do not themselves keep the precepts of God."[120] Compare this to the case of Muḥammad, who sees sinners whose lips and tongues are cut. After asking Gabriel about them, Muḥammad is told that "these are the preachers of your community, the preachers that cause sedition (*khuṭabāʾ al-fitna*), who say what they do not do themselves."[121]

Here is not the place to study the deep historical connections between the Prophet's Ascension and other Near and Middle Eastern otherworldly journeys. What concerns us is the observation that the Prophet's Ascension, certainly in its popular manifestations, remained amenable to both inner developments and external influences. Storytellers of virtually all times and regions, building on a basic skeletal frame, could add to the narrative, drawing from their own imagination and acquaintance with otherworldly narratives. Beyond the Prophet's journey to Jerusalem and ascent through the heavens, the story's paradise and hell sections open up vistas onto two new other worlds, two arenas that were especially conducive towards processes of creative amplification, towards the growth of paradise and hell as spaces of the imagination.

115 *Ardāvirānāmak*, tr. Gignoux, *Le livre d'Ardā Vīrāz*, 177. Cf. Segal, *Life after death*, 195–6. The punishment is also found in the seventh/thirteenth-century Persian adaptation by Zartusht-i Bahrām, the *Ardāvīrāfnāma-yi manẓūm*, 79 (vv. 1336–44).

116 Schrieke, "Himmelsreise," 18n1; Horovitz, "Muhammeds Himmelsfahrt," 173–4.

117 Late Antique and medieval Jewish and Christian apocalyptic literature knows a great number of otherworldly journeys of saints and prophets. For surveys, see Himmelfarb, *Ascent to heaven*; eadem, *Tours of hell.* According to the Babylonian Talmud, four celebrated rabbis entered paradise alive (see *BT, Ḥagigah* 14b, tr. XX, 90–1), eleven according to various Jewish legends compiled by Louis Ginzberg. See Ginzberg, *Legends*, V, 96.

118 Suyūṭī, *La'ālī*, I, 74.

119 *Apocalypse of Paul* 21 (tr. 628).

120 *Apocalypse of Paul* 36 (tr. 634–5).

121 Ṭabarī, *Jāmiʿ*, XV, 12 (*ad* Q 17:1).

The Prophet's Ascension was no doubt the most popular otherworldly journey that Muslim preachers and storytellers related, but it was not the only one. Muḥammad is not the only prophet in Islam credited with a tour of the otherworld. As in Jewish tradition, a visit to hell and a heavenly ascent was also attributed to the prophet Idrīs (Enoch) whom God, according to the Qur'ān (19:57) "raised to a high position." In one version of the story, that which is contained in the *Tales of the Prophets* (*Qiṣaṣ al-anbiyā'*) of al-Kisā'ī (*fl.* third/ninth c. [?]),[122] Idrīs asks God for permission to take a look at hell and, guided by the angel Mālik, arrives at the brink of the hell-funnel to inspect the horrors below. Having returned to earth, Idrīs finds no sleep and almost fails to eat, "out of fear of the punishment that he had witnessed." To remedy this state, he now asks to be allowed a look into paradise. At first, the angel Riḍwān, the guardian of paradise, does not want to indulge him, stating that "nobody may enter paradise while still alive on earth," but God then orders a branch from the paradisiacal tree of Ṭūbā to lower itself towards Idrīs. He grabs it, and is lifted up. Perched atop a tree in paradise, Idrīs now refuses to move, quoting the Qur'ān that the inhabitants of paradise "reside in it eternally" (Q 20:76). Angered by Idrīs's insolence, the angel of death complains to God that Idrīs has escaped his claws. "My servant Idrīs has already reasoned with you about this (*ḥājjaka fī l-kalām*)," God rebukes him, "so let him be in My Garden and do him no harm!"[123] One can easily picture how such stories both chilled and delighted audiences, and it has been suggested that texts such as al-Kisā'ī's *Tales* are in fact no more than manuals for storytellers, upon which actual performances improvised freely,[124] as in the case of certain versions of the Ascension narrative.

Another example of the appeal that paradise and hell exerted on popular religious tales is the story of Jesus and the skull. Though included in only some of the collections of *Tales of the Prophets*, this narrative circulated widely in the Islamic later middle period, as can be seen from its numerous attestations in manuscripts.[125] The earliest version that has come down to us is that preserved by Abū Nu'aym from Isfahan (d. 430/1038), who traces it back to Ka'b al-Aḥbār.[126] In the seventh/thirteenth century, Farīd al-Dīn 'Aṭṭār dedicated a small epic in rhyme to the story, the *Book of the*

[122] The identity of al-Kisā'ī is unknown. The oldest manuscript of his *Qiṣaṣ al-anbiyā'* dates from the seventh/thirteenth century. See Tottoli, *Biblical prophets*, 151–2.

[123] Kisā'ī, *Qiṣaṣ*, I, 81–5. The story is also transmitted separately. See the MS Bibliothèque Nationale de France Arabic 1947, *Qiṣṣat Idrīs* (copied *ca.* 905/1500).

[124] Shoshan, "High Culture," 85.

[125] For a survey of the substantial scholarship on, and a discussion of the history of this text, as well as a study of the spread of the relevant manuscripts, see Tottoli, "The Story of Jesus and the Skull."

[126] Abū Nu'aym, *Ḥilya*, VI, 10–12. For an English translation, see Khalidi, *The Muslim Jesus*, 154–7. Abū Nu'aym also relates one of the earliest versions of the "Colloquy of Moses with God" (*Munājāt Mūsā*), likewise traced back to Ka'b al-Aḥbār, and likewise containing a detailed vision of the otherworld. See Abū Nu'aym, *Ḥilya*, VI, 37–42.

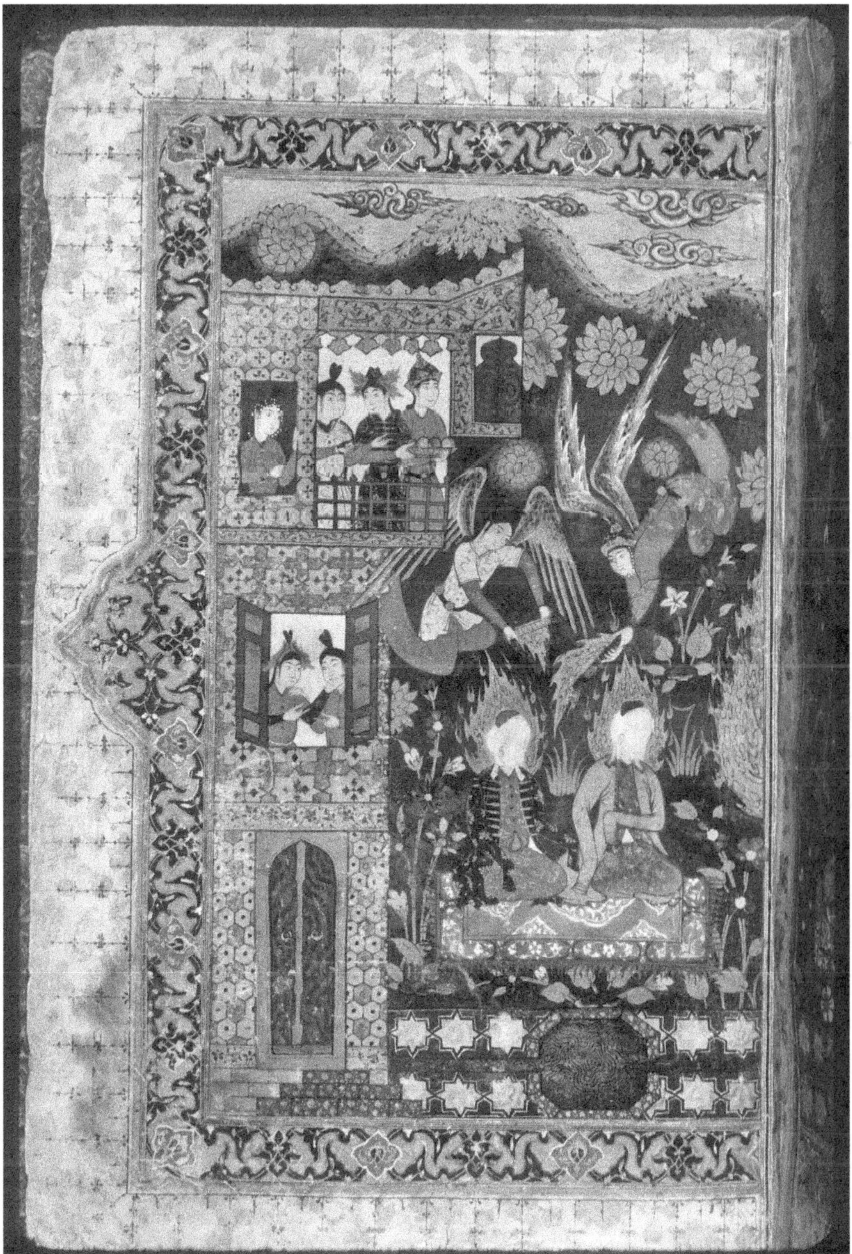

FIGURE 5. Two prophetic figures in paradise. From al-Nīshāpūrī, *Qiṣaṣ al-anbiyā'* (*Tales of the Prophets*), Qazwin/Persia (?), 984/1577. The New York Library, Astor, Lenox and Tilden Foundations. MS Spencer Persian 46, fol. 176v.

Skull (*Jumjumanāmeh*).[127] Jesus, the story has it, stumbles upon a skull that miraculously begins to speak to him, relating "with eloquent tongue" what happened to its former carrier's soul at death, including the judgement by terrifying angels and a vision of paradise and hell. After enumerating the seven layers of hell and a short description of the classes of sinners consigned to them, the skull entreats Jesus to intercede with God so that it may be reunited with its soul and thus be brought back to life. God grants this wish, the skull is resurrected, "and then it remained twelve years worshipping God with Jesus." The skull, the story ends, "died a true believer, and God in His mercy placed it among the people of paradise."[128]

One of the most fantastic of all tales providing a look into the otherworld is that of Bulūqiyā, told in the *Tales of the Prophets* of al-Thaʿlabī (d. 427/1035),[129] but also, and with greater attention to eschatological detail, in the *Arabian Nights*.[130] Bulūqiyā, who is described as a prince of the Israelites in Cairo, sets out on a journey over the seven seas in search for Muḥammad, about whose coming he has been foretold. Stranded on an island, he meets serpents "as big as camels and palm trees" that glorify the names of God and of Muḥammad. They explain to Bulūqiyā that they are residents of hell, where their task is to punish the unbelievers. Twice a year, when Jahannam exhales to relieve itself of its heat, they are squeezed out of hell to the surface of the earth, while much bigger snakes – so big that "were the biggest of us to pass over their nostrils they would not feel it" – remain trapped under the earth.[131] Later on in his travels, on a different island, Bulūqiyā encounters Sakhr, king of the jinn, who describes to him the seven layers of hell and its valleys and cities. Sakhr also tells of two punisher angels, lionlike Khalīt and wolflike Malīt, whose tails end in copulating genitals, thus siring hell's snakes and scorpions.[132] Popular tales skirting the otherworld such as the story of Bulūqiyā, or the Arabic versions of the Alexander romance,[133] or the Persian tale of Salāmān and Absāl, were, in a sense, religiously sanctioned, because traditionist literature usually affirmed the presence of paradise and hell on earth, on the

[127] For an Italian translation, Pennachietti, "Il racconto di Giomgiomé." Cf. Ritter, *Meer*, 100–1.

[128] Abū Nuʿaym, *Ḥilya*, VI, 12.

[129] Thaʿlabī, *ʿArāʾis*, 288–94.

[130] For a comparison between the two versions, see Horovitz, "Bulūqjā." For possible vestiges of ancient Near Eastern lore (in particular the Gilgamesh epic) in the story of Bulūqiya, see Dalley, "Gilgamesh in the Arabian Nights." Cf. also the references provided in Fudge, "Underworlds," 259n6.

[131] *Arabian Nights*, II, 370. Cf. Suyūṭī, *Budūr*, 428.

[132] *Arabian Nights*, II, 381–2.

[133] See Ott, "Paradise, Alexander the Great, and the *Arabian Nights*." According to the twelfth/eighteenth-century *Sīrat al-malik Iskandar Dhū l-Qarnayn*, Alexander approaches the northeastern edge of the world, where "above the high mountains is paradise hanging between heaven and earth like a huge town." See *Sīrat al-malik Iskandar*, fol. 74v.

far periphery of the terrestrial world.[134] In these stories, the interest in the spectacular and marvellous predominates over scholarly or even moralising and parenetic aims.

With this, we have reached the end of the spectrum of narrative literature on paradise and hell surveyed in this and the previous chapter. The journey has taken us from the learned handbooks of eschatological hadith, which combine attention to the question of the authenticity of eschatological hadith with an encyclopaedic interest in completeness, to the parenetic works, which strive to strike the right balance between encouraging hope in, or fear of, the afterlife, and finally, to the popular literature on paradise and hell, which in its commitment to telling a good story, oscillates over into the marvellous and fantastic. Along the way, some glimpses of the contents of the Muslim otherworld have been offered. However, a comprehensive topography of the otherworld as one encounters it in Muslim narrative literature has not been provided. Therefore, before examining some of the theological, philosophical, and mystical responses to the rich storehouse of Muslim eschatological images and ideas, the following chapter unfolds a full tableau of paradise and hell in Islam.

[134] Cf. Suyūṭī, *Sharḥ al-ṣudūr*, 242; Baḥrānī, *Maʿālim*, II, 95, 96, 100–2. For other traditions locating paradise and hell on earth, see the following text, pp. 131, 246–57.

4

The Imagination Unbound: Two Late Medieval Muslim Scholars on Paradise and Hell

As we noted in previous chapters, the adage that the otherworld is filled with things "that no eye has seen, no ear has heard and no human mind has conceived" enjoys great prominence in Muslim eschatological literature.[1] Nonetheless, there are myriad works of the traditionist kind, some impressively large, that purport to know a great deal about paradise and hell. This contradiction was facilitated by the agglutinative nature of traditionist literature. Eschatology being one of the most fertile fields for the religious imagination, numerous traditions (*akhbār*, sg. *khabar*) gradually came into circulation from the early centuries of Islam onwards. Given the low standards of admissibility especially for eschatological hadiths, collectors of *khabar*s were relatively free in compiling the material. Gradually, but inexorably, traditions added up to more complex scenes, and scenes were combined into detailed tableaux. From this process emerged encyclopaedic works of eschatology that built on and developed "a canon [that] imagines the unimaginable."[2]

Chapters 1 through 3 of this book have traced the scriptural and textual history of the (Sunni) Muslim imagery of paradise and hell. Building on this foundation, this chapter offers a broad panoply of the Muslim paradise and hell, outlining the topography of both realms and providing an inventory of their contents. Two Late Medieval compilations of eschatological hadith will serve as our main witnesses, the *Shining Full Moons of Eschatology* (*al-Budūr al-sāfira fī ʿulūm al-ākhira*) of the Sunni polymath al-Suyūṭī (Egypt, d. 911/1505), and the chapters on the otherworld contained in volumes six through eight of the *Oceans of Lights* (*Biḥār al-anwār*) of the Shiʿi traditionist and theologian al-Majlisī (Persia, d. 1110/1699). Both al-Suyūṭī and al-Majlisī are major contributors to the genre. As such, their biographies receive separate discussion in other

[1] See the preceding text, pp. 2–3, 21–2, 73, 83, 91.

[2] Al-Azmeh, "Rhetoric," 218.

chapters of this book.[3] To complement these two sources, and to achieve a wider geographical spread, reference will also be made to the eschatological handbooks of the Sunni commentator and jurist al-Qurṭubī (al-Andalus/Egypt, d. 621/1273) and the Shiʿi traditionist and exegete Hāshim b. Sulaymān al-Baḥrānī (Bahrain, d. 1107/1695 or 6), two scholars whose biographies likewise receive greater attention elsewhere in this book.[4] What will occupy us in the pages that follow is not the place of these compilers in the history of Muslim eschatological literature but the morphology of paradise and hell that emerges from a synchronic reading of their works. We enter into novel territory here, because none of these four sources have previously been made the object of detailed analysis; in general, to date there are no attempts in the scholarly literature, to the best of my knowledge, to survey the full arsenal of Late Medieval Muslim eschatological hadiths; neither have the differences between the Sunni and Shiʿi contributions to the genre been examined.[5]

The aim of this chapter is to grasp the organisational principles and key concerns that shape Late Medieval traditionist eschatology, and in the process to show the wide spectrum of ideas and images in which eschatologists traded. For lack of space, broader contextual questions can only be dealt with in passing. For example, there can be no doubt that the otherworld that one encounters in the texts under discussion here is conceived from the point of view of a patriarchal and often misogynist tradition of male scholarship. In fact, the point seems so abundantly clear as to be in no need of elaboration – the texts speak for themselves. However, in this chapter, the question of the gender dynamics of Late Medieval Islamic eschatology, for reasons of space, can only be alluded to. Similarly, the political, social, and ethical agendas of the four eschatologists must largely be left out of the picture. It is clear that these four compilers promote a discourse on virtues and sins that is ripe with claims to religious authority as well as with attacks on those accused of lacking correct religion and morality. Yet this chapter does not investigate the historical conditions that enabled this discourse to flourish, nor shall we study how it worked in practice. Where appropriate, references to studies pursuing such questions will be made in the footnotes; for the rest, readers are invited to turn to the relevant discussions in later chapters of this book.

[3] For al-Suyūṭī, see the preceding text, pp. 88–9. For al-Majlisī, see the following text, pp. 204–5.

[4] For al-Qurṭubī, see the preceding text, pp. 87–8. For al-Baḥrānī, see the following text, pp. 205–9.

[5] For surveys of Muslim traditionist eschatology, see, e.g., Asín, *Escatologia*, 99–232; El-Saleh, *La vie future*, 25–53; Smith and Haddad, *The Islamic understanding*, 85–91; Rustomji, *The Garden and the Fire*, 63–97 and passim.

A Prelude to the Otherworld

Before we turn to paradise and hell as two discrete otherworldly spaces, we need to take stock of a number of eschatological traditions that feature paradise and hell in a somewhat coincidental way. By this I mean those chapters in Muslim traditionist eschatology that talk of the presence of paradise and hell (1) in the *barzakh*, that is, the isthmus between death and resurrection, and (2) on the Day of Judgement.

The concept of *barzakh* as a separate, third space between this world and the otherworld, while absent in the Qur'ān (where the word *barzakh* denotes a "barrier" between two worlds, cf. Q 23:100), had an extraordinarily successful career in Islam, spawning many treatises and collections of hadiths.[6] In this literature, graves are described as entry gates to the otherworld; they are called "the first way-station (*manzil*) of the otherworld."[7] People on earth, in this perspective, live their lives on top of countless mini-entries to paradise and hell. The ground, especially in cemeteries, is perforated with holes, like a sieve. Through these holes, the otherworld beckons large.

Certain cemeteries, such as the al-Qarāfa cemetery in Cairo, were declared to be a part of paradise in their entirety. For example, the historian al-Maqrīzī (d. 845/1442) writes that from the time of the conquest of Egypt, Muslims desired to be put to rest on al-Qarāfa, because the foot of the Muqaṭṭam mountain, over which the vast burial ground extends, was said to be a garden (*janna*) in which God had planted the seeds of the trees of paradise (*ghirās al-janna*).[8] However, eschatologists like al-Suyūṭī and al-Majlisī relate from the Prophet that the grave is "a garden of paradise" only for some; for others, it is "a pit in hell."[9] In one of the stories of the Persian mystic, Farīd al-Dīn ʿAṭṭār (d. 627/1230), the holy fool Bahlūl walks barefoot to the graveyard in winter, crossing puddles of ice-cold water.

[6] The fundamental study remains Eklund, *Life*. The pertinent chapters in Leor Halevi's study of the genesis of Muslim burial rites focuses on the transition from the Qur'ānic concept of *barzakh* as a "boundary line" between the here and the hereafter to that of *barzakh* as a "boundary space" identified with the grave, i.e., from seeing *barzakh* as a "liminal gateway" to seeing it as a "halfway house," a shift he dates to the early second/eighth century. See Halevi, *Muhammad's grave*, 197–240. Halevi's study should be read in conjunction with the impressive work of Diem and Schöller, *The living and the dead*, esp. II, 107–45. Earlier studies include Mehren, "Muhammedansk Eschatologi"; Carra de Vaux, "Fragments," 18–23; *EI2*, s.v. Barzakh, I, 1071 (Carra de Vaux). See also *EI3*, s.v. Barzakh (Ch. Lange); *Encyclopaedia Islamica*, s.v. Barzakh (A. Pakatchi and Gh. Ebrahimi Dinani); Rebstock, "Das Grabesleben." Postmortem communication with the dead is a "routine" notion in early Rabbinic Judaism (see Avery-Peck, "Resurrection of the body," 255), from where the Islamic *barzakh* may have taken its cue. On communication between the dead and the living in the Islamic literature on graves, see Smith, "Concours"; Kinberg, "Interaction."

[7] Qurṭubī, *Tadhkira*, I, 110; Baḥrānī, *Maʿālim*, II, 36; Majlisī, *Biḥār*, VI, 424.

[8] Maqrīzī, *Mawāʿiẓ*, I, 50, 233–4.

[9] Suyūṭī, *Sharḥ al-ṣudūr*. 168, 213–4; Majlisī, *Biḥār*, VI, 398, 441, VIII, 408; Baḥrānī, *Maʿālim*, II, 35, 62–3. See also Qummī, *Tafsīr*, 451 (*ad* Q 23:99–100); Ghazālī, *Kīmiyā*, 91.

When asked where he is going, he answers that he is on his way to the grave of a tyrant, to warm his feet on the fire with which the tyrant is punished in his subterranean abode.[10]

Whilst in the *barzakh*, the dead come into contact with paradise and hell on separate occasions. In his work on the *barzakh*,[11] al-Suyūṭī begins the chapter entitled "Where the Souls Reside" (*B. maqarr al-arwāḥ*) by citing numerous hadiths that suggest that the souls of the dead, after separation from their bodies, pass into paradise and hell immediately, that is, without spending time in the grave.[12] "The souls of the believers," the Prophet allegedly declared, "are in the crops of green birds that roam paradise, eat its fruits, drink its waters, and reside in golden lamps [that hang] underneath the Throne." The souls of unbelievers, however, "are in the crops of black birds, eat and drink fire, and reside in a chasm in hell."[13] Such traditions are akin to the Qur'ān[14] in the sense that they do not express a specific awareness of rewards and punishments in the grave, let alone of the *barzakh* as a separate, third time-space unit between this world and the otherworld.[15] The Companion ʿAbdallāh b. ʿUmar (d. 73/693) consoled the grieving Asmāʾ bt. Abī Bakr, standing beneath the cross bearing the corpse of her crucified son, the countercaliph ʿAbdallāh b. al-Zubayr (d. 73/692), by saying: "The souls are in heaven with God; this is but a cadaver."[16] "Death is resurrection, who dies is resurrected," asserted the traditionist and erstwhile servant of the Prophet, Anas b. Malik (d. *ca.* 91–3/709–11).[17] In Shiʿi sources, the Imam Jaʿfar al-Ṣādiq (d. 148/765) is repeatedly attributed the view that paradise and hell, "ever since they were created," have been filled with the souls of the believers and unbelievers.[18] According to one story, Jaʿfar once passed a mountain to the left of the road from Mecca to Medina, explaining to his companions that he heard the voices of those tortured in hell rising from this mountain, sitting on top of one of the valleys of hell.[19] Jaʿfar, one might add,

[10] Ritter, *Meer*, 100.

[11] This work is entitled *The Opening of Hearts by Means of Explaining the Condition of the Dead and the Graves* (*Sharḥ al-ṣudūr bi-sharḥ ḥāl al-mawtā wa-l-qubūr*). In this work, al-Suyūṭī cites more than eleven thousand traditions on the authority of various collectors, primarily Ibn Abī l-Dunyā (quoted some three hundred times), al-Bayhaqī (*ca.* 170), Ibn ʿAsākir (*ca.* 150), Ibn Ḥanbal, Ibn Abī Shayba, Abū Nuʿaym, and al-Ṭabarānī (each *ca.* 100). See Eklund, *Life*, 26. Abridgements of the *Sharḥ* include one ascribed to al-Suyūṭī (*Bushrā l-kaʾīb bi-liqāʾ al-ḥabīb*), as well as a work entitled *al-Taḥrīr al-murassakh* by Muḥammad Ibn Ṭulūn al-Ṣāliḥī (d. 953/1546).

[12] Suyūṭī, *Sharḥ al-ṣudūr*, 304–13.

[13] Ibid., 310; Baḥrānī, *Maʿālim*, II, 74.

[14] See the preceding text, p. 40.

[15] Cf. Halevi, *Muḥammad's grave*, 206.

[16] Suyūṭī, *Sharḥ al-ṣudūr*, 311.

[17] Ibn Abī l-Dunyā, *Mawt*, 36 (#35). Cf. *TG*, IV, 526–8.

[18] Baḥrānī, *Maʿālim*, II, 79; Majlisī, *Biḥār*, VI, 419, 444.

[19] Baḥrānī, *Maʿālim*, II, 91–2.

refused to believe that postmortem souls reside in the crops of birds. Such a thing, he reckoned, would not befit the Prophet and the members of his family, who instead must be imagined to have humanlike bodies in paradise.[20]

Al-Suyūṭī devotes considerable space to traditions such as these, traditions that ostensibly affirm that paradise and hell are entered without delay, and lastingly, after death. This suggests that this view continued to reverberate over the centuries. Al-Suyūṭī attributes it, among others, to Ibn Ḥanbal (d. 241/855), and states that scholars through the ages continued to disagree about the question.[21] However, the view that al-Suyūṭī champions – by and large the standard position of both Sunni and Shiʿi authors – is that only special classes of people enter paradise right after death. These people, which al-Suyūṭī identifies as "those who are brought near" (*al-muqarrabūn*), are the prophets, martyrs, and those believers who are not *mukallafūn*, that is, subject to the revealed law, such as the underage children of Muslims.[22] (Conversely, as the literature on jihad at times affirms, the unbelievers killed in the armed struggle with Muslims go immediately to hell.)[23] Al-Baḥrānī, as a Shiʿi, adds the Prophet's family to the list, as well as a number of other figures, such as Khadīja, Moses's sister Kulthūm, Pharaoh's wife Āsiya, and Mary.[24]

As for all others, they are afforded only a brief foretaste of the otherworld. At death, they are separated from their bodies temporarily and taken on a summary tour of paradise and hell by the angels.[25] They are then returned to the *barzakh* on earth. This return can mean one of two things. One possibility is that souls are confined to an earthly waiting room, such as, for example, the well of Zamzam in Mecca or the well of Barhūt in

[20] Majlisī, *Biḥār*, VI, 415, 443. Baḥrānī, *Maʿālim*, II, 72–4, attributes this view to ʿAlī b. Abī Ṭālib.

[21] Suyūṭī, *Sharḥ al-ṣudūr*, 328. Halevi notes that the "classical" Sunni collectors of hadith generally shunned the term *barzakh*, as if they felt uncomfortable with the "novel interpretation of al-barzakh as an independent dimension of space-time." See Halevi, *Muḥammad's grave*, 217.

[22] Suyūṭī, *Sharḥ al-ṣudūr*, 314, 325–7; Qurṭubī, *Tadhkira*, I, 183–8 and 188–91 (with definitions of who counts as a martyr, or *shahīd*); Baḥrānī, *Maʿālim*, II, 109–10 (the children in paradise are brought up by Fāṭima and fed by Abraham); Majlisī, *Biḥār*, VI, 416 (ditto). On martyrs passing into paradise immediately after death, see Ibn Hishām, *Sīrat*, 604–6 (battle of Uḥud).

[23] In the *K. al-Jihād* of ʿAlī b. Ṭāhir al-Sulamī (d. 500/1106), composed at Damascus in reaction to the arrival of the crusaders in the Levant, it is related that ʿUmar b. al-Khaṭṭāb told his enemy Abū Sufyān at the Battle of Uḥud in 3/625 that those killed on the side of the unbelieving Meccans "are in the Fire, being punished." See Sulamī, *Jihād*, 9b, quoted in Christie, "Paradise and hell in the *K. al-jihād*," at n9.

[24] Baḥrānī, *Maʿālim*, II, 82–5.

[25] Suyūṭī, *Sharḥ al-ṣudūr*, 165–6, 170–1, 178; Qurṭubī, *Tadhkira*, I, 144; Majlisī, *Biḥār*, VIII, 407–8; Baḥrānī, *Maʿālim*, II, 76. On the tour of the otherworld of the souls of the dead, cf. Smith and Haddad, *Islamic understanding*, 39–40; Halevi, *Muhammad's grave*, 207–10; Seidensticker, "Der rūḥ," 144.

Hadramawt valley (for believers and unbelievers, respectively),[26] or a certain hill on the outskirts of Kufa where, according to Shiʿi tradition, ʿAlī clairvoyantly observed the dead sitting around in circles, talking to each other.[27] The other possibility, which enjoys greater popularity in traditionist literature, is that souls are rejoined with their bodies in the grave, and then undergo questioning about the tenets of faith by two fearsome angels called Munkar and Nakīr. Depending on whether they are able to provide the correct answers, Munkar and Nakīr then open a door in the grave through which some catch a glimpse of their future seat (*maqʿad*) in paradise, while others are shown hell.[28] Until the Day of Resurrection, these doors are opened twice a day, in the morning and evening,[29] except that the door leading to hell remains shut on Fridays, as a token of God's mercy.[30]

Paradise and hell, however, are not just distant vistas for the inhabitants of the graves. In numerous traditions, both colonise the inside of tombs. The grave of the believer thus becomes a paradisiacal chamber of delights. In their spacious subterranean garden pavilions, the walls of which are "painted with their religious knowledge (*ʿilm*)," believers rest on couches bedecked with green silk and cushions of gold brocade.[31] While lamps bathe them in the light of paradise, they enjoy food, dress, and perfume brought to them from the eternal garden.[32] To alleviate their loneliness, they are allowed to visit the other dead;[33] or their good works, incarnated in a host of handsome folk, keep them company; and in case they wish to read, they are provided a copy of the Qurʾān.[34] By contrast, the unbelievers in their graves, into which they are squeezed "like the blade of a spear is squeezed into its shaft,"[35] feed on the hellish plants of Zaqqūm and *ḍarīʿ*; are dressed in garments of fire; are bitten by snakes, scorpions, and vermin; and are mercilessly flogged by the angels of the grave, who wield whips with thick knotted ends.[36]

[26] Suyūṭī, *Sharḥ al-ṣudūr*, 312, 317–8, 329.

[27] Baḥrānī, *Maʿālim*, II, 72; Majlisī, *Biḥār*, VI, 424–5, 442.

[28] Suyūṭī, *Sharḥ al-ṣudūr*, 166, 178; Baḥrānī, *Maʿālim*, II, 39, 47, 51; Majlisī, *Biḥār*, VI, 413, 439–40.

[29] Suyūṭī, *Sharḥ al-ṣudūr*, 340; Qurṭubī, *Tadhkira*, I, 181–2; Majlisī, *Biḥār*, VI, 432.

[30] Suyūṭī, *Sharḥ al-ṣudūr*, 209.

[31] Ibid., 183, 213, 219; Baḥrānī, *Maʿālim*, II, 39, 45, 49.

[32] Suyūṭī, *Sharḥ al-ṣudūr*, 183, 220; Majlisī, *Biḥār*, VI, 410, 439, VIII, 407; Baḥrānī, *Maʿālim*, III, 106.

[33] Qurṭubī, *Tadhkira*, I, 120. One should note, however, the strong current in Islamic hortatory literature and epigraphy stressing the solitude and forlornness (*waḥda, waḥsha*) of the grave. See Diem and Schöller, *The living and the dead*, II, 134–9.

[34] Suyūṭī, *Sharḥ al-ṣudūr*, 178, 183; Majlisī, *Biḥār*, VI, 412, 419; Baḥrānī, *Maʿālim*, II, 46. Cf. Halevi, *Muhammad's grave*, 199; Carra de Vaux, Fragments, 20.

[35] Baḥrānī, *Maʿālim*, II, 47.

[36] Suyūṭī, *Sharḥ al-ṣudūr*, 192, 223; Majlisī, *Biḥār*, VI, 405, 408, 440; Baḥrānī, *Maʿālim*, II, 47.

FIGURE 6. The angels of the grave, Munkar and Nakīr, torturing an inhabitant of the grave. From an anonymous *Ḥajjnāma*. India, twelfth/eighteenth century (?). MS Bodleian Pers. d. 29, fol. 25r.

Unsurprisingly, the fact that the dead were thought to reside either in their graves or in various terrestrial paradises and hells caused some confusion. The Damascene Ibn Qayyim al-Jawziyya (d. 751/1350), whose *Book of the Soul* (*K. al-rūḥ*) sums up traditionist notions about *barzakh* while also offering attempts at harmonisation, proposed that souls in the *barzakh* are capable of bilocality, of being present simultaneously in several places, in the manner of sun rays.[37] Thus they travel, with the speed of light as it were, between different locations. This idea, too, was clothed in the form of hadiths. Al-Baḥrānī relates that the souls of the believers rise from their graves in the evening, hover in the air for awhile, then fly to the terrestrial paradise in the west, to return to their graves at dawn. Similarly, the unbelievers' souls, during the night, travel to "a fire in the east," or to Barhūt.[38] According to al-Suyūṭī, the Syrian traditionist al-Awzāʿī (d. 157/774) was once asked about certain black birds that rise from the Mediterranean in the morning and return in the evening. He responded that these birds, whose feathers he said were scorched by hellfire, carried the wicked souls of the "people of Pharaoh" to their nests.[39] One presumes that he thought them to spend the night in hell – the sea, according to a fairly widespread tradition,[40] is the top layer of hell – and the day in the vicinity of their graves.

The period of the *barzakh* comes to an end when the dead are resurrected and assembled on the Place of Gathering (*arḍ al-maḥshar*), which al-Suyūṭī locates in Jerusalem.[41] During the apocalyptic upheaval that precedes this final moment of human history, creation is undone. As the Qurʾān puts it, paradise is "brought near" and hell is "brought out" (Q 26:90–91; cf. 81:11–13). Both, in other words, are now in plain sight of everybody, while previously, in the *barzakh*, they were visible only occasionally and at some distance. Inspired by the Qurʾānic verse that "on that day, Jahannam will be brought forth" (Q 89:23), hell makes a particularly dramatic appearance. The hell-monster Jahannam raises its neck (*ʿunuq*) from the flames and, led by legions of angels, circles the assembly of humankind, then proceeding to interrogate individual sinners.[42] As it roars, the mountains melt, and everybody, including the angels and the prophets, fall to their knees to plead for their lives. Only the prophet Muḥammad steps up to confront the monster, demanding that his community (*umma*) be saved.[43] According to a Shiʿi

[37] Ibn Qayyim al-Jawziyya, *Rūḥ*, 127. Cf. Suyūṭī, *Sharḥ al-ṣudūr*, 316. On Ibn [al-]Qayyim's *K. al-rūḥ*, see now Langermann, "Ibn al-Qayyim's *Kitāb al-Rūḥ*," 125–45, esp. 139.

[38] Baḥrānī, *Maʿālim*, II, 77–8.

[39] Suyūṭī, *Sharḥ al-ṣudūr*, 341.

[40] Idem, *Budūr*, 411–13; Qurṭubī, *Tadhkira*, II, 101–2.

[41] Suyūṭī, *Budūr*, 91; Qurṭubī, *Tadhkira*, I, 234–5.

[42] Suyūṭī, *Budūr*, 411; Majlisī, *Biḥār*, VIII, 464; Qurṭubī, *Tadhkira*, II, 96–100; Baḥrānī, *Maʿālim*, III, 357–9. A version of the narrative appears as early as in Muqātil's (d. 150/767) *tafsīr* (*ad* 84:1); cf. Sinai, *Fortschreibung und Auslegung*, 221–4.

[43] Suyūṭī, *Budūr*, 68, 149–52, 227; Baḥrānī, *Maʿālim*, II 545, 547, 550–2, III, 106; Majlisī, *Biḥār*, VII, 95–6.

tradition, Muḥammad delegates the taming of Jahannam to his son-in-law ʿAlī, first of the Imams, who grabs the beast's reins and mounts its backside, while holding in his hands the keys to paradise and hell.[44] Once judged, the resurrected pass over the Bridge (*ṣirāṭ*), spanning the hell-funnel, that leads towards paradise. As a Shiʿi tradition declares, nobody traverses the Bridge without a written pass (*jawāz*) issued by ʿAlī.[45] Both those who tumble into the abyss and those who make it to the other side have now reached their final destination.[46]

Time, Space, and Vision in the Muslim Paradise and Hell

As we have just seen, according to the literature on the *barzakh*, paradise and hell coexist with this world, and some of the rewards and punishments meted out in them predate the final judgement at the end of time. This synchronicity is likewise presumed in the traditionist literature dedicated to paradise and hell proper. Writers and compilers working in this genre hardly seem to have reflected on the implied contradiction. They do not hesitate to relate traditions that speak of the final judgement *and* the creation of paradise and hell at the beginning of time.[47] Al-Suyūṭī, for example, reports that when hell was created, the angels' hearts were overcome with dismay (*ṭārat afʾidatuhā*), only to be calmed when God fashioned Adam.[48] (However, not all the angels fully recovered from the shock. The archangels Gabriel and Michael never laughed again.)[49] Numerous traditions transmitted by al-Suyūṭī and al-Majlisī refer to the prophet Muḥammad's visit of paradise and hell during his ascension. From this, too, readers were invited to infer that both abodes were already in place and operative.[50] Some traditions make the point explicitly and categorically.[51]

The preapocalyptic and the postapocalyptic paradise and hell are not in all respects the same, however. After the final judgement, a momentous change in the temporality of the otherworld occurs. According to a much-commented-upon hadith,[52] once the blessed and the damned have

44 Majlisī, *Biḥār*, VII, 243.

45 Baḥrānī, *Maʿālim*, III, 100–1. Cf. ibid., 159.

46 On the *ṣirāṭ*, see Suyūṭī, *Budūr*, 341–8; Majlisī, *Biḥār*, VIII, 304–9, 470; Qurṭubī, *Tadhkira*, II, 26–37; Baḥrāni, *Maʿālim*, II, 545–52.

47 God created paradise before hell, in the same way in which He created mercy before wrath, light before darkness, and life before death. See Suyūṭī, *Budūr*, 489; Baḥrānī, *Maʿālim*, III, 7. Cf. Majlisī, *Biḥār*, VIII, 480.

48 Suyūṭī, *Budūr*, 410; Qurṭubī, *Tadhkira*, II, 86.

49 Suyūṭī, *Budūr*, 409.

50 Majlisī, *Biḥār*, VIII, 344–5; Baḥrānī, *Maʿālim*, III, 253–4; Baḥrānī, *Nuzhat*, 40.

51 Majlisī, *Biḥār*, VIII, 354, 402, 407–8, 463 and passim.

52 Bukhārī, *Ṣaḥīḥ*, *k. al-riqāq* 51 (*b. ṣifat al-janna wa-l-nār*), IV, 207; cf. Ibn Ḥajar, *Fatḥ al-bārī*, XI, 420–2 (#6182). See also Muslim, *Ṣaḥīḥ*, *k. al-janna* 40–3, IV, 2188–9; cf. Nawawī, *Sharḥ*, XVII, 156. For further references in the hadith, see *CTM*, II, 172b. On the meaning of *amlaḥ*

arrived at their final destination, death is brought forth in the form of a white ram, made to stand on the wall between paradise and hell (or on the *ṣirāt* bridge according to other traditions), and slaughtered by an angel. A caller (*munādī*) then announces: "O people of paradise! Death is no more! O people of hell! Death is no more!"[53] How exactly death takes the form of a white ram is the object of some discussion among the eschatologists. Al-Qurṭubī opines that God creates a ram that He then names Death, which serves to remind the inhabitants of paradise and hell that eternity has begun.[54] Others suggest that the ram in question is no other than the angel of death, whose service is longer required.[55] Opinions seem to have settled, however, on accepting that death has a form (*ṣūra*) in the hereafter, in the same way in which people's good or bad actions, according to various hadiths, acquire a visible shape at judgement.[56] In fact, in the Muslim eschatological imagination, paradise and hell are populated by numerous true allegories of this sort, examples of which shall be mentioned later in this chapter.[57]

As they leave the framework of history and are ushered into that of eternity, paradise and hell shift into full gear as institutions of perpetual reward and punishment. It is not the case, as Muslim theologians occasionally imagined, that all activity in the otherworld is frozen in one eternal moment.[58] Rather, the events in paradise and hell enter into circles of endless repetition, as in a perpetuum mobile. The inhabitants of paradise and hell, who never sleep, serve as the wheels in this unceasing, self-renewing clockwork.[59] Thus, when the blessed pluck a fruit from a tree in paradise, a new fruit grows immediately in its place.[60] When they see a bird whose

as "white," see Fischer, *Farb- und Formbezeichnungen*, 252–3. Al-Suyūṭī devoted a short separate epistle to the question, the *Risāla fī dhabḥ al-mawt*. See also the extended discussions in Ibn Qayyim al-Jawziyya, *Ḥādī*, 288–90; Majlisī, *Biḥār*, VIII, 509–16.

[53] Suyūṭī, *Budūr*, 472–3; Qurṭubī, *Tadhkira*, II, 155–6. On the origin of this hadith, cf. *ECḤ*, 90.

[54] Qurṭubī, *Tadhkira*, II, 158.

[55] Ibn Ḥajar, *Fatḥ al-bārī*, XI, 420; Suyūṭī, *Risāla fī dhabḥ al-mawt*, fol. 292r, ult.

[56] Idem, *Budūr*, 143, 475; Ibn Qayyim al-Jawziyya, *Ḥādī*, 289; Baḥrānī, *Maʿālim*, I, 247, III, 372. Already Ibn al-Mubārak relates a tradition according to which prayer and fasting intercede on behalf of those who practice them on the Day of Judgement. See Ibn al-Mubārak, *Musnad*, 58–9 (#96). A Zoroastrian background to this idea seems likely. In the Avesta, "religious belief" (*daēnā*) appears to the dead as a guide to the afterlife, either in the form of a beautiful young woman or an ugly hag. See Hutter, "The impurity of the corpse," 23–4; Boyce, *Textual sources*, 80.

[57] Qurṭubī, *Tadhkira*, II, 76: this world (*al-dunyā*) appears on the Day of Resurrection in the form of a grotesquely ugly old hag. Baḥrānī, *Maʿālim*, III, 31: the good action precedes his owner (*ṣāḥibuhu*) to paradise and prepares his resting place there, just as the servant (*ghulām*) does in this world. Cf. Suyūṭī, *Maʿānī*, wherein he argues that abstract ideas possess corporeality in the presence of God.

[58] See the following text, p. 169.

[59] No sleep in paradise: Suyūṭī, *Budūr*, 596–7; Baḥrānī, *Maʿālim*, III, 126. No sleep in hell: Majlisī, *Biḥār*, VIII, 457, 471.

[60] Suyūṭī, *Budūr*, 528, 533; Majlisī, *Biḥār*, VIII, 356, 410; Qurṭubī, *Tadhkira*, II, 174.

meat they wish to eat, it falls readily roasted into their hands, and when they are finished with it, it regains its former shape and flies away.[61] When they deflower one of the heavenly maidens, a houri, her virginity is restored right after congress.[62] In fact, not only are the houris recursively virginal, they grow like fruit on trees or like plants on the shore of a river in paradise, "and whenever one of them is taken [by one of the inhabitants of paradise], a new one springs forth in her place."[63] *Mutatis mutandis*, the damned in hell are recursively mutilated and annihilated. The fire in hell ravages their skins, but these are immediately replaced with new skins "as white as paper."[64] The sinners drown in a sea of fire, but when they seek refuge on the shore, they are attacked by giant snakes and scorpions and driven back into a vicious circle.[65] Others climb a mountain so hot that it melts their hands and feet, but these, too, grow back immediately, and once they have reached the summit they are thrown down to the foot of the mountain to begin their painful ascent anew.[66] Yet others swirl through the entire hell edifice in one big circular movement, as they are propelled upwards, "flying like sparks," from the bottom to hell's upper layer, and then cast back into the abyss.[67]

Turning to the spatial characteristics of the traditionist otherworld, one finds the conflicting notions that there are four or seven paradise gardens, that paradise has one hundred or more layers (*darajāt*), and that paradise has eight gates (instead of seven, as one might expect), or even seventy-one gates.[68] Al-Suyūṭī harmonises these notions by declaring that the gardens are subdivided in a variety of ways.[69] In fact, the space that stretches from one gate of paradise to the next is enormous. It is "like that which is between the heaven and the earth," or like the distance covered in forty years of travel.[70] Similarly, a journey from one gate of hell to the next lasts five hundred years,[71] and a stone thrown from the brim into the hell-pit falls seventy

[61] Suyūṭī, *Budūr*, 537, 580–1; Majlisī, *Biḥār*, VIII, 319, 337; Qurṭubī, *Tadhkira*, II, 208; Baḥrānī, *Maʿālim*, III, 129, 172.

[62] Suyūṭī, *Budūr*, 571–2; Majlisī, *Biḥār*, VIII, 357, 411, 430; Baḥrānī, *Maʿālim*, III, 110.

[63] Majlisī, *Biḥār*, VIII, 346, 354–5, 358. Cf. Suyūṭī, *Budūr*, 541; Qurṭubī, *Tadhkira*, II, 235 (virgins spring forth from a river); Baḥrānī, *Maʿālim*, III, 110, 135 (recursive virginity). I borrow the phrase "recursively virginal" from al-Azmeh, "Rhetoric," 225.

[64] Suyūṭī, *Budūr*, 451–2; Majlisī, *Biḥār*, VIII, 430.

[65] Suyūṭī, *Budūr*, 443; Qurṭubī, *Tadhkira*, II, 119.

[66] Suyūṭī, *Budūr*, 417, 420–1, 466; Majlisī, *Biḥār*, VIII, 453.

[67] Qurṭubī, *Tadhkira*, II, 113; Suyūṭī, *Budūr*, 434–5; Majlisī, *Biḥār*, VIII, 439.

[68] Suyūṭī, *Budūr*, 494, 496, 502; Majlisī, *Biḥār*, VIII, 358, 362, 373, 414; Qurṭubī, *Tadhkira*, II, 178–81, 183–4, 227. Majlisī, *Biḥār*, VIII, 346, reserves two of the gates to the prophets and martyrs, five to the Shiʿa, and one to all other virtuous Muslims. On the notion of eight gates, see Lange, "The 'eight gates of paradise'-tradition."

[69] Suyūṭī, *Budūr*, 496.

[70] Ibid., 496, 508.

[71] Qurṭubī, *Tadhkira*, II, 93.

years before it hits the bottom.[72] The size of otherworldly phenomena is recurrently measured in exceedingly large time units. The valleys and mountain gorges in hell, for example, are so deep that the sinners who are pushed into them fall forty years before they reach the ground;[73] the branches of the Ṭūbā tree in paradise cover an expense that a rider cannot traverse in a hundred years;[74] the height of paradise's "raised couches" (cf. Q 56:34) is five hundred years;[75] the punisher angels in hell are giants, with shoulders one hundred years apart;[76] and so on and so forth. Unhinged from earthly constraints of time and space, the imagination is pushed to an extreme. This results in a discourse on the otherworld in which the temporal and spatial dimensions of paradise and hell are fathomless in one sense but in another, they remain commensurate with human categories of thought; a discourse that approaches eternity and infinity asymptotically.

Al-Suyūṭī and al-Majlisī report several traditions about the location of paradise and hell, not all of which are easily pictured or indeed mutually reconcilable. On the one hand, paradise is said to be located in the seventh heaven, or right below God's Throne, while hell is in the lowest earth.[77] As was noted previously, the sea, in this vertically oriented model, functions as the lid covering the subterranean fires. One tradition even declares it to be *jahannam*, that is, the top layer of the hell edifice.[78] On the other hand, the otherworld is imagined to surround (*yuḥīṭu*) the inhabited world, in the manner of horizontally arranged concentric rings.[79] Both paradise and hell have seven layers, or compartments, each of which is accessible through a separate gate. The seven layers, or gardens, of paradise are called Dār al-Jalāl ("the Abode of Glory"), Dār al-Salām ("the Abode of Peace"), Dār al-Khuld ("the Abode of Eternity"), Jannat ʿAdn ("the Garden of Eden"), Jannat al-Ma'wā ("the Garden of the Refuge"), Jannat al-Naʿīm ("the Garden of Bliss"), and, the highest of them all, Jannat al-Firdaws ("the Garden of Firdaws").[80] Mirroring this structure, the seven layers of hell are

72 Suyūṭī, *Budūr*, 424–5. Cf. Qurṭubī, *Tadhkira*, II, 111, for the enormously long chain (*silsila*) hanging from hell's roof to its bottom.

73 Suyūṭī, *Budūr*, 417.

74 Ibid., 525–6; Majlisī, *Biḥār*, VIII, 337, 344; Qurṭubī, *Tadhkira*, II, 172.

75 Suyūṭī, *Budūr*, 551.

76 Ibid., 415.

77 Ibid., 411; Majlisī, *Biḥār*, VIII, 347, 350–1; Baḥrānī, *Maʿālim*, III, 120–1, 163. Al-Suyūṭī also reports the opinion of the early Qur'ān commentator al-Ḍaḥḥāk that both paradise and hell are in heaven (*samā'*).

78 Suyūṭī, *Budūr*, 411. Cf. Qurṭubī, *Tadhkira*, II, 105.

79 Suyūṭī, *Budūr*, 411; Baḥrānī, *Maʿālim*, III, 166: *al-ākhira muḥīṭa bi-l-dunyā*. Al-Majlisī, who consistently seeks to place the eschatological paradise in the heavens, opines that only the flames of the subterranean hell "surround" the earth, one presumes like the flames around a kettle. See Majlisī, *Biḥār*, VIII, 376. Cf. ibid., VIII, 350–1.

80 Suyūṭī, *Budūr*, 496; Qurṭubī, *Tadhkira*, II, 227. Cf. Q 6:127, 18:107, 38:50, 41:28, 53:15, 56:89. Only Dār al-Jalāl is not mentioned in the Qur'ān. A tradition in Baḥrānī, *Maʿālim*, III, 169, adds an eighth garden, the "Garden of Light" (*jannat al-nūr*).

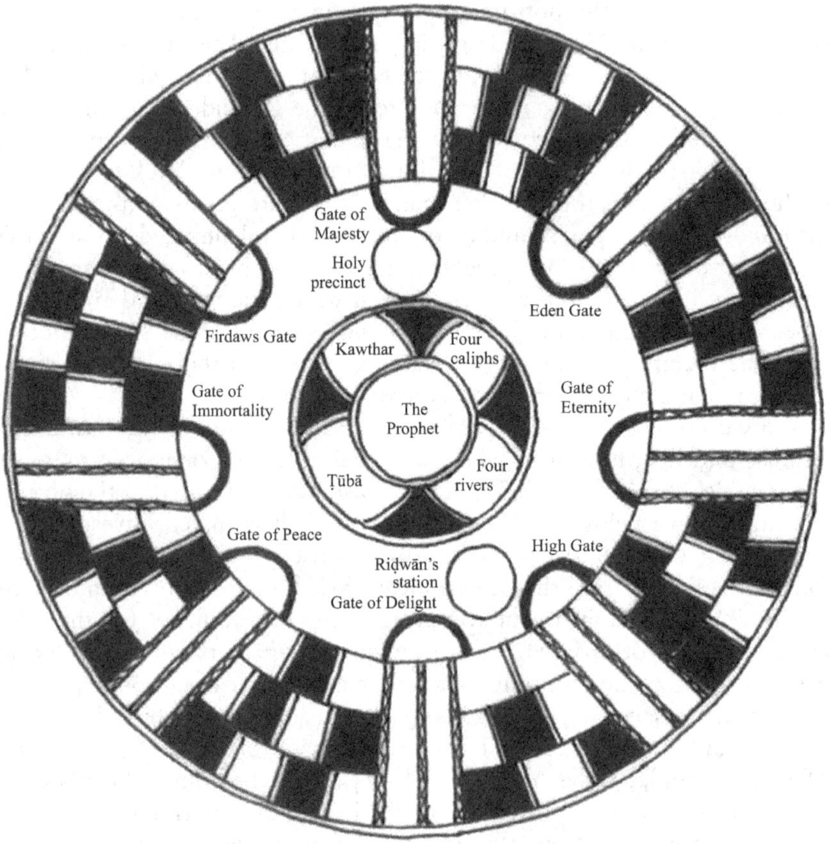

FIGURE 7. The eight gates and gardens of paradise. Adapted from Ḥusām al-Dīn Bursawī (d. 1042/1632–3), *Mir'āt al-kā'ināt* (*The Mirror of Created Things*). Turkey, before 1147/[1735]. MS Staatsbibliothek Berlin, Or. quart 1837, fol. 10v.

called Jahannam ("Gehenna"), al-Sa'īr ("the Blaze"), Laẓā ("Fierceflame"), al-Ḥuṭama ("Glutton" [?]), Saqar ("Raging Fire"), al-Jaḥīm ("Hellfire"), and, the lowest of them all, al-Hāwiya ("the Abyss").[81]

As noted, Firdaws is usually designated as the most central and highest garden, so close to God on top that its inhabitants can hear the creaking sound (*aṭīṭ*) of the divine Throne.[82] According to a divergent tradition related by al-Majlisī, Jannat 'Adn is the most central and the highest of

[81] Suyūṭī, *Budūr*, 413; Qurṭubī, *Tadhkira*, II, 93–4. Again, all these names are taken from the Qur'ān. See Q 2:119, 2:206, 4:10, 54:48, 70:15, 104:4–5, 101:9, and passim. A tradition in Majlisī, *Biḥār*, VIII, 434, reverses the order: *hāwiya*, *sa'īr*, *jaḥīm*, *saqar*, *al-ḥuṭama*, *laẓā*, *jahannam*.

[82] Suyūṭī, *Budūr*, 496–7. Cf. Majlisī, *Biḥār*, VIII, 322.

the gardens of paradise; here live the messengers, prophets, Imams, and martyrs.[83] Here, too, are located the springs of Zanjabīl, Salsabīl, and Tasnīm, from which flow the four rivers of water, honey, milk, and wine.[84] These rivers disappear through a hole, presumably at the bottom of paradise, and then reemerge on earth as the rivers Sayḥān, Jayḥān, Nile, and Euphrates.[85] In addition to these four, numerous other rivers are mentioned by al-Suyūṭī and al-Majlisī, including the rivers al-Kawthar and Jaʿfar.[86] These rivers flow amidst meadows of saffron that grow on a ground of ambergris strewn with pearls and rubies, while dunes of musk line the horizon, serving as miradors to the blessed who take a leisurely seat on them.[87] As for the buildings that dot this fantastic landscape, no effort is spared to describe their sumptuousness. Their bricks are solid gold or silver, or massive precious stones, while the mortar that binds them is a blend of musk and incense.[88] While some of the blessed reside in castles[89] – a Shiʿi tradition singles out the castle of ʿAlī b. Abī Ṭālib,[90] a Sunni one that of ʿUmar b. al-Khaṭṭāb[91] – even the meekest of the paradise dwellers live in canopies or houses carved from single giant pearls.[92]

Hell, in contrast to the sprawling meadows and gently flowing rivers of paradise, is vertically oriented. While paradise has no depth – its rivers do not run in beds but rather, they flow flatly over the surface of the earth[93] – hell is a vertigo-inducing abyss, a craggy landscape scarred by deep ravines and mountain gorges, on top of which are perched fearsome prison citadels.[94]

[83] Ibid., VIII, 319, 394. According to Suyūṭī, *Budūr*, 584, Jannat ʿAdn is for the prophets, martyrs, and righteous ones (*ṣiddīqūn*). Elsewhere, Jannat al-Maʾwā is reserved for the martyrs. See *EQ*, s.v. Paradise, IV, 12a-20a, at 14a (L. Kinberg).

[84] Suyūṭī, *Budūr*, 496–7, 540, 542; Majlisī, *Biḥār*, VIII, 321–2; Qurṭubī, *Tadhkira*, II, 170. According to Qurṭubī, *Tadhkira*, II, 168, the four rivers spring from al-Kawthar in paradise. There are also rivers in paradise that spring from mountains of musk. See Suyūṭī, *Budūr*, 538; Qurṭubī, *Tadhkira*, II, 167.

[85] Suyūṭī, *Budūr*, 539.

[86] Majlisī, *Biḥār*, VIII, 348, 374 (al-Kawthar and al-Raḥma); Majlisī, *Biḥār*, VIII, 374 (Jaʿfar); Suyūṭī, *Budūr*, 540 (al-Baydaj); Suyūṭī, *Budūr*, 541 (al-Rayyān); Majlisī, *Biḥār*, VIII, 372 (Khayr).

[87] Suyūṭī, *Budūr*, 491, 510–12, 582; Majlisī, *Biḥār*, VIII, 414.

[88] Suyūṭī, *Budūr*, 490–1, 515–6; Majlisī, *Biḥār*, VIII, 319, 342–3.

[89] Suyūṭī, *Budūr*, 515, 517; Majlisī, *Biḥār*, VIII, 330, 368.

[90] Ibid., VIII, 384.

[91] Qurṭubī, *Tadhkira*, II, 189.

[92] Suyūṭī, *Budūr*, 516, 546, 553; Majlisī, *Biḥār*, VIII, 336. In the *Midrash Ha-Gadol* (Bereshit 2:8), in a Midrash on Ezekiel 28:13 ("You were in Eden the garden of God; every precious stone was your covering"), God is said to have created canopies of precious stones for Adam. See also Qurṭubī, *Tadhkira*, II, 216–8, for the palaces of the lowest inhabitants of paradise.

[93] Suyūṭī, *Budūr*, 511–12, 539; Majlisī, *Biḥār*, VIII, 337, 340; Qurṭubī, *Tadhkira*, II, 174; Baḥrānī, *Maʿālim*, III, 124.

[94] Suyūṭī, *Budūr*, 417–24; Qurṭubī, *Tadhkira*, II, 116 (a fortress called al-Hawāʾ, cf. Q 20:81: *fa-qad hawā*).

Instead of rivers and springs, valleys (*awdiya*) and deep wells (*ajbāb*) are characteristic of hell. There is a rather large number of the latter in particular,[95] and their names tend to be derived, by an interpretive process of turning abstract nouns into concrete toponyms,[96] from the Qur'ān. For example, when the Qur'ān declares that the sinners "will meet error (*ghayy*)" (19:59) and that they "will meet the price of sin (*athām*)" (25:68), in the eschatological imagination of the exegetes, Ghayy and Athām become the proper names of two wells, located at the bottom of hell, into which the pus of the tortured inhabitants of hell is collected.[97] One could adduce numerous other examples of this typical exegetical technique of reification.[98]

Eschatologists like al-Suyūṭī and al-Majlisī relate numerous traditions that describe the various modalities of traversing paradisiacal space, whether by means of the entire body or with the eye alone, and the impossibility of traversing hellish space. The freedom of movement in paradise is unlimited, while in hell it is severely restricted. The blessed undertake pleasure excursions on winged horses and camels to visit each other,[99] covering great distances in the blink of an eye.[100] The damned in hell, by contrast, are in chains and pinned to the ground "like nails in the wall,"[101] while others are imprisoned in iron trunks.[102] Similarly, the gaze of the inhabitants of paradise wanders freely, while the damned see nothing at all. This is so if only because there is no night in paradise,[103] while there is no light in hell. Not even the flames of the ever-burning hellfire illuminate the hellish landscape.[104] God fanned the fire of hell with his breath over a period of several thousand years, so that it changed its colour from white to red and, eventually, to black.[105]

95 See also Suyūṭī, *Budūr*, 422 (al-Ḥuzn), Suyūṭī, *Budūr*, 423 (al-Mansā); Qurṭubī, *Tadhkira*, II, 116 (Habhab). Cf. Lange, *Justice*, 128.

96 Cf. Raven, "Hell in popular Muslim imagination." On its application in ascension narratives, see Colby, *Narrating*, 21–2.

97 Suyūṭī, *Budūr*, 419; Majlisī, *Biḥār*, VIII, 441.

98 Suyūṭī, *Budūr*, 418 (Wayl), 419 (Ghayy), 420–1 (Ṣa'ūd), 421 (al-Falaq); Majlisī, *Biḥār*, VIII, 444 (Ghassāq), 459, 472 (al-Falaq), and passim; Qurṭubī, *Tadhkira*, II, 115–6 (Yaḥmūm, Mawbiq, Ghayy, al-Falaq, Ṣa'ūd). Consider also the case of the river al-Kawthar ("abundance") in paradise, a name derived from Q 108:1. Cf. Birkeland, *The Lord guideth*, 56–76; Saleh, *Formation*, 119–24; Gilliot, "L'embarras d'un exégète," 37–48. The name of the angel, Riḍwān ("satisfaction"), is probably derived from Q 3:15. See *EI2*, s.v. Riḍwān (W. Raven), VIII, 519a; Budge, *Angels in Islam*, 74.

99 Suyūṭī, *Budūr*, 525, 580, 597–8; Qurṭubī, *Tadhkira*, II, 211.

100 Baḥrānī, *Ma'ālim*, III, 109.

101 Suyūṭī, *Budūr*, 432, 456. As in the grave, they are "squeezed like the blade of spear into the shaft." See Suyūṭī, *Budūr*, 456; Majlisī, *Biḥār*, VIII, 441, 444.

102 Suyūṭī, *Budūr*, 423; Majlisī, *Biḥār*, VIII, 431, 460, 472; Qurṭubī, *Tadhkira*, II, 90; Baḥrānī, *Ma'ālim*, III, 328.

103 Suyūṭī, *Budūr*, 537.

104 Ibid., 410, 428–9.

105 Ibid., 410, 426; Majlisī, *Biḥār*, VIII, 460; Qurṭubī, *Tadhkira*, II, 104–5; Baḥrānī, *Ma'ālim*, III, 363. The (predominant) colour of paradise, by contrast, is white. See Suyūṭī, *Budūr*, 492.

The vision of the inhabitants of paradise stands in contrast not only to that of those in hell but also to the scopic régime in place in the present world.[106] According to a tradition, the ground in paradise is a silver mirror,[107] and in general the conditions of visibility in paradise are absolutely pristine. Vision reaches far indeed. The people of paradise can spot the white hairs in the black beards of men from a distance of one thousand years.[108] When they look up to the windows of the castles in paradise, they can see the faces of the prophets and the other religious exemplars who inhabit them "like stars on the horizon."[109] An eerie transparency is characteristic of paradise as a whole. The houses and castles in paradise have walls "whose inside can be seen from the outside, and whose outside can be seen from the inside";[110] the silver bottles in which wine is served to the paradise dwellers are so exquisite that one can see through them like through a glass;[111] the men's gaze pierces through the seventy thousand fine veils worn by the houris, as well as through their skin, so that they see the marrow in their shank bones like a thread running through a ruby, or like red drink in a white glass, or like a coin tossed into clear water.[112] However, as if to assuage concerns that such unrestrained visibility might undermine people's right to privacy, both al-Suyūṭi and al-Majlisī also quote traditions that assert that there are rooms inside the houses in paradise reserved for the inner family (and particularly, the women) of the owner of the house, who are shielded from sight.[113]

Plants, Animals, and Spiritual Beings

The Islamic otherworld is home to a variety of remarkable plants. On several occasions already, we have come across the tree in paradise whose shadow a rider cannot cross in a century. This tree is usually referred to as Ṭūbā,[114] another instance in which an abstract concept in the Qur'ān (13:29: "those who believe and do righteous deeds will have bliss [*ṭūbā*]") is reified into a concrete phenomenon in paradise and hell. According to tradition, the Prophet was the first to suggest that the word *ṭūbā* signifies a paradisiacal

[106] The pioneering study of this phenomenon is O'Meara, "Muslim visuality." According to Lamaṭī, *Ibrīz* (tr. O'Kane/Radtke), 909, the Prophet stated that "the body's vision in Paradise doesn't halt at any limit."

[107] Suyūṭī, *Budūr*, 511. See also Baḥrānī, *Ma'ālim*, III, 109, where people see their own faces in the walls of the houses.

[108] Suyūṭī, *Budūr*, 592.

[109] Ibid., 513; Majlisī, *Biḥār*, VIII, 383.

[110] Suyūṭī, *Budūr*, 513; Majlisī, *Biḥār*, VIII, 344; Baḥrānī, *Ma'ālim*, III, 109, 120.

[111] Majlisī, *Biḥār*, VIII, 339.

[112] Suyūṭī, *Budūr*, 555, 560; Qurṭubī, *Tadhkira*, II, 202; Majlisī, *Biḥār*, VIII, 346, 356, 411; Baḥrānī, *Ma'ālim*, III, 109–10.

[113] Suyūṭī, *Budūr*, 553, 556; Majlisī, *Biḥār*, VIII, 336; Qurṭubī, *Tadhkira*, II, 235.

[114] However, this tree is also identified as the "Jujube tree of the Boundary" (*sidrat al-muntahā*). See Suyūṭī, *Budūr*, 526; Qurṭubī, *Tadhkira*, II, 172

tree.[115] Both al-Suyūṭī and al-Majlisī provide plenty of additional information. Ṭūbā, planted by God,[116] has branches that cover the entire width of paradise; in fact they reach into the houses of all the blessed and even hang over the wall that surrounds paradise.[117] On every leaf sits an angel who praises God.[118] On command, Ṭūbā produces precious robes of silver and gold brocade as its fruit (which are lowered down to the ground in baskets), or beautifully bridled horses and camels, or even houris, as well as a great variety of fruits and heavenly victuals.[119] In Shiʿi eschatology, Ṭūbā acquires a number of distinctive characteristics. Al-Majlisī relates traditions according to which the tree has its roots in the mansion of ʿAlī in paradise,[120] although elsewhere it is stated that ʿAlī's shares his heavenly palace with the prophet Muḥammad.[121] When the Prophet ate a date (or an apple) from Ṭūba during his ascension, this date became a drop of semen in his tailbone, from which Khadīja eventually conceived Fāṭima.[122]

There are other trees and plants in paradise, even though they are quite literally overshadowed by Ṭūbā. In a hadith, a Bedouin challenges the Prophet to explain how it is that, as the Qur'ān affirms, there are Jujube (*sidr*) trees in paradise, the Jujube having thorns,[123] and thus the ability to hurt people? The Prophet answers that, as is stated in the Qur'ān (56:28), it is a "broken Jujube" (*sidr makhḍūd*), that is, a tree whose thorns God has broken off and replaced with seventy-two different kinds of fruit.[124] Of other species, the *ṭalḥ* (cf. Q 56:29) is named, a kind of acacia, which on occasion is identified with a banana-bearing tree growing in the Yemen and the Ḥijāz, "the most beautiful tree to look at."[125] Other marvellous trees and palms abound, with trunks of green emerald and red gold, and fruits (dates, bananas, pomegranates, and grapes) that are whiter than milk, sweeter than honey, and softer than butter, "like the breasts of virgins."[126] Other trees double as musical

[115] Ibn Ḥanbal, *Musnad*, III, 71, IV, 183–4. Cf. N. R. Reat, "The tree symbol in Islam," in *Studies in Comparative Religion* 9 (1975), 164–82.

[116] Suyūṭī, *Budūr*, 526; Majlisī, *Biḥār*, VIII, 383; Baḥrānī, *Maʿālim*, III, 68.

[117] Suyūṭī, *Budūr*, 526; Majlisī, *Biḥār*, VIII, 344, 353, 383; Baḥrānī, *Maʿālim*, III, 67, 134.

[118] Majlisī, *Biḥār*, VIII, 415.

[119] Suyūṭī, *Budūr*, 528; Majlisī, *Biḥār*, VIII, 344, 357–8; Qurṭubī, *Tadhkira*, II, 176.

[120] Majlisī, *Biḥār*, VIII, 345, 352, 361; Baḥrānī, *Maʿālim*, III, 62. Cf. Shīrāzī, *Ḥikma*, tr. Morris, 232–3.

[121] Majlisī, *Biḥār*, VIII, 365; Baḥrānī, *Maʿālim*, III, 66.

[122] Majlisī, *Biḥār*, VIII, 345, 367; Baḥrānī, *Maʿālim*, III, 64, 70.

[123] According to Linnaean classification, this is *ziziphus spina-christi*, or Christ's Thorn Jujube. Cf. Dafni, Levy, and Lev, "The ethnobotany of Christ's Thorn Jujube."

[124] Suyūṭī, *Budūr*, 527; Qurṭubī, *Tadhkira*, II, 173. Cf. Majlisī, *Biḥār*, VIII, 337.

[125] Suyūṭī, *Budūr*, 527; Majlisī, *Biḥār*, VIII, 337. According to Qurṭubī, *Tadhkira*, II, 174, the banana is the only fruit on earth that resembles the fruits of paradise. On *ṭalḥ*, cf. Toelle, *Le Coran revisité*, 43.

[126] Suyūṭī, *Budūr*, 526, 530; Majlisī, *Biḥār*, VIII, 415. Cf. Qurṭubī, *Tadhkira*, II, 177; Baḥrānī, *Maʿālim*, III, 125.

instruments. God orders a wind to blow through their branches, which are studded with bells, and this produces tunes "the likes of which no creature has ever heard before."[127]

The hellish counterpart to the paradisiacal Ṭūbā is the tree of Zaqqūm. Zaqqūm grows at the bottom of hell on a slippery rock that the damned have to climb repeatedly, much in the manner of Sisyphus.[128] Its seventy thousand branches reach up into the seven levels of hell, while its roots feed on fire instead of water.[129] The inhabitants of hell are forced to eat Zaqqūm's fruits. According to the Qur'ān (37:65), these fruits are "heads of devils" (*ru'ūs al-shayāṭīn*), and in the exegetical literature it is explained that these fruits are hard like stones and stink worse than cadavers.[130] In fact, they are so poisonous that were a drop of their juice to fall to the earth, it would melt the mountains and corrupt humankind's livelihood.[131] When the damned approach Zaqqūm, the "heads of devils" snap back at them and, reversing the hellish food chain, take a bite.[132] Not much else besides Zaqqūm grows in hell, for obvious reasons. Some traditions identify the *ḍarīʿ* and *ghislīn*, which are mentioned as the food of the sinners in the Qur'ān (88:6, 69:36), as thorny desert shrubs that get stuck in the throats of the damned as they chew them. Elsewhere they are declared to be the fruit, or a different name, of Zaqqūm.[133] On the brink of the top layer of hell, where life becomes almost bearable, grows cress (*jarjarīr*).[134]

The prophet Muḥammad's archenemy Abū Jahl, according to a tradition related by al-Majlisī, poked fun at the idea that there are plants growing in hell.[135] Al-Majlisī counters this by asserting that it is entirely plausible to imagine that Zaqqūm survives the flames of hell, just like the snakes and scorpions and other things in hell are not destroyed by it.[136] Reportedly, Abū Jahl also declared that Zaqqūm was the name of a sweet dish made of dates and butter, which he cheerfully and publicly proceeded to eat as a mockery of the Prophet. This story reflects a certain exegetical uncertainty surrounding the etymology of the tree's name. The exegetes, in the end, came to identify Zaqqūm with a disgustingly bitter plant growing in the Tihāma region of southern Arabia.[137] This corresponds to a tendency to establish

[127] Majlisī, *Biḥār*, VIII, 350, 399. Cf. Suyūṭī, *Budūr*, 575.
[128] Majlisī, *Biḥār*, VIII, 490.
[129] Ibid., VIII, 443, 490; Qurṭubī, *Tadhkira*, II, 133.
[130] Majlisī, *Biḥār*, VIII, 443.
[131] Suyūṭī, *Budūr*, 437; Majlisī, *Biḥār*, VIII, 477.
[132] Suyūṭī, *Budūr*, 437; Qurṭubī, *Tadhkira*, II, 133.
[133] Suyūṭī, *Budūr*, 437, 439.
[134] Ibid., 480; Majlisī, *Biḥār*, VIII, 479.
[135] Ibid., VIII, 443. Cf. ibid., VIII, 484.
[136] Ibid., VIII, 443. Cf. Radscheit, "Höllenbaum," 99.
[137] Ibn al-Jawzī, *Zād al-masīr*, VII, 62. The botanist Abū Ḥanīfa al-Dīnawārī (*fl.* second half of the third/ninth c.) describes the Zaqqūm tree in detail and asserts that it is a terrestrial

earthly analogues for the things in the otherworld.[138] Al-Suyūṭī reports, for example, that the al-Ḥawra tree that one finds in Syria resembles Ṭūbā, albeit it only in shape.[139] If pressed, however, both al-Suyūṭī and al-Majlisī remain cautious about the geomorphisation of the otherworld. Al-Majlisī reports that "some say Zaqqūm is a tree on earth that the Arabs know," but also points out that others deny this.[140] And while al-Suyūṭī relates that all the fruits on earth derive from the seeds that Adam took with him when he was expelled from paradise,[141] he also quotes a tradition according to which "there is nothing in this world that partakes in paradise, except names."[142] As for Abū Jahl, he is among the unhappy sinners in hell who are forced to eat the fruit of Zaqqūm.[143]

The animate but nonhuman inhabitants of paradise and hell fall into two groups: those animals and spiritual beings that serve to bring either pleasure or pain to the blessed and the damned; and those that are rewarded or punished. Regarding, first, the animals,[144] al-Suyūṭī reports that they are resurrected, bear testimony against humans who maltreated them, and are rewarded and punished on the Day of Judgement. For example, horned goats that injured their hornless fellow goats suffer a talionic punishment. Then, however, God turns all animals to dust (*yajʿaluhā turāban*).[145] One infers from this that the animals in paradise and hell are not the resurrected animals of this world, but newly created, otherworldly animals. As such, they are appropriately marvellous.[146] The horses in paradise, including a horse named Rafraf (cf. Q 55:76),[147] are made of rubies and have wings, and they do not defecate or urinate,[148] while the birds there are "whiter than snow" and big as mules, with seventy thousand soft feathers each.[149] There is also a place in paradise for camels, as well as sheep and

species found on the South Arabian coast. See Dīnawārī, *Nabāt*, 204 (tr. 37). Cf. Radscheit, "Höllenbaum," 100–1; Toelle, *Le Coran revisité*, 47–8.

138 Reinhart maintains that "[t]he wondrous analogies to this world [in Islamic eschatology] ... make the hereafter more, rather than less, remote." Similarly, Reinhart, "The here and the hereafter," 18. I do not agree with this assessment but reserve a discussion of this point to other chapters of this book. See, in particular, the introduction and conclusion.

139 Suyūṭī, *Budūr*, 533.

140 Majlisī, *Biḥār*, VIII, 443.

141 Suyūṭī, *Budūr*, 534. A tradition extolling the paradisiacal qualities of water melons in Qurṭubī, *Tadhkira*, II, 175.

142 Suyūṭī, *Budūr*, 532.

143 Majlisī, *Biḥār*, VIII, 443. Cf. ibid., 484.

144 For a survey, see Canova, "Animals."

145 Suyūṭī, *Budūr*, 266–7.

146 It deserves noting here that certain angels were imagined to have the form of animals. See Sublet, "Nommer l'animal," 60.

147 El-Saleh, *Vie future*, 37. On the many interpretations of the word *rafraf*, see Qurṭubī, *Tadhkira*, II, 164–5, 235.

148 Suyūṭī, *Budūr*, 579–80.

149 Ibid., 580–1.

goats.[150] The snakes in hell are as big as elephants or as thick as the necks of Bactrian camels, while the scorpions have fangs as long as palm trunks.[151] Al-Suyūṭī also reports the tradition that "all flying insects are in hell, except bees,"[152] and he mentions that all animals that inflict pain on people in this world continue to do so in the next.[153] However, he does not fully endorse this view, perhaps because of his earlier denial of the continued existence of worldly animals in the otherworld.

Ashʿarite theologians, al-Suyūṭī being one of them, stressed the voluntarist principle that God places people in paradise and hell only in function of His inscrutable will.[154] In consequence, they were averse to the idea, known as a core tenet of Muʿtazilite theology, that God is constrained by His justice to requite good actions with reward, and evil deeds with punishment.[155] Some Muʿtazilites, keen to follow this idea through to its logical conclusions, applied it also to animals.[156] This meant that, according to the Muʿtazilites, the entire animal kingdom is, in principle, resurrected and experiences pleasure or misery in paradise or hell. One of the famous Muʿtazilites of Baghdad, Abū l-Hudhayl (d. 227/841?), for example, reasoned that all the animals that are either ugly or hurt people in this world, that is, all animals of prey, domestic animals, reptiles, and insects (again with the exception of bees) go to hell. There they will continue to do what they did on earth, although as in the case of the angels of punishment, this task will not be a burden on them.[157] By contrast, horses, gazelles, peacocks, and pheasants delight people in this life and, therefore, are rewarded with paradise.[158]

It seems no coincidence, therefore, that the Shiʿi collectors of eschatological hadith, who as Shiʿis were sympathetic to Muʿtazilite theology, included hadiths in their works that specify a reward for good animals in paradise. For example, the mule on which one performs the pilgrimage to Mecca seven times is assured a place in the eternal grazing grounds.[159] A story is told by

[150] For camels, see Suyūṭī, *Budūr*, 597. The sheep, goats, and even cattle are the beasts of burden (*dawābb*) in paradise. See Suyūṭī, *Budūr*, 581; Qurṭubī, *Tadhkira*, II, 213.

[151] Suyūṭī, *Budūr*, 442–4; Majlisī, *Biḥār*, VIII, 435; Baḥrānī, *Maʿālim*, III, 364, 374.

[152] Suyūṭī, *Budūr*, 444. Cf. al-Jāḥiẓ, *Ḥayawān*, III, 121; Nābulusī, *Ahl al-janna*, 75. The bees, however, do not produce the honey in paradise; rather, it is created by God directly. See Canova, "Animals," 65.

[153] Suyūṭī, *Budūr*, 445.

[154] Cf. Gardet, *Dieu*, 91–4.

[155] On this debate, see Chapter 5, pp. 176–8.

[156] Cf. Goldziher, *Richtungen*, 160. For various arguments in the debate, see Ashʿarī, *Maqālāt*, 254–5. Al-Naẓẓām is attributed the view that animals are recipients of divine mercy in the same way in which sinless children are. See Shahrastānī, *Milal*, 41.

[157] Jāḥiẓ, *Ḥayawān*, III, 122–3.

[158] Ibid., III, 122.

[159] Baḥrānī, *Maʿālim*, III, 232. Also Mullā Ṣadrā discusses the issue. See Shīrāzī, *Ḥikma*, tr. Morris, 245–9.

al-Baḥrānī that the fourth Imam ʿAlī Zayn al-ʿĀbidīn (d. *ca.* 95/713), on his deathbed, exhorted his son Muḥammad al-Bāqir (d. *ca.* 115/733) to bury the she-camel on which he had performed the hajj, so that she would not be eaten by wild animals, and enter paradise intact.[160] The horses of those fighting in jihad accompany those who ride them into paradise.[161] Animals that suffered unjustly, such as the donkey of Balʿam b. Bāʿūra, flogged to death by his cruel owner, and the she-camel of the prophet Ṣāliḥ, wounded by the treacherous and godless people of Thamūd (cf. Q 7:77), enjoy a happy afterlife.[162] While al-Baḥrānī and al-Majlisī report lists of three and four animals in paradise, elsewhere, ten are named: the camel of Ṣāliḥ, the calf of Abraham, the ram of Ismāʿīl, the cow of Moses, the fish of Jonah, the donkey of ʿUzayr, the ant of Solomon, the hoopoe of Bilqīs, the she-camel of Muḥammad, and the dog of the People of the Cave.[163] Occasionally it was suggested that these animals would be given a new form (*ṣūra*) in paradise, namely that of a human, or of a ram (*kabsh*).[164] However, eschatologists who followed the line of Abū l-Hudhayl and the other Muʿtazilites insisted that animals enter the otherworld with the bodies they had on earth.[165]

That the jinn enter paradise or hell, depending on their belief, was a widely accepted notion.[166] The Qurʾān suggests as much in sura 55, a sura that details the joys of paradise and horrors of hell, and is addressed, seemingly, to both humans and jinn (*al-thaqalān*, cf. Q 55:31). Accordingly, al-Suyūṭī and al-Majlisī report the opinion that there are two types of maidens "untouched before by either men or jinn" (Q 55:74) for the blessed in paradise, one humanlike for humans and, another, jinnlike for the jinn.[167] Al-Suyūṭī relates, too, that the Muslim jinn (*muslimū l-jinn*) will not mix with the human believers but instead reside on the wall of paradise (*al-aʿrāf*), amply provided with water, trees, and fruits.[168] The unbelieving, evil jinn, the "hosts of Iblīs, all of them" (Q 26:95), by contrast, are punished in

160 Baḥrānī, *Maʿālim*, III, 232.

161 Ibid., III, 131, 232.

162 Majlisī, *Biḥār*, VIII, 399; Baḥrānī, *Maʿālim*, III, 241.

163 *Daqāʾiq al-akhbār*, 73 (tr. Wolff, 130). See also the anonymous *Zakhr al-ʿābidīn*, fol. 237b. Cf. Ahlwardt, *Handschriften-Verzeichnisse*, II, 655. In both sources, the tradition is attributed to Muqātil, but it does not appear in the published version of his *tafsīr*. A tradition in al-Majlisī suggests that the camel of ʿĀʾisha, on which she rode in the Battle of the Camel, is punished in hell. See Majlisī, *Biḥār*, VIII, 476.

164 See, e.g., Burūsawī, *Rūḥ*, V, 174 (*ad* Q 18:18), who quotes a poem by Saʿdī stating that the dog of the People of the Cave "became human" (*mardum shud*), but corrects this by affirming that the dog "entered paradise with the people in the shape of a ram" (*yaʿnī bā mardumān dākhil-i jannat shud dar ṣūrat-i kabsh*).

165 Jāḥiẓ, *Ḥayawān*, III, 122.

166 Cf. Meier, "The ultimate origin," 100–1.

167 Suyūṭī, *Budūr*, 408; Majlisī, *Biḥār*, VIII, 334.

168 Suyūṭī, *Budūr*, 407. Cf. Baḥrānī, *Maʿālim*, III, 288–9.

hell. In fact, Iblīs and his troops are the "first to enter hell,"[169] and in Sunni stratificatory models they reside in the lowest layer.[170] Al-Baḥrānī, however, relates that ʿUmar b. al-Khaṭṭāb finds himself in an even lower spot, and that Iblīs looks down on him, cursing him.[171]

Traditionists like al-Suyūṭī and al-Majlisī do not dwell much on the otherworldly fate of jinn and devils. They devote far more attention to the spiritual beings that form the personnel of the Islamic otherworld: the angels that serve the denizens of paradise, the houris, and the punisher angels in hell. Angels, like the rest of creation, perish in the apocalypse and are resurrected.[172] Because they are not subject to desire (*shahwa*) and thus incapable of sin, they are, in principle, assured a place in paradise, but their immunity vis-à-vis sin also makes them subservient to the blessed, whom they continuously praise for having resisted desire during their earthly lives.[173] Some exegetes even suggest that only humans enjoy the privilege of seeing God, but not the angels, even though al-Suyūṭī does not endorse this view, citing a number of traditions about the vision of God by the angels.[174] Be that as it may, the angels in paradise serve the human inhabitants in several ways. The angel Riḍwān is the "guardian of the garden" (*khāzin al-janna*).[175] Other angels guide the newcomers in paradise to their mansions, where their wives await them,[176] and they facilitate meetings, or marriages, between the inhabitants of paradise and the houris.[177] God uses angels to send messages to the blessed,[178] and they wait on them during heavenly banquets and provide them with precious robes.[179] The angels are also the masons of paradise: while the believers on earth perform good deeds or pronounce pious formulas such as *al-ḥamdū li-llāh!* ("God be praised!") or *lā ilāha illā llāh!* ("There is no god but God!"), the angels erect pavilions made of gold and silver bricks for them, but when the believers interrupt their invocations, they stop laying bricks.[180]

169 Ibid., III, 308.
170 Thaʿlabī, *ʿArāʾis*, 10. According to Lamaṭī, *Ibrīz* (tr. O'Kane/Radtke), 922, the jinn in hell are not punished with fire, "because fire is [their] nature and causes [them] no harm," but rather, with severe frost (*zamharīr*).
171 Baḥrānī, *Maʿālim*, III, 312. On Shīʿi vilification of the first two caliphs, see Kohlberg, "Some Imāmī Shīʿī views," esp. 160–7.
172 Suyūṭī, *Budūr*, 67.
173 Majlisī, *Biḥār*, VIII, 360.
174 Suyūṭī, *Budūr*, 616–7.
175 Idem, *Ḥabāʾik*, 67 (§ 237); Baḥrānī, *Maʿālim*, III, 63.
176 Majlisī, *Biḥār*, VIII, 371.
177 Suyūṭī, *Budūr*, 517; Majlisī, *Biḥār*, VIII, 372.
178 Ibid., VIII, 372.
179 Ibid., VIII, 414.
180 Suyūṭī, *Budūr*, 520; Majlisī, *Biḥār*, VIII, 347–8; Qurṭubī, *Tadhkira*, II, 215; Baḥrānī, *Maʿālim*, III, 133. The Egyptian al-Shaʿrānī, in the early tenth/sixteenth century, strongly

The Qur'ān mentions that the blessed are served by male servants (*ghilmān*, 52:24) and immortal young boys (*wildān*, Q 56:17, 76:19), but neither al-Suyūṭī nor al-Majlisī have much to say about them. Both note that according to some exegetes, these are the children of the unbelievers.[181] Al-Suyūṭī relates that there are large numbers of them, anything between one thousand and fifteen thousand for even the lowest-ranking inhabitant of paradise.[182] A great deal more is said about the houris. It should be noted, however, that there is some confusion, both in al-Suyūṭī's and al-Majlisī's account, about whether the descriptions of these female companions refer to the rejuvenated wives of the believers or to creatures of the otherworld. Al-Suyūṭī, for example, reports traditions about both in the same lengthy chapter he devotes to the "wives of the people of paradise" (*azwāj ahl al-janna*).[183]

As for traditions in which the houris are explicitly named, al-Majlisī relates that they are created from a mixture of earth (*turāb*) and saffron (as opposed to humans, who are created from earth only).[184] The dominant view, which emphasises their otherworldly nature, asserts that the houris are made of fragrant substances such as musk, camphor, and saffron, or even light.[185] Their hair, "longer than the wings of eagles,"[186] is beautifully braided; their faces shine like the moon; their bosoms are crescent shaped like those of young girls; and they are exquisitely dressed, while their bodies remain perfectly visible and transparent.[187] The houris are confined (*maḥbūsāt*) in their dwellings in paradise,[188] but at the same time they are defined by their availability – they grow on trees, after all, or rain down on the blessed from a cloud whenever desire piques them.[189] The idea of availability also finds expression in the large quantity of houris awaiting each believer. Characteristically, numbers remain

promoted the so-called *maḥyā*, a night-long vigil between Thursday and Friday in which the invocation of blessings upon the Prophet (*taṣliyya*) was performed without interruption, and whose rewards included remission of sins, a great number of heavenly wives, and a high rank in paradise. The practice spread to other lands and continued to flourish for centuries. See Meier, *Bemerkungen*, I, 54. In the Muḥammad-focused piety of authors of later centuries, the invocation of blessings on the Prophet is likewise said to "increase paradise in size." See Lamaṭī, *Ibrīz* (tr. O'Kane/Radtke), 904–5.

181 Suyūṭī, *Budūr*, 402–3; Majlisī, *Biḥār*, VIII, 337.

182 Suyūṭī, *Budūr*, 578–9.

183 Ibid., 554–61. Similarly Majlisī, *Biḥār*, VIII, 335, 411; Baḥrānī, *Ma'ālim*, III, 109.

184 Majlisī, *Biḥār*, VIII, 347.

185 Suyūṭī, *Budūr*, 559; Qurṭubī, *Tadhkira*, II, 205–6. The description in Baḥrānī, *Ma'ālim*, III, 175–6, stresses the luminous character of the houris.

186 Suyūṭī, *Budūr*, 560.

187 Ibid., 555–6; Qurṭubī, *Tadhkira*, II, 201, 206.

188 Suyūṭī, *Budūr*, 556; Majlisī, *Biḥār*, VIII, 411; Baḥrānī, *Ma'ālim*, III, 109.

189 Suyūṭī, *Budūr*, 563.

unstable, ranging from two[190] to seventy or seventy-two,[191] five hundred[192] or multiples thereof.[193]

There can be little doubt that the houris of Late Medieval traditionist literature are imagined as ideal courtesans. Not only their physical appearance is agreeable, but so is their submissive way of addressing and talking to the believers[194] and of entertaining them with song.[195] According to a tradition related by al-Suyūṭī, a houri known as Coquette (*al-Ghanija*) resides in a mansion called the High Abode. The angel Gabriel serves as the messenger between her and her suitors. When she is called, she appears in a procession, accompanied by four thousand maid-servants.[196] In a somewhat coarser version of this motif, the inhabitants of paradise descend from their castles to visit the houris in their tents, which are located at the shore of a river. There the houris sit to wait, "their large posteriors rising over the edges of their seats" (*kharajat ʿajīzatuhā min jawānib al-kursī*).[197] In some instances, specific houris are reserved for specific men. During his ascension, the Prophet meets houris who declare that they are waiting for the Prophet's adopted son Zayd b. Ḥāritha, or for his son-in-law ʿAlī b. Abī Ṭālib.[198] A houri known as Wide-in-the-Eyes (*al-ʿAynāʾ*) is destined for those who practice the ethical duty of "commanding right and forbidding wrong" (*al-amr bi-l-maʿrūf wa-l-nahy ʿan al-munkar*) while on earth, and a houri called Plaything (*al-Luʿba*) awaits all those who are obedient to God.[199] Such traditions are variations on the theme that good deeds on earth are the bride money (*mahr*) that males bring with them to paradise in order to celebrate nuptials there with the houris.[200] Again pious actions, by a process of reification, acquire a concrete form, that of the houris, a motif that appears regularly in traditionist eschatology, especially in the context of the Day of Judgement, where one's

190 Ibid.; Majlisī, *Biḥār*, VIII, 346; Baḥrānī, *Maʿālim*, III, 118.

191 Suyūṭī, *Budūr*, 562. Muslim *isnād* criticism considered the tradition to be weak. See on this point, Brown, *Misquoting Muhammad*, 302–5.

192 Suyūṭī, *Budūr*, 562–3; Majlisī, *Biḥār*, VIII, 411; Baḥrānī, *Maʿālim*, III, 111.

193 Suyūṭī, *Budūr*, 515. According to Baḥrānī, *Maʿālim*, III, 119, ʿAlī b. Abī Ṭālib enjoys the company of seventy thousand houris.

194 Suyūṭī, *Budūr*, 558; Qurṭubī, *Tadhkira*, II, 200; Majlisī, *Biḥār*, VIII, 346; Baḥrānī, *Maʿālim*, III, 119.

195 Suyūṭī, *Budūr*, 574; Majlisī, *Biḥār*, VIII, 364, 399; Baḥrānī, *Maʿālim*, III, 122.

196 Suyūṭī, *Budūr*, 517.

197 Ibid., 561. It should be noted, with Geert Jan van Gelder and Gregor Schoeler, that ""[h]eavy posteriors are part of the ideal beauty in classical Arabic love poetry." See van Gelder and Schoeler (trans.), *Epistle of forgiveness*, 354n486. For other examples of descriptions of the large posteriors of the houris, though with an ironical twist, see Maʿarrī, *Risāla*, 224, 156 (tr. 225, 157).

198 Majlisī, *Biḥār*, VIII, 348, 395.

199 Suyūṭī, *Budūr*, 566; Qurṭubī, *Tadhkira*, II, 201.

200 Qurṭubī, *Tadhkira*, II, 202–5. Cf. Majlisī, *Biḥār*, VIII, 401.

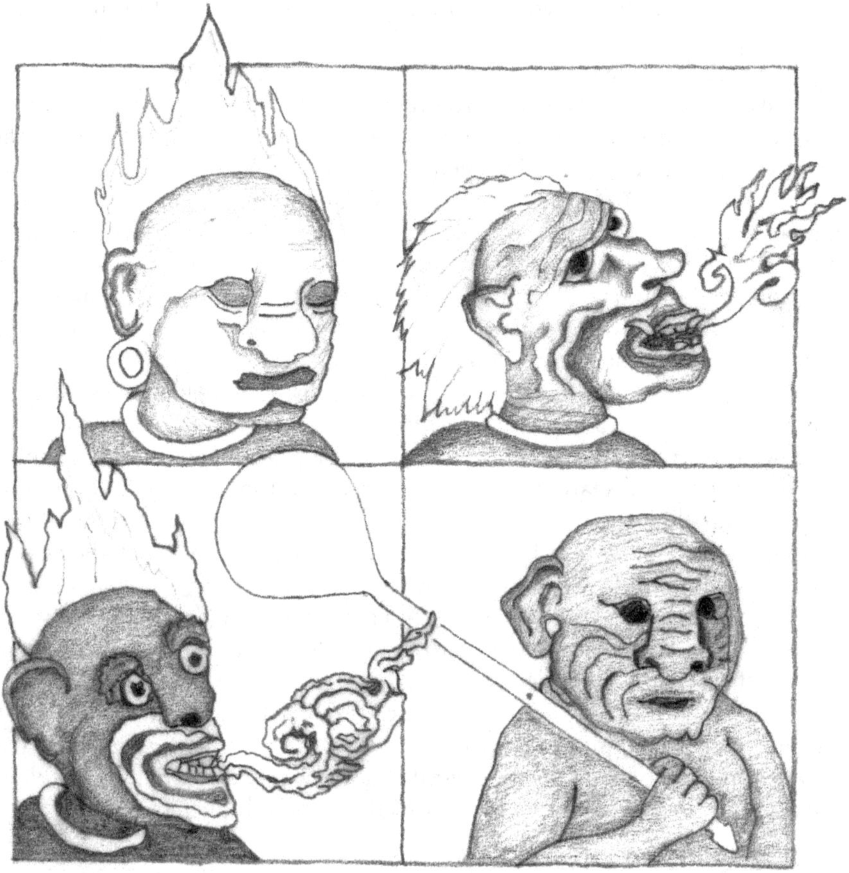

FIGURE 8. Hell's angels. Adapted from the Uighur *Miʿrājnāma* (*Book of Ascension*). Herat/Afghanistan, ninth/fifteenth century. MS Bibliothèque nationale de France Supplément Turc 190, fols. 53v, 59r, 59v, 61r (details).

good deeds (*ḥasanāt*) and bad deeds (*sayyiʾāt*) acquire a visible form and act as witnesses against those who committed them.[201]

Just as the tree of Ṭūbā is mirrored by the tree of Zaqqūm, the houris have their counterparts in the myrmidons of hell, the angels of punishment. Their appearance is nothing short of monstrous. They have eyes like flashing lightning, protruding teeth in the shape of cow's horns, lips hanging down to their feet, and they spit fire and exude a foul-smelling breath.[202] As one tradition puts it, if hell's angels were to show themselves on earth everybody would die from the shock of seeing their faces and smelling their

[201] Suyūṭī, *Budūr*, 295.
[202] Majlisī, *Biḥār*, VIII, 453. Cf. Suyūṭī, *Ḥabāʾik*, 66 (§ 233).

stench.[203] They are giants, with shoulders that are miles apart and enormous claws with which they clutch multitudes of the damned in a single moment.[204] The arsenal of tortures they visit upon their victims includes dragging them around by their forelocks through puddles of boiling water (*ḥamīm*)[205] and chaining their various body parts together, thus forcing them into painfully contorted positions.[206] They are merciless floggers who beat people to pulp (*ṭaḥīn*),[207] wielding a great variety of weapons, from whips to iron hooks, rods, clubs, and big hammers, the likes of which are used by blacksmiths.[208]

As in the case of the heavenly houris, there is some difference of opinion regarding how many hell's angels there are. Exegetes attempt in more than one way to circumvent the statement in the Qur'ān that only "nineteen [angels] are set over it [hell]" (74:31). Either they argue that each of the nineteen has so many arms and fingers that all those punished in hell are taken care of; or that the "nineteen" guard only one of the compartments of hell, while numerous other angels of punishment are in charge of the other compartments; or that each of the damned is tortured by nineteen angels; or that "nineteen" is simply a shorthand for nineteen thousand.[209] In the end, the eschatologists' tendency to approach infinity, albeit asymptotically, also comes to bear on this question, resulting in the dominant view that there are nineteen chief angels of punishment, each of whom is served by myriad lower-ranking angels, "whose number is only known to God."[210]

While little if any distinction is made between the terms used in the Qur'ān to denote the various classes of punisher angels in hell,[211] the traditionist literature on hell puts specific angels into more relief. This is particularly the case with Mālik, the chief guardian of hell.[212] In stories about Muḥammad's journey to the otherworld, related both by al-Suyūṭī and al-Majlisī, Mālik opens the door of hell to the Prophet. Muḥammad is in awe of his unsmiling face and wrathful temper, and after being granted a vision of hell, does

203 Suyūṭī, *Budūr*, 410; Majlisī, *Biḥār*, VIII, 460, 479; Baḥrānī, *Ma'ālim*, III, 365.
204 Suyūṭī, *Budūr*, 416; Majlisī, *Biḥār*, VIII, 453.
205 Ibid., VIII, 447, 458.
206 Ibid., VIII, 451.
207 Suyūṭī, *Budūr*, 416. Cf. idem, *Ḥabā'ik*, 66 (§ 231).
208 Suyūṭī, *Budūr*, 415, 438; Majlisī, *Biḥār*, VIII, 439, 473, 487.
209 Suyūṭī, *Budūr*, 415–6; idem, *Ḥabā'ik*, 65 (§ 119), 66 (§ 234); Majlisī, *Biḥār*, VIII, 453–4; Qurṭubī, *Tadhkira*, II, 100; Baḥrānī, *Ma'ālim*, III, 381.
210 Suyūṭī, *Budūr*, 416.
211 See the preceding text, pp. 53, 64, 113, 116.
212 Al-Majlisī also mentions the angel Saḥqaṭā'īl. See Majlisī, *Biḥār*, VIII, 487. A number of other infernal angels appear in Shī'i mi'rāj narratives, as in general the nomenclature of Islamic angelology, in later centuries, incorporated Persian names for angels. See, e.g., Gruber, *Ilkhanid Book of Ascension*, 54. Cf. Burge, *Angels in Islam*, 49; Colby, "Fire in the upper heaven."

not laugh again for the remainder of his life.[213] While Mālik, in the ascension narratives, usually stands at the entry gate of hell, exegetes sometimes also imagined him sitting on a raised platform in the middle of hell, like in a panopticon.[214] He is the angel of punishment, after all, to whom the sinners in hell address their complaints and calls for mercy (cf. Q 43:77). However, he does not answer them for forty years or longer. Then, rather than coming to their succour, he ushers them to the infernal banquet of Zaqqūm.[215]

Otherworldly Bodies

How does the traditionist literature on paradise and hell picture the state of the blessed and the damned? What do they look like, and how do they behave? What are their rewards and punishments, and what virtues and sins determine their destiny? One should note at the beginning that, on the Day of Resurrection, people revert to a primordial, precivilisational body, regardless of whether they are destined for paradise or hell. "As We began the first creation," it is stated in the Qur'ān, "We shall bring it back again" (21:104), and the expression "first creation" is taken by the traditionists to refer to the primordial creation of humankind in paradise, when all of Adam's progeny was extracted from his loins and made to testify their belief in God. Accordingly, a tradition asserts that people are resurrected "naked, barefoot and with foreskins intact."[216] This creates room for the eschatological imagination to make two crucial moves. First, the passage into paradise is described as a second initiation, after life on earth, into civilisation, albeit into a higher, ultimate form thereof. (Hell, by contrast, is in many respects the opposite of civilisation, as will become clear.) Secondly, while bodies in the otherworld are essentially the same that people possessed in their previous lives[217] and in fact from the beginning of time, these bodies are remodelled and enhanced so as to reflect their owners' new circumstances. They are made impeccable in the case of the blessed, abominable in the case of the damned.

Regarding, first, the inhabitants of paradise, one encounters the notion that they are as tall as Adam (sixty ells), as old as Jesus when he was taken

[213] Majlisī, *Biḥār*, VIII, 463, 468; Baḥrānī, *Maʿālim*, III, 445.

[214] Ṭabarī, *Jāmiʿ*, XVIII, 71 (*ad* Q 23:105–6). According to the anonymous *Daqā'iq al-akhbār*, Mālik "sits on a minbar of fire in the middle of Jahannam." See *Daqā'iq*, 100 (tr. 178).

[215] Suyūṭī, *Budūr*, 438; Majlisī, *Biḥār*, VIII, 443, 448, 478.

[216] Suyūṭī, *Budūr*, 116. An exception is made for martyrs, who are allowed to dress in their burial shrouds. See ibid., 118. Cf. Majlisī, *Biḥār*, VIII, 362.

[217] There are exceptions to this pattern. Famously, Jaʿfar b. Abī Ṭālib (d. 8/629), "the man of the two wings," was seen by the Prophet in a vision, flying through paradise with two wings that replaced the two arms he had lost when martyred during the raid on Mu'ta in Syria. See *ECḤ*, 250.

FIGURE 9. Mālik, the guardian of hell. From an anonymous *ʿUqūbāt al-ʿuṣāt* (*The Punishments of the Sinners*). India, thirteenth/nineteenth century (?). MS Leiden Or 26545, fol. 10r.

to the heavens (thirty-three years), and as beautiful as Joseph, while their inheritance from Muḥammad is that they all speak Arabic.[218] In addition to their ideal proportions, age, and eloquence, they do not spit, belch, blow their

[218] Suyūṭī, *Budūr*, 591, 593; Majlisī, *Biḥār*, VIII, 414, 464; Baḥrānī, *Maʿālim*, III, 123, 158.

noses, urinate, defecate, or, in the case of women, menstruate or parturate.[219] Digestion is by way of a sweet-smelling light sweat.[220] This physical impeccability (by the standards of the Islamic purity code) comes about as the result of their drinking from a spring in paradise, which purges their bodies from all inconveniences, including the urge to sleep.[221] A similar but rather more dramatic rite of purification is undergone by the Muslim sinners who receive a temporary punishment in hell and are only *then* admitted into paradise. These sinners are cast down, like bricks of coal (*faḥm*), on the shores of the River of Life (*nahr al-ḥayāt*) in paradise, sprinkled with water, and then sprout forth spontaneously "like seeds on a layer of fertile mud borne by a torrent."[222] Their flesh, skin, hair, and brains grow back on them.[223] In other words, when crossing the threshold leading into paradise the bodies of the blessed, while modelled on a residual core that preserves their identity, are profoundly enhanced (*yazdādūna jamālan wa-ḥusnan*).[224] They now exist in a state of perpetual ritual purity, unaffected by bodily functions such as digestion, menstruation, or sleep, in pronounced opposition to the situation on earth.

According to a tradition rooted in Islamic asceticism, the human need to defecate arose after Adam and Eve ate from the tree in paradise. Because paradise was not the proper place for this, they were expelled from it.[225] Humankind, "the sons of Adam" (*banū Ādam*), are "hollow" (*ajwaf*) creatures, possessing bellies that need to be filled and thus give rise to worldly desires and greed, which in turn occasions ritual impurity. By contrast, according to a tradition related by al-Suyūṭī, heavenly bellies shrink back (*ḍamara*) to their primordial state.[226] This makes the inhabitants of paradise curiously compact, a condition that reflects their proximity to God, one of whose famously enigmatic Qur'ānic epithets is "the Solid" (*al-ṣamad*, cf. Q 112:2).[227] The inhabitants of hell, by contrast, continue in their penetrable

[219] Suyūṭī, *Budūr*, 536, 554, 590; Majlisī, *Biḥār*, VIII, 332, 347, 356, 365; Qurṭubī, *Tadhkira*, II, 197; Baḥrānī, *Maʿālim*, III, 121, 135.

[220] Ibid.

[221] Suyūṭī, *Budūr*, 586, 596; Baḥrānī, *Maʿālim*, III, 126, 187.

[222] Qurṭubī, *Tadhkira*, II, 150. Similarly, Suyūṭī, *Budūr*, 479.

[223] Baḥrānī, *Maʿālim*, III, 245–6.

[224] Ibid., III, 121.

[225] Thaʿlabī, *ʿArāʾis*, 17. See also Makkī, *Qūt al-qulūb*, quoted in Gramlich, *Weltverzicht*, 109. According to al-Shaʿrānī, Adam's eating of unlawful food also led God to impose laws on humankind. See Shaʿrānī, *Mīzān*, II, 207–10; cf. Winter, *Society and religion*, 159–60. However, more positive Sufi interpretations of Adam's fall also existed. Cf. the following text, p. 171.

[226] Suyūṭī, *Budūr*, 535; Qurṭubī, *Tadhkira*, II, 208.

[227] See the discussion in Katz, *Body of text*, 176–8. For the meaning of "solid" for *ṣamad* in Qur'ān 112:2, cf. Paret, *Kommentar*, 530. Ṭabarī, *Jāmiʿ*, XXX, 420 (*ad* Q 112:2), quotes the opinion that "*al-ṣamad* means someone who is not hollow (*laysa bi-ajwaf*) and who does not eat or drink." Cf. ibid., XXX, 422: "*Al-ṣamad* means someone from whom nothing exits (*lā yakhruju minhu shayʾ*)." As Josef van Ess notes, the anthropomorphistic meaning

"hollow" state, in fact they hunger and thirst much more than they used to during their lives on earth.[228] Bodies in hell are grotesquely inflated and mutilated. The inhabitants of hell, who speak a form of Old or Middle Persian (*al-majūsiyya*),[229] have seventy layers of coarse and thick skin through which enormous worms carve their way, roaring like wild beasts.[230] The molar teeth of the damned are as big as the mountain of Uḥud, and their legs resemble the mountains of Wariqān and al-Bayḍā'.[231] They have snouts like the trunks of elephants, which they drag over the ground.[232] Their tongues are a mile or more long, and the other people in hell trample on them.[233] Lips are shrivelled by the fire, so that teeth are bared like those of "grilled [sheep] heads."[234]

Much of the violence in hell is directed against the face, the "noblest part of the human body" in al-Majlisī's phrase.[235] Faces are not only disfigured as described in the preceding text, but charred black, beaten with whips, and bitten by snakes, while hell's angels drag people over the ground on them.[236] According to some traditions, the fire peels the skin off the damned's faces, and this is just one of many instances in which body boundaries are violated and corporal integrity is destroyed.[237] Iron chains are forced through the mouths of the damned and extracted from their rears,[238] and the boiling drinks of *ḥamīm* and *ṣadīd* dissolve their entrails, which exit their bodies by the same route.[239] In fact, the bodies of the inhabitants of hell hold no liquids at all. Their brains, dissolved by the heat, flow out from their nostrils,[240] and they weep blood so profusely that ships could sail in the stream pouring forth from their eyes.[241] Their genitals leak vast amounts of pus, which others are

of *al-ṣamad* as "the Solid" was overwhelmingly rejected in the later centuries of Muslim exegesis. See van Ess, *The youthful god*, 5.

228 Suyūṭī, *Budūr*, 438; Majlisī, *Biḥār*, VIII, 476.

229 Ibid., VIII, 464; Baḥrānī, *Ma'ālim*, III, 158. According to a tradition related by al-Qurṭubī and al-Suyūṭī, people speak Syriac (*al-suryānī*) in the graves. See Suyūṭī, *Budūr*, 593; Qurṭubī, *Tadhkira*, II, 200. Ibn Ḥanbal reports that people are resurrected "naked, uncircumcised and speaking a foreign language (*buhman*, sg. *abham*)," although in the same hadith there is a gloss explaining that *buhman* means "without having anything with them." See Ibn Ḥanbal, *Musnad*, III, 495. This, however, is a meaning of *abham* that is not found in the classical dictionaries.

230 Suyūṭī, *Budūr*, 444, 448; Majlisī, *Biḥār*, VIII, 489; Baḥrānī, *Ma'ālim*, III, 373.

231 Suyūṭī, *Budūr*, 447–8; Majlisī, *Biḥār*, VIII, 489; Qurṭubī, *Tadhkira*, II, 123.

232 Suyūṭī, *Budūr*, 447–8; Majlisī, *Biḥār*, VIII, 489.

233 Suyūṭī, *Budūr*, 448; Qurṭubī, *Tadhkira*, II, 124.

234 Suyūṭī, *Budūr*, 452–3; Majlisī, *Biḥār*, VIII, 439, 469.

235 Majlisī, *Biḥār*, VIII, 445. For faces in Islamic eschatology, see further Lange, "On that day."

236 Suyūṭī, *Budūr*, 423, 463; Majlisī, *Biḥār*, VIII, 489.

237 Suyūṭī, *Budūr*, 438, 440, 453; Majlisī, *Biḥār*, VIII, 435, 439, 466.

238 Suyūṭī, *Budūr*, 432.

239 Ibid., 435, 439; Majlisī, *Biḥār*, VIII, 433, 466.

240 Baḥrānī, *Ma'ālim*, III, 373.

241 Suyūṭī, *Budūr*, 454; Majlisī, *Biḥār*, VIII, 433, 466; Qurṭubī, *Tadhkira*, II, 139.

forced to drink as a punishment.[242] Disgusting though their nourishment is, the damned gobble it down like camels suffering from a burning thirst.[243] A bestialisation of those punished in hell occurs also in other ways, for they are said to bray like donkeys[244] or howl like dogs and wolves.[245] In some instances, sinners are turned, by punitive metamorphosis, into dogs, swine, apes, or donkeys.[246] Characterisations of the damned as animals demonstrate the instability or even loss of identity they suffer, but they also accentuate their metabolic hollowness, that is, their beastly preoccupation with filling their stomachs. In sum, while the inhabitants of hell have abominable stomachs that condemn them to eternal incontinency and impurity, the denizens of paradise, unencumbered by digestion as they are, have none at all.

The material riches and pleasures, both bodily and spiritual, of the blessed in paradise are a spectacular continuation and amplification of the most refined traits of medieval Islamic civilisation. There is certainly no trace of any sort of *nudisme eschatologique* in the Late Medieval Muslim paradise.[247] Not only are the men in paradise circumcised (recall that right after resurrection, they are not), their otherworldly bodies are made up and coiffured in multiple other ways. Eyes are lined with collyrium, hair is neatly trimmed, and all body hairs (including beards) are removed.[248] With regards to facial hair, exceptions are sometimes made in the traditionist literature. Prophets such as Adam and Moses, for example, are allowed to keep their honorific beards; in other hadiths it is even argued that wearing a beard in paradise is a privilege that all Muslims will enjoy.[249] Numerous traditions speak of the luxurious silk robes, jewellery, and crowns of the blessed,[250] and descriptions of the precious cushions and beds on which they rest go to considerable length.[251] Mention has already been made of the delicious victuals they eat; this is complemented by fresh and cool water and an array of exquisite wines, which come mixed with a number of exotic spices.[252] As for hors d'œuvres, both al-Suyūṭī and al-Majlisī relate a curious tradition according to which the first food that the inhabitants of paradise will be given to eat is the "lobe of fish liver" (*ziyādat kibd al-ḥūt*),[253] a notion that

[242] Suyūṭī, *Budūr*, 442; Majlisī, *Biḥār*, VIII, 433, 466.

[243] Suyūṭī, *Budūr*, 440; Majlisī, *Biḥār*, VIII, 452.

[244] Ibid., VIII, 438, 491.

[245] Ibid., VIII, 461.

[246] Ibid., VIII, 481–2; Baḥrānī, *Maʿālim*, III, 326. On punitive metamorphosis in Islam, see further Rubin, "Apes."

[247] Cf. Eliade, "Les Américains en Océanie et le nudisme eschatologique."

[248] Suyūṭī, *Budūr*, 591; Majlisī, *Biḥār*, VIII, 415; Qurṭubī, *Tadhkira*, II, 198; Baḥrānī, *Maʿālim*, III, 125.

[249] Suyūṭī, *Budūr*, 591–2; Qurṭubī, *Tadhkira*, II, 198; Nājī, *Ḥuṣūl*.

[250] Suyūṭī, *Budūr*, 545–9; Majlisī, *Biḥār*, VIII, 351, 410; Baḥrānī, *Maʿālim*, III, 125.

[251] Majlisī, *Biḥār*, VIII, 415; Baḥrānī, *Maʿālim*, III, 173–4.

[252] Suyūṭī, *Budūr*, 542–3; Majlisī, *Biḥār*, VIII, 341, 355.

[253] Suyūṭī, *Budūr*, 538; Majlisī, *Biḥār*, VIII, 383. See also Baḥrānī, *Maʿālim*, III, 137.

resonates with rabbinical teachings about the food of the righteous in the world to come.[254]

The material culture of paradise, though not lacking in fantastic elements, is thoroughly worldly. Traditionist literature delights in stressing the correspondences between earthly and otherworldly pleasures and pains, while asserting time and again that they are not of the same intensity. The most significant difference, however, is that the inhabitants of paradise have the otherworldly capacity for unceasing enjoyment of pleasure. Their desire for food and sex, in stark contrast to the situation on earth, is endless.[255] It is a desire, one should add, that is always and immediately consummated. This makes it a "virtual desire," that is, a desire eradicated by the "endless capacity" and the "total and unbending empowerment" of the inhabitants of paradise.[256] A banquet in paradise, as one tradition puts it, lasts as long as the earth exists (*ayyām al-dunyā*).[257] The male inhabitants of paradise have the potency of a hundred young men,[258] and coitus in paradise therefore lasts for forty or even one hundred years, without genitals tiring or becoming sore from the effort.[259] Orgasm, it follows, is absent in paradise. There is uninterrupted, frenetic shoving (*daḥm*) but no ejaculation, whether of male semen or female semen.[260] This implies that the inhabitants of paradise do not conceive children.[261] However, al-Suyūṭī, who devotes a separate chapter to the question, supports hadiths declaring that this is up to the blessed: if they desire offspring, their wish is granted, but pregnancy, parturition, and childhood all take place within a single hour.[262]

Although neither al-Suyūṭī nor al-Majlisī do so, some medieval Muslim theologians openly speculated that there would be sex between men in paradise.[263] Some argued that sodomy (*liwāṭ*) was, like wine, forbidden only

254 The fingerlike appendix of fish liver was used for burning incense offerings in the Jerusalem Temple. See Exodus 29:13, 29:22; Leviticus 3:4, 3:10, 3:15, 4:9, 7:4, 8:16, 8:25, 9:10, 9:19. According to the Mishnah, after the slaying of Leviathan, God preserved the giant fish's flesh, and "He will in time to come make a banquet for the righteous from the flesh of Leviathan." See *BT*, *Baba Bathra*, 75a (tr. XXI, 299). In the hadith preserved by al-Suyūṭī and al-Majlisī, tellingly it is the Jews who challenge Muḥammad to tell them what the first food in paradise will be. See also Ibn Hishām, *Sīra*, tr. Guillaume, 255–6, where the Prophet demonstrates his knowledge about Jewish food laws concerning the "two lobes of the liver."

255 Suyūṭī, *Budūr*, 535; Majlisī, *Biḥār*, VIII, 332, 340.

256 Al-Azmeh, "Rhetoric," 220, 224. Cf. Rosenthal, "Reflections on love," 248–9.

257 Majlisī, *Biḥār*, VIII, 389; Baḥrānī, *Maʿālim*, III, 191.

258 Suyūṭī, *Budūr*, 535, 562; Majlisī, *Biḥār*, VIII, 332, 411; Qurṭubī, *Tadhkira*, II, 207–8.

259 Suyūṭī, *Budūr*, 570–1; Majlisī, *Biḥār*, VIII, 351; Baḥrānī, *Maʿālim*, III, 142.

260 Suyūṭī, *Budūr*, 569, 571. As Al-Azmeh notes, "medieval [Muslim] physiology believed both sexes produced their respective types of semen, both required for conception." See al-Azmeh, "Rhetoric," 223.

261 Suyūṭī, *Budūr*, 571.

262 Ibid., 572–3. Cf. Qurṭubī, *Tadhkira*, II, 209, who leaves the question open.

263 Cf. El-Rouayheb, *Before homosexuality*, 128–37.

in the present life, but allowed in the next.[264] This was premised on the assumption that the desire for anal intercourse, like the appreciation of wine, is natural among men, an idea that was defended by Muslim thinkers of various stripes and colours.[265] Others, however, contended that the desire for anal sex was reprehensible and abhorrent in itself, and therefore nonexistent in paradise.[266] Even if one admitted that the two cases of wine and anal intercourse were in principle analogous, recourse could be made to the argument that the blessed have no anuses, seeing that they do not defecate, and that therefore the occasion for sodomy would not present itself anyway.[267]

Al-Suyūṭī's chapters on sexuality lead over directly into a chapter devoted to the music (*samāʿ*) in paradise, as in general the salience of genital carnality does not preclude other sensual and indeed spiritual pleasures.[268] The transitions from sexual to culinary, auditive, and disembodied or spiritual pleasures occur in seamless fashion in both al-Suyūṭī and al-Majlisī. In fact, "the sexual and the sacred are integrated" in the Islamic paradise.[269] The blessed are entertained by the sweet song of the houris and their wives, as well as by the sounds produced by trees in the breeze.[270] The most spectacular of all concerts, however, takes place during the reception before God's Throne, which occurs every Friday, the "Day of Surplus" (*yawm al-mazīd*), thereby following "a rhythm roughly equivalent to the mundane rhythm of prayer rituals."[271] Here it is the psalmist David, standing next to the Throne, who performs to an enraptured audience.[272] This reception, it is repeatedly affirmed, is the greatest of all pleasures in paradise, as it culminates in the vision of God.[273] The blessed are invited by a caller (*munādī*) to gather in God's estate, the Abode of Peace (*dār al-salām*). When they arrive there, they take a seat on dunes of musk in a beautiful valley, while God descends, hidden

264 Ibn ʿĀbidīn, *Ḥāshiya*, IV, 28, referring back to a fifth/eleventh-century debate among the Baghdad *ʿulamāʾ*.

265 Lange, *Justice*, 211–12. In al-Maʿarrī's *Risālat al-ghufrān*, Satan maliciously insinuates that there is homosexual activity in paradise involving the *wildān*. See Maʿarrī, *Risālat al-ghufrān*, 248 (tr. 249).

266 See, notably, Jāḥiẓ, *Rasāʾil*, III, 43–4.

267 See Ḥamawī (Ḥanafī, *fl.* 1098/1687), *Ghamz*, I, 287, quoted in El-Rouayheb, *Before homosexuality*, 130.

268 On sensual pleasures in the Muslim paradise, cf. Maḥmūd, *Jughrāfiyyat al-maladhdhāt*. On acoustic pleasures (*al-maladhdhāt al-samʿiyya*), see ibid., 327–42. On Dhū l-Nūn's heavenly *samāʿ*, see Ebstein, "D̲ū l-Nūn," 591.

269 Al-Azmeh, "Rhetoric," 227. Cf. Bouhdiba, *Sexuality*, 80–1.

270 Suyūṭī, *Budūr*, 574–5; Majlisī, *Biḥār*, VIII, 399; Baḥrānī, *Maʿālim*, III, 122, 144, 243. A Prophetic hadith in defence of both earthly and heavenly music is found in Sirjānī, *Bayāḍ*, #741.

271 Al-Azmeh, "Rhetoric," 228. On the *yawm al-mazīd*, see Goitein, "Beholding."

272 Suyūṭī, *Budūr*, 574. This tradition appears to go back to the Egyptian Dhū l-Nūn. See Abū Nuʿaym, *Ḥilya*, X, 82–3. Cf. *TG*, IV, 412.

273 Cf. on this reception, al-Azmeh, "Rhetoric," 228–31.

behind veils, from al-ʿIlliyyūn, the pinnacle of paradise, His Throne surrounded by pulpits on which sit the prophets, martyrs, and righteous.[274] A lavish banquet follows, catered by the angels, at the end of which the veils are lowered, and the blessed are granted a vision of God's face. Al-Majlisī, reflecting the Shiʿi-Muʿtazilī aversion to thinking about God in anthropomorphic terms, relates traditions that emphasise that the blessed only see the light that emanates from God.[275] God then sends his guests back to their homes, parting from them with the promise that their every wish will be fulfilled. According to some versions, on their way back they pass through a marketplace (*sūq*) in which "nothing is sold or bought except the forms (*ṣuwar*) of men and women." The only currency, as it were, that is used in this market is the power of imagination, for "whether man or woman, when one of them desires a form, he enters into it (*dakhala fīhā*) and becomes the owner of the form."[276] The market in paradise epitomises a theme that is recurrent in Islamic paradise literature, that is, the ability of the blessed to bring the objects of their desire into being by sheer force of the imagination. The Shiʿi sources, in particular, provide examples of this. "When the thought of a bird occurs to them," states one tradition, "it takes shape (*yaṣīru mumaththalan*) in their hands according to how they desired it."[277] The inhabitants of paradise imagine delicacies that they are unable to name (*ghayr an yusammā*), but which are promptly delivered to them.[278] "When the believers desire a river to flow," one reads in another hadith, "they draw a line [on the ground], and from there springs water, flowing incessantly."[279]

Such unlimited, spectacularly creative powers are, of course, denied to the inhabitants of hell, whose punishments are aimed to systematically divest them of their identity, honour, and agency. Their desire for respite is endless, but unlike the desire for pleasure of the blessed, it is recurrently thwarted, as the minions of hell either ignore their pleas or cruelly inflict on them the opposite of their wishes. In a mocking reversal of the precious accessories provided in paradise, the damned dress in rags of sulphur or fire, or in long black robes (*qalansuwwa*),[280] or in fact the "veils" that protect their naked bodies are ripped apart (*hutikat ʿanhum al-sutūr*), so that their privacy is destroyed.[281] They are made to wear bracelets and crowns of fire.[282] According to al-Majlisī,

274 Suyūṭī, *Budūr*, 602–9.

275 Majlisī, *Biḥār*, VIII, 412, 416. A figurative interpretation of the expression "God's face" in Baḥrānī, *Maʿālim*, III, 116.

276 Suyūṭī, *Budūr*, 582–3, 611; Majlisī, *Biḥār*, VIII, 364. A slightly different version in Qurṭubī, *Tadhkira*, II, 192 (a *gharīb* tradition from al-Tirmidhī).

277 Majlisī, *Biḥār*, VIII, 337.

278 Baḥrānī, *Maʿālim*, III, 89.

279 Majlisī, *Biḥār*, VIII, 339. The idea also occurs in Lamaṭī, *Ibrīz* (tr. O'Kane/Radtke), 894.

280 Suyūṭī, *Budūr*, 430; Majlisī, *Biḥār*, VIII, 466, 483, 489; Baḥrānī, *Maʿālim*, III, 373.

281 Ibid., III, 371.

282 Suyūṭī, *Budūr*, 431; Majlisī, *Biḥār*, VIII, 489.

the hellish diet of Zaqqūm and thorny shrubs is complemented by the tears of the angels shed over the killing of al-Ḥasan and al-Ḥusayn. These tears are collected by the myrmidons of hell, who add them to an explosive cocktail of boiling water and pus and feed it to those who rejoiced over the demise of the two Imams.[283] Naturally, there is no music in hell, only the cacophony of the braying sounds and cries of pain produced by the tortured. Likewise, there is no vision of God, as in general the damned lack the ability to see, imprisoned as they are in eternal darkness.

Fire is by no means "the source of all suffering" in hell, as has been claimed.[284] The catalogue of punishments in the Muslim hell is extensive, and corresponds in many respects to the arsenal of punishments characteristic of medieval Islamic legal culture. Thus, there are a variety of capital punishments (decapitation, stoning, gibbeting, throwing off cliffs or high buildings, and trampling by animals) and physical tortures (flogging, cutting, branding, and other forms of maiming).[285] A kind of ignominious parading takes places when the sinners, their faces blackened, are resurrected with a symbol of their transgression dangling around their necks and are then called to appear before God's Throne to receive their judgement in front of the assembly of humankind. Those who usurped sheep and cattle, for instance, are resurrected carrying the stolen animals on their backs.[286] Those who built a house above the permitted height, thereby transgressing against the right to privacy of their neighbours, are forced to carry their house on their shoulders.[287] The drunkard is resurrected with a wine jug hanging from his neck.[288] Finally, hell's punishments also consist in punitive imprisonment and in banishment.[289] The deeper the sinners are cast into the abyss, the further they are distanced from God. This, in fact, is "the worst punishment of the people of hell."[290]

The Blessed and the Damned

The traditionist literature on paradise and hell doubles as a moral catechism. As such, it overlaps not just with the Ascension narratives,[291] but with Islamic religious ethics and the literature on virtues, sins, and expiation. However, given the agglutinative character of the traditionist genre, the treatment of virtues and sins unfolds in a far less systematic way. The different gates, or compartments (*abwāb*), of paradise and hell are assigned,

283 Ibid., VIII, 483.
284 El-Saleh, *Vie future*, 51.
285 A fuller discussion of this can be found in Lange, *Justice*, 144–50.
286 Suyūṭī, *Budūr*, 131–4.
287 Ibid., 135.
288 Qurṭubī, *Tadhkira*, I, 236.
289 For prisons in hell, see Qurṭubī, *Tadhkira*, II, 115 (al-Falaq), 117 (Būlus).
290 Ibn Rajab, *Takhwīf*, 153.
291 On ascension narratives as didactic tales, see Vuckovic, *Heavenly journeys*.

in certain traditions, to eight or, respectively, seven classes of believers and sinners. The gates through which those who fight in the jihad and those who fast enter paradise are often named.[292] Such traditions indicate the attempt to bring some order into the rather chaotic moral landscape of paradise and hell. However, Late Medieval traditionist eschatology features a much greater number of virtues and sins. For example, generosity, as one tradition asserts, is the name of a tree in paradise whose branches hang down to earth, and that one must grab to be lifted up.[293] Various speech acts, such as reciting the Qur'ān, pious formulas, or performing the call to prayer, are likewise promised a reward in paradise.[294] Shi'i traditions specify that those who visit (*zāra*) the graves of the Prophet and his family in this world will be granted the privilege of visiting them in paradise, too.[295]

The discourse on sin embedded in the traditionist literature on hell is even more productive. The only sin that is punished eternally is *shirk*, the act of assigning associates to God,[296] but a plethora of lesser sins also result in a sojourn in hell, albeit a temporary one. A core group comprises grave sins such as murder, fornication, consumption of wine, slander, and suicide, but the list of sins threatened with requital in hell extends down to more ordinary transgressions such as inattentiveness in ritual ablution, cursing, or the use of gold and silver cups.[297] A number of sins receive a contrapasso punishment. Thus, vainglorious people are dragged on their faces,[298] obscene speech has its perpetrators leak blood and pus from the mouth, and those who slandered others – those who "ate the flesh of others," as the Arabic phrase has it – are forced to practice autosarcophagy.[299]

Of particular interest are borderline cases of sinfulness. Unbelievers (*kuffār*) are generally denied entry into paradise,[300] but al-Majlisī reports the opinion that some of them, "on account of their good deeds" (*a'māluhum al-ḥasana*), are not punished in the conventional way. They reside in hell untouched by the flames, but nonetheless suffer from the psychological strain of witnessing the pain of others.[301] This corresponds in certain respects to the widespread idea that *jahannam*, hell's upper layer, is populated by Muslim

[292] Suyūṭī, *Budūr*, 496, 502; Majlisī, *Biḥār*, VIII, 380, 393, 402 (jihad); Suyūṭī, *Budūr*, 502; Majlisī, *Biḥār*, VIII, 380, 398 (fasting). See Baḥrānī, *Ma'ālim*, 273–7, for a long hadith about the virtues and sins inscribed on the eight gates of paradise and the seven gates of hell.

[293] Majlisī, *Biḥār*, VIII, 381.

[294] Ibid., VIII, 396, 402 (reciting the Qur'ān); Suyūṭī, *Budūr*, 477, 507; Majlisī, *Biḥār*, VIII, 385, 393 (pious formulas); ibid., VIII, 397 (call to prayer).

[295] Baḥrānī, *Ma'ālim*, III, 234–8.

[296] Majlisī, *Biḥār*, VIII, 427, 493.

[297] Suyūṭī, *Budūr*, 423, 461–9; Majlisī, *Biḥār*, VIII, 353, 402.

[298] Suyūṭī, *Budūr*, 463.

[299] Ibid., 467; Majlisī, *Biḥār*, VIII, 460.

[300] Baḥrānī, *Ma'ālim*, III, 217–8.

[301] Majlisī, *Biḥār*, VIII, 472.

sinners, who are therefore called *jahannamiyyūn*. Several traditions point out that the faces of the *jahannamiyyūn* in hell are not blackened.[302] According to other traditions, the heat from which they suffer is no more than the heat one experiences in a bathhouse (*ḥammām*),[303] or their only punishment is seeing what happens in the lower strata of hell.[304] From their privileged position, the *jahannamiyyūn* eventually ascend to the lowest level of paradise,[305] this being a prerogative not enjoyed by any of the unbelievers. They take a purificatory bath in the River of Life in paradise, and although their bodies are from then on as pleasantly refurbished as those of the other paradise dwellers, they are marked by an inscription on their foreheads that reads: "We are those whom God manumitted (*ʿutaqāʾ Allāh*)."[306]

As for those who lived before the age of revelation or otherwise had no access to it, the so-called People of the Interval (*ahl al-fatra*), one comes across conflicting reports. Al-Suyūṭī relates traditions that suggest that the People of the Interval are predestined to either paradise or to hell.[307] He is also known to have composed several works in which he aims to prove that the parents of the prophet Muḥammad, although deceased before the coming of revelation, reside in paradise.[308] Al-Baḥrānī is emphatic in affirming that all the prophets, from Abraham to Jesus, belong to the "party" (*shīʿa*) of Muḥammad and are therefore saved.[309] Only half of the inhabitants of paradise, one reads in a tradition quoted by al-Qurṭubī, are Muslims.[310] Elsewhere, Khadīja is reported to have asked the Prophet about two of her adult sons who died before the advent of Islam. Much to her displeasure, the Prophet answers that they are in hell; he adds, however, that their rank (*makān*) there is such that Khadīja need not worry too much.[311] Some traditions specify that the "lightest punishment" in hell consists in standing in a shallow (*ḍaḥḍāj*) of fire that only reaches up to the ankles, or in wearing "sandals of fire." This results in an intense headache, or "boiling brains." This is the fate of the Prophet's uncle and paternal protector Abū Ṭālib and, according to al-Majlisī, of ʿAbdallāh Ibn Judʿān, a proverbially generous philanthropist of pre-Islamic Mecca.[312] There is also the category

302 Suyūṭī, *Budūr*, 483; Majlisī, *Biḥār*, VIII, 493; Baḥrānī, *Maʿālim*, 215. According to Qurṭubī, *Tadhkira*, II, 90, the Muslim sinners residing in the top layer of hell are called *Muḥammadiyyūn* (from al-Ḍaḥḥāk).

303 Suyūṭī, *Budūr*, 460.

304 Ibid., 459.

305 Ibid., 479–80. Cf. Pagani, "Vane speranze."

306 Suyūṭī, *Budūr*, 479–80.

307 Ibid., 405–7.

308 Cf. Ahlwardt, *Handschriften-Verzeichnisse*, II, 649b-651a.

309 Baḥrānī, *Maʿālim*, III, 226–9.

310 Qurṭubī, *Tadhkira*, II, 84.

311 Suyūṭī, *Budūr*, 400.

312 Ibid., 458; Majlisī, *Biḥār*, VIII, 471, 487. Cf. Baḥrānī, *Maʿālim*, III, 361. On Ibn Judʿān, see *EI2*, s.v. ʿAbdallāh b. Djudʿān, I, 44b-45a (Ch. Pellat).

of those who, either because of their age or because of a mental handicap, cannot be considered accountable for their actions. In this context, al-Suyūṭī relates the tradition according to which "most of the people of paradise are simpletons (*bulh*)."[313] He is equally optimistic in regard to children: the children of Muslims keep their parents company,[314] while the children of the unbelievers are looked after by the patriarch Abraham and his wife Sarah.[315]

The case of the *jahannamiyyūn*, who occupy first the highest layer of hell and then the lowest level of paradise, suggests a certain hierarchisation within both paradise and hell. This is the final structural principle that defines the morphology of paradise and hell in traditionist literature. There are different degrees of exultation in paradise. A basic, probably early division is that between two upper gardens (Jannat ʿAdn and Jannat al-Naʿīm according to a tradition in al-Qurṭubī) and two lower gardens (Firdaws and Jannat al-Maʾwā); the former populated by "those who are brought near" (*al-muqarrabūn*), the latter by "the companions of the right" (*aṣḥāb al-yamīn*).[316] Further processes of differentiation take place. The top garden, whether called Jannat ʿAdn or Firdaws, is reserved for prophets, martyrs, and the righteous, while ordinary Muslims dwell in lower spheres and the *jahannamiyyūn* at the bottom of paradise. In Shiʿi versions of this motif, the heights of paradise are occupied by Muḥammad and the Twelve Imams,[317] or by Muḥammad and his extended family,[318] and only the Shiʿites enjoy the privilege of visiting them there.[319] The "well-built chambers upon chambers" mentioned in the Qurʾān (*ghuraf min fawqihā ghuraf mabniyya*, 39:20) are usually considered to be elevated places of special privilege in paradise; they are assigned to different classes of the blessed, from the prophets down to the most pious among ordinary Muslims.[320] Conversely, there are different degrees of degradation in hell. Muslims are on top while non-Muslim sinners reside at the bottom, around Zaqqūm. Neither paradise nor hell, in other words, are classless societies. Both are stratified, and both reflect and inculcate an ideology of moral and social order. This happens along the three

[313] Suyūṭī, *Budūr*, 594; Qurṭubī, *Tadhkira*, II, 71.

[314] Suyūṭī, *Budūr*, 400, 404, 500. Cf. ibid., 504: There is gate to paradise called the "Gate of Joy" (*bāb al-faraḥ*), reserved for those who made children happy. See also Baḥrānī, *Maʿālim*, III, 187.

[315] Suyūṭī, *Budūr*, 401. But see the tradition in the preceding text, n182, in which they are said to serve the believers. Cf. Majlisī, *Biḥār*, VIII, 336. See also Sulaymān al-Baḥrānī (d. 1120/1708?), *Fī walad al-zinā*, an epistle in which it is argued, following earlier Shiʿi authorities such as Muḥammad b. Idrīs al-Ḥillī (d. 598/1202), that children born out of wedlock may be admitted to paradise, provided they believe and are pious.

[316] Qurṭubī, *Tadhkira*, II, 162–3.

[317] Majlisī, *Biḥār*, VIII, 394.

[318] Baḥrānī, *Maʿālim*, III, 190.

[319] Majlisī, *Biḥār*, VIII, 383.

[320] Suyūṭī, *Budūr*, 512–4; Qurṭubī, *Tadhkira*, II, 185–8.

lines of gender, power, and orthodoxy. In conclusion to this chapter, let us review each of these three areas.

The paradise traditions reported by al-Suyūṭī and al-Majlisī are not exclusively unfavourable towards women.[321] Like their male companions, women are rejuvenated upon entering the eternal garden, and their virginity is restored.[322] If married more than once, women in paradise enjoy the privilege of choosing as their otherworldly partner the husband they like best,[323] even though it is nowhere intimated that the male young servants of paradise entertain them in the same ways in which the houris give pleasure to the men. It is repeatedly made clear that Muslim women occupy a higher rank in the hereafter than the houris because of the good deeds they did on earth. Muḥammad's wife Hind, according to a tradition reported by both al-Suyūṭī and al-Majlisī, once begged the Prophet to explain the meaning of the Qurʾānic phrase *ḥūr ʿīn* to her. The Prophet launched into a long description of the houris, to which Hind, understandably worried, replied with the question: "Are the women of this world better (*afḍalu*), or the houris?" The Prophet reassured Hind that "the women of this world are better than the houris, just as the outside (*ẓihāra*) is superior to the inside (*biṭāna*)," explaining that this is "on account of their prayers and their fasting."[324] Because every man in paradise is granted two wives, commentators usually conclude that there are more women in paradise than men.[325] Female exemplars from among non-Islamic peoples and from early Islamic history receive special mention. Āsiya is accorded her own mansion in paradise, as are Mary and Khadīja.[326] According to a Shiʿi tradition, Āsiya, Mary, Khadīja, and Fāṭima are "the best of the women of paradise."[327]

At the same time, there is no shortage of patriarchal, at times overtly misogynist statements about women sinners in hell. At its most blunt, this is exemplified by the saying attributed to the Prophet that "most people in hell are women,"[328] an assertion that seems to contradict the notion that there are more women than men in paradise. Some exegetes, however, argue that

[321] Also the Qurʾān has an egalitarian vision of access to paradise, stating that both men and women will be rewarded by God with "a great wage" (33:35). See the similar remarks by Rosenthal, who however also notes, correctly, that "[n]early all the fantasies about Paradise are meant for men." See Rosenthal, "Reflections on love," 254.

[322] Suyūṭī, *Budūr*, 557; Majlisī, *Biḥār*, VIII, 338.

[323] Suyūṭī, *Budūr*, 559.

[324] Ibid., 558; Majlisī, *Biḥār*, VIII, 411; Baḥrānī, *Maʿālim*, III, 109.

[325] This is already suggested in Muslim, *Ṣaḥīḥ*, *k. al-janna* 14 (*b. awwalu zamra tadkhulu l-janna*), IV, 2178–9. See further Suyūṭī, *Budūr*, 561; al-ʿAynī, *ʿUmdat*, XII, 305, quoted in Reinhart, "The here and the hereafter," 17.

[326] Suyūṭī, *Budūr*, 585.

[327] Majlisī, *Biḥār*, VIII, 386–7; Baḥrānī, *Maʿālim*, III, 160.

[328] Bukhārī, *Ṣaḥīḥ*, *k. al-riqāq* 51 (*b. ṣifat al-janna wa-l-nār*), IV, 207; Suyūṭī, *Budūr*, 460–1, 594; Qurṭubī, *Tadhkira*, II, 74. On this, probably ancient, tradition, see Juynboll, "Some *isnād*-analytical methods," 362–9.

the hadith is not about female unbelievers but about female Muslim sinners, whose purgative punishment in hell creates a temporary female majority there.[329] Indeed, women tend to be in hell not because of their unbelief (*kufr bi-llāh*) but because of their ungratefulness vis-à-vis their husbands (*kufr bi-l-ʿashīr*), to which is added the alleged female propensity to following passion blindly and being distracted easily from the demands of religion.[330] Descriptions of the punishment of female sinners do not make for pleasant reading. According to a tradition related by al-Majlisī, they are hung up by their hair, tongues, thighs, and feet, tortured with red-hot pincers, or transformed into bitches and sodomised by fire, for offenses that include indecent dressing and makeup, lascivious behaviour vis-à-vis men, failure to perform the ritual washing after menstruation, and pandering.[331] Women who wear too much jewellery in this life, according to a tradition reported by al-Suyūṭī, are made to wear necklaces of fire in the next.[332] However, as has been noted, such statements should not be seen as "the considered conclusion of Muslim theologians ... but rather [as] the attempt to legitimate forms of social control over women" specific to traditionist literature and to the scholars who produced and transmitted it.[333]

The perspective of a male traditionist milieu of origin also comes across rather clearly in traditions that express a deep-seated aversion against rulers and the representatives of the repressive state apparatus. There is no blanket condemnation of rulers, but numerous traditions specify that tyrants will receive their due punishment in the otherworld.[334] Shiʿi traditions add specificities. Al-Baḥrānī devotes more than thirty pages (in the printed edition) to traditions detailing the punishment of the political enemies of the Shiʿa.[335] The Umayyads, for example, are assigned their own compartment in hell,[336] and the caliphs Abū Bakr, ʿUmar, Muʿāwiya, and ʿAbd al-Malik, as well as ʿĀʾisha "and all the other people of the [Battle of] the Camel," receive separate mention.[337] Eschatological factionalism is by no means peculiar to Shiʿi literature, but rather should be seen in analogy to traditions exalting the heroes of Sunni salvation history, such as "the ten who were given glad tidings" (*al-ʿashara al-mubashshara*), members of the Meccan Quraysh and intimates of the first Umayyad caliph ʿUthmān

329 Qurṭubī, *Tadhkira*, II, 199.
330 Suyūṭī, *Budūr*, 460–1; Qurṭubī, *Tadhkira*, II, 74–5.
331 Majlisī, *Biḥār*, VIII, 481–2.
332 Suyūṭī, *Budūr*, 464.
333 Smith and Haddad, *Understanding*, 163. On the issue, see also the balanced remarks by Rosenthal, "Reflections on love," 251–2.
334 Suyūṭī, *Budūr*, 422, 469; Majlisī, *Biḥār*, VIII, 473.
335 Baḥrānī, *Maʿālim*, III, 314–45, 351–7.
336 Majlisī, *Biḥār*, VIII, 463–4.
337 Ibid., VIII, 476, 483. According to Baḥrānī, *Maʿālim*, III, 242, paradise "longs for" (*tashtāqū ilā*) ʿAlī, ʿAmmār, Salmān, Abū Dharr, and al-Miqdād.

b. ʿAffān (r. 23–5/644–56) to whom the Prophet had allegedly promised paradise.[338] As for government officials, a dire end is predicted for evil viziers and local superintendents (*ʿurafāʾ*),[339] as well as for the collectors of illegitimate taxes (*maks*), policemen (*shuraṭ*, *muḥtasib*s), and "all helpers of tyranny."[340] Corrupt or incompetent judges, as well as their enforcers, the court-sheriffs (*jalāwiza*, sg. *jilwāz*), are regularly threatened with punishment in hell.[341] "The first to enter hell," states a tradition, "are the professional floggers (*al-sawwāṭūn*)."[342]

According to a tradition preserved by al-Suyūṭī, the blessed will continue to consult scholars (*ʿulamāʾ*) in paradise; they need their fatwas in order to learn from them the proper etiquette when directing requests to God.[343] Many traditions featuring men of religion, however, consist in warnings to the bad apples among them, such as different kinds of corrupt or vainglorious scholars and Qurʾān reciters,[344] or preachers "who say what they do not do themselves."[345] Those who learn to speak and argue "in the manner of the Jews and Christians" (*man yataʿallamu kalām al-yahūd wa-l-naṣāra*), doing so "without properly explaining what they mean," are banished to the farthest depths of hell.[346] It is hardly surprising that hell also serves as the place of residence for heretics, schismatics, and other enemies of the faith. The apostle Paul (*Bawlus*), according to a tradition preserved by al-Majlisī, is in hell,[347] presumably because he was thought to be responsible for falsifying the true teachings of the prophet Jesus. The atheists (*dahriyya*)[348] and antipredestinarian Qadarites of early Islam keep him company.[349] Shiʿi tradition consigns Ibn Muljam, the murderer of ʿAlī, and his fellow Khārijite Dhū l-Thadya to a box of fire in the infernal well of Falaq,[350] while the murderers

[338] See, e.g., Nābulusī, *Ahl al-janna*, 17. On the *ḥadīth al-ʿashara al-mubashshara*, see Yazigi, "Ḥadīth al-ʿashara"; *EI2*, s.v. al-ʿAshara al-mubashshara, I, 693a-694a (A. J. Wensinck); *TG*, I, 21–2; van Ess, *Fehltritt*, 172–3.

[339] Majlisī, *Biḥār*, VIII, 483; Qurṭubī, *Tadhkira*, II, 76.

[340] Suyūṭī, *Budūr*, 469; Majlisī, *Biḥār*, VIII, 353, 402; Qurṭubī, *Tadhkira*, II, 77. Cf. Baḥrānī, *Maʿālim*, III, 292. On *muḥtasib*s in hell, see Lange, *Justice*, 159.

[341] For examples, see Tillier, "The *qāḍī* before the Judge"; Lange, *Justice*, 157–9.

[342] Suyūṭī, *Budūr*, 457; Qurṭubī, *Tadhkira*, II, 130. Cf. the tradition in Qurṭubī, *Tadhkira*, II, 71, 73, threatening those wielding unduly thick whips with hell.

[343] Suyūṭī, *Budūr*, 595. Several traditions about scholars going to paradise in Baḥrānī, *Maʿālim*, III, 76–81.

[344] Suyūṭī, *Budūr*, 463; Majlisī, *Biḥār*, VIII, 482–3.

[345] Qurṭubī, *Tadhkira*, II, 129.

[346] Suyūṭī, *Budūr*, 425; Qurṭubī, *Tadhkira*, II, 91. The canonical version of the hadith is more generally directed against all forms of idle talk. See Muslim, *Ṣaḥīḥ*, *k. al-zuhd wa-l-riqāq* 6 (*b. al-takallum bi-l-kalima*), V, 2290: *al-ʿabd la-yatakallamu bi-l-kalima mā fīhā yatabayyanu*. Cf. Nawawī, *Sharḥ*, IX, 93.

[347] Majlisī, *Biḥār*, VIII, 483.

[348] Qurṭubī, *Tadhkira*, II, 92.

[349] Suyūṭī, *Budūr*, 423; Majlisī, *Biḥār*, VIII, 353; Baḥrānī, *Maʿālim*, III, 292.

[350] Majlisī, *Biḥār*, VIII, 472.

of al-Ḥusayn and his sons are in the lowest hell.[351] The eighth Imam of the Twelver Shiʿites, ʿAlī al-Riḍā (d. 293/818), is on record for declaring that one of the schismatics asserting that the line of Imams had ended after the seventh Imam "has entered hell."[352] Issues surrounding Muslim morality, but also questions relating to gender, worldly power, and orthodoxy are prime concerns of traditionist eschatology. How eschatologists such as al-Suyūṭī, al-Majlisī, al-Qurṭubī, and al-Baḥrānī identified and classified the blessed and the damned reflects how they understood and, by reproducing traditions that underpinned them, perpetuated the moral and political hierarchies of the communities they lived in.

With this, our tour of paradise and hell has come to an end. It should be emphasised that the picture that has emerged is far from complete. Like a moving spotlight that illuminates selected spots on a theatre stage, we have skimmed the surface of the Islamic otherworld as it is presented in Late Medieval traditionist literature. Here and there, we have drilled some holes. In conclusion to this chapter, some synthetic observations suggest themselves. Both al-Suyūṭī and al-Majlisī anchor their texts in the eschatological data of the Qurʾān. Al-Suyūṭī presents a topical selection of Qurʾānic verses at the beginning of each of his chapters; al-Majlisī proceeds by prefacing his comprehensive chapters on paradise and hell with a complete inventory of the verses bearing on the topic. In the traditions that follow upon these selections, several exegetical techniques are at play. First, by a process of midrashic elaboration, Qurʾānic themes, such as the width and depth of paradise and hell, are amplified, and oftentimes enriched with materials originating from non-Islamic backgrounds such as were circulated in Islamic milieus by the popular preachers (*quṣṣāṣ*). Secondly, there is what I have identified as a tendency towards reification, whereby abstract Qurʾānic concepts become concrete phenomena or bodies in the otherworld, a technique that is also applied more generally and not just on the basis of Qurʾānic terminology, thus resulting in the corporal presence of "true allegories" in the otherworld. Thirdly, while much of the information provided by al-Suyūṭī and al-Majlisī is generic – think of the descriptions of the houris – there is also a manifest drive towards specification, such that certain places, gates of paradise and hell, buildings, or indeed houris are singled out, given a name, and ascribed a set of particularities.

The communalities between the Sunni and the Shiʿi sources by far outweigh the differences. The otherworld of Shiʿi traditionists is hardly more disembodied than the Sunni one.[353] However, some characteristic divergences there are. Most striking, perhaps, is the role enjoyed, in Shiʿi literature, by the Imams on the Day of Judgement, and their exalted position,

351 Ibid., VIII, 382.

352 Ibid., VI, 424. Cf. Halm, *Schia*, 38–9.

353 See the defence of a physical afterlife in Majlisī, *Biḥār*, VIII, 403.

together with that of the extended family of the Prophet, that is, "the people of the house" (*ahl al-bayt*), in paradise. The Sunni and Shiʿi collectors diverge on certain theological questions, and on salient figures of the early history of Islam. However, a more thorough examination of these issues must be reserved to the following two chapters, in which the properly theological Sunni and Shiʿi literature on paradise and hell is studied.

In conclusion, it might be observed that the imagination that unfolds in traditionist eschatology is not completely unbound, contrary to what the title of this chapter suggests. After all, collectors such as al-Suyūṭī, al-Majlisī, al-Qurṭubī, and al-Baḥrānī were answerable to the criteria of medieval Muslim hadith criticism, as described in Chapter 2. Al-Qurṭubī, to provide an example, warns against laxity in accepting unsound eschatological traditions, stating that "in the books of renunciation and of exhortations that stir the hearts of the audience (*kutub al-zuhd wa-l-raqāʾiq*), the names of the layers [of hell] and of the religious communities [residing therein] are arranged in a way that is not confirmed by sound tradition."[354] In this sense, the imagination that unfolds in traditionist eschatology does not measure up to the kind of unfettered imagination one comes across in popular works on cosmogony,[355] in certain Late Medieval works about the "Marvels of Creation" (*ʿajāʾib al-makhlūqāt*),[356] or in poetic imaginations of the otherworld.[357] However, while Late Medieval traditionist eschatology moulds the imagination rather than allowing it complete freedom, it is still remarkably inclusive of the rare and the recondite. The overall impression is decidedly rich. To some, the accumulated layers of medieval traditionist eschatology may seem rather like cobwebs covering an old master's painting stored on a dusty attic, redundant baroque embellishments and gothic horror images concealing and at times barring access to the layers of spirituality below. Rather than swiping these cobwebs aside, in this chapter I have attempted to map out their compositional principles and thereby to develop an understanding of the concerns that structure them. In the chapters that follow, I shall turn to the theological, philosophical, and mystical dimensions that lie underneath.

354 Qurṭubī, *Tadhkira*, II, 90.

355 For paradise and hell in popular cosmography, see the anonymous *K. al-ʿAẓama* studied by Raven, "A Kitāb al-ʿAẓama"; idem, "Hell in popular Muslim imagination."

356 See Walid Saleh's study of *The Delight of Onlookers and the Signs for Investigators* (*Bahjat al-nāẓirīn wa-āyāt al-mustadillīn*) of the Egyptian Marʿī ibn Yūsuf al-Karmī (d. 1033/1624), a popular work that Islamises the *ʿajāʾib* genre by including descriptions of eschatological phenomena, a feature that is missing from, e.g., the *ʿAjāʾib al-makhlūqāt* of al-Qazwīnī (d. 682/1262). See Saleh, "Paradise in an Islamic *ʿajāʾib* work."

357 For poetic works, see the examples of al-Maʿarrī, *Risālat al-ghufrān*, and al-Wahrānī, *al-Manām*, discussed in the following text, pp. 279–80. Cf. Abou-Deeb, *The imagination unbound*, 17–30.

PART II

DISCOURSES AND PRACTICES: DEBATING THE OTHERWORLD

5

The Otherworld Contested: Cosmology, Soteriology, and Ontology in Sunni Theology and Philosophy

Theological thinking about the otherworld in Islam unfolded in three main areas: cosmology, soteriology, and ontology.[1] That is to say, Muslim theologians debated how paradise and hell are situated in space and in time; they discussed the conditions for, and the various modalities of, salvation and damnation in the afterlife; and they sought to define in what sense the otherworld is "real," whether it is spiritual or corporeal, or both, or something else altogether. While the first, cosmological tradition of theological thinking connects to mythic repertoires of picturing the otherworld, the second, soteriological one is rooted in the discipline of dialectic theology (*kalām*), the trading of arguments between different schools of thought. Finally, in their discussions of the ontological status of the otherworld, Muslim theologians came to interact with Islamic philosophy, or *falsafa*, which gave rise, in the later Middle Ages, to new philosophical-theological syntheses.[2] The aim of this chapter is to trace each of these traditions of thought and in the process also critically put to the test three common – and in my view, not entirely correct – scholarly perceptions of Sunni theological eschatology: firstly, that it rigorously divorces the otherworld from earthly, ordinary space and time; secondly, that it unfailingly professes a high degree of salvation certainty; and thirdly, that it has a straightforward, materialistic conception of the otherworld.[3]

The Location, Creation, and Duration of Paradise and Hell

In the early centuries of Islam, Muslim theologians disagreed as to whether paradise and hell were located on earth or in the otherworld. The question

[1] I draw inspiration here from the taxonomy provided by Martin, *La vie future*.

[2] For surveys of Islamic theological eschatology, see Gardet, *Dieu*, 231–346; Martin, *La vie future*; Smith and Haddad, *Islamic understanding*, 63–97; *TG*, IV, 543–61 and passim.

[3] Shi'i theologians and philosophers also debated these issues, and they did so no less comprehensively. See Chapter 6.

seems to have been somewhat less controversial with regard to hell. After all, the Qur'ān speaks of "seven earths" (65:12), while also describing hell as a trench or subterranean pit, a netherworld, divided into seven compartments. The standard notion, therefore, was that hell coincides with the subterranean layers of the earth, or that it is "inside the earth,"[4] while being connected to the surface by a number of gateways, usually imagined as leading through deep wells.[5] Exegetes commonly associated the mysterious *sijjīn* mentioned in the Qur'ān, a place in hell where "the record of the reprobates" is kept (Q 83:7–9), with a rock, situated in the lowest earth, on which the whole universe rests.[6]

As for the location of paradise, the Qur'ān, as we saw in Chapter 1, leaves some room for interpretation, seemingly placing it at the nexus of earth and heaven. In early Muslim theology as well as in later centuries, the standard position was that Adam's and Eve's paradise, to which all their descendants will one day return, was on earth.[7] The Baghdad littérateur and traditionist, Ibn Qutayba (d. 276/889), in his *Book of Knowledge* (*K. al-Maʿārif*), collected a number of Adamic legends from which arguments for the earthly location of the primordial garden could be inferred. For instance, Adam and Eve, when dwelling in the garden, were told to "multiply and fill the earth" – *not* the heavens; when Adam came to die, he asked his sons to fetch him some grapes from the garden – which therefore must have been within reach on the surface of the earth; and so forth.[8] It was also argued that when in the Qur'ān, Adam is commanded to "go down" (*ihbiṭ*) from the garden, this does not indicate a vertical movement, or "fall" from paradise. Rather, the expression refers to horizontal dislocation, as in another Qur'ānic verse in which Moses, annoyed at the Israelites' recalcitrance, tells them to "go down to Egypt" (*ihbiṭū Miṣr*, 2:61).[9]

The arguments of those who, on such evidence, insisted on the earthly location of the eschatological paradise were premised on the assumption

[4] See already, Asad, *Zuhd*, 66. See further Suyūṭī, *Budūr*, 411; Majlisī, *Biḥār*, VIII, 460. Cf. El-Saleh, *La vie future*, 45. It appears that the notion was openly called into question only from the nineteenth century onwards. According to Ibrahīm al-Bājūrī (d. 1860), "the correct attitude is to refer oneself to God" in this regard. See Bājurī, *Tuḥfat al-murīd*, 107, quoted in Gardet, *Dieu*, 328.

[5] In the anonymous *Qurrat al-ʿuyūn* (see the preceding text, pp. 105–7) it is related from "one of the pious forefathers" that the well of Barhūt in the Hadramawt valley in Yemen is the entry (*fam*) to *jahannam*. See *Qurrat al-ʿuyūn*, 104. Cf. *EI2*, s.v. Barhūt, I, 1045a (G. Rentz); *TG*, IV, 522. On Barhūt and other entries to hell (as well as paradise), see following text, pp. 256–7.

[6] Ibn Ḥanbal, *Musnad*, IV, 288; Ibn Qayyim al-Jawziyya, *Rūḥ*, 112. Cf. Heinen, *Islamic cosmology*, 88, 143.

[7] Cf. *TG*, IV, 550.

[8] Ibn Qutayba, *Maʿārif*, 11–15, 19. Cf. Ibn Qayyim al-Jawziyya, *Ḥādī*, 26.

[9] This was the view of the Muʿtazilites Abū l-Qāsim al-Balkhī (d. 319/931) and Abū Muslim al-Iṣfahānī (d. 322/934). See ibid., 24.

that the garden to which the believers will return at the end of times is identical with Adam's and Eve's garden.[10] As a gradual process of sublimating paradise into a transcendent, otherworldly realm set in, some severed this connection. The Cordovan scholar Mundhir b. Saʿīd (d. 355/966) is remembered as one of the most outspoken deniers of the identity of the two gardens.[11] His line of reasoning centred on the idea that the eschatological paradise has a degree of perfection that the primordial garden lacks. Existence in the future paradise, Mundhir asserted, never ends, whereas Adam's and Eve's sojourn in Eden *did* come to an end. Besides, there are no trials or tribulations in paradise; in fact, as the Qurʾān explicates, there is not even idle talk in the future abode of the blessed (52:23). It results that Satan, the idlest of all talkers, could only whisper lies to Adam and Eve in "their" garden.[12] Neither is there sleep in the eternal garden. Adam, however, slept in "his" garden when Eve was created from his rib.[13]

Others, including the Iraqi Ḍirār b. ʿAmr (d. *ca.* 180/796), strove to disassociate the otherworld from this world not only in spatial but also in temporal terms. Accordingly, they argued that paradise and hell will only be created at the end of time, after this world has been undone. Ḍirār's motifs in making this claim are not easy to reconstruct,[14] but in the generations following him, members of the theological movement to which he adhered, Muʿtazilism (*fl.* second-fifth/eighth-eleventh c.), averred that it made no sense to assume that this world and the otherworld existed simultaneously. Imagine, reasoned the Muʿtazilites, a king who built a splendid palace filled with all sorts of beautiful things to delight the senses, and then let nobody enter it – would this not be a pointless exercise? However, as the argument continued, everything that God does, He does on purpose. He creates paradise and hell in order to reward or punish people. Therefore, paradise and hell will only be created after the final judgement has been passed on the Day of Resurrection.[15]

[10] Some arguments in favour of the identity of the protological and eschatological garden are listed in Pazdawī, *Uṣūl al-dīn*, 170.

[11] Ibn Qayyim al-Jawziyya, *Ḥādī*, p. 25. Cf. *TG*, IV, 553. Mundhir also denied that Adam's and Eve's garden was on earth.

[12] Ibn Qayyim al-Jawziyya, *Ḥādī*, 31–34.

[13] Ibid., 32. When the Prophet was once asked whether the inhabitants of paradise sleep he answered that they do not, because "sleep is the brother of death." See Ibn al-Kharrāṭ, *ʿĀqiba*, 325. More arguments against the identity of the protological and the eschatological garden are gathered in Ibn Hishām, *Tījān*, 11. See the translation in *TG*, V, 244–5. Cf. ibid., III, 53–4, IV, 553–4.

[14] *TG*, III, 53.

[15] Shahrastānī, *Milal* (ed. M. F. Badrān), 110 (from Hishām al-Fuwaṭī [d. *ca.* 218/833], translated in *TG*, VI, 233 [text #36]). See further Sibṭ b. al-Jawzī, *Mirʾāt al-zamān*, I, 199; Ibn Abī l-ʿIzz, *Sharḥ al-ʿaqīda al-Ṭaḥāwiyya*, 420; Āmidī, *Abkār al-afkār*, III, 248; Majlisī, *Biḥār*, VIII, 406. Cf. Abrahamov, "The creation and duration," 91; van Ess, "Das begrenzte Paradies," 115.

Even among the Muʿtazilites, however, this postponement of the creation of paradise and hell was a matter of dispute, For example, Bishr b. al-Muʿtamir (d. 210/825) and Abū l-Hudhayl (d. 227/841?), both from Baghdad, disagreed.[16] In the long run, the notion was unable to impose itself on a broad basis.[17] Just like theologians of later centuries generally opined that Adam's and Eve's garden was identical with the future paradise, they also insisted that paradise and hell, as the creeds' phrase has it, are "already created."[18] The accumulated weight of tradition was, perhaps, too heavy to ignore. Did not the Qurʾān promise that martyrs would enter paradise immediately after death? Had not the Prophet, during his ascension, *already* seen paradise and hell, both filled with all kinds of people?[19] And were there not plenty of hadiths that detailed that the dead in their graves are shown paradise and hell, or are even taken on a preliminary tour of them, as a foretaste of what awaits them after the final judgement on the Day of Resurrection?[20] Besides, rational arguments could be marshalled. The Transoxanian preacher and theologian Abū l-Layth al-Samarqandī (d. 373/983), for example, reasoned that the present existence of paradise and hell serves the purpose of inspiring hope and fear; therefore, the synchronicity of this world and the otherworld was not nearly as pointless as Muʿtazilite thinkers claimed.[21]

More lastingly disputed was the question regarding whether paradise and hell will *continue* to exist forever, or whether both, or one of the two, will eventually come to an end. The spark that ignited this debate appears to

[16] *TG*, III, 107, IV, 552, and the text translated ibid., V, 324 (#56). In addition, Abrahamov names al-Jubbāʾī (d. 303/915) and Abū l-Ḥusayn al-Baṣrī (d. 436/1044). See Abrahamov, "The creation and duration," 91.

[17] A concurrent development occurs regarding the "punishment of the grave" (*ʿadhāb al-qabr*). Early detractors included Jahm b. Ṣafwān and the Khārijites, and Muʿtazilites from the early third/ninth century such as Ḍirār b. ʿAmr (d. *ca.* 180/796) and Bishr al-Mārisī (d. 218/833) likewise denied the reality of such a punishment, which is not mentioned in the Qurʾān. However, half a century later, "the skeptics," in Leor Halevi's words, "had been cowed," as can be seen in the example of the Muʿtazilite al-Shaḥḥām (d. after 257/871). See Halevi, *Muḥammad's grave*, 218. The "punishment of the grave" is affirmed as real (*ḥaqq*) in the anonymous Testament of Abū Ḥanīfa (*waṣiyyat Abī Ḥanīfa*, written *ca.* middle of the third/ninth century) and in the document known as al-Fiqh al-akbar II. See Wensinck, *Islamic creeds*, 59 (#18), 67 (#23). See also Ashʿarī, *Maqālāt*, I, 127, II, 430.

[18] Pazdawī, *Uṣūl al-dīn*, 170; Ījī, *Mawāqif*, 375; Jurjānī, *Sharḥ al-mawāqif*, VIII, 328–9. Also the creeds from the third/ninth to the eighth/fourteenth centuries collected by W. Montgomery Watt unanimously reproduce the formula that paradise and hell are "already created" (*makhlūqa*). See Watt, *Islamic creeds*, 31 (Ibn Ḥanbal), 36, 46 (al-Ashʿarī), 54 (al-Ṭaḥāwī), 60 (al-Fiqh al-akbar I), 66 (al-Fiqh al-akbar II), 71 (Ibn Abī Zayd), 82 (al-Nasafī), 88 (al-Ījī). The single exception is the creed of al-Ghazālī, which remains silent on the issue.

[19] This argument appears in the creed attributed to Aḥmad b. Ḥanbal. See ibid., 31 (#12).

[20] See Eklund, *Life*, 5, 7–8, with examples from the hadith collections of al-Bukhārī, Ibn Ḥanbal, and Abū Dāwūd.

[21] Samarqandī, *Sharḥ al-fiqh al-absaṭ*, 186; Juwaynī, *Irshād*, 319. Cf. Abrahamov, "The creation and duration," 90–1.

have been the doctrine of Jahm b. Ṣafwān (East Iran, d. 128/746) that both paradise and hell perish because both are part of God's creation and therefore finite.[22] In the words of the Qur'ān, "everything will perish except His face" (Q 28:88). Jahm concluded that only God, "the First and the Last" (Q 57:3), exists eternally outside of creation. This view had to be reconciled, of course, with those scriptural passages that emphasised the everlastingness of paradise and hell. Jahm taught that the Qur'ānic expression "they dwell in it [i.e., paradise] forever (*khālidīna fīhā*, 3:15 and passim)" should be understood as a hyperbole. He also thought the finite duration of paradise and hell was implied in the statement that the sinners in hell remain there "as long" – to mean: only as long – "as the heaven and the earth" (11:107).[23] According to a formula attributed to Jahm and his followers, God does not punish *in* the Fire (*fī l-nār*) but *during* the Fire (*ʿinda l-nār*) – that is, as long as it exists.[24]

Although maligned in later times, Jahm's view initially found a substantial number of followers.[25] The Muʿtazilite Abū l-Hudhayl leant in this direction, although he did not go so far as to conclude that paradise and hell (and with them, their inhabitants) perish in the physical sense. Rather, he reasoned that merely the movements (*ḥawādith*) of the dwellers in the otherworld, and with them, time, come to an end. From then on, he argued, the blessed and the damned remain motionless, petrified in perpetual pleasure or pain, in a perfectly unmoved landscape.[26] This is a rare and strange view that few supported in later centuries, whether Muʿtazilites or not.[27] Some poked fun at it. Hishām al-Fuwaṭī (d. *ca.* 230/845), for example, imagined that, were Abū l-Hudhayl right, believers would be frozen with both arms outstretched, reaching out with their left to grab a fruit and receiving with their right a cup of wine, thus remaining fixated in the undignified position of a crucified man.[28] At any rate, the standard creeds and textbooks of Sunni theology usually assert that "paradise and hell will never disappear or cease

[22] Ibn Ḥanbal, *al-Radd ʿalā l-zanādiqa wa-l-Jahmiyya*, 325; Pazdawī, *Uṣūl al-dīn*, 171; Ibn Qayyim al-Jawziyya, *Ḥādī*, 255. Cf. *TG*, II, 505–6, IV, 552, 554.

[23] Ashʿarī, *Maqālāt*, 164. See the translation in *TG*, V, 217 (#13).

[24] Thus in the creed of the Ḥanbalī popular preacher al-Barbahārī (d. 329/941). See Ibn Abī Yaʿlā, *Ṭabaqāt*, III, 52. I owe this reference to Christopher Melchert.

[25] *TG*, IV, 554.

[26] Ashʿari, *Maqālāt*, 485. See the translation in *TG*, V, 407. See also Ibn Qayyim al-Jawziyya, *Ḥādī*, 255, 259. Cf. *TG*, III, 255–6; Frank, "The divine attributes," 473–5.

[27] Among those who seem to have defended a version of Abū l-Hudhayl's theory is al-Shaḥḥām (d. after 257/871). See *TG*, IV, 49.

[28] Hishām al-Fuwaṭī's ironical comment is reported in Khayyāṭ, *Intiṣār*, 57. See the translation in *TG*, V, 417 (#95), and the discussion ibid., III, 259. According to the creed of al-Barbahārī (see preceding text), Hishām followed Jahm's view on the limited duration of hell. Cf. Majlisī, *Biḥār*, VIII, 361, where the argument is traced back to Ibn Qutayba and levelled at al-Naẓẓām (d. *ca.* 230/845), who supposedly shared the view of his contemporary Abū l-Hudhayl on the matter.

to exist."[29] The Spaniard Ibn Ḥazm, in the fifth/eleventh century, claimed that this was the consensus (*ijmāʿ*) of Muslim scholars, which one had to accept or else risk being called an unbeliever.[30]

A renewed challenge to this dominant view came in the work of the Damascene scholars Ibn Taymiyya (d. 728/1328) and his student Ibn Qayyim al-Jawziyya (d. 751/1350). Both held a more narrow definition of *ijmāʿ* than Ibn Ḥazm, considering only the consensus of the first generations of Muslims, the *salaf*, to be binding. Ibn Taymiyya, as reported by Ibn Qayyim al-Jawziyya, stated that the early Muslims were known to have disagreed on the matter, particularly in regard to the eternal duration of hell. (Paradise, they were happy to concede, continues to exist forever.) The second caliph ʿUmar b. al-Khaṭṭāb, as well as early authorities such as Ibn Masʿūd and Abū Hurayra, held the view that God eventually destroys hell and that punishment therein thus comes to an end.[31] Also, Ibn Taymiyya pointed out, the threat of eternal punishment is accompanied in the Qurʾān by important qualifications: firstly and most importantly in Q 11:107, the passage, already used by Jahm, that states that sinners are in hell "as long as the earth and the heaven"; and secondly in Q 6:128, where the unbelievers are promised an infinite sojourn in hell "except as God wills." Similar exceptions, Ibn Tayimyya and Ibn Qayyim al-Jawziyya observed, do not occur in verses that speak of the eternal joys of paradise. To the contrary, some verses, such as Q 11:108, emphatically underline that paradise is a "gift never cut off." Finally, Ibn Taymiyya and Ibn Qayyim al-Jawziyya added two theological arguments. First, they asserted that God's mercy precludes the idea of perpetual punishment. Secondly, they reasoned that everlasting chastisement is impossible because it contradicts God's wise purpose (*ḥikma*): the aim of hell is to reform and purify the sinners, not to inflict pain. Therefore, they concluded, once this aim has been achieved, all inhabitants of hell will be moved to paradise, and hell must perish.[32]

In the centuries after Ibn Taymiyya and Ibn Qayyim al-Jawziyya, this inclusivist view of salvation, according to which everybody is eventually saved, did not catch on among Muslim theologians. Rather, several refutations of their argument about "hell's perdition" (*fanāʾ al-nār*) were written.[33] A well-known rejoinder is that of the Egyptian Ashʿarite theologian Taqī al-Dīn al-Subkī (d. 756/1355), who reasserted the consensus

[29] For a sample, see Watt, *Islamic creeds*, 54 (Ṭaḥāwī), 66 (Fiqh akbar II), 82 (Nasafī), 88 (Ījī).

[30] Ibn Ḥazm, *Marātib al-ijmāʿ*, 267–8.

[31] Ibn Qayyim al-Jawziyya, *Ḥādī*, 259.

[32] Ibid., 266–80. Cf. Hoover, "Islamic universalism," 188–91; Abrahamov, "The creation and duration," 96–8.

[33] See, e.g., Subkī, *Iʿtibār*; Ṣanʿanī, *Rafʿ al-astār*. Muḥammad Nāṣir al-Dīn al-Albānī, who is also the editor of al-Ṣanʿānī's eighteenth-century work, held that Ibn Taymiyya wrote the *Fanāʾ al-nār* before he had fully mastered the religious sciences, while still holding a favourable view of Ibn al-ʿArabī. See Khalil, *Islam and the fate of others*, 87.

view affirmed by Ibn Ḥazm, and insisted that punishment is as much a part of God as His mercy.[34] Al-Subkī's critique, written in 749/1348, effectively sunk Ibn Taymiyya's and Ibn Qayyim al-Jawziyya's project. As others have noted, in his last work Ibn Qayyim al-Jawziyya, possibly under the influence of al-Subkī, reneged from the view he held earlier, briefly noting that unbelievers will suffer eternal punishment in hell.[35] In spite of this apparent retraction, in later times there were some attempts, such as that by the Yemeni traditionalist Ibn al-Wazīr (d. 840/1436), to declare *both* doctrines compatible with Islamic orthodoxy. This agnostic viewpoint, however, left important questions unanswered, for example, whether punishment in hell serves reform or retribution.[36]

Salvation in Sunni Theology

Scholars writing about the history of Islamic eschatology have often asserted that Sunni Islam offers its adherents a supreme degree of salvation certainty.[37] In this context, it is relevant to note that exegetes of the Qur'ānic Adam story generally downplay Adam's transgression and instead underscore his sinlessness (*ʿiṣma*) as prophet; the notion that he and Eve bequeathed an essential human deficiency to their descendants is largely alien to the tradition.[38] Adam's and Eve's expulsion from paradise, accordingly, was not seen in terms of a punishment. As Ibn Qayyim al-Jawziyya asserts at the beginning of his treatise on theodicy, *The Key to Happiness* (*Miftāḥ al-saʿāda*), their settling on earth was the result of divine wisdom (*ḥikma*). Had Adam and Eve not experienced the hardships of life on earth, they would not have been able fully to appreciate the glory of paradise, their natural destination; had they not fathered offspring on earth, there would have been no prophets and saints through whom God could have given expression to His love for His creation; had Adam's and Eve's progeny not populated the earth, God could not have manifested the full range of His attributes (his "beautiful names," *al-asmāʾ al-ḥusnā*), His forgiveness and kindness, but also His might and awe-inspiring power; and so forth.[39]

[34] Subkī, *Iʿtibār*, 196–8 and passim. Cf. Khalil, *Islam and the fate of others*, 89–92; idem, "Is hell truly everlasting?"

[35] See Hoover, "Withholding judgment." Cf. Ibn Qayyim al-Jawziyya, *Zād al-maʿād*, I, 68.

[36] Ibn al-Wazīr, *ʿAwāṣim*, VI, 357–63, quoted in Hoover, "Withholding judgment."

[37] Goldziher speaks of the "pure optimism" of "Islamic orthodoxy" in this regard, while van Ess calls this the "guiding principle of later Sunni theology." See Goldziher, *Richtungen*, 160; van Ess, *Flowering*, 42. Smith and Haddad choose to go even further, stating that "popular belief chose to see that all but the most sinful will be saved." See Smith and Haddad, *The Islamic understanding*, 81.

[38] See Kister, "Ādam," 147–54; Schöck, *Adam*, 92–4, 123–5.

[39] Ibn Qayyim al-Jawziyya, *Miftāḥ*, 5–7 and passim. For similar arguments in the thought of the Sufi Aḥmad Samʿānī (d. 534/1140), see Chittick, "The myth of Adam's Fall."

Further to this essentially positive view of human nature, the Sunni certainty of salvation is supposed to result from the belief that faith by and large ensures paradise, a salvific optimism enhanced by the idea that repentance and good actions wipe out sins; that the punishment of Muslim sinners will only be temporary; and that, importantly, they will benefit from the Prophet's intercession (*shafāʿa*) on their behalf. Each of the key terms in this summary of Sunni soteriology, however, has its own history of contestation in Islamic theology. The following remarks serve to sketch the contours of these controversies, and thereby to reassess the degree of salvation certainty that can plausibly be attributed to Sunni theology.

If it ever existed at all, unconditional *certitudo salutis* was characteristic only of the community of believers (*muʾminūn*) guided by the prophet Muḥammad and his immediate successors, the first caliphs.[40] Those who fell on the battlefield during the charismatic early age of Islam were assured a place in paradise by virtue of the Qurʾānic promise that those who are killed "in God's way" are "not dead but alive with their Lord and provided for" (3:169). This promise was soon supplemented by the statement, attributed to the Prophet, that "all those who say with a pure heart 'There is no god but God' enter paradise without being touched by hell-fire."[41] However, in the second half of the first century of Islam, the enthusiastic conviction that all believing Muslims were the elect "people of paradise" (*ahl al-janna*) was called into question by two events. On the one hand, the experience of two disastrous civil wars (35–40/656–661 and 64–73/683–92) undermined the view that all Muslims were equally deserving of a joyful afterlife. On the other, a theological reaction set in, spearheaded by ascetically minded non-Arab clients (*mawālī*) of the conquerors, particularly in the Iraqi city of Basra, the home of the pious renunciant Ḥasan al-Baṣrī (d. 110/728). Rather than the feeling of communal electedness, Ḥasan emphasised individual awareness of sins. Condemning the arrogance of those who took paradise for granted, he claimed that the Prophet had taught that "only those who say 'I'll be in hell' are believers" while "those who say 'I'll be in paradise' go to hell."[42]

With this, the so-called verses of threat (*āyāt al-waʿīd*) of the Qurʾān moved into focus, verses that predicted punishment in hell not only for the unbelievers (as in, e.g., Q 9:68), but also addressed all kinds of sinners, regardless of belief. For example, Q 4:10 states that "those who consume the property of orphans wrongfully will roast in a blaze." Muʿtazilite theologians stressed that such verses had to be understood in the general (*ʿāmm*) sense and must not be relativised by attributing a particular

[40] Here I follow the outlines of the development sketched by van Ess, *Fehltritt*, 97–108, 172–6; *TG*, I, 20–22, II, 4, 45, 87 (on Baṣra and al-Ḥasan al-Baṣrī).

[41] Ibn Ḥanbal, *Musnad*, V, 236.

[42] Ṭabarī, *Tahdhīb*, 681 (#1025), quoted in van Ess, *Fehltritt*, 105. Cf. *TG*, I, 20.

(*khāṣṣ*) meaning to them, for instance, by making them applicable only to non-Muslims. In fact, the affirmation of both the "divine promise" (*al-waʿd*) *and* the "divine threat" (*al-waʿīd*) became one of the five key tenets (*uṣūl*) of the Muʿtazilite school.[43] The Muʿtazilites further reasoned that punishment for grave sins is perpetual,[44] and that grave sinners should not be considered as believers. However, neither should grave sinners be declared unbelievers; rather, they are "transgressors" (*fussāq*, sg. *fāsiq*) against God, a position that came to be described as "the status between the two statuses (*al-manzila bayna l-manzilatayn*)," another of the five *uṣūl* of the Muʿtazilites.[45]

It is important to stress here that theologians usually argued that punishment in hell would be meted out only as a recompense for grave sins (*kabāʾir*, sg. *kabīra*), to the exclusion of minor sins (*ṣaghāʾir*, sg. *ṣaghīra*). In the Qurʾān (4:31), they pointed out, it is stated that "if you avoid the grave sins that are forbidden to you, We will acquit you of your evil deeds, and admit you by the gate of honour [into paradise]." Peccadillos, it was inferred, would be forgiven. But just how one was to conceive of grave sins, and how many such grave sins there were, never ceased to be a matter of disagreement.[46] Some Muʿtazilites rejected the possibility of the distinction between minor and grave sins outright.[47] Among the other theological schools, various definitions were traded, but these remained vague. Ibn ʿAbbās was reported to have taught, rather tautologically, that a grave sin is "every sin for which God has decreed hell-fire, [His] displeasure, [His] curse, or punishment [on earth],"[48] a formula that remained popular.[49] One consequence of this was that the more hadiths about punishment in hell one was prepared to accept, the longer one's list of grave sins became. As we have seen in preceding chapters, over the centuries the hadith literature on the topic grew to considerable proportions.

Quantitative definitions of grave sins reflect this dynamics. While al-Ṭabarī, in the fourth/tenth century, collects the opinions of those who counted three, four, seven, or nine sins,[50] he also relates the opinion, again of Ibn ʿAbbās, that the grave sins are closer to seven hundred than to seven.[51] Two generations

[43] *EI2*, s.v. al-Waʿd wa ʿl-waʿīd, XI, 6b-7a (U. Rudolph).

[44] See the creed of al-Zamaksharī (d. 538/1144) in Schmitke, *Muʿtazilite creed*, 76. See also Pazdawī, *Uṣūl*, 135. Cf. Gardet, *Dieu*, 303; Vasalou, *Moral agents*, 121–32.

[45] Pazdawī, *Uṣūl*, 135. For Muʿtazilite and Zaydi references, see Kalisch, "Anmerkungen zu Jenseitsvorstellungen," 87–104, esp. at 92.

[46] Stehly, "Un problème," 174. Cf. *EQ*, s.v. Sin, Major and Minor, V, 19a-28a (M.Q. Zaman).

[47] See Schmidtke, *Theology*, 228n25, quoting ʿAbd al-Jabbār, *Mughnī*, XIV, 393.

[48] Ṭabarī, *Jāmiʿ al-bayān*, V, 52.

[49] For Ibn Ḥanbal, see Laoust, *La profession de foi*, 100n2. See also Ibn Ḥazm, *Risālat al-talkhīṣ*, 90; Ghazālī, *Iḥyāʾ*, IV, 24; Ibn al-Jawzī, *Zād al-masīr*, II, 66; Dhahabī, *Kabāʾir*, 8.

[50] Ṭabarī, *Jāmiʿ al-bayān*, V, 48–52.

[51] Ibid., V, 52.

later, Abū Ṭālib al-Makkī (d. 386/996) lists seventeen grave sins.[52] Ibn Ḥazm (d. 456/1064) breaks off an incomplete list at thirty-nine.[53] In later centuries, al-Dhahabī (d. 748/1348), in what remains a standard work on the topic, enumerates seventy-five,[54] and Ibn Ḥajar al-Haythamī (d. 974/1567) ups the ante to 467.[55] This trend is paralleled, and indeed counteracted, by a proliferation of ways to expiate grave sins. After all, God was supposed to have stated, in a divine saying, that "for every [sinful] act, there is an expiatory act (*kaffāra*, pl. *kaffārāt*)."[56] Alongside the increase in grave sins, a casuistry of the *kaffārāt* developed that significantly softened the damnatory impact of grave sins.[57] Some traditions that circulated to this effect express a kind of *carte blanche* mentality. For example, in a tradition extolling the expiatory efficacy of performing the hajj, one reads that "whoever circumambulates this House [the Kaaba] seven times, prays two prostration cycles behind Abraham's Station and drinks from the water of Zamzam, his sins will be forgiven, however numerous they may be."[58] According to another hadith, forty grave sins could be expiated by carrying the bier in a funeral procession.[59]

Such extravagant promises, however, were met with regular disapproval. Late Medieval critics thought the hadith about carrying the funeral bier to be forged (*mawḍūʿ*). Ibn Ḥajar al-Haythamī denied that the hajj could expiate grave sins, a view that "plunged people into despair" according to an observer writing a generation later.[60] In fact, theologians tended to argue that the *kaffārāt*, or in fact all good deeds (*ḥasanāt*), could only atone for minor sins, but not grave sins.[61]

[52] Makkī, *Qūt al-qulūb*, tr. Gramlich, III, 215–24. Al-Makkī is followed in this by al-Ghazālī, *Iḥyāʾ*, IV, 25–6.

[53] Ibn Ḥazm, *Risālat al-talkhīṣ*, 89–90.

[54] Dhahabī, *Kabāʾir*.

[55] Ibn Ḥajar al-Haythamī, *Zawājir*.

[56] Bukhārī, *Ṣaḥīḥ, k. al-tawḥīd* 50 (*b. dhikr al-nabī [eulogy] wa-riwāyatihi ʿan rabbih*), IV, 460; Ibn Ḥanbal, *Musnad*, II, 457, 467, 504: *li-kulli ʿamal kaffāra.*

[57] See, e.g., the extended discussion of the *kaffāra* for *ẓihār* in Māwardī, *Ḥāwī*, XXIII, 353–450. Al-Māwardī discusses, *inter alia*, the kind of slave that one may or may not manumit, the appropriate times of the year for expiatory fasting, and the kind of food that one may or may not distribute when choosing to feed sixty of the poor. He devotes similarly extended discussions to the *kaffāra* for homicide (ibid., XVI, 308–17) and the *kaffāra* for false oaths (ibid., XIX, 353–401).

[58] See Katz, "Ḥajj," 129, quoting Sakhāwī, *Maqāṣid*, 417. Also Gardet notes that "according to certain Muslim traditions," grave sins may be wiped out by actions such as the pilgrimage to Mecca, or participation in jihad. See Gardet, *Dieu*, 310.

[59] Suyūṭī, *Laʾālī*, II, 405.

[60] For Ibn Ḥajar's view, see Ibn ʿĀbidīn, *Ḥāshiya*, II, 623. For ʿAlī al-Qārī's (d. 1014/1606) comment, see Ḥanafī, *Irshād*, 322. Both sources are quoted in Katz, "The ḥajj," 106.

[61] See Pazdawī, *Uṣūl*, 147. This was the view of some Muʿtazilites, including Jaʿfar b. Mubashshir (d. 234/849) and al-Zamakhsharī. See *TG*, IV, 64; Ibrahim, "The concept of iḥbāṭ," 117–21. Cf. Mensia, "L'acte expiatoire," 126, 133, 139.

In the theologians' view, the only efficient mechanism to make amends for grave sins was the act of "turning back" (*tawba*), that is, repentance in the *forum internum* of the individual's consciousness. Believers may have felt encouraged by the fact that, as they read in the Qur'ān (4:48), "God does not forgive others being associated with Him; but He forgives anything short of that to those whom He wishes." From this, it was plausible to infer that *all* sins could be forgiven, to the exception of polytheism (*shirk*).[62] Repentance remained, in principle, the most promising strategy to earn such forgiveness.[63] Opinions only differed with regard to the question whether God *had* to forgive grave sinners after their repentance (this was the position of the Muʿtazilites)[64] or whether it remained theoretically possible for Him not to do so (the position of the Ashʿarites and Māturīdites).[65]

Muslim theologians also acknowledged, however, that true repentance is not achieved easily.[66] What counts, they maintained, is the context in which repentance occurs. While in some hadiths, a lenient position is taken, and some authors had a rather permissive view of the issue,[67] most thought repentance (and by the same token, conversion to Islam) right before death to be invalid, as in the case of Pharaoh who, chasing the Israelites across the Red Sea, declared his belief in God only "when the drowning overtook him" (Q 10:90; cf. 4:18).[68] In addition, repentance, it was asserted, has to be sincere (*naṣūḥ*, cf. Q 66:8) and must include the clear determination not to lapse, qualities that the scrupulously pious would never claim lightheartedly.[69] According to some, repentance also differed according to the kind of sin committed: the graver the sin, the more demanding the requirements for atonement.[70] Finally, Muslim theologians emphasised that repentance is a

[62] Some held that also (intentional) murder was unforgivable, a view that found confirmation in the Qur'ān (4:93) and in the hadith that "God may forgive all sins, except when someone dies as an unbeliever or kills a believer intentionally." See Abū Dāwūd, *Sunan, k. al-fitan* 6 (*b. fī taʿẓīm qatl al-muʾmin*), II, 505; Ibn Ḥanbal, *Musnad*, I, 240. Cf. *TG*, II, 112–3.

[63] On cases of public repentance, particularly that of government officials, in the high medieval period, see Pomerantz, "Muʿtazilī theory in practice."

[64] ʿAbd al-Jabbār, *Mughnī*, XIV, 337–44.

[65] Pazdawī, *Uṣūl al-dīn*, 235. Cf. Gardet, *Dieu*, 308.

[66] For an overview, though largely focusing on Sufi and Shiʿi conceptions, see Ayoub, "Repentance." Cf. *TG*, IV, 579–90. On the Muʿtazilī doctrine of repentance, see also Pomerantz, "Muʿtazilī theory in practice," 476–81.

[67] See Tirmidhī, *Jāmiʿ*, *k. al-daʿawāt* 98, V, 547; Ibn Ḥanbal, *Musnad*, II, 132 and passim: "God accepts repentance as long as the believer does not yet gurgle [in his terminal delirium] (*mā-lam yugharghir*)." Abū Ṭālib al-Makkī thought that repentance was possible until the moment when the soul, departing from the body, reaches one's throat and one starts to see the angels. See Makkī, *Qūt*, tr. Gramlich, III, 222. Ibn al-ʿArabī argued that Pharao was saved by his repentance and acceptance of Islam. See Ibn al-ʿArabī, *Fuṣūṣ al-ḥikam*, 201. Al-Qārī al-Harawī condemned this view. See Qārī, *Farr al-ʿawn*, quoted in *TG*, IV, 581.

[68] Cf. Ormsby, "The faith of Pharao."

[69] For a conspicuous example, see Muḥāsibī, *Aḥkām al-tawba*.

[70] Ibn Ḥazm, *Risālat al-takhlīṣ*, 133. Cf. Lange, "Ibn Ḥazm on sins and salvation," 437–41.

mutual relationship between the individual and God:[71] God must agree to grant (*manaḥa*) it, and He is free not to do so (again, according to all but the Muʿtazilites).[72]

What, then, of unrepentant grave sinners? Here we enter into the heart of Islamic soteriology. As we saw, the Muʿtazilites held that unrepentant Muslim sinners would be punished with perpetual hellfire, even though they tended to grant that the punishment of these "transgressors" would be lighter than that of the unbelievers.[73] This struck most theologians of the early centuries as too radical.[74] Around the fourth/tenth century, a compromise emerged and found widespread acceptance among non-Muʿtazilī theologians according to which "God is free to either punish whomever He likes from among the believing grave sinners with hell-fire and then let them enter paradise, or to pardon them and let them enter paradise [immediately], without punishing them."[75] This middle position between *certitudo salutis* and the doctrine of perpetual punishment of grave sinners is usually connected to the theological school of the Murjiʾa. From here, the two dominant Sunni theological schools of the later centuries, the Ashʿarites and the Māturīdites, took their cue. It should be stressed that the Murjiʾite view of the Muslim grave sinner only refuses to countenance *perpetual* punishment for Muslim believers; below this threshold, however, it leaves all options open for the "divine threat" to become manifest. Therefore, as has been noted, to describe the Murjiʾa (or the theological schools that followed their lead) "as raising excessive hope for divine forgiveness ... is basically mistaken,"[76] despite the fact that later Sunni authors retrospectively accused the Murjiʾa of laxity in the question.[77]

The emphasis in theological discussion now shifted to the question of how violent, how long, and how likely temporary punishment of the Muslim grave sinner was. The more rigorous position in this debate was that of the Māturīdites, heirs of the Muʿtazilites in this regard.[78] An important step in this direction was taken by the Central Asian theologian, Abū l-Muʿīn al-Nasafī (d. 508/1114), a contemporary of al-Ghazālī, who distinguished between a corrupt (*khabīth*) and a correct form of Murjiʾism. The former, he averred, was to claim that "no Muslim is ever punished for a grave sin,

[71] This is a Qurʾānic idea. See *EQ*, s.v. Repentance and penance, IV, 426b-427a (U. Rubin).

[72] See *TG*, IV, 579–80.

[73] See Pazdawī, *Uṣūl*, 135.

[74] See *TG*, IV, 547; Gardet, *Dieu*, 303.

[75] Ibn Ḥazm, *Fiṣal*, IV, 45. See the translation in *TG*, V, 47. On the emergence of the doctrine of temporary punishment in hell (of a group of people called *jahannamiyyūn*), the roots of which the author traces back to the early second/eighth century, see Hamza, "To hell and back." See also *ECḤ*, 665–6, for the oldest traces of the *jahannamiyyūn* in the hadith literature.

[76] *EI2*, s.v. Murdji'a, VII, 607a (W. Madelung).

[77] See Ibn al-Jawzī, *Talbīs*, 125; Jurjānī, *Sharḥ al-mawāqif*, VIII, 340.

[78] See Lange, "Sins, expiation," 160–7.

and that, in the same way in which a good deed is to no avail if there is no faith, an evil deed does not do any harm when there is faith."[79] The correct way of approaching the question, as another Māturīdite theologian put it a generation later, was to stress that "the punishment for some sinful believers is in accordance with God's knowledge and will."[80] Later Māturīdite authors moved from affirming the logical possibility that God will punish Muslim grave sinners, towards stating the logical impossibility that He will not. There simply can be no "reneging on the divine threat" (*khulf al-waʿīd*), they reasoned. This, as the Ottoman theologian ʿAbd al-Raḥmān b. ʿAlī Shaykhzādeh (d. 944/1537) explained, "would be a change (*tabdīl*) of [God's] word," while He has stated clearly that "what I [once] said, will not be changed" (Q 50:29). God does not lie when He pronounces a threat.[81] The Meccan Māturīdī scholar al-Qārī al-Harawī (d. 1014/1605), who dedicated an epistle to the question of *khulf al-waʿīd*, likewise affirmed the general necessity for God to punish Muslim grave sinners, while also stressing that He is not obliged to punish them in each case, thus drawing a line between himself and the Muʿtazilites, with whom he agreed in other respects (asserting, e.g., the *ʿāmm* character of the verses of threat).[82]

Most scholarly accounts of the history of Islamic theology tend to pass over the doctrinal differences between Ashʿarite and Māturīdite theologians and regard them as inconsequential.[83] Such judgements seem influenced by the attempts of a sizeable group of Muslim scholars, such as the Egyptian Tāj al-Dīn al-Subkī (d. 771/1370) and the Ottoman scholar, Abū ʿUdhba (fl. 1125/1713), to harmonise Ashʿarite and Māturīdite positions.[84] However, in particular from the sixth/twelfth century onwards, Māturīdism was characterised by a "distinctly rationalist flavor" that was aimed, *inter alia*, against Ashʿarite salvific optimism.[85] With regard to the question of the punishment of the grave sinner, there is a notable

[79] Nasafī, *Tabṣirat al-adilla*, II, 766.

[80] See Watt, *Islamic creeds*, 82 (Abu Ḥafṣ al-Nasafī).

[81] Shaykhzādeh, *Naẓm*, 212.

[82] Qārī, *Qawl*, 46–7. I have not been able to see the recent study of *khulf al-waʿīd* by Dreher, *Maṭāliʿ al-nūr*.

[83] Goldziher argued that it was "not worth going into the petty differences of these two closely related doctrines." See Goldziher, *Vorlesungen*, 117. Cf. the summary of this question in Rudolph, *Māturīdī*, 13.

[84] Ibid., 8–10. On the processes of harmonisation between Ashʿarite and Māturīdite positions by Ottoman scholars in the wake of al-Subkī, see Badeen, *Sunnitische Theologie*.

[85] Madelung, "Spread of Māturīdism," 134–5. Al-Ashʿarī espouses a basic voluntarism, writing that Muslims ought to believe that "if God wills, He punishes them [the grave sinners], and if He wills, He forgives them." See Ashʿarī, Ibāna, 9–13 (tr. Watt, *Islamic creeds*, 41–7, at 44). Cf. the similar creed in idem, *Maqālāt*, 290–7; Jurjānī, *Sharḥ al-Mawāqif*, VIII, 340. In a recent study of al-Ghazālī's soteriology, Pisani stresses that mercy (*raḥma*) precedes wrath in al-Ghazālī's thought, and that for al-Ghazālī there is salvation for all those who have hope including, notably, the parents of the Prophet. See Pisani, "Hors de l'Islam point de salut?" For a Late Medieval example of salvific optimism, see Abū ʿUdhba, *Rawḍa*, 115: "God is

divergence between the two schools.[86] The Māturīdites' scepticism with regard to the human capacity to achieve salvation was never as extreme as that of the Muʿtazilites, but at least some of the latters' "pessimistic view of the hereafter"[87] survived in their theology and continued to play a role in Late Medieval Sunni eschatological thought, notwithstanding the attempts to silence the issue.[88]

One final aspect of Sunni soteriology that deserves mention, albeit briefly, is the notion of intercession (*shafāʿa*), by which God may be persuaded to let people enter paradise without further reckoning. The Qurʾān, as we saw in Chapter 1, does not allocate the power of intercession to Muḥammad in unequivocal terms; in fact, on the whole, it does not seem to favour the idea.[89] In the hadith, by contrast, this power is explicitly granted. In a variant of the hadith quoted in the preceding text, Muḥammad is made to say that "my intercession is for all those who testify with a pure heart that there is no god but God."[90] More specifically, in apparent reaction against those who predicted punishment for Muslim grave sinners, another hadith states that "my intercession is for the grave sinners from among my community."[91] The Muʿtazilites refused to accept these hadiths.[92] Faithful to their stress on individual accountability, they denied that the Prophet could influence God's judgement of the grave sinners; at best, they suggested, he might see to it that the believers who are already in paradise will be moved up a rank.[93]

However, the majority of Sunni theologians came to agree that the Prophet is in fact able to intercede on behalf of the grave sinners. Various creeds from the third/ninth century onwards include this belief among the core tenets of Islam.[94] Gradually, the scope of those with the power to practice *shafāʿa* widened. Later creeds simply speak of the possibility of the "intercession of

generous for the sake of the servants, because He does that which is good, by abandoning punishment (*jāda fī ḥaqq al-ʿibād bi-l-iḥsān … bi-tark al-ʿiqāb*)."

86 See Gardet, *Dieu*, 304.

87 See Goldziher, *Richtungen*, 155–69.

88 Neither al-Subkī's nor Abū ʿUdhba's treatise dedicated to the differences (*ikhtilāfāt*) between the Ashʿarites and the Māturīdites gives much attention to the issue of *khulf al-waʿīd*, preferring instead to emphasise the "orthodoxy" of both groups.

89 Wensinck, *Muslim creed*, 180–1; *EQ*, s.v. Intercession, II, 551a-555b (V. Hoffman). Also leaning in this direction is Rahman, *Major themes*, 31–2.

90 Ibn Ḥanbal, *Musnad*, II, 307, 518.

91 Tirmidhī, *Jāmiʿ*, *k. al-qiyāma* 11, IV, 625; Ibn Māja, *Sunan*, *k. al-zuhd* 37 (*b. dhikr al-shafāʿa*), III, 541; Ibn Ḥanbal, *Musnad*, II, 70, 82; cf. *CTM*, s.v. sh-f-ʿ, III, 151b. See also Rāzī, *Shafāʿa*, 51. Cf. Huitema, *Voorspraak*, 35–6.

92 They argued, e.g., that the hadith was a single-strand tradition (*khabar al-wāḥid*). See Rāzī, *Shafāʿa*, 51, 54–5.

93 See the reports in Ashʿarī, *Maqālāt*, 474:3–5; Rāzī, *Shafāʿa*, 39; Jurjānī, *Sharḥ al-Mawāqif*, VIII, 341. Cf. Huitema, *Voorspraak*, 41–2, 86–8; Hamza, "To hell and back," 159–61; *EI2*, s.v. Shafāʿa. 1. In official Islam, IX, 178b (A. J. Wensinck and D. Gimaret).

94 See Watt, *Islamic creeds*, 31 (§ 11, Ibn Ḥanbal), 44 (§ 26, al-Ashʿarī), 60 (§ 25, Wāṣiyat Abī Ḥanīfa), 71 (§ 20, Ibn Abī Zayd al-Qayrawānī [d. 386/996]), 88 (§ 19, al-Ījī [d. 756/1355]).

intercessors,"[95] or attribute intercession to prophets and "the élite" (*al-khāṣṣ*) in general.[96] Al-Ghazālī, writing towards the end of the fifth/eleventh century, extends *shafāʿa* to "the prophets, then the scholars, then the martyrs, then the other believers, each according to his dignity and his rank in the sight of God."[97] Such a broad conceptualisation opened the door to the notion, announced already by al-Ashʿarī (d. 324/935–6), that prayers of any believer for the deceased are efficacious in improving the dead's chances for salvation.[98] Here as elsewhere, however, the development was not linear. In particular, Ibn Taymiyya (d. 728/1328), and following him, the Wahhābīs, campaigned relentlessly against the practice of praying at the graves of saints (*awliyāʾ*) for their intercession.[99] Ibn Taymiyya granted that people appealed for the Prophet's intercession while he was alive; at Resurrection, they may do so again. However, in the intervening period, visiting the Prophet's grave in Medina and seeking his intercession is against Islam.[100]

The Reality of the Afterlife

Earlier in this chapter, in the discussion of the cosmological coordinates of the Muslim otherworld, we have observed the efforts of certain theologians to stress the distance, both spatial and temporal, that separates this world from paradise and hell. Similar concerns also applied to the modality, or rather, the reality, of otherworldly existence. Such concerns were motivated by a particular transcendentalist understanding of the nature of God. "There is nothing like Him," states the Qurʾān (42:11), a verse that became the shibboleth of those, identified by later tradition as the "emptiers" (*muʿaṭṭila*), who insisted that God cannot be understood in terms derived from the observation of this-worldly phenomena. One of the earliest representatives of this view, the Iranian Jahm b. Ṣafwān, is said to have advocated that God has no boundary (*ḥadd*), limit (*ghāya*), or end (*nihāya*), let alone a body or body parts like human beings.[101]

Anthropomorphic descriptions of God in the Qurʾān, later followers of this line of thought taught, ought to be interpreted figuratively. For example, when the Qurʾān mentions God's hand, this should be understood as a metaphor for God's generosity in distributing His bounties to the created world. Likewise,

[95] See ibid., 36 (§ 7, later Ḥanbalite creed)

[96] See ibid., 66 (§ 20, Fiqh akbar II), 82 (§ 19, Abū Ḥafṣ ʿUmar al-Nasafī, d. 537/1142): "the messengers and the élite (*khāṣṣ*)."

[97] Ghazālī, *Iḥyāʾ*, I, 12 (tr. Watt, *Islamic creeds*, 78 [§ 24]). Cf. ibid., V, 153 (tr. Winter, 215).

[98] Gardet, *Dieu*, 313n11. Cf. Goldziher, *Richtungen*, 170–1.

[99] Laoust, *Essai*, 185, 621.

[100] Ibn Taymiyya, *Qāʾida*, 75–6. I owe this reference to Arjan Post.

[101] Frank, "The neoplatonism of Jahm ibn Ṣafwān," 400, 414. See also the translation of Ibn Ḥanbal's *al-Radd ʿalā l-zanādiqa wa-l-Jahmiyya* in *TG*, V, 222–3. On Jahm in general, cf. *TG*, II, 493–507.

the Qur'ānic notion that God sits on a throne carried by angels (cf. 32:4, 69:17) was interpreted by Jahm's acolytes, the Jahmiyya, as indicating God's encompassing power over the universe.[102] It seems safe to project that, if the Throne's corporeality could be denied, denying the corporeality of other eschatological phenomena, including the corporal pleasures of paradise and torments in hell, must have seemed a natural next step. From here, one might easily have inferred that bodies were not needed in the afterlife, and that resurrection was, in consequence, a purely spiritual affair.

However, in the formative period of Muslim theology, the otherworld was never fully spiritualised. Not even the Mu'tazilites, who shared with the Jahmiyya the insistence on God's transcendent otherness, and therefore the inclination towards metaphorical interpretation of the scriptural data, went the full distance.[103] It is true that one hears on occasion about the aversion or even the sarcasm with which they reacted to the sensual picture of paradise painted in Qur'ānic exegesis and in the hadiths. Al-Naẓẓām, for example, expressed a low opinion of those who took the word *wayl* in Q 83:1 (*waylun li-l-muṭaffifīn*, "Woe to the stinters!") to refer to a valley in hell, "and then start to describe this valley."[104] Hishām al-Fuwaṭī (d. *ca.* 218/833) denied that virgins are deflowered in paradise.[105] "How strange!," a Mu'tazilite of the late third/ninth century is reported to have exclaimed, marvelling at the idea that the inhabitants of paradise continuously eat, drink, and fornicate. "Is this not a very boring and suffocating state," he maliciously inquired, "and will they not be annoyed to the point of throwing up?"[106] One should also note that certain Mu'tazilites refused to accept the existence of eschatological particulars such as the Bridge, the Pool in front of the entry to paradise, and the Scales on which deeds are weighed on the Day of Judgement.[107] Like the Jahmiyya, the Mu'tazilites also denied that the inhabitants of paradise see God "by a vision of the eyes" (*bi-l-abṣār*).[108]

[102] Dārimī, *Radd*, 16, quoted in Nagel, *Geschichte*, 104.

[103] Cf. *EI2*, s.v. Djanna, II, 449a-b (L. Gardet).

[104] Jaḥīẓ, *Ḥayawān*, I, 168. Cf. Goldziher, *Richtungen*, 111–2.

[105] Baghdādī, *Farq*, 150. See the translation in *TG*, VI, 233 (text #37).

[106] The quote occurs in the thirty-fifth *muqābasa* ("On the strange situation of the people of paradise, and how it is that they do not get bored of the pleasure, the food, &c.") of the *K. al-Muqābasāt* by Abū Ḥayyān al-Tawḥīdī (d. 414/1023), and is attributed to "the theologian" (*al-mutakallim*) Abū Isḥāq al-Naṣībī, a servant (*ghulām*) of the Mu'tazilī al-Ju'al (d. 299/911–2). See Tawḥīdī, *Muqābasāt*, fol. 38b, quoted in Goldziher, "Geschichte," 3n2. Cf. the discussion of this passage in Rosenthal, "Reflections on love," 249.

[107] Ḍirār b. 'Amr was the last Mu'tazilite who defended such positions "out of principle." See *TG*, IV, 560–1. A general swipe at the deniers of the corporeality of the Balance is found in Ash'arī, *Maqālāt*, 472.

[108] The question of the vision of God is comprehensively treated in 'Abd al-Jabbār, *Mughnī*, IV, 33–240. Some Mu'tazilites allowed a vision of God "with the heart" (*bi-l-qalb*), but most affirmed with the Jahmiyya that God cannot be seen, only mentally understood. See *TG*, IV, 413–4. Cf. Gardet, *Dieu*, 338–49; Isutzu, *Concept of belief*.

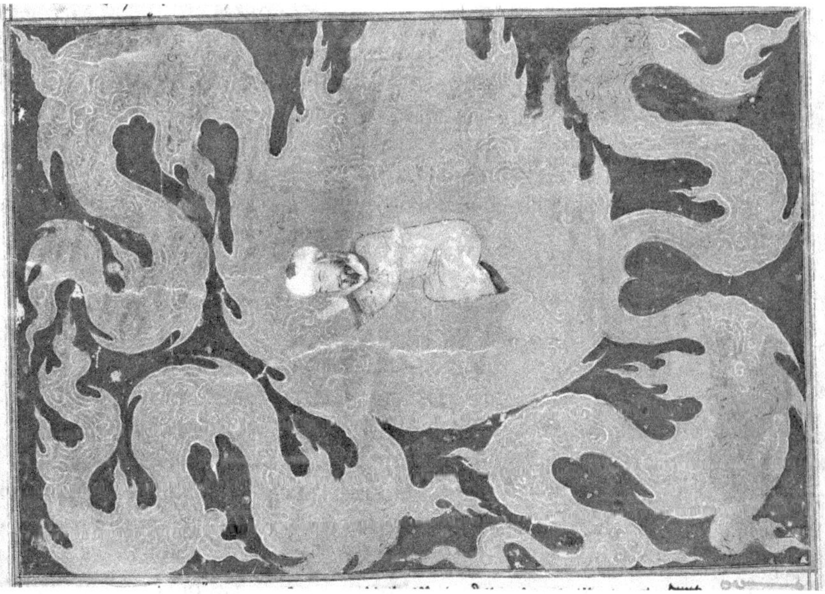

FIGURE 10. Muḥammad, during his heavenly journey, prostrates before God. From the Uighur *Miʿrājnāma* (*Book of Ascension*). Herat/Afghanistan, ninth/fifteenth century. MS Bibliothèque nationale de France Supplément Turc 190, fol. 36v.

Unsurprisingly, although generally uninterested in hadith, they quoted the unfathomability tradition. Al-Zamakhsharī (d. 538/1144), in his famous Muʿtazilite Qurʾān commentary, cites an expanded, tellingly softened version: "I have prepared for my believing servants things no eye has seen nor any ear has heard, in excess of what I have told them about (*balha mā aṭlaʿtuhum ʿalayhā*)."[109]

The example of al-Zamakhsharī demonstrates the kind of concessions the Muʿtazilites were ready to make. Generally speaking, they did not deny the corporeality of paradise and hell; some even affirmed the bodily existence of animals there (horses, gazelles, peacocks, and pheasants in paradise, snakes, scorpions, flies, and other vermin in hell).[110] In sum, it may be true

[109] Zamakhsharī, *Kashshāf*, III, 497 (ad 32:17). Cf. Bayḍāwī, *Anwār*, II, 235. This expanded version, an attempt to reconcile the unfathomability tradition with the traditionist imagery of paradise and hell, is already found in the *Muṣannaf* of Ibn Abī Shayba (X, 136), where, however, the addition *balha mā aṭlaʿakum* is cited as an explanation provided by the Prophet to the *ḥadīth qudsī*. At the beginning of the paradise chapter in Muslim's *Ṣaḥīḥ* the phrase is merged into the hadith as the very word of God. See Muslim, *Ṣaḥīḥ*, *k. al-janna* 3, IV, 2174. As such it also appears later in the Sufi Qurʾān commentaries of Ismail Haqqi Bursawi and al-Ālūsī, as well as the *Risālat al-ghufrān* of al-Maʿarrī. See Maʿarrī, *Risālat*, 224 (tr. 225).

[110] See Goldziher, *Richtungen*, 160; *TG*, II, 53, III, 87, IV, 32, 555.

that Muʿtazilite thinkers were less forthcoming than others in embracing the descriptions of the otherworld in the Qurʾān and hadith; but they generally conceded, as did for example Abū l-Hudhayl, that the corporeal existence of beings and things in the afterworld was a proposition that did not clash with the criteria of reason.[111] The absolute transcendence of God, not that of paradise and hell, was what occupied the theologians. Arguably, paradise and hell, "crammed with images" as they were, escaped the general trend towards transcendentalism.[112]

Nonetheless, the challenge of the Jahmiyya and the Muʿtazila was strong enough to propel the traditionalist majority to emphatically underscore that the resurrection of bodies,[113] the Bridge, the Pool, and indeed paradise and hell as a whole are real (*ḥaqq*), as the Sunni creeds from the third/ninth century onwards consistently put it.[114] Also the ocular vision of God was affirmed.[115] The view that the systematic theologians (*mutakallimūn*) settled on, however, was that all props on the otherworldly stage are corporeal in a way that, in the final analysis, eludes human understanding. "The question of God's sitting on the Throne is subtle," one reads in a creed, written probably in the fifth/eleventh century, "it is better not to engage in discussions regarding this subject."[116] The ultimate reality of the eschatological phenomena, like the question of God's body, remains fathomless and must, according to a famous Ashʿarī principle, simply be accepted *bi-lā kayf*, "without asking how."

To repeat, a thorough spiritualisation of paradise and hell did not occur in early Muslim theology. The otherworld sketched out by the Qurʾān and the hadith may have been too concrete to allow for this, in the same way that the Qurʾānic concept of the "soul" (*nafs*, pl. *anfus*) is not exactly spiritual, for in most instances *anfus* simply translates as "people." When the

[111] Jurjanī, *Sharḥ*, 350:1–6. Cf. Gardet, *Dieu*, 314–5.

[112] See now the summary of this development by van Ess, "Zum Geleit," from whom I borrow the phrase "crammed with images" ("mit Bildern vollgestellt").

[113] Discussions unfolded about the exact modality of resurrection, i.e., whether a "gathering of scattered parts" (*jamʿ al-ajzāʾ al-mutafarriqa*) would take place, or a return of a previously annihilated body (*iʿādat al-maʿdūm*). See, e.g., Juwaynī, *Irshād*, tr. Walker, *Guide*, 205; Āmidī, *Abkār*, IV, 267. Cf. *TG*, III, 255 and passim; Gardet, *Dieu*, 268–73.

[114] Ashʿarī, *Maqālāt*, 293. See also Watt, *Islamic creeds*, 44 (§ 17, al-Ashʿarī), 52 (§ 18, al-Ṭaḥāwī), 60 (§§ 20–2, Wāṣiyat Abī Ḥanīfa), 66 (§ 21, Fiqh akbar II), 71 (§23, al-Qayrawānī), 77–8 (§§ 17–21, al-Ghazālī), 82 (§ 17, al-Nasafī), 88 (§ 18, al-Ījī). The characteristic phrase that the Bridge, Pool, and so forth are real (*ḥaqq*) is not yet to be found in the creed of Aḥmad b. Ḥanbal, although the ocular vision of God in paradise is affirmed there. See ibid., 30–2. Numerous canonical hadith collections also state the paradise and hell are real (*al-janna ḥaqq wa-l-nār ḥaqq*). See *CTM*, s.v. j-n-n, I, 377a (Bukhārī, Abū Dāwūd, Nasāʾī, Ibn Māja, Mālik b. Anas).

[115] Watt, *Islamic creeds*, 65–6 (§ 17, Fiqh akbar II). Cf. Gilliot, "Vision de Dieu," 244–5; *ECḤ*, 161. Seeing God and seeing paradise, of course, are different things. In traditions affirming ocular vision in the afterlife, God is in paradise; in traditions denying ocular vision, He is beyond paradise, while paradise may still be seen.

[116] Wensinck, *Muslim creed*, 266 (§ 12, Fiqh akbar III).

Qur'ān refers to *nafs* as the "inner person," the word is used to designate a subtle but nonetheless physical part of the body.[117] This understanding was also dominant among Muslim theologians.[118] While Late Antique Christian authors, following in the footsteps of Origen, speculated about a purely spiritual or intellectual afterlife of the soul, the impact of such Hellenic ideas was less pronounced in Islam.[119]

This impact only came to be felt, and then only in certain corners, when Muslim peripatetic philosophy entered into its era of flourishing from the fourth/tenth century onwards.[120] A different and more radical challenge to the dominant discourse on the corporeality of the afterlife was now mounted by figures such as the celebrated Avicenna (Iran, d. 428/1037). A physician as well as a philosopher, Avicenna championed a Neoplatonic cosmology centred on the notion of the intellect (*ʿaql*, pl. *ʿuqūl*), the highest part of the human soul, which connects the individual with a hierarchy of heavenly intellects whose apex is God, from whom the First Intellect emanates. It is characteristic of Avicenna's program as a philosopher operating within the Islamic tradition that he clothes his ideas about the gradual perfection of the human intellect, which alone constitutes true felicity (*saʿāda*),[121] in terms of an ascension (*miʿrāj*) towards God. This allows him, notably in his *Book of the Ascension* (*Miʿrājnāma*), to allegorise the traditional account of the prophet Muḥammad's tour of the otherworld as the successful philosophical journey towards the highest forms of intellection.[122] Also Avicenna's rejection of metempsychosis, the transmigration of the soul to another body after death, can be interpreted as a part of his project to Islamise Neoplatonic philosophy, in which metempsychosis features prominently.[123]

Avicenna's thoughts on death and the afterlife are laid out in several of his works, most comprehensively in his *Epistle, Written on the Feast of Sacrifice, on the Return* (*al-Risāla l-aḍḥawiyya fī l-maʿād*). In the same way in which he denies that the Prophet's ascension was corporeal,[124] Avicenna denies that there is a bodily resurrection and afterlife. "True human happiness," he writes, following Neoplatonic ideas but also developing his own perspective,[125] "is contrary to the soul's existence in the body; bodily

[117] *EQ*, s.v. Soul, V, 80b-84b (Th. E. Homerin); Rahman, *Major themes*, 112; Picken, "Tazkiyat al-nafs," 106.

[118] Gardet, *Dieu*, 345.

[119] *TG*, IV, 555.

[120] Ibid.

[121] See Stroumsa, "True felicity," 56–7, 59–61.

[122] Ibn Sīna (= Avicenna), *Miʿrājnāma*, tr. Heath, *Allegory*, 111–43. Cf. Hughes, "Miʿrāj and the language of legitimation," 172–91; Nünlist, *Himmelfahrt*.

[123] See Adamson, "Correcting Plotinus," 70–1.

[124] Ibn Sīna, *Miʿrājnāma*, tr. Heath, *Allegory*, 125. Cf. Buckley, *The night journey*, 89–92.

[125] Cf. Plotinus, *Enneads*, 339–91 (chapter IV.7: "On the immortality of the soul"), at 385 and passim; *Uthūlūjiyā Arisṭāṭālis*, 54–5, 84, 91 and passim. On Avicenna's reception of

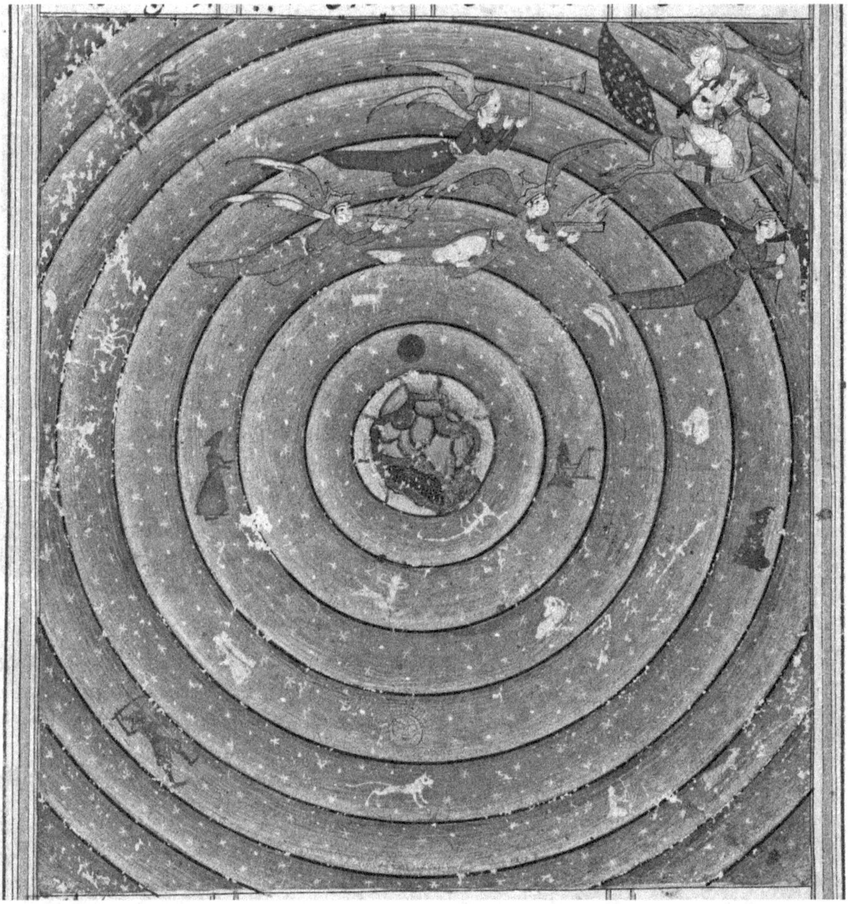

FIGURE 11. The Prophet's ascension. From Niẓāmī, *Makhzan al-asrār* (*The Treasury of Secrets*). Persia, 1076/[1665–6]. MS British Library Ad 6,613, fol. 3v.

pleasures are not true pleasures; it would be a punishment for the soul to return to dwell in the body [after death]."[126] Praise and blame, and therefore a happy or miserable afterlife, attach to the soul, not the body. According to the *Epistle on the Return*, it is not only that bodies are not needed in the afterlife: Avicenna squarely refuses to acknowledge that they exist at all.[127]

Neoplatonic psychology, see Adamson, "Correcting Plotinus," esp. 63–4, 74. On spiritual resurrection in Christian thought, especially Origen, and its Platonic forerunners, see Segal, *Life after death*, 572–4.

[126] Ibn Sīna, *Risāla*, 53. On the controversy over Avicenna's "mysticism," see Gutas, "Avicenna's Eastern ('Oriental') philosophy."

[127] For discussions of the various arguments used by Avicenna, see Jaffer, "Bodies, souls and resurrection," 164–71; Michot, *Destinée de l'homme*, 14–8.

Faced with the task of reconciling this view with the evidence in Islamic scripture speaking of bodies in paradise and hell, Avicenna posits another major modification of the traditional Islamic understanding of the afterlife. In his view, there are two different kinds of paradise and hell, one that is intellectual and one that is imagined.

According to Avicenna, there is, on the one hand, an otherworldly realm in which souls enter into conjunction (*ittiṣāl*) with the heavenly intellects and experience intellectual fulfilment and happiness. This type of otherworldly existence is reserved for those souls who have attained intellectual perfection during their life on earth.[128] Conversely, there are the souls of those who, during their earthly lives, have an understanding of humankind's desire for intellectual perfection but deliberately do not develop it. Having passed into the next world, such souls suffer an immense "pain of frustrated intellectual desire,"[129] because having lost their bodily senses, and thereby the capacity for cognition and learning, they can no longer achieve true (intellectual) happiness.[130]

On the other hand, there is the sizeable group of souls of people unaware of the sheer possibility of intellectual perfection. This is the group of the "simple-minded people" (*bulh*), the nonphilosophical masses, those who, during their earthly lives, do nothing to actualise their souls' potential because they do not know better.[131] It is for this particular group that the descriptions of the corporeal delights and torments of the otherworld, inculcated by means of the Qurʾān and the hadith, retain value. People in this group, Avicenna appears to say, carry mental representations of a corporeal afterlife with them into their postmortem existence, where their souls *imagine*, by strength of the imaginative faculty (*al-quwwa al-mutawahhima*), that bodily experiences are taking place. The souls of virtuous "simple-minded people" will envision and experience the pleasures of paradise; the souls of wicked people will have an imaginative experience of the torments of hell. They will not, however, attain absolute happiness or absolute misery.[132] The imagery of the divine "promise and threat" (*al-waʿd wa-l-waʿīd*) contained in the revealed scriptures thus continues to enjoy a function, albeit one limited to the imagination.[133]

[128] Ibn Sīna, *Risāla*, 120–1. Avicenna actually makes room for a subcategory of "perfect souls that lack moral perfection" (*nufūs kāmila ghayr munazzaha*), who also partake in the purely spiritual felicity, but have to undergo a period of purification before they attain it. Cf. Davidson, *Alfarabi*, 111–2.

[129] Ibid., 111.

[130] Ibn Sīna, *Risāla*, 121:2–4.

[131] Ibid., 121:5–13. I am simplifying Avicenna's argument here, as he foresees more nuanced gradations between souls that have reached intellectual perfection and those that are utterly clueless.

[132] Ibid., 124–5.

[133] See also Michot, *Destinée de l'homme*, esp. 190–218; Davidson, *Alfarabi*, 109–16; Marmura, "Paradise in Islamic philosophy."

Imagining the Otherworld

Avicenna's notion of a non-material, imagined hereafter initially met with little success.[134] However, as we just noted, contrary to the purely disembodied, intellectualist eschatology of other Muslim philosophers (such as al-Fārābī [d. 339/950] or Ibn Bājja/Avempace [d. 533/1139]),[135] Avicenna's view left some room for the traditional picture of an embodied afterlife, and did not relegate this traditional imagery to the sphere of mere metaphor. This seems to have facilitated its survival and resurgence in the thought of some Late Medieval thinkers, in particular al-Suhrawardī (d. 587/1191) and his school. Before we turn to al-Suhrawardī, however, we must note that Muslim theologians of the centuries following Avicenna generally insisted on the imperative to believe in bodily resurrection. Al-Ghazālī, in his *Incoherence of the Philosophers* (*Tahāfut al-falāsifa*), declared those to be unbelievers who taught that bodies are not resurrected and not joined to the souls that formerly inhabited them, so as to experience bodily pleasures and pains.[136] It is noteworthy, however, that Avicenna's notion of an imagined hereafter is never directly the target of criticism in the *Incoherence of the Philosophers*. In fact, in some of his other writings, al-Ghazālī appears to adopt elements of the idea.

In a passage in *The Revivification of the Religious Sciences (Iḥyāʾ ʿulūm al-dīn)* dealing with the torture in the grave by snakes and scorpions,[137] al-Ghazālī explains that eyes are not fit to perceive the things in the "World of Sovereignty" (*malakūt*), the realm in which postmortem existence unfolds. On the most fundamental level, he asserts, believers must simply believe that the snakes in the grave exist and that they bite. A more advanced understanding, however, is to compare the torture in the grave to seeing a snake in a dream and feeling pain as a result. The dreamer, al-Ghazālī reasons, "is *truly* seeing these things, which he derives from his own soul, and may

[134] On the reception history of the *Risāla aḍḥawiyya*, particularly in the work of Ibn Taymiyya, see Michot, "A Mamluk theologian's commentary."

[135] Cf. Marmura, "Paradise in Islamic philosophy." Al-Fārābī believed that the souls of the nonphilosophical masses would perish after death, although he also seems to have accepted a kind of collective immortality of the world intellect. His views of the afterlife are not free of ambivalences. See Fakhry, *Al-Fārābī*, 11; Rudolph, "Abū Naṣr al-Farābī," 440–2. According to Ibn Miskawayh (d. 421/1030), the sensual view of paradise is only held by ignorant degenerates and uncouth commoners. It is dangerous, because it spoils people's motivation for correct behaviour in this life. See Ibn Miskawayh, *Tahdhīb al-akhlāq*, 42–3. Other philosophers, such as al-ʿĀmirī (d. 381/992), Ibn Rushd (d. 595/1198), and Ibn al-Nafīs (d. 687/1288), accept that revelation describes the afterlife in corporeal terms, but reserve these descriptions for the rough, uncouth Muslims. For al-ʿĀmirī, see Rowson, *Muslim philosopher*, 167 (§ 10), 320–1. For Ibn Rushd, see Ibn Rushd, *Kashf*, 240–7 (tr. 121–7). For Ibn al-Nafīs, see Meyerhof and Schacht, *Autodidactus*, 57.

[136] Ghazālī, *Tahāfut*, 226. Cf. idem, *Fayṣal al-tafriqa*, 191.

[137] Idem, *Iḥyāʾ*, V, 113–4 (tr. Winter, 139–40).

suffer just as much as a man awake."[138] The most advanced understanding is to realise that the pain is not caused by the snake but by the venom that enters the body of the tortured; this venom, al-Ghazālī asserts, is what sinners bring with them to the otherworld, namely, the character traits that condemn them to perdition (*al-ṣifāt al-muhlikāt*).[139]

It is the second level, that of experiencing otherworldly punishment in a way that does not involve the outer senses, that interests us here. Al-Ghazālī reprises and elaborates this idea in the introduction to *The Alchemy of Happiness* (*Kīmiyā-yi sa'ādat*), his Persian abridgment of *The Revivification of the Religious Sciences*. "The senses we use in this world," he states there, "are incapable of grasping the pleasures of paradise; the senses pertaining to the otherworld are of another kind (*ḥawāss-i ān jahānī khud-i dīgar ast*)."[140] Again, the inner sense activated in dreams offers the aptest analogy, except that dreamers wake up and then refer to that which they have seen as imagined (*khayālī*). "The dead, however, remain in this state, for death has no end."[141] The imagination that is at work in the otherworld, in other words, is more permanent than that which humans ordinarily enjoy during their earthly lives. All things seen in the afterlife are permanently real in this sense. For example, on the Day of Judgement, the world (*dunyā*) appears in the form of an ugly old hag,[142] the Qur'ān in that of a handsome young man, and Friday, the day of prayer, is seen as a beautiful bride led in procession. "On earth," writes al-Ghazālī, "they are not understood to have individuality, but in the otherworld, they do."[143] As noted, in several places al-Ghazālī stresses that it is best to accept the existence of such entities in the spirit of the Ash'arite principle of *bi-lā kayf*; but in a certain reading of his thought, al-Ghazālī can be said to go beyond this agnosticism and replace it with a more substantial theory, one that is grounded in the concept of the imagination.[144]

In al-Ghazālī's thought, the question of the reality of the otherworld is interwoven closely with his division of the cosmos into realms according to the means of perception and understanding that prevail in them. Al-Ghazālī makes a fundamental distinction between the "World of Dominion" (*mulk*) and the "World of Sovereignty" (*malakūt*), the sensible and the intelligible world, to use philosophical terminology.[145] The concept of *mulk* denotes the

[138] Ibid., V, 114:9–10 (tr. Winter, 140).

[139] Ibid., V, 114:21 (tr. Winter, 140). Cf. Majlisī, *Biḥār*, VI, 449, who cites al-Ghazālī approvingly on all three accounts.

[140] Ghazālī, *Kīmiyā*, 93.

[141] Ibid., 98.

[142] Ibid., 105.

[143] Idem, *Durra*, 107–8.

[144] The anonymous scholar (*muḥaqqiq*) praised by Mullā Ṣadrā in his *Ta'līqāt* for preceding him in *khayālī* eschatology has been identified by Landolt as no other than al-Ghazālī. See Landolt's introduction in Badakhchani (ed. and trans.), *Paradise of submission*, 247n31.

[145] For studies of al-Ghazālī's cosmology, see Wensinck, "Ghazālī's cosmology"; Nakamura, "Imām Ghazālī's cosmology." The following paragraphs are based mainly on Nakamura's

physical world of the here and now, while *malakūt* refers to the ineffable and everlasting otherworld, a world of pure intelligibles over which God presides, a realm from which originates revelation and, by the divine command, creation as a whole. Only the realm of *malakūt* is fully and truly real (*ḥaqq*), argues al-Ghazālī, while the realm of *mulk* relates to it rather like the shadow relates to the body; in his phrase, it is no more than "the world of falsehood (*zūr*) and delusion (*ghurūr*)."[146] The conceptual pair *mulk/malakūt* corresponds to the Qurʾānic binary of *dunyā/ākhira*, in the sense that human beings pass into the world of *malakūt* after death, while also being able to glimpse aspects of it in visions and dreams.

It is noteworthy that in select passages of his œuvre, al-Ghazālī expands this basic scheme into a tripartite model, allowing for a third realm to intervene between *mulk* and *malakūt*. In a commentary he adds to a passage in his *Revivification of the Religious Sciences*, he states that "the 'World of Might' (*jabarūt*) lies between the two worlds, resembling the world of *mulk* externally but being conjoined to the world of *malakūt* by the eternal power [of God]."[147] From this, one gathers that al-Ghazālī posits the existence of a third cosmological domain. Then again, in other passages, he appears to say that the concept of *jabarūt* refers to no more than a particular mode of apprehending the otherworld, one that is connected to the imaginative faculty (*al-quwwa al-wahmiyya*).[148] While the human sensory apparatus provides knowledge of *mulk*, and while the spirit and intellect aim to grasp the realities of *malakūt* directly,[149] the knowledge connected to the realm of *jabarūt* is of the order of "awe, fear, joy, dread, and similar feelings."[150] It is a higher form of understanding than that provided by the external senses, one that engages the internal senses and the faculty of imagination in particular, in order to grasp the realities of the otherworld. However, it does not reach the level of prophetic or saintly insight into the "World of the Sovereignty." Therefore, in *The Alchemy of Happiness*, al-Ghazālī can affirm that in the afterlife, prophets, saints, and all "pure Muslims" (*pārsāyān-i muslimānān*) will be able to dispense of the imagination;[151] not unlike Avicenna's philosophers, they will experience purely spiritual felicity.

study. The concept of *malakūt*, a calque on Syriac *malkutā*, occurs in the expression "the kingdom of heaven" (*malakūt al-samawāt*) in the Qurʾān (6:75, 7:185). In the thought of Dhū l-Nūn, it denotes a realm close to God in which the spirits of the "friends of God" (*awliyāʾ*) are free to travel. See Ebstein, "D̲hū l-Nūn," 584–6.

146 Ghazālī, *Arbaʿīn*, 53–4, 56. Cf. Nakamura, "Imām Ghazālī's cosmology," 34; Wensinck, "Ghazālī's cosmology," 198. Avicenna speaks of the sensible world as the "world of corruption and the graves." See Avicenna, *Ithbāt*, 89 (tr. Marmura, 119–20).

147 Ghazālī, *Imlāʾ*, 187. Cf. the translation in Wensinck, "Ghazālī's cosmology," 195.

148 Ghazālī, *Imlāʾ*, 183–4.

149 Ibid., 190.

150 Idem, *Arbaʿīn*, 49.

151 Idem, *Kīmiyā*, 99.

In consequence, it has been proposed that *jabarūt*, for al-Ghazālī, is an experiential, or epistemological, rather than an ontological category.[152] It is only in the centuries after al-Ghazālī, and in particular in the so-called illuminationist (*ishrāqī*) school of thought (as well as in the mystical thought of Ibn al-ʿArabī, which will be dealt with in a later chapter), that the "world of imagination" becomes a fully independent, intermediate world. The seminal thinker in this tradition is al-Suhrawardī al-Maqtūl (d. 587/1191), the "Master of Illumination" (*shaykh al-ishrāq*), a Persian-born philosopher executed in Aleppo on the order of the sultan Saladin (whence his sobriquet *al-maqtūl*, "the killed one").[153] Instead of speaking, like Avicenna, of a succession of intellects connecting God with the human soul, al-Suhrawardī envisions a hierarchy of lights, an idea that may have contributed to the impression that his thought is that of a mystic.[154] In the highest sphere, which al-Suhrawardī terms *jabarūt* (thereby reversing al-Ghazālī's sequence), resides God, the "light of lights" (*nūr al-anwār*); it is filled with pure intelligibles. The intermediate sphere of *malakūt* is home to the "victorious lights" (*al-anwār al-qāhira*) corresponding roughly to Avicenna's supralunar intellects; in it are the angels and postmortem souls of humans. In the sublunar world of *mulk*, which al-Suhrawardī calls "the world of bodies" (or "barriers," *barāzikh*), darkness prevails, were it not for the "regent lights" (*al-anwār al-mudabbira*), that is, the human souls, which control the "fortresses" of their bodies and are connected to the lights of the higher spheres, be it temporarily (in visions, dreams, ascensions, and so forth) or lastingly after death.[155] In the Suhrawardian tradition, a certain insight into the otherworld is possible on strength of the human imagination. It is worth highlighting, however, that for al-Suhrawardī, like for Avicenna before him, the imagination is a deficient source of knowledge, the ideal remaining a direct communion with pure intelligibles.[156]

152 Nakamura, "Imām Ghazālī's cosmology," 46.

153 On al-Suhrawardī's notion of a "world of image," see Marcotte, "Suhrawardī's realm of the imaginal."

154 E.g., in his mystical work, *The Niche of Lights* (*Mishkāt al-anwār*), al-Ghazālī states that God is "the True Light" (*al-nūr al-ḥaqq*). See Ghazālī, *Mishkāt*, 4. Cf. Lazarus-Yafeh, *Studies*, 264–348 ("Ch. IV: Symbolism of Light in Al-Ghazzālī's Writings"). The relatedness of the *Mishkāt al-anwār* and al-Suhrawardī's *Ḥikmat al-ishrāq* is also noted by Davidson, *Intellect*, 164, 170. Henry Corbin, however, has argued for a predominantly Zoroastrian background that would have given rise to a specifically "Iranian Islam" in the thought of al-Suhrawardī and his followers. See Corbin, *Spiritual body*, xiv, 12, and passim. Hossein Ziai, by contrast, warns that al-Suhrawardī's thought should not be confused with the "subjective" use of philosophical concepts by the Sufis, seeing in al-Suhrawardī the key philosopher of late medieval Islam. See *EI2*, s.v. al-Suhrawardī, Shihāb al-Dīn Yaḥyā, IX, 782a-784b.

155 This is a simplified summary of al-Suhrawardī's metaphysics as one finds it in discourses one to three of the second part of his *Ḥikmat al-ishrāq*, §§ 107–93 (tr. Walbridge, 77–123). A useful summary can be found in Sinai, "Kommentar," 283–92.

156 In one place, al-Suhrawardī calls the imagination "an obstructing mountain between our souls and the world of the intellect." See Suhrawardī, *Alwāḥ*, ed. Corbin, in *Oeuvres*

At death, the "regent lights" leave their terrestrial bodies and move into the heavenly spheres of light.[157] Here, al-Suhrawardī embraces the idea, hesitatingly proposed by Avicenna,[158] that the postmortem souls of the nonphilosophical masses become attached to celestial bodies in the hereafter, which allows them to activate their imagination and experience pleasure and pain. This doctrine seeks to take into account that imagination is not a purely intellectual effort; the imaginative faculty requires a material substrate to be activated, whether in this world (where this substrate is the human body, and the brain in particular) or in the afterlife. Al-Suhrawardī states that, while the perfect souls (of which, as in Avicenna's model, there are few) join themselves immediately to the pure lights of the intelligible world,[159] common people's souls enter into the intermediate "world of suspended images" (*ʿālam al-muthul al-muʿallaqa*).[160] The phrase "suspended images" refers to a category of things that *appear* in certain places, but do not exist in them in a conventional sense. The example al-Suhrawardī cites repeatedly is that of images in a mirror.[161] This, in fact, is how al-Suhrawardī pictures the reality of the eschatological phenomena described in Islamic scripture: they subsist externally in celestial bodies, which function as their "places of appearance" (*maẓāhir*, sg. *maẓhar*). In this way, paradise and hell, as well as the pleasures and punishments that are experienced in them, are provided an ontological status more real than that which can be claimed for invented mental representations.[162] In one place, al-Suhrawardī even states that the "resurrection of bodies" (*baʿth al-ajsām*) is made possible through the "suspended images."[163]

The "world of suspended images" proved to be a fertile concept in the later centuries of Islamic thought, particularly in what came to be known as

philosophiques, IV, 95. Cf. the discussion in van Lit, "Eschatology and the world of image," 216.

157 Suhrawardī, *Ḥikmat al-ishrāq*, §§ 243, 250 (tr. 148, 151). Al-Suhrawardī also appears to play with the idea that impure souls can be reincarnated in animals and thus remain imprisoned in the sublunar "world of barriers." He relates, e.g., that some philosophers teach reincarnation in other terrestrial bodies and connects this to Q 32:20, according to which every time the sinners in hell "seek to get out of it, are returned to it." See Suhrawardī, *Ḥikmat al-ishrāq*, § 235 (tr. 144). Metempsychosis is an important topic in *ishrāqī* philosophy, but cannot be dealt with here in any exhaustive fashion. Cf. Freitag, *Seelenwanderung*; Jambet, *Mort et résurrection*, 111–49; Schmidtke, "Doctrine of transmigration"; Walbridge, *Science*, 141–9, 157–8.

158 Ibn Sīna, *Shifāʾ*, tr. Marmura, 356. Cf. Stroumsa, "True felicity," 63–4.

159 Suhrawardī, *Ḥikmat al-ishrāq*, § 240 (tr. 146–7).

160 Ibid., §§ 244, 250 (tr. 148–9, 151).

161 Ibid., §§ 104, 243, 247 (tr. 72–3, 148, 150).

162 Cf. Rahman, "Dreams, imagination," 170. More careful in this respect is Arnzen, *Platonische Ideen*, 149.

163 Suhrawardī, *Ḥikmat al-ishrāq*, ed. Corbin (Oeuvres Philosophiques), II, 234. In their edition, Ziai and Walbridge prefer to base their text on a manuscript that reads "resurrection of images" (*baʿth al-amthāl*). See Suhrawardī, *Ḥikmat al-ishrāq*, 150. For a discussion of this telling editorial choice, see the discussion in van Lit, "Eschatology and the world of image," 219n128.

the illuminationist (*ishrāqī*) tradition of philosophy. Al-Suhrawardī's writings spawned several commentaries and super-commentaries, notably those of al-Shahrazūrī (*fl.* late seventh/thirteenth c.) and Quṭb al-Dīn al-Shīrāzī (d. 710/1311).[164] Particularly al-Shahrazūrī amplifies al-Suhrawardī's notion of a realm of "suspended images" into that of an ontologically independent "world of image and the imagination" (*ʿālam al-mithāl wa-l-khayāl*), located as a third world between the sensible and the intelligible world.[165] This world of image, states al-Shahrazūrī, has many layers, every layer being filled with infinite individuals. Some of these layers are "illumined, pleasure-bestowing, and noble"; these are "the layers of the Gardens that the mid-ranked of the people of paradise (*al-mutawassiṭūn min ahl al-janna*) enjoy." Other layers of the world of image, however, are "dark and cause pain"; these are "the layers of hell (*jaḥīm*) in which suffer the people of hell."[166]

The impact of al-Suhrawardī's eschatological ideas on Sunnī *kalām* works, however, was minimal.[167] His pedigree as a peripatetic philosopher, who defined true bliss in purely intellectual terms, hindered a more thorough reception of his ideas. In any event, the view that became enshrined in the textbooks was that the phenomena of the otherworld are "real without further interpretation" (*ḥaqq bi-lā taʾwīl*).[168] The corporeality of the afterlife was conceived to be different from this-worldly sensible experience only in degree, not in kind. It was in different contexts, in Shiʿism and Sufism, that Avicenna's, and in particular al-Ghazālī's and al-Suhrawardī's concept of an imaginable afterlife found more congenial audiences. It is to these two traditions that we turn in the next two chapters.

[164] Shahrazūrī, *Sharḥ*; Shīrāzī, *Sharḥ*; idem, *Risāla*. On the development of the commentary tradition on al-Suhrawardī's œuvre, and on his eschatological thought in particular, see now van Lit, "Eschatology and the world of image."

[165] See the epistle on the topic contained in Shahrazūrī, *Shajara*, III, 457–71, at 457. Cf. idem, *Sharḥ*, 509. Shahrazūrī's key contribution in this context is discussed in van Lit, "Eschatology and the world of image," 229–72. See also the forthcoming translation and study of this epistle by van Lit and Lange.

[166] Shahrazūrī, *Shajara*, III, 465.

[167] An important exception is the *Sharḥ al-maqāṣid* of al-Taftāzānī (d. 793/1390), a *kalām* work that reprises a key passage on the world of image from al-Shīrāzī's *Sharḥ Ḥikmat al-ishrāq*. See Taftāzānī, *Sharḥ al-maqāṣid*, III, 372. While al-Taftāzānī's famous older and younger contemporaries, al-Ījī (d. 756/1355) and al-Jurjānī (d. 816/1413) ignored the idea, al-Taftāzānī's text, states Eric van Lit, "became one of the primary hubs for the transmission of the idea of a world of image," particularly as the idea migrated to Twelver-Shiʿi thought. See van Lit, "Eschatology and the world of image," 305. On al-Taftāzānī's eschatological thought, see now Würtz, "The orthodox conception." Würtz also emphasises al-Taftāzānī's indebtedness to philosophical eschatology.

[168] Jurjānī, *Sharḥ al-Mawāqif*, VIII, 348.

6

Otherworlds Apart: Shiʿi Visions of Paradise and Hell

Having ended the preceding chapter with an examination of the eschatological thought of al-Suhrawardī, we begin the present chapter with the observation that his ideas found a particularly receptive audience in Shiʿism. Shiʿi thinkers, in many instances, developed al-Suhrawardī's concept of a "world of suspended images" and took it to a new level, by consistently framing it in terms of an autonomous, and often spatially defined, "world of image" (*ʿālam al-mithāl*). Most contemporary scholarship on Shiʿi teachings about the afterlife in fact focuses almost exclusively on the world of image, particularly as it was developed in the thought of the so-called School of Isfahan (*fl.* eleventh/seventeenth c.) and of the Shaykhi and Babi movements of later centuries. However, one should not underestimate the important strands of traditionist, that is, hadith-based, thinking about the otherworld in Shiʿism. Neither must we fail to pay attention to the eschatological doctrines of Shiʿi dialectic theology (*kalām*). The first three sections of this chapter, then, survey Shiʿi philosophical, traditionist, and *kalām* views of the otherworld as they were formulated in Imami (or Twelver Shiʿi) writings. The concluding section is devoted to the philosophical eschatology of Ismaʿilism (or Sevener Shiʿism). The Shiʿi paradise and hell, it should be noted, is a topic so rich that it would deserve a separate book-length investigation. Here, we must restrict ourselves to highlighting some of its salient features. In the process, we shall not only review a number of Shiʿi doctrines on the afterlife, but also sketch the general contours of the history of Shiʿi literature on paradise and hell.

The World of Image in Shiʿi Thought

In the centuries following al-Suhrawardī, the thinkers referring back to him sought to elaborate and conceptually consolidate the "world of suspended images," the world of image (*ʿālam al-mithāl*), as they came to call it.[1] In the Shiʿi world, an illustration of this process can be found in the exegesis of the Qurʾānic verse "the people of the garden today are happy in what occupies them" (36:55) by Mullā Ṣadrā of Shīrāz (d. 1050/1640).[2] Ṣadrā infers from this verse that the blessed in paradise determine the pleasures they experience on the strength of their imagination. This, he maintains, is also implied by the Prophetic tradition about the market in paradise (*sūq al-janna*), in which the believers freely acquire images and "enter into them."[3] Like Avicenna and al-Suhrawardī before him, Ṣadrā argues that souls in the otherworld create their own paradises and hells, while also insisting on the existence, external to the faculty of the imagination, of the imagined phenomena in paradise and hell. However, while al-Suhrawardī had speculated that the realities in paradise and hell occur in celestial bodies that function as their heavenly places of manifestation (*maẓāhir*), Ṣadrā believed that the souls in paradise and hell need no such *maẓāhir* to imagine the world of image into being.[4] According to Ṣadrā, as it were, every postmortem soul creates its *own* world of image.[5] This, arguably, puts the coherence of this world as a third, intersubjective world in doubt.[6] Some scholars, however, will stress that the world of image, in Ṣadrā's take, becomes "an absolute ontological one, independent of the soul,"[7] a "different order of reality."[8]

[1] Corbin, *Spiritual body*, 87. Corbin makes the ontological claim that the "creative imagination" that he sees at work in the *ʿālam al-mithāl* "does not *construct* something unreal, but *unveils* the hidden reality." See Corbin, *Spiritual body*, 12 and passim. For a "delocalised" (and deontologised) interpretation of al-Suhrawardī's cosmology, akin to Nakamura's identification of al-Ghazālī's terms *mulk*, *malakūt*, and *jabarūt* with epistemological categories, see now van Lit, "Eschatology and the world of image," 201–2.

[2] On Mullā Ṣadrā's eschatological thought, see Corbin, *En islam iranien*, IV, 84–115; Morris, *Wisdom*, 76–85; Rahman, *Philosophy*, 247–62; Jambet, *Mort*; Rustom, "Psychology"; idem, *Triumph*, chs. 6 and 7 (on soteriology). See now also Kutubi, *Mulla Sadra and eschatology*; Landolt, "Being-towards-resurrection."

[3] Ṣadrā, *Tafsīr*, V, 189–92. On the market in paradise, cf. the preceding text, p. 153.

[4] Ibid., V, 201–2. Corbin refers to this ability as the "eschatological function of the creative imagination." See Corbin, *En Islam iranien*, IV, 106–15.

[5] For a succinct statement of this position, see Principle #10 announced at the beginning of the chapter on bodily return in Ṣadrā's *Four Principles* (*Al-Asfār al-arbaʿa*), translated in Landolt, "Being-towards-resurrection." Landolt reads Ṣadrā's "response" to al-Suhrawardī as a "critique rather than a confirmation of an eschatology that ends up in a purely *imaginal* world." See ibid.

[6] See van Lit, "Eschatology and the world of image," 249, quoting Ṣadrā, *Taʿlīqāt*, II, 530; idem, *Mabdaʾ*, 545; idem, *Shawāhid*, 268.

[7] Rahman, *Philosophy of Ṣadrā*, 261. Cf. Jambet, *Mort et résurrection*, 186.

[8] Rustom, "Psychology," 12. Here, I can only summarise Ṣadrā's complex doctrine of paradise and hell, for which one should also consult his *al Mabdaʾ wa-l-maʿād* and *al-Ḥikma al ʿarshiyya* (particularly Part II.C §§ 10–17 [tr. 215–58]), alongside the works of Corbin, Jambet, Landolt, Rustom, and others.

Other Shiʿi authors talk about the world of image as a separate continent, called Hūrqalyā. The name Hūrqalyā is already used by al-Suhrawardī, who leans on earlier Islamic mythical geographies that speak of an eighth climate (*iqlīm*), situated beyond the seven climates in the vicinity of the mountain of Qāf, which marks the boundary of the known world.[9] Hūrqalyā becomes a pivotal concept in the thought of Aḥmad al-Aḥsāʾī (d. 1241/1826), a Shiʿi scholar from al-Baḥrayn who was active in Iraq and Persia, where he emerged as the eponymous leader of the theological-mystical school that is known as Shaykhism. Hūrqalyā, in al-Aḥsāʾī's system, denotes the inter-world (or *barzakh*) between the visible, material world and the abstract world of intelligibles.[10] According to al-Aḥsāʾī, the spirits of the inhabitants of paradise and hell, both of which are located in Hūrqalyā, possess a special kind of body that is neither material nor immaterial.

Al-Aḥsāʾī illustrates this idea with the following comparison. Silica and potash are opaque substances; however, when they are liquified and fused, they become transparent glass. A similar process of purification happens to human beings after death: their terrestrial, corruptible bodies of flesh disappear due to natural decay; however, an invisible "body of spiritual flesh" survives.[11] The human spirit, in the meantime, leaves the body; it is only reunited with the "body of spiritual flesh" on the day of resurrection, when together they enter paradise and hell in Hūrqalyā.[12] The ascension of the prophet Muḥammad to Hūrqalyā, al-Aḥsāʾī contends, took place in his "body of spiritual flesh." Rising up through the higher spheres, he gradually shed the elements of his terrestrial body and continued the journey in his subtle, "Hūrqalyian" body. However, he did not ascend in his spirit alone.[13]

[9] Al-Suhrawardī names the cities Jābalaq, Jābaraṣ, and Hūrqalyā among the "wondrous cities" of the "eighth climate." See Suhrawardī, *Ḥikmat al-ishrāq*, § 273 (tr. Walbridge, 160). Cf. Muqātil, *Tafsīr*, IV, 476 (*ad* Q 73:9, from Ibn ʿAbbās); Yāqūt, *Muʿjam*, I, 90–1. See also the anonymous Ilkhanid *Miʿrājnāma* (tr. Gruber, 72–3), where the Prophet visits the two cities at the end of his night journey. Al-Suhrawardī's commentator al-Sharazūrī explains that the cities of Jābalaq and Jābaraṣ in the world of image have "a thousand gates and uncountable creatures in it," and that "the world of image is parallel to the ever-moving world of sense." See Shahrazūrī, *Sharḥ*, 554. Cf. the translation in van Lit, "Eschatology and the world of image," 253–4. Quṭb al-Dīn al-Shīrāzī (d. 710/1311) states that the world of image is "the world of the subtle bodies, which alone are able to rise to heaven." See Shīrāzī, *Sharḥ Ḥikmat al-ishrāq*, § 273, tr. Corbin, *Spiritual body*, 127.

[10] Corbin, *Spiritual body*, 191–7, translating Aḥsāʾī, *Jawāmiʿ al-kalim*, I/3, 8–10 [= pp. 153–4] (ninth *risāla*). On al-Aḥsāʾī's conception of a world of image, see also Lawson, "Shaykh Aḥmad al-Aḥsāʾī," 22–9.

[11] Corbin, *Spiritual body*, 180–9, at 183, translating Aḥsāʾī, *Sharḥ al-ziyāra*, 369–70.

[12] This is a simplified summary, space not permitting a fuller discussion of al-Aḥsāʾī's idea of the two essential and two accidental bodies (*ajsād* and *ajsām*, respectively). Cf. *EI3*, s.v. al-Aḥsāʾī, Shaykh Aḥmad (*M. A.* Amir-Moezzi); *EIr*, s.v. Aḥsāʾī, Shaikh Aḥmad, I, 674–9 (*D. M.* MacEoin); *Encyclopaedia Islamica*, s.v. al-Aḥsāʾī (Zeinolabedin Ebrahimi and Jawad Qasemi). The standard account remains Corbin, *Spiritual body*, 90–105.

[13] Aḥsāʾī, *Jawāmiʿ al-kalim* I/2, pp. 144–66, question 26 ("al-Resāla al-Qaṭīfīya"). Cf. Buckley, *Night journey*, 109–111, 143, who states, incorrectly it seems to me, that al-Aḥsāʾī

In sum, although the many dimensions of this development deserve a much-fuller treatment, what we see in the eschatological thought of the followers of Avicenna and al-Suhrawardī up to the early modern period is a gradual process of ontologisation of a philosophical and spiritual concept of paradise and hell. The philosophers' disembodied intellects thus become material, though subtle, "bodies of spiritual flesh" that populate the otherworld; the objects and experiences in paradise and hell that for Avicenna were dreamlike figments of the imagination turn into properly spatial and corporeal phenomena that are external to the perceiving subject; the very concept of the imagination is reified into a special, third kind of otherworldly being and knowing, in between the sensible and the intelligible; and the world of image becomes a geomorphic continent, Hūrqalyā. The philosophical-spiritual eschatology that results from this process is an original system that diverts from standard theological formulations regarding the materiality and corporeality of the otherworld but manages, at the same time, to incorporate many elements of the traditional picture of paradise and hell. This acknowledgement of received opinion did not necessarily protect its proponents from the attack of the traditionalists. Al-Aḥsāʾī's doctrine of the afterlife and of resurrection led to his condemnation as an unbeliever (*takfīr*) by the Shiʿi religious authorities of his day. Chased from Persia and Iraq, he died on the road to Mecca, finding his final resting place on the al-Baqīʿ cemetery in Medina, the burial ground of the four Imams al-Ḥasan b. ʿAlī, ʿAlī Zayn al-ʿĀbidīn, Muḥammad al-Bāqir, and Jaʿfar al-Ṣādiq.[14]

The Shiʿi Imams, in fact, play a prominent role in al-Aḥsāʾī's (and also, Mullā Ṣadrā's) eschatological thought.[15] Next to the paradise situated in the world of image, Mullā Ṣadrā posits a higher garden, a purely intelligible garden (*janna maʿqūla*) inhabited by beings free from all association with corporeality and possessed of true knowledge. These beings, Mullā Ṣadrā says, are the "ones who are brought near" (*al-muqarrabūn*) mentioned in the Qurʾān (56:11), that is, angels, but also the revered figures of Shiʿi soteriology: Muḥammad, Fāṭima, ʿAlī, al-Ḥasan, and al-Ḥusayn.[16] It is a truism that Shiʿi religious thought revolves around the concept of the Imamate. The Shiʿi Imams, descendants of the prophet Muḥammad through his daughter Fāṭima and his son-in-law ʿAlī, serve as the Shiʿites' supreme spiritual guides and exemplars of pious and lawful behaviour. Moreover, in the person of the Mahdi, the "hidden" Imam who will return at the end of

"maintained that it [the *miʿrāj*] was a spiritual event." Cf. against this perception Corbin, *En Islam iranien*, IV, 226.

14 On the persecution and death of al-Aḥṣāʾī, see ibid., IV, 227. On the significance of Medina's al-Baqīʿ cemetery in Shiʿism, cf. Ende, "Steine des Anstoßes," 181–200.

15 On Ṣadra, see Rizvi, *Mullā Ṣadrā and metaphysics*, 130; but cf. the comment made by Mohammed Rustom in his review of Rizvi's study (p. 412), casting doubt on the centrality of the Imams in Ṣadrā's eschatology.

16 Jambet, *Mort*, 176–82, at 178.

time to restore the rightful leadership of the Prophet's family (*ahl al-bayt*), they betoken the Shi'ites' future communal salvation. Accordingly, in Shi'i eschatology, the Imams are placed in the highest echelons of the otherworld. In Shaykhi thought, the twelve Imams, the prophet Muḥammad, and his daughter Fāṭima, that is, "the fourteen immaculate ones," are elevated into the rank of manifestations of the divine attributes. In Corbin's phrase, they are "theophanic persons." As such, they are thought to reside above the intermediate world of Hūrqalyā, in intimate proximity to God.[17]

Traditionalism and Rationalism in Shi'i Eschatology

Imamology and eschatology are intertwined not only in the thought of the theorists of the world of image, but also in Shi'i traditionalism and rationalist theology. It has been suggested that the messianic figure of the Mahdi (or Qā'im, "Resurrector," as he is also known) has played so dominant a role that paradise and hell are "almost entirely absent from Imami eschatological literature."[18] There may be some truth in this, but it should be noted that it was not before the mid-fourth/tenth century that the Imami belief in the apocalyptic return of the Mahdi-Imam came to dominate.[19] During the three preceding centuries, Imami authors made regular contributions to the growing traditionist literature on paradise and hell. Also in later centuries, as we will see presently, Shi'i authors made ample recourse to this literature, or even expanded it.

Early Shi'i collections of eschatological hadith only occasionally convey a markedly Shi'i flavor. In fact, the earliest known version of the Prophet's *mi'rāj* compiled by a Shi'i author (around the middle of the second/eighth century) "contains no distinctly Shi'i elements."[20] In the *Book of Renunciation* (*K. al-Zuhd*) of al-Ahwāzī (d. middle of third/ninth c. [?]),[21]

[17] Corbin, *Spiritual body*, 58–9; idem, *En Islam iranien*, IV, 207. The Qā'im dwells in Hūrqalyā and will return from there ("Risālat Mollā Moḥammad-Ḥosayn Anṣārī" in Aḥṣā'ī, *Jawāmi' al-kalim* I/3, pp. 8–10 [153–4]; "Resāla-ye Rashtiyya," ibid., I/2, pp. 68–114, question 28).

[18] *EIr*, s.v. Eschatology. iii. Imami Shi'ism (M. A. Amir-Moezzi).

[19] Kohlberg, "From Imāmiyya to Ithnā-'Ashariyya," 521.

[20] See Buckley, *Night journey*, 303n113. This *mi'rāj* is attributed to Hishām b. Sālim al-Jawālīqī (d. 179/795), who transmitted hadiths from the Imams Ja'far al-Ṣādiq and Mūsā al-Kāẓim. On al-Jawālīqī, cf. van Ess, *TG*, I, 342–8. The text is preserved in the *tafsīr* of 'Alī al-Qummī (alive in 307/919). See Qummī, *Tafsīr*, 369–75 (*ad* Q 17:1), tr. Buckley, *The night journey*, 6–18. Cf. Modarressi, *Tradition*, I, 269.

[21] In the *K. al-Zuhd*, al-Ahwāzī, a native of Kufa who lived in Qum most of his life, quotes directly from Muḥammad Ibn Abī 'Umayr al-Azdī (d. 217/832), an influential Shi'i from Baghdad (he served as the representative [*wakīl*] of Mūsā al-Kāẓim there) and a student of Hishām al-Jawālīqī (see the preceding footnote). See *TG*, I, 384–6. On al-Ahwāzī's *K. al-Zuhd*, cf. *GAS*, I, 539. Many *zuhd* traditions about paradise and hell can also be found in the *Nahj al-balāgha*. See *Nahj*, I, 71–2, 211–2, II, 15, 75–6, 90, 131, 160 (*contemptus mundi* and praise of the otherworld), I, 67, II, 3, III, 30 (paradise praised in the context of jihad).

FIGURE 12. Muḥammad with ʿAlī, al-Ḥusayn and al-Ḥasan in paradise. Punjab, 1097/1686. From Muḥammad Ibn Ḥusām Khūsifī Bīrjandī (d. 875/1470), *Khāwarānnāma*. MS British Library Add. 19776, fol. 362v.

Shiʿi motifs are likewise rare. None of the traditions al-Ahwāzī collects in his chapter on intercession (*shafāʿa*) mentions that the Imams are possessed of this power.[22] In the chapter on paradise and hell, however, one reads that

[22] Ahwāzī, *Zuhd*, 174–8.

Muḥammad, ʿAlī, and the Imams up to Jaʿfar al-Ṣādiq (from whom the tradition is related), are invited by God on the Day of Judgement to confirm that they brought the true religion to their unbelieving contemporaries, many of whom deny this and are sent to hell.[23] A degree more exuberant is a tradition attributed to the eighth Imam ʿAlī al-Riḍā (d. 203/818), which declares that al-Ḥasan (d. 50/670 or 58/678) and al-Ḥusayn (d. 61/680), the second and third Imam, respectively, are the "two lords of the youths of paradise (*sayyidā shabāb ahl al-janna*)," while their father ʿAlī b. Abī Ṭālib is "even better than they (*khayrun minhumā*)."[24]

Several works bearing the title *What Paradise and Hell are like* (*Ṣifat al-janna wa-l-nār*) were written by Shiʿi scholars in the early third/ninth century.[25] The work of the Kufan Saʿīd Ibn Janāḥ, a non-Arab client (*mawlā*) and resident of Baghdad who claimed to have received the text, through an intermediary, from Jaʿfar al-Ṣādiq, seems to be the earliest extant example.[26] Ibn Janāḥ's text makes only oblique reference to the imamate. For example, the angels Munkar and Nakīr, when interrogating the believer in the grave, are reported to ask: "Who is your Prophet? And who is your leader (*imām*)?" Rather than jumping on the occasion and promptly proclaiming his allegiance to the Shiʿi Imams (a move that becomes standard in the

[23] Ibid., 186–7.

[24] ʿAlī al-Riḍā, *Musnad*, #24. That al-Ḥasan and al-Ḥusayn are the "leaders among the youth of paradise" is also affirmed in later Shiʿi sources. See, e.g., *Nahj al-balāgha*, III, 32; Baḥrānī, *Maʿālim*, III, 63, 72–4. Sunni authors also occasionally relate the notion. See Tirmidhī, *Jāmiʿ*, *k. al-manāqib* 30 (*b. manāqib al-Ḥasan wa-l-Ḥusayn*), V, 656; Ibn Ḥanbal, *Musnad*, III, 3 and passim; Ibn Jubayr, *Riḥla*, 114; Nābulusī, *Ahl al-janna*, 18. A Sunni answer to this claim is the tradition in which the Prophet tells ʿAlī that Abū Bakr and ʿUmar are the "lords of the middle-aged people of paradise" (*sayyidā kuhūl ahl al-janna*). See Ibn Abī Shayba, *Muṣannaf*, VI, 350; Ibn Ḥanbal, *Musnad*, I, 80; Ibn Māja, *Sunan*, *k. al-muqaddima* 11, I, 73–4 (#95); Tirmidhī, *Jāmiʿ*, *k. al-manāqib* 16 (*b. fī manāqib Abī Bakr*), V, 611. For a Sufi interpretation of this hadith, see Sulamī, *Masāʾil*, 73–4.

[25] In addition to the work of Saʿīd b. Janāḥ discussed in the text, there is the *K. Ṣifat al-janna wa-l-nār* of Ibn al-Qaddāḥ (*fl.* second half second/eighth century), a servant of the sixth Imam Jaʿfar al-Ṣādiq (d. 148/765). See Najāshī, *Fihrist*, ed. Maktabat al-Dāwarī, 148. Cf. Modarressi, *Tradition*, I, 145–50. Another compiler of a treatise with this title is Ḥanān al-Ṣayrafī ("the moneylender"), who transmitted hadith from Jaʿfar al-Ṣādiq and his successor Mūsā al-Kāzim (d. 183/799). Fragments of this text are known from later works such as Ibn Bābūya's *Thawāb al-aʿmāl*. See Modarressi, *Tradition*, I, 240–42. Finally, mention should be made of the *K. al-janna wa-l-nār* of Abū l-Ḥasan ʿAlī b. al-Ḥasan al-Kūfī, an associate of the eighth Imam ʿAlī al-Riḍā (d. 203/818). See Ibn Shahrashūb, *Maʿālim al-ʿulamāʾ*, 57.

[26] Al-Majlisī notes that Saʿīd b. Najāḥ transmitted his *K. Ṣifat al-janna wa-l-nār*, as well as a *K. Qabḍ rūḥ al-muʾmin wa-l-kāfir*, on the authority of a certain "unknown" (*majhūl*) ʿAwf b. ʿAbdallāh, who would have received both texts from Abū ʿAbdallāh, i.e., Jaʿfar al-Ṣādiq. See Majlisī, *Biḥār*, VIII, 416 (with further biographical information on Ibn Najāḥ, including the fact that he was said to have transmitted hadith from Mūsā al-Kāẓim and ʿAlī al-Riḍā). Ibn Najāḥ's text is preserved in Mufīd, *Ikhtiṣāṣ*, 345–65; Majlisī, *Biḥār*, VIII, 407–16.

following century and in later Shiʿi texts[27]), the believer answers that his "leader" and "protector" (*muhaymin*) is the Qurʾān.[28] At the same time, Ibn Najāḥ relates that the blessed in paradise witness festive public processions of the prophets Adam, Abraham, Moses, Jesus, and Muḥammad, followed by the crowning appearance of another, unidentified prophetic figure. Asked about him, the angels explain that this is "the comrade [lit. brother] of God's messenger in this world and the otherworld (*akhū rasūl Allāh fī l-dunyā wa-l-ākhira*)" – that is, ʿAlī.[29]

During the third/ninth century, then, ʿAlī and the other Imams gradually gain in importance in Shiʿi eschatological hadith. Writing around 269/882, the Muʿtazilī theologian al-Khayyāṭ accuses the Shiʿa of claiming intercessory powers for the descendants of ʿAlī.[30] This tendency becomes fully manifest in traditionist works compiled after the beginning of the period of occultation (*ghayba*) of the twelfth Imam in 260/874. Among the Shiʿi authors of the fourth/tenth century, Ibn Bābūya from Qum (d. 306/991) is particularly eloquent in respect to paradise and hell.[31] In his *Epistle on the Tenets of Faith* (*Risālat al-iʿtiqādāt*), the first comprehensive creed of Imami Shiʿism, Ibn Babūya states that the prophet Muḥammad and his "executors" (*awṣiyāʾ*), that is, the twelve Imams, will stand on the wall (*aʿrāf*) between paradise and hell, and only those who recognise them and acknowledge their leadership will be allowed to enter the eternal garden.[32] As Ibn Bābūya relates elsewhere, the Prophet, during his Ascension, saw written on the Throne of God that ʿAlī is his helper and brother.[33] In Shiʿi versions of the *miʿrāj* that have recourse to Ibn Bābūya's *K. al-Miʿrāj*, the explicit designation by God of ʿAlī as Muḥammad's successor (*khalīfa*) takes centre stage.[34]

[27] Kūlīnī, *Kāfī*, I, 376; Baḥrānī, *Maʿālim*, II, 39–41, 61, and passim; Majlisī, *Biḥār*, VI, 377, 404–5, 408.

[28] Mufīd, *Ikhtiṣāṣ*, 347–8; Majlisī, *Biḥār*, VIII, 408. Cf. Baḥrānī, *Maʿālim*, II, 50.

[29] Mufīd, *Ikhtiṣāṣ*, 355; Majlisī, *Biḥār*, VIII, 413.

[30] See Hamza, "To hell and back," 162–3.

[31] Ibn Bābūya is, notably, the author of a work entitled *The Reward and Punishment for [Good and Bad] Actions* (*Thawāb al-aʿmāl wa-ʿiqāb al-aʿmāl*), a work that lists some two hundred virtuous and another eighty sinful actions, and their respective rewards and punishments in paradise and hell. Also his *K. al-Khiṣāl*, a work on numerology, includes many eschatological traditions. See, e.g., Ibn Bābūya, *Khiṣāl*, 331 (one of the seven gates of hell is reserved for the Umayyads). Ibn Bābūya also transmitted (and possibly, expanded) the *K. Ṣifat al-janna wa-l-nār* of Saʿīd b. Janāḥ. See *GAS* I, 549; Al-Tihrānī, *Dharīʿa*, V, 164.

[32] Ibn Bābūya, *Risālat al-iʿtiqādāt*, 66 (§ 25). Cf. ibid., 63 (§ 21). A similar tradition appears in al-Kulaynī's *al-Kāfī*. See Kulaynī, *Kāfī, k. al-ḥujja, b. maʿrifat al-Imām*, ed. Shams al-Dīn, I, 235 (#9). See further *Nahj al-balāgha*, II, 40–1; Majlisī, *Biḥār*, VIII, 507; Baḥrānī, *Maʿālim*, II, 377–91. On Mullā Ṣadrā's esoteric interpretation of the tradition in al-Kulaynī, see Corbin, *En Islam iranien*, I, 310–20.

[33] Ibn Bābūyā, *Khiṣāl*, 189. Elsewhere it is stated that ʿAlī's name is written on all the veils in paradise. See Baḥrānī, *Maʿālim*, III, 51.

[34] Amir-Moezzi, "L'Imām dans le ciel," 99–116; Buckley, *Night journey*, 155–63; *TG*, IV, 393.

FIGURE 13. A Shiʿi Judgement scene. Persian rug, *ca.* 1900–1930. National Museum van Wereldculturen Amsterdam, Coll. no. TM-3070-12.

ʿAlī now becomes the "divider" (*qasīm*) between paradise and hell, that is, at Judgement, he holds the keys to paradise and hell, deciding who enters one or the other.[35]

With al-Shaykh al-Mufīd (Baghdad, d. 413/1022), a student of Ibn Bābūya, Shiʿi eschatology, and Shiʿi theology in general, takes a rationalist turn, approaching in many areas the teachings of the Muʿtazilites.[36] Arguably, already Ibn Bābūya and the authorities he quotes had leant in that direction. For example, Ibn Bābūya thought that Adam's garden was a terrestrial garden devoid of any connection with the transcendent paradise; the latter is "the garden of eternity" (*jannat al-khuld*), but Adam's

[35] Ḥillī, *Muḥtaḍar*, 69. Cf. *TG*, IV, 547, 594; Amir-Moezzi, "Some Remarks," 117–8. See also Ṭūsī, *Mabdaʾ*, 65 (§34); Majlisī, *Biḥār*, VII, 243, VIII, 505; Baḥrānī, *Maʿālim*, II, 262–76; Kāshānī, *Kalimāt*, 208–10.

[36] Madelung, "Imamism"; Halm, *Schia*, 62–73.

and Eve's sojourn in "their" garden was not eternal.[37] Like the Muʿtazilites, Ibn Bābūya also denied the ocular vision of God.[38] This is in line with later Imami theology.[39] According to al-Majlisī, for example, when God manifests Himself (*tajallā*), the believers see only the "lights of His majesty and the effects of His mercy and kindness," but not God Himself.[40] Later Imami theologians applied reason-based arguments to eschatological doctrines. For example, they asserted that reason alone, irrespective of revelation, can show that there is perpetual reward in paradise for obedient believers.[41] They also stressed the importance of works in addition to correct belief. ʿAlī, according to a Shiʿi tradition, was once asked whether someone who professed the *shahāda* should be considered a Muslim. "What of the obligations due to God (*farāʾiḍ Allāh*)?" was his curt reply.[42]

Some of the Shiʿi Muʿtazilites argued for the future creation of paradise and hell, though not all: Al-Shaykh al-Mufīd, for example, pronounced himself against Ḍirār's theory of future creation, arguing that people do not yet inhabit paradise, but that angels do, a view that was also endorsed in traditionist circles.[43] The dominant Shiʿi theologians of the centuries following al-Shaykh al-Mufīd, men such as al-Sharīf al-Murtaḍā (Baghdad, d. 436/1044) and al-ʿAllāma al-Ḥillī (Tabriz, d. 726/1325), did

[37] See Majlisī, *Biḥār*, VIII, 403. Note, however, that al-Majlisī also quotes views in support of the opinion that Adam's paradise and the eschatological garden are the same. See ibid., VIII, 406.

[38] Ibn Bābūya, *Creed*, 30 (§ 1): The inhabitants in paradise will look at the rewards of God, not at Himself, despite the plain meaning of Q 75:22–3. For a later, standard Imami creed, see Watt, *Islamic creeds*, 100 (al-ʿAllāma al-Ḥillī). Cf. Madelung, "Imamism," 19. Some extreme Shiʿis (*ghulāt*) denied the existence of paradise and hell altogether, claiming instead that they were allegories for states of bliss and misery in this world. This was the teaching, e.g., of Abū Manṣūr al-ʿIjlī, a companion of the fifth Imam, Muḥammad al-Bāqir (d. *ca.* 115/733). By contrast, Abū Manṣūr claimed to have ascended to heaven and to have been patted on his head by God. See Daftary, *Ismāʿīlīs*, 69–70. A short creed of Ibn Bābūya, contained in his *K. Ṣifāt al-Shīʿa*, enumerates belief in the ascension, the questioning in the grave, the Pond, intercession, the createdness of paradise and hell, the Bridge, the Scales, (bodily) resurrection, and reward and punishment among the tenets of Shiʿi faith. See Baḥrānī, *Maʿālim*, II, 70–1; III, 254. Cf. Majlisī, *Biḥār*, VIII, 400.

[39] On the vision of God in Shiʿism, see Amir-Moezzi, "Pre-existence of the Imam," 44–55; Georges Vajda, "Le problème," 31–54.

[40] Majlisī, *Biḥār*, VIII, 350. Cf. ibid., VIII, 416.

[41] Schmidtke, *Theologie*, 234–5.

[42] Baḥrānī, *Maʿālim*, III, 213.

[43] Mufīd, *Ajwiba*, 123; Majlisī, *Biḥār*, VIII, 427. Cf. *TG*, IV, 553. Ibn Bābūya, *Creed*, 73 (§ 29), states that paradise and hell have been created, i.e., they are coterminous with this world. However, the garden of Adam is not the eschatologial paradise. See ibid., 74 (§ 29). Thus also in a tradition attributed to Jaʿfar al-Ṣādiq: "Had it [Adam's garden] been one of the gardens of the otherworld, he would never have left it." See *Mawsūʿat al-Imam al-Ṣādiq*, XI, 102 (quoting Kulaynī, *Kāfī*, III, 247). However, al-Majlisī relates the opinion of the sixth Imam, ʿAlī al-Riḍā (d. 203/818), that paradise must have been created *ab initio*, for otherwise, "where would Adam's paradise have been?" See Majlisī, *Biḥār*, VIII, 363.

not categorically deny the corporeal particulars of the otherworld but tended to downplay their importance, a fact that accords with their general preference for reason-based (*ʿaqlī*) theology and their distrust of the traditionist (*naqlī*) sciences.[44] This may also explain the dearth of Shiʿi traditionist literature dedicated to paradise and hell in the period from the fifth/eleventh to the tenth/sixteenth century. One only has to compare this to the continued production of such works by Sunni authors, as discussed in Chapters 2 and 3. When pushed, however, Shiʿi theologians vigourously defended the existence of physical pleasures in the afterlife. In the words of al-Mufīd,

> there is no-one in paradise who does not enjoy food and drink and what the senses perceive. The claim that there are people in paradise whose joy consists in praising and sanctifying [God], to the exception of food and drink, leads astray from the religion of Islam. It is [a position] derived from the faith of the Christians, who claim that those who are obedient in this life become angels in paradise who do not eat, drink or have sexual intercourse. However, God in His book has indicated that this position is wrong: He stimulates people's desire for food, drink and sexual intercourse [in paradise].[45]

Al-Majlisī comments that not all corporeal pleasures are experienced in the same way, which explains the existence of different gradations of pleasure in paradise. An ignoramus who is served a sweet dish by a king does not feel any different when served from a stall in the marketplace. The connoisseur, however, "he who understands a thing or two about the grandeur of the ruler (*ʿaẓamat al-sulṭān*)," derives much greater joy from the experience.[46]

However, there were also points on which Shiʿi theologians conspicuously and consistently departed from Muʿtazilite teachings. These differences concerned core tenets of their eschatology. They rejected the doctrine of *al-waʿīd*, that is, they refused to countenance perpetual punishment of unrepentant Muslim sinners – instead, they emphasised the possibility of God's forgiveness in such cases;[47] as noted, they mostly taught that paradise and

[44] Halm, *Schia*, 86.

[45] Majlisī, *Biḥār*, VIII, 403.

[46] Ibid., 404.

[47] Ibn Bābūya, *Creed*, 63–4 (§ 22); Majlisī, *Biḥār*, VIII, 427, 493. Cf. *TG*, IV, 548; Madelung, "Imamism," 16, 20, 23, 37; Schmidtke, *Theology*, 230–1, 235–6. Among the Shiʿis only the Zaydīs believe in perpetual punishment for Muslim sinners, and the Imams, whose function is defined in primarily political terms, lose their ability to intercede. See Madelung, "Imamism," 28. Abū l-ʿAtāhiya (Zaydī/Iraq, d. *ca.* 210/825) thought that punishment for grave sinners in hell is perpetual. See *TG*, I, 448; Kalisch, "Anmerkungen zu Jenseitsvorstellungen," 92 (quoting Sharafī, *ʿUdda*, II, 313ff.). A maverick universalist position, arguing that God would have to forgive even the unbelievers, was taken by the Basran Shiʿi Muʿtazilite, Abū Saʿīd al-Ḥaḍrī (*fl.* second half of third/ninth c.); his view, however, remained peripheral. See *TG*, IV, 91–2; V, 344; Crone, "Abū Saʿīd al-Ḥaḍrī."

FIGURE 14. The prophet Muḥammad, during his heavenly journey, visits paradise. From Shujāʾī Mashhadī, *Miʿrājnāma* (*Book of Ascension*). Persian lithograph dated 1271/1854. Image courtesy of Ali Boozari.

hell were "already created";[48] and they insisted on the efficacy of the Imams' intercession (i.e., on behalf of the Shiʿites).[49] Al-ʿAllāma al-Ḥillī reasoned that the sins committed during a lifetime are finite and that, therefore, it would be

[48] Majlisī, *Biḥār*, VIII, 318 (referring to Q 3:133: *uʿiddat li-l-muttaqīn*), 463; Baḥrānī, *Maʿālim*, II, 205 (from Ibn Bābūya): *khalq al-janna wa-l-nār* is one of the tenets of faith.

[49] Ibn Bābūya, *Creed*, 63 (§ 21); Mufīd, *Awāʾil al-maqālāt*, 52 (tr. Sourdel, "L'Imamisme," 284); Majlisī, *Biḥār*, VIII, 504. Cf. Hamza, "To hell and back," 161–4; Madelung, "Imamism," 27–9; *TG*, I, 276; McDermott, *Theology*, 254–5; Schmidtke, *Theology*, 238–9; eadem,

an act of injustice to inflict infinite punishment on sinners in the afterlife. It is a different matter, he however added, in the case of unbelief, "which is the gravest of sins, equaling infinite sinning."[50]

The Akhbārī Revival of Eschatology

Eleventh/seventeenth-century Shiʿism witnessed the emergence of the so-called Akhbārī school, characterised by the renewed commitment to collecting the sayings (*akhbār*) of the Imams and recognising them as revealed scripture, and the concomitant rejection of the rationalist outlook of thinkers in the tradition of al-ʿAllāma al-Ḥillī and his forerunners, who came to be referred to as Uṣūlīs. While the Uṣūlīs, who thrived under the patronage of the Safavid Shahs of Persia (r. 907–1135/1501–1722), eventually proved victorious in the conflict, Akhbārī ideas stimulated a renaissance of traditionist literature. This is certainly true in the area of eschatological hadith. The most extensive premodern collection of Shiʿi hadith, the *Oceans of Lights* (*Biḥār al-anwār*) of the court theologian and inquisitor Muḥammad Bāqir al-Majlisī (d. 1110/1699), may be invoked here as exemplifying a number of Akhbārī principles, in particular the notion of a "less stringent application of *isnād* criticism," typical of the Akhbārīs' "attempt to maximise the revelatory material."[51] The sixth to eighth of the 110 volumes of al-Majlisī's collection are devoted to eschatology (*maʿād*), covering the events in the *barzakh*, at resurrection and judgement, and in paradise and hell. These three volumes surpass not only all previous Shiʿi handbooks of eschatological hadith, but also the Sunni compilations.[52] The section on paradise and hell in the *Oceans of Light* is roughly one and a half times as long as, for example, the works of al-Qurṭubī and al-Suyūṭī.

Al-Majlisī, however, is not simply a collector of hadith. His survey of Muslim eschatology features regular discussions of a theological and even philosophical kind. Rather than suggesting a comparison with the works of al-Qurṭubī and al-Suyūṭī, this makes al-Majlisī's approach akin to that of the Sunni compiler-*cum*-theologian Ibn Qayyim al-Jawziyya (d. 751/1350), whose

Theologie, 262–3. For Shiʿi traditions about the intercession of the Imams, see Majlisī, *Biḥār*, VIII, 500–9; Baḥrānī, *Maʿālim*, II, 187–92.

[50] Ḥillī, *Manāhij*, translated in Schmidtke, *Theology*, 235.

[51] Gleave, *Scripturalist Islam*, 264. As Gleave notes, al-Majlisī is claimed by both the Akhbārīs and the Uṣūlīs as one of their own, while al-Majlisī stated that he pursued a "middle way" between the two schools. See ibid., 44, 155, 201. Cf. Halm, *Schia*, 126.

[52] Majlisī, *Biḥār*, VIII, 309–417, deals with paradise, comprising Qurʾānic verses (pp. 309–15), exegesis (pp. 315–42), and *akhbār* (pp. 342–417), culled to a large extent from Ibn Bābūya's works (*K. al-Amālī*; *K. al-Khiṣāl*; *K. Thawāb al-aʿmāl*) and to a lesser from al-Kulaynī's *K. al-Kāfī*, but also from the *K. al-Zuhd* of al-Ahwāzī, the *K. al-Ikhtiṣāṣ* of al-Mufīd (which contains the *K. Ṣifat al-janna wa-l-nār* of Ibn Janāḥ), the *Nahj al-balāgha*, as well as numerous Shiʿi *tafsīrs*. For hell, see ibid., 417–96, again comprising Qurʾānic verses (pp. 417–26), exegesis (pp. 426–59), and *akhbār* (pp. 460–96).

Urging Souls Forwards to the Lands of Happiness (*Ḥādī l-arwāḥ ilā bilād al-afrāḥ*), though rigorously examining the scriptural bases for eschatological beliefs, frequently delves into questions of systematic theology.[53] Al-Majlisī, for example, presents a lengthy refutation of philosophical eschatology. It is striking that this refutation names Avicenna and al-Fārābī, but not al-Suhrawardī.[54] Either al-Majlisī simply chose to ignore al-Suhrawardī as a maverick, or he sympathised, to some degree at least, with the idea of an imaginable existence after death. Some passages in the *Oceans of Light* seem to suggest as much, even though al-Majlisī appears to restrict the applicability of the concept to the period between death and resurrection, that is, the *barzakh*, and then only to certain individuals. Those who are pure in belief, asserts one tradition he quotes, are moved from their earthly form (*haykal*) to another form (*ṣūra*). It is in this latter form that they have an experience of paradise and hell until the Day of Resurrection.[55] Elsewhere it is stated that most people experience the punishment of the grave in their original physical bodies (*al-ajsād al-aṣliyya*), but that the souls of others attach themselves to "subtle imaginable bodies" (*al-ajsād al-mithāliyya al-laṭīfa*) that "resemble" the original bodies. In these imaginable bodies, souls have the ability to fly through the air, or appear to relatives in visions; they are the same bodies that one inhabits in dreams.[56]

Arguably the most important contribution to Akhbāri eschatological literature is that of Hāshim b. Sulaymān al-Baḥrānī (d. 1107/1695 or 6). Al-Baḥrānī was born in the village of al-Tūblī on the main island of al-Baḥrayn, the east Arabian coast having come under the dominion of the Safavids in 1010/1610. After a period of study with Akhbārī masters in Iraq and Persia he returned to his home island and became judge and censor of public morals (*muḥtasib*) there.[57] Akhbārism flourished on the margin of the Safavid Empire more than in its centre,[58] and al-Baḥrānī is the founder of one of "the many Bahrayni Akhbārī networks which emerge in the [eleventh/seventeenth] century."[59] Venerated after his death at a "well-known shrine" (*mazār maʿrūf*) in al-Tūblī,[60] he is perhaps best remembered as the author of a large Akhbārī commentary on the Qurʾān.[61] Imami historians praise

[53] Cf. the previous chapter, in which frequent recourse is had to Ibn Qayyim al-Jawziyya's *Ḥādī l-arwāḥ*.

[54] Majlisī, *Biḥār*, VIII, 494–6.

[55] Ibid., VI, 432.

[56] Ibid., VI, 444–5.

[57] For a biography of al-Baḥrānī and lists of his teachers and students, see Yūsuf al-Baḥrānī's (d. 1186/1772) *Luʾluʾat al-Baḥrayn*, 63–6. See also *EIr*, s.v. Baḥrānī, Hāšem (W. Madelung).

[58] Halm, *Schia*, 125, 132.

[59] Gleave, *Scripturalist Islam*, 169.

[60] Baḥrānī, *Luʾluʾat al-Baḥrayn*, 63–4.

[61] Al-Baḥrānī's *al-Burhān fī tafsīr al-Qurʾān* was completed in 1094/1683 and dedicated to the Ṣafavid Sulaymān I (r. 1077–1105/1666–94). Another *tafsīr*, the *K. al-Hādī*, remains unpublished. On al-Baḥrānī's *tafsīr*, see Lawson, "Akhbārī Shīʿī approaches"; Gleave, *Scripturalist Islam*, 228–32.

al-Baḥrānī for collecting hadiths to a degree matched only by al-Majlisī, and for transmitting them from books that do not figure among the sources of the *Oceans of Light*, such as the *K. al-Miʿrāj* of Ibn Bābūya.[62]

Two of al-Baḥrānī's collections of eschatological hadith interest us in particular. The more extensive of the two, his *Signposts of Nearness [to God] in the Knowledge of This Life and the Next* (*Maʿālim al-zulfā fī maʿārif al-nashʾa al-ūlā wa-l-ukhrā*), is a *summa* of eschatological traditions, published (in its modern edition) in three large volumes and easily surpassing the eschatological portions of the *Oceans of Light* in length.[63] Al-Baḥrānī's work includes numerous traditions about the topography of paradise and hell, the prominence of the Shiʿi Imams in the afterworld, and the state of the blessed and the damned, often in long versions enriched by copious narrative details. There are also many lengthy stories of a legendary and fantastic kind. He relates, for example, a Shiʿi version of the story of Jesus and the skull that differs from the Sunni version[64] in several intriguing ways. This time, it is not Jesus who is the hero of the story but ʿAlī, who in fact finds and revivifies two, rather than one, skulls. One belongs to the pre-Islamic Persian king Chosroe Anushirvan, who reports that God has placed him in hell because of his unbelief, but that the flames do not touch him because he was a just ruler. The other skull belongs to the evil king Parviz b. Hurmuz who relates his gruesome tortures at the hands of the *zabāniya* in hell. According to the story, upon hearing of ʿAlī's wondrous conversation with the dead, many Zoroastrians convert to Islam.[65]

Also noteworthy, and in certain respects more remarkable, is al-Baḥrānī's *Entertainment of the Godly People and the Lighthouse of Inspection of the Createdness of Paradise and Hell* (*Nuzhat al-abrār wa-manār al-anẓār fī khalq al-janna wa-l-nār*). As al-Baḥrānī writes in his introduction, when he compiled traditions for the eighty-second chapter of his *Signposts of Nearness*, a chapter dealing "with the creation, in this world, of paradise and hell," he realised he had a great deal more to say than could be fitted into the text. Hence he penned a separate compilation, the *Entertainment of the Godly People*, featuring 252 traditions.[66] This is a work that focuses on the theme of the interfusion of this world and the otherworld, highlighting both their temporal and spatial overlaps. The text stands as a monument against all attempts to emphasise the ontological gap between this world and the otherworld. Against the philosophers, who talk about the otherworld in terms of a realm of pure intelligibles, and against the rationalist theologians, who stress the aspect of God's transcendent unfathomability,

[62] See ʿĀmilī, *Aʿyān al-shīʿa*, X, 249.
[63] Baḥrānī, *Maʿālim*.
[64] See the preceding text, pp. 116–8.
[65] Ibid., II, 100–3.
[66] Idem, *Nuzhat*, 39. Cf. idem, *Maʿālim*, III, 253–72 (with nineteen traditions).

the *Entertainment of the Godly People* foregrounds the notion that this world and the otherworld are in multiple ways connected, not separate. Al-Baḥrānī quotes a tradition traced to ʿAlī, according to which "this world is in the otherworld (*al-dunyā fī l-ākhira*), and the otherworld encompasses this world (*muḥīṭa bi-l-dunyā*)." This is not to say that they are identical. As the tradition continues,

this world is ephemeral, while the otherworld is [truly] alive and stable. The likeness of this is someone who is sleeping. The body sleeps but the spirit does not sleep. The body dies but the spirit dies not. God said: *The otherworld: that is truly life – did they but know!* [Q 29:64] This world is the vestige of the otherworld (*al-dunyā rasmu l-ākhira*), and the otherworld is the vestige of this world. Yet this world is not the otherworld, and the otherworld is not this world. When the spirit leaves the body, each of them returns to that from which it originated and from which it was created. Likewise [i.e., like the spirit exists both in the body and in the otherworld], paradise and hell are present both in this world and in the otherworld.[67]

Like body and soul are interfused, so are this world and the otherworld. Each leaves vestiges, or traces, in the other; each thereby becomes observable in the other. Similarly, Muḥsin Fayḍ Kāshānī (d. 1091/1680), a son-in-law of Mullā Ṣadrā and follower of his ontology, states that "the abode of existence is one; this world and the otherworld complement each other."[68]

Characteristically, it is the "people of the house" (*ahl al-bayt*) who act as intermediaries between the two realms, and the first third or so of al-Baḥrānī's work is dedicated to them. The Prophet, whose *miʿrāj* is taken as evidence for the simultaneous existence of this world and the otherworld, is quoted as saying:

When I was lifted up into heaven, Gabriel took me by the hand and made me enter paradise, where he offered me one of its ripe dates. I ate it, and it became a sperm [deposited] in my tailbone (*ṣulb*). After descending to earth, I had intercourse with Khadīja, and she became pregnant with Fāṭima. Fāṭima, therefore, is a human houri (*ḥawrāʾ insāniyya*). Whenever I long for the scent of paradise, I smell the scent of my daughter Fāṭima.[69]

According to another tradition, Fāṭima existed before heaven and earth were created, as a light attached to God's Throne. During the Prophet's *miʿrāj*, she was transformed into an apple and eaten by him, and then reborn in human form on earth.[70] The idea that Fāṭima was conceived in paradise applies equally to the other "people of the house," particularly to the Imams. The mother of ʿAlī, according to a story related by al-Baḥrānī, was miraculously

[67] Ibid., III, 166–7, 273.
[68] Kāshānī, *Kalimāt*, 165.
[69] Baḥrānī, *Nuzhat*, 40 (#1). Cf. ibid., 113–49 (##17–30); idem, *Maʿālim*, III, 254–5. Also in Majlisī, *Biḥār*, VIII, 345.
[70] Baḥrānī, *Nuzhat*, 113–4 (#17).

FIGURE 15. ʿAlī offers Muḥammad an apple in paradise. From Shujāʿī Mashhadī, *Miʿrājnāma (Book of Ascension)*. Persian lithograph dated 1271/1854. Image courtesy of Ali Boozari.

swallowed by the Kaaba, a wall of which opened up and closed behind her. Three days later, she emerged, carrying the infant ʿAlī, telling people that she had been eating the fruits of paradise while giving birth to her son.[71]

However, the stuff of paradise is embodied in this world not only in the Imams. Certain objects and tools used on earth derive from paradise:[72] The blade of ʿAlī's sword (the famous *dhū l-fiqār*) is a leaf from an otherworldly myrtle tree; the prophets Abraham and Joseph wore fabric tailored in paradise; Moses's staff was cut from a heavenly boxthorn bush.[73] Creation is peppered with paradise, like scattered pearls: the Black Stone of the Kaaba and other precious stone, fine sorts of camels and of palm trees, or the drops of dew on the leaves of wild chicory.[74] In every pomegranate there is a seed from paradise, "and if an unbeliever eats it, God sends an angel to pick it out [i.e., before he can swallow it]."[75] Most daringly of all, it is stated (on the authority of Jaʿfar al-Ṣādiq) that "God creates all believers from the earth of paradise (*ṭīnat al-janna*), all the unbelievers from the earth of hell."[76]

It is when quoting traditions such as the last one that al-Baḥrānī, in the second half of his work, comes close to embracing mystical ideas. In fact,

71 Ibid., 94–5 (#13).

72 The notion is not unique to Shiʿi hadith. See, e.g., the list of a "traditions about non-human, paradisiacal things that are in this world and in paradise" in Nābulusī, *Ahl al-janna*, 44–55, and 74–7 (similarly, but in regard to hell).

73 Baḥrānī, *Nuzhat*, 227 (#85), 271–5 (##122–25), 390 (#221).

74 Ibid., 287–9 (##136–8), 289 (#139), 294 (#141), 304 (#150).

75 Ibid., 303 (#146). A version of this tradition is also found in Suyūṭī, *Budūr*, 534. According to Majlisī, *Biḥār*, VIII, 352, five are the fruit of paradise in this world: pomegranates, apples, quinces, grapes, and dates.

76 Baḥrānī, *Nuzhat*, 44 (#6).

there are several examples of Akhbārī scholars who declared themselves to be Sufis.[77] In this context, one should recall that in certain respects Imami Shi'ism is characterised by a certain affinity to Sufi traditions. One thinks, for example, of the insistence on the concepts of *walāya,* the loving devotion to the Imam, and of *ta'wīl*, the "spiritual hermeneutics" used to derive the inner (*bāṭin*) meaning of scripture.[78]

Isma'ili Eschatology

The concept of *ta'wīl*, the extraction of revelation's inner (*bāṭin*) meaning, which crowns its contingent outward (*ẓāhir*) meaning, is central to the thought of the Isma'ili Shi'a, the second-largest Shi'i community after the Imamis. The Isma'ilis, especially in the work of foundational thinkers of the tradition such as al-Sijistānī (d. after 361/971) and al-Kirmānī (d. after 311/1021), wed this hermeneutical principle with cosmological speculations about a hierarchy of celestial intellects, and with the belief that the Prophets, the Imams, and their representatives on earth act as intermediaries between these celestial intellects and the intellects of humans. Their eschatological thought tends towards Neoplatonic philosophy, in fact it is at times barely distinguishable from it. The philosophical eschatology of the Isma'ilis, a description of which concludes this chapter, can be considered a fourth mode of conceptualising paradise and hell in Shi'i Islam, next to the systems professed by the adherents of the Uṣūlī, Akhbārī, and Ishrāqī/Shaykhī schools among the Imami Shi'ites.

As scholars of Isma'ilism have noted, Isma'ili texts about resurrection, judgment, paradise, and hell are as obscure as they are rare, not to mention the fact that Isma'ili *ta'wīl* is notoriously ambivalent and subtle, refusing to attribute a single meaning to verses of the Qur'ān.[79] On occasion the impression arises that Isma'ili authors deliberately tried to obfuscate their traces.[80] Besides being sworn to secrecy within a hierarchical system of religious leadership, they may have felt compelled to do so out of a concern for their safety, for it was particularly the eschatological aspects of Isma'ili doctrine that elicited the most aggressive responses from their Sunni (and also Imami) opponents. In his polemical treatise entitled *The Vices of the People of Inner Meaning* (*Faḍā'iḥ al-bāṭiniyya*), al-Ghazālī declared the Isma'ilis to be guilty of manifest unbelief because they taught that the pleasures and punishments

77 See Kohlberg, "Aspects of Akhbari thought," 145–6.

78 The semantic range of the term *walāya* is wide. In a sense shared by Sufis and Shi'ites, *walāya* expresses the loving submission of initiates to their spiritual guide. See Amir-Moezzi, "Notes à propos de la *walāya*," 729, 735–8. On "spiritual hermeneutics" and Shi'ism's relationship to Sufism, see Nasr, "Le shī'isme et le soufisme," 215–33.

79 Cf. Poonawala, "Ismā'īlī *ta'wīl*."

80 Badakhchani, "Introduction," 9; De Smet, "Isma'ili-Shi'i visions of hell," 241-2.

of the hereafter are purely spiritual and not corporeal, based on an allegorical interpretation (*ta'wīl*) of the Qur'ān. Al-Ghazālī also reminds his readers, fatally, that in the time of the Companions, such blasphemy was punishable by death.[81] Under the patrons of al-Ghazālī, the Seljuq rulers of Iraq and Persia, persecutions of Isma'ilis were a common occurrence. At times, they escalated into mob lynchings and public burnings in pits.[82]

In the course of the third/ninth century, the Isma'ilis formed a revolutionary opposition movement to the Sunni caliphs of Baghdad, culminating in the establishment, around the turn of the century, of an Isma'ili countercaliphate in Ifriqiya (modern-day Tunisia), that of the Fāṭimids (r. 297–567/909–1171). The Fāṭimid caliphs claimed the title of Imam, arguing that they were the direct descendants of Ismā'īl (d. 138/755), the seventh Imam and son of Ja'far al-Ṣādiq, and therefore the rightful heirs of the Imamate. It was not before the fourth/tenth century, however, that Isma'ili authors laid the foundations of the mature, philosophical Isma'ili system of thought, harmonising their commitment to the leadership of the Isma'ili Imam (the Fāṭimid caliph who resided, from 358/969 onwards, in Cairo) with gnostic and Neoplatonic teachings, particularly as they were known to them in the form of the so-called *Theology of Aristotle* (*Ūthūlūjiya Arisṭāṭālis*), an Arabic paraphrase of Books 4–6 of Plotinus's *Enneads*.[83]

A central role in the construction of this intellectual edifice was played by the eastern missionaries (*dā'ī*s) of the Fāṭimids, prominently by Abū Ya'qūb al-Sijistānī (d. after 361/971), a *dā'ī* in Persia and Sijistan, who is considered "the major philosophical theologian of Ismā'īlī Shī'ism in the mid-fourth/tenth century."[84] Al-Sijistānī squarely denies the resurrection of bodies,[85] and he is followed in this doctrine by prominent Isma'ili thinkers of later times, such as the *dā'ī* Ḥamīd al-Dīn al-Kirmānī (d. after 311/1021). Resurrection is a spiritual event. Pure souls, al-Sijistānī teaches, are illuminated at the end of time by the teaching of the Qā'im, the awaited messianic Imam; impure and dark souls, by contrast, remain imprisoned in ignorance and darkness.[86] According to al-Sijistānī's *Book of Wellsprings* (*K. al-Yanābī'*), "the reward in the Abode of Permanence is knowledge (*'ilm*), not sensation and

[81] Ghazālī, *Faḍā'iḥ al-bāṭiniyya*, 151–4 (tr. 267). On al-Ghazālī's involvement in the sectarian politics of the Seljuqs, see Mitha, *Al-Ghazālī*, 1–27; Safi, *The politics of knowledge*, 105–24.

[82] Ibn al-Athīr, *Kāmil*, VIII, 450 (s.a. 494). Cf. Lange, *Justice*, 68–9.

[83] Daftary, *Ismā'īlīs*, 223–5. Other Neoplatonic texts in Arabic translations influenced the early Isma'ili *da'wa*, such as pseudo-Ammonius and the *Discourse on the Pure Good* (*Kalām fī maḥḍ al-khayr*), another pseudo-Aristotelian work based on a paraphrase of the *Elements of Theology* of Proclus, known to medieval Europe as the *Liber de causis* (*Book of Causes*). Cf. Halm, *Reich*, 262–5.

[84] *EI3*, s.v. Abū Ya'qūb al-Sijistānī (*P. E.* Walker). Cf. Walker, "Introduction," 17.

[85] Sijistānī, *Kashf*, 120 (§ 7.2.3), 122–4 (§ 7.3); idem, *Maqālīd*, 183–8. I thank Paul Walker for drawing my attention to the *K. al- Maqālīd* and Daniel de Smet for providing me with a copy of the passage in question.

[86] Idem, *Risāla*, 45, 48–9; idem, *Iftikhār*, 196–205 (*b. fī ma'rifat al-ba'th*).

not sensual things." This, al-Sijistānī explains, is because sensual pleasures (such as the feeling of satiation) are finite; they exhaust themselves and thus are by definition defective. This makes them incompatible with paradise. Knowledge, however, never lessens, it can only increase.[87]

Al-Sijistānī at times intimates that those who achieve full knowledge in this life partake in paradise *already*, that before the "Great Resurrection" (*al-qiyāma al-kubrā*) at the end of time, certain adepts of Isma'ilism enjoy a kind of proleptic resurrection and are "reborn" into an existence of pure spiritual bliss.[88] Paradise is called a garden (*bustān*), he declares, because gardens are adorned by trees, fruits, fountains, and other properties that cause the senses tranquility and serenity. Similarly, knowledge is a garden of the intellect, adorned with the Prophets – the Isma'ilis reckon that six "Speaking-Prophets" (*nuṭaqā'*) have appeared so far, that is, Adam, Noah, Abraham, Moses, Jesus, and Muḥammad – and the (Isma'ili) Imams, whose teachings, if properly understood, bring joy and felicity.[89] Those, therefore, who comprehend the true, or inner, (*bāṭin*) aspects of revelation as brought by the Prophets and taught by the Imams and the hierarchy of dignitaries serving them, already enjoy the pleasures of paradise. However, those who stick to the outward (*ẓāhir*) meaning of revelation suffer the torments of hell during their earthly lives.[90] After death, they may even undergo metempsychosis as punishment, the soul's rebirth in another body or lower material form.[91]

The point is not made explicit by al-Sijistānī himself;[92] other Isma'ili authors are more forthcoming. In a fourth/tenth-century Isma'ili text, for example, one finds the following esoteric interpretation (*ta'wīl*) of the Qur'ānic verse 4:56 that states that "those who do not believe in Our signs" will be punished in the Fire and given "new skins every time their skins are consumed." These new skins, it is explained, are new bodies into which the

[87] Idem, *Yanābī'*, 65–7 (§§ 18–30, tr. 88–9). For al-Sijistānī's spiritual interpretation of reward and punishment, see idem, *Iftikhār*, 206–14 (*b. fī ma'rifat al-thawāb wa-l-'iqāb*). On al-Sijistānī's doctrine of paradise, as well as its continuation in the thought of al-Mu'ayyad fī l-Dīn al-Shīrāzī (d. 471/1078), see now Alexandrin, "Paradise as the abode of pure knowledge."

[88] See, e.g., Sijistānī, *Kashf*, 123 (§ 7.4.3).

[89] Idem, *Yanābī'*, 67:7–11 (§ 131, tr. 89). On the *nuṭaqā'*, see Halm, *Kosmologie*, 18–34.

[90] A sixth/twelfth-century heresiographical source, the *'Aqā'id al-thalāth wa-l-sab'īna firqa* (written *ca.* 540/1145–6) of Abū Muḥammad al-Yamanī, attacks the Carmathian *dā'ī* Abū Tammām (*fl.* fourth/tenth c.) for having declared in his *Shajarat al-dīn* that the strict observance of the Sharī'a in everyday life is hell for the ordinary Muslim. See Walker, "Abū Tammām," 346.

[91] Cf. Walker, "The doctrine of metempsychosis"; Freitag, *Seelenwanderung*.

[92] Al-Sijistānī states that after death, souls are reborn into *barzakh*s, which he explains to be bodies in which the dead await resurrection. See Sijistānī, *Risāla*, 40, 46–7. Cf. de Smet, "Isma'ili-Shi'i visions of hell," 252–3. The forty-fourth chapter of al-Sijistānī's *K. al-Maqālīd* is a refutation of the belief in metempsychosis, specifically the rebirth in animals. See Sijistānī, *Maqālīd*, 200–4. Cf. Poonawala, "Al-Sijistānī and his *K. al-Maqālīd*," 282.

souls of the uninitiated are reborn after death, thus continuing to suffer from their ignorance on earth.[93] This belief in metempsychosis is propounded in particular by the Ṭayyibīs, a branch of the Isma'ilis in Yemen that flourished there from the sixth/twelfth century onwards.[94] Ṭayyibī authors teach that impure souls may be reborn in darker, less noble bodies, first in those of blacks, Berbers, and Turks, then in those of animals, from edible ones down to the lowest insect, and, finally, in plants. Shortly before the advent of the Imam-Qā'im, these plants are eaten by unbelievers and thus become a part of them. At Judgement, the unbelievers are punished with confinement to Sijjīn (cf. Q 83:7), a rock in the middle of the earth, the darkest place on earth where matter is most dense.[95]

The Brethren of Purity (*Ikhwān al-Ṣafā'*), an anonymous group of philosophers from Basra (*fl.* probably second half of the fourth/tenth c.),[96] also deserve mention in this context. The central concern of the *Epistles of the Brethren of Purity* (*Rasā'il ikhwān al-ṣafā*), an encyclopaedic collection of fifty-two treatises dealing with topics in mathematics, physics, psychology, and metaphysics, is the soul's happiness in the world to come.[97] This is achieved, the Brethren maintain, by gradually purifying one's soul from all attachments to material things. While the Brethren do not openly support the claims of the Fāṭimid caliph, their *Epistles* overlap with Isma'ili eschatological doctrines in significant respects,[98] including the belief in the transmigration of impure souls after death into new, earthly bodies.[99] Hell, in their definition, is no other than the world of bodies (*'ālam al-ajsām*), while paradise is the world of spirits (*'ālam al-arwāḥ*), attained by the pure souls when they are released from their bodies at death.[100] Resurrection (*qiyām*) in fact occurs at this very moment, "when the soul rises from its grave, that is, from the body in which it was previously."[101]

[93] (Pseudo-)'Abdān, *Shajarat al-yaqīn*, 134. This work should not be attributed to 'Abdān but rather, to the Carmathian *dā'ī* in Khorasan, Abū Tammām (*fl.* fourth/tenth c.). See De Smet, "Isma'ili-Shi'i visions of hell," 244.

[94] *EI2*, s.v. Ṭayyibiyya, X, 403a-404a (F. Daftary).

[95] De Smet, "Isma'ili-Shi'i visions of hell," 263.

[96] For a summary of discussions surrounding the dating of the *Rasā'il*, see de Smet, "Religiöse Anwendung," 533–4.

[97] Goldziher, *Richtungen*, 189; Marquet, *La philosophie*, 383–403; *EI2*, s.v. Ikhwān al-Ṣafā', III, 1071a-1076b, at 1074a (Y. Marquet).

[98] The extent to which the Brethren were affiliated with or even gave rise to Isma'ili teachings continues to be a point of contention among scholars. Cf. Daftary, *The Ismā'īlīs*, 234–7. Their influence on later Isma'ili literature, by contrast, is beyond dispute. See Daftary, *Isma'ilis*, 236.

[99] Ikhwān al-Ṣafā', *Jāmi'a*, 176. Not all Isma'ili thinkers espoused metempsychosis, however, Nāṣir-i Khusraw (d. after 465/1072) being an important exception. See Corbin, *En Islam iranien*, IV, 89n119.

[100] Ikhwān al-Ṣafā', *Rasā'il*, III, 397.

[101] Ibid., III, 398. Cf. Marquet, "Imāmat, résurrection et hiérarchie"; Baffioni, "Bodily resurrection."

It is instructive at this point to provide some further examples of Isma'ili *ta'wīl* of eschatological verses in the Qur'ān. "O soul at peace," the Qur'ān promises its audience, "return to your Lord, pleased and pleasing, enter among my righteous servants, enter my Paradise" (89:27–30). The *ta'wīl* of this verse that one encounters in the *Book of Unveiling* (*K. al-Kashf*), an Isma'ili text originating probably as early as the second half of the third/ninth century,[102] consists in a relatively straightforward act of specification: The "soul at peace," the *Book of Unveiling* affirms, is, of course, the soul of the (Isma'ili) believer; "your Lord" refers not to God but to the "Commander of the Faithful" 'Alī, the pivotal figure in the early history of Shi'ism; the "righteous servants" are the "Speaking-Prophets" and the Imams; and finally, the phrase "enter my Paradise" is interpreted as an invitation to submit to the person known as *ḥujja* ("proof"), in this instance most likely a reference to the awaited Imam, the Qā'im.[103]

A later Isma'ili author who provides us with a number of examples of *ta'wīl* of eschatological verses is Naṣīr al-Dīn Ṭūsī (d. 672/1274), a polymath scholar and politician who served for a while at the courts of local Isma'ili lords in Persia. The treatise in which these examples occur is called *The Origin and the Return* (*al-Mabda' wa-l-ma'ād*), a title that proved popular among philosophically minded eschatologists of all times and places.[104] A fairly conventional allegorisation that Ṭūsī proposes is that the four rivers of paradise mentioned in the Qur'ān (47:15) represent four different types of religious knowledge. The river of water, Ṭūsī avers, is basic religious knowledge acquired in sermons and through the advice given to commoners; the river of milk is more refined: it corresponds to the exoteric religious knowledge of the educated elite; the river of honey is only for the elite of the elite (*khāṣṣ al-khawāṣṣ*): it equals the insight into "obscure issues" achieved after instruction (*ta'līm*) by Isma'ili authorities; finally, the river of wine is

[102] See Velji, "Fashioning empires," 34. The text was edited and published by Muṣṭafā Ghālib in 1984.

[103] *K. al-Kashf*, 72. Cf. Velji, "Fashioning empires," 76–8.

[104] The popularity, among philosophers, of the antonyms *mabda'* and *ma'ād* resonates with the fact that they occur in the Qur'ān in a context that is appropriately abstract and devoid of eschatological particulars: "He is the one who originates and returns" (*innahu huwa yubdi'u wa-yu'īd*, 85:13). The noun *ma'ād* occurs only once in the Qur'ān (28:85). Earlier examples of works entitled *al-Mabda' wa-l-ma'ād* include an unedited work by al-Sijistānī (see *GAS*, I, 575) and one by Avicenna. See Ibn Sīna, *al-Mabda' wa-l-ma'ād*. Later contributors include Bābā Afḍal (d. prob. 619/1213–4), 'Azīz-i Nasafī (*fl.* mid-seventh/thirteenth c.), Mullā Ṣadrā and the Sufi master of Mughal India, Shaykh Aḥmad Sirhindī (d. 1034/1624). See Bābā Afḍal, *Jāvidān-nāma*, chs. 3 and 4 (on *mabda'* and *ma'ād*, respectively); Nasafī, *Kashf al-ḥaqā'iq* (fifth epistle, fols. 290a ff.); Ṣadrā, *al-Mabda' wa-l-ma'ād*; Sirhindī, *Mabda' wa-ma'ād*. *Mabda'* and *ma'ād*, according to Halm, are key terms of the Isfahān school of theosophy. See Halm, *Schia*, 118. One might also mention the *K. al-Mabda' wa-l-ma'ād* of the Ṭayyibī author Ibn al-Walīd (d. 667/1268), in addition to numerous other works.

divinely inspired knowledge gained in direct communication with the higher intellects.[105]

More daring is Ṭūsī's explanation of Qur'ān 74:30 ("Over it [hell] are nineteen"). The nineteen *zabāniya* or "administrators" (*mudabbirān*) of the "upper *barzakh*s," he states, are the seven planets and the twelve signs of the zodiac.[106] The idea here seems to be that there is a kind of hell in the celestial sphere where impure souls, after the "Greater Resurrection," remain imprisoned in bodies (which Ṭūsī calls *barzakh*s), rather than experiencing salvation in a purely intellectual existence.[107] There are also the "lower *barzakh*s," however, that is, earthly bodies inhabited by impure souls. These are likewise governed by nineteen evil forces, that is, the faculties that orient the human being towards material and sensual concerns. These include the five senses, but also the internal senses of fancy [*wahm*] and imagination [*khayāl*], among others.[108] If, Ṭūsī writes, one is prey in one's earthly life to these nineteen faculties, one will pass from this world's prison (*sijn*) to the hell of *sijjīn* in the next life.[109] The Qur'ānic counterparts of the *zabāniya*, the heavenly houris, are likewise the object of Ṭūsī's *ta'wīl*. He affirms that they are the forms (*ṣuwar*) in which the spiritual realities of the otherworld appear to the (Isma'ili) initiate. The houris are, as it were, knowledge items from the beyond. The "marriage" that takes place between them and the believers (Q 44:54) is nothing but the believer's cognitive assimilation of these knowledge items, which remain inaccessible to the exotericists and the enemies of the Isma'ilis ("the people of opposition," *ahl-i taḍādd*). For, as Ṭūsī reminds us, "they [the houris] are touched neither by man nor jinn" (Q 55:74).[110]

What these exegetical passages have in common is that they suggest that paradise and hell are close at hand, on account of their being spiritual realities, not otherworldly spaces pertaining to the end of time. The "people of [wrong] opinion" (*ahl-i gumān*) – a term Ṭūsī uses to designate the detractors of Isma'ilism – "think that Resurrection is far away both in time and place ... but the people of certainty (*ahl-i yaqīn*) know that it is near." Does not the Qur'ān state that "they think it is far away; we think it is near"

[105] My summary elides Ṭūsī's explanations in *Mabda'*, 74–5 (§§ 70–4, tr. 79–80) and *Rawḍat al-taslīm*, 151 (§ 454). Cf. al-Qāḍī al-Nu'mān, *Ta'wīl al-da'ā'im*, 127, for an earlier example of this allegorisation.

[106] In the cosmology of the early Ismā'iliyya, which builds on ancient Mesopotamian astral cults, nineteen angels, seven cherubs (*karūbiyya*), and twelve "spirits" (*rūḥāniyya*) are associated with the seven planets and the twelve signs of the zodiac. See Halm, *Kosmologie*, 91–100.

[107] That the *barzakh* is constituted by bodies in which impure souls are reincarnated is an idea that goes back to al-Suhrawardī. See Chapter 5, p. 189.

[108] An idea also found in Ṣadrā, *Ḥikma*, tr. Morris, 226–7.

[109] Ṭūsī, *Mabda'*, 72–3 (§§ 67–8, tr. 78–9).

[110] Ibid., 81–2 (§§ 86–7, tr. 85–6). The text is also edited and translated by Berthels, "Die paradiesischen Jungfraun," 274–5.

(70:6–7)? And did not the Prophet, Ṭūsī adds, demonstrate the proximity and accessibility of the otherworld when he stretched out his hand and obtained a fruit from paradise?[111]

Here may in fact lie part of the explosive promise of Ismaʿilism, one of the reasons why its mission (*daʿwa*), through much of medieval Islamic history, appealed to the many, particularly among the learned.[112] The third/ninth-century *dāʿīs* Ḥamdan Qarmaṭ and ʿAbdān, who were active in Iraq, levied a special contribution from new converts, "receipt of which was acknowledged by the *dāʿī* with a meal of sweets supposed to have originated literally in Paradise, and to have been sent down by the Mahdi himself."[113] Al-Qāḍī al-Nuʿmān (d. 363/974), the illustrious head of the Ismaʿili *daʿwa* in the second half of the fourth/tenth century, wrote that in the realm of *bāṭin* (*fī l-bāṭin*), the *daʿwa* is the likeness (*mathal*) of paradise; the word for paradise, *janna*, is derived from a root meaning "concealment" (*ijtinān*), and the *daʿwa* is likewise a "veiled" (*mastūra*) activity by and for the elect; the knowledge that is imparted by the teaching of the *dāʿīs* corresponds to the four rivers flowing in paradise.[114] Ismaʿili thought, thus, plays with the idea that felicity is accessible in the here and now. This felicity is made available through the proper understanding of secret doctrines, which are propagated by the *dāʿīs*, through submission to the leadership of the Ismaʿili Imam, and through the belief in the appearance of the messianic Imam-Qāʾim.

Much of the polemics and slander levelled at Ismaʿilis directly targets their notion of a realised eschatology. The most conspicuous example, at least in the West, is the legend of the Old Man of the Mountain, which Marco Polo, in the late seventh/thirteenth century, claimed to have heard from natives of Eastern Persia.[115] According to this legend, well known ever after to European writers on the Islamic Middle East, the Ismaʿili militias of Persia (whom Polo calls the "Ashishin," "Assassins" in the usual spelling of later times, a bowdlerised version of Arabic *ḥashīshiyyūn*, "consumers of hashish") were

[111] Ṭūsī, *Mabdaʾ*, (§ 21, tr. 58–9). The Prophet once sat with his Companions on the mountain of Rabāb, when a pomegranate appeared above his head, dangling down from paradise. He grabbed it, split it open, and shared it with ʿAlī, while Abū Bakr was denied it. See Baḥrānī, *Maʿālim*, III, 281; idem, *Nuzhat*, 198–9. Al-Ghazālī denies that the Prophet actually brought paradisiacal fruits down to earth; he only had a vision (*kashf*) of the heavenly grapes. See Ghazālī, *Kīmiyā*, 92. According to a tradition in Muslim, *Ṣaḥīḥ, k. al-khusūf* 3 (*b. mā ʿaraḍa al-nabī fī ṣalāt al-khusūf*), II, 722, when seeing paradise and hell in the *qibla* wall of the Medina mosque, the Prophet reached out to take a fruit but failed to reach it (*qaṣurat yadī ʿanhu*). Cf. *ECH*, 17–8, 179, 315, 706.

[112] Halm, *Reich*, 265.

[113] Ibid., 52.

[114] Al-Qāḍī al-Nuʿmān, *Taʾwīl al-daʿāʾim*, 127. I owe the knowledge of this text, and a copy of the passage in question, to Jamel Velji. On the equation of the Ismaʿili *daʿwa* with paradise, see also Lewis, "An Ismaili interpretation," 695. On the hermeneutical principle of *al-mathal wa-l-mamthūl* in Ismaʿilism, see Poonawala, "Ismāʿīlī *taʾwīl*," 212.

[115] Hodgson, *Order*, 133–9; Daftary, *The Assasin legends*, 1–7, 95–120, and passim.

brainwashed and made ready for selfless service by an elaborate hoax. Their commander, the Old Man of the Mountain, would have built a lush, secret garden adjacent to his fortress, ordering that his sleeping adepts be carried into it. There, they would awake to the company of beautiful damsels serving them wine and other delicacies. Transported back, after a while, into the real world, the Old Man would promise them a speedy return to paradise if they sacrificed their lives in suicide attacks carried out against the enemies of the Isma'ilis.[116] While this story finds no corroboration in the contemporary Muslim chronicles (whether Isma'ili or not) and therefore is almost certainly ahistorical,[117] it cannot be said to be a baseless invention either. Rather, it should be regarded a hostile parody of an enduring Isma'ili theme, that is, the restoration, here and now, of the "true religion" (*dīn al-ḥaqq*), Adam's primordial religion in paradise, in which there were no prohibitions or laws.

The expectations of the early followers of the Isma'ili imamate that the advent of the Mahdi was imminent, that paradise would be (re-)established on earth in the present, were gradually channelled by the Fāṭimid and later Isma'ili rulers into more durable forms of political organisation, in which the coming of the Imam-Qā'im was postponed to the future. However, at intervals, the latent millenarianism of the Isma'ilis spectacularly surged to the surface.[118] In one dramatic instance, an Isma'ili ruler openly declared himself to be the expected Imam-Qā'im who would inaugurate paradise on earth. This was Ḥasan II (r. 557–61/1162–66), a ruler of the Nizārī branch of the Isma'ilis in Northern Persia. In the month of ritual fasting, on 17 Ramadan 559/8 August 1164, Ḥasan staged the "Great Resurrection" (*al-qiyāma al-kubrā*), a solemn ceremony in front of the mountain fortress of Alamut, the Nizārī Isma'ilis' stronghold and seat of government in Persia, delivering a public address to his followers in which he proclaimed that from now on, all *bāṭin* knowledge would be revealed and made openly available. In this way, in the words of Marshal Hodgson, he had "actualized the Paradise that some individual Isma'ilis had been able to approach in potentiality." From now on, "men could see God directly, with their spiritual eyes, as was appropriate to Paradise."[119] In a dramatic break with the Islamic community in

[116] Polo, *Book of Ser Marco Polo*, I, 139–46.

[117] The seventh/thirteenth-century historian al-Juwaynī, who inspected the Isma'ili fortress of Alamūt shortly after its fall to the Mongols, makes no mention of a secret garden there or elsewhere in the Nizārī-Isma'ili realm. See Daftary, *The Ismā'īlīs*, 18.

[118] Halm, *Reich*, 224; idem, *Kalifen von Kairo*, 282. Followers of the Fāṭimid caliph al-Ḥākim (r. 386–411/996–1021), later known as the Druzes, believed that al-Ḥākim had ushered in the end of time and abrogated the Shari'a, and that the beatific vision of God was possible on earth because God manifested Himself in the person of the caliph. See ibid., 283–4. Another instance is the public restoration of the "religion of paradise" by the Isma'ili Carmathians of the east coast of the Arabian peninsula in 319/931, which led to the temporary enthronement of a beardless youth from Persia as the incarnate God. See Halm, *Reich*, 230–6; van Ess, "Schönheit und Macht," 27–32. For an overview, see Hajnal, "The events of paradise."

[119] Hodgson, *Order*, 155.

whose midst the Nizārī Ismaʿilis had tried, more or less successfully, to carve out an existence, Ḥasan II declared the Shariʿa to be abrogated and thus the fall from paradise to be reversed, inviting his audience to join him, in broad daylight, to a banquet, there to break the fast, once and for all.[120] The five obligatory prayers were abandoned. The "true prayer" (*namāz-i ḥaqīqī*) that henceforth replaced the older "outward" ritual, was to carry God in one's heart at all times.[121]

The charismatic, "resurrected" community inaugurated by Ḥasan II did not last long, at least in its pure state. A mere year and half after his declaration of the Great Resurrection, Ḥasan II was murdered by his brother-in-law, an Imami Shiʿite. Ḥasan's son and successor, Nūr al-Dīn Muḥammad (r. 561–607/1166–1210), devoted his reign to a reformulation of his father's doctrine of resurrection. The main innovation he introduced, which healed the rift caused by Ḥasan II's premature passing and thus ensured the survival of Nizārī identity, was that *every* successive Imam of the Nizārīs should be considered an Imam-Qāʾim. The beatific vision of God, the supreme pleasure of paradise, Nizārī authors of the post-Resurrection period affirmed, occurs by witnessing the present and living Imam.[122] This placed the Imam at the very heart of Ismaʿili devotion. The exaltation of the Imam, his veneration as the manifestation of the divine word, and thus his elevation to a position of cosmic importance (a quality that previously, Shiʿis had only granted to the Prophet and the early Imams), from then on became the hallmark of Nizārī Ismaʿilism.

In sum, the propensity to bring paradise (and hell) down to earth, to insist on the many ways in which both are or can be made present in this life, is a salient characteristic of the Ismaʿili tradition. However, as shown in the preceding text, it also applies to important strands within Shiʿi eschatology, more generally speaking. In this respect, the Shiʿi tradition bears similarities to certain trends within Islamic mysticism, or Sufism. For example, the cosmic position of the Imam – which is particularly pronounced in Nizārī Ismaʿilism, but also present in other Shiʿi traditions – is mirrored in the idea of the Perfect Man (*al-insān al-kāmil*), which occurs in the thought of, prominently, Ibn al-ʿArabī (d. 638/1240). As previously noted, Shiʿi theorists also share with Sufi authors an interest in *taʾwīl*, the "decoding" of the data of revelation and the extraction of their "inner" (*bāṭin*) meaning. The Ismaʿili distinction between a lesser and a greater resurrection recalls the Sufi notion of "voluntary" and "compulsory return." Like certain Sufi thinkers,

120 See the translations from the seventh/thirteenth-century chronicle of Rashīd al-Dīn al-Juwaynī and the ninth/fifteenth-century Ismaʿili text known as *Haft Bāb-i Abī Isḥāq* in Hodgson, *Order*, 148–50.

121 Daftary, *The Ismāʿīlīs*, 360. On the whole incidence of the Niẓārī "Great Resurrection," see Jambet, *La grande résurrection*.

122 Hodgson, *Order*, 162–6; Daftary, *The Ismāʿīlīs*, 363–5.

Shiʿi theologians such as Ibn Najāḥ (who related a description of paradise on the authority of Jaʿfar al-Ṣādiq) stressed that the object of the *visio beatifica* was a vision of the divine light, or gnosis (*maʿrifa*).[123] Needless to say, Sufi eschatology is a wide field. Like Shiʿism, it knows of several modes of interpreting the relationship between this world and the otherworld, and these modes of eschatological thought deserve full and systematic study. In the next chapter we turn, therefore, to an analysis of these Sufi modes of approaching paradise and hell.

[123] Majlisī, *Biḥār*, VIII, 416.

7

The Otherworld Within: Paradise and Hell in Islamic Mysticism

Asceticism and mysticism were part of Islam from its inception, as the Qur'ān gives rise to a vocabulary of renunciation and religious experience.[1] As we saw in Chapter 1, the Qur'ān is a text pregnant with eschatological ideas, which it frames in terms that, if not fully mystical, are conducive towards conceiving this world and the otherworld as a unity, rather than as ontologically separate realms. In the gradual unfolding of what later came to be referred to by the umbrella term Sufism (*taṣawwuf*), the relationship between this world and the otherworld occupied centre stage. One should note at the outset, however, that there is a remarkable historical diversity of Sufi attitudes towards the otherworld. By charting a typology of these attitudes, this chapter seeks to trace how the Sufis' conceptualisations of the otherworld reflected and reinforced their understandings of human existence and of the moral and spiritual status of the present world. Concomitantly, this chapter examines how Sufi thinkers described the nature, function, and ultimate value of the otherworld. What, in Sufi thought, is the relevance of belief in the two otherworldly abodes, and how is one to picture them? What constitutes felicity in paradise and misery in hell?[2]

Fear and Longing in Early Sufism

In the collections of sayings attributed to the renunciants and mystics of the formative period of Sufism (third-sixth/ninth-twelfth centuries), one can identify four noticeable attitudes towards paradise and hell: fear of the otherworld; hope and longing for the otherworld; and dismissal of the

[1] Massignon, *Essai*, 139; Nwyia, *Exégèse*, 24.

[2] Overviews of Sufi eschatology are rare in the secondary literature, but see El-Saleh, *Vie future*, 91–120; Chittick, "Muslim eschatology"; idem, "Eschatology in Islamic thought," 238–57. For a recent study of Sufi teachings about paradise and hell in works of *tafsīr* of the classical period, see now Coppens, "Seeing God," ch. 1.

otherworld, of which there is a cold (or "sober") and a hot (or "intoxicated") variant. These four basic attitudes do not follow upon one another in a neat chronological order. Rather, they overlap, sometimes even within the thought of a single individual. While many of the fourth/tenth- and fifth/eleventh-century handbooks of Sufism, such as al-Sarrāj's (d. 378/988) *Book of Flashes* (*K. al-Lumaʿ*) or al-Kalābādhī's (d. *ca.* 384/994) *Introduction to the Doctrines of the Sufi School* (*K. al-Taʿarruf li-madhhab ahl al-taṣawwuf*), preserve traces of all four of them, they tend to privilege sober dismissal over other modes of experiencing the otherworld. This makes reconstruction of the developments of earlier times difficult and complicates attempts at periodisation. Late Medieval synthetic works of Sufism, such as Jalāl al-Dīn Rūmī's (d. 672/1273) great didactic poem, the *Mathnawī*, or the esoteric Qurʾān commentary of the Ottoman scholar, Ismail Haqqi Bursawi (Bursalı İsmaʿil Hakkı, d. 1137/1725), present the four different Sufi modes of experiencing the otherworld side by side, while also featuring conceptualisations of a more speculative, monistic kind.

The point of departure for the renunciants and mystics of the early centuries was the idea that the hereafter is unspeakably better than this life, and that therefore the truly pious should focus all their attention on the otherworld, *al-ākhira*. It could be claimed that this idea was anchored in the Qurʾān, particularly in those verses with an ascetic, world-denying tinge. "This lower life," the Qurʾān proclaims in one verse, "is but sport and play, but the distant abode: that is truly life" (29:64).[3] Sufi thinkers emphasised that the prophet Muḥammad lived his life in constant awareness of what was to come after death. "What do I have to do with this world?" he was reported to have quipped.[4] Bāyazīd Basṭāmī (d. 234/848 or 261/875) averred that after thinking a great deal he had come to the realisation that this world is a cadaver, over which it is appropriate to say four times *Allāhu akbar*, as one does when someone is buried.[5] This form of *contemptus mundi* (*dhamm al-dunyā*) is regularly attributed to the renunciants (*zuhhād*) of the first three centuries of Islam, but it continued to be a dominant theme also in the works of mystical authors of later times.[6]

The *zuhhād* seem to have emphasised one aspect of the afterworld in particular, namely hell. Their sayings, as they are preserved in the handbooks and hagiographical sources, reveal a visceral fear, an expectation that hell will seize them at any moment.[7] They are said to have wept a great deal, and

[3] According to Goldziher's classic exposition, world denial is a feature particularly of the Meccan period (to which this verse is commonly attributed), while in Medina the tone of the Qurʾān becomes more pragmatic and worldly. See Goldziher, *Introduction*, 116.

[4] Sarrāj, *Lumaʿ* (tr. Gramlich), 166. Collectors of hadith addressing issues of renunciation (*zuhd*) often quoted this tradition. See, e.g., Ibn Ḥanbal, *Zuhd*, 29, 37, 40 (##34, 62, 71).

[5] Massignon, *Essai*, 276.

[6] See Ritter, *Meer*, 34.

[7] Cf. Melchert, "Exaggerated fear," 283–300; idem, "Locating hell," 103, 105–8 and passim.

generally to have behaved as if "God's threats only apply to them, while His promises are only for others."[8] For example, Ḥasan al-Baṣrī (d. 110/728), the most famous representative of early Islam's renunciant movement, was continuously sad because he was afraid that God would cast him into hell "without asking much."[9] Reportedly, the fixation of the *zuhhād* on hell was sometimes rather extreme, to the point of putting them in physical danger. Several of the *zuhhād* of the first two centuries of Islam allegedly wept, fainted, or even died on the spot when passing blacksmiths working a forge, overwhelmed by the thought of hellfire.[10] ʿAlī b. al-Ḥusayn Zayn al-ʿĀbidīn (d. *ca.* 95/713), whom the Shiʿites revere as their fourth Imam, kept praying although his house in Medina had caught fire. When asked why he had not left the house to save his life, he said: "The Great Fire made me oblivious of this fire."[11] Less life-threatening side effects included cross-eyes. The third/ninth-century Baghdad renunciant Sarī al-Saqaṭī reportedly squinted at his nose once every day. He explained that he did this in order to check whether his face had turned black, in anticipation of the charring of faces in hell.[12] In sum, *zuhd* and the fear of hell were considered "twins,"[13] and even though *zuhd* was gradually assimilated into less austere forms of contemplative life, a measure of this anxiety-driven outlook on the human condition survived into later Sufism.[14]

During the second/eighth and third/ninth centuries, an increasing number of mystics seem to have settled on the opinion that not only hell but also paradise should form the object of pious devotion. In other words, fear should be accompanied by hope (*rajāʾ*) and longing (*shawq*) for paradise. Al-Dārānī (d. 215/830), a renunciant from Iraq (?) who settled in Dārāyā near Damascus towards the end of his life,[15] is on record for teaching that too much fear moves people towards despairing of God, which he thought

[8] Kalābādhī, *Taʿarruf*, tr. Arberry, 38. See also Shaʿrānī, *Ṭabaqāt*, I, 31–2.

[9] Ritter, "Ḥasan al-Baṣrī," 15.

[10] See the examples given in Melchert, "Locating hell." Such behaviour relates closely to a Qurʾānic injunction: "Have you not considered the fire that you ignite? ... We have made it a reminder (*tadhkira*)!" (Q 56:71–3). Cf. the cases of *zuhhād* who passed away upon hearing the Qurʾān's hell verses recited to them, as in the biographies collected in al-Thaʿlabī's (d. 427/1035) *Qatlā l-Qurʾān*. See Kermani, *Gott ist schön*, 378–9; Meier, *Abū Saʿīd*, 196–7. Famous among the "verses of threat" (*āyāt al-waʿīd*) were 4:37, 23:104, 39:46, 54:46, as well as sūras 67 and 102.

[11] Qushayrī, *Risāla*, 69 (tr. 92). As a later Sufi poet mused, "he who *is* fire – how shall he burn"? See Kalābādhī, *Taʿarruf*, tr. Arberry, 89.

[12] Ibid., 38; Qushayrī, *Risāla*, 130 (tr. 147).

[13] Shaqīq al-Balkhī, *Ādāb al-ʿibādāt*, 18. Cf. Nwyia, *Exégèse*, 222.

[14] Al-Shiblī (d. 334/945–6), upon gazing at a succulent lamb in an oven, is said to have defended himself by saying that "I was merely thinking that all other living beings enter the fire only after they have died, whereas we enter it alive!" See Ibn al-Qāriḥ, *Risāla*, 60 (tr. 61).

[15] On al-Dārānī and his circle, cf. Knysh, *Islamic mysticism*, 36–9; *TG*, I, 142–3; *EIsl*, s.v. Abū Sulaymān al-Dārānī (Gh. Ghaya and F. Negahban).

was a grave sin, or even a form of polytheism (*shirk*).[16] As Sahl al-Tustarī (*fl.* late third/ninth century) puts it, "fear is male, and hope is female,"[17] that is, both complement each other and form an integrated whole. In the later handbooks of Sufism, this became the standard view.[18] In his classical exposé of the question, al-Makkī (d. 386/996) stated that "hope and fear ... are two qualities supporting faith (*waṣfānī li-l-īmān*), like the two wings that carry the bird."[19]

If it was acceptable, then, to hope for paradise, was it also acceptable to delight in imagining its sensual pleasures? Al-Dārānī, it is related, told a friend that he regularly saw the houris of paradise in his dreams, but begged him, slightly embarrassed by his nightly visions, not to pass this information on to others. Perhaps in an attempt to tame his fascination with the beautiful maidens of paradise, he developed a habit of counting the number of houris awaiting him in paradise by counting the tears and prayers in his earthly life.[20] He is also reported to have distinguished between the licit gazing at beautiful women with "the eyes of the heart" (i.e., seeing in them but a reminder of the promised houris of paradise) and illicit looking at them with "the eyes of the head" (i.e., with lust and earthly desire).[21] The Basran ʿAbd al-Wāḥid b. Zayd (d. *ca.* 150/767), a student of Ḥasan al-Baṣrī, also dreamed of the houris and claimed that they had cured him from a disease.[22] Inspired by their teacher's

[16] Hujwīrī, *Kashf*, tr. Nicholson, 112–3. At the same time, al-Dārānī was remembered as saying that "the root of everything that is good in this life and the next is the fear of God." See Abū Nuʿaym, *Ḥilya*, IX, 259. Compare also his saying that "if hope becomes preponderant in the heart, the heart will perish." See Qushayrī, *Risāla*, 128 (tr. 145). Cf. Sviri, "Between fear and hope," 334n71; Rosenthal, "*Sweeter than hope*," 142n788.

[17] Kalābādhī, *Taʿarruf*, tr. Arberry, 89.

[18] Cf. Meier, *Abū Saʿīd*, 148. For variants of al-Tustarī's saying, all underscoring the need to balance hope and fear, cf. Sviri, "Between fear and hope," 328–9. The idea is also clothed in the form of a Prophetic hadith. See Sirjānī, *Bayāḍ*, #586.

[19] Makkī, *Qūt al-qulūb*, I, 483. Similarly in Ghazālī, *Iḥyāʾ*, III, 571. Cf. Sviri, "Between fear and hope," 330; Rosenthal, "*Sweeter than hope*," 144–5.

[20] Abū Nuʿaym, *Ḥilya*, IX, 259. Cf. Massignon, *Essai*, 219–20. Massignon notes that al-Dārānī's attempt to reconcile theological orthodoxy with renunciant ideals was liked neither by the mystics nor the jurists. On al-Dārānī's condemnation of marriage as an obstacle to spiritual life, see Schimmel, "I take off the dress of my body," 270. Al-Dārānī, however, was not entirely opposed to marriage, although he advised that one should take an ugly or aged wife. See Gramlich, *Weltverzicht*, 260–1. Cf. *EI3*, s.v. al-Dārānī, Abū Sulaymān (J. van Ess). Al-Dārānī was also remembered as the transmitter of a rather explicit hadith about the houris of paradise. See Suyūṭī, *Budūr*, 561; and the preceding text, p. 143.

[21] Kalābādhī, *Taʿarruf*, tr. Arberry, 112–3. Towards the end of his life, al-Dārānī is said to have taught that the thought of paradise should not divert one's attention away from God. See Abū Nuʿaym, *Ḥilya*, IX, 270, quoted in *TG*, I, 143. Al-Muḥāsibī criticised those who looked at beautiful women in order to feel reminded of the houris of paradise. See Meier, *Abū Saʿīd*, 206.

[22] Abū Nuʿaym, *Ḥilya*, VI, 161,11ff. ʿAbd al-Wāḥid is also reported to have approved of dream visions of houris if they motivated his followers to fight with him in the jihad against the Byzantines. Thus in the eleventh story in ʿAfīf al-Dīn al-Yāfiʿī's (d. 768/1367) collection of stories about Sufi saints, the *Rawḍat al-rayāḥīn* (ed. and trans. Berthels, "Die paradiesischen

example, some of his followers concluded that paradise could be experienced on earth, glowingly reporting back to him that they had met the houris during nightly sessions in the desert. Annoyed at his followers' unbridled enthusiasm, ʿAbd al-Wāḥid responded that the houris they had encountered had hooves as their feet.[23]

Scholars have noted that "[u]nambiguous statements stressing hope over fear do not seem to be easily available"[24] in the history of early Sufism. However, there *are* instances in which the hope and longing for paradise was seen as something entirely positive, with the potential to cover up, though not obliterate, the fear of hell. The Khorasanian devotee Shaqīq al-Balkhī (d. 195/810) viewed renunciation, the fear of hell and the longing for paradise as three successive stations (*manāzil*, sg. *manzil*) on the Sufi path towards God. Shaqīq is one of the earliest Sufi theorists of spiritual "states" and "stations," and it is noteworthy that he locates the hope of paradise on a more advanced level than *zuhd* and fear, even though he advises that even higher levels should be aspired to.[25] Unlike al-Dārānī, Shaqīq had no qualms to openly admit that longing for paradise "is to nourish in oneself the desire for the houris of the beautiful eyes and the desire for constant and perpetual happiness."[26] Yaḥyā b. Muʿādh (d. 258/872) is known to have emphasised hope to the detriment of fear; he even developed his own particular "science of hope" (*ʿilm al-rajāʾ*), although this earned him the rebuke of his contemporaries as well as of later authors.[27] Towards the end of his life, Abū Saʿīd b. Abī al-Khayr (d. 440/1049) decided he would only read verses of the Qurʾan that spoke of God's mercy and the rewards meted out in paradise, but not the "verses of threat" (*āyāt al-waʿīd*). Criticised by a fellow dervish

Jungfrauen," 281–7). He also figures prominently as one of the early transmitters (from Ḥasan al-Baṣrī) of the divine saying (*ḥadīth qudsī*) according to which "He [God] desires me and I desire Him" (*ʿashiqanī wa-ʿashiqtuhu*). See Abū Nuʿaym, *Ḥilya*, VI, 165, 7. On Sufi visions of the houris in combination with *zuhd*, see further Meier, *Abū Saʿīd*, 205–6.

23 Sarrāj, *Lumaʿ*, 429, tr. Gramlich 593–4. On ʿAbd al-Wāḥid b. Zayd, see *TG*, II, 96–100. Al-Ashʿarī relates from "a group among the Sufis" that they "thought it possible that … the fruits of the Garden come to them in this world so that they [could] eat them, and that they could have sexual intercourse with the houris in this world." See Ashʿarī, *Maqālāt*, 438; Malaṭī, *Tanbīh*, 73. On the likely Tantric background to this, see Crone, *Nativist prophets*, 266.

24 Rosenthal, "*Sweeter than hope*," 144.

25 Shaqīq al-Balkhī, *Ādāb al-ʿibādāt*, 17–21. The fourth *manzil* in Shaqīq's model is love for God, *al-maḥabba li-llāh*. See ibid., 20. Cf. Nwyia, *Exégèse*, 215. Shaqīq stresses that the station of "desire for paradise" does not abrogate *zuhd* and *khawf* but rather encompasses them, in the same way in which a stronger light englobes another, weaker one. Ibid., 224, 226. Cf. Knysh, *Islamic mysticism*, 35. In later Sufi models, the dyad fear/hope is usually relegated to the lowest stage on the Sufi path. Cf. Sviri, "Between fear and hope," 337–44.

26 Shaqīq al-Balkhī, *Ādāb al-ʿibādāt*, 19. Cf. Nwyia, *Exégèse*, 224.

27 Meier, *Abū Saʿīd*, 167–77; Rosenthal, "*Sweeter than hope*," 143; Sviri, "Between hope and fear," 332.

FIGURE 16. Allegory of heavenly drunkenness. Illustration from a *Dīwān* of Ḥāfiẓ made for the Safavid prince Sām Mīrzā, signed by Sulṭān-Muḥammad. Tabriz/Persia 933/[1526–7]. Harvard Art Museums/Arthur M. Sackler Museum, The Stuart Cary Welch Collection, Gift of Mr. and Mrs. Stuart Cary Welch in honor of the students of Harvard University and Radcliffe College, jointly owned by the Harvard Art Museums and the Metropolitan Museum of Art, 1988.460.2.

for his selective reading, he replied in a verse that "today I shall drink wine, for it is the time of joy!"[28]

The prophet Muḥammad, as certain hadiths affirmed, had actively encouraged his followers to cultivate the joyful expectation of paradise. "Does nobody long for paradise?" he was said to have wondered, and then exclaimed: "By the Lord of the Kaaba, paradise is a quivering basil stem, a constantly flowing river, and a beautiful spouse!"[29] According to a story from the early fourth/tenth century, a sage (*ḥakīm*) in Mosul is asked by another sage whether he longs for the houris. No, is the sage's curt reply, whereupon his companion commends him to "long for them, for the light of their faces derives from the light of God Exalted!" Struck by these words, the sage looses consciousness and has to be carried home, where he remains ailing for a month.[30] Also in later centuries, one occasionally comes across Sufi personalities who express a kind of joy mysticism, celebrating the prospect of God's mercy and of otherworldly reward.[31] For example, Bahā' al-Walad (d. 628/1231), Rūmī's father, extolled the beauty of the houris, gardens, and palaces of paradise in his sermons, and although much of his use of these ideas points in the direction of a spiritual and interiorised understanding (a Sufi mode of talking about the otherworld about which more will be said in the following text), a naïve, joyful optimism that paradise was for him to enter is an indelible part of his message.[32]

Contemptus Ultramundi

In response, it seems, to the extremes to which the fear of hell and longing for paradise could lead, some Sufis decided to forsake interest in the otherworld altogether, an attitude that at times went hand in hand with the rejection of the present world; it was then referred to as *al-takhallī min al-kawnayn*, "throwing off both worlds."[33] There was a cold and a hot mode of this *contemptus ultramundi*.

[28] Meier, *Abū Sa'īd*, 198, citing Abū Sa'īd's hagiography, the *Asrār al-tawḥīd* of Ibn al-Munawwar (*fl.* 574–88/1178–92), 216. Al-Būṣīrī compares the Qur'ān to water that quenches the flames of hell, and to the basin in which sinners wash their faces clean before they enter paradise. See Būṣīrī, *Burda*, 22 (vv. 100–1).

[29] Ibn Abī l-Dunyā, known for his piety and for his *zuhd*, opens his *Ṣifat al-janna* with this tradition. See Ibn Abī l-Dunyā, *Ṣifat al-janna*, 184. For more such comparisons, see Ibn Māja, *Sunan, zuhd* 39, II, 1448–9 (#4332); Sarrāj, *Luma'*, tr. Gramlich, 117; Qurṭubī, *Tadhkira*, II, 165.

[30] Ibn Abī l-Dunyā, *Ṣifat al-janna*, 272 (#307).

[31] For examples, see Meier, *Abū Sa'īd*, 468–516.

[32] See Meier, *Bahā'-i Walad*, 244–60, esp. 245, 255.

[33] Ibn Adham is quoted in Massignon, *Essai*, 257. For *al-takhallī min al-kawnayn*, see Qushayrī, *Risāla*, 163 (tr. 179, from Basṭāmī); Ghazālī, *Mishkāt al-anwār*, 30, 32; Lamaṭī, *Ibrīz* (tr. O'Kane/Radtke), 906. Cf. Goldziher, *Richtungen*, 199–200 (Ghazālī); Christensen, *Recherches*, 108 (Khayyām, Nāṣir-i Khusraw, 'Aṭṭār, Ḥāfiẓ). Metonymically, Sufis also spoke of "throwing off the two sandals" (*khal' al-na'layn*). See, e.g., the work of the same title by

The proponents of the cold mode saw the preoccupation with paradise and hell first and foremost as an intellectual problem. They worried that it diverted too much attention from what really mattered, that is, the devotion to God. The renunciant ʿĀmir b. ʿAbd Qays (*fl.* 35/65), a semilegendary figure, was said to have pleaded with God that all his worries might become just one, namely, the concern for God.[34] Figures such as Jaʿfar al-Ṣādiq (d. 148/756) and Maʿrūf al-Karkhī (d. *ca.* 200/815), as well as later Sufis picked up on this motif, arguing that one should only focus on the reality that lies *behind* the pleasures of paradise and the punishments of hell: God Himself.[35] The followers of Sufis, relates Abū l-Ḥasan al-Sirjānī (d. *ca.* 470/1077), must "sell paradise for the sake of their object [of devotion, i.e. God] and not fear hell while serving Him."[36]

This does not mean that the existence of paradise and hell was denied. Al-Muḥāsibī (d. 243/857) and al-Ghazālī (d. 505/1111), to name two famous examples, wrote at length about the physical contents of paradise and hell; but their works, as we saw in Chapter 3, both end with the assertion that the highest, indeed the only true pleasure in paradise is the company and the vision of God, while the worst punishment in hell is the feeling of distance from God.[37] On the whole, Sufis in this line of thought showed themselves to be unimpressed by hell; they considered the pain of not seeing God, of being far away from Him, to be worse than any of the other punishments that could possibly be inflicted on them. Likewise, they were unimpressed by the pleasures that were in store in paradise; the joy of seeing God, to them, seemed a far greater promise.[38] This was the position adopted by those Sufis who later came to be considered the forefathers of orthodox Sufism, figures such as al-Junayd, Abū Ṭālib al-Makkī, and particularly, al-Ghazālī, who did much to enshrine this view in his version of a moderate, law-abiding mystical outlook on life.

However, next to this cool indifference to paradise and hell, there were also those who showed a more emotional response. "I would be ashamed before

the Portuguese Ibn Qasī (d. 546/1151), to which Ibn al-ʿArabī devoted a commentary. In later centuries, dervish groups such as the Qalandars also stressed the need "to throw off both worlds," which, combined with their latent antinomianism, earned them the ire of their contemporaries. See Karamustafa, *God's unruly friends*, 2, 14, 40–2, referring to the hagiographic account of the life of the Qalandar Jamāl al-Dīn Sāwī by Khāṭib Fārisī (written in 748/1347–8).

[34] According to Benedikt Reinert, ʿĀmir was deeply involved in the "ascetic problem of paradise and hell." See Reinert, *Lehre*, 65. A collection of ʿĀmir's sayings can be found in Ibn Ḥanbal, *Zuhd*, 331–42.

[35] See Jaʿfar's commentary on Q43:71, in which he distinguishes between paradisiacal vision and the fulfilment of (corporeal) desires in paradise, clearly privileging the former. Sulamī, *Ḥaqāʾiq*, II, 236. I owe this reference to Pieter Coppens, who is however critical of the attribution to Jaʿfar. On Maʿrūf, see El-Saleh, *Vie future*, 97–8.

[36] Sirjānī, *Bayāḍ* #381.

[37] See the preceding text, pp. 99, 154. Cf. Massignon, *Essai*, 218; El-Saleh, *Vie future*, 99–100.

[38] For a later example, see Lamaṭī, *Ibrīz* (tr. O'Kane/Radtke), 894. Cf. Ritter, *Meer*, 523.

God," a sage (*ḥakīm*) is quoted in a second/eighth-century collection of pious sayings, "if I served Him in the hope of paradise, for then I'd be like a worker who only works for a wage and does not work when he does not receive it."[39] Shame could lead to a more visceral, hot response, at times even a passionate dislike of paradise and hell, expressed in hyperbolical or even ecstatic speech (*shaṭḥ*). An early representative of this kind of attitude is Ibn Adham (d. 160/776–7), a renunciant from Khorasan who is reported to have stated that "in my eyes paradise is not worth the wing of a fly," and to have prayed to God that if only He bestowed His love on him, He might as well "give paradise to whomever else You please."[40]

Rābiʿa of Basra (d. 185/801) is another example of this high-strung dismissal of the otherworld. On the one hand, Rābiʿa was much occupied with paradise and hell, and pictured the two frequently. She is said to have been prey to the same intense fear of hell from which her *zuhhād* contemporaries in Basra suffered. According to one story, she fainted at the mere mention of hell.[41] She is also reported to have had visions of paradise.[42] On the other hand, there are many stories attributing to her a passionate desire to pass beyond paradise and hell. One of her famous maxims is *al-jār thumma l-dār*, "the neighbour first, then the house!"[43] For Rābiʿa, the "house" (i.e., the afterworld) is a barrier set up in front of its owner, the "neighbor," that is, God. In one of her prayers she says, "O Lord, if I worship You out of fear of hell, burn me in hell; and if I worship You in the hope of paradise, forbid it to me. However, if I worship You for Your own sake, do not deprive me of Your eternal beauty!"[44]

A degree or two more radical in his rejection of paradise and hell is Bāyazīd Basṭāmī,[45] a lone figure from northern Persia who does not seem to have been affiliated with any of the mystical or theological circles of his day. His fame results, among other things, from being the first Sufi to claim a spiritual ascension (*miʿrāj*) to heaven, in emulation of Muḥammad's famous heavenly journey.[46] Paradise, however, is not where Basṭāmī's *miʿrāj*

[39] Khuttalī, *Maḥabba*, tr. Radtke, 91–2 (#88).

[40] Abū Nuʿaym, *Ḥilya*, VIII, 35.

[41] Shaʿrānī, *Ṭabaqāt*, I, 72. As Meier notes, the Ottoman pious scholar and preacher, Mehmet Efendi Birgiwî (Muḥammad b. Pīr ʿAlī al-Birkawī, d. 981/1573), was of the opinion that Rābiʿa had stressed fear over hope. See Meier, *Abū Saʿīd*, 164, quoting Birgiwî, *Ṭarīqa*, 67.

[42] Sarrāj, *Lumaʿ*, 121.

[43] See al-Ghazālī, *Iḥyāʾ*, IV, 45, 453; ʿAṭṭār, *Tadhkirat al-awliyāʾ*, tr. Sells (with Paul Losensky), *Early Islamic mysticism*, 166. Cf. El-Saleh, *Vie future*, 96.

[44] ʿAṭṭār, *Tadhkirat al-awliyāʾ*, tr. Sells (with Paul Losensky), *Early Islamic mysticism*, 169.

[45] For a collection of his sayings about paradise and hell, see Ritter, "Aussprüche des Bāyezīd Bisṭāmī," 237–8.

[46] The text has been edited by R. A. Nicholson, "An early Arabic version." Cf. Knysh, *Islamic mysticism*, 69. For a recent translation, see Sells, *Early Islamic mysticism*, 244–50. Pierre Lory has argued that Basṭāmī was attributed a *miʿrāj* in order to justify the full-fledged mystical ascensions of later centuries (such as the one claimed by Ibn al-ʿArabī), but that he did not himself relate a coherent *miʿrāj* à la Muḥammad. See Lory, "Le *miʿrāǧ* d'Abū

is headed: "My spirit," he relates in his visionary account of his visit to the higher realms, "looked at nothing and gave no heed, though paradise was displayed to it."[47] Basṭāmī's goal is God, not paradise, which, echoing Rābiʿa, he labels the "supreme veil." "Those who are in paradise are not in God," he declares, and then he adds, almost with a measure of scorn: "Let them be fooled, these simpletons!"[48] When the truly pious see paradise "and its adornment," they will cry out in horror, like the sinners in hell cry out from the pain they suffer.[49] A couple of centuries later, the Persian mystic ʿAṭṭār (d. 627/1230) wrote that some pious men, when resurrected, have to be dragged into paradise with chains.[50]

Basṭāmī's attitude towards hell is equally dismissive. He asserts that God's fire of love burns a thousand times more intensely than the fire of hell; in fact, God's love fire has the oxymoronic power to burn hell. As Basṭāmī puts it, God will take the foot of the hell-monster and dip it into the fire of His love, and hellfire will then be consumed and obliterated.[51] Basṭāmī, in his moments of ecstasy, felt vastly superior to hell. He is said to have claimed that he would be able to smother hell with the tip of his frock, thereby redeeming the rest of humankind from punishment.[52]

Yazīd Basṭāmī." Moderate Sufi authors such as al-Qushayrī (d. 465/1072) regularly warned against false claims to heavenly journeys. See Qushayrī, *Rasāʾil*, 1–49. Under the Egyptian Mamluks, a Sufi called Abū l-ʿAbbās al-Mulaththam boasted a *miʿrāj*; he was declared insane and imprisoned. See Geoffroy, *Le soufisme*, 434. Geoffroy (ibid. 434n160) notes that there are few historical examples of Sufis who openly claimed to have experienced a *miʿrāj*, referring to the "very discrete" way in which ʿAbd al-Karīm al-Jīlī (d. *ca.* 832/1428) alludes to his ascension in his *al-Insān al-kāmil*. Later examples of Sufis purporting to have undertaken a *miʿrāj* include Muḥammad al-Ghawth in eighth/sixteenth-century Hindustan. See Kugle, "Heaven's witness." Also Ibn al-ʿArabī (d. 638/1240) and Aḥmad Sirhindī (d. 1034/1624) claimed a spiritual ascension. See Ibn al-ʿArabī, *K. al-Isrāʾ*; Sirhindī, *Mabdaʾ wa-maʿād*, 33:17–34:5 (where Sirhindī performs a heavenly *ṭawāf* with the angels). Cf. ter Haar, *Sirhindī*, 56; Morris, "Spiritual ascension"; Vakily, "Some notes."

47 The translation is from Arberry, *Sufism*, 54. Cf. Basṭāmī's saying in Sells, *Islamic mysticism*, 236: "Paradise is of no concern to the people of love."

48 Badawī, *Shaṭaḥāt*, 22. Cf. Bayhaqī, *Shuʿab*, II, 57: "Most of the inhabitants of paradise are fools (*akthar ahl al-janna al-bulh*)." The hadith is a favourite trope in Sufi eschatology, quoted, among others, by ʿAṭṭār in his *Muṣībatnāmeh*. See Ritter, *Meer*, 24. Cf. Qurṭubī, *Tadhkira*, II, 72–3; Suyūṭī, *Budūr*, 594.

49 Ritter, *Meer*, 523 (from ʿAṭṭār); idem, "Aussprüche des Bāyezīd Bisṭāmī," 237. According to Sahl al-Tustarī, the blessed in paradise cry out as soon as they are veiled from God, and be it only for the "twinkling of an eye." See Tustarī, *Tafsīr*, tr. Keeler, 120 (*ad* Q 19:61). Cf. Böwering, *The mystical vision*, 170. For a similar tradition ascribed to Basṭāmī, see Suyūṭī, *Budūr*, 615.

50 Quoted in Ritter, *Meer*, 523. Ritter (ibid.) also relates that according Yaḥyā b. Muʿādh al-Rāzī (d. 258/872), paradise is the "prison" of those possessed by mystical knowledge. This inverts the well-known hadith that "the world (*al-dunyā*) is the prison of the believer (*al-dunyā sijnu l-muʾmin*)." See *CTM*, I, 377a (Tirmidhī, Ibn Māja, Ibn Ḥanbal).

51 Sarrāj, *Lumaʿ*, tr. Gramlich, 529–30.

52 See Ritter, "Aussprüche des Bāyezīd Bisṭāmī," 237.

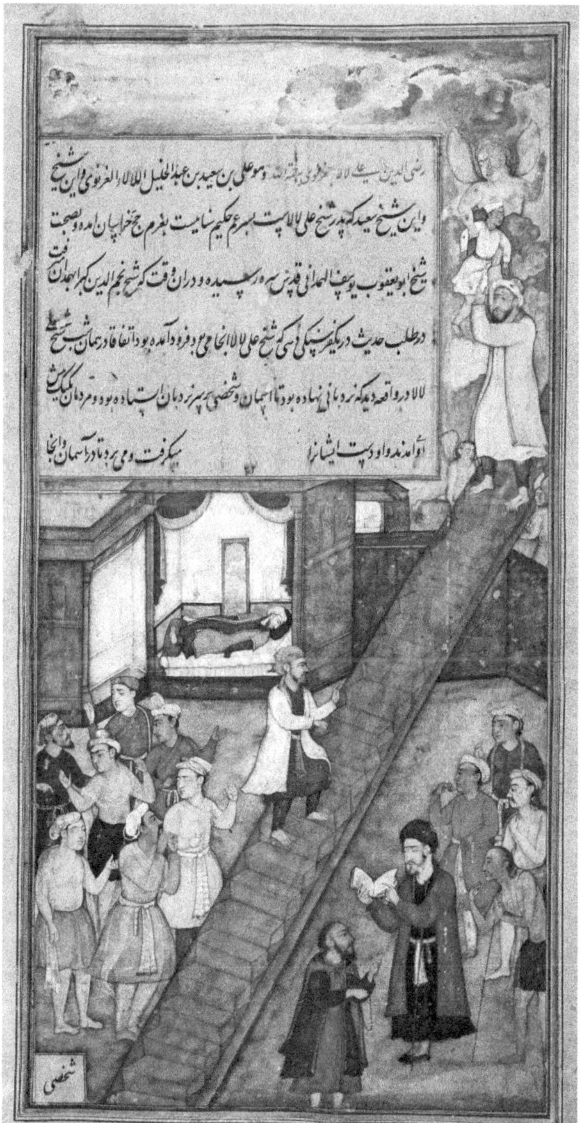

FIGURE 17. A dream vision of Najm al-Dīn Kubrā's ascension. From Jāmī, *Nafaḥāt al-uns (The Scents of Intimacy)*. Agra/India, 1012/1603. MS British Library Or 1362, fol. 271v.

Elsewhere, he seems to give hell instructions or even threaten it. In one of his inspired utterances (*shataḥāt*), he addresses hell in the following way: "If you … punish the damned too harshly I will let them know that paradise is a game for children!" Telling the people in hell that paradise is an inconsequential pleasure, one gathers, will alleviate their disappointment of not having entered it.[53]

Abū Bakr al-Shiblī (d. 334/946) and Muḥammad b. ʿAbd al-Jabbār al-Niffarī (d. 350/961 or *ca.* 366/977) may serve as another two examples of the hot response to the fixation on paradise and hell characteristic of the earlier renunciants and Sufis. Al-Shiblī was one of the love-drunk, ecstatic Sufis for whom the city of Baghdad, in the first half of the fourth/tenth century, had become home. Issuing from an affluent background, al-Shiblī had found Sufism relatively late in his life, but then embraced it with fiery passion.[54] According to his biographer ʿAṭṭār, al-Shiblī was once met in the streets of Baghdad with two torches in his hand. When asked what he intended to do with them, he responded that he had set out to burn paradise and hell.[55] (A later, expanded version of this story features Rābiʿa as the heroine, carrying a bucket of water to extinguish hell and a torch to put fire to paradise.[56]) Hell, for al-Shiblī, holds no horrors. "What am I to do with flame and hell?" he quipped. "In my opinion, flame and hell are but sugar in comparison with being separated [from God]."[57] Al-Shiblī also remarked, full of contempt, that he could extinguish the fire of hell if he spat on it.[58]

A similar feeling of superiority over hell is voiced by the enigmatic figure of al-Niffarī, an ecstatic mystic from Niffar in lower Iraq, who proclaimed that the Sufis are encouraged by God "to enter the Fire, because then the Fire will be extinguished."[59] In al-Niffarī's thought, the Sufis' willingness to enter hell becomes the hallmark of their election. While paradise will only be populated by "slaves," the "truly free," al-Niffarī states, are in hell.[60] In a daring move, al-Niffarī claims that God made him stand in the Fire, and that he saw it consume religious knowledge, works, the wisdom produced by intellects (*ʿuqūl*), and even the knowledge of mystics about stations and states on the mystical path. In the love of God, all this becomes mere firewood.[61] As the biographers do not fail to note, al-Shiblī's and al-Niffarī's utterances aroused the suspicion and criticism

[53] Badawī, *Shaṭaḥāt*, 22. Cf. Massignon, *Essai*, 283.

[54] People even thought he was mentally deranged, and for a period in his life, he was detained in one of Baghdad's asylums for the mad. He may have affected madness, however, to elude the kind of persecution that cost the life of his friend al-Ḥallāj (d. 309/922). See Knysh, *Islamic mysticism*, 65. On Shiblī's life and teachings, see now Avery, *Shiblī*.

[55] ʿAṭṭār, *Tadhkira*, II, 163.

[56] See Massignon, *Recueil*, 8.

[57] Sarrāj, *Lumaʿ*, tr. Gramlich, 547–8. Al-Sarrāj explains that "those whom God punishes with separation are tortured more than those whom He punishes with flame and hell." Cf. the commentary by Baqlī, *Sharḥ*, 254 (#455): "This means that [. . .] the pain of separation is one thousand times more difficult for me than the torment of the people of hell."

[58] See Sarrāj, *Lumaʿ*, tr. Gramlich, 548.

[59] Niffarī, *Mawāqif*, 81 (#50).

[60] Ibid., 76 (#47).

[61] See Nwyia, *Trois oeuvres*, 203. I owe this reference to Pieter Coppens.

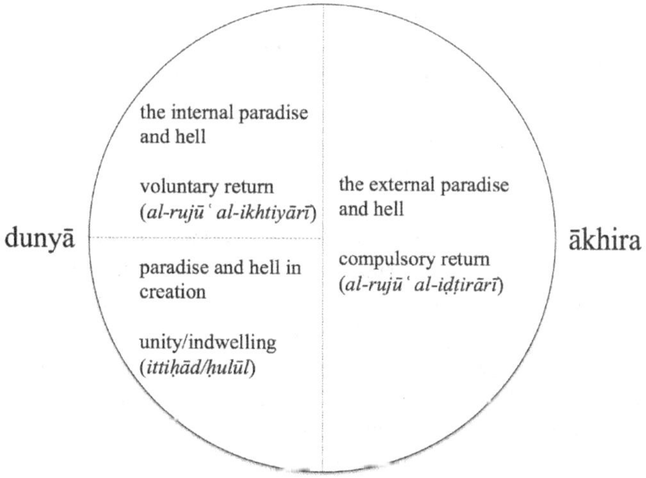

CHART 4. Three types of unitive conceptualisations of the *dunyā/ākhira* relationship.

of their contemporaries,[62] who feared the deleterious effects of such ideas on the broader public. While Sufi authors liked to quote the Prophetic hadith that hell, on the Day of Judgement, will tell every believer to "pass on, for your light has quenched my flame!" scholars such as the hadith critic ʿAbd al-Raʾūf al-Munāwī (d. 1031/1621) warned that "such hadiths must not be told to the commoners, nor should they be related from the pulpits or on the occasion of religious festivals, rather one should strongly censure those [who do so]."[63]

The Immanentist View

Already before the time of al-Ghazālī, some Sufi authors had begun to develop what could be considered a fifth mode of apprehending the otherworld in Sufi thought: the tendency to regard paradise and hell as immanent in creation. This approach, which for convenience we may characterise as unitive, can be divided into three dominant strands, as is visualised in Chart 4.

The first of these three trends revolves around the idea that the otherworld is present in the physical world of the here and now, in the sense of foreshadowing, reflecting, or indeed sharing in paradise and hell. While extreme proponents of this line of thought would speak of the encompassing overlap, or "unity" (*ittiḥād*), of the otherworld and this world, detractors accused them of teaching the "indwelling" (*ḥulūl*) of God in creation. Opinions are

[62] Sarrāj, *Lumaʿ*, tr. Gramlich, 548 (on al-Shiblī).
[63] The hadith is related by Sarrāj, ibid. Cf. the criticism in Munāwī, *Fayḍ*, XII, 172.

divided as to how significant this doctrine was within Sufism. What seems relatively clear is that while the roots of this attitude stretch back to the formative period of Sufism, it only fully came to flourish under the influence of the unitive metaphysics developed by a number of Andalusian Sufis,[64] particularly Ibn al-ʿArabī of Murcia (d. 638/1240), and the Persian mystic from Konya in Anatolia, Rūmī (d. 672/1273).[65]

Sufis of this kind liked to invoke hadiths according to which the prophet Muḥammad had seen, tasted, and heard paradise in the external world. According to one such tradition, he witnessed paradise and hell not just during his otherworldly journey, the *miʿrāj*, but he saw paradise and hell in the *qibla* wall of the mosque in Medina.[66] Some also related that he ate the grapes of paradise and encountered the houris during prayer.[67] According to another hadith, he told his companions: "When you pass by the gardens of paradise, alight and graze there!" When asked what these gardens were, he answered: "The gatherings at which God is remembered (*ḥilaq al-dhikr*)."[68] Certain Sufi authors took this to refer to the Sufis' communal sessions of ritual remembrance (*dhikr*) and music sessions (*samāʿ*), and to the peak moments of joy and spiritual realisation that they experienced in their course.[69]

As early as the third/ninth century, mystics like the Egyptian Dhū l-Nūn (d. 245/859 or 248/862) challenged the renunciants' contempt for the world and instead praised nature, "the voices of the beasts or the rustle of the trees, the splashing of the waters or the song of the birds," as a "testimony" to God's unity and omnipotence.[70] The Persian mystic, Sahl al-Tustarī

[64] Before Ibn al-ʿArabī, mention should be made of Ibn Masarra of Cordoba (d. 319/931) and Ibn Barrajān of Seville (d. 536/1141). On Ibn Masarra, positing an Ismāʿīlī background to the cosmological teachings of the line of Andalusian mystics beginning with Ibn Masarra, see Ebstein, *Mysticism and philosophy.* On Ibn Masarra's hermeneutical concept of *iʿtibār* ("the deciphering of the Divine signs in creation") and on his theory of mystical ascension, see ibid., 219–22, 228–9, at 222. On Ibn Barrajān's pivotal concept of *ʿibra*, or "crossing-over" from this world to the otherworld as a spiritual discipline, see now Casewit, "The forgotton mystic," 385–98.

[65] See Karamustafa, *God's unruly friends*, 29.

[66] See *CTM*, s.v. j-n-n, I, 376b (Bukhārī, Muslim, Nasāʾī, Ibn Ḥanbal): *ʿuriḍat ʿalayya l-jannatu wa-l-nāru ānifan fī ʿurḍi hādhā l-ḥāʾiṭ*. Cf. Ritter, *Meer*, 187; O'Meara, *Space*, 20–1. Cf. the following text, ch. 8, p. 250.

[67] The hadith is quoted, *inter alia*, in ʿAṭṭār's *Asrārnāmeh*. See Ritter, *Meer*, 187.

[68] Tirmidhī, *Jāmiʿ*, *k. al-daʿawāt* 83, V, 532; Ibn Ḥanbal, *Musnad*, III, 150. However, there are no *dhikr* sessions in paradise, made superfluous by the the fact that the blessed have God in their minds constantly. See Sirjānī, *Bayāḍ*, #670. According to another version of the hadith, the Prophet would have answered that the gardens were the "learned colloquia" (*majālis al-ʿilm*). See Ṭabarānī, *Muʿjam*, XI, 95.

[69] Qushayrī, *Risāla*, 222 (tr. 233).

[70] Abū Nuʿaym, *Ḥilya*, IX, 342. Cf. Schimmel, "The celestial garden," 24. To Dhū l-Nūn, however, are also attributed sayings expressive of an unmitigated attitude of *dhamm al-dunyā*. See Ibn al-ʿArabī, *Kawkab*, tr. Deladrière, 319 (#185). On Dhū l-Nūn's asceticism, see also Ebstein, "D̲ū l-Nūn," 572–4.

(d. 283/896), who derived his spiritual genealogy (*silsila*) from Dhū l-Nūn, is perhaps the earliest authority to play openly with the possibility of experiencing paradise on earth, in the manner of the prophet Muḥammad. In his esoteric Qur'ān commentary, he relates a story about a "friend of God" (*walī*) who meets a man on the seashore, holding in his hand a large pomegranate. When asked about it, the man says: "It is a pomegranate that I saw in paradise and that I desired, so God granted it to me, but when He placed it before me I regretted my haste for having it while still in this world." The "friend of God" cheerily proceeds to grab the pomegranate, eating most of it, upon which the man remarks with astonishment: "I did not know your [spiritual] rank before you ate it; no one eats of the food of paradise in this life except the people of paradise."[71]

Al-Tustarī's story, it may be observed, presents us with two different kinds of God-seekers: those who see the pleasures of paradise before them but dare not consume them, akin to al-Tustarī's older contemporary al-Dārānī who, as noted previously, had visions of the houris but felt rather embarrassed by them; and others with a heart (and indeed a mouth) big enough to embrace the pleasures of paradise already in this life. When asked by his friends whether he knew how the fabulous pomegranate of the story actually tasted, al-Tustarī gave a detailed answer; his friends and followers therefore suspected that al-Tustarī was really himself the story's "friend of God."[72]

While al-Tustarī perhaps presents us with an allegorical tale, referring to inner rather than external taste buds, a certain Abū Ḥulmān al-Fārisī (*fl.* second half third/ninth c.), who may have been influenced by al-Tustarī's teachings, took things a step further. He called upon his followers in Damascus, the so-called Ḥulmāniyya, "to prostrate themselves before handsome individuals, beautiful plants, animals or other objects," arguing "that the perfection of their forms was a corporeal reflection of God's eternal beauty, and, as such, must be worshipped by all believers."[73] As some related, Muḥammad had seen God during his night journey in the form of a beardless adolescent (*amrad*) adorned with golden sandals, sitting in a green meadow in paradise.[74] Allegedly, also Basṭāmī declared that he had seen

[71] Tustarī, *Tafsīr*, tr. Keeler, 15. The story is also translated in Karamustafa, *Sufism*, 39. I have slightly altered the translation by Keeler.

[72] Tustarī, *Tafsīr*, tr. Keeler, 15–6 (*ad* Q 2:25). Cf. Ibid., 260 (*ad* Q 76:21), where Sahl claims to have tasted the wine of paradise when reciting Q 76:21 during prayer ("The Lord will give them a pure drink").

[73] Knysh, *Islamic mysticism*, 85. Cf. *TG*, I, 144; Ritter, *Meer*, 452–3, quoting Baghdādī, *Farq*, 245.

[74] Al-Khaṭīb al-Baghdādī, *Ta'rīkh Baghdād*, XIII, 311, disapprovingly attributes this tradition to Nu'aym b. Ḥammād (Eastern Iran and Egypt, d. 228/843), a disciple of Ibn al-Mubārak (see the preceding text, ch. 2, pp. 75–6). Cf. Ritter, *Seele*, 445. Various versions of this hadith can be found in Suyūṭī, *La'ālī*, I, 29–30.

God in the form of a beardless boy.[75] After all, did not a hadith assert that "God created man in His image," and was it not possible, therefore, that certain beardless adolescents, if properly appreciated, provided a glimpse of paradise?[76] Some Sufis devotees, wrote the Iraqi heresiographer al-Ashʿarī in the fourth/tenth century, taught that God could "inhabit a human being or even an animal [. . . .] They see a beautiful thing and say: Who knows, perchance God has taken up residence in it."[77]

Such immanentist conceptions were rejected not just by theologians wishing to stress God's transcendence, but also by most Sufis, including, of course, those who held that the focus on paradise and hell was a distraction and that, if indeed there was a vision of God, it would not be experienced before the Day of Resurrection.[78] Hujwīrī, for example, strongly condemned the practice of gazing at beautiful youths and declared those to be unbelievers who considered it licit.[79] However, later Sufi poetry abounds with allusions to beautiful youths as "witnesses" (*shuhadā'*, sg. *shāhid*) of the otherworld.[80] In the words of ʿAbd al-Karīm al-Jīlī (d. *ca.* 832/1428), "had God not created a bit of paradise and hell in this world, intellects would not be able to reach knowledge about them, because nothing would compare to them (*li-ʿadam al-munāsib*); in consequence, belief in them would not be obligatory."[81] One also encounters the idea that paradise and hell can be seen in creation in disguise. For ʿAṭṭār, the otherworld is hidden in creation, or rather, it exists on earth *in potentia*, while otherworldly existence is a continuation of earthly life in amplified form. However, certain inferences about paradise may be gleaned from the observation of beauty in nature. Thus, a dervish marvelling at the night sky is quoted as saying: "God, if the roof of your prison is so beautiful, how much more beautiful will then be the roof of your Garden!"[82]

[75] Aflākī, *Manāqib al-ʿārifīn*, II, 637.

[76] Cf. Baqlī, *ʿAbhar al-ʿāshiqīn*, § 79: "The face of Adam is the *qibla* of the lovers." On this topic, see Ritter, *Meer*, 449–51 and passim; van Ess, *The youthful god*, 10–1. For later centuries, see Karamustafa, *God's unruly friends*, 22.

[77] Ashʿarī, *Maqālāt*, 13–4. Al-Ashʿarī classifies such people among the Shiʿi "extremists" (*ghulāt*). The Sufi Yaḥyā' b. Muʿādh al-Rāzī (d. 258/872) described a Sufi séance in which the vision of God in paradise as a beautiful youth was theatrically preenacted. See van Ess, "Schönheit und Macht," 24–5. In later times, antinomian Sufis were suspected of, and ridiculed for, declaring beautiful youth to be the houris and beardless boys of paradise, or even to seek intercourse with them, thus in the eleventh/seventeenth-century parody of life in rural Egypt by Yūsuf al-Shirbīnī. See Shirbīnī, *Hazz*, II, 180–1.

[78] Cf. *TG*, IV, 411–5. Karamustafa argues that in the second half of the third/ninth century, the Sufis of Basra and Baghdad "repositioned themselves closer to the social mainstream by taming their radical approach to issues such as experiencing paradise on earth." See Karamustafa, *Sufism*, 172. For a sketch of early Sufis' positions with regard to the possibility of seeing God in this world, see Chodkiewicz, "The vision of God," 33–7.

[79] Hujwīrī, *Kashf*, tr. Nicholson, 416.

[80] See the examples adduced by Schimmel, "I take off the dress," 274–7; Ritter, *Meer*, 443–67.

[81] Jīlī, *Insān*, 246.

[82] ʿAṭṭār, *Asrārnāmeh*, quoted in Ritter, *Meer*, 50, 187.

Rūmī develops these ideas further, even though his massive oeuvre is by no means limited to the immanentist approach to the otherworld. In fact, his writings encompass the full spectrum of Sufi attitudes towards the *dunyā/ākhira* relationship: one finds the rejection of the world as ephemeral; the downgrading of the physical paradise and hell as inconsequential; the notion that things appear in an imaginable form in the hereafter (an idea that will be further explored in the following text); and the simile of the human heart as the garden of paradise (see the following text). It should also be noted that Rūmī is careful to avoid an explicit espousal of monism, of which he has sometimes been accused, the encompassing equation of this world with God. He makes it clear that the earthly garden is "but a leaf" of the eternal garden,[83] a statement that chimes with the mainstream notion that the pleasure of sexual union, for example, is but a faint foretaste of the pleasures experienced in paradise, or that the pain caused by earthly fire is inconsequential in comparison with that caused by the flames in hell.[84] Yet Rūmī, "the most eloquent master in the field of truly mystical interpretation of nature,"[85] also waxes powerful about the ways in which paradise and hell are experienced in the external world.

One of the central motifs in the work of Rūmī is the divine saying (*ḥadīth qudsī*) that "I was a hidden treasure and wanted to be known."[86] This means, as Rūmī paraphrases it: "I created the whole of the universe, and the goal in all of it is to make Myself manifest, sometimes through gentleness and sometimes through severity."[87] Creation, albeit imperfectly, mirrors God's beauty and gentleness, but also His awe-inspiring, severe side; the seeing eye of the Sufi perceives both. Among Rūmī's favourite imagery is the paradisiacal spring garden and its opposite, autumn and winter, natural phenomena that he likens to a hellish "torture chamber" and interprets as a reminder of "God's threat and intimidation."[88] The sweet wind of the first warm days of the year, by contrast, blows like the trumpet that announces the resurrection of the dead. When the first green leaves appear, one is reminded of the *sabzpūsh*, "those dressed in green," that is, the angels and houris in paradise.[89] "Spring and the garden are messengers from the paradise of the unseen," states Rūmī, and quoting the Qur'ān, he urges his audience to listen, "since 'It is only for the messenger to deliver the message [5:99].' "[90]

Nature is thus invested with the status of revelation, apt by its own example to convince doubters of the reality of paradise and hell. In Rūmī's

83 Rūmī, *Mathnawī*, book 2, v. 3231 (tr. II, 389).
84 Ghazālī, *Iḥyā'*, V, 158, tr. Winter, 223.
85 Schimmel, "The celestial garden," 27.
86 On the background: *TG*, IV, 456; Schimmel, *The triumphal sun*, 225–47.
87 Rūmī, *Fīhi mā fīhi*, 176–7 (tr. 184–5).
88 Idem, *Mathnawī*, book 2, vv. 2959–60 (tr. II, 375)
89 On garden imagery in Rūmī, see the translations in Chittick, *Sufi path of love*, 280–5. Cf. Schimmel, *The triumphal sun*, 82–93; eadem, "The celestial garden," 27–30.
90 Chittick, *Sufi path of love*, 282.

retelling of the story of the encounter between Moses and Pharaoh, the latter mockingly asks for proof of the exact location of hell, with which the prophet has threatened him. Moses answers that God brings hell into being wherever He wants: "Your teeth may hurt so much that you will say: 'This is hell and [the bite of] a snake.'" By contrast, a kiss between lovers, Moses lectures Pharaoh, is pure bliss: "He makes the spittle of your mouth as honey, so that you say: 'This is paradise and [heaven's] adornment.'"[91] However, not everyone is capable of correctly interpreting the traces of the otherworld in this world. Rūmī, as the story goes, was once criticised for his passionate interest in music. "The sound of the rebec (*rubāb*) is the squeaking of the door of paradise," he had ventured. "We hear it, too," came the ironic reply of one of the people listening, "but why is it that we do not feel as warm (*garm*) because of it as our Mawla?" – to which Rūmī retorted: "We hear the door as it opens, while he hears it being closed."[92]

Compulsory Return

A related but different unitive mode of viewing the otherworld is the spiritualisation and the interiorisation of paradise and hell. It was usually suggested by thinkers in this tradition that the macrocosmic paradise and hell are paralleled in the microcosm of the human being. Thus, al-Tustarī had distinguished between two paradises, "one of them is [the macrocosmic] paradise itself, the other is life with Life itself (*ḥayāt ba-ḥayāt*) and subsistence in Subsistence (*baqāʾ ba-baqāʾ*)."[93] The aim was to enter paradise, as it were, twice: once in the afterlife and once before death, by actualising it in the self. Sufi theorists such as Ibn al-ʿArabī spoke of two modes of "returning" to God: a compulsory one (*al-rujūʿ al-iḍṭirārī*), which results from the natural unfolding of individual and cosmic eschatology, and another, voluntary one (*al-rujūʿ al-ikhtiyārī*) that mystics can achieve already during their lifetime.

Sufi authors of the post-Ghazālian period largely focused on the "voluntary return," the return to the otherworld within,[94] but also their explorations of the transcendent realities encountered during the "compulsory return" marked a new departure. Nowhere is this new conceptualisation of the otherworld more extensively discussed than in the work of Ibn al-ʿArabī,

[91] Rūmī, *Mathnawī*, book 4, vv. 2811–3 (tr. IV, 427).

[92] Quoted by Jāmī, *Nafaḥāt*, 462. On Rūmī's imagery of music and dance, see Schimmel, *The triumphal sun*, 210–22.

[93] Tustarī, *Tafsīr*, tr. Keeler, 284 (*ad* Q 89:30). Cf. Böwering, *The mystical vision*, 172. In a similar vein, al-Tustarī states that "there is a Paradise and a Hellfire in this life. Paradise is safety (*ʿāfiya*), and safety is that God takes care of your affairs, and Hellfire is tribulation (*balwā*). Tribulation is when He leaves you in charge of your self." See Tustarī, *Tafsīr*, tr. Keeler, 253–4 (*ad* Q 73:9).

[94] Chittick, "Muslim eschatology," 138, 144.

whose thoughts on the topic are so complex that only a general impression of the picture he paints can be given here.[95] While earlier Sufis, as discussed in the previous sections, had tended to accept the physicality of the otherworld but had, largely *because* of this physicality, dismissed paradise and hell as inconsequential, Ibn al-ʿArabī revalidated the two postmortem abodes as necessary intermediate stages on the individual's progress towards that which is fully true and real, namely, God.

Developing an idea that was, as we saw in the two preceding chapters, foreshadowed by Avicenna and al-Ghazālī and consequently pursued by thinkers operating in the illuminationist (*ishrāqī*) tradition, Ibn al-ʿArabī posits that the phenomena in the otherworld are neither material nor immaterial; rather, they possess a different reality, a *third* kind of reality, which he refers to as "imaginal" (*khayālī*) or "interstitial" (*barzakhī*). God, in Ibn al-ʿArabī's vision, created the world to serve as a reflection or mirror of Himself, providing humans the opportunity to become conscious of their Creator. With an individual's passage – whether after death or before, during visionary moments – into the *barzakh* and, eventually, into paradise and hell,[96] the self-disclosure of God reaches a more intense level, because the search in the phenomenal world for signs of the immaterial beyond now becomes significantly easier. This is because, in Ibn al-ʿArabī's vision, the realities that man witnesses in the imaginal world are direct representations of the truths that lie hidden behind the surface of things on earth. In the imaginal world, the resurrected individual sees formerly inward, spiritual qualities in corresponding outward forms: for example, mystical knowledge attaches itself to the imaginal body of a saint in the form of a bright light,[97] or is drunk in the form of milk, honey, or wine by the inhabitants of paradise,[98] while sins take the form of chains and fetters weighing down on the sinners.[99] The human soul thus "becomes embodied in an imaginal form appropriate to its own attributes; likewise, all its works, character traits, knowledge, and aspirations appear to it in appropriate forms."[100]

95 I base the following largely on William Chittick's fundamental study, "Death and the World of Imagination." Maurice Gloton has produced a French translation of the central eschatological chapters (##61–5) of Ibn al-ʿArabī's *al-Futūḥāt al-Makkiyya*, which I have gratefully consulted.

96 As Chittick, "Death," 65, notes, "[i]t is not easy to discern the exact difference between the Isthmus [*barzakh*] and the next world from Ibn al-ʿArabī's writings." In one instance, he calls *barzakh* "the first way-station (*manzil*) of the next world." See Ibn al-ʿArabī, *Futūḥāt*, IV, 282.13. In another place, he likens death to awakening from a dream within a dream, resurrection then being the real wake-up call. See ibid., II, 313.6.

97 Ibid., II, 296.10.

98 Ibid., I, 306.13; II, 311.14; IV, 418.3.

99 Ibid., I, 306.13, IV, 418.3.

100 Chittick, "Death," 63. Rūmī likens mystical experience (*dhawq-i jan*) to the well-guarded houris. See Rūmī, *Mathnawī*, book 5, v. 3292 (tr. VI, 198). Cf. Chittick, *Sufi path of love*, 106. Shahzad Bashier notes how widespread the concept of "spiritual bodies" in the *ʿālam al-mithāl* is in Persianate Sufi literature. See Bashier, *Sufi bodies*, 38.

The imaginal entities in Ibn al-ʿArabī's interstitial world also include fundamental religious ideas: the concept of "Islam" thus appears as a strong pillar, and the Qurʾān is presented to the blessed as butter and honey.[101] Hell is no other than the interstitial embodiment of God's anger at humankind's failure to pay Him proper service. As Ibn al-ʿArabī states, God created hell as a manifestation (*tajallī*) of the divine saying: "Though I was hungry you did not feed Me, though I was thirsty you did not quench My thirst, though I was sick you did not visit Me!"[102] God is manifest in an imaginal body that the blessed see in paradise, where He appears to them as a beautiful young man.[103] It may well be that Ibn al-ʿArabī's view of the imaginal reality of the phenomena of the otherworld opened the door for Sufi literature to rehabilitate, and in fact reappropriate, traditional notions of an embodied afterlife. In the centuries after Ibn al-ʿArabī, one finds several examples of Sufi authors who compiled eschatological works in the traditionist genre.[104]

Ibn al-ʿArabī's writings are also ripe with cosmological speculations about the location and topology of paradise and hell. All of creation, in Ibn al-ʿArabī's expression, is God's exhalation, "the Breath of the All-Merciful" (*nafas al-raḥmān*), descending from the transcendent top to the sublunar world, thus creating a hierarchy of levels of existence, marked by increasing differentiation and distance from God. In this scheme, paradise fills the upper half of the sphere of the fixed stars, its roof demarcating the boundary to the sphere of the zodiac, while hell occupies the lower, bottom half of the sphere of the fixed stars. The sphere of the zodiac, in turn, is placed directly under the footstool (*kursī*) of God's throne (*ʿarsh*). According to Ibn al-ʿArabī, God puts His two feet on the footstool, and paradise and hell, as one infers, derive organically from this juxtaposition of right and left, that is, God's mercy and wrath. As such, they are so intimately bound to God that they survive the reordering of the cosmos at resurrection, when everything below the sphere of the fixed stars disintegrates into nothingness.[105]

Ibn al-ʿArabī goes to some length to show that the suffering in hell is a function of its inhabitants, not of hell. For example, he relates a vision in which he inspects hell and comes to witness the quarrelling that goes on among the damned. "I realised something astonishing," he writes, "the quarreling is itself their punishment … and [even though it] is *in* hell, it does not result *from* hell."[106] Ibn al-ʿArabī insists that the divine anger that is manifest in hell is caused by the damned, while God's relationship to hell

[101] Ibn al-ʿArabī, *Futūḥāt*, I, 306.13, IV, 418.3.

[102] Ibid., I, 297.26–7.

[103] Ibid., I, 306.13; IV, 418.3.

[104] See the preceding text, pp. 87–8.

[105] For this, see chs. 198 and 371 of the *Futūḥāt*. Cf. Ibn al-ʿArabī, *Futūḥāt*, tr. Gloton, 39, 64. Cf. Chittick, *Imaginal worlds*, 111–2; idem, *Sufi path of knowledge*, 359–61; Rustom, *Triumph*, 107–9.

[106] Ibn al-ʿArabī, *Futūḥāt*, I, 299.3–4.

is one of mercy. This corresponds to his view that punishment in hell is not eternal: because God is essentially merciful, His anger, which is accidental to His essence, will eventually come to an end.[107] This accords with the divine saying, popular among Sufis such as Ibn al-ʿArabī, that "My mercy outweighs My wrath (*inna raḥmatī taghlibu ghaḍabī*)."[108]

However, for Ibn al-ʿArabī, this does not mean that God eventually destroys hell, or that those who are condemned to eternal damnation – those he identifies as the haughty (*mutakabbirūn*), idolaters (*mushrikūn*), deniers of God's attributes (*muʿaṭṭila*) and hypocrites (*munāfiqūn*) – are allowed a way out of hell into paradise. After they have received their due punishment, the damned simply lose the ability to feel pain, helped by the fact that they grow thicker skins each time that they have been burned (cf. Qur'ān 4:56).[109] At any rate, Ibn al-ʿArabī ventures, knowing what they have done, the damned would feel humiliated were they let into paradise, whereas they do not suffer from such humiliation in hell.[110] In sum, their eternal residence in hell is "good news" (*bushrā*) for them.[111] In the words of Mullā Ṣadrā, whose soteriology is inspired by that of Ibn al-ʿArabī, "the punishment (*ʿadhāb*) will become sweetness (*ʿadhb*)"[112] – even though, as Ibn al-ʿArabī puts it, this "sweet suffering" is no more than an "imagined well-being" (*naʿīm khayālī*).[113]

Voluntary Return

As noted in the preceding text, the imaginal otherworld, as Ibn al-ʿArabī describes it, is accessible not just after death, but also during dreams and in states of mystical "unveiling" (*kashf/mukāshafa*) such as those that Ibn

[107] This is an idea embraced by a number of post-Akbarian thinkers, prominently Mullā Ṣadrā. See Rustom, *Triumph of mercy*, 86, 99, 110, 113, and passim.

[108] Bukhārī, *Ṣaḥīḥ*, *k. al-tawḥīd* 15 (*b. qawl Allāh [eulogy]*), IV, 421. For variants of this hadith, see Graham, *Divine word*, 184–5. Cf. Sviri, "Between fear and hope," 335.

[109] Ibn al-ʿArabī, *Futūḥāt*, I, 303.21–23. On Ibn al-ʿArabī's hell, see now Pagani, "Ibn ʿArabī and political hell." See also the summary of Ibn al-ʿArabī's doctrine of a "paradisiacal hell" in Khalil, *Islam*, 62–7.

[110] Ibn al-ʿArabī, *Futūḥāt*, I, 301.15.

[111] Ibid., I, 301.13.

[112] See Rustom, *Triumph of mercy*, 113, quoting from Ṣadrā, *Tafsīr*, I, 70–1. For Mullā Ṣadrā's soteriology, see ibid., 85–115.

[113] Ibn al-ʿArabī, *Futūḥāt*, I, 303.22. ʿAbd al-Karīm al-Jīlī (d. *ca.* 832/1428), a follower of Ibn al-ʿArabī, taught that "for the people in Hell God creates a natural pleasure of which their bodies become enamoured; Hell at last will be extinguished and replaced by a tree named D̲j̲ird̲j̲īr; Iblīs will return to the presence and grace of God; all infidels worship God according to the necessity of their essential natures and all will be saved, etc." Al-Jīlī also reported visions of an otherworldly journey through paradise and hell. See *EI2*, s.v. al-D̲j̲īlī, I, 71a-71b (H. Ritter). Cf. the preceding text, n46. The tree Jirjīr seems related to the notion that watercress (*jarjarīr*) grows in the upper regions of hell. See the preceding text, p. 137.

al-ʿArabī claimed for himself and attributed to other Sufis he knew.[114] Such explorations of realities of the cosmic paradise and hell were paralleled by Sufi forays into the inner paradise and hell, a movement *ab intra* that Ibn al-ʿArabī referred to as the "voluntary return" and that gestures back to the inward turn of Muslim mystics in the second half of the third/ninth century, particularly in the city of Baghdad.[115] Indeed, centuries before Ibn al-ʿArabī, Sufis had begun to liken inner spiritual states to experiencing paradise or suffering the torments of hell. Abū l-Ḥasan al-Nūrī (d. 295/907–8) of Baghdad, in a celebrated passage, likened the Sufi's heart to the Kaaba, Islam's holiest place, "cleansed of idolatry, doubt, hypocrisy and discord" by the "wind of God's magnamity," a place in which blossom "all kinds of plants such as certainty, trust, sincerity, fear, hope and love," as well as "the tree of knowledge." From this inner Kaaba, according to al-Nūrī, God opens a door "to the garden of His mercy and sows there many kinds of fragrant herbs of praise, glorification, exaltation and commemoration ... making waters of the ocean of guidance flow to these plants through the river of kindness."[116] Paradise, in this vision, is accessed through the human heart.[117]

The Persian mystic Hujwīrī (d. 465/1073 or 469/1077) writes that man's lower soul (*nafs*), the seat of carnal appetites, corresponds to hell, while man's spirit or higher soul (*jān*) corresponds to paradise, "of which it is a type in this world."[118] Already ʿAbd al-Wāḥid b. Zayd contended that contemplative contentment (*riḍā*) with God's ordering of the world and of one's life, whatever it may be, is "the greatest door of God, and paradise on earth."[119] Al-Qushayrī (d. 465/1072) notes that the Iraqi Sufis hold that *riḍā* is a state (*ḥāl*) that cannot be actively sought by the Sufis; rather it overcomes them as a mercy bestowed on them by God. The Khorasanian Sufis, however, argue that *riḍā* is actively acquired; it is a station (*maqām*) on the mystical path towards union with God.[120] It may be true that it was a hallmark of Sufis of the Persian-speaking world to theorise about the active conquest of the paradise within.

[114] Ibn al-ʿArabī relates that the Andalusian mystic Ibn Barrajān (d. 536/1141) saw hell in the form of a buffalo (*jāmūs*) in a state of mystical unveiling (*kashf*), while his contemporary Ibn Qasī (d. 546/1151) saw it as a snake. See Ibn al-ʿArabī, *Futūḥāt*, I, 297.24–5.

[115] On the "inward turn," see Karamustafa, *Sufism*, 1–7, 20–1, and passim.

[116] See Nwyia, *Exégèse*, 325–30. On Nūrī, see further Gramlich, *Alte Vorbilder*, I, 381–446; Karamustafa, *Sufism*, 11–5; Knysh, *Islamic mysticism*, 60–3.

[117] Similarly in Jaʿfar al-Ṣādiq's (d. 148/765) *Tafsīr*, 224, tr. Mayer, 157 (*ad* Q 55:11), where the hearts of God's friends are declared to be "the meadows of His intimacy" (*riyāḍ unsih*). Ibn al-ʿArabī states that the human heart is the Throne of God in the microcosmos, as can be argued on the basis of the divine saying: "My earth and my heaven do not contain Me, but the heart of My believing servant contains Me." See Ibn al-ʿArabī, *Futūḥāt*, III, 249.31. Cf. Chittick, *The self-disclosure of God*, 351.

[118] Hujwīrī, *Kashf*, tr. Nicholson, 199. See also ʿAyn al-Quḍāṭ (d. 525/1131), *Tamhīdāt*, 288–90.

[119] Qushayrī, *Risāla*, 192–7, at 194 (tr. 205–10, at 207).

[120] Ibid., 193 (tr. 206). Cf. Meier, *Abū Saʿīd*, 4.

The Khorasani ʿAzīz-i Nasafī (*fl.* middle of seventh/thirteenth century), a relatively well-known figure in the Western study of Sufism,[121] may serve as an example.[122] His most famous work, *The Perfect Man* (*Insān-i kāmil*), includes a chapter on paradise and hell.[123] Nasafī begins this chapter by defining paradise and hell in the abstract, as harmony (*muwāfaqat*) and opposition (*mukhālafat*), a formulation he seems to borrow from Ibn al-ʿArabī.[124] Nasafī acknowledges the future otherworld, but he points out that "presently there is a paradise and hell within us as well."[125] In the remainder of his text, this general definition is spelled out on three levels, as Nasafī successively discusses an ethical, noetic, and spiritual otherworld within.

With regard to the first, ethical level, Nasafī states that "all the approved words and deeds and all the praiseworthy manners are the gates of paradise," while "all the disapproved words and deeds and all the blameworthy manners are the gates of hell."[126] A drawing contained in a manuscript of

[121] The first English publication devoted to Sufism, Edward Henry Palmer's *Oriental mysticism* (1867), was a paraphrase of one of Nasafī's works, the *Maqṣad-i aqṣā*. Fritz Meier devoted two comprehensive studies to Nasafī's thought. See Meier, *Das Problem der Natur*; idem, "Die Schriften des ʿAzīz-i Nasafī." See also Landolt, "Le soufisme"; Ridgeon, *ʿAzīz Nasafī*.

[122] One may also compare this to Najm al-Dīn al-Rāzī (d. 654/1256), who writes that the Sufis "have died a true death before the occurrence of material death … [t]hey reside in this world in outward appearance, but in reality they have transcended the eight paradises." See Rāzī, *Mirṣād*, tr. Algar, 375. On the theme of the hadith "die before you die" (*mūtū qabla an tamūtū*), see Ritter, *Meer*, 583; Rosenthal, "Reflections on love," 247–8; Karamustafa, *God's unruly friends*, 16, 21. Also in the thought of ʿAbd al-Razzāq al-Qāshānī (d. 730/1329), a follower of Ibn al-ʿArabī and author of an esoteric commentary (the *Taʾwīlāt al-Qurʾān*) regarded, for a long time, as the work of his master, there is a "complete coincidence" between spiritual accomplishment of the Sufi and eschatological salvation. See Lory, *Commentaires*, 107. In addition to the passages from al-Qāshānī's Qurʾān commentary discussed by Lory, see Qāshānī, *Majmūʿa-yi rasāʾil*, in particular "Risāla-yi mabdaʾ va-maʿād" (ibid., pp. 302–6) and "al-Risāla al-maʿādiyya" (ibid., pp. 307–11).

[123] Nasafī, *Insān*, 294–309. For a fuller discussion of this epistle, see Lange, "A Sufi's paradise and hell."

[124] See Ibn al-ʿArabī, *Futūḥāt*, IV, 14.34. Cf. Chittick, "Death," 80. Felicity in paradise, for Nasafī, is "finding that which is desired" (*yāftan-i murād*), while the misery of hell is its opposite, i.e., not finding that which is willed. See Nasafī, *Insān*, 295.

[125] Ibid., 294.

[126] The idea that the gates of paradise and hell correspond to specific virtuous and sinful actions is found in the hadith, e.g., Bukhārī, *Ṣaḥīḥ*, *k. al-ṣawm* 4 (*b. al-rayyān li-l-ṣāʾimīn*), I, 488, where prayer, fasting, charity, jihad, and so forth are the gates of paradise. Al-Ḥakīm al-Tirmidhī (d. between 295/905 and 300/910) allocates those who distinguish themselves by pious works (*aʿmāl*), such as steadfastness (*ṣabr*) and gratefulness (*shukr*), to nine different ranks (*darajāt*) in paradise. See al-Ḥakīm al-Tirmidhī, *Masʾala*, fol. 43b, l. 1–2. I thank Bernd Radtke for providing me with a scan of this text. In this context belong Sufi understandings of the hadith that "this world is the sowing field (*mazraʿa*) of the otherworld. See, e.g., Jīlī, *Insān*, 226. Al-Ghazālī notes that there are eight virtues, and hence eight gates of paradise, as opposed to the seven cardinal sins and the seven gates of hell. See Ghazālī, *Iḥyāʾ*, IV, 536, tr. Winter, 235. According to Schimmel, "traditional Sufi leaders recognized

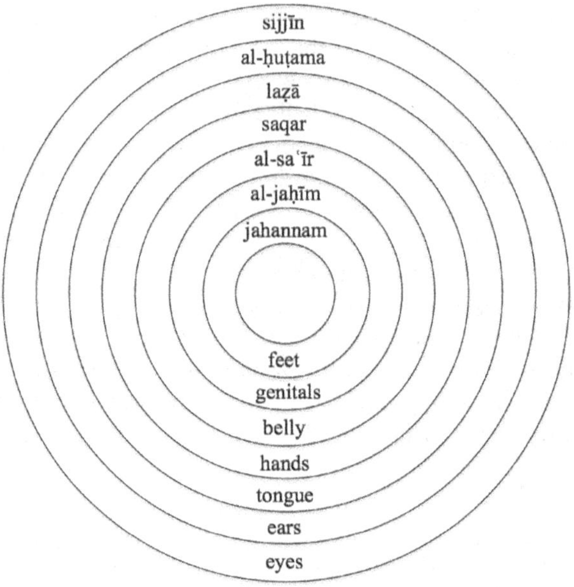

CHART 5. Ibn al-ʿArabī's ethical hell.
Note: This is a simplified version of the diagram offered by Ibn al-ʿArabī, who further subdivides the seven concentric circles into quadrants comprising unbelievers, polytheists, atheists, and hypocrites. See Ibn al-ʿArabī, *Futūḥāt*, III, 557.

Ibn al-ʿArabī's *Meccan Openings* (*al-Futūḥāt al-Makkiyya*) visualises this idea, correlating the traditional names of the seven concentric layers of hell with the seven body parts that are instrumental in committing sins, both externally in practice and internally in thought (see Chart 5).[127]

According to Nasafī, "every affliction and misery that befalls man results from disapproved words and deeds ... while every moment of ease and happiness that a man encounters results from approved words and deeds and from praiseworthy manners."[128] One notices in this passage that Nasafī does not distinguish between the felicity or misery attained in this world and in the otherworld. For him, they seem collapsed into one. The same phenomenon occurs on the level of the noetic paradise and hell that Nasafī describes. Paradise, he says, comes about if there is balance between the human faculties of perception and understanding: the five outer senses as well as the inward faculties of imagination (*khayāl*), fancy (*wahm*), and reason (*ʿaql*). If reason controls the other seven faculties, together they are the eight gates to

seven gates to hell: pride, cupidity, lust, anger, envy, avarice, and hatred." See Schimmel, "I take off the dress," 265, quoting R. A. Nicholson in *Mathnawī*, Commentary, VII, 68.

127 See the discussion in Asín, *La escatologia*, 118–9.

128 Nasafī, *Insān*, 295.

paradise. If, by contrast, reason is absent and the remaining seven faculties are out of balance, they equal the seven gates of hell.[129]

The third kind of paradise, following upon the paradises of ethical and intellectual perfection, is a spiritual state of mystical insight. It is reserved for the Sufis alone and represents the highest degree of human perfection. Nasafī describes a gradual "ascension" of the Sufi through the paradises of praiseworthy character and manners (*khuluq*, *akhlāq-i nīk*), ordinary knowledge (*ʿilm*), and inspired knowledge (*maʿrifat*), a journey culminating in the "paradise of light" and the "paradise of direct encounter (*liqā*)" with God. In this state, the Sufi has achieved the "true paradise" (*bihisht-i ḥaqīqī*), a state of perfect comprehension in which "nothing in the worlds of *mulk*, *malakūt* and *jabarūt* remains veiled" from him.[130]

Nasafī's ascension model appears to lean on Ibn al-ʿArabī, who had divided paradise into a "Garden of Works" (entered on account of one's good actions), a "Garden of Inheritance" (housing those Muslims who deserve paradise on account of their belief, albeit after temporary punishment in hell), and a "Garden of Election" (occupied by "the people who have knowledge of God's unity," but also by children to the age of six, the mentally impaired, and by those who did not receive the message of a messenger of God).[131] However, in Nasafī's epistle, these types of gardens are consistently located within the human individual. Thus, a kind of paradise and hell on earth can be experienced even by those people who remain on the level of ethical or noetic "harmony" (or "opposition") but do not reach the rank of all-round "perfect" human beings. Overall, although Nasafī engages to some extent with the centuries of Sufi and philosophical eschatology that precedes him, in many respects his project is a new departure. Nasafī's radical interiorisation of the otherworld, which parallels and complements Ibn al-ʿArabī's concept of the "imaginal" otherworld, can be read as a response to the decentring of paradise and hell in the thought of the Sufis of earlier centuries, as an attempt to reinsert paradise and hell into Sufi discourse by sublimating them and locating them within mundane human experience.

To conclude, the typology of Sufi attitudes that this chapter has mapped out helps us to nuance two common assumptions about the Sufis' view of the relationship between this world and the otherworld. First, it would be

[129] Ibid., 295–6. The same idea occurs in Ṭūsī, *Mabdaʾ*, 77–8 (§§ 65–6); Kashānī, *Kalimāt*, 210–1 (quoting Ṭūsī).

[130] Nasafī, *Insān*, 304. Nasafī also alludes to the existence of a "ninth paradise," reserved for the "Perfect Man" (*insān-i kāmil*), a figure who possesses the miracle-mongering ability called *himmat* ("spiritual energy"). *Himmat* enables one to create effects of the otherworld in this world, and to partake simultaneously in both. See ibid., 307–8. The idea goes back to Ibn al-ʿArabī, *Futūḥāt*, II, 385. It also occurs in the School of Isfahan, e.g., in the thought of Muḥsin Fayḍ Kāshānī. See Kāshānī, *Kalimāt*, 180–3 and 208–10, where the "Perfect Man" is identified with ʿAlī.

[131] Ibn al-ʿArabī, *Futūḥāt*, I, 317–8.

a simplification to argue that for Sufi authors concerned with grasping the reality of the otherworld the present life had no value at all.[132] The ways in which Sufis wrote about how this world and the otherworld relate to one another suggest a far more complex and dynamic understanding. Secondly, it may be true that Sufis throughout the centuries accepted the physicality of the afterlife as a given.[133] More important, however, is the observation that Sufi authors interpreted this physicality in ways that were radically different from the discourse of Muslim traditionists, theologians and, though to a lesser degree, philosophers. Some dismissed it as inconsequential while others despised it actively; others again located paradise and hell (or parts thereof) on earth. In the later period, the focus of Sufi eschatology shifted to an explicit interiorisation of paradise and hell. This shift occurred next to, but not to the exclusion of, discussions of the external paradise and hell. In this arena of eschatological thought, Sufi thought increasingly came to interact with philosophical discussions about the human imagination as the true *locus* of paradise and hell, as was discussed in Chapters 5 and 6 of this book. Particularly in the thought of Ibn al-ʿArabī and his followers, paradise and hell took on characteristics of an imaginal world, thus claiming a distinct reality of their own.

[132] El-Saleh, *Vie future*, 91.

[133] See ibid., 101. El-Saleh, however, also notes that there were Sufis who eschewed all talk about the physical paradise and hell. Al-Ḥallāj appears to be an example of this.

8

Eschatology Now: Paradise and Hell in Muslim Topography, Architecture, and Ritual

In the preceding chapters of this book much of our attention has been occupied by textual spadework. The dearth of previous scholarship devoted to the Muslim literature on paradise and hell invited this approach, in fact it necessitated it. Now that we have laid some textual foundations, we shall examine how the literary representations of paradise and hell translated into tangible spatial and material phenomena. As I argue in this chapter, paradise and hell were world-making ideas in the history of Islamic civilisation not just in the sense of giving rise to abstract cosmological, theological, or mystical systems of thought. Rather, in certain contexts, they provided a concrete blueprint for the interpretation of this-worldly realities and for the organisation of Muslim society on earth. This chapter highlights three areas in which the Muslim discourse on paradise and hell became operative in this way: topography, architecture, and ritual. An analysis of these three fields of cultural production brings to light an eschatological worldview, by which I mean the conceptual framework in which otherworldly phenomena are made to be present in this world in a regularised and sustained fashion in order to provide everyday life with layers of ultimate meaning. In this framework, paradise and hell are not distant repositories of truth and justice but immediate targets to which present concerns are addressed. Furthermore, as I argue in this chapter, the mode in which paradise and hell are made to be present in this world is not referential. It is not that certain worldly spaces, objects, and rituals symbolise, refer to, or gesture towards an otherworld that is absent, although they may often do this, too. Rather, what emerges from the sources understudy here is the sense that these phenomena are truly and fully here on earth. They claim to be the thing itself, not signs of it. They indicate presence, not likeness.

Eutopia/Dystopia

"The entire world is a place for us to worship (*juʿilat la-nā al-arḍ kulluhu masjidan*)," the Prophet is reported to have said.[1] In this view, the world as a whole is sanctified in the sense that it gives access to the divine. It is clear, at the same time, that certain spaces, such as mosques, cities, and sacred landscapes enjoy a privileged status, while others, such as bathhouses and marketplaces, are devalued and declared unfit for ritual.[2] Paradise and hell were mapped onto such spaces in processes of constructing this-worldly eutopias and dystopias. I prefer to use the term *eutopia* ("good place") here, the true antonym of *dystopia* ("bad place"), in order to indicate that I am talking about places of ideal well-being that one may practically aspire to, in contrast to *utopias* ("no-places"), which are impossible to attain (though they may be conceived to exist in the mythic past or future).

It is true that medieval Islamic maps, such as the one produced by the Sicilian scholar al-Idrīsī in the sixth/twelfth century, unlike some medieval Christian world maps, show neither paradise nor hell. At best, as in the case of the world map of al-Kāshgharī (Baghdad, fifth/eleventh c.), they indicate the spot were Adam fell to the earth after his expulsion from the Garden, a place that was usually identified with Sri Lanka (Arab. Sarandīb).[3] In general, cosmological maps that represent the structure of the universe, including paradise and hell, appear to be a rare and late (post-eighteenth c.) phenomenon, the two specimen included in the Ottoman scholar-mystic İbrahim Hakkı's encyclopaedia, *The Book of Knowledge* (*Maʿrifetnāma*, written in 1170/1756–7), providing perhaps the most spectacular illustration.[4] However, perhaps one should not make too much of the absence of eschatological features on premodern Islamic maps.[5] Cartography, in this respect, may turn out to be the exception to the rule. For, as previous chapters of this book have demonstrated, there are important strands in the exegetical, traditionist, theological, philosophical, and mystical literature of Sunni and Shiʿi Islam that *do* allow for multiple ways of conceiving the

[1] Muslim, *Ṣaḥīḥ, k. al-masājid* 4 [no *bāb*], I, 371; Ibn Ḥanbal, *Musnad*, V, 383.

[2] Cf., e.g., the tradition that states that mosques are the "gardens of paradise," and that people should "alight and graze" there. See Tirmidhī, *Jāmiʿ*, *k. al-daʿawāt* 83, V, 532; Nābulusī, *Ahl al-janna*, 53. Another tradition declares that "the best place[s] on earth are mosques, and the worst place[s] on earth are market-places." See Fākihī, *Akhbār Makka*, II, 34 (#1090). On the ambiguous eschatological symbolism of bathhouses, see Pagani, "Un paradiso in terra." See also a poet's description of the bathhouse ("its pleasantness recalls Eden, its heat hell; its servants are houris working next to *zabāniya*") in Bākharzī, *Dumya*, II, 856, quoted in Szombathy, "Come hell or high water," 166.

[3] Ibn Qutayba, *Maʿārif*, 15; Thaʿlabī, *ʿArāʾis*, 33. On al-Kāshgharī's map, see Savage-Smith, "In medieval Islamic cosmography."

[4] On Hakkı's maps, see Savage-Smith, "In medieval Islamic cosmography."

[5] *Pace* van Ess, who states, rather apodictically, that in Islam, paradise and hell are defined "in purely temporal terms." See *TG*, IV, 552.

presence of paradise and hell on earth. Sometimes, as in the case of geographical works devoted to the "merits" (*faḍā'il*) or "wondrous qualities" (*'ajā'ib*) of specific cities and regions of the Islamic world, authors discuss the precise location of paradise and hell on earth, and they indicate ways of traversing into them.

To begin with what is perhaps the most well-known example, Muslim eschatologists often asserted that Jerusalem was the site of the future earthly paradise, a Jewish notion that was taken up in Islam.[6] However, Jerusalem, especially the Temple Mount, or "Noble Sanctuary" (*al-ḥaram al-sharīf*), already *is* paradise, or at least very close to it, "the closest place on earth to heaven," as was related from Ka'b al-Aḥbār.[7] The "Story of the Leaves," quoted in the introduction of this book, is a case in point. "Praying in Jerusalem," states a hadith, "is like praying in heaven."[8] From Jerusalem the prophets Jesus and Muḥammad ascended into the heavens. The Temple Mount is where heaven and earth meet.[9]

It might be objected that the Muslim literature on the Prophet's ascension usually situates paradise in a realm that is beyond this world: Muḥammad climbs up a ladder until he reaches the ceiling, so to speak, of the world, where angels let him pass through a gate, emerging into the first heaven as if through a hole in the roof; it is only in the higher celestial spheres that he catches a glimpse of paradise and hell.[10] However, there is also the notion that the Temple Mount is immediately contiguous with paradise. Thus, texts composed in praise of Jerusalem specify that the Rock sits on top of one of the gates of paradise, or indeed the Rock is called the gate to paradise.[11] The four paradisiacal rivers, Sayḥān, Jayḥān, Euphrates, and Nile, are said to spring from underneath the Rock,[12] or the Rock is pictured to sit atop a palm tree that has its roots in one of the rivers of paradise.[13] Jerusalem, in these traditions, appears as the navel of the world, the vertical point of

6 *TG*, IV, 395. Cf. van Ess, "'Abd al-Malik and the Dome of the Rock," 89: the Rock is the "holiest of all places." Cf. Suyūṭī, *Budūr*, 91, for traditions specifying that the Judgement takes place in Jerusalem.

7 Qurṭubī, *Tadhkira*, I, 235. Ibn Taymiyya, by contrast, seeks to refute superstitious beliefs in the holiness of the site, particularly if they are based on *isrā'īliyyāt* transmitted from Ka'b al-Aḥbār. See Ibn Taymiyya, *Iqtiḍā'*, II, 817–24, passim.

8 Yāqūt, *Buldān*, s.v. al-Maqdis, V, 166b.

9 Kaplony, *The Ḥaram*, 359.

10 Some versions of the *mi'rāj*, however, seek to preserve the idea that paradise and hell are on earth. See the preceding text, pp. 112–3.

11 Ibn 'Abd Rabbih, *'Iqd*, VII, 256,19f. (tr. LeStrange, *Palestine*, 164); Nābulusī, *Ahl al-janna*, 48. Cf. Elad, *Medieval Jerusalem*, 79. See the references in Kaplony, *The Ḥaram*, 511.

12 Wāsiṭī, *Faḍā'il*, 68 (#110). Cf. Kaplony, *The Ḥaram*, 359. Cf. Psalm 46.5; Ezekiel 47.1–12.

13 Wāsiṭī, *Faḍā'il*, 67 (#108). In a dream in the night of 'Āshūrā of 335/10–1 August 946, 'Abd Allāh b. Muḥammad al-Ḥawlī sees the Rock shining like ruby (*yāqūta*), and four rivers coming out from beneath it, and it is explained to him that these are the rivers of Paradise. See Ibn al-Murajjā, *Faḍa'il*, 268, 6–8 (#407), cited in Kaplony, *The Ḥaram*, 512.

contact between this world and the life-giving reservoir of subterranean sweet water.[14] There is also a horizontal dimension, however, as if the otherworld enters the world through a vertical conduit but then spreads out to cover a wider stretch of space, that of the Temple Mount, like water gushing forth from a hole in the ground, forming a reservoir. In fact, the entire area of the Temple Mount becomes an eschatological theatre. Thus, the east wall of the Temple Mount, adorned by the "Gate of Mercy" (*bāb al-raḥma*), was sometimes equated by exegetes of the Qur'ān with the barrier between paradise and hell, "inside it will be mercy, and outside it, in front of it, punishment" (Q 57:13), while the valley east of the Temple Mount was identified as the "valley of hell" (*wādī jahannam*).[15]

The Temple Mount in Jerusalem, however, was not the only earthly paradise known in early Islam. In the first century of the Islamic era, the sacred precinct (*ḥaram*) of Thaqīf near al-Ṭā'if in the Hijaz, in the Wajj valley, was said to have been the place where God had set His last step (*ākhir waṭ'*) on earth.[16] Hence some thought Wajj to be the primordial paradise.[17] It has been suggested that this notion was circulated in the Hijaz in order to oppose the claim of the Umayyad caliphate (r. 41–132/661–750) that the earthly paradise was located in Syria.[18] Though Wajj's career as paradise soon came to an end it may have set a precedent to think about earthly paradises in other local contexts. The sacred geography of the Hijaz, in particular, offers examples, many of which centre on the oasis of Medina.

As one learns from a noncanonical hadith that entered into the geographical and historiographical literature, the two mountains of Uḥud and ʿAyr, located on opposite ends of Medina, sit on top of the gates of paradise and hell, respectively.[19] Buṭḥān, one of the three valleys forming the

[14] *EQ*, s.v. Springs and fountains (M. Radscheidt), V, 121b-128b, at 127a.

[15] Ibn ʿAbd Rabbih, *ʿIqd*, VII, 256, 7–9 (tr. LeStrange, *Palestine*, 174).

[16] *Musnad ʿUmar b. ʿAbd al-ʿAzīz*, 421; Yāqūt, *Muʿjam*, s.v. Wajj, V, 361b; Ibn al-Jawzī, *Dafʿ*, 56.

[17] See Lammens, "La cité arabe de Ṭā'if," 139–40; Kister, "Some reports concerning al-Ṭā'if," 18.

[18] See *TG*, IV, 396.

[19] According to a Prophetic tradition reported by al-Ṭabarānī, Uḥud is on top of one of the gates of paradise, the mountain of ʿAyr is on top of one of the gates of hell. See Ṭabarānī, *al-Muʿjam al-kabīr*, IX, 202. Also in Yāqūt, *Buldān*, s.v. Uḥud, I, 109b; Ibn Kathīr, *al-Bidāya wa-l-nihāya*, s.v. *Ghazwa Uḥud*, IV, 9; Suyūṭī, *Budūr*, 512 (where one should correct to *ʿAyr* instead of *Ghayr*); Nābulusī, *Ahl al-janna*, 47–8, 74. Al-Majlisī relates the statement of Jaʿfar al-Ṣādiq that the souls of the believers gather on the mountain of Raḍwā, where they see the members of the family of the Prophet and eat, drink, and talk with them until the arrival of the Qā'im-Mahdī at the end of time. See Majlisī, *Biḥār*, VI, 425. Raḍwā is at a distance of a day's journey from Medina, in the direction of Mecca. See Yāqūt, *Buldān*, s.v. Raḍwā, III, 51a. Al-Suyūṭī reports the view that Uḥud is "one of the pillars (*arkān*) of paradise," which connects Uḥud with a heavenly rather than a subterranean paradise. See Suyūṭī, *Budūr*, 512. According to a tradition preserved ibid., 539, the four mountains of paradise in this world are Uḥud, Sinai, the Lebanon, and Wariqān (near al-ʿArj between Mecca and Medina).

1 - The prayer niches (*miḥrābs*) of the prophets
2 - The pulpit (*minbar*) of Muḥammad
3 - The fountain of al-Kawthar
4 - The Balance of Deeds (*mizān-i aʿmāl*)
5 - The Dome of the Rock
6 - The Path of Ṣirāṭ (*sabīl-i ṣirāṭ*)
7 - The Gate of Paradise (*dar-i bihisht*)

FIGURE 18. An eschatological map of the Temple Mount in Jerusalem. Mecca, *ca.* 967/1559 (1 – The prayer niches [*miḥrābs*] of the prophets; 2 – The pulpit [*minbar*] of Muḥammad; 3 – The fountain of al-Kawthar; 4 – The Balance of Deeds [*mīzān-i aʿmāl*]; 5 – The Dome of the Rock; 6 – The Path of Ṣirāṭ [*sabīl-i ṣirāṭ*]; 7 – The Gate of Paradise [*dar-i bihisht*]). Adapted from Sayyid ʿAlī al-Ḥusaynī, *Shawqnāma*. Haifa, The National Maritime Museum, Inv. no. 4576, fol. 49r.

Medina oasis, is located atop one of the pools of paradise.[20] The sacred precinct, or *ḥaram*, of Medina, is particularly pregnant territory; it may have been associated with the otherworld from the earliest days of the nascent Muslim community.[21] In the *ḥaram*'s mosque, the ground between the prophet Muḥammad's house (*bayt*), where he lies buried, and the pulpit (*minbar*) from which he used to preach, is, in the Prophet's own words, "one of the gardens of the gardens of paradise" (*rawḍa min riyāḍ al-janna*).[22] In the same way in which the Rock in Jerusalem was believed to throne above the subterranean waters of paradise, the Prophet's pulpit in the mosque of Medina was declared to sit on top of a water course (*turʿa*), or indeed the Pool (*ḥawḍ*), of paradise.[23] The presence of the otherworld in the Medinan mosque presumably explains how Muḥammad was able to see a reflection of paradise and hell in the *qibla* wall.[24] The hadith that reports this vision tallies with the decoration of the mosque's walls with mosaics during the reign of the Umayyad caliph al-Walīd I (r. 86–96/705–15). According to a chronicle dating to the late second/eighth century, a craftsman employed in the production of these mosaics related that "we made them according to the images of the trees and palaces of paradise."[25]

In Syria, by contrast, Jerusalem was not the only city in the race for Eden. Damascus, the chosen capital of the Umayyad caliphs, also boasted a special connection with the eternal garden.[26] The mosaic panels gracing the inner walls of the Umayyad mosque (also built under al-Walīd I), which resemble the mosaics in the southeastern annex floor in the Church of the Holy

[20] Suyūṭī, *Budūr*, 540. Cf. Yāqūt, *Buldān*, s.v. Buṭḥān, I, 446b-447a; Nābulusī, *Ahl al-janna*, 48.

[21] Busse, "Die Kanzel des Propheten," 107–8. I take the following examples from Busse's article. On Medina's sanctity, see also von Grunebaum, "The sacred character of Islamic cities," 31.

[22] Ibn Saʿd, *Ṭabaqāt*, I, 250, 252, 254; Bukhārī, *Ṣaḥīḥ*, *K. faḍl al-ṣalāt fī masjid Makka wa-l-Madīna* 5 (*b. faḍl mā bayna l-qabr wa-l-minbar*), I, 320; Ibn Ḥanbal, *Musnad*, II, 401–2, 412, 534, IV, 41 and passim. See also Ibn Jubayr, *Riḥla*, 192 (tr. 200); Nābulusī, *Ahl al-janna*, 45. The hadith also occurs in the *Guidelines to blessings* (*Dalāʾil al-khayrāt*) of the Moroccan mystic al-Jazūlī (d. 870/1465), a litany of blessings over the Prophet that is "one of the most successful books in Sunni Islam, after the Qurʾān itself." See Witkam, "The battle of images," 67. G. H. A. Juynboll (*ECḤ*, 313) suggests that the tradition originates with the famous Medinan scholar Mālik b. Anas (d. 179/795).

[23] Ibn Saʿd, *Ṭabaqāt*, I, 250, 252.

[24] See Bukhārī, *Ṣaḥīḥ*, *k. al-mawāqīt* 11 (*b. waqt al-ẓuhr ʿinda l-zawāl*), I, 174 and passim; Muslim, *Ṣaḥīḥ*, *k. al-kusūf* 3 (*b. mā ʿaraḍa ʿalā l-nabī [eulogy] fī ṣalāt al-kusūf*), II, 722; Ibn Ḥanbal, *Musnad*, II, 159, 688: *ʿuriḍat ʿalayya l-jannatu wa-l-nāru ānifan fī ʿurḍi hādhā l-ḥāʾiṭ*. Cf. *CTM*, I, 376b.

[25] See Sauvaget, *Mosquée omeyyade*, 81. The quote is preserved in Ibn al-Najjār (*fl.* 593/1196), *K. al-Durra l-thāmina fī akhbār al-Madīna*, MS BNF Ar. 1630, fol. 31v. Ibn Najjār takes it from the (lost) *History of Medina* of Muḥammad b. al-Ḥasan Ibn Zabāla, written in 199/814. Ibn Zabāla is also quoted in al-Samhūdī's (d. 911/1506) *Wafāʾ al-wafāʾ*, I, 367. See Leisten, *Architektur*, 79n10.

[26] On the sanctity of Damascus, see Kister, "Sanctity," 21–6; Khalek, *Damascus*, 135–55.

Cross (built in 559 CE) of the northern Syrian city of Ruṣāfā/Sergiopolis, bring paradise, as it were, right into the cultic centre of the Umayyad seat of government.[27] The entire oasis, or Ghūṭa, of Damascus was declared to be an otherworldly garden. Umayyad poets such as Ibn Qays al-Ruqayyāt (*fl.* 70/690) and Jarīr (d. *ca.* 110/728) celebratingly referred to the Ghūṭa, the fertile valley of Damascus, as a eutopian, paradisiacal space.[28]

These ideas reverberated in later centuries, long after the capital of the Islamic empire had moved to other regions. The geographer Yāqūt (d. 626/1229) considered the Ghūṭa the "most exalted" of the "four [paradise] gardens on earth (*jinān al-arḍ al-arbaʿ*)."[29] In a eulogy composed after his visit to the city, his contemporary, the Spanish traveller Ibn Jubayr (d. 614/1217) wrote that Damascus is "the paradise of the east" (*jannat al-mashriq*),

> garnished with the flowers of sweet-scented herbs, and bedecked by gardens [as if] in brocaded vestments. In the realm of beauty she [Damascus] holds a sure position, and on her nuptial chair she is most richly adorned ..., [she lies at] a hill having meadows and springs [Q 23:50] with deep shade and water of Salsabīl, whose rivulets twist like serpents through every way, and the perfumed zephyrs of flower gardens breathe life to the soul. ... To those who contemplate her she displays herself in a pure white dress calling to them: "Come to the halting place of beauty, and take the midday repose" [Q 18:33]. ... By God, they spoke truth who said: "If paradise is on the earth then Damascus is without a doubt in it. If it [paradise] is in the sky, then it [Damascus] vies with it and shares its glory."[30]

Ibn Jubayr's depiction is a charming piece of Arabic rhetoric, ripe with quotations from, and allusions to, the Qurʾān's paradise passages. Damascus is likened to a bride embracing the visitor, a houri in the eternal garden awaiting the believer with outstretched arms. The smell of flowers and herbs, vegetation as lush and dark as brocaded cloth, the well of Salsabīl and rivulets of water crisscrossing the landscape: all these are images traditionally associated with the Muslim paradise.[31] There is a great deal of hyperbole

[27] Cf. Ulbert, *Die Basilika des heiligen Kreuzes*. Cf. Brisch, "Observations." One should note, however, that the interpretation of the mosaics remains a matter of scholarly debate. See Ettinghausen et al., *Islamic art*, 26.

[28] Yāqūt, *Buldān*, s.v. Yabrīn, V, 427, quoting Jarīr: "How far is Yabrīn [a sandy region in eastern Arabia] from the Gate of Paradise (*min bāb al-farādīs*)!"; ibid., s.v. al-Ghūṭa, IV, 219b, quoting Ibn Qays: "They may not inhabit the paradise gardens (*aqfarat minhum al-farādīs*), but the *ghūṭa* has beautiful villages and offers shade." Cf. Horovitz, "Das koranische Paradies," 61–2.

[29] Yāqūt, *Buldān*, s.v. al-Ghūṭa, IV, 219a. The other three paradise gardens on earth, according to Yāqūt, are al-Ṣughd (i.e., Samarqand and its surroundings), al-Ubulla (in the Euphrates-Tigris delta), and Shiʿb Bawwān (fifty miles northwest of Shīrāz). Cf. ibid., s.v. Bawwān, I, 503b-505b; al-Ṣughd, III, 409a-410b; al-Ubulla, I, 76b-78a.

[30] Ibn Jubayr, *Riḥla*, 240, ed. Wright and de Goeje, 260–1. I follow, with slight modifications, the translation by Broadhurst, *The travels of Ibn Jubayr*, 271–2.

[31] On the political subtext of Ibn Jubayr's eschatological framing of Damascus, see Dejugnat, "Voyage au centre du monde," 196–205.

and poetic convention in Ibn Jubayr's sentences,[32] but it is not clear that he writes in a purely metaphorical vein. In fact, the end of the passage suggests the possibility that Damascus is truly and fully a paradise on earth – even if some, as Ibn Jubayr does not fail to note, locate paradise "in the sky."

The likely context out of which traditions about the special cosmological and eschatological importance of Jerusalem, Damascus, and Medina (as well as Mecca, for which see the following text) arose is the struggle in the first century of Islam over the question whether political and spiritual authority attached primarily to Syria, the Umayyads' base of power, or the homeland of the Prophet, the Hijaz.[33] However, the list of paradise cities continued to expand, as different political formations and local communities in the Islamic world developed their own visions of paradise on earth.[34]

Note that in addition to Damascus, the "paradise of the east," Ibn Jubayr implies the existence of a "paradise of the west" – one presumes this to be Cordoba, the capital of his patrons, the Almohad dynasty. The Almohads (r. 524–668/1130–1269), rulers over Cordoba from 543/1148 onwards, attempted to link their claims to authority back to the Spanish Umayyads (r. 138–422/756–1031), as whose heirs they styled themselves. However, Cordoba, which together with the adjacent palace city of Madīnat al-Zahrā', had been the Spanish Umayyads' splendid capital,[35] was past its prime as early as the late fifth/eleventh century. Other places, such as Seville and Granada, had taken its place as the foremost cities of al-Andalus, receiving lavish praise as terrestrial paradises by poets.[36] Also Valencia, the city

[32] It was commonplace of ʿAbbāsid geographers to liken cities to a heavenly bride. See Miquel, *La géographie humaine*, IV, 179. Spanish poets regularly compared al-Andalus and its urban centres to paradise. For a number of examples, rather similar to Ibn Jubayr's poem, see Pérès, *La poésie andalouse*, 115–57. Al-Thaʿālibī (d. 429/1038), in his anthology of two-word phrases and clichés, the *Thimār al-qulūb*, lists twelve such phrases involving the garden of paradise, providing examples for each. See Thaʿālibī, *Thimār al-qulūb*, 694–7.

[33] Kister, "'You shall only set out for three mosques"; Elad, *Medieval Jerusalem*, 6–22; Cobb, "Virtual sacrality," 37, 50–1; Khalek, *Damascus*, 162–5; Shoemaker, *Death of a prophet*, 231–40. See also the notion that the souls of believers gather in al-Jābiya, the former residence of the Ghassānids in Jawlān, some eighty kilometres south of Damascus. See Suyūṭī, *Sharḥ al-ṣudūr*, 312. Cf. Eklund, *Life after death*, 41, 97, 107–8; *TG*, IV, 522; *EI2*, s.v. al-Djābiya (H. Lammens and J. Sourdel-Thomine), II, 360. Known for its healthy climate and as a place of refuge during plagues, al-Jābiya played a significant role during the conquest of Syria and during the Marwānid restoration after the second civil war, hosting several meetings.

[34] See Antrim, *Routes & realms*, for a study of the "discourse of place," as she terms it, that emerges in a variety of Muslim geographical and historiographical sources, primarily of the third/ninth to sixth/twelfth centuries. Paradise and hell, however, are referred to only peripherally by Antrim.

[35] On the paradise symbolism of Madīnat al-Zahrā', see the following text. On Ibn Jubayr's relation to the Almohads, see Dejugnat, "La méditerranée come frontière," 150, 160–1, 166; idem, "Voyage au centre du monde," 196–200.

[36] See Pérès, *La poésie andalouse*, 134–9 (Seville), 146–7 (Granada).

of birth of Ibn Jubayr, was likened to paradise. In the fifth/eleventh century, the poet Abū Jaʿfar Ibn Masʿada al-Gharnāṭī called Valencia the paradise garden (*firdaws*) on earth; a little later, around the turn of the century, Ibn al-Zaqqāq wrote that that it was "the most splendid of all cities ... clothed by the Lord into the brocade of beauty."[37]

In Egypt, local legend elevated Cairo to the rank of a paradise garden.[38] The fact that the Nile was held to be one of the four rivers of paradise was duly exploited in the literature praising the "merits" (*faḍāʾil*) of Cairo.[39] The geographer al-Muqaddasī (d. *ca.* 380/990), for example, reports that the honey of paradise flows in the Nile.[40] Further east, from the context of the jihad fought during the early years of Muslim expansion into Iran and Central Asia emerged a tradition according to which the Prophet had instructed his followers to "make a raid on Qazwin, for it is one of the highest gates of paradise!"[41] One of the eight gates of paradise, according to a hadith, is called the Gate of Jihad (*bab al-jihad*). It may have been a short step, then, to identify this gate with Qazwin, serving as it did as a base camp for Iraqi raids into the coastal plains of the Caspian Sea in the time of the Muslim conquests.[42] Other frontier settlements that played an important role in the era of early Muslim expansion were likewise declared to be "gates to paradise."[43] The historian al-Maqqarī (d. 1042/1632) relates a famous address, supposedly delivered by the general Ṭāriq b. Khālid (d. 92/711), in which he promises his Muslim soldiers "beautiful houris ... well-guarded in royal palaces" (*al-ḥūr al-ḥisān ... al-maqṣūrāt fī quṣūr al-mulūk*) should

37 Ibid., 117–8, 154.

38 Maqrīzī, *Khiṭaṭ*, I, 48, 50.

39 Ibid., I, 95.

40 See Muqaddasī, *K. Aḥsan al-taqāsīm*, 193. For references to further comparisons of Cairo (and of Egypt as a whole) with paradise, see Antrim, *Routes & realms*, 133n82.

41 The local historian al-Rāfiʿī (d. 623/1226), at the beginning of the first part (*al-qism al-awwal*) of his *al-Tadwīn fī akhbār Qazwīn*, makes an explicit connection with jihad. See also Muttaqī, *Kanz*, XII, 477; Nābulusī, *Ahl al-janna*, 48–9. According to Yāqūt, the Prophet would have said: "Qazwin is to the world what Eden is to paradise." See Yāqūt, *Buldān*, s.v. Qazwīn, IV, 343b. Cf. Kister, "Sanctity," 43, with further traditions linking Qazwin with paradise. The fact that Qazwin was known in medieval Islam for its rich orchards and vineyards may also have contributed to its Edenification. See Mustawfī, *Nuzhat al-qulūb*, 58, 222. Cf. *EI2*, s.v. Ḳazwīn, i. Geography and history, IV, 857a-862b (A. K. S. Lambton). Also into the context of jihad belongs the hadith that "paradise lies under the tips of spears" (*al-janna taḥta aṭrāf al-ʿawālī*). See, e.g., *Nahj al-balāgha*, II, 3.

42 Yāqūt notes that Qazwin, in the time of the Kufan governor Saʿīd b. al-ʿĀṣ b. Umayya (r. 29–34/649–55), was the base camp for Kufan raids into Daylam. See Yāqūt, *Buldān*, s.v. Qazwīn, IV, 343a. On the apocalyptical importance attached to Qazwin, see Cook, *Muslim apocalyptic*, 260–1.

43 Consider, e.g., the case of Hims in Syria. See Rabaʿī, *Faḍāʾil al-Shām*, 28 (from Kaʿb). Hims is also mentioned as one of the paradise cities on earth in a tradition attributed to Kaʿb al-Aḥbār. See Fasawī, *Maʿrifa*, II, 304, quoted in Kister, "Sanctity," 24. See ibid., 44, for traditions declaring ʿAbbādān to be among the gates to paradise.

they overcome their enemies and conquer al-Andalus; if they meet death on the battlefield, such seems to be the implication, they will be recompensed by the same token in heaven.[44]

For the Shiʿites, the plain of Kerbela, the place where the Imam al-Ḥusayn had suffered martyrdom, was "the purest and holiest plot of land on earth" and a "part of the richly watered plains of paradise" (*min baṭḥāʾ al-janna*).[45] "God created Kerbela," one reads in another tradition, "24,000 years before He created the Kaaba," and as such "it is the best piece of land in paradise."[46] Al-Ḥusayn's grave is "a garden of paradise," and a ladder ascends from it to heaven. Throngs of angels scuttle up and down this ladder to visit the site.[47] The tomb of ʿAlī b. Abī Ṭālib in Najaf was likewise considered to be a part of paradise,[48] as was Tus, the burial ground of the Imam ʿAlī al-Riḍā.[49] ʿAlī b. Abī Ṭālib was said to have visited the vicinity of his future grave, to have stretched out flat on the earth, and to have pronounced that the souls of all the believers haunted the place, sitting together in circles and talking to each other.[50] Shiʿite traditions also bestowed a special eschatological status to the mosque of Kufa, a fulcrum of early Shiʿi propaganda. "Four are the palaces of paradise in this world," ʿAlī was reported to have said, "the mosque of Mecca, the mosque of Medina, the mosque of Jerusalem and the mosque of Kufa."[51] The central courtyard of the mosque (*waṣatuhu*) was considered to lie "atop a garden of paradise," and three paradisiacal springs were said to be found in it.[52] It is noteworthy that the early Islamic traditions about terrestrial paradises, whether in the Hijaz, Syria, Iraq, or elsewhere, do not declare these spaces or cities to be "like" paradise; nor does one encounter the idea that these places "foreshadow" the paradise to come. Rather, they *are* paradise, or rather, "one of its gardens." Paradise in these traditions is pictured as being simultaneously present in the otherworld *and* this world.

So much for the earthly paradise; but where on earth is hell? Al-Qurṭubī, the seventh/thirteenth-century Andalusian collector of eschatological hadith,

44 Maqqarī, *Nafḥ al-ṭīb*, ed. ʿAbbās, I, 241. I owe this reference to Vahid Behmardi. Cf. Jones, *The power of oratory*, 33.

45 Majlisī, *Biḥār*, XLV, 126 (a revelation of Gabriel to the Prophet). On the superiority of Kerbela over the Kaaba, see Majlisī, *Biḥār*, LIII, 11; Baḥrānī, *Maʿālim*, III, 239.

46 Ibid.

47 Ibid., II, 12.

48 Ibid., II, 9.

49 Ibid., II, 13.

50 Majlisī, *Biḥār*, VI, 424–5, 442. The place is described as an elevation (*ẓahr*) that one reaches after passing al-Ghariyyān in the outskirts of Kufa. Cf. Yāqūt, s.v. al-Ghariyyān, IV, 196b. Yāqūt notes that al-Ghariyyān is the name given to two hermitages (*ṣawmaʿatān*) in the vicinity of ʿAlī's tomb. For a similar tradition about ʿAlī, identifying this place as the Valley of Peace (*wādī l-salām*), see Baḥrānī, *Maʿālim*, II, 72.

51 Ṭūsī, *Amālī*, I, 379, quoted in Kister, "An early tradition," 190n84. Cf. Baḥrānī, *Maʿālim*, II, 72, III, 239.

52 Yāqūt, *Buldān*, s.v. Kūfa, IV, 492b. Cf. Kister, "Sanctity," 33.

devotes a section of his *Memoir* to the fact that, as he phrases it, "hell is in the earth (*fī l-arḍ*)."[53] In this section he relates, for example, a Prophetic hadith that warns against travelling over the sea, or using seawater for ritual ablutions, because it is a layer of hell – one presumes the top layer.[54] As for where the entry gate to hell is to be found, one of the more popular ideas seems to have been that the passageway into the netherworld was in the Wādī Jahannam in Jerusalem, the biblical valley of Hinnom, which runs between the eastern wall of the Temple Mount and the Mount of Olives.[55] In the early centuries, hell seems to have been inextricably linked to paradise, so that both appear on earth in tandem, as in the cases of Jerusalem and Medina considered in the preceding text.

Other traditions, by contrast, show a tendency to push the earthly hell to the margins of the Islamic world, or into non Muslim territories. Medieval Muslim geographers and travellers subtly deployed eschatological imagery in their descriptions of the world, in order to map out a cosmos divided into heavenly and hellish realms. Ibn Jubayr's travelogue, for example, has been read as "transfiguring the borderlands [of Islam] into the marches of hell, contiguous with the tenebrous regions of the universe and forming the reverse image of the luminous lands of Islam, illuminated by the presence of God."[56] One sees an early example of this strategy to divide the world into realms of light and darkness in the tradition attributed to the Prophet that states that Medina, Mecca, Damascus, and Jerusalem are "four of the cities of paradise on earth" (*mudun al-janna fī l-dunyā*), while Constantinople, Rome, Antioch, and Sanaa are "four of the cities of hell on earth."[57] The ʿAbbāsid emissary from Baghdad, Ibn Faḍlān (*fl.* early fourth/tenth c.), having travelled up the Volga River into Slavic territory, remarked that he had arrived at a place so cold that he thought he had approached the gate of *zamharīr*.[58]

[53] Qurṭubī, *Tadhkira*, II, 101.

[54] Ibn Abī Shayba, *Muṣannaf*, I, 122; Abū Dāwūd, *Sunan*, III, 6; Qurṭubī, *Tadhkira*, II, 101–2; Nābulusī, *Ahl al-janna*, 74. Cf. Melchert, "Locating hell," n15. According to a similar tradition, the Prophet interdicted bathing in hot mountain springs, "for they flow from hell." See Majlisī, *Biḥār*, VIII, 486.

[55] Monfarrer Sala, "A propósito," 152. Cf. 2 Kings 23:10; Jer. 19:6; Is. 30:32. According to al-Wāsiṭī, the nephew of Kaʿb al-Aḥbār, a man called Nawf al-Bikālī, told the caliph ʿAbd al-Malik that in a verse of the Bible, God said to Jerusalem: "There are within you six things: my residence, my judgment place, my gathering place, my paradise, my hell and my balance." See Wāsiṭī, *Faḍāʾil*, 23.

[56] Dejugnat, "La méditerranée comme frontière," 160.

[57] Suyūṭī, *Laʾālī*, II, 86. Cf. Kister, "Sanctity," 24, including a number of alternative lists. Al-Ḥakīm al-Tirmidhī and Ibn Manda related a tradition on the authority of Kaʿb al-Aḥbār according to which the souls of the unbelievers gather in Sanaa after death. See Suyūṭī, *Sharḥ al-ṣudūr*, 313. See also the many references in Livne-Kafri, "Jerusalem," 58 n58.

[58] See Ibn Faḍlān, *Riḥla*, 114. On *zamharīr*, see the preceding text, pp. 10, 141n170. Cf. Tottoli, "The case of *zamharīr*," 145.

Particularly inhospitable places invited their identification with the netherworld. An old idea was that the foul-smelling sulphurous well of Barhūt in the Wādī Barhūt in Hadramawt in Yemen was the gate to hell.[59] In a Shiʿi tradition, the Imam Muḥammad al-Bāqir meets an Arab bedouin (*aʿrābī*) at the Prophet's Mosque in Medina. The bedouin reports that he has arrived in Medina "from the furthest regions of the earth," and he describes how on the way he has traversed a vermin-infested dark valley inhabited by a miserable people meagrely subsisting on goat milk as their only nourishment. Muḥammad al-Bāqir explains that the bedouin has been to the valley of Barhūt, where the souls of the unbelievers reside, including that of the accursed Cain and his kinfolk.[60] Here again, one sees how the otherworld, hell in this case, enters this world through a conduit (the well of Barhūt) but then branches out to occupy a greater area (the valley of Barhūt).[61] It may also be that in stories such as this, an urban fear of the desert is at play. Deserts, in fact, offered an obvious analogy to hell. The Moroccan traveller Ibn Baṭṭūṭa (d. 770/1368–9 or 779/1377), on his way from Damascus to Mecca to perform the pilgrimage, passed through al-Ukhayḍir valley, some sixty kilometres north of Mecca. In it, he relates in his travelogue, a great deal of pilgrims perish because of the hot and venomous wind called *samūm*, "as if it is the Valley of Hell, may God protect us from it."[62]

Further east, a Persian work of the mirabilia genre from the sixth/twelfth century locates the entry to hell in a gorge, appropriately called Wādī Jahannam, in the neighbourhood of Balkh in Afghanistan. The author writes about this sinister venue saying it "sinks steeply into the ground, and the fearless and ruthless joke that it goes down so deeply that if one throws a stone into the cavity one cannot see it reaching the bottom."[63] He also notes that "in this cavity, strange birds have countless nests," an observation that accords with the notion that the souls of infidels and sinners haunt the gate to hell in the bellies of black birds.[64] In this account, one also hears echoes

59 Al-Fākihī states that the souls of the unbelievers gather in the well of Barhūt. The well is covered with locustlike vermin and filled with a puslike liquid that gushes forth in the morning but dries up in the evening. See Fākihī, *Akhbār Makka*, II, 41, 43 (#1106, 1110). Baḥrānī, *Maʿālim*, II, 75, relates from ʿAlī that Barhūt is the "worst well in hell." See also *Qurrat al-ʿuyūn*, 104, where the notion is related from "one of the pious forefathers"; Suyūṭī, *Sharḥ al-ṣudūr*, 312–3, 317–8, 330, with several anecdotes, including one about a Muslim convert who visits Barhūt to talk to the soul of his unbelieving father. A philosophical explanation is found in Ṣaarā, *Mabdaʾ*, 473–84 (with references to other earthly locations of hell and paradise); idem, *Ḥikma*, tr. Morris, 218. Cf. *EI2*, s.v. Barhūt, I, 1045a (G. Rentz); *TG*, IV, 522.

60 Baḥrānī, *Maʿālim*, II, 76–7, 87. Cf. ibid., II, 86–7, a story about a man who walks through the valley of Barhūt and finds that Cain is dangling from a chain around his neck above him in the air, beseeching him for water.

61 According to a tradition in Majlisī, *Biḥār*, VIII, 464, Barhūt is "one of the valleys of hell."

62 Ibn Baṭṭūṭa, *Riḥla*, 112. Cf. Waines, *The odyssey of Ibn Battuta*, 34.

63 Ṭūsī, *ʿAjāyib*, 293–4.

64 Suyūṭī, *Sharḥ al-ṣudūr*, 310; Baḥrānī, *Maʿālim*, II, 74. Cf. *TG*, IV, 523.

of eschatological hadiths that describe the extreme depth of the hell funnel, where a stone thrown from the bridge of Ṣirāṭ falls for seventy years before hitting bottom.[65] At times, hell is pushed even farther away, to the farthest reaches of the world. A tradition attributed to Wahb b. Munabbih, which reprises a common Near Eastern theme, locates the entry to the netherworld behind the legendary mountain range of Qāf. Qāf surrounds the terrestrial world; its snow-capped peaks serve to cool hellfire down so that life on earth becomes bearable.[66] As we saw in Chapter 3 of this book, some versions of the Prophet's *miʿrāj* locate hell in heaven; but this seems due, first and foremost, to the narrative convenience of placing the Prophet's visit to hell *after* his journey through the heavens, rather than at its beginning or in its middle. In fact, several important Late Medieval *miʿrāj* narratives revert to the old idea of a subterranean location of hell: in these versions, the Prophet, after his audience with God, looks down from heaven and sees the earth split open, revealing the bowels of hell.[67]

Architectural Visions of Paradise

The eutopian and dystopian traditions surveyed up until here all express the feeling that paradise and hell are part of this world. This notion is perhaps most conspicuous in the Islamic literature on *barzakh*, the intermediary state between death and resurrection in the grave. As was noted in Chapter 4, the graves of pious Muslims were regarded as dwellings in paradise; hence, one gathers, the practice of referring to graves and mausolea as "gardens" (*riyāḍ*, sg. *rawḍa*). This appellation is attested especially from the sixth/twelfth century onwards, and at first seems to have been used primarily to designate the graves of Muḥammad and the members of his family, in whose vicinity people, in consequence, wanted to be buried.[68] The tombs of the Shiʿi Imams are an obvious example. The desert plain west of the Shrine tombs of Kerbela, before being swallowed by the growing city, was covered with graves, and the dead would be carried long distances to find their final resting place near the Imams.[69] The *translatio mortuorum* (*naql al-mawtā*)

[65] Tirmidhī, *Jāmiʿ*, *k. ṣifat jahannam* 2 (*b. mā jā'a fī ṣifat qaʿr jahannam*), IV, 680.

[66] Thaʿlabī, *ʿArā'is*, 8; Qurṭubī, *Tadhkira*, II, 102; Suyūṭī, *Budūr*, 412. On Qāf, see *EI2*, s.v. Ḳāf, IV, 400a–402b (M. Streck and A. Miquel). According to a teaching of the Babylonian Talmud, hell (*gehinnom*) "is above the firmament; some, however, say that [it] is behind the Mountains of Darkness [in Africa]." See *BT*, *Tamid* 32b (tr. XXXII, 29). One should also note the belief that the gate to heaven is just above Simurgh's nest on top of Qāf. See, e.g., the Persian *Daqā'iq al-ḥaqā'iq* (Anatolia, written 675/1276), fols. 107r–107v.

[67] *Majlis dar Qiṣṣa-yi Rasūl*, 307; Bakrī, *Ḥadīth al-miʿrāj*, fol. 81v.

[68] Leisten, *Architektur für Tote*, 80–81; Diem and Schöller, *The living and the dead*, II, 48–50. By the eighth/fourteenth century in Iran, the term was applied to almost any tomb building or mausoleum, "with no particular sense of garden." See Bloom, "Paradise as a garden," 40.

[69] See Nöldeke, *Heiligtum*, 8.

FIGURE 19. The entry to heaven on top of mount Qāf. From an anonymous *K. Daqā'iq al-ḥaqā'iq* (*Book of Subtleties and Realities*). Turkey, 675/[1276]. MS Bibliothèque nationale de France Persan 174, fol. 107r.

was a common Shiʿi practice. Caravans to the holy shrines (*ʿatabāt*) in Iraq, especially from Iran, would at times carry hundreds of corpses.[70] Corpses were also transported to the al-Baqīʿ cemetery in Medina (also called *Jannat al-Baqīʿ*, "the [paradise] garden of al-Baqīʿ"), which adjoined the grave of the Prophet.[71] Sunni jurists, when discussing the licitness of relocating (previously unburied) corpses, usually agreed that the practice was better avoided, but that a transport over one or two leagues was tolerable, especially when destined towards the holy cities of Mecca and Medina.[72]

Rather than letting one's corpse be carried to paradisiacal ground, one could seek to bring paradise to one's own grave, by building tomb shrines that suggested to visitors that those who lay buried there already enjoyed the joys of the otherworld. This tactic, of course, was available only to the extravagantly rich. It was seen with scepticism by scholars of religion, who resented funerary structures because of their assumed incompatibility with Islamic egalitarian principles.[73] Although the tombs of rulers were conceptually linked to paradise from the early centuries of Islam onwards,[74] an important precedent, architecturally speaking, was set by the mausoleum of the Seljuq sultan Sanjar (r. 511–52/1118–57) at Merv (Turkmenistan), a building that was known as *dār al-ākhira*, "the palace of the otherworld."[75] In later times, splendid mausolea modelled on Sanjar's tomb were built by the Timurid rulers of Transoxania and Persia (r. 771–913/1370–1507) and the Mughal emperors of India (r. 932–1274/1526–1858).

Without doubt the most famous of all these mausolea is the Taj Mahal (Arab. "the crown of the realm"). This imposing structure is set in a garden comprising fountains, water channels, trees, gates, and mosques that are spread out over forty-two acres on the bank of the Jumna, the river that

70 Donaldson, *Shiʿite religion*, 97.

71 Cf. the examples given in Leisten, *Architektur*, 24n201, including Sunni dignitaries.

72 Ibn Nujaym, *al-Baḥr al-rāʾiq*, V, 59. For the Shāfiʿites, who take a somewhat more restrictive view, see Nawawī, *Rawḍat al-ṭālibīn*, II, 205. The Shāfiʿī jurist from Baghdad, al-Māwardī (d. 450/1058), in his treatise on public law, allocates the power to interdict the "translation of the dead" (*naql al-mawtā*) to the market inspector and censor of public morals (*muḥtasib*), whose duties included the supervision of the cemeteries. See Māwardī, *Aḥkām*, 338. On the *muḥtasib*'s relationship with cemeteries, see Klein, "Between public and private." The controversy continues to this day. In 2010, the Fatwa Council (*lajnat al-iftāʾ*) of Saudi-Arabia declared that to carry corpses from abroad to Mecca or Medina was prohibited. See *Arab News*, 28 May 2010 ("Sending bodies to holy cities for burial banned"), quoted in Ende, "Stein," 183–4.

73 See Leisten, "Between orthodoxy and exegesis."

74 Leisten notes, e.g., that the tombs of the Umayyads of Cordoba were referred to as *al-riyāḍ al-mabniyya*, "[well-]built gardens." See Leisten, *Architektur*, 80n11. The name recalls Q 39:20, which promises the believers "[well-]built chambers" (*ghuraf mabniyya*). The term *rawḍa* (pl. *riyāḍ* or *rawḍāt*) in the sense of an eschatological garden occurs twice in the Qurʾan (30:15, 42:22).

75 On Sanjar's mausoleum, "a dry run for the Tāj Mahal," see Hillenbrand, "Seljuq monuments," 295–303.

flows through the Mughal capital city of Agra, some two hundred kilometres to the southeast of Delhi. Mumtaz Mahal, "the choice of the realm," the favourite wife of the Mughal emperor Shāh Jahān (r. 1037–68/1628–58), lies buried here. After twenty-five years of marriage, Mumtaz died in 1040/1631 after giving birth to her fourteenth child, whereupon the emperor issued orders for the construction of the Taj Mahal. What his architects and builders created is, by all appearances, a monumental allegory of the last judgement and of paradise.[76] What exactly propelled Shāh Jahān to commission the Taj Mahal is a matter of scholarly debate. The idea that he was driven by the grief over his wife's passing, a notion dear to the European romantic imagination, should be nuanced, to say the least; to the same, probably even to a more important degree, the Taj Mahal was a political *coup de propagande*, loudly proclaiming to the world its builder's exalted status and his connectedness to otherworldly realms.[77]

At the foot of the wide platform on which the Taj Mahal rests lies a *chahārbāgh* (Pers. "fourfold garden"), divided into quarters by broad water channels that converge in a raised marble tank. Although the *chahārbāgh* can be traced back to pre-Islamic Iranian prototypes that carry no observable eschatological meaning,[78] it is not implausible to think that this particular type of garden became layered, in specific instances, with paradisiacal overtones. Whether by coincidence or because it is inspired by prototypes of fourfold gardens, the Qur'an speaks of four gardens (55:46–58), as well as of the four rivers of paradise (47:15). This Qur'anic theme was picked up and woven into later Muslim literature on terrestrial gardens. It became a standard trope of Persian poetry to liken gardens in general, and Mughal garden tombs in particular, to paradise.[79] An inscription over the entry gate to the tomb garden of the Mughal emperor Akbar (r. 964–1014/1556–1605), the grandfather of Shāh Jahān, makes the connection clear: "These are the gardens of Eden," the inscription proclaims, "enter them to live for ever!"[80] It is plausible, therefore, to see in the four water channels running in front of the Taj Mahal an allusion to the four rivers of the Islamic paradise, and to think that the marble tank upon which these channels converge is a replica of the celestial pool of al-Kawthar.

It can be argued, however, that more was intended by the construction of the Taj Mahal than to create a mere "replica" or "allegory" of paradise, that

[76] *EI2*, s.v. Tādj Maḥall, X, 58b-60a (E. Koch).

[77] Cf. Begley, "The myth of the Taj Mahal."

[78] See *EIr*, s.v. Čahārbāḡ (D. Stronach); Pinder-Wilson, "The Persian garden."

[79] See Schimmel, "The celestial garden"; Hanaway, "Paradise on earth." See also the Persian poems dedicated to palaces and their paradisiacal gardens. See Meisami, "Palaces and paradises," 24 (Farrukhī), 27 ('Unṣurī), 31–2 (Azraqī), 34 (Mukhtarī), 36, 38 (Anwarī), 38 (Khāqānī), 40–1 (Ibn-i Yamīn). For Arabic poems dedicated to the caliphal palace at Samarra, see eadem, "The palace-complex as emblem."

[80] See Smith, *Akbar's tomb*, 35.

the aim was to make paradise present in a fuller sense, to suggest that the Taj Mahal does not refer to paradise, but rather, that it has a share in it. The Qur'anic inscriptions that scroll over the arches and walls of the Taj Mahal and the buildings surrounding it make it explicit that the Taj Mahal *is* the gate to heaven. For example, written over the south facade of the gateway is sura 89, a text replete with eschatological imagery that culminates in the words: "O soul in repose ... enter My Garden" (89:27–30). One scholar of the Taj Mahal, basing himself on a comparison with tenth/sixteenth- and eleventh/seventeenth-century Persian and Mughal paintings, has argued that the monumental tomb building, with its four characteristic minarets, is a marble version of the Mughal imperial throne. In its otherworldly loftiness and grandeur, the building suggests an analogy with, rather than an allegory of, the celestial throne of God.[81] Tradition places this throne directly above the heavenly gardens, in the same way in which the Taj Mahal is situated not in the middle of the *chahārbāgh* (as is common in other Mughal tomb complexes), but next to it at its top. The same divine authority sanctions and sanctifies both thrones.

Imperial paradise architecture in Islam is found not only in the form of tomb shrines. Muslim rulers also had palaces, sometimes entire cities built as harbingers of the world to come. However, lest we overreach interpretively, a word of caution is in order here. It has become a standard scholarly tactic to question the facile assumption that Islamic art and architecture, and garden architecture in particular, intend to create paradise on earth. "Without a specific indication that a particular garden or motif was meant to represent paradise, it seems best to tread cautiously," opines a leading historian of Islamic art.[82] For example, the assertion that the Alhambra in Granada, together with its splendid gardens, was built to mirror the heavenly paradise rests on close to no archaeological or textual evidence. In fact, medieval Muslim writers very seldom offer symbolic interpretations of architecture, even in the case of buildings that appear ripe with eschatological connotations. Overall, Western interpreters of Islamic buildings and gardens seem to have been keener to speculate about such connotations than Muslim authors. Behind this Western penchant towards symbolic interpretation, as has been suggested, lies a reductionist agenda to decontextualise works of Islamic art and posit instead a single dominant rationale for it, namely, a certain irrational otherworldliness. Muslims, in this view, would be unable to appreciate art purely for art's sake.[83]

[81] Begley, "Myth of the Taj Mahal," 16. On the analogy between the celestial throne of God and earthly thrones, see Lange, "Sitting by the ruler's throne."

[82] Bloom, "Paradise as a garden," 47. Cf. Lohlker and Nowak, "Das islamische Paradies," 212–6.

[83] One of the most eloquent attacks on such reductionist interpretations of Islamic art has come from Terri Allen. See Allen, "Imagining paradise in Islamic art." See also Leaman, *Islamic aesthetics*, 121–3.

If one wishes to write about the eschatological meaning of Islamic architecture one is well-advised to take such criticisms seriously. One should also remain open to the possibility that architectural associations with paradise were playful rather than meant literally. The Persian couplet inscribed on the walls at both ends of the private audience hall (*dīwān-i khāṣṣ*) of the Red Fort, Shāh Jahān's palace in Delhi, which states that "if there is a paradise on earth, it is here, it is here, it is here" (*agar firdaws ast dar jahān, īnjā-st īnjā-st īnjā-st*),[84] is perhaps a case in point. There are examples of imperial buildings, however, which clearly invite a more thorough eschatological interpretation. This is the case with the palace complex of Madīnat al-Zahrā', built on the order of the Spanish Umayyad caliph 'Abd al-Raḥmān III (r. 300–50/912–61), arguably the most sustained and systematic effort to create a paradise city that was ever undertaken in the history of Islam. There is enough contextual evidence available to make a plausible case that 'Abd al-Raḥmān III intentionally sought to create a paradise on earth – regardless of his ulterior reasons, which were more likely political than spiritual.[85]

Madīnat al-Zahrā' is located some seven kilometres west of Cordoba, in the foothills of the Sierra Morena overlooking the Guadalquivir valley to the south. It covers a rectangular area of roughly 1,500 by 750 metres and is spread out over three stratified large terraces. The caliphal palace and living quarters occupy the highest of the three terraces, while the second terrace is dominated by 'Abd al-Raḥmān III's large audience hall, the Salón Rico. The urban hamlets of the city complex are located on the third and lowest terrace. In 316/929, 'Abd al-Raḥmān III, a descendant of the Umayyads, had declared himself caliph, God's representative on earth, both the religious and political leader of all Muslims. This declaration served to stake out his supreme authority in the face of two other dynasties claiming the caliphate, that of the venerable house of the 'Abbāsids in Baghdad (r. 132–656/750–1258) and that of the Fāṭimids (r. 297–567/909–1171), the rising Shi'i-Isma'ili power in North Africa and Egypt. For the first ten years of his reign, 'Abd al-Raḥmān III's imperial city had been Cordoba, then the largest city in Europe. Madīnat al-Zahrā' was built as a separate city, complete with its own palace, congregational mosque, jurisdiction, and police. Yet it was not meant to supersede Cordoba, nor was its function secondary to it. In the words of its foremost interpreter, Madīnat al-Zahrā' was "a whole new type of city, representing a new esthetics"[86] – in fact, as one might add, a different (though not so new) type of otherwordly space. Thus, Cordoba and Madīnat al-Zahrā' formed "a single capital with a double pole."[87]

[84] Sanderson, *Guide to the buildings*, 42.
[85] Fierro, "Madīnat al-Zahrā'."
[86] Ruggles, *Gardens*, 53.
[87] Fierro, *'Abd al-Rahman III*, 112.

Construction began in 327/939 shortly after the battle of Simancas against a coalition of Navarre and León, a military defeat that redirected ʿAbd al-Raḥmān III's energies from territorial expansion to ideological representation of his empire. A significant moment in the building process was the addition of the Salón Rico between 341/953 and 345/957. The year 341/953 had marked the enthronement of a new Fāṭimid caliph, to which the construction of the Salón therefore appears to respond.[88] This new Fāṭimid caliph, al-Muʿizz (r. 341–65/953–75), styled himself as a messianic figure who would usher in the promised end of time. ʿAbd al-Raḥmān III's intention in building the splendid centrepiece of his new city may well have been to bring paradise, as it were, back home.

Madīnat al-Zahrāʾ, and the Salón in particular, evoked paradise in several ways: the Salón, like the eternal garden, had eight doors; in its centre was a large tank of mercury that produced dazzling light effects, thus conjuring up the heavenly pool of al-Kawthar; and surrounding the building were the two pairs of the upper gardens and the lower gardens, in a manner of quoting the Qurʾān, which speaks of two pairs of paradise gardens sitting on top of each other (55:46–58). In the upper pair of gardens, as the Qurʾān states, are "from each kind fruit two varieties" (*min kulli fākiha zawjān*, 55:52), an expression that the exegetes often took to refer to fantastic plants producing two different kinds of fruit at the same time. As has been suggested, it is precisely such asymmetrical, otherworldly plants that the stucco panels covering the inside of the Salón depict, showing as they do "an astonishing proliferation of floral and vegetal motifs [which are] arranged alongside stems [and are] asymmetrical, each side being different from its mirror counterpart." In fact, it is the deliberate attempt to create an analogy between the Salón and the Qurʾanic upper paradise that "explain[s] the asymmetry in the pairs of floral and vegetal motifs found in the decoration of the Hall."[89]

In sum, the ideological program of ʿAbd al-Raḥmānn III in building Madīnat al-Zahrāʾ and the Salón in particular would have been to demonstrate that "the caliph ensures salvation and therefore [that] it was as if Paradise already existed in this world, in the town built by the caliph."[90] For reasons that should have become obvious by now, I agree with this interpretation to the exception of the phrase "as if." Contextual data suggest that the construction of Madīnat al-Zahrāʾ provoked not just symbolic associations with paradise. ʿAbd al-Raḥmān III's own passionate involvement in the construction went to such extremes that he failed to show up for Friday prayer in Cordoba's congregational mosque on a number of occasions. This promptly earned him a public dressing-down from Cordoba's

[88] Eadem, "Madīnat al-Zahrāʾ," 301.

[89] Eadem, *ʿAbd al-Rahman III*, 115–6. Cf. Fierro's detailed discussion of this point in "Madīnat al-Zahrāʾ," 307–8.

[90] Eadem, *ʿAbd al-Raḥmān III*, 116.

judge, Mundhir b. Saʿīd (d. 355/966).[91] Since the year 338/949, Mundhir had been one of the most high-ranking legal and religious authorities in al-Andalus. He also acted as a close advisor of ʿAbd al-Raḥmān III, which however did not prevent him from airing his criticism.[92] In his rebuke, "full of allusions to the culpable behaviour of the monarch ... and in particular to the criticisms addressed to him directly after he had built a pavilion covered with tiles gilded in gold and silver," Mundhir even accused ʿAbd al-Raḥmān III of "allowing himself to be seduced by Satan to the point of acting like an infidel."[93]

Mundhīr's most important disagreement may have been with the excessive luxury of Madīnat al-Zahrāʾ, but as has been suggested, he may also have taken issue with ʿAbd al-Raḥmān III's hubris in desiring to build a paradise on earth.[94] Mundhir, as we saw in Chapter 5, was among the theologians who most vociferously argued that the eschatological and protological paradise were not the same, and that the protological paradise inhabited by Adam and Eve was not on earth.[95] To see his monarch try to bring paradise down to the hills of Cordoba may have provoked his theological sensibilities. In this respect, the story of the legendary city of Iram "of the columns" could have served him as a warning.[96] According to the exegetes commenting on Qurʾan 89:6–8 ("Have you not seen how the Lord dealt with ... Iram with its pillars, the like of which had not been created in the land?"), a king named Shaddād had once arrogantly resolved to build a city to rival paradise, "with palaces made of gold and silver, pillars cut from chrysolite and ruby, filled with different kinds of trees, and crossed by perenially flowing rivers." God, to punish Shaddād, promptly sent a natural disaster from the heaven (*baʿatha ... ṣayḥa min al-samāʾ*), "and they [all] perished."[97] Muslim exegetes, in fact, often suggested that the city of Iram was no other than the Umayyad capital, Damascus.[98] Shaddād's sudden demise, the moment when

91 Maqqarī, *Nafḥ al-ṭīb*, I, 375; idem, *Azhār al-riyāḍ fī akhbār ʿiyād*, II, 270. Cf. Ruggles, *Gardens*, 60.

92 *EI2*, s.v. (al-)Mundhir b. Saʿīd', VII, 569a-570a (Ch. Pellat).

93 Ibid.

94 Fierro, "Madīnat al-Zahrāʾ," 325.

95 See p. 167.

96 Ibn al-ʿArabī (d. 543/1148) from Seville suggests that the story of Iram serves a cautionary purpose (*taḥdhīr*), and that "the building of excessively high buildings is one of the signs of the apocalypse (*ashrāṭ al-sāʿa*)." See Ibn al-ʿArabī, *Aḥkām*, IV, 362.

97 Qurṭubī, *Jāmiʿ*, XX, 47. See also Yāqūt, *Buldān*, s.v. Iram, I, 155a-157b, at 155b-156b. Cf. *EI2*, s.v. Iram, III, 1270a-b (W. M. Watt); *EQ*, s.v. Iram, II, 559a-b (P. Cobb); Wheeler, *Mecca and Eden*, 113.

98 See Ṭabarī, *Jāmiʿ*, XXX, 212–3; Ibn al-ʿArabī, *Aḥkām*, IV, 361; Qurṭubī, *Jāmiʿ*, XX, 46. Cf. Yāqūt, *Buldān*, s.v. Dimashq. Cobb finds that Damascus is also equated with Iram in works devoted to the "merits" (*faḍāʾil*) of Damascus, such as al-Rabaʿī's fifth/eleventh-century *Faḍāʾil al-Shām wa-Dimashq* (pp. 20 [#36], 21 [#38]). See Cobb, "Virtual sacrality," 46; *EQ*, s.v. Iram, II, 559b (P. Cobb). The anti-Umayyad gist of the tradition, which, to me at least, seems clear, may have been forgotten in later centuries.

FIGURE 20. The city of Iram. From Rashīd al-Dīn, *Jāmiʿ al-tawārīkh* (*Comprehensive History*), Tabriz/Persia, *ca.* 705/[1306] or 714/[1314–15]. Edinburgh University Library, Centre for Research Collections, MS Edinburgh Or. 20, fol. 1r.

the angel of death descends upon him, was a popular motif of Islamic painters of the later medieval period; it appears in royal copies of the so-called *Books of Omens* (*Fālnāmas*).[99]

Memories of Umayyad transgressions may have lingered in Cordoba. The local historians related that the practice of planting trees in the courtyards of congregational mosques had been brought to al-Andalus in the second/eighth century from Syria,[100] and such memories harkened back to the Syrian Umayyads' efforts to make sites such as the Temple Mount in Jerusalem and the Umayyad Mosque in Damascus into earthly paradises. In the fourth/tenth century, under ʿAbd al-Raḥmān III and his successors, there were trees in the courtyard of the Great Mosque of Cordoba, and the famous mosaics of the prayer niche, commissioned by ʿAbd al-Ḥakam II (r. 350–66/961–76), were designed to emulate the paradise decoration of the Umayyad Mosque in Damascus.[101] However, the theologians and jurists seem to have viewed the use of such iconography with unease, whether in the context of palaces or of mosques. In the fifth/eleventh century, a number of prominent jurists from Cordoba, such as Muḥammad Ibn ʿAttāb (d. 462/1070) and the judge ʿĪsā Ibn Sahl (d. 486/1093), began to speak out against the practice of planting trees in mosque courtyards. Existing trees should not be cut, they argued, but ordinary believers must be prohibited from eating their fruit[102] – lest they feel they had tasted paradise on earth?

[99] See Farhad, *Falnama*, 10, 169, 279.

[100] *Wathāʾiq fī shuʾūn al-ʿumrān*, 49–50. I am grateful to Maribel Fierro for providing me with a copy of Ibn Sahl's *fatwā*.

[101] Fierro, "En tomo a la decoración con mosaicos de las mezquitas omeyas."

[102] *Wathāʾiq fī shuʾūn al-ʿumrān*, 50.

FIGURE 21. The angel of death grabbing the soul of the king Shaddād. From the Rotterdam *Fālnāma* (*Book of Omens*). India (?), probably eleventh/seventeenth century. MS Museum voor Volkenkunde Rotterdam 17803, fol. 33.

Otherworldly Rituals

As if approaching the centre of concentric circles, let us proceed from the examination of topographical and architectural constructions of the otherworld on earth to a consideration of the human body as the site of transgression into paradise and hell. For paradise and hell are made to be present not only in landscapes, cities, and buildings, but in bodies as well. The arena in which this typically happens is ritual. In certain rituals, ordinary Muslims are not denied but encouraged, and sometimes forced, to switch from this-worldly to otherworldly existence.[103] In these rituals, the human body becomes the vehicle for crossing the boundary between this world and the eutopian (or indeed the dystopian) otherworld. Here I shall foreground the pilgrimage to Mecca, which is particularly illustrative because it combines topographical, architectural, and ritual aspects, but I shall also reflect on fasting and prayer, and certain rituals of punishment.[104]

The pilgrimage to Mecca is a tour of paradise already in the sense that the city is considered otherworldly territory, and quite literally so. Next to Jerusalem, Damascus, and Medina, Mecca is one of the paradise cities of early Islam. As a local chronicle puts it, "God built Mecca on this-worldly hardships (*makrūhāt al-dunyā*) and on the layers of paradise (*darajāt al-janna*),"[105] suggesting that, although life in the city may be difficult,[106] it is a part, in fact the highest part, of the eternal garden. The Kaaba, which medieval Islamic maps regularly put at the centre of the world, is also connected upwards to paradise, as the Kaaba is mirrored by its heavenly counterpart, the "Enlivened House" (*al-bayt al-maʿmūr*, cf. Q 52:3) in heaven,

103 It is noteworthy in this respect that common definitions of the term *ʿibādāt* ("rituals, acts of devotion") draw explicit attention to the fact that the *ʿibādāt* are "norms of the Law that are connected to the otherworld" (*al-aḥkām al-sharʿiyya al-mutaʿalliqa bi-amr al-ākhira*). See Tahānawī, *Kashshāf*, 1161. Cf. Reinhart, "Ritual action," 57–8, 95.

104 In a classical formulation of Charles J. Adams, "there are data for the investigator in these realms [of Islamic myth and ritual] to consider, but in comparison with the Hindu tradition or that of the ancient Near East, it is very much less in both quantity and significance." See Adam, "The study of religions," 182. In 1983, William Graham could still assert that there was no significant scholarly interest in "study[ing] of Muslim ritual on its own terms," and that scholars of Islam were mostly interested in locating the "essence" of Muslim "orthoprax" ritual in its pre-Islamic origins. See Graham, "Islam in the mirror of ritual," 58–9. Several decades later, the mythical and eschatological aspects of Islamic ritual have, with few exceptions, still not been sufficiently studied to prove the correctness or incorrectness of Adams's assertion.

105 Fākihī, *Akhbār Makka*, II, 313 (#1572). Cf. the notion that "paradise is surrounded with hardships" (*ḥuffat bi-l-makārih*). See Muslim, *Ṣaḥīḥ*, *k. al-janna* 1, IV, 2174 (cf. *CTM*, VI, 7a [Bukhārī, Abū Dāwūd, Tirmidhī, Nasāʾī, Dārimī, and Malik]); Samarqandī, *Tanbīh*, 35; Qurṭubī, *Tadhkira*, II, 61.

106 Ismāʿīl would have complained to God about the heat in Mecca and received the reply: "I have opened a door for you from paradise in the Ḥijr; the spirit (*rūḥ*) flows from it over you until the Day of Resurrection." See Azraqī, *Akhbār Makka*, 229.

circled by the angels. According to the literature devoted to the "merits" (*faḍā'il*) of Mecca, the patch of land between the stone in the ground known as Abraham's Station (*maqām Ibrāhīm*) and the Black Stone in the eastern corner of the Kaaba is particularly sacred; it is "one of the gardens of paradise."[107] Abraham's Station and the Black Stone, as numerous texts assert, are "two precious stones" (*jawharatānī*) or "two sapphires" (*yāqūtatāni*) from paradise, though their former brilliance is dimmed by the sins of humankind.[108] The so-called Yemeni Corner of the Kaaba is "one of the gates of paradise."[109] The well of Zamzam, which is immediately adjacent to the area, feeds off the subterranean waters of paradise.[110] In the space between Zamzam, Abraham's Station, and the Black Stone are buried many prophets, including Ismāʿīl,[111] and according to tradition, the well is the abode of the souls of the believers during their existence in *barzakh*.[112] (The souls of unbelievers, as will be recalled, reside in the well of Barhūt in Hadramawt.) In fact, the entire sanctuary (*ḥaram*) of Mecca enjoys a special, otherworldly status.[113] Tradition declares this to be sacred, paradisiacal ground, and the rituals performed on it are held to be particularly efficacious.[114]

Muslim jurists, both classical and modern, usually take the view that the hajj rituals should simply be understood as acts of devotion (*ʿibādāt*) that are due to God, and that it is moot to seek to comprehend their logical, historical, or mythic underpinnings.[115] However, sober views of this kind

[107] Fākihī, *Akhbār Makka*, I, 468 (#1032); Ibn Jubayr, *Riḥla*, 56 (tr. Broadhurst, 80–1). Cf. Kister, "Maqām Ibrāhīm," 482. According to Fākihī, *Akhbār Makka*, I, 360–1 (#1011), the Prophet had a vision of paradise unfolding before him between the *maqām* and the Kaaba, after praying there with forty-two of his Companions.

[108] Azraqī, *Akhbār Makka*, 227–8 and passim; Fākihī, *Akhbār Makka*, I, 82, 84–5 (##1, 6–9) and passim. See also Ghazālī, *Iḥyā'*, I, 402; Nābulusī, *Ahl al-janna*, 46–7. Cf. Kister, "Maqām Ibrāhīm," 481; Lory, "Lieux saints," 30.

[109] Azraqī, *Akhbār Makka*, 240.

[110] Fākihī, *Akhbār Makka*, II, 35 (#1092): The spring of Shiloah (*ʿayn Silwān*) and Zamzam are "from paradise." Cf. *EQ*, s.v. Springs and fountains, V, 121b-128b, at 127a (M. Radscheit).

[111] Fākihī, *Akhbar Makka*, II, 34 (#1090). Cf. Rubin, "Kaʿba," 111.

[112] Suyūṭī, *Sharḥ al-ṣudūr*, 329 and passim. Cf. Eklund, *Life between death and resurrection*, 43 (from Ibn Abī l-Dunyā); Rubin, "Kaʿba," 111–2.

[113] When Adam fell to the earth, one reads in the local chronicles, he missed his joyful existence in paradise so much that God, in order to console him, sent him to Mecca where, under the protection of guardian angels circling over the perimeter of the *ḥaram*, Adam established the House of God and the rites performed around it. See Azraqī, *Akhbār Makka*, 7–8; Fākihī, *Akhbār Makka*, I, 82, II, 274–6, III, 219 (##1, 1514, 1517, 2007) and passim.

[114] Recently, this point has been supported by Marion Katz, who states that "the traditions on the merits (*faḍā'il*) of the ḥajj ... are centrally concerned with the core Islamic themes of sin and salvation ... the purging of sin is a constant and pervasive theme." See Katz, "The Ḥajj," 103.

[115] Graham refers to al-Ghazālī as an important witness to this position, while also noting that al-Ghazālī simultaneously made "as beautiful and coherent sense of the 'mysteries' of hajj symbolism as has ever been done." See Graham, "Islam in the mirror of ritual," 56, 68–9. Jurists subsumed the *ʿibādāt* under a special category of nonrational legal norms, namely,

coexisted at all times with more imaginative interpretations, which are preserved in a variety of genres of Islamic literature.[116] Sufi authors in particular wrote about the pilgrimage as a journey towards the hereafter, and about Mecca as a version of paradise on earth. Al-Ghazālī, closely echoing the third/ninth-century Egyptian Dhū l-Nūn (d. 246/861), provides an influential reading along these lines.[117] The pilgrims, he asserts, leave their homes realising that they have set out on a journey "unlike the journeys on earth," a journey that is "directed toward the angel of death." When traversing the inhospitable deserts on their way to Mecca, they feel as if they have entered the *barzakh* between death and resurrection: the brigands that threaten them on the road remind them of the fearsome angels Munkar and Nakīr, and the beasts of the wilderness prefigure the scorpions and snakes in the grave. When, finally, the pilgrims enter Mecca, they are reassured that now "they are safe, on account of entering [Mecca], from God's punishment."[118] A century later, Ruzbihān-i Baqlī (d. 606/1209) compares the hills of Ṣafā and Marwa to the tents and palaces in the realms of Malakūt and Jabarūt, stating that they surround Mecca like veils. Ruzbihān construes a simile of Mecca's famous landmarks as the heavenly veils that separate the inhabitants of paradise from God: Ṣafā and Marwa veil Mecca, Mecca veils the sacred mosque, and the mosque veils the Kaaba in its midst, in which God is present.[119] In later centuries, illustrated guides to the Hijaz were produced that framed the visit to the holy sites in terms of a journey to the otherworld. For example, a richly though crudely illustrated late-Mughal (?) manuscript presents a dozen maps and depictions of specific buildings (showing, e.g., the *ḥaram* in Mecca and the al-Baqīʿ cemetery in Medina) and then switches seamlessly to a series of some fifty images of the Judgement, the pleasures of paradise, and the torments of hell. There is also a view of a mountain (presumably the mountain of ʿAyr) sitting on top of hell, circled by black birds in which are the souls of sinners.[120]

the "divinely ordained norms" (*muqaddarāt*), "whose purpose cannot be apprehended" (*lā yumkinu taʿaqqul al-maʿnā*). See Āmidī, *Iḥkām*, IV, 65. For further references, see Lange, "Sins, expiation, and non-rationality," 153–6.

116 *Pace* Kevin Reinhart who questions approaches to Islamic ritual that are not based on legal texts, "the genre of ritual prescription" in Islam. According to Reinhart, the meanings provided by extra-fiqh texts are "unstable, quite variable, contested, and often contradictory," and therefore "secondary." See Reinhart, "What to do with ritual texts."

117 For Dhū l-Nūn's eschatological interpretation of the pilgrimage, see Sulamī, *Ḥaqāʾiq al-tafsīr*, II, 20–21. I owe this reference to Pieter Coppens. On Dhū l-Nūn's pilgrimage, see the references given in Ebstein, "Ḏū l-Nūn," 567.

118 Ghazālī, *Iḥyāʾ*, I, 440–42. Cf. Campo, "Authority, ritual and spatial order," 82–4; Katz, "Ḥajj," 121–2. In a similar vein, Maybudī likens the excitement that seizes the pilgrim before his departure from home to the state of agitation and anxiety before death. See Maybudī, *Kashf al-asrār*, 552, cited in Masud, "Sufi understanding of hajj," 283.

119 See Maybudī, *Kashf al-asrār*, 430, cited in Masud, "Sufi understanding of hajj," 288.

120 *Ḥajjnāma*, MS Bodleian Pers. d. 29.

FIGURE 22. The mountain of ʿAyr. From an anonymous *Ḥajjnāma*. India, probably late twelfth/eighteenth century. MS Bodleian Pers. d29, fol. 57r.

The imagery of this manuscript taps into a standard iconographic repertoire, and like other such manuscripts seems to have been produced for a popular audience of prospective or former pilgrims.[121] However, the conceptual links between Islamic rituals and the otherworld are pervasive also in texts commonly considered to be scholarly, and not only in regard to the pilgrimage. For example, the historian and theologian Ibn al-Jawzī (d. 597/1201), a detractor of popular religion and of Sufism if ever there was one, muses at length over the similarity (*shibh*) between the Day of the Feast of Sacrifice and the Day of Resurrection. He notes that in the congestion of the feast, celebrated in the public arena of the city, people stand on each others' feet, as they do on the Day of Judgement, and the flags hissed during the feast remind Ibn al-Jawzī of the flags of the righteous unfurled at the Resurrection.[122] Or consider the case of the Islamic ablution rites (*wuḍū'*). Performed repeatedly over the course of the day, ablution (and also the full-body lustration, *ghusl*) functions to remove the ritual impurity incurred through the acts of defecating, urinating, ejaculation, menstruation, parturition, and sleep or loss of consciousness, with the ultimate aim of making bodies fit for prayer.[123] It is striking that none of these acts and states of being apply to the inhabitants of paradise, as one learns from the traditionist literature. Not even sex is an exception here, for while there is uninterrupted congress in the eschatological paradise, there is no ejaculation.[124] Muslim purity laws, as has been observed, cannot be reduced "to any single generating principle,"[125] and my argument here is not that the essence of these laws is that they aim to establish paradise on earth. I merely wish to point out that *one* noteworthy aspect of Islamic purity laws is that they seem designed to (pre-)enact the bodily state of the paradise dwellers. Other universal rituals in Islam appear to invite similar processes of assimilating this-worldly to otherworldly bodies. "Fasting," the Prophet is reported to have said, "is a protection from hell" (*al-ṣawm junna min al-nār*), adding that the breath of a person who fasts smells better than musk, the perfume of paradise.[126] The doors of hell are shut close, and the doors of paradise are opened according to the number of days one fasts in the month of Rajab;[127] fasting on every

[121] Cf. *'Uqūbāt al-'uṣāt*, MS Leiden Or. 26.545, attributed to Ja'far al-Ṣādiq. The Leiden and Bodleian manuscripts seem closely related. See, e.g., the representation of Mālik as an Indian deity with sixteen arms in Ms. Bodleian Pers. d.29, fol. 55r and Ms. Leiden Or. 26.545, fol. 10a. On the genre of illustrated hajj manuscripts, see Milstein, "*Kitāb Shawq-Nāma*"; Graves and Junot, *Architecture*, 62–3.

[122] Ibn al-Jawzī, *Ṣayd al-khāṭir*, 477–8.

[123] A convenient summary can be found in Reinhart, "Impurity/No Danger," 3–18. See also Gauvain, "Ritual rewards," 339–42.

[124] 'Abd al-Razzāq, *Muṣannaf*, *b. al-janna wa-ṣifatihā*, XI, 421 (#20890); Suyūṭī, *Budūr*, 536. Cf. Azmeh, "Rhetoric for the senses," 223–4.

[125] Katz, *Body of texts*, 24.

[126] Tirmidhī, *Jāmi'*, *k. al-īmān* 8 (*b. mā jā'a fī faḍl al-ṣawm*), III, 136 (#764).

[127] Majlisī, *Biḥār*, VIII, 380–1.

day in the month of Ramadan accumulates multiple rewards in paradise.[128] "When the servant takes up the standing position in prayer (*idhā qāma fī l-ṣalāt*)," states another tradition, "the Gardens are opened for him, the veils separating him from his Lord are removed, and the houris receive him, as long as he does not blow his nose or clear this throat."[129]

There are different ways of interpreting the sense of slippage between this world and the otherworld that these rituals establish. It has been proposed, for example, that the hajj, by gesturing back to the prelapsarian state of Adam and Eve, serves to remind the participants that the utopia of paradise is lost, and in consequence to make "an absolute distinction ... between heaven and earth."[130] This, as the argument goes, would have cemented the power of the jurists of Islam, as the guardians of the legal rules regulating the pilgrimage. However, the correspondences between the pilgrimage to Mecca and the eschatological paradise seem at least as strong, perhaps even stronger, than the links with the lost protological garden. I would suggest that in Muslim literature the hajj rites are interpreted not so much as a ritual repetition of acts performed in Adam's garden but as a ritual (pre-)enactment of the state of believers in the hereafter. The future garden, after all, betokens a joyous return, not a traumatic expulsion, and pilgrims usually do not report a feeling of loss and sadness when they reflect on their experience, but rather, one of joy and spiritual elation.

A related way of looking at the ḥajj rituals is to see them serve a "monitory" purpose, that is, by giving the participants an impression of the future paradise, they function to move participants to an "edifying reflection" on how to reform their lives on earth.[131] It is striking, however, that the classical sources on the hajj do not, as a rule, talk about the hajj in terms of a system of signs or symbols gesturing towards an absent (future) paradise. According to these sources, as been correctly observed, "The Black Stone does not merely represent a fragment of Paradise or bring to mind the pernicious effects of sin; it *is* a fragment of Paradise...."[132] The sense that emerges from these texts, as in the case of the topographical and architectural traditions considered in the preceding text, is that eschatology is *now*. This world

[128] Ibid., VIII, 390–1.

[129] Suyūṭī, *Budūr*, 568. A similar tradition in Majlisī, *Biḥār*, VIII, 392.

[130] Wheeler, *Mecca and Eden*, 132. Wheeler argues that the pilgrims' experience is modelled on the precivilisational conditions of the protological garden (where there was no sewn clothing, shaving of hair, use of perfume and henna, or hunting). See ibid., 64–7. A convenient summary of the prohibitions during the pilgrimage, the details of which cannot be rehearsed here in any exhaustive fashion, is found in Jazīrī, *Fiqh*, I, 541–51.

[131] Katz, "Ḥajj," 122.

[132] Ibid., 125. Katz's observation, correct to my mind, stands in some tension to her earlier assertion that the hajj rituals' otherworldly connotation are of a "purely monitory" kind. See the preceding footnote.

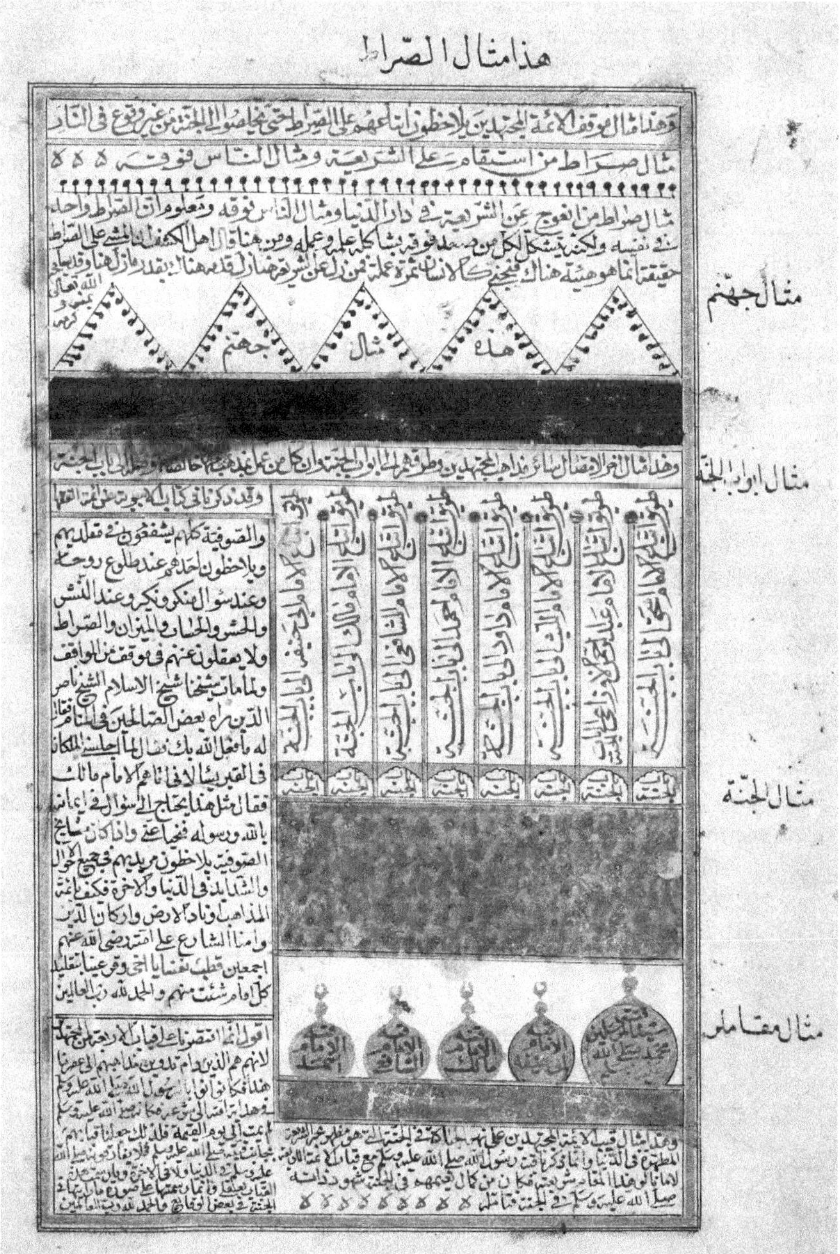

FIGURE 23. The Bridge, the valleys and mountains of hell, the eight gates of paradise, and the residences therein of the Prophet and the eponyms of the four Sunni schools of law. From *Akhlāq-i rasūl Allāh* (*The Manners of the Messenger of God*). Turkey, twelfth/eighteenth century. MS Staatsbibliothek Berlin Or. Oct. 1602, fol. 39v.

and the otherworld are intermeshed. Paradise and hell are imagined to cut through this present life in a seamless synchronicity of events.

Hell fully deserves mention in this context; for it is not only paradise that is ritually enacted. In public rituals of punishment Muslim rulers of the premodern period took at face value the traditional belief that hell is on earth, and with devastating effect.[133] Perhaps one could object that public spectacles of punishment ought to be considered political, not religious rituals. The distinction collapses quickly, however. In the same way in which religious rituals such as burial rites, communal prayer, or the pilgrimage were bearers of political meaning, political rituals such as royal processions, acts of investiture, or indeed rituals of justice invariably relied on religious repertoires of signification and justification. The punishments meted out in hell served as the "brooding metaphysical context"[134] within which earthly acts of violence could be understood.

The most obvious instance, perhaps, of punishments designed to suggest to onlookers that they were witnessing acts of otherworldly justice was death by fire. "Only God punishes with fire," declares a Prophetic hadith,[135] but evidence found in the chronicles from the early centuries to the late Islamic Middle Period suggests that rulers did not feel deterred by such warnings, but rather stood to benefit from usurping the divine prerogative over the stake.[136] Two examples, both from the sixth/twelfth century, can serve to illustrate this point. When a number of Ismaʿilis were burned at Isfahan in 494/1101, the man in charge of the burning pits was nicknamed Mālik by the people,[137] in reference to the angel who guards the entry to hell, ushering sinners into the Fire.[138] As was noted in Chapter 4, the gaolers of hell are angels and, as such, "good" agents of God's terrifying but ultimately just use of punishment. Ostensibly, the name Mālik served to drive home the point that the Ismaʿilis' punishment was a religiously sanctioned expression of the ruler's duty to prosecute unbelieving enemies. The Ḥanbalī judge Ibn ʿAqīl (Baghdad, d. 513/1119) is on record for comparing his sentencing Ismaʿilis to death to God's sentencing sinners to hell.[139]

133 In the following paragraphs, I summarise an argument that I have laboured elsewhere. See Lange, *Justice*, 168–75; idem, "Ignominious parading," 104–6; idem, "Where on earth is hell?"

134 I borrow this phrase from Warner, *Fantastic metamorphoses*, 39.

135 Bukhārī, *Ṣaḥīḥ*, *k. al-jihād wa-l-siyar* 107 (*b. al-tawdīʿ*), II, 249; Ibn Ḥanbal, *Musnad*, II, 307, 338, 453. See also *CTM*, s.v. ʿ-dh-b, IV, 164a-b, with variants. Cf. *EI1*, s.v. Murtadd, 6:736b-738a ([W.] Heffening); van Ess, *Das* K. al-Nakṭ, 50–1; Kraemer, "Apostates, rebels and brigands," 40.

136 See the copious examples given by Al-Shāljī, *Mawsūʿat al-ʿadhāb*, VI, 187–204. Gerald Hawting discusses a number of burnings, mostly of heretics, in the Umayyad period. See Hawting, "Jaʿd." See also the cases cited by Kraemer, "Apostates, rebels and brigands," 44–6. A Fāṭimid *dāʿī* was burned in Mecca in 420/1029. See Ṣafadī, *Wāfī*, XXVII, 114.

137 Ibn al-Athīr, *Kāmil*, VIII, 450.

138 Ghazālī, *Durra*, 99.

139 See Griffel, *Apostasie*, 282.

Ibn al-Jawzī, whose particular interest in hell was noted in Chapter 3, relates a public burning that took place in the year 530/1135. A woman convicted of an unspecified crime "although she was deemed good" was made to stand in a reed basket in the courtyard of the Friday mosque in East Baghdad. Then an official entrusted with handling naphta (*naffāṭ*) proceeded to put fire to the basket. Miraculously, Ibn al-Jawzī continues, the woman managed to escape the basket, naked and only partially burned, whereupon she was pardoned.[140] From this passage, not only does one gather that there was a habitual pattern, a ritualised technique for public burnings in the penal theatre of the Congregational Mosque, but also, that such events were framed in eschatological terms. The aborted attempt at incineration reported by Ibn al-Jawzī corresponds to stories in the eschatological literature in which Muslim sinners, scorched partially by the flames of hell, escape into the presence of God, to be forgiven and washed clean of their burning marks in the river of life at the entry to paradise.[141]

Another hellish ritual of punishment, more widespread and more characteristic of premodern Islamic penal practice, was ignominious parading (*tashhīr*, "to make well-known, notorious").[142] To judge by the chronicles, *tashhīr* parades were a common sight in the cities of the Islamic world until at least the nineteenth century; it is also one of the most frequently mentioned punishments in the *Arabian Nights*.[143] Offenders were led through the city sitting backwards on donkeys, camels, or oxen, their faces blackened with soot or embers, their bodies decorated with demeaning signs and objects, and their crimes called out to the public. During their ordeal, the mob pelted them with stones and abused them verbally. If Islamic rituals generally show a great concern with purity, *tashhīr* is the closest one comes in Islamic legal culture to a rite of pollution. It is a ritual of purity (*ṭahāra*) turned on its head.

The Arabic idiom "to blacken someone's face" (*sawwada wajhahu*) connotes the idea of dishonouring, or shaming. However, black faces also carry an obvious eschatological meaning, recalling the Qurʾānic verses that speak of the black faces, scorched and covered in dust, of the sinners who are led before God on the Day of Resurrection (3:106, 39:60, 80:40–2). Eschatological hadiths and Qurʾān commentaries improvise amply on this theme;[144] in fact the idea circulated so widely that one may legitimately

140 Ibn al-Jawzī, *Muntaẓam*, XXVII, 310. On this incident, see Lange, *Justice*, 68, 146–7. Cf. the long story in Baḥrānī, *Maʿālim*, III, 441–2, according to which ʿAlī ordered the burning of a sodomite, who was likewise saved by the intervention of divine mercy.

141 Ghazālī, *Durra*, 100. Cf. the variants in Tirmidhī, *Jāmiʿ*, *k. ṣifat jahannam* 10, IV, 714; Abū Nuʿaym, *Ḥilyat al-awliyāʾ*, IV, 285.

142 Lange, "Ignominious parading"; Rowson, "Reveal and conceal."

143 Rescher, "Studien," 69–70.

144 See, e.g., Tirmidhī, *Jāmiʿ*, *k. ṣifat jahannam* 4 (*b. mā jāʾa fī ṣifat sharāb ahl al-nār*), IV, 705; *Daqāʾiq al-akhbār*, 59 (tr. Wolff, 145); Ghazālī, *Durra*, 56.

assume that eschatological punishment was on the minds of those who witnessed, enacted, or indeed suffered ignominious parading and the face blackening that came with it. Other constitutive elements of the practice also suggest that *tashhīr* processions were theatrical performances of otherworldly justice. Offenders were frequently displayed to the public with a sign of their crime dangling around their necks. The Ottoman Criminal Code promulgated under Süleyman the Magnificent (r. 927–74/1520–66) stipulates that a person convicted of stealing a chicken is to be paraded with the stolen chicken hanging from his neck, while fraudulent merchants must be led around with their faulty goods hanging from a thread fastened to their pierced noses.[145] Compare this to the Qur'ānic verse that states "that which they held on to will be tied to their necks on the Day of Resurrection" (3:180). The eschatological manuals give multiple examples: As the sinners convene before God's court of justice, their sins are recognisable by the signs they carry around their necks. A jug will be hung from the neck of the drunkard,[146] while thieves carry the stolen object around their necks,[147] and so forth.

Often, during ignominious parades, the victims were followed by a government agent charged with flogging them, thus driving them on to continue their unhappy journey through the city.[148] In 431/1040, when Bādīs, the ruler of Granada, had his vizier Abū l-Futūḥ al-Jurjānī paraded, a "harsh and fat black servant" (*aswadu faẓẓun ḍakhmun*) followed Abū l-Futūḥ, slapping him without interruption.[149] Surely the thought of the *zabāniya*, ushering people into hell and beating them with iron rods,[150] was close at hand. One cannot assume, of course, that *tashhīr* processions were always and everywhere staged and understood in eschatological terms. Rather, like the examples discussed in the preceding text of garden architecture or hajj rites, the ritual came with a built-in ambiguity: one *could* interpret it in an otherworldly framework, but one never *had* to. On occasion, however, there was little choice in the matter. Under the Egyptian Fāṭimids, as the historian al-Maqrīzī reports referring to an incident in Cairo in 521/1127, *tashhīr* processions were accompanied by "torch-bearers in the guise of angels" – an unmistakable reference to the fire-guarding punisher angels in hell.[151]

145 Peters, *Crime and punishment*, 98.
146 *Daqā'iq al-akhbār*, 71 (tr. Wolff, 175).
147 Muttaqī, *Kanz al-ʿummāl*, V, 222.
148 Ibn al-Athīr, *Kāmil*, VIII, 337; Ibn al-Jawzī, *Muntaẓam*, XVI, 295, XVII, 172, 264, XVIII, 152.
149 Ibn al-Khaṭīb, *Iḥāṭa*, 462–6.
150 Ghazālī, *Iḥyā'*, V, 176 (tr. Winter, 220). Cf. idem, *Durra*, 99 (Mālik driving people into the Fire).
151 Maqrīzī, *Ittiʿāẓ*, III, 119, cited in Buckley, "The Muḥtasib," 110.

Interfused Worlds

To be sure, such explicitly eschatological framings of rituals of punishment are rare in the chronicles. In fact, a similar observation applies to all the examples adduced in this chapter, all of which, as is readily admitted, are chosen selectively. Ranging from Spain to India, and from early Islam to early modernity, it is easy to criticise this chapter for covering so much ground as to make synthetic conclusions gratuitous. It is not my intention, however, to argue that the agenda to bring paradise and hell down to earth informed the construction and the perception of sacred topographies, funerary buildings, palaces, or rituals at all times and in all places. Rather, the purpose of this chapter has been to highlight a number of instances in which, to my mind at least, the translation of eschatological images and ideas into tangible spatial, architectural, and ritual phenomena is incontrovertible. However, even then a certain ambiguity remains, for these phenomena generally invite eschatological readings but do not impose them.

A second point to be made in conclusion to this chapter concerns the mode in which the relationship between the terrestrial and the otherworldly paradise and hell is conceived. Several times over the course of the foregoing discussion I have stressed that symbolic interpretations of certain spaces, buildings, or rituals as paradisiacal or infernal do not tell the full story. As I have highlighted, these spaces, buildings, and rituals often do not *refer* to the otherworld but rather, they *claim a share* in it. Therefore, rather than of a referential or symbolic relationship, I would prefer to speak of mimetic communion, to capture the sense of the true and full presence of paradise and hell on earth, not as a prefiguration of the world to come, but as its simultaneous realisation. Put differently, the examples that I have discussed show the interfusion of the otherworld throughout the terrestrial world.[152] What is more, I argue that this interfusion occurs in a great variety of Islamically encoded spaces, material practices, and ritualised forms of behaviour, in the same way in which it can be observed in a wide and diverse range of Islamic textual traditions, a phenomenon that has been highlighted repeatedly in previous chapters of this book. This does not mean that the relationship between the otherworld and its terrestrial manifestations was never analysed and understood in symbolic terms. As seen in the preceding text, writers like al-Ghazālī, Ibn al-Jawzī, or Ibn Baṭṭūṭa preferred to talk about certain places, objects, and rituals in the conditional, "as if" they were a part of paradise or hell. However, the dominant impression that arises from the sources considered in this chapter is one of enacted presence, not of symbolised absence.

A final issue to be raised concerns the sociopolitical causes and functions of this participatory relationship. It would be wrong to suggest that there is

[152] I borrow the term *interfusion* from Coleridge, who defines *mimesis* as "the interfusion of the same throughout the radically different." See Coleridge, *Biographia Literaria*, I, 72. On Coleridge's theory of imagination, see Iser, *Das Fiktive und das Imaginäre*, 316–31.

a single answer to this question. How and why sacred spaces, architecture, and objects are created, and what function(s) ritual serves, remains a highly contested field of scholarly debate. Several of the examples discussed in this chapter suggest the involvement of institutions of power in the construction of paradise and hell on earth. The mosques of Damascus and Medina, the "palace of the otherworld" of Sanjar and the Taj Mahal at Agra, Madīnat al-Zahrā', and the palaces of rulers built adjacent to the Meccan sanctuary all demonstrate the attempts of political authorities to associate themselves, by a suggestive play of analogy, with God's ultimate sovereignty on earth.[153] The rulers of Islamic history, however, were not the only ones concerned with exploiting the meaning-making potential of these sites and bringing it under their discursive control. The scholars, the guardians of Islamic law, likewise claimed authority over the terrestrial paradise and hell; a point that is perhaps most easily made in regard to the ritual laws that framed the experience of the pilgrims to Mecca,[154] but that can also be observed in the scholars' attempts to regulate state rituals of power such as executions by burning or ignominious parades.

Ordinary Muslims may have misrecognised the claims to mundane power that lurked behind the Edenification or infernalisation of certain spaces, objects, and rituals, and thus become submissive to these claims.[155] Paradise and hell would have appeared to them subject to the will and mercy of others, whether God, the earthly ruler, or the community of scholars. It is also possible, however, that practitioners drew their own conclusions from the encounter with the otherworld on earth. The experience of the interfusion of this world and the otherworld is likely to have stimulated a variety of psychological responses. One the one hand, this experience could have been received as a life-affirming impetus for the active conquest of paradise; on the other, it could have been interpreted as a reminder of the fragility and precariousness of human existence, of how quickly life descends into hellish misery. Reactions thus may have ranged from an optimistic embrace of both this-worldly *and* otherworldly existence to dejection and fear of this life and the next. In sum, the notion of the otherworld's interfusion in this world, so widespread in Islamic discursive, material, and practical traditions, heightened awareness of the eutopian and dystopian potential of life on earth, and thus contributed to giving human existence a particular eschatological depth.

153 Campo, "Authority, ritual and spatial order." On the "play of analogy," see Azmeh, *Muslim kingship*, 155; Lange, "Sitting by the ruler's throne." For a critique, see Kalmar, *Imagined Islam*.

154 Wheeler, *Mecca and Eden*, 12, 47, 70 and passim; Katz, "Ḥajj," 129.

155 Catherine Bell goes as far as to speak of this kind of "misrecognition" as one of the defining elements of ritual. See Bell, *Ritual theory*, 82–3.

Epilogue

> I looked around hell, and didn't see
> an ignorant person, or one who wasn't thoughtful.
> For the ignorant dwell in the Gardens...
> Jamīl Ṣidqī al-Zahāwī, *Thawra fī l-jaḥīm*[1]

When, in 1931, the Iraqi poet and philosopher Jamīl Ṣidqī al-Zahāwī (d. 1936) published his satirical poem, *Revolution in Hell* (*Thawra fī l-jaḥīm*), he met with public outrage. From the pulpits in Baghdad, al-Zahāwī was denounced as a heretic and atheist.[2] According to al-Zahāwī's visionary tour of the otherworld, which is presented as a dream occasioned by a dish seasoned with watercress,[3] hell is where the philosophers and rationalists are, the forward-thinking spirits that Islam traditionally condemns to eternal punishment: Avicenna, Ibn Rushd, and Naṣīr al-Dīn Ṭūsī, but also Socrates, Epicurus, Voltaire, and Spinoza, to name just a few. Fired up by the passionate address of a young revolutionary, and with the aid of infernal weaponry developed by a group of empirical scientists, the inhabitants of hell storm heaven and threaten to topple God's Throne. At that moment, the poet wakes up.

Modern Continuities and Discontinuities

While al-Zahāwī frames his poem in modern, scientific terms, his irreverent attitude towards traditional eschatology is hardly novel. *Revolution in Hell* gestures back to earlier literary tours of the otherworld, in

1 Zahāwī, *Thawra*, 731–2 (tr. 69).

2 See Widmer, "Der ʿirākische Dichter," 13. Cf. van Leeuwen, "Literature and religious controversy."

3 Zahāwī, *Thawra*, 739 (tr. 79). Watercress is the only edible plant that grows in the Muslim hell, i.e., in *jahannam*, hell's uppermost layer where life becomes just about bearable. See Suyūṭī, *Budūr* 480; Majlisī, *Biḥār* viii, 479.

particular al-Maʿarrī's (Syria, d. 449/1058) *The Epistle of Forgiveness* (*Risālat al-ghufrān*) and al-Wahrānī's (d. 575/1179) *The Great Dream* (*al-Manām al-aʿẓam*). In certain respects, al-Zahāwī's two medieval forerunners even surpass him in their outré brazenness and penchant for provocation. Al-Zahāwī imagines the houris in paradise with slender waists and backsides "so heavy that they can hardly move them,"[4] but in al-Maʿarrī's ironic take on the topic, the posterior of one of the heavenly maidens is enlarged to the size of hills, whereupon the protagonist of his narrative, the Aleppine poet Ibn al-Qāriḥ, entreats God "to reduce the bum of this damsel to one square mile, for Thou hast surpassed my expectations with Thy measure!"[5] The angels of the grave, in al-Zahāwī's poem, torture the poet when he declares his belief in God as an abstract natural principle, "ether" (*athīr*).[6] In *The Great Dream*, the angel Mālik grabs al-Wahrānī and drags him towards hell, and when the poet protests, Mālik unleashes a diatribe against him for being "one of the most skilled sodomites around" and for recording the names of his young male lovers in a special register, "arranged in alphabetical order."[7] Neither al-Maʿarrī nor al-Wahrānī, it is true, dare to picture the overthrow of the entire eschatological order; by contrast, al-Zahāwī, in terms reminiscent of the Marxist class struggle, has al-Maʿarrī, one of his revolutionary firebrands in hell, whip up the crowd with the slogan: "You only have miserable huts of fire, while the simpletons (*bulh*) in paradise live in castles!"[8]

While al-Zahāwī playfully flirts with the destruction of received eschatology, other Muslim modernists do not go quite as far, even though they undertake to dismantle the traditional preoccupation with the otherworld, "anxious to reinstate what they understand to be the true Islamic emphasis on the importance of *dunyā* as well as of *ākhira*, and on the strength and potential of the community in this life."[9] Mohamed Arkoun (Algeria/France, d. 2010), for example, takes issue with al-Ghazālī's allegorical interpretation of the hajj as a journey towards the afterlife. In Arkoun's view, the mentality al-Ghazālī promotes is a *maladie à la mort*, a fatal attitude that Muslims must abandon lest they privilege death over human creativity, freedom, and life.[10] Ḥassan Ḥanafī (Egypt, b. 1935), commenting on the last of the forty books in al-Ghazālī's *The Revivification of the Religious Sciences*, questions "the purpose of all this detailed description of death and life after

[4] Zahāwī, *Thawra*, 728 (tr. 64).
[5] Maʿarrī, *Risālat al-ghufrān*, 224 (tr. 225). Heavy posteriors are the typical ideal of classical Arabic poetry.
[6] Zahāwī, *Thawra*, 725 (tr. 61–2).
[7] Wahrānī, *Manām*, 29–30. On Wahrānī's *The Great Dream*, a scatological masterpiece, cf. Abu-Deeb, *The imagination unbound*, 19–30.
[8] Zahāwī, *Thawra*, 736 (tr. 76).
[9] Smith and Haddad, *The Islamic understanding*, 100.
[10] Arkoun, *Lectures du Coran*, 168.

death," suggesting that it is all about "narratives, not reason." Though granting that "to frighten and to excite are two ways in the logic of persuasion," Ḥanafī insists that "development thinking," the kind of thought he believes will help Islam to overcome its modern predicament, "is concerned with life rather than with death, with living people in urban areas in big cities such as Cairo and not with those in the grave."[11] Humankind's salvation, in the thought of modernists like Arkoun and Ḥanafī, is something that should be striven for *within* this world; narratives about the joys in heaven and the tortures in hell are an unwelcome, unsavoury distraction.[12]

This view notwithstanding, when surveying the nineteenth- and twentieth-century Muslim literature on paradise and hell, it is impossible to overlook the important continuities with the premodern tradition. These continuities, in fact, often seem as important as the discontinuities, despite the manifold challenges levelled at traditional eschatology by Western and Muslim critics steeped in modern scientism, empiricism, and rationalism.[13] One way of maintaining continuity with tradition is to reiterate and, at times, to adapt spiritual and interiorised interpretations of paradise and hell. In the Shiʿi world, for example, the eschatological thought of Mullā Ṣadrā, to this day, enjoys great, perhaps even increasing, popularity.[14] In the Sunni world, the Pakistani reformer Muhammad Iqbal (d. 1938) deserves mention. Just as al-Zahāwī updates al-Maʿarrī with terms borrowed from modern science, so Iqbal combines the eschatological thought of Ibn al-ʿArabī and Rūmī with the thought of twentieth-century Western philosophers such as Henri Bergson (d. 1941). Iqbal sees paradise and hell primarily as metaphors for the inner psychic and intellectual developments of the individual. For example, according to Iqbal, when the Quran announces that "the fire of God, kindled, ... rises over the hearts [of people]" (Q 104:6–7), this refers to no other than the painful realisation of one's failure as a human being. Paradise and hell, in Iqbal's phrase, are "states, not localities."[15]

Modern Muslim theologians seeking a closer alignment with traditional Islamic theology have tended to find Iqbal's proposals insufficiently grounded in the tradition. In the words of Fazlur Rahman (Pakistan/United States, d. 1988), "the structural elements of [Iqbal's] thought are too contemporary to be an adequate basis for an ongoing Islamic metaphysical endeavor."[16] Rahman is more sympathetic to Muḥammad ʿAbduh's (Egypt, d. 1905) attempt to "resurrect ... rationalism," an attitude he attributes to

[11] Ḥanafī, "Mysticisme et dévelopment," 181.

[12] See Hirschkind, *The ethical soundscape*, 146. The "banishment of death" as a feature of industrialised and urbanised (Western) modernity is famously described in Phillipe Ariès's *L'homme devant la mort* (1977).

[13] For a more extended discussion, see Smith and Haddad, *The Islamic understanding*, 127–46.

[14] Cf. the summary comments made by Meisami, *Mulla Sadra*, 124–6.

[15] Iqbal, "Reconstruction," 98. Cf. Smith and Haddad, *The Islamic understanding*, 138.

[16] Rahman, *Islam and modernity*, 132.

the Mu'tazila.[17] 'Abduh, in his *Epistle of Unity* (*Risālat al-tawḥīd*), judged that Muslims are not required to believe in the corporeal particulars of the afterlife, even if these are recorded in "clear" (*ẓāhir*) traditions. In his view, a general affirmation of the doctrine of life after death, including postmortem rewards and punishment, is enough, in his view, to qualify someone as a "true believer" (*mu'min ḥaqq*). A thorough rationalisation and demythologisation of traditional eschatology, however, should only be practiced by the intellectual elite (*'uqūl al-khāṣṣa*).[18] 'Abduh's student, the Salafi writer Rashīd Riḍā (d. 1935), popularised this notion in a 1921 *fatwā* published in his journal *The Lighthouse* (*al-Manār*), in a response to the question of a reader regarding how the findings of modern geography can be reconciled with the hadith stating that the Nile and Euphrates spring from paradise. Riḍā's answer is that some scholars "have suggested that the hadith construes an analogy between the sweetness, goodness and blessedness of the waters of the Nile and Euphrates and the water of paradise, by way of a rhetorical figure of speech (*'alā ṭarīq al-mubālagha*)." In Riḍā's view, "there is nothing unnatural or constrained (*takalluf*) in interpreting the hadith in this way."[19] As for the detailed descriptions of the physical contents of paradise and hell in the Qur'ān and the hadith, 'Abduh adopts a position of *bi-lā kayf*, stressing the unfathomability of these phenomena. "We believe in [paradise and hell] in terms of the World of the Unseen (*al-ghayb*)," he explains, "and we do not speak about the reality of these two matters. We do not wish to add anything categorical concerning these, because the World of the Unseen is not understood by analogy."[20]

Other modern and contemporary eschatologists in the Islamic world follow the well-trodden, traditionist path of collecting hadiths, even if they tend to align this endeavour with the linguistic, esthetic, moral, and sectarian conventions familiar to their audiences. In this genre, the work of the Ibāḍī scholar from the Mzab, Muḥammad Iṭfayyish (Algeria, d. 1917), entitled *The Shelter in the Description of Paradise* (*al-Junna fī waṣf al-janna*), is one of the most creative contributions, a verse-by-verse commentary on a sixth/twelfth-century poem on paradise, enriched with citations from the Qur'ān and the hadith, some poetry, as well as sayings of early pious figures such as Ḥasan al-Baṣrī.[21] The *Waystations of the Otherworld* (*Manāzil al-ākhira*) of

[17] Ibid. 153.

[18] 'Abduh, *Risālat al-tawḥīd (b. al-taṣdīq bi-mā jā'a bihi Muḥammad)*, 178.

[19] Riḍā, "Khurūj al-Nīl wa-l-Furāt," 262. Characteristically, Riḍā only accepts the oldest and simplest versions of the hadith, while rejecting the more elaborate and flowery traditions of Late Medieval literature, e.g. certain popular versions of the *mi'rāj*. Cf. Stieglecker, *Glaubenslehren*, 796–8.

[20] 'Abdūh, *Tafsīr*, I, 231–2 (*ad* Q 2:25), quoted in Smith and Haddad, *The Islamic understanding*, 140.

[21] Iṭfayyish, *Junna*. The poem Iṭfayyish comments on is *al-'Ābiriyya fī waṣf al-janna* by Muḥammad b. Ibrāhīm al-Kindī (d. 507/1114). On these two works, see Custers, *Al-Ibāḍiyya*, I, 230, II, 132.

FIGURE 24. Book cover of Manṣūr ʿAbd al-Ḥakīm, *Khāzin al-nār Mālik* (*The Guardian of Hell Mālik*). Damascus-Cairo 2008.

the Shiʿi scholar from Qum, ʿAbbās al-Qummī (Iran, d. 1941), compiler of the much used prayer book entitled *Keys of the Gardens* (*Mafātīḥ al-jinān*), is another noteworthy example. Conceiving of his work as a pious guide to the afterlife, al-Qummī does not devote much attention to paradise and hell as such, but arranges Shiʿi hadiths and exhortatory stories around the various stations traversed by the believer at the moment of death, life in the *barzakh*, resurrection, the Scales, and so forth.[22] Perhaps what one sees in al-Qummī's treatment is a "modern" turn towards praxis, where the way to get to paradise is more important than the destination.

In comparison, neo-Salafi works of traditionist eschatology, written around the turn of the twentieth century, stick more closely to premodern patterns. Since at least the 1980s, a great number of such works have been published, both in a popular and a scholarly vein.[23] *The Last Day* (*al-Yawm*

[22] Qummī, *Manāzil*.

[23] A noteworthy recent publication is the glossy *Encyclopaedia of the Otherworld* (*Mawsūʿat al-ākhira*) of the Emirati scholar Māhir Aḥmad Ṣūfī (2007), which seems based on a flurry of earlier publications by the same author. Cf. Lohlker and Nowak, "Das islamische

al-ākhir) of ʿUmar Sulaymān al-Ashqar (d. 2012), a Palestinian professor of Sharia law in Kuwait and Amman, can serve to illustrate a couple of points.[24] The arrangement of topics in *The Last Day*, as well as the combination of Qurʾānic verses, hadiths, and some commentary, is not much different from, say, al-Qurṭubī's *Memoir* or al-Saffārīnī's *Swelling Oceans*.[25] In other respects, however, there are some innovations in al-Ashqar's treatment. Showing the influence of his teacher, the prominent Salafi thinker Muḥammad al-Albānī (d. 1999), al-Ashqar breaks with centuries of previous scholarship in the sense that hadiths, for him, are simply either true or false. There is no room for grading hadiths into numerous categories of soundness according to the reliability of their *isnād*s. Further, though he looks up to Ibn Qayyim al-Jawziyya as a forefather of modern Salafism, al-Ashqar rejects the doctrine of the "demise of hell" (*fanāʾ al-nār*).[26] By contrast, ʿAbduh and Riḍā were advocates of *fanāʾ al-nār*, an idea that is also embraced by the likes of Ismail Hakkı İzmirli (Turkey, d. 1946), Mawlana Muhammad Ali (India, d. 1951), Elija Muhammad (United States, d. 1975), and, more recently, Yūsuf al-Qaraḍāwī (Egypt/Qatar, b. 1926) and Muḥammad Ḥabash (Syria, b. 1962).[27]

Al-Ashqar interprets the hadith that there are seventy-three confessional groups (*firaq*) in Islam, of which only one goes to paradise, in view of his own sectarian beliefs. To the one saved group (*al-firqa al-nājiya*), according to him, belong all those who hold fast to the Qurʾān and the Sunna. Some of the remaining seventy-two groups, such as the Muʿtazilites, Khārijities, and Twelver Shiʿites suffer a temporary punishment in the hereafter; only "extreme" groups such as the Ismaʿilis, Druze, and Alevites are forever in

Paradies," 221–2. Also specialised works of eschatological hadiths continue to be compiled. See Shinnāwī, *Mashāhir nisāʾ ahl al-nār*; idem, *Nisāʾ ahl al-janna*; ʿAṭā, *ʿUlamāʾ fī l-janna wa-ʿulamāʾ fī l-nār*; ʿAbd al-Ḥakīm, *Khāzin al-nār*.

[24] According to al-Ashqar, when *The Last Day* was first published in 1986 (in Kuwait), the print run of five thousand copies was sold out within a couple of months, so that a second print run of ten thousand was issued. In 1998, a Saudi-based publisher, al-Dār al-ʿĀlamiyya li-l-Kitāb al-Islāmī, agreed with al-Ashqar that *The Last Day* would be translated into twenty-five languages. See Ashqar, *Ṣafaḥāt*, 145. The English translation of *The Last Day*, first published in 1999, went into its fourth edition in 2003. There are also translations into Spanish (2003) and French (2007). See further, Lange, "Contemporary Salafi literature."

[25] See the preceding text, Chapter 2, pp. 87, 89–90.

[26] Ashqar, *Yawm*, 44–6. On attempts by contemporary Muslim theologians to argue that Ibn Taymiyya and Ibn Qayyim al-Jawziyya actually affirmed the eternity of hell, see Hoover, "Against Islamic Universalism."

[27] On Riḍā and al-Qaraḍāwī, see Ryad, "Eschatology." On Hakkı, see Kaya, "İzmirli Ismail Hakkı." On Muhammad Ali and Elijah Muhammad, see Khalil, *Islam and the fate of others*, 102–6. James Robson's 1938 article "Is the Moslem hell eternal?" is a response to Muhammad Ali's view, as expressed in his 1936 *The religion of Islam*. On Ḥabash, see Heck, "Religious renewal in Syria." Also Maḥmūd, *Jughrāfiyyat al-maldhdhāt*, 408, defends the idea vigourously.

hell.[28] In his discussion of the hadith that "most of the inhabitants of hell are women," al-Ashqar first quotes a long passage from al-Qurṭubī, in which he rehearses the stock repertoire of arguments regarding why women are less likely to enter paradise: they suffer from a deficiency in intellectual ability (*nuqṣān al-ʿuqūl*); are too attached to the ephemeral world of the here and now; are subject to uncontrollable passions; and so forth. Al-Ashqar then adds that, "in spite of this, many women are good and pious (*ṣāliḥāt*) ... and a great number of them enter paradise, including those who are superior to many a man in terms of the soundness of their belief and their pious actions."[29] Such lip service to female emancipation does little to veil the chauvinism of neo-Salafi thought. In comparison, even al-Saffārīnī's explanation, quoted in Chapter 2, seems more balanced.[30]

In many modern and contemporary publications, one observes a certain prudishness regarding the sexual joys in paradise. ʿAbduh, for example, undertakes to sanitise the houris, declaring them to be no other than the rejuvenated earthly wives of the believers, even though, in a typical move, he also allocates them to the order of the fathomless.[31] An editorial footnote in the 1968 Saudi edition of *The End of the Beginning* (*Nihāyat al-bidāya*) of Ibn Kathīr[32] explains that "the Prophet's answer to the question whether the people in Paradise would touch their wives was omitted from this edition because it contains coarse language which the Prophet would never have used."[33] In 1984, the Egyptian journalist Muḥammad Jalāl Kishk (d. 1993) published a book in which he openly affirmed the existence of bisexual relations in paradise; the authorities of al-Azhar University in Cairo quickly tried to suppress Kishk's work.[34] As for al-Ashqar, he simply shuns any discussion of the question of homosexuality in paradise.

In sum, modern and contemporary traditionist works of eschatology, especially those written by Salafi and traditionalist authors, reproduce much of what is found in the premodern literature, but they also indulge the preferences of their modern readerships, making traditional teachings more easily digestible by simplifying *isnād*s and insisting on the transparency of the sources, and by interpreting hadiths in such a way as to buttress their moral and sectarian convictions. Finally, it should be mentioned that medieval works of eschatology like the anonymous *Subtle Traditions* (*Daqāʾiq al-akhbār*), *Causing Fear of the Fire* by Ibn Rajab al-Ḥanbalī, and

28 Ashqar, *Yawm*, 63.

29 Ibid., 83–4. Similarly in Ṣūfī, *Mawsūʿat al-ākhira*, III, 294; Ṭahṭāwī, *Naʿīm*, 27.

30 See the preceding text, p. 90.

31 ʿAbduh, *Tafsīr*, I, 233. ʿAlī al-Ṭahṭāwī, a professor at al-Azhar University, in his chapter on the "women in paradise," only refers to the "purified" earthly wives of the believers. See Ṭaḥṭāwī, *Naʿīm*, 51. Cf. Smith and Haddad, *The Islamic understanding*, 166.

32 On this work, see the preceding text, Chapter 2, pp. 85–6.

33 Ibn Kathīr, *Bidāya*, II, 292–3. Cf. Rosenthal, "Reflections on love," 248n7.

34 Kishk, *Khawāṭir*, 114. Cf. Massad, *Desiring Arabs*, 203–4; al-Azmeh, "Rhetoric," 216.

the *Memoir* of al-Qurṭubī are republished frequently in Arabic lands and beyond, and are widely on sale in bookshops and on street corners all over the Islamic world.[35] In fact, traditionist eschatology appears to be a particularly apt illustration of the fact, easily observable by even the casual visitor of bookshops in Casablanca, Cairo, or Tehran, that medieval Arabic books continue to claim a dominant place in contemporary Muslim publishing.

The Disappearing Boundary

Here is not the place to study the full gamut of the modern and postmodern permutations of the traditional picture of paradise and hell, a topic that, as I noted in the introduction, invites fuller treatment in a separate book. My aim in the preceding paragraphs has been to offer a brief sketch of the directions in which discussions in Islam, specifically, the Arabic-speaking parts of the Islamic world have moved over the last two hundred years or so. As I noted, the major, premodern approaches to the otherworld find continued expression. One encounters ironic and playful literary engagements, the move towards allegorical and spiritualised interpretations, and the stress on the unfathomability of the otherworld; but also one sees the insistence on the belief in the apparent sense of the Qur'ān and hadith corpus. The only fundamental break with the tradition is the proposal of some thinkers to relativise radically the belief in paradise and hell, not in order to deny the reality (*ḥaqq*) of the otherworld but to subvert the logical and moral primacy of *al-ākhira* over *al-dunyā*. However, whether this new perspective amounts to a full paradigm shift, or whether it remains limited to (semi-)secularised, peripheral groups, is unclear. Whether the contemporary Islamic world will undergo a further secularisation in this respect, or whether traditional positions will become more entrenched, I am in no position to predict. In my view, contemporary Muslim terrorists, who trade in promises of immediate entrance to heaven for getting killed fighting so-called infidels, are not driven by the thought of paradise, at least not primarily. Political, not eschatological motives best explain their violence, a fact that is occasionally obscured by the attention that observers lavish on the houris that allegedly await these terrorists.[36]

The purpose of this book has been to take stock of the many different imaginings of paradise and hell that have developed in the course of Islamic religious history until the age of modernity. In conclusion, let me highlight, once more, the larger narratives that shape common perceptions

[35] Also digests of classical works continue to be published, see, e.g., Zāyid, *Mukhtaṣar al-Tadhkira*. A compilation of *ṣaḥīḥ* hadiths on paradise and hell is Bālī, *Waṣf al-janna wa-l-nār*.

[36] For examples of contemporary jihad rhetoric that taps into traditional paradise imagery, see Lohlker and Nowak, "Das islamische Paradies," 200–3.

of Islamic eschatology, and the ways in which this book may help us to think about them.

First of all, readers will notice that I have devoted considerable attention in my account to hell. Not only have I felt the need to rehabilitate the Muslim hell as a subject worthy of scholars' attention, but also the sources have suggested this approach. This casts doubt on the common assumption that Muslims of all times and places have enjoyed an overwhelming certainty of salvation. Of course, salvific optimism remains a strong characteristic of the tradition, particularly in Ashʿarī and, to a lesser extent, Māturīdī *kalām*. However, when writing a thematic history of Islamic religious history, such as the one proposed here, one must not fall hostage to a *kalām*-centred approach. When we broaden our range of sources and historical contexts of study, as I have attempted in this book, things quickly become a great deal more complex. Salvific optimism and the fear of hell never existed in pure form, but were always entangled with each other according to different ratios, depending on time and place.

Secondly, as I noted in the introduction, the question of the somaticity of the Muslim afterlife has exercised commentators for centuries. That much of Islamic eschatology uses sensual imagery, and that it does so in remarkably unabashed and also creative ways, has, I hope, become clear during the course of this book. That this use of sensual imagery is phallocentric and at times misogynist should require no reiteration. What, in addition, I have sought to highlight is that there was vigourous debate, in various Muslim intellectual traditions, about the modality of the "reality" (*ḥaqq*) of the sensual pleasures and pains of paradise and hell, as well as of the otherworld as a whole. A salient development in these discussions is the emergence of the imagination (*khayāl*) as a key concept in Muslim understandings of the otherworld. If, as stated in the introduction, the theme of boundary crossing between *al-dunyā* and *al-ākhira* runs like a bass line through this book, the concept of the imagination is its recurring leitmotif. This is so in two different but related ways. First, as I have maintained throughout this book, paradise and hell are theatres of and for the imagination, canvasses upon which Muslim eschatologists projected their hopes for a better life and their fears of enduring misery. If we are willing momentarily to listen to this symphony, a concert of heavenly voices in some instances, a hellish cacophony in others, we will be able to lay aside once and for all the notion that the Islamic eschatological imagination is impoverished in comparison with that of other religious traditions, in particular the Christian one. Second, the rise to prominence of the imagination as an ontological and epistemological concept in Muslim eschatology led to it becoming entangled with the developing canon of eschatological imagery in complex ways. While the older, alternative conceptualisations of the otherworld that stressed its corporeality, incorporeality, or unfathomability continued to flourish, the idea that the particulars of the otherworld possessed their own kind of imaginal reality gradually spread from the seminal writings of Avicenna, a-Ghazalı, al-Suhrawardī, and Ibn al-ʿArabī into more mainstream eschatological thought, particularly, but not exclusively, in the Shīʿi world. Broadening our sources not just by including materials other than *kalām* and hadith narratives, but by pushing our study into the Late Medieval and early modern centuries of Islamic religious history, has helped us to excavate this important strand of thought.

The imagination is a human faculty located in between the concrete and the abstract. It does not produce pure thought, because its characteristic *modus operandi* is *bricolage*: the combination of visual perceptions, stored in the brain, into new images. This in-betwixt nature of the imagination also determines its role in eschatological thought, where it serves to bridge the space between this world and the otherworld. In the introduction, I proposed a list of go-betweens, that is, of objects and substances that Muslim traditions picture as moving back and forth between *al-dunyā* and *al-ākhira*. In the course of this book, I provided some more examples. To this list, we may now add the imagination, a faculty that epitomises the pervasive sense of slippage between the here and the hereafter that I have highlighted in this book. In my account, I have repeatedly suspended the binary *dunyā/ākhira* and instead emphasised the continuous exchange and overlap between the two realms, stressing what connects the two realms, not what separates them. Although others will prefer different readings of the evidence, I suggest that this slippage is characteristic of the sources, not of my own preconceived ideas about them.

The Qurʾān, as I have argued, plays a formative role in this. Its eschatological tenor is to see this world and the otherworld as a *merismos*, an integrated whole. The traditionist and exegetical literature, in its striking propensity to conceive of this world and the otherworld as temporally synchronous and spatially contiguous realms, follows suit. This is particularly conspicuous in traditions about the *barzakh*, but the sense of interconnectedness is also visible in traditions that describe instances of boundary crossing between *al-dunyā* and *al-ākhira*, or showcase what I have called, in Chapter 4, the geomorphisation of the otherworld. It is true, collectors of eschatological traditions such al-Suyūṭī and al-Majlisī remain ambivalent about this issue, and they do relate reports that militate against the erosion of the boundary between this world and the next. However, they also provide numerous examples of how this world and the otherworld overlap. For example, while the bodies of the blessed and the damned are in many respects unreal – think of their perpetual purity, or their capacity for endless pleasure and pain – the bodily adornments, architecture, material culture, and rituals of pleasure and punishment that they experience add up to a decidedly worldly environment, a milieu in which the markers of human civilisation on earth are writ large. While there is unrestricted visibility and sexual availability in paradise, in contrast to the scopic and sexual régimes that are in place on earth, the Islamic paradise and hell also demonstrate the concern with privacy and protection of the family (or the lack thereof, respectively). And while social injustices will be put right in the otherworld – tyrants will be punished, the poor will enter paradise before the rich, and so forth – it is clear that the social and moral taxonomies that govern medieval Islamic society are mimicked in paradise and hell. In sum, the society of the living and the society of the dead are knit together closely.

The continuum between *al-dunyā* and *al-ākhira* that I am driving at is, in the majority of cases, not made explicit by the Muslim eschatologists, who will prefer, if pressed, to assert the diachronic succession of *al-dunyā* and *al-ākhira* and talk about paradise and hell as uncertain realities in the distant future. Such is certainly the case for the discourse of *kalām*, even if, as I showed in Chapter 5, the contiguity and synchronicity of paradise, hell, and this world was generally upheld. However, I plead for thinking about Islamic eschatology in terms broader than the tradition of *kalām* ostensibly allows for. Discourses on the otherworld in Islam are, to reprise a term I used in the introduction, teleographies. Certain clusters of eschatological hadiths (Chapter 4), not to mention traditions of realised eschatology in Islamic mysticism and philosophy (Chapters 5 through 7), in addition to the topographical, architectural, and ritual realisations of paradise and hell on earth (Chapter 8), all add up to the impression that in much of premodern Muslim thought, the boundary between *al-dunyā* and *al-ākhira* is permeable. This permeability, or even the recurring disappearance of this boundary, is what merits more sustained attention by scholars studying Islamic eschatology; not the fact that it seals this world off from the otherworld. Arguably, modern criticisms of the "otherworldliness" of traditional Islam, in this perspective, miss the point. In much of premodern Islamic eschatology, *al-ākhira* does not aim to eclipse *al-dunyā*. Rather, it informs the present and provides it with layers of religious meaning. In Islam, the enduring promise of paradise and hell is not the escape to an unreal world of dreams, nor is it the apocalyptic imminence of the world to come, but the ability of the otherworld to sanctify life in the here and now.

Primary Sources

Non-Muslim

1 Enoch. Translated by E. Isaac. In *OTP*, Vol. 1, pp. 5–89.
2 Enoch. Translated by F. I. Andersen. In *OTP*, Vol. 1, pp. 91–221.
3 (Hebrew) Enoch. Translated by P. Alexander. In *OTP*, Vol. 1, pp. 223–302.
4 Ezra. Translated by B. M. Metzger. In *OTP*, Vol. 1, pp. 517–60.
Acts of Thomas, Translated by J. K. Elliott. In *ANT*, pp. 439–511.
Apocalypse of Abraham. Translated by R. Rubinkiewicz. In *OTP*, Vol. 1, pp. 681–706.
Apocalypse of Paul. Translated by J. K. Elliott. In *ANT*, pp. 616–44.
Apocalypse of Peter. Translated by J. K. Elliott. In *ANT*, pp. 593–612.
Aphrahat, *Homilies*. Translated by G. Bert. *Aphrahat's des persischen Weisen Homilien*. Leipzig: J. C. Hinrichs, 1888.
Ardāvīrāfnāmak. Transliterated and translated by Philippe Gignoux. *Le livre d'Ardā Vīrāz*. Paris: Éditions recherche sur les civilisations, 1984.
Cave of Treasures. *See Meʿarrat gazze.*
Derek ereẓ-zuṭa. In *The minor tractates of the Talmud*. Translated by A. Cohen. London: Soncino Press, 1965, Vol. 2, pp. 567–98.
Ephrem. *Commentary on Genesis*. In Edward G. Mathews and Joseph P. Amar (trs.). *The Fathers of the Church:* Vol. 91: *St. Ephrem the Syrian: Selected prose works*. Washington, DC: The Catholic University of America Press, 1994, pp. 67–216.
"Eine Rede der Zurechtweisung des Mar Ephräm, des Seligen." In Edmund Beck (tr.). *Des heiligen Ephraem des Syrers Sermones* (Corpus scriptorum Christianorum Orientalium v. 312, Scriptores Syri t. 135), Leuven: Secrétariat du Corpus SCO, 1970, Vol. 2, pp. 54–71.
Hymns of paradise. Translated by Sebastian Brock. Crestwood, NY: St. Vladimir's Seminary Press, 1990.
"Letter to Publius." In Edward G. Mathews and Joseph P. Amar (trs.). The Fathers of the Church, Vol. 91: *St. Ephrem the Syrian: Selected prose works*. Washington, DC: The Catholic University of America Press, 1994, pp. 335–55.
Nisibene Hymns. Translated by J. T. Sarsfield Stopford. In *A select library of the Nicene and post-Nicene fathers of the Christian Church, Second series*, Vol.

XIII: *Gregory the Great (II), Ephraim Syrus, Aphrahat*. Edited by Ph. Schaff and H. Wace. First published 1890–1900. Grand Rapids, MI: W. B. Eerdmanns, 1978–9, pp. 165–219.

"Poem about the Judgment and Resurrection of the Dead." In *Chrestomathia Syriaca*. Edited by Emil Roediger. Halle: Sumtibus Orphanotropei, 1868, pp. 77–84.

"Sermo in pretiosam et vivificam crucem." In *Sancti patris nostri Ephraem Syri, opera omnia*. 6 vols. Edited by J. S. Assemani. Rome: Ex Typographia Vaticana, 1743–6, Vol. 2, pp. 247–58.

Ethiopic Apocalypse of Baruch. Translated by Wolf Leslau. *Falasha anthology*. New Haven, CT: Yale University Press, 1951, pp. 64–76, 162–72.

Genesis Rabbah. In *Midrash Rabbah*. 10 vols. Translated under the editorship of H. Freedman. London: Soncino Press, 1939–51, vols. 1–2.

Gospel of Nicodemus. Translated by by J. K. Elliott. In *ANT*, pp. 169–204.

Goethe, Johann Wolfgang von. *West-östlicher Divan*. 2 vols. Frankfurt am Main: Deutscher Klassiker Verlag, 1994.

Jacob of Serugh. *Quatre homélies métriques sur la création*. Translated by Khalil Alwan. Leuven: Peeters, 1989.

Łewond, *History*. Translated by Zaven Arzoumanian. *History of Lewond the eminent Vardapet of the Armenians*. Wynnewood, PA: St. Sahag and St. Mesrob Armenian Church, 1982.

Meʿarrat gazze. 2 vols. Edited and translated by Su-Min Ri. *La Caverne des trésors. Les deux recensions syriaques*. Louvain: Peeters, 1987.

Montesquieu, *Lettres persanes*. First published 1721. Paris: Éditions Gallimard, 1973.

Narsai. *Homélies de Narsaï sur la création*. Edited and translated by Phillipe Gignoux. Turnhout and Paris: Brepols, 1968.

Numbers Rabbah. In *Midrash Rabbah*. 10 vols. Translated under the editorship of H. Freedman. London: Soncino Press, 1939–51, vols. 5–6.

Persius. *Satires*. Edited by A. Perreau. *A. Persius Flaccus cum interpretatione Latina*. Paris: Colligebat N. E. Lemaire, 1830.

Pius II (Aeneas Silvius Piccolomini). *Epistola ad Mahomatem* (*Epistle to Mehmed II*). Edited and translated by Albert R. Baca. New York: Peter Lang, 1990.

Plotinus. *Enneads IV, 1–9*. Translated by A. H. Armstrong. Cambridge, MA: Harvard University Press, 1984.

Polo, Marco. *The Book of Ser Marco Polo, the Venetian*. Edited and translated by Henry Yule. 2 vols. 3rd rev. ed. by Henri Cordier. New York: Scribner, 1903.

Sybilline Oracles. Translated by J. J. Collins. In *OTP*, Vol. 1, pp. 317–472.

Uthūlūjiyā Arisṭāṭālīs. In *Aflaṭūn ʿinda l-ʿarab*. Edited by ʿAbd al-Raḥmān Badawī. Cairo: Maktabat al-Nahḍa al-Miṣriyya, 1955.

Zartusht-i Bahrām. *Ardāvīrāfnāma-yi manẓūm*. Edited by Raḥīm ʿAfīfī. Mashhad: Chāpkhāna-yi Dānishgāh-i Mashhad, 1343sh/[1964].

Muslim

ʿAbd al-Ḥakīm, Manṣūr. *Khāzin al-nār Mālik ʿalayhi l-salām*. Damascus and Cairo: Dār al-Kitāb al-ʿArabī, 2008.

ʿAbd al-Jabbār b. Aḥmad al-Asadābādī. *Al-Mughnī fī abwāb al-tawḥīd wa-l-ʿadl.* Cairo: Wizārat al-Thaqāfa wa-l-Irshāf al-Qawmī, [195-?]–[196-?].
ʿAbd al-Razzāq al-Ṣanʿānī. *Al-Muṣannaf fī l-ḥadīth.* Edited by Ḥabīb al-Raḥmān al-Aʿẓamī. 11 vols. Beirut: Al-Maktab al-Islāmī, 1970.
ʿAbduh, Muḥammad. *Risālat al-tawḥīd.* First publ. 1897. Beirut: Dār al-Shurūq, 1414/1994.
Tafsīr al-Qurʾān al-karīm. Cairo: s.n., 1927.
Abū Dāwūd, Sulaymān b. al-Ashʿath. *Sunan.* Edited by Muḥammad Muḥyī l-Dīn ʿAbd al-Ḥamīd. 4 vols. in 2. Cairo: Al-Maktaba al-Tijāriyya al-Kubrā, [1935?].
Abū Nuʿaym al-Iṣfahānī, Aḥmad b. ʿAbdallāh. *Ḥilyat al-awliyāʾ wa-ṭabaqāt al-aṣfiyāʾ.* 10 vols. Cairo: Maktabat al-Khānjī, 1352–7/1932–8.
Ṣifat al-janna. Edited by ʿAlī Riḍā b. ʿAbdallāh b. ʿAlī Riḍā. 3 vols. in 1. Beirut: Dār al-Maʾmūn li-l-Turāth, 1410/1995, 2nd ed.
Abū ʿUdhba al-Ḥasan b. ʿAbd al-Muḥsin. *Al-Rawḍah al-bahiyyah fī-mā bayna l-Ashāʿirah wa l Māturīdiyyah.* In *Al-Musāʾil al-khilāfiyyha bayna Ashaʿirah wa-l-Māturīdiyyah.* Edited by Bassām ʿAbd al-Wahhāb al-Jābī. Limassol: al-Jaffān wa-al-Jābī lil-Ṭibāʿah wa-al-Nashr; Beirut: Dār Ibn Ḥazm, 2003, pp. 79–163.
Aflākī, Shams al-Dīn Aḥmad. *Manāqib al-ʿārifīn.* Edited by Taḥsīn Yāzijī. 2 vols. Ankara: Chāpkhāna-yi Anjuman-i Tārīkh-i Turk, 1959–61.
al-Aḥsāʾī, Shaykh Aḥmad. *Jawāmiʿ al-kalim.* 2 vols. Tabriz: s.n., 1273–6/1856–9.
K. Sharḥ al-ziyāra. 2 vols. Tabriz: s.n., 1276/1859.
Aḥwāl al-qiyāma. See Daqāʾiq al-akhbār.
al-Ahwāzī, al-Ḥusayn b. Saʿīd. *K. al-Zuhd.* Edited by Mahdī Ghulāmʿalī. Qum: Dār al-Ḥadīth, 1384sh/[2005–6].
Aḥwāl-i qiyāmat. MS KK Hofbibliothek Vienna 1700, fols. 31v–48r.
Aḥwāl-i qiyāmat. MS Staatsbibliothek Berlin Or. Oct. 1596.
Alf layla wa-layla. See The Arabian Nights.
ʿAlī al-Riḍā b. Mūsā. *Musnad al-Riḍā.* Edited by Jawād al-Ḥusaynī al-Jalālī. Qum: Maktab al-Iʿlām al-Islāmī, 1418/[1998].
ʿAlwān (Shaykh), ʿAlī b. ʿAṭiyya. *Nasamāt al-asḥār fī manāqib al-awliyāʾ.* MS Damascus 8460.
al-Āmidī, ʿAlī b. Abī ʿAlī. *Abkār al-afkār fī uṣūl al-dīn.* Edited by Aḥmad Muḥammad al-Mahdī. 5 vols. Cairo: Dār al-Kutub wa-l-Wathāʾiq al-Qaymiyya, 2002.
Al-Iḥkām fī uṣūl al-aḥkām. Edited by Sayyid al-Jumaylī. 4 vols. in 2. Beirut: Dār al-Kitāb al-ʿArabī, 1404/1983.
al-ʿĀmilī, Muḥsin al-Ḥusaynī. *Aʿyān al-shīʿa.* Edited by Ḥasan al-Amīn. Beirut: Maṭbaʿat al-Inṣaf, 1960–.
al-Anṣārī, ʿAbdallāh. *Risāla-yi Qalandarnāma.* In *Rasāʾil-i jāmiʿ-i ʿārif-i qarn-i chahārum-i hijrī Khwāja ʿAbdallāh Anṣārī.* Edited by Vahīd Dastgirdī. Tehran: Majalla-yi Armaghān, 1347sh/1968, pp. 92–9.
Arkoun, Mohamed, *Lectures du Coran.* Paris: G.-P. Maisonneuve et Larose, 1982.
Asad b. Mūsā. *K. al-Zuhd.* Edited by Rudolf Leszynski. *Mohammedanische Traditionen über das Jüngste Gericht. Eine vergleichende Studie zur jüdisch-christlichen und mohammedanischen Eschatologie.* Phd Heidelberg 1909. Also edited by Raif Georges Khoury. *Kitāb al-zuhd. Nouvelle édition, corrigée et augmentée de tous les certificats de lecture d'après les deux copies de Berlin et de Damas avec une étude sur l'auteur.* Wiesbaden: O. Harrassowitz, 1976.

al-Ashʿarī, ʿAlī b. Ismāʿīl. *Al-Ibāna ʿan uṣūl al-diyāna*. Hyderabad: Dāʾirat al-Maʿārif al-Niẓāmiyya, 1321/[1903]).

Maqālāt al-Islamiyyīn. Edited by Helmut Ritter. Istanbul: Devlet Matbaasi, 1929–30.

al-Ashqar, ʿUmar Sulaymān. *Ṣafaḥāt min ḥayātī*. Amman: Dār al-Nafāʾis li-l-Nashr wa-l-Tawzīʿ, 1430/2010.

Al-yawm al-ākhir, Vol. III: *Al-janna wa-l-nār*. Amman: Dār al-Nafāʾis li-l-Nashr wa-l-Tawzīʿ, 1991.

ʿAṭā, Rabīʿ ʿAbd Ribḥ. *ʿUlamāʾ fī l-janna wa-ʿulamāʾ fī l-nār*. Cairo: Markaz al-Rāyah, [1998].

ʿAṭṭār, Farīd al-Dīn. *Tadhkirat al-awliyāʾ*. Edited by Reynold A. Nicholson. *Memoirs of the saints*. London: Luzac, 1905–7.

al-ʿAynī, Maḥmūd b. Aḥmad. *ʿUmdat al-qārī sharḥ al-Bukhārī*. 25 vols. Cairo: Idārat al-Ṭibāʿa al-Munīriyya, 1983.

Avicenna. *See* Ibn Sīna.

ʿAyn al-Quḍāt al-Hamadhānī. *Tamhīdāt*. Tehran: Dānishgāh-i Tihrān, 1341sh/[1962].

al-Azraqī, Muḥammad b. ʿAbdallāh. *Akhbār Makka sharrafahā Allāhu taʿāla wa-mā jāʾa fīhā min al-akhbār*. Edited by Ferdinand Wüstenfeld. *Die Chroniken der Stadt Mekka, Bd. 1*. Leipzig: Brockhaus, 1858.

Bābā Afḍal al-Dīn, Muḥammad Maraqī Kāshānī. *Jāvidān-nāma*. In *Muṣannafāt-i Afḍal-al-Dīn Muḥammad Maraqī Kāshānī*. Edited by Mujtabā Mīnuvī and Yaḥyā Mahdawī. 2 vols. Tehran: Dānishgāh-i Tihrān, 1331–7sh/[1952–8], pp. 259–326.

al-Badawī, ʿAbd al-Raḥmān. *Shaṭaḥāt al-Ṣūfiyya: Juzʾ 1: Abū Yazīd al-Basṭāmī*. Cairo: Maktabat al-Nahḍa al-Miṣriyya, 1949.

al-Baghdādī, ʿAbd al-Qāhir b. Ṭāhir. *Al-farq bayna l-firaq*. Edited by Muḥammad Badr. Cairo: Maṭbaʿat al-Maʿārif, 1328/[1910].

al-Baghdādī, Ismāʿīl Bāshā. *Hadiyat al-ʿārifīn, asmāʾ al-muʾāllifīn wa-āthār al-muṣannifīn*. Istanbul: s.n., 1955–7.

al-Bahrānī, Hāshim b. Sulaymān. *Maʿālim al-zulfā fī maʿārif al-nashāt al-ūlā wa-l-ukhrā*. Edited by Muʾassasat Iḥyāʾ al-Kutub al-Islāmiyya. 3 vols. Qum: Intishārāt-i Nawrūḥī, 1430/[2009].

Nuzhat al-abrār wa-manār al-anẓār fī khalq al-janna wa-l-nār. Edited by Fāris Ḥassūn Karīm. Qum: Maktabat Fadak li-Iḥyāʾ al-Turāth, [2007].

al-Baḥrānī, Sulaymān b. ʿAbdallāh al-Baḥrānī. *Fī walad al-zinā wa-mā warada fīhi*. MS Staatsbibliothek Berlin Pm 505, fols. 10a–12a.

al-Bājūrī, Ibrāhīm b. Muḥammad. *Tuḥfat al-murīd ʿalā Jawharat al-tawḥīd*. Cairo: Muṣṭafā al-Bābī al-Ḥalabī, 1358/[1939].

al-Bākharzī, ʿAlī b. al-Ḥasan b. ʿAlī. *Dumyat al-qaṣr fī ʿuṣrat ahl al-ʿaṣr*. Edited by Muḥammad al-Tūnjī, 3 vols. Beirut: Dār al-Jīl, 1414/1993.

al-Bakrī, Abū l-Ḥasan Aḥmad b. ʿAbdallāh (attr.). *Ḥadīth al-miʿrāj ʿalā l-tamām wa-l-kamāl*. MS Istanbul Süleymaniye Kütüphanesi, Amcazade Hüsayın Paša 95–2.

Bālī, Waḥīd ʿAbd al-Salām. *Waṣf al-janna wa-l-nār min ṣaḥīḥ al-akhbār*. Beirut: Dār al-Kutub al-ʿIlmiyya, 1407/1987.

Baqlī, Ruzbihan. *Sharḥ-i shaṭḥiyyāt*. Edited by Henry Corbin. *Commentaire sur les paradoxes des soufis*. Tehran and Paris: Departement d'iranologie de l'institut franco-iranien, 1966.

ʿAbhar al-ʿāshiqīn. Edited by H. Corbin and M. Moen. *Le jasmin des fidèles d'amour*. Tehran and Paris: Département d'iranologie de l'institut franco-iranien, 1958.

Basṭāmī, Abū Yazīd. *See* al-Badawī, *Shataḥāt*; Ritter, "Aussprüche."

al-Bayḍāwī, ʿAbdallāh b. ʿUmar. *Anwār al-tanzīl wa-asrār al-taʾwīl*. 2 vols. Cairo: Muṣṭafā al-Bābī al-Ḥalabī, 1388/1968.

al-Bayhaqī, Aḥmad b. al-Ḥusayn. *K. al-Baʿth wa-l-nushūr*. Edited by ʿĀmir Aḥmad Ḥaydar. Beirut: Markaz al-Khidmāt wa-l-Abḥāth al-Thaqāfiyya, 1406/1986.

Dalāʾil al-nubuwwa wa-maʿrifat aḥwāl ṣaḥib al-sharīʿa. Edited by ʿAbd al-Muʿṭī Qalʿajī. 7 vols. Beirut: Dār al-Kutub al-ʿIlmiyya, 1405/1985.

Ithbāt ʿadhāb al-qabr wa-suʾāl al-malakayn. Edited by Abū Hājir M. al-Saʿīd al-Zaghlūl and Abū l-Fidāʾ ʿAbdallāh al-Qāḍī. Cairo: Maktabat al-Turāth al-Islāmī, [1986].

Shuʿab al-īmān. Edited by M. Basyūnī Zaghlūl. 7 vols. Beirut: Dār al-Kutub al-ʿIlmiyya, 1410/1990.

Al-Sunan al-kubrā. Edited by Muḥammad ʿAbd al-Qādir ʿAṭā. 11 vols. Beirut: Dār al-Kutub al-ʿIlmiyya, 1993–4.

al-Zuhd al-kabīr. Edited by ʿĀmir Aḥmad Ḥaydar. Beirut: Dār al-Jinān, 1408/1987.

Birgiwî, Mehmet Efendi. *Al-Ṭarīqa al-muḥammadiyya aw al-sīra al-Aḥmadiyya*. Istanbul: s.n., 1307/[1889].

al-Bukhārī, Muḥammad b. Ismāʿīl. *Al-Ṣaḥīḥ*. Edited by Ṭaha ʿAbd al-Raʾūf Saʿd. 4 vols. Al-Mansura: Maktabat al-Īmān, 1419/1998.

al-Burūsawī, Ibrāhīm Ḥaqqī b. Muṣṭafā. *Rūḥ al-bayān*. 10 vols. Beirut: Dār Iḥyāʾ al-Turāth al-ʿArabī, n.d.

al-Būṣīrī, Muḥammad b. Saʿīd. *Qaṣīdat al-burda*. Edited and translated by C. A. Ralfs. *Die Burda: Ein Lobgedicht auf Muhammad*. Vienna: KK Hof- und Staatsdruckerei, 1860.

Daqāʾiq al-akhbār fī dhikr al-janna wa-l-nār. Cairo: Maktabat al-Taḥrīr, n.d. = *Aḥwāl al-qiyāma*. Edited and translated by Moritz Wolff. *Muhammedanische Eschatologie*. Leipzig: Brockhaus, 1872, repr. Hildesheim, Zürich, and New York: Olms, 2004 = *Shajarat al-yaqīn*. Attributed to Abū l-Ḥasan Aḥmad b. Muḥammad al-Ashʿarī. Edited and translated by Concepción Castillo Castillo. *Kitāb Šaŷarat al-yaqīn. Tratado de eschatología musulmana*. Madrid: Instituto Hispano-Arabe de Cultura, 1987 = *K. al-Ḥaqāʾiq wa-l-daqāʾiq*. Attributed to Abū l-Layth al-Samarqandī. Partially edited and translated, based on MS Leeds 264, by John MacDonald. "Islamic Eschatology I-VI." *IS* 3 (1964), pp. 285–308, 485–519; 4 (1965), pp. 55–102, 137–79; 5 (1966), pp. 129–97, 331–83.

Daqāʾiq al-ḥaqāʾiq. MS Bibliothèque Nationale de France Persan 174, fols. 51r–132r.

al-Dārimī, ʿUthmān b. Saʿīd. *Al-Radd ʿalā l-Jahmiyya*. Edited by Gösta Vitestam. Lund: C. W. K. Gleerup, 1960.

al-Daylamī, Shīrwayh b. Shahrdār. *Firdaws al-akhbār bi-maʾthūr al-khiṭāb*. Edited by al-Saʿīd b. Basyūnī Zaghlūl. Beirut: Dār al-Kutub al-ʿIlmiyya, 1406/1986.

al-Dhahabī, Muhammad b. Aḥmad. *K. al-Kabāʾir*. Beirut: al-Maktaba al-Umawiyya, 1389/1970.

Mīzān al-iʿtidāl fī naqd al-rijāl. Edited by ʿAlī Muḥammad al-Bajāwī. Cairo: ʿĪsā al-Bābī al-Ḥalabī, 1382/1963–4.

Tadhkirat al-ḥuffāẓ. Edited by Zakariyyā ʿUmayrāt. 5 vols. Beirut: Dār al-Kutub al-ʿIlmiyya, 1998.

al-Dīnawārī, Abū Ḥanīfa Aḥmad b. Dāwūd. *K. al-Nabāt*. Edited and translated by Bernhard Lewin. *The book of plants*. Uppsala: Uppsala Universites Arsskrift, [1953].

al-Durar al-ḥusān fī l-baʿth wa-naʿīm al-jinān, apud *Daqāʾiq al-akhbār fī dhikr al-janna wa-l-nār*. Cairo: Maktabat al-Taḥrīr, n.d.

al-Fākihī, Abū ʿAbdallāh Muḥammad b. Isḥāq. *Akhbār Makka fī qadīm al-dahr wa-ḥadīthihi*. Edited by ʿAbd al-Malik b. ʿAbdallāh b. Dhuhaysh. 6 vols. in 3. Beirut: Dār Khiḍr li-l-Ṭabāʿa wa-l-Nashr wa-l-Tawzīʿ, 1414/1994, 2nd ed.

al-Fasawī, Yaʿqūb b. Sufyān. *K. al-Maʿrifa wa-l-taʾrīkh*. Edited by Ḍiyāʾ al-Dīn al-ʿUmarī. [Baghdad: Al-Jumhuriyya al-ʿIrāqiyya, 1976–?].

al-Ghazālī, Abū Ḥāmid Muḥammad. *K. al-Arbaʿīn fī uṣūl al-dīn*. Cairo: al-Maktaba al-Tijāriyya al-Kubrā, 1344/1925.

Al-Durra al-fākhira fī ʿulūm kashf al-ākhira. Edited by Lucien Gautier. *La perle précieuse*. Geneva, 1878. Reprint Amsterdam: Oriental Press, 1974. Translated by Jane Idleman Smith. *The precious pearl*. Missoula, MT: Scholars Press, 1979.

Faḍāʾiḥ al-bāṭiniyya wa faḍāʾil al-mustaẓhiriyya. Edited by ʿAbd al-Raḥmān Badawī. Cairo: Al-Dār al-Qawmiyya li-l-Ṭibāʿa wa-l-Nashr, 1964. Translated by Richard J. McCarthy. *Freedom and fulfillment: An annotated translation of al-Ghazālī's* al-Munqidh min al-ḍalāl *and other relevant works of al-Ghazālī*. Boston: Tawyne Publishers, 1980, pp. 175–286.

Fayṣal al-tafriqa bayna l-Islām wa-l-zandaqa. Cairo: ʿĪsā al-Bābī al-Ḥalabī, 1961.

Iḥyāʾ ʿulūm al-dīn. Edited by Muḥammad ʿAbd al-Malik al-Zughbī. 5 vols. [Cairo]: Dār al-Manār, n.d. Books 31–6 translated by Richard Gramlich. *Muḥammad al-Ġazzālī's Lehre von der Stufen zur Gottesliebe: Die Bücher 31–36 seines Hauptwerks*. Wiesbaden: Steiner, 1984. Book 40 translated by T. J. Winter. *The remembrance of death and the afterlife: Book XL of the Revival of the religious sciences*. Cambridge: Islamic Texts Society, 1989.

K. al-Imlāʾ fī ishkālāt al-Iḥyāʾ. *Apud* idem, *Iḥyā ʿulūm al-dīn*. Cairo: Muṣṭafā al-Bābī al-Ḥalabī, 1346/[1927].

Al-Iqtiṣād fī l-iʿtiqād. Edited by Ḥusayn Ātāyī and Ibrāhīm Chubūqchī. Ankara: Nur Matbaası, 1962.

Kīmiyā-yi saʿādat. Edited by Ḥusayn Khadīvjam. 2 vols. First published 1352 sh/[1974]. Tehran: Shirkat-i Intishārāt-i ʿIlmī wa-Farhangī, 1380sh/[2001], 9th ed.

Mishkāt al-anwār. Edited and translated by David Buchman. *The Niche of Lights*. Provo, UT: Brigham Young University Press, 1998.

Tahāfut al-falāsifa. Edited and translated by Michael Marmura. *The incoherence of the philosophers*. Provo, UT: Brigham Young University Press, 2000.

al-Ghayṭī, Muḥammad b. Aḥmad. *Al-Miʿrāj al-kabīr*. Cairo 1324/1906. Translated by Arthur Jeffery. In *A reader on Islam: Passages from standard Arabic writings illustrative of the beliefs and practices of Muslims*. 'S-Gravenhage: Mouton and Co., 1962, pp. 621–39.

Ḥājjī Khalīfa [Kātip Çelebi]. *Kashf al-ẓunūn ʿan asāmī l-kutub wa-l-funūn*. 7 vols. Edited by Gustav Flügel. London: R. Bentley for the Oriental Translation Fund of Great Britain and Ireland, 1835–58.

Ḥajjnāma. MS Bodleian Pers. d. 29.

al-Ḥakīm al-Tirmidhī. *Masʾala*. MS Ankara Saib 1571, fols. 43r–44r.

al-Ḥākim al-Naysābūrī, Muḥammad b. ʿAbdallāh. *Al-Mustadrak ʿalā l-ṣaḥīḥyan*. 4 vols. Hyderabad: Dārʾirat al-Maʿārif al-ʿUthmāniyya, 1917–25.

al-Hamadhānī, Badīʿ al-Zamān. *Al-Maqāmāt*. Edited by Muḥammad ʿAbduh. Beirut: Dār al-Mashriq, 1993, 9th ed.al-Ḥamawī, Aḥmad b. Muḥammad. *Ghamz ʿuyūn al-baṣāʾir sharḥ al-Ashbāh wa-l-naẓāʾir*. Apud Ibn Nujaym, Zayn al-Dīn Ibrāhīm. *Al-Ashbāh wa-l-naẓāʾir*. [Istanbul]: Dār al-Maṭbaʿa al-ʿĀmira, 1290/[1873–4].

Hammām b. Munabbih. *Al-Ṣaḥīfa*. Edited by Rifʿat Fawzī ʿAbd al-Muṭṭalib. Cairo: Maktabat al-Khānjī, 1406/1985.

Ḥanafī, Ḥassan. "Mysticisme et dévelopment: Un dialogue entre la «vivification des sciences de la foi» (Iḥyâʾ ʿulûm al-Dîn) de Ghazâlî et une «vivification des sciences du monde» (Iḥyâʾ ʿulûm al-dunyâ)." In *Ghazali: La raison et le miracle*. Paris: Éditions Maisonneuve et Larose, 1987, pp. 169–82.

al-Ḥanafī, Ḥusayn b. Muḥammad Saʿīd. *Irshād al-sharīʿa ilā manāsik al-mullā ʿAlī al-Qārī*. Beirut: Dār al-Kutub al-ʿArabiyya, n.d.

Hannād b. al-Sarī, Abū l-Layth Muḥammad. *K. al-Zuhd*. Edited by ʿAbd al-Raḥmān Ibn ʿAbd al-Jabbār al-Faryawāʾī. 2 vols. Kuwait: Dār al-Khulafāʾ li-l-Kitāb al-Islāmī, 1406/1985.

al-Ḥaqāʾiq wa-l-daqāʾiq. See Daqāʾiq al-akhbār.

al-Ḥillī, Muḥammad al-Ḥasan b. Sulaymān. *Al-Muḥtaḍar*. Edited by Muḥammad ʿAlī al-Awradabādī al-Gharawī [?]. Najaf: al-Maṭbaʿa al-Ḥaydariyya, 1951.

al-Hujwīrī, ʿAlī b. ʿUthmān. *Kashf al-maḥjūb*. Edited by V. A. Zukovskij. Leningrad, 1926. Translated by Reynold A. Nicholson. *The "Kashf al-Maḥjūb," the oldest Persian treatise on Sufism*. London: Luzac, 1911. Reprint London: Luzac, 1959, 1976.

Ibn ʿAbd Rabbih. *Al-ʿIqd al-farīd*, eds. Muḥammad Saʿīd al-ʿAryān et al., 4 vols. in 8. Cairo, 1372/1953.

Ibn Abī l-Dunyā, ʿAbdallāh b. Muḥammad. *Ṣifat al-janna wa-mā aʿadda llāhu li-ahlihi*. Edited by ʿAlī al-Ṭaḥṭāwī. Beirut: Dār al-Kutub al-ʿIlmiyya, 2006, 2nd ed.

K. al-Mawt wa-K. al-qubūr. Edited by Leah Kinberg. [Haifa]: University of Haifa, 1983.

Ṣifat al-nār. Edited by Muḥammad Khayr Ramaḍān Yūsuf. Beirut: Dār Ibn Ḥazm, 1427/1997.

Ibn Abī Ḥajala al-Tilimsānī, Aḥmad b. Yaḥyā. *Salwat al-ḥazīn fī mawt al-banīn*. Edited by Mukhaymar Ṣāliḥ. Amman: Dār al-Fayḥāʾ, n.d.

Ibn Abī Ḥātim al-Rāzī, ʿAbd al-Raḥmān b. Muḥammad. *Taqdimat al-maʿrifa li-Kitāb al-jarḥ wa-l-taʿdīl*. Hyderabad: Dāʾirat al-Maʿārif al-ʿUthmāniyya, 1371/1952.

Ibn Abī l-ʿIzz, ʿAlī b. ʿAlī. *Sharḥ al-ʿaqīda al-Ṭaḥānawiyya*. Edited by Muḥammad Nāṣir al-Dīn al-Albānī et al. Beirut: Al-Maktab al-Islāmī, 1414/1984.

Ibn Abī Shayba, ʿAbdallāh b. Muḥammad. *Al-Muṣannaf*. 9 vols. Edited by Saʿīd al-Laḥḥām. Beirut: Dār al-Fikr, 1409/1989.

Ibn Abī Yaʿlā, Muḥammad b. Muḥammad. *Ṭabaqāt al-Ḥanābila*. Edited by ʿAbd al-Raḥmān Ibn Sulaymān al-ʿUthaymin. 3 vols. [Riyadh]: Al-Mamlaka al-ʿArabiyya al-Saʿūdiyya, 1999.
Ibn ʿĀbidīn, Muḥammad Amīn b. ʿUmar. *Ḥāshiyat radd al-muḥtār ʿalā al-Durr al-mukhtār*. 8 vols. [Cairo]: Muṣṭafā al-Bābī al-Ḥalabī, 1386/1966. Repr. Beirut: Dār al-Fikr, 1421/2000.
Ibn ʿAdī, ʿAbdallāh. *Al-Kāmil fī ḍuʿafāʾ al-rijāl*. Edited by ʿĀdil Aḥmad ʿAbd al-Mawjūd and ʿAlī Muḥammad Muʿawwaḍ. Beirut: Dār al-Kutub al-ʿIlmiyya, 1997.
Ibn ʿAjība, Aḥmad. *Miʿrāj al-tashawwuf ilā ḥaqāʾiq al-taṣawwuf*. Edited and translated by Mohamed Fouad Aresmouk and Michael Abdurrahman Fitzgerald. *The book of the ascension to the essential truths of Sufism: A lexicon of Sufi terminology*. Louisville, KY: Fons Vitae, 2011.
Ibn al-ʿArabī, Muḥammad b. ʿAbdallāh. *Aḥkām al-Qurʾān*. Edited by ʿAlī Muḥammad al-Bijāwī. Beirut: Dār Iḥyāʾ al-Turāth al-ʿArabī, 1421/2001.
Ibn al-ʿArabī. Muḥammad b. ʿAlī. *Fuṣūṣ al-ḥikam*. Edited by Abū l-ʿAlāʾ ʿAfīfī. [Cairo]: ʿĪsā al-Bābī al-Ḥalabī, 1365/1946.
Al-Futūḥāt al-Makkiyya. 4 vols. Cairo 1329. Repr. Beirut: Dār Ṣādir, [1968]. Partial translation (chs. 61–5) by Maurice Gloton. *Ibn ʿArabī: De la mort à la resurrection*. Beirut: Albouraq, 2009.
K. al-Isrāʾ ilā maqām al-asrā. In *Rasāʾil Ibn ʿArabī*. Edited by Muḥammad ʿAbd al-Karīm al-Nimrī. Beirut: Dār al-Kutub al-ʿIlmiyya, 1421/2001, pp. 132–83.
Al-Kawkab al-durrī fī manāqib Dhī l-Nūn al-Miṣrī. Translated by Roger Deladrière. *La vie merveilleuse de Dhû-l-Nûn l'Egyptien*. Paris: Editions Sindbad, 1988.
Ibn ʿAsākir, ʿAlī b. al-Ḥasan. *Taʾrīkh madīnat Dimashq*. 80 vols. Edited by ʿAlī Shīrī. Beirut: Dār al-Fikr, 1995–2001.
Ibn al-Athīr, ʿIzz al-Dīn. *Al-Kāmil fī l-taʾrīkh*. Edited by ʿUmar ʿAbd al-Salām Tadmurī. 11 vols. Beirut: Dār al-Kitāb al-ʿArabī, 1417/1997.
Ibn Bābūya, Muḥammad b. ʿAlī al-Shaykh al-Ṣaddūq. *Al-Khiṣāl*. Najaf: Manshūrāt al-Maṭbaʿa al-Ḥaydariyya, 1391/1971.
Risālat al-iʿtiqādāt. Tabriz: s.n., 1371/1951. Translated by Asaf A. A. Fyzee. *A Shīʿite creed: A translation of Risālatuʾl Iʿtiqādāt of Muḥammad b. ʿAlī Ibn Bābawayhi al-Qummī known as Shakh Ṣadūq* (London and New York: Oxford University Press, 1942. Rev. ed. Tehran: World Organization For Islamic Services, 1420/1999.
Thawāb al-aʿmāl wa-ʿiqāb al-aʿmāl. Najaf: Al-Maṭbaʿa al-Ḥaydariyya, 1392/1972.
Ibn Baṭṭūṭa. *Riḥla*. Beirut: Dār Ṣādir, 1384/1964, 1418/1998, 2nd ed.
Ibn Faḍlān. *Riḥla*. Beirut: Dār al-Fikr, 1992.
Ibn al-Farrāʾ, Muḥammad b. Abī Yaʿlā. *Al-Muʿtamad fī uṣūl al-dīn*. Beirut: Dār al-Mashriq, 1974.
Ibn Ḥabīb, ʿAbd al-Malik. *Kitāb al-Taʾrīkh*. Edited by Jorge Aguadé. Madrid: CSIC, 1991.
Waṣf al-firdaws. Edited by ʿAbd al-Laṭīf Ḥasan ʿAbd al-Raḥmān. Beirut: Dār al-Kutub al-ʿIlmiyya, 1427/2006, 2nd ed.
Ibn Ḥajar al-ʿAsqalānī, Aḥmad b. ʿAlī. *Fatḥ al-bārī bi-sharḥ Ṣaḥīḥ al-Bukhārī*. Edited by Aḥmad b. ʿAlī al-Shāfiʿī. 13 vols. Beirut: Dār al-Maʿrifa, 1379/[1959–60].
Ibn Ḥajar al-Haythamī, Aḥmad b. Muḥammad. *Al-Zawājir ʿan iqtirāf al-kabāʾir*. Beirut: Dār al-Maʿrifa, 1998.

Ibn Ḥanbal, Aḥmad b. Muḥammad. *K. al-Musnad.* 6 vols., Cairo: Muʾassasat Qurṭuba, n.d.

Al-Radd ʿalā l-zanādiqa wa-l-Jahmiyya. Edited by Daghash al-ʿAjamī. Kuwait: Gharās, 1426/2005.

Al-Musnad. Edited by Aḥmad Muḥammad Shākir. Cairo: Dār al-Maʿārif, 1368–75/1948–56.

K. al-Zuhd. Edited by ʿIṣam Fāris al-Ḥaristānī and Muḥammad Ibrāhīm al-Zughbī. Beirut: Dār al-Jīl, 1414/1994.

Ibn Ḥazm, ʿAlī b. Aḥmad. *Al-Fiṣal fī l-milal wa-l-ahwāʾ wa-l-niḥal.* 5 vols. in 1. Cairo: s.n., 1317/[1899–1900].

Marātib al-ijmāʿ. Edited by Ḥasan Aḥmad Asīr. Beirut: Dār Ibn Ḥazm, 1419/1998.

Risālat al-talkhīṣ li-wujūh al-takhlīs. Edited by Abū ʿAbdallāh al-Shammarī al-Ẓāhirī. Riyadh: Ibn Ḥazm, 1427/2005.

Ibn Hishām, ʿAbd al-Malik. *Sīrat rasūl Allāh.* Edited by Ferdinand Wüstenfeld. *Das Leben Muhammed's nach Muhammed Ibn Ishâk bearbeitet von Abd el-Malik ibn Hischâm.* 2 vols. Göttingen: Dieterichsche Universitätsbuchhandlung, 1858–60. Translated by A. Guillaume. *The Life of Muhammad.* London, New York, and Toronto: Oxford University Press, 1955.

K. al-Tījān fī mulūk Ḥimyar. Hyderabad: Maṭbaʿat Majlis Dāʾirat al-Maʿārif al-ʿUthmāniyya, 1347/[1928–9].

Ibn al-Jawzī, ʿAbd al-Raḥmān. *Dafʿ shubhat al-tashbīh wa-l-radd ʿalā l-mujassima.* [Damascus]: Maṭbaʿat al-Taraqqī, 1345/[1926–7].

K. al-Mawḍūʿāt. Edited by ʿAbd al-Raḥmān Muḥammad ʿUthmān. 3 vols. Medina: al-Maktaba al-Salafiyya, 1386–8/1966–8.

Al-Muntaẓam fī tawārīkh al-mulūk wa-l-umam. 10 vols. Beirut: Dār Ṣādir, 1358.

K. al-Muqliq. Edited by Majdī Fatḥī al-Sayyid. Ṭanṭā: Dār al-Ṣaḥāba li-l-Turāth, 1991/1411.

K. al-Quṣṣāṣ wa l-mudhakkirīn. Edited by Merlin Swartz. Beirut: Dar El-Machreq, 1986.

Ṣayd al-khāṭir. Edited by ʿAbd al-Qādir Aḥmad ʿAṭā. Beirut: Dār al-Kutub al-ʿIlmiyya, 1412/1992.

Ṣifat al-ṣafwa. Edited by Maḥmūd Fākhūrī and Muḥammad Rawwās Qalʿajī. 4 vols. Beirut: Dār al-Maʿrifa, 1399/1979.

Al-Taḥqīq fī aḥādīth al-khilāf. Edited by Masʿad ʿAbd al-Ḥamīd al-Saʿdānī and Muḥammad Fāris. 2 vols. Beirut: Dār al-Kutub al-ʿIlmiyya, 1994.

Talbīs Iblīs. Edited by Muḥammad al-Ṣabbāḥ. Beirut: Dār Maktabat al-Ḥayāt, 1409/1989.

Zād al-masīr fī ʿilm al-tafsīr. [Damascus]: al-Maktab al-Islāmī, 1964–8.

Ibn Jubayr, Muḥammad b. Aḥmad. *Riḥla.* Edited by William Wright. 2nd rev. ed. by M. J. de Goeje. Leiden: Brill, 1907. Translated by R. J. C. Broadhurst. *The travels of Ibn Jubayr.* London: J. Cape, [1952].

Ibn Kathīr, Ismāʿīl b. ʿUmar. *Al-Bidāya wa-l-nihāya.* 14 vols. in 7. Cairo: Dār al-Manār, 1321/2001.

Nihāyat al-bidāya wa-l-nihāya fī l-fitan wa-l-malāḥim. Edited by Muḥammad Fahīm Abū ʿAbiyya, 2 vols. Riyadh: Maktabat al-Naṣr al-Ḥadītha, 1968.

Ibn al-Kharrāṭ, *K. al-ʿĀqiba aw al-mawt wa-l-ḥashr wa-nushūr.* Edited by ʿUbaydallāh al-Muḍarī al-Atharī. Ṭanṭā: Dār al-Ṣaḥāba li-l-Turāth, 1410/1990.

Ibn al-Khaṭīb, Muḥammad b. Saʿīd. *Al-Iḥāṭa fī akhbār Gharnāṭa*. Cairo: Dār al-Maʾārif, 1973.
Ibn Lahīʿa, ʿAbdallāh. *Ṣaḥīfa*. Edited by Raif Georges Khoury. *ʿAbd Allāh b. Lahīʿa (97–174/715–790): juge et grand maître de l'école égyptienne*. Wiesbaden: Harrassowitz, 1986.
Ibn Māja, Muḥammad b. Yazīd. *Sunan*. Edited by Fuʾād ʿAbd al-Bāqī. 2 vols. Cairo: Dār Iḥyāʾ al-Kutub al-ʿArabiyya, 1952–4. Repr. in 4 vols. Cairo: Dār al-Ḥadīth, 1419/1998.
Ibn al-Mibrad, Yūsuf b. Ḥasan. *Al-Jawhar al-munaḍḍad fī ṭabaqāt mutaʾakhkhirī aṣḥāb Aḥmad*. Edited by ʿAbd al-Raḥmān b. Sulaymān al-ʿUthaymīn. Cairo: Maktabat al-Khānjī, 1987.
Ibn Miskawayh, Aḥmad b. Muḥammad. *Tahdhīb al-akhlāq*. Edited by Qusṭanṭīn Zurayq. Beirut: s.n., 1966.
Ibn al-Mubārak, ʿAbdallāh. *Musnad*. Edited by Ṣubḥī al-Badrī al-Sāmmarāʾī. Riyadh: Maktabat al-Maʿārif, 1407/1987.
K. al-Zuhd wa-l-raqāʾiq. Edited by Ḥabīb al-Raḥmān al-Aʿẓamī. First publ. 1966. Repr. Beirut: Muḥammad ʿAfīf al-Zughbī, 1971.
Ibn al-Munawwar, Muḥammad b. Nūr al-Dīn. *Asrār al-tawḥīd fī maqāmāt al-shaykh Abī Saʿīd*. Edited by Dhabīḥullāh Ṣafā. Tehran: Amīr Kabīr, 1332sh/1953.
Ibn al-Murajjā, al-Musharraf b. Ibrāhīm. *Faḍāʾil Bayt al-Maqdis wa-l-Khalīl wa-Faḍāʾil al-Shām*. Edited by Ofer Livne-Kafri. Shifāʾ ʿAmr [Shfaram]: Dār al-Mashriq, 1995.
Ibn al-Nadīm, Muḥammad b. Isḥāq. *K. al-Fihrist*. Edited by Gustav Flügel. Leipzig: F. C. W. Vogel, 1871–2.
Ibn Nujaym, ʿUmar b. Ibrāhīm. *Al-Baḥr al-rāʾiq*. Edited by Aḥmad ʿIzzū ʿInāya. 3 vols. Beirut: Dār al-Kutub al-ʿIlmiyya, 1422/2002.
Ibn al-Qāriḥ, ʿAlī b. Manṣūr. *Risāla*. Edited and translated by Geert Jan van Gelder and Gregor Schoeler. *The Epistle of Forgiveness or A pardon to enter the Garden, by Abū l-ʿAlāʾ al-Maʿarrī. Vol. 1: A vision of Paradise and Hell, preceded by Ibn al-Qāriḥ's Epistle*. New York and London: New York University Press, 2013, pp. 2–63.
Ibn Qasī, Aḥmad b. al-Ḥusayn. *Khalʿ al-naʿlayn wa-iqtibās al-nūr min mawḍiʿ al-qadamayn*. Edited by Aḥmad Farīd al-Mazīdī. [Cairo]: Dar Rītāj, 2011.
Ibn Qayyim al-Jawziyya, Muḥammad b. Abī Bakr. *Ḥādī l-arwāḥ ilā bilād al-afrāḥ*. Edited by Zakariyyāʾ ʿUmayrāt. Beirut: Dār al-Kutub al-ʿIlmiyya, 1428/2007.
Miftāḥ al-saʿāda wa-manshūr wilāyat al-ʿilm wa-l-irāda. Edited by ʿAbd al-Raḥmān b. Ḥasan b. Qāʾid. 3 vols. Mecca: Dār ʿĀlam al-Fawāʾid, 1432/[2010–11].
K. al-Rūḥ. Edited by Ṣāliḥ Aḥmad al-Shāmī. Beirut, Damascus, and Amman: Al-Maktab al-Islāmī, 1425/2004.
Zād al-maʿād fī hudā khayr al-ʿibād. Edited by Shuʿayb al-Arnaʾūṭ and ʿAbd al-Qādir al-Arnaʾūṭ. 6 vols. Beirut: Muʾassasat al-Risāla, 1994.
Ibn Qutayba, ʿAbdallāh b. Muslim. *K. al-Maʿārif*. Edited by Saroite Okacha. [Cairo]: s.n., 1960.
Ibn Rabbān al-Ṭabarī, ʿAlī b. Sahl. *K. al-Dīn wa-l-dawla*. Edited by ʿĀdil Nuwayhid. Beirut: Dār al-Āfāq al-Jadīda, 1973.
Ibn Rajab, ʿAbd al-Raḥmān b. Aḥmad. *Al-Takhwīf min al-nār wa-l-taʿrīf bi-ḥāl dār al-bawār*. Edited by ʿAbdallāh Salām. Beirut: Dār al-Kutub al-ʿIlmiyya, 1423/2002.

Sharḥ ʿilal al-Tirmidhī. Edited by Nūr al-Dīn ʿItr. 2 vols. [Lebanon]: Dār al-Mallāḥ, 1398/1978.

Ibn Rushd, Abū l-Walīd. *Al-Kashf ʿan manāhij al-adilla fī ʿaqāʾid al-milla*. Edited by Maḥmūd Qāsim. Cairo: The Anglo-Egyptian Library, 1964. Translated by Ibrahim Y. Najjar. *Faith and reason in Islam: Averroes' exposition of religious arguments*. Oxford: Oneworld, 2001.

Ibn Saʿd, Muḥammad. *Al-Ṭabaqāt al-kubrā*. Edited by Iḥsān ʿAbbās. 9 vols. Beirut: Dār Ṣādir, 1957–68.

Ibn al-Ṣalāḥ al-Shahrazūrī, ʿUthmān b. ʿAbd al-Raḥmān. *ʿUlūm al-ḥadīth*. Edited by Nūr al-Dīn ʿItr. 2 vols. Damascus 1986. Translated by Eerik Dickinson. *Introduction to the science of the Ḥadith*. Reading, UK: Garnet, 2005.

Ibn Shahrashūb, Muḥammad b. ʿAlī. *Maʿālim al-ʿulamāʾ fī fihrist kutub al-Shīʿa*. Edited by ʿAbbāṣ Iqbāl. Tehran: Maṭbaʿat Fardīn, 1353/[1934–5].

Ibn Sīna. *Ithbāt al-nubuwwāt*. Edited by Michael Marmura. Beirut: Dar al-Nahar li-l-Nashr, 1991, 2nd ed. Translated by Michael Marmura. "On the proof of prophecies." In *Medieval political philosophy: A sourcebook*. Edited by Ralph Lerner and Muhsin Mahdi. Ithaca, NY: Cornell University Press, 2005, pp. 112–21.

K. al-Mabdaʾ wa-l-maʿād. Edited by ʿAbdallāh Nūrānī. Tehran: Intishārāt-i Muʾassasa-yi Muṭālaʿāt-i Islāmī, 1343sh/1984.

Miʿrājnāma. Edited by N. Māyil Hiravī. Mashhad: Āstān-i Quds-i Radavī, 1986. Translated by Peter Heath. *Allegory and philosophy in Avicenna (Ibn Sīnā), with a translation of the book of the Prophet Muhammad's ascent to heaven*. Philadelphia: University of Philadelphia Press, 1992.

Risāla aḍḥawiyya fī amr al-maʿād. Edited by Sulaymān Dunyā. Cairo: Dār al-Fikr al-ʿArabī, 1368/1949. Also edited and translated by Francesca Lucchetta. *Avicenna, Epistola sulla vita futura*. Padua: Antenore, 1969.

K. al-Shifāʾ. Translated by Michael Marmura. *The metaphysics of healing*. Provo, UT: Brigham Young University Press, 2005.

Ibn Taymiyya, Aḥmad b. ʿAbd al-Ḥalīm. *Iqtiḍāʾal-sirāṭ al-mustaqīm li-mukhālafat aṣḥāb al-jaḥīm*. Edited by Nāṣir b. ʿAbd al-Karīm al-ʿAql. 2 vols. Riyadh: Maktabat al-Rushd, 1998.

Majmūʿ fatāwā shaykh al-islām Ibn Taymiyya. Edited by ʿAbd al-Raḥmān b. Muḥammad al-ʿĀṣimī. 37 vols. Riyadh: Maṭābiʿ al-Riyāḍ, 1381–6/1967.

Qāʾida jalīla fī l-tawassul wa-l-wasīla. Edited by Rabīʿ b. Hādī al-Madkhalī. Cairo: Dār al-Imām Aḥmad, 2010.

Ibn Ṭulūn al-Ṣāliḥī, Muḥammad b. ʿAlī. *Al-Taḥrīr al-murassakh fī aḥwāl al-barzakh*. Edited by Abū ʿAbd al-Raḥmān al-Miṣrī al-Atharī. Tanta: Dār al-Ṣaḥāba li-l-Turāth, 1991.

Ibn Wahb, ʿAbdallāh. *Al-Jāmiʿ*. Edited by Jean David-Weill. *Le Djâmiʿ d'Ibn Wahb*. 3 vols. Cairo: Imprimerie de l'IFAO, 1939–48.

Ibn al-Walīd, al-Ḥusayn b. ʿAlī b. Muḥammad. *K. al-Mabdaʾ wa-l-maʿād*. Edited and translated by Henry Corbin. *Trilogie ismaelienne: Textes edités avec traduction française et commentaire*. Tehran: Institut franco-iranien, 1961, pp. 99–130 (Arabic text), 129–200 (transl.).

Ibn al-Wazīr, Muḥammad b. Aḥmad. *Al-ʿAwāṣim wa al-qawāṣim fī al-dhabb ʿan sunnat Abī al-Qāsim*. Edited by Shuʿayb al-Arnaʾūṭ. 9 vols. Beirut: Muʾassasat al-Risāla, 1412/1992, 2nd ed.

Ibn al-Zamlakānī, ʿAbd al-Wāḥid b. ʿAbd al-Karīm. *Al-Tibyān fī ʿilm al-bayān*. Edited by Aḥmad Maṭlūb and Khadīja al-Ḥadīthī. Baghdad: Maṭbaʿat al-ʿĀnī, 1383/1964.

al-Ījī, ʿAḍud al-Dīn ʿAbd al-Raḥmān. *Al-Mawāqif fī ʿilm al-kalām*. Cairo: Maktabat al-Mutanabbī, [1983?].

Ikhwān al-Ṣafāʾ. *Rasāʾil Ikhwān al-Ṣafāʾ*. Edited by Muṣṭafā Ghālib. 4 vols. Beirut: Dār Ṣādir, 1957.

Risālat jāmiʿat al-jāmiʿa. Edited by ʿĀrif Tāmir. Beirut: Dār Maktabat al-Ḥayāt, [2]1970.

Īlkhānid *Miʿrājnāma*. MS Istanbul Ayasofya 3441, fols. 2v–75r. Edited and translated by Christiane Gruber, *The Ilkhanid Book of Ascension: A Persian-Sunni devotional tale*. London and New York: I. B. Tauris, 2010.

Iqbal, Muhammad. *The reconstruction of religious thought in Islam*. First publ. 1930. Edited by M. Saeed Sheikh. Lahore: Institute of Islamic Culture, 1986.

Iṭfayyish, Muḥammad b. Yūsuf. *Al-Junna fī waṣf al-janna*. [Muscat]: Wizārat al-Turāth al-Qawmī wa-l-Thaqāfa, 1405/1985.

Jaʿfar al-Ṣādiq. *Tafsīr*. Edited by Paul Nwyia. "Le tafsīr mystique attribué a Ǧaʿfar Ṣādiq." *Mélanges de l'Université Saint-Joseph* 43,4 (1968), pp. 181–230. Translated by Farhana Mayer. *Spiritual gems: The mystical Qurʾān commentary ascribed to Jaʿfar al-Ṣādiq as contained in Sulamī's* Ḥaqāʾiq al-tafsīr *from the text of Paul Nwyia*. Louisville, KY: Fons Vitae, 2011.

al-Jāḥiẓ, ʿAmr b. Baḥr. *K. al-Ḥayawān*. 4 parts in 2 vols. [Cairo]: Maṭbaʿat al-Taqdīm, 1324/1906.

Rasāʾil al-Jāḥiẓ. Edited by ʿAbd al-Salām Muḥammad Hārūn. 4 vols. Cairo: Maktabat al-Khānjī, 1964–79.

Jāmī. *Nafaḥāt al-uns*. Edited by Mahdī Tawḥīdīpūr. Tehran: Saʿdī, 1336sh/[1958].

al-Jazīrī, ʿAbd al-Raḥmān. *K. al-Fiqh ʿalā l-madhāhib al-arbaʿa*. 5 vols. Beirut: Dār al-Fikr, 1422/2002.

al-Jīlī, ʿAbd al-Karīm. *Al-Insān al-kāmil fī maʿrifat al-awākhir wa-l-awāʾil*. Edited by Ṣalāḥ b. Muḥammad b. ʿUwayḍa. Cairo: Al-Hayʾa al-ʿĀmma li-Quṣūr al-Thaqāfa, 2012.

al-Jurjānī, ʿAlī b. Muḥammad. *Sharḥ al-Mawāqif fī ʿilm al-kalām*. Edited by Maḥmūd ʿUmar al-Dimyāṭī. Beirut: Dār al-Kutub al-ʿIlmiyya, 1433/2012.

al-Juwaynī, Imām al-Ḥaramayn. *K. al-Irshād ilā qawāṭiʿ al-adilla fī uṣūl al-iʿtiqād*. Edited by Asad Tamīm. Beirut: Muʾassasat al-Kutub al-Thaqafiyya, 1985. Translated by Paul E. Walker. *A guide to the conclusive proofs for the principles of belief*. Reading, UK: Garnet, 2000.

al-Kalābādhī, Muḥammad b. Ibrāhīm. *K. al-Taʿarruf*. Translated by Arthur Arberry. *The doctrine of the Ṣūfīs*. Cambridge: Cambridge University Press, 1935.

Kāshānī, Muḥsin Fayḍ. *Al-Kalimāt al-maknūna*. Edited by ʿAlīriḍā Aṣgharī. Tehran: Madrasat-i ʿĀlī-yi Shahīd-i Muṭṭaharī, 1387sh, 4rth ed./[2008].

al-Khaṭīb al-Baghdādī, Aḥmad b. ʿAlī. *Taʾrīkh Baghdād*. 14 vols. Cairo: Maktabat al-Khānjī, 1349/1931.

al-Khayyāṭ, ʿAbd al-Raḥīm b. Muḥammad. *K. al-Intiṣār wa-l-radd ʿalā Ibn al-Rāwandī al-mulḥid*. Edited and translated by Albīr Naṣrī Nādir. *Le livre du triomphe et de la réfutation d'Ibn al-Rāwandī l'hérétique*. Beirut: Al-Maṭbaʿa al-Kāthūlīkiyya, 1957.

al-Khuttalī, Abū Isḥāq Ibrāhīm b. ʿAbd Allāh b. al-Junayd. *K. al-Maḥabba*. Edited by ʿAbd al-Karīm Zuhūr ʿAdī. *RAAD* 58 (1983) and 59 (1984). Transcribed and translated by Bernd Radtke. *Materialien zur alten islamischen Frömmigkeit*. Leiden: Brill, 2009, pp. 47–194.

Kitāb al-Kashf. Edited by Muṣṭafā Ghālib. Beirut: Dār al-Andalus, 1984.

al-Kisāʾī, Muḥammad b. ʿAbdallāh. *Qiṣaṣ al-anbiyāʾ*. Edited by Isaac Eisenberg. *Vita prophetarum*. 2 vols. Leiden: Brill, 1922–3.

Kishk, Muḥammad Jalāl. *Khawāṭir Muslim fī l-masʾala al-jinsiyya*. First publ. 1984. Beirut and Cairo: Dār al-Jīl and Maktab al-Turāth al-Islāmī, 1992.

al-Kūlaynī, Muḥammad b. Yaʿqūb. *Al-Kāfī*. Edited by ʿAlī Akbar al-Ghaffārī. 8 vols. Tehran: Dār al-Kutub al-Islāmiyya, 1377–81/[1957–61]. Also edited Muḥammad Jaʿfar Shams al-Dīn. 8 vols. Beirut: Dar al-Taʿāruf li-l-Maṭbūʿāt, 1430/2009.

al-Lamaṭī, Aḥmad b. al Mubārak. *Al-Dhahab al-ibrīz min kalām sayyidī ʿAbd al-ʿAzīz al-Dabbāgh*. Translated by John O'Kane and Bernd Radtke. *Pure gold from the words of Sayyidī ʿAbd al-ʿAzīz al-Dabbāgh*. Leiden and Boston: Brill, 2007.

Liber scalae. See Livre de l'Eschiele.

Livre de l'Eschiele Mahomet = Liber scalae Machometi. Edited by Enrico Cerulli. *Il "Libro della scala" e la questione delle fonti arabo-spagnole della Divina Commedia*. Città del Vaticano: Biblioteca Apostolica Vaticana, 1949, pp. 24–225.

al-Maʿarrī, Abū l-ʿAlāʾ. *Risālat al-ghufrān*. Edited and translated by Geert Jan van Gelder and Gregor Schoeler. *The Epistle of Forgiveness*. Vol. 1: *A vision of heaven and hell*. New York and London: New York University Press, 2013.

Majlis dar qiṣṣa-yi rasūl. Edited by Muḥammad Pārsānasab. Tehran: Markaz-i Pizhūhishī-yi Mīrāth-i Maktūb, 1390sh/2011.

al-Majlisī, Muḥammad Bāqir b. Muḥammad. *Biḥār al-anwār*. Edited by Lajna min al-ʿulamāʾ. 110 fasc. in 66 vols. Beirut: Muʾassasat al-Aʿlamī li-l-Maṭbūʿāt. 1429/2008.

al-Makkī, Abū Ṭālib. *Qūt al-qulūb*. 2 vols. Cairo: Al-Maktaba al-Tawfīqiyya, n.d. Translated by Richard Gramlich. *Die Nahrung der Herzen*. Stuttgart: Franz Steiner, 1992–5.

al-Malaṭī, Muḥammad b. Aḥmad. *K. al-Tanbīh wa l-radd ʿalā ahl al-ahwāʾ wa-l-bidaʿ*. Edited by Sven Dedering. Istanbul: Maṭbaʿat al-Dawla, 1936.

al-Maqdisī, ʿAbd al-Ghanī b. ʿAbd al-Wāḥid. *Dhikr al-nār*. Edited by Adīb Muḥammad al-Ghazāwī. Beirut: Dār al-Bashāʾir al-Islāmiyya, 1994/1415.

al-Maqdisī, Aḥmad b. Muḥammad. *Muthīr al-gharām bi-faḍāʾil al-Quds wa-l-Shām*. Edited by Aḥmad Sāmiḥ al-Khālidī. Jaffa: Maktabat al-Ṭāhir Ikhwān, 1365/1946.

al-Maqdisī, Muḥammad b. ʿAbd al-Wāḥid. *Ṣifat al-janna*. Edited by Ṣabrī b. Salāma Shāhīn. Riyadh: Dār Balansiyya li-l-Nashr wa-l-Tawzīʿ, 1423/2002.

al-Maqqarī, Aḥmad b. Muḥammad. *Azhār al-riyāḍ fī akhbār ʿIyāḍ*. Edited by Muṣṭafā al-Saqqā et al. 2 vols. Cairo: Maṭbaʿat Lajnat al-Taʾlīf wa-l-Tarjama wa-l-Nashr, 1939.

Nafḥ al-ṭīb min ghuṣn al-Andalus al-raṭīb wa-dhikr wazīrihā Lisān al-Dīn Ibn al-Khaṭīb. Edited by R. Dozy et al. 2 vols. Leiden: Brill, 1855–61. Reprinted Amsterdam: Oriental Press, 1967. Also edited by Iḥsān ʿAbbās. 8 vols. Beirut: Dār Ṣādir, 1968.

al-Maqrīzī, Aḥmad b. ʿAlī. *Ittiʿāẓ al-ḥunafāʾ bi-akhbār al-āʾimma al-Faṭimiyyīn al-khulafāʾ*. Edited by Shamāl al-Dīn Shayyāl. Cairo: s.n., 1967–73.

K. al-Mawāʿiẓ wa-l-iʿtibār bi-dhikr al-khiṭaṭ wa-l-āthār. Edited by Khalīl al-Manṣūr. 4 vols. Beirut: Dār al-Kutub al-ʿIlmiyya, 1418/1998.

al-Marākushī, Muḥammad b. ʿAbd al-Malik. *Al-dhayl wa-l-takmila li-kitābay al-Mawṣūl wa-l-Ṣila*. Edited by Iḥsān ʿAbbās. 5 vols. Beirut: Dār al-Thaqāfa, [1964–].

al-Māturīdī, Muḥammad b. Muḥammad. *Taʾwīlāt al-Qurʾān*. Edited by Ahmet Vanlioğlu. 18 vols. Istanbul: Mizan Yayınevi, 2010.

al-Māwardī, ʿAlī b. Muḥammad. *Al-Aḥkām al-sulṭāniyya*. Kuwait: Maktabat Dār Ibn Qutayba, 1409/1989.

Al-Ḥāwī al-kabīr. Edited by Muḥammad Musṭafā et al. 24 vols. Beirut: Dār al-Fikr, 1994.

Mawsūʿat al-Imām al-Ṣādiq. Edited by Muḥammad Kāẓim Qazwīnī. 42 vols. Qum: s.n., 1414/1994–.

Maybudī, Abū l-Fādl Rasdhīd al-Dīn. *Kashf al-asrār wa-ʿuddat al-abrār*. Tehran: Intishārāt-i Dānishgāh-i Tihrān, 1331–9sh/[1952–61].

al-Mizzī, Yūsuf b. al-Zakī. *Tahdhīb al-kamāl fī asmāʾ al-rijāl*. Edited by Bashshār ʿAwād Maʿrūf. 35 vols. Beirut: Muʾassasat al-Risāla, 1400/1980.

al-Mufīd, Muḥammad b. Muḥammad = al-Shaykh al-Mufīd. *Ajwibat al-masāʾil al-ḥājibiyya*. Edited and introduced by Martin J. McDermott. "Al-Shaykh al-Mufīd answers the Ḥājib: A Shīʿite theologians interprets Quran and Tradition." *Mélanges de l'Université Saint-Joseph* 51 (1990), pp. 91–164.

Awāʾil al-maqālāt fī l-madhāhib al-mukhtārāt. Edited by ʿAbbāsqulī Wajdī. Tabriz: Maktabat Ḥaqīqat, 1371/[1951–2].

Al-Ikhtiṣāṣ. Edited by ʿAlī Akbar al-Ghaffārī. Tehran: Maktabat al-Ṣadūq, 1379/[1959–60].

al-Muḥāsibī, al-Ḥārith b. Asad. *K. Aḥkām al-tawba*. Edited by ʿAbd al-Qādir Aḥmad ʿAṭāʾ. [Cairo]: Dār al-Iʿtiṣām, [1982].

K. al-Tawahhum. Edited and translated André Roman. *Une vision humaine des fins dernières*. Paris: Klincksieck, 1978.

al-Munāwī, ʿAbd al-Raʾūf b. Tāj al-ʿĀrifīn. *Fayḍ al-qadīr*. Edited by Aḥmad ʿAbd al-Salām. 6 vols. Beirut: Dār al-Kutub al-ʿIlmiyya, 1415/1994.

al-Muqaddasī, Muḥammad b. Aḥmad. *K. Aḥsan al-taqāsīm fī maʿrifat al-aqālīm*. Edited by Michael Jan de Goeje. Leiden: Brill, 1967.

Muqātil b. Sulaymān. *Tafsīr al-Qurʾān al-karīm*. Edited by ʿAbdallāh Muḥammad Shaḥāta. 5 vols. [Cairo]: Al-Hayʾa al-Miṣriyya al-ʿĀmma li-l-Kitāb, 1979–89.

Muslim b. al-Ḥajjāj. *Al-Ṣaḥīḥ*. Edited by Muḥammad Fuʾād ʿAbd al-Bāqī. 5 vols. [Cairo]: ʿĪsā al-Bābī al-Ḥalabī, 1374–5/1955–6. Reprinted Beirut: Dār al-Fikr, 1419/1999.

Musnad ʿUmar b. ʿAbd al-ʿAzīz. Edited by A. H. Harley. *Journal of Asiatic Society of Bengal*, New Series 20 (1924), pp. 391–488.

Mustawfī, Ḥamd Allāh. *Nuzhat al-qulūb*. Partially edited by Guy Le Strange. 2 vols. Leiden: E. J. Brill and London: Luzac, 1915–19.

al-Muttaqī al-Hindī, ʿAlī b. ʿAbd al-Malik. *Kanz al-ʿummāl fī sunan al-aqwāl wa-l-afʿāl*. 16 vols. in 8. Beirut: Dār al-Kutub al-ʿIlmiyya, 1419/1998.
al-Nābulusī, ʿAbd al-Ghanī b. Ismāʿīl. *Ahl al-janna wa-ahl al-nār*. Cairo: Maktabat al-Turāth al-Islāmī, 2002.
Nahj al-balāgha. With a commentary by Muḥammad ʿAbduh. 4 vols. in 1. [Cairo]: Maktabat al-Naḥda al-ʿArabiyya, n.d.
al-Najāshī, Aḥmad b. ʿAlī. *Fihrist asmāʾ muṣannifī l-Shīʿa*. First published 1317sh/[1899]. Qum: Maktabat al-Dāwarī, [1977].
al-Nājī, Ibrāhīm b. Muḥammad. *Al-Ḥuṣūl al-bāghiya li-l-sāʾil hal li-aḥadin min ahl al-janna liḥya*. MS Staatsbibliothek Berlin We 409, fols. 11v–13v.
al-Nasafī, Abū l-Muʿīn. *Tabṣirat al-adilla*. Edited by Claude Salamé. Damascus: IFEAD, 1990–3.
Nasafī, ʿAzīz-i. *Al-Insān al-kāmil*. Edited by Marijan Molé. *Le livre de l'homme parfait*. Tehran. Chāpkhāna-yi Taban, 1962.
Kashf al-ḥaqāʾiq. MS Istanbul Nuru Osmaniye 4899, fols. 220v–314r.
al-Nasāʾī, Aḥmad b. Shuʿayb. *Al-Sunan al-kubrā*. Edited by ʿAbd al-Ghaffār Sulaymān al-Bundārī and Sayyid Kisrawī Ḥasan. 6 vols. Beirut: Dār al-Kutub al-ʿIlmiyya, 1411/1991.
al-Nawawī, Yaḥyā b. Sharaf. *Rawḍat al-ṭālibīn*. Edited by Aḥmad ʿAbd al-Mawjūd. Beirut: Dār al-Kutub al-ʿIlmiyya, n.d.
Riyāḍ al-ṣāliḥīn. Edited by Māhir Yāsīn al-Faḥl. Damascus and Beirut: Dār Ibn Kathīr, 1428/2007.
Sharḥ Ṣaḥīḥ Muslim. Edited by Ṭaha ʿAbd al-Raʾūf. 18 fasc. in 9 vols. [Cairo]: Al-Maktaba al-Tawfīqiyya, n.d.
al-Niffarī, Muḥammad b. ʿAbd al-Jabbār. *Al-Mawāqif wa l-mukhāṭabāt*. Edited and translated by Arthur J. Arberry. *The Mawáqif and Mukhátabát of Muḥammad b. ʿAbd al-Jabbár Al-Niffarí*. London: Luzac, 1935.
al-Nuwayrī, Aḥmad b. ʿAbd al-Wahhāb. *Nihāyat al-arab fī funūn al-adab*. Cairo: Dār al-Kutub al-Miṣriyya, 1342/1923.
al-Pazdawī, Abū l-Yusr Muḥammad b. Muḥammad. *Uṣūl al-dīn*. Edited by Hans Peter Lins. Cairo: Dār Iḥyāʾ al-Kutub al-ʿArabiyyah, 1963.
(Pseudo-)ʿAbdān. *K. Shajarat al-yaqīn*. Edited by ʿĀrif Tāmir. Beirut: Dār al-Āfāq al-Jadīda, 1982.
al-Qāḍī, ʿAbd al-Raḥīm (attr.). *Daqāʾiq al-akhbār*. *See Daqāʾiq al-akhbār*.
al-Qāḍī ʿIyāḍ b. Mūsā. *Ikmāl al-muʿlim bi-fawāʾid Muslim*. Edited by Yaḥyā Ismāʿīl. 9 vols. Mansoura: Dār al-Wafāʾ, 1998.
Tartīb al-madārik wa-taqrīb al-masālik li-maʿrifat aʿlām madhhab Mālik. Rabat: Wizārat al-Awqāf, 1983.
al-Qāḍī al-Nuʿmān = Abū Ḥanīfa Nuʿmān b. Muḥammad. *Taʾwīl al-daʿāʾim*. Edited by ʿĀrif Tāmir. 3 vols. in 2. Beirut: Dār al-Aḍwāʾ, 1995.
al-Qārī al-Harawī, ʿAlī b. Sulṭān. *Farr al-ʿawn min muddaʿī īmān Firʿawn*. Edited by Ibn al-Khaṭīb. [Cairo]: Al-Maṭbaʿa al-Miṣriyya wa-Maktabatuhā, [1383/1964].
Al-Muqaddima al-sālima fī khawf al-khātima. Tanta: Dār al-Ṣaḥāba li-l-Turāth, 1412/1992.
Al-Qawl al-sadīd fī khulf al-waʿīd. Ṭanṭā: Dār al-Ṣaḥāba li-l-Turāth, 1412/1992.
al-Qāshānī, ʿAbd al-Razzāq. *Majmūʿa-yi rasāʾil wa-muṣannafāt*. Edited by Majīd Hādīzādeh. Tehran: Mirāth-i Maktūb, 2000.

Qiṣṣat Idrīs. MS Bibliothèque Nationale de France Arabe 1947.
al-Qummī, ʿAbbās b. Muḥammad Riḍā. *Manāzil al-ākhira*. Arabic translation by Ḥusayn Kūrdī. [Beirut]: Dār al-Taʿāruf li-l-Maṭbūʿāt, 1413/1993, 3rd ed.
al-Qummī, ʿAlī b. Ibrāhīm. *Al-Tafsīr*. Beirut: Muʾassasat al-Aʿlamī li-l-Maṭbūʿāt, 1428/2007.
al-Qurʾān al-karīm. Cairo 1924. Translated by M. A. S. Abdel Haleem. *The Qurʾān*. Oxford and New York: Oxford University Press, 2008; Arthur Arberry. *The Koran interpreted*. New York: Macmillan, 1955; Jacques Berque. *Le Coran*. Paris: Sindbad, 1990; Alan Jones. *The Qurʾān*. [Cambridge]: Gibb Memorial Trust, 2007; Fred Leemhuis. *De Koran*. Houten: Het wereldvenster, 1990; Rudi Paret. *Der Koran: Übersetzung*. Stuttgart: W. Kohlhammer, 1979.
Qurrat al-ʿuyūn wa-mufriḥ al-qalb al-maḥzūn. Apud al-Shaʿrānī, ʿAbd al-Wahhāb b. Aḥmad. *Mukhtaṣar tadhkirat al-Qurṭubī*. Cairo: Maṭbaʿat Muṣṭafā al-Bābī al-Ḥalabī, 1358/1939.
al-Qurṭubī, Muḥammad b. Aḥmad. *Al-Jāmiʿ li-aḥkām al-Qurʾān*. Riyadh: Dār ʿĀlam al-Kutub, 1423/2003.
Al-Tadhkira fī aḥwāl al-mawtā wa-umūr al-ākhira. Edited by Aḥmad Ḥijāzī al-Saqqā. 2 vols. in 1. Cairo: Maktabat al-Kulliyāt al-Azhariyya, 1980.
al-Qushayrī, Abū l-Qāsim ʿAbd al-Karīm. *Al-Rasāʾil al-Qushayriyya*. Edited by Muḥammad Ḥasan. Karachi: Al-Maʿhad al-Markazī li-l-Abḥāth al-Islāmiyya, 1964.
Al-Risāla al-Qushayriyya fī ʿilm al-taṣawwuf. Edited by Maʿrūf Muṣṭafā Zurayq. Beirut: Al-Maktaba al-ʿAṣriyya, 1426/2005. Translated by Alexander Knysh. *Al-Qushayrī's epistle on Sufism*. Reading, UK: Garnet Publishing, 2007.
al-Rabaʿī, ʿAlī b. Muḥammad. *Faḍāʾil al-Shām wa-Dimashq*. Edited by Ṣalāḥ al-Dīn al-Munajjid. Damascus: Maṭbaʿat al-Turkī, 1950.
al-Rāfiʿī, ʿAbd al-Karīm b. Muḥammad. *Al-Tadwīn fī akhbār Qazwīn*. Edited by ʿAzīz Allāh al-ʿAṭaridī. Hyderabad: Al-Maṭbaʿa al-ʿAzīziyya, 1984.
Rahman, Fazlur. *Islam and modernity: Transformation of an intellectual tradition*. Chicago: University of Chicago Press, 1982.
al-Rāzī, Fakhr al-Dīn. *Al-Shafāʿa al-ʿuẓmā fī yawm al-qiyāma*. Edited by Aḥmad Ḥijāzī Aḥmād al-Saqā. Cairo: al-Maktaba al-Azhariyya li-l-Turāth, 1409/1989.
al-Rāzī, Najm al-Dīn Dāya. *Mirṣād al-ʿibād min al-mabdaʾ ilā l-maʿād*. Translated by Hamid Algar. *The path of God's bondmen from origin to return*. North Haledon, NJ: Islamic Publications International, 1980.
Riḍā, Rashīd. "Khurūj al-Nīl wa-l-Furāt min Sidrat al-Muntahā wa-kawnuhumā min al-janna." *Majallat al-manār* 22,4 (March 1921), pp. 260–2.
Rūmī, Jalāl al-Dīn. *Fīhi mā fīhi*. Edited by Badīʿ al-Zamān Furūzānfar. Tehran: Intishārāt-i Dānishgāh, 1330sh/[1951], 2nd ed. Translated by Arthur Arberry. *Discourses of Rūmī*. London: John Murray, 1961.
Mathnawī. Edited, with critical notes, translation, and commentary by Reynold A. Nicholson. *The Mathnawí of Jalálu'ddín Rúmí*. 8 vols. London: Luzac and Co., 1925–40.
Ṣadrā, Mullā = al-Shīrāzī, Ṣadr al-Dīn Muḥammad Mullā Ṣadrā. *Al-Ḥikma al-ʿarshiyya*. Edited by Fātin M. Kh. al-Labūn and Fuʾad Dakār. Beirut: Muʾassasat al-Tārīkh al-ʿArabī, 2000. Translated by James Winston Morris. *The wisdom of the throne: An introduction to the philosophy of Mulla Sadra*. Princeton, NJ: Princeton University Press, 1981, pp. 89–258.

Al-Mabda' wa-l-ma'ād. Edited by Jalāl al-Dīn Āshtiyānī. Tehran: Imperial Iranian Academy of Philosophy, 1976. Repr. Tehran: Būstān-i Kitāb Publishers, 2008.
Al-Shawāhid al-rubūbiyya. Edited by Jalāl al-Dīn Āshtiyānī. Mashhad: Chāpkhāna-yi Dānishgāh-i Mashhad, 1967.
Tafsīr al-Qur'ān al-karīm. 7 vols. Qum: Intishārāt-i Bīdār, 1366–69sh/1987–90.
Ta'līqāt Ṣadr al-muta'allihīn. Printed *apud* al-Shīrāzī. *Sharḥ Ḥikmat al-ishrāq*. Edited by S. M. Musavi. 2 vols. Tehran: Mu'assasa-yi Intishārāt-i Ḥikmat, 2010.
al-Ṣafadī, Khalīl b. Aybak. *Al-Wāfī bi-l-wafayāt*. Edited by Aḥmad Arna'ūṭ and Turkī Muṣṭafā. 29 vols. Beirut: Dār Iḥyā' al-Turāth al-'Arabī, 1420/2000.
al-Saffārīnī, Muḥammad b. Aḥmad. *Al-Buḥūr al-zākhira fī 'ulūm al-ākhira*. Edited by 'Abd al-'Azīz Aḥmad b. Muhammad b. Ḥammūd al-Mushayqiḥ. Riyadh: Dār al-'Āṣima li-l-Nashr wa-l-Tawzī', 2009.
al-Sakhāwī, Muḥammad b. 'Abd al-Raḥmān. *Al-Maqāṣid al-ḥasana fī bayān kathīr min al-aḥādīth al-mushtahira 'alā l-alsina*. Edited by 'Abdallah Muḥammad al-Ṣiddīq. Beirut: Dār al-Kutub al-'Ilmiyya, 1399/1979.
al-Samarqandī, Abū l-Layth. *Sharḥ al-fiqh al-absaṭ li-Abī Ḥanīfa*. Edited by Hans Daiber. *The Islamic concept of belief in the 4th/10th century*. Tokyo: Institute for the Study of Languages and Cultures of Asia and Africa, Tokyo University of Foreign Studies, 1995.
(attr.). *Al-Ḥaqā'iq wa-l-daqā'iq. See Daqā'iq al-akhbār.*
(attr.). *Qurrat al-'uyūn. See Qurrat al-'uyūn.*
Tafsīr [= *Baḥr al-'ulūm*]. Edited by Maḥmūd Maṭrajī. 3 vols. Beirut: Dār al-Fikr, n.d.
Tanbīh al-ghāfilīn. Edited by Haytham Khalīfat al-Ṭu'aymī. Ṣaydā-Beirut: Al-Maktaba al-'Aṣriyya, 1427/2006.
al-Samhūdī, 'Alī b. Aḥmad. *Wafā' al-wafā' bi-akhbār dār al-muṣṭafā*. Edited by M. Muḥyī al-Dīn 'Abd al-Ḥamīd. 4 parts in 2 vols. Cairo: 1374/1955.
al-Ṣan'ānī, 'Abd al-Razzāq. *See* 'Abd al-Razzāq.
al-Ṣan'ānī al-Mu'ayyad bi-llāh, Muḥammad b. Ismā'īl. *Raf' al-astār li-ibṭāl adillat al-qā'ilīn bi-fanā' al-nār*. Edited by Muḥammad Nāṣir al-Dīn al-Albānī. Beirut: Al-Maktab al-Islāmī, 1984.
al-Sarrāj, 'Abdallāh b. 'Alī. *K. al-Luma' fī al-taṣawwuf*. Edited by Reynold Nicholson. Leiden: Brill, 1914. Translated by Richard Gramlich. *Schlaglichter über das Sufitum: Abū Naṣr as-Sarrāğs* Kitāb al-luma'. Stuttgart: F. Steiner, 1990.
al-Shahrastānī, Muḥammad b. 'Abd al-Karīm. *K. al-Milal wa-l-niḥal*. Edited by William Cureton. London: Society for the Publication of Oriental Texts, 1842–6.
al-Shahrazūrī, Shams al-Dīn Muḥammad b. Maḥmūd. *Al-Shajara al-ilāhiyya fī 'ulūm al-ḥaqā'iq al-rabbāniyya*. Edited by Najafqulī Habibi. Tehran: Mu'assasa-yi Pizhuhūhishī-yi Ḥikmat wa-Falsafa, 1383sh/[2004–5].
Sharḥ Ḥikmat al-ishrāq. Edited by Hossein Ziai. Tehran: Mu'assasa-yi Muṭāla'āt wa-Taḥqiqāt-i Farhangī, 1372sh/[1993].
Shajarat al-yaqīn. See Daqā'iq al-akhbār.
Shaqīq al-Balkhī. *Ādāb al-'ibādāt*. Edited by Paul Nwyia. *Trois oeuvres inédites de mystiques musulmans*. Beirut: Dar al-Machreq, 1973, pp. 17–22.
al-Sharafī, Aḥmad b. Muḥammad b. Ṣalāḥ. *'Uddat al-akyās fī sharḥ ma'ānī al-Asās*. 2 vols. Ṣan'ā': Dār al-Ḥikma al-Yamaniyya, 1995.
al-Sha'rānī, 'Abd al-Wahhāb b. Aḥmad. *Mukhtaṣar Tadhkirat al-imām Abī 'Abdillāh al-Qurṭubī*. Cairo: 'Īsā al-Bābī al-Ḥalabī, 1358/1939.
Al-Mīzān al-kubrā. 2 vols. in 1. Cairo: Muṣṭafā al-Bābī al-Ḥalabī, [1940].

Al-Ṭabaqāt al-kubrā. 2 vols. Cairo: s.n., 1299/[1881].

Shaykhzādeh, ʿAbd al-Raḥīm b. ʿAlī Ibn al-Muʾayyad. *Naẓm al-farāʾiḍ wa-jamʿ al-fawāʾid*. In *Al-Masāʾil al-khilāfiyyha bayna Ashāʿirah wa-l-Māturīdiyyah*. Edited by Bassām ʿA. al-Jābī. Limassol: al-Jaffān wa-al-Jābī lil-Ṭibāʿah wa-al-Nashr; Beirut: Dār Ibn Ḥazm, 2003, pp. 167–266.

al-Shinnāwī, ʿAbd al-ʿAzīz. *Mashāhir nisāʾ ahl al-nār*. Cairo: Maktabat al-Turāth al-Islāmī, 1990.

Nisāʾ ahl al-janna. Cairo: Maktabat al-Turāth al-Islāmī, 1990.

al-Shīrāzī, Quṭb al-Dīn Maḥmūd b. Masʿūd. *Risāla fī taḥqīq ʿālam al-mithāl*. Edited and translated by John Walbridge. *The science of mystic lights: Quṭb al-Dīn al-Shīrāzī and the illuminationist tradition in Islamic philosophy*. Cambridge, MA: Harvard University Press, 1992.

Sharḥ Ḥikmat al-ishrāq. Edited by ʿAbdallāh Nūrānī and Mahdī Muḥaqqiq. Tehran: Muʾassasa-yi Muṭālaʿāt-i Islāmī, 2001.

al-Shirbīnī, Yūsuf. *Hazz al-quḥūf bi-sharḥ qaṣīd Abī Shādūf*. Edited and translated by Humphrey Davies. 2 vols. Leuven: Peeters, 2007.

Sibṭ b. al-Jawzī, Yūsuf b. Qizughlī. *Mirʾāt al-zamān fī tārīkh al-aʿyān*. Edited by Iḥsān ʿAbbās. Beirut: Dār al-Shurūq, 1405/1985.

Ṣiddīq Ḥasan Khān, Muḥammad. *Yaqaẓat ūlī l-iʿtibār mimmā warada fī dhikr al-nār wa-aṣḥāb al-nār*. Beirut: Dār Ibn Ḥazm, 1426/2005.

Jahannam: aḥwāluhā wa-ahluhā. Amman: al-Maktabah al-Islāmīyah, 1408/[1987–8].

al-Sijistānī, Abū Yaʿqūb. *K. al-Iftikhār*. Edited by Ismail K. Poonawala. Beirut: Dār al-Gharb al-Islāmī, 2000.

Kashf al-maḥjūb. Translated by Henry Corbin. *Le dévoilement des choses cachées*. Lagrasse: Éditions Verdier, 1988.

K. al-Maqālīd al-malakūtiyya. Edited by Ismail K. Poonawala. Tunis: Dār al-Gharb al-Islāmī, 2011.

K. al-Yanābīʿ. Edited by Henry Corbin. *Trilogie ismaelienne: Textes edités avec traduction française et commentaire*. Tehran: Institut franco-iranien, 1961, pp. 1–92. Translated by Paul Walker. *The wellsprings of wisdom: A study of Abū Yaʿqūb al-Sijistānī's Kitāb al-Yanābīʿ including a complete English translation with commentary and notes on the Arabic text*. Salt Lake City: University of Utah Press, 1994, pp. 37–112.

Al-Risāla al-bāhira. Edited by B. Hīrjī. *Taḥqīqāt-i islāmī* 7 (1371sh/1992), pp. 37–50.

Sīrat al-malik Iskandar Dhū l-Qarnayn. MS Bibliothèque Nationale de France Arabe 3687.

Sirhindī, Shaykh Aḥmad. *Mabdaʾ wa-maʿād*. Delhi: s.n., n.d.

al-Sirjānī, Abū l-Ḥasan. *K. al-Bayāḍ wa-l-sawād min khaṣāʾiṣ ḥikam al-ʿibād fī naʿt al-murīd wa-l-murād*. Edited by Bilal Orfali and Nada Saab. *Sufism, black and white*. Leiden: Brill, 2012.

al-Subkī, Taqī al-Dīn ʿAlī b. ʿAbd al-Kāfī. *K. al-Iʿtibār bi-baqāʾ al-janna wa-l-nār*. In *al-Rasāʾil al-Subkiyya fī l-radd ʿalā Ibn Taymiyya wa-tilmīdhihi Ibn Qayyim al-Jawziyya*. Beirut: ʿĀlam al-Kutub, 1983.

al-Ṣūfī, Māhir Aḥmad. *Mawsūʿat al-ākhira*. 3 vols. Beirut: al-Maktaba al-ʿAṣriyya, 1426/2007.

al-Suhrawardī, Yaḥyā b. Ḥabash. *Alwāḥ-i ʿimādī*. In *Oeuvres philosophiques et mystiques*, Vol. 3. Edited by Henry Corbin. Istanbul: Maarif Matbaasi, 1945–.

Ḥikmat al-ishrāq. Edited and translated by John Walbridge and Hossein Ziai. *The philosophy of illumination*. Provo, UT: Brigham Young University Press, 1999.

al-Sulamī, Abū ʿAbd al-Raḥmān. *Ḥaqāʾiq al-tafsīr: tafsīr al-qurʾān al-ʿazīz*. 2 vols. Edited by Sayyid ʿUmrān. Beirut: Dār al-Kutub al-ʿIlmiyya, 2001.

Masāʾil wa-taʾwīlāt ṣūfiyya. Edited by Bilal Orfali and Gerhard Böwering. Beirut: Dār al-Mashriq, 2012, 2nd ed.

al-Sulamī, ʿAlī b. Ṭāhir. *K. al-Jihād*. MS Asad Library Damascus (no cataloguing information available), formerly MS Ẓāhiriyya 3796, fols. 172–237, and 4511, fols. 1–20.

al-Suyūṭī, Jalāl al-Dīn ʿAbd al-Raḥmān. *Al-Budūr al-sāfira fī ʿulūm al-ākhira*. Edited by Abū ʿAbdallāh Muḥammad al-Shāfiʿī. Beirut: Dār al-Kutub, 1416/1996.

Bushrā l-kaʾīb bi-liqāʾ al-ḥabīb. Edited by Majdī al-Sayyid Ibrāhīm. Cairo: Maktabat al-Qurʾān, [1986].

al-Suyūṭī, Jalāl al-Dīn ʿAbd al-Rahmān (attr.). *Al-Durar al-ḥusān*. *See al-Durar al-ḥusān*.

al-Suyūṭī, Jalāl al-Dīn ʿAbd al-Raḥmān. *Al-Durr al-manthūr fī l-tafsīr bi-l-maʾthūr*. 6 vols. Cairo: Al-Maṭbaʿa al-Maymaniyya, 1314/[1897]. Repr. Beirut: Dār al-Maʿrifa, [1972?].

Faḍl al-jalad fī faqd al-walad. MS Staatsbibliothek Berlin Spr 724, fols. 1r–28v.

Al-Ḥabāʾik fī akhbār al-malāʾik. Edited by Muḥammad Zaghlūl. Beirut: Dār al-Kutub al-ʿIlmiyya, 1985. Partially translated by Stephen R. Burge. *Angels in Islam: Jalāl al-Dīn al-Suyūṭī's al-Ḥabāʾik fī akhbār al-malāʾik*. London and New York: Routledge, 2012, pp. 114–74.

Isbāl al-kisāʾ ʿalā l-nisāʾ and Tuḥfat al-julasāʾ bi-ruʾyat Allāh li-l-nisāʾ. Beirut: Dār al-Kutub al-ʿIlmiyya, 1405/1985.

Al-Laʾālī al-maṣnūʿa. 2 vols. Cairo: al-Maktaba al-Tijāriyya al-Kubrā, n.d. Repr. Beirut: Dār al-Maʿrifa, 1401/1981.

Al-Maʿānī al-daqīqa fī idrāk al-ḥaqīqa. MS Staatsbibliothek Berlin Pm 407, fols. 226r–232v.

Masālik al-ḥunafāʾ fī wāliday al-muṣṭafā. MS Staatsbibliothek Berlin We 1725, fols. 12–32.

Al-Muzhir fī ʿulūm al-lugha wa-anwāʿihā. Edited by Muḥammad Aḥmad Jādd al-Mawlā, Muḥammad Abū l-Faḍl Ibrāhīm, and ʿAlī Muḥammad al-Bajāwī. [Cairo]: Dār Iḥyāʾ al-Kutub al-ʿArabiyya, [1958].

Risāla fī dhabḥ al-mawt. MS Staatsbibliothek Berlin Pm 407, fols. 291r–293v.

Sharḥ al-ṣudūr. Damascus and Beirut: Dār Ibn Kathīr, 1429/2008, 5th ed.

Taʾyīd al-ḥaqīqa al-ʿaliyya wa-tashyīd al-ṭarīqa al-Shādhiliyya. Edited by ʿAbdallāh b. Muḥammad b. al-Ṣiddīq al-Ghumarī al-Ḥasanī. [Cairo]: Al-Maṭbaʿa al-Islāmiyya, 1934.

al-Ṭabarānī, Sulaymān b. Aḥmad. *Al-Muʿjam al-kabīr*. 28 vols. Edited by Ḥamdī b. ʿAbd al-Majīd al-Salafī. Mosul: Maktabat al-ʿUlūm, 1404, 2nd ed./1983.

al-Ṭabarī, Muḥammad b. Jarīr. *Jāmiʿ al-bayan ʿan taʾwīl āy al-Qurʾān*. Edited by Maḥmūd Shākir Ḥaristānī and ʿAlī ʿĀshūr. 30 vols. in 16. Beirut: Dār Iḥyāʾ al-Turāth al-ʿArabī, [2011?].

Tahdhīb al-āthār wa-tafṣīl al-thābit ʿan rasūl Allāh min al-akhbār. Edited by Maḥmūd Muḥammad Shākir. 3 vols. Cairo: Maṭbaʿat al-Madanī, [1982–3].
al-Taftāzānī, Masʿūd b. ʿUmar. *Sharḥ al-maqāṣid*. Edited by ʿAbd al-Raḥmān ʿUmayra. 5 vols. Beirut: ʿĀlam al-Kutub, 1989.
al-Tahānawī, Muḥammad ʿAlī. *Kashshāf iṣṭilāḥāt al-funūn wa-l-ʿulūm*. Edited by ʿAlī Daḥrūj. 2 vols. Beirut: Maktabat Lubnān Nāshirūn, 1996.
al-Ṭahṭāwī, ʿAlī ʿAbd al-ʿĀl. *Naʿīm ahl al-janna wa-ʿadhāb ahl al-nār*. [Cairo]: Al-Maktaba al-Tawfīqiyya, n.d.
al-Tawḥīdī, Abū Ḥayyān. *Al-Imtāʿ wa-l-muʾānasa*. Edited by Aḥmad Amīn and Aḥmad al-Zayn. 3 vols. in 1. Beirut: Al-Maktaba al-ʿAṣriyya, 1373/1953.
Al-Muqābasāt. MS Leiden 1443.
al-Thaʿālibī, ʿAbd al-Malik b. Muḥammad. *Thimār al-qulūb fī l-muḍāf wa-l-mansūb*. Edited by Muḥammad Abū l-Faḍl Ibrāhīm. Cairo: Dār Naḥdat Miṣr, 1965.
al-Thaʿālibī, ʿAbd al-Raḥmān. *K. al-ʿulūm al-fākhira fī l-naẓar fī umūr al-ākhira*. 2 vols. in 1. [Cairo]: al-Maṭbaʿa al-Ḥamīdiyya al-Miṣriyya, 1317/[1899].
al-Thaʿlabī, Aḥmad b. Muḥammad. *ʿArāʾis al-majālis*. Beirut: Dār al-Fikr, 1324/2004.
Al-Kashf wa-l-bayān. Edited by Abū Muḥammad Ibn ʿĀshūr. 10 vols. Beirut: Dār Iḥyāʾ al-Turāth al-ʿArabī, 1422/2002.
The Arabian nights. Translated by Malcom C. Lyons. 3 vols. London: Penguin, 2008.
al-Tirmidhī, Muḥammad b. ʿĪsā. *Al-Jāmiʿ al-ṣaḥīḥ*. Edited by Aḥmad Muḥammad Shākir, Muḥammad Fuʾād ʿAbd al Bāqī, and Ibrāhīm ʿAṭwa ʿIwaḍ. 5 vols. Cairo: Muṣṭafā al Bābī al Ḥalabī, 1356–95/1937–75.
al-Ṭūsī, Muḥammad b. al-Ḥasan. *Al-Amālī*. 2 vols. Baghdad: Al-Maktaba al-Ahliyya, 1964.
Ṭūsī, Muḥammad b. Maḥmūd. *ʿAjāyib al-makhlūqāt*. Edited by Manūchihr Sotūda. Tehran: Nashr-i Kitāb, [1345sh/1966].
Ṭūsī, Naṣīr al-Dīn Muḥammad b. Muḥammad. *Al-Mabdaʾ wa-l-maʿād* [= *Aghāz-u anjām*]. Translated by S. J. Badakhchani. *Shiʿi interpretations of Islam: Three treatises on Islamic theology and eschatology*. London: I. B. Tauris, 2010, pp. 45–88.
Rawḍat al-taslīm. Edited and translated by S. J. Badakhchani. *Paradise of submission: A medieval treatise on Ismaili thought*. London: I. B. Tauris, 2005.
al-Tustarī, Sahl b. ʿAbdallāh. *Tafsīr*. Translated by Annabel Keeler and Ali Keeler. Louisville, KY: Fons Vitae, 2011.
Uighur *Miʿrājnāma*. Transcribed and translated by Max Scherrberger. *Das Miʿrāǧnāme. Die Himmel- und Höllenfahrt des Propheten Muḥammad in der osttürkischen Überlieferung*. Würzburg: Ergon Verlag, 2003.
al-ʿUlaymī al-Ḥanbalī, Mujīr al-Dīn. *Al-Uns al-jalīl bi-tārīkh al-Quds wa-l-Khalīl*. 2 vols. Cairo: al-Maṭbaʿa al-Wahbiliyya, 1283/[1866].
al-Wahrānī, Muḥammad b. Muḥammad. *Al-Manām al-aʿẓam*. In *Manāmāt al-Wahrānī wa-maqāmātuhu wa-rasāʾiluhu*. Edited by Ibrāhīm Shaʿlān and Muḥammad Naghsh. Cairo: Dār al-Kātib al-ʿArabi li-l-Ṭibāʿa wa-l-Nashr, 1387/1968, pp. 17–60.
Wakīʿ, Muḥammad b. Khalaf. *Akhbār al-quḍāt*. Edited by ʿAbd al-ʿAzīz Muṣṭafā al-Marāghī. 3 vols. Cairo: Maṭbaʿat al-Istiqāma, 1366–9/1947–50.
al-Wāsiṭī, Abū Bakr Muḥammad b. Aḥmad. *Faḍāʾil al-Bayt al-Muqaddas*. Edited by Isaac Hasson. Jerusalem: Hebrew University/The Max Schloessinger Memorial Series, 1979.

Wathā'iq fī shu'ūn al-'umrān fī l-Andalus: al-masājid wa-l-dūr. Edited by Muḥammad 'Abd al-Wahhāb Khallāf. Cairo: Al-Markaz al-'Arabī al-Dawlī li-l-I'lām, 1983.

Yāqūt b. 'Abdallāh al-Hamawī. *Mu'jam al-buldān*. 7 vols. Beirut: Dār Ṣādir, 1993.

al-Zahāwī, Jamīl Ṣidqī. "Thawra fī al-jaḥīm." First publ. 1931. Republ. in idem. *Dīwān Ṣidqī al-Zahāwī*. Beirut: Dār al-'Awda, 1972, Vol. 1, pp. 715–36. Translated by G. Widmer. "Der 'irāqische Dichter Ǧamīl Ṣidqī az-Zahāwī aus Baghdad." *Die Welt des Islams* 17, 1–2 (1935), pp. 1–79, at pp. 50–79.

Zakhr al-'ābidīn. MS Staatsbibliothek Berlin Mq 115, fols. 221r–237v.

al-Zamakhsharī, Muḥammad b. 'Umar. *Al-Kashshāf 'an ḥaqā'iq ghiwāmiḍ al-tanzīl wa-'uyūn al-aqāwīl fī wujūh al-tanzīl*. Edited by Muḥammad 'Abd al-Salām Shāhīn. 4 vols. Beirut: Dār al-Kutub al-'Ilmiyya, 2009.

al-Zarkashī, Muḥammad b. Bahādur. *Al-Burhān fī 'ulūm al-Qur'ān*. 4 vols. [Cairo]: Dār Iḥyā' al-Kutub al-'Arabiyya, 1957–58.

Zāyid, Shiḥāṭa. *Mukhtaṣar al-Tadhkira fī aḥwāl al-mawtā wa-umūr al-ākhira*. Cairo: Al-Mukhtār al-Islāmī, 1988.

Secondary Sources

Abrahamov, Binyamin. "The creation and duration of paradise and hell in Islamic theology." *Der Islam* 79 (2002), pp. 87–102.

Abu-Deeb, Kamal. *The imagination unbound:* Al-adab al-ʿajāʾibī *and the literature of the fantastic.* London: Saqi, 2007.

Adam, Charles J. "The study of religions and the study of Islam." In *The History of religions: Essays on the problem of understanding.* Edited by Joseph M. Kitagawa. Chicago: Chicago University Press, 1967, pp. 177–93.

Aguadé, Jorge. "*Inna lladī yaʾkulu wa-yašrubu takūnu lahū l-ḥāğa*: Ein Beitrag zur jüdisch-christlichen Polemik gegen den Islam." *Welt des Orients* 10 (1979), pp. 61–72.

Ahlwardt, W. Die Handschriften-Verzeichnisse der Königlichen Bibliothek zu Berlin. Vol. 7–9: *Verzeichnis der arabischen Handschriften.* 3 vols. Berlin: A. W. Schade's Buchdruck, 1887.

Ahmed, Waleed. "The characteristics of paradise (*ṣifat al-janna*): A genre of eschatological literature in medieval Islam." In Günther and Lawson, eds. *Roads to paradise*, forthcoming.

Ahrens, Karl. *Muhammad als Religionsstifter.* Leipzig: DMG in Kommission bei F.A. Brockhaus, 1935.

Al-Azmeh, Aziz. *Muslim kingship: Power and the sacred in Muslim, Christian and pagan polities.* London and New York: I. B. Tauris, 1997.

"Preamble." *The Medieval History Journal* 9,1 (2006), pp. 17–36.

"Rhetoric for the senses: A consideration of Muslim paradise narratives." *Journal of Arabic Literature* 26,3 (1995), pp. 215–31.

Al-Najdī, Muḥammad b. ʿAbdallah. *Al-Suḥub al-wābila ʿalā ḍarāʾiḥ al-Ḥanābila.* 3 vols. Beirut: Muʾassasat al-Risāla, 1996.

Al-Shāljī, ʿAbbūd. *Mawsūʿat al-ʿadhāb.* 7 vols. Beirut: al-Dār al-ʿArabiyya li-l-Mawsūʿāt, 1980.

Al-Tihrānī, Āghā Buzurg. *Al-Dharīʿa ilā taṣānīf al-Shīʿa.* 25 vols. Tehran and Najaf: Maṭbaʿat al-Gharrā, 1936–78.

Alexandrin, Elizabeth. "Paradise as the abode of pure knowledge: Reconsidering al-Mu'ayyad's 'Isma'ili Neoplatonism.'" In Günther and Lawson, eds. *Roads to paradise*, forthcoming.

Allen, Terri. "Imagining Paradise in Islamic Art." In *Five Essays on Islamic Art* (1988). Online publication (http://www.sonic.net/~tallen/palmtree/ip.html).

Almond, Philip C. *Heretic and hero: Muhammad and the Victorians*. Wiesbaden: Harrassowitz, 1989.

Amir-Moezzi, Mohammad Ali, ed. *Le voyage initiatique en terre d'Islam: Ascensions célestes et itinéraires spirituels*. Louvain: Peeters, 1996.

"L'Imām dans le ciel: Ascension et initation (Aspects de l'Imāmologie Duodécimaine III)." In Amir-Moezzi, ed. *Le voyage initiatique*, pp. 99–116.

"Notes à propos de la walāya Imamite (aspects de l'Imamologie duodécimaine, X)." *JAOS* 122 (2002), pp. 722–41.

The divine guide in early Shi'ism: The sources of exotericism in Islam. Translated by David Streight. Albany, NY: SUNY Press, 1994.

"Some remarks on the divinity of the Imam." In *The divine guide*, pp. 103–21.

"The pre-existence of the Imam." In *The divine guide*, pp. 29–59.

Anawati, Georges C. "La notion de 'péché originel' existe-t-elle en Islam?" *SI* 31 (1970), pp. 29–40.

And, Metin. *Minyatür*. Istanbul: Türkiye İş Bankası, 2002.

Minyatürlerle Osmanlı-İslâm mitologyası. Istanbul: Akbank, 1998.

Anderson, G. "The cosmic mountain: Eden and its interpreters in Syriac Christianity." In *Genesis 1–3 in the history of exegesis*. Edited by G. A. Robbins. Lewiston, NY: Mellen, 1988, pp. 187–223.

Andræ, Tor. *Die Person Mohammed in Lehre und Glauben seiner Gemeinde*. Stockholm: Kungl. boktryckeriet. P. A. Norstedt & söner, 1917. Translated by Theophil Menzel. *Mohammed: The man and his faith*. First published 1936. Mineola, NY: Dover Publications, 2000.

Der Ursprung des Islams und das Christentum. Uppsala and Stockholm: Almquist, 1926. Translated by J. Roche. *Les origines de l'islam et le christianisme*. Paris: Adrien-Maisonneuve, 1955.

Antrim, Zayde. *Routes and realms: The power of place in the early Islamic world*. Oxford: Oxford University Press, 2012.

Arberry, Arthur. "Introduction." In idem, ed. *K. al-Tawahhum*. Cairo: Lajnat al-Ta'līf wa-l-Tarjama wa-l-Nashr, 1937.

Sufism: An account of the mystics of Islam. London: George Allen and Unwin Ltd., 1950.

Ariès, Phillipe. *L'homme devant la mort*. Paris: Éditions du Seuil, 1977.

Arkoun, Mohamed. "Peut-on parler de merveilleux dans le Coran?" In Mohamed Arkoun, Jacques Le Goff, Tawfiq Fahd, and Maxime Rodinson. *L'étrange et le merveilleux dans l'islam médiéval*. Paris: Editions J. A., 1978, pp. 1–24 (followed by a transcript of the "discussion du rapport," pp. 25–60).

Arkoun, Mohamed, Le Goff, Jacques, Fahd, Tawfiq, and Rodinson, Maxime, eds. *L'étrange et le merveilleux dans l'Islam médiéval*. Paris: Editions J. A., 1978.

Arnzen, Rüdiger. *Platonische Ideen in der islamischen Philosophie: Texte und Materialien zur Begriffsgeschichte von* ṣuwar aflaṭūniyya *und* muthul aflāṭūniyya. Berlin and Boston: de Gruyter, 2011.

Asín Palacios, Miguel. *La espiritualidad de Algazel y su sentido cristiano*. 4 vols. Madrid: Maestre, 1934–.

La escatologia musulmana en la Divina comedia. Madrid: E. Maestre, 1919. Rev. ed. *La escatologia musulmana en la Divina comedia: Seguida de, Historia y crítica de una polémica*. Madrid: Hiperión, 1984, 2nd ed.

Assmann, Jan. *Tod und Jenseits im alten Ägypten*. Munich: C. H. Beck, 2001.

ʿAthamina, Khalil. "Al-Qasas: Its emergence, religious origin and its socio-political impact on early Muslim society." *SI* 76 (1992), pp. 53–74.

Attar, Samar. "An Islamic *paradiso* in a medieval Christian poem? Dante's *Divine Comedy* revisited." In Günther and Lawson, eds. *Roads to paradise*, forthcoming.

Aune, David. *The cultic setting of realized eschatology in early Christianity*. Leiden: E. J. Brill, 1972.

Avery, Kenneth. *Shiblī: His life and thought in the Sufi tradition*. Albany, NY: SUNY Press, 2014.

Avery-Peck, Alan J. "Resurrection of the body in early Rabbinic Judaism." *Deuterocanonical and Cognate Literature Yearbook* (2009), pp. 243–66.

Ayoub, Mahmoud. "Repentance in the Islamic tradition." In *Repentance: A comparative perspective*. Edited by Amitai Etzioni and David E. Carney. Lanham, MD: Rowman and Littlefield, 1997, pp. 96–121.

Azaiez, Mehdi. "Les contre-discours eschatologiques dans le Coran et le traité de Sanhédrin. Une réflexion sur les formes de la polémique coranique." In *Les origines du Coran, le Coran des origines*. Edited by François Deroche, Christian Julien Robin, and Michel Zink. Paris: Académie des Inscriptions et Belles-Lettres, 2015, pp. 111–27.

Badakhchani, S. J. "Introduction." In idem, trans. *Shīʿi interpretations of Islam: Three treatises on theology and eschatology: A Persian edition and English translation of Tawallā wa tabarrā, Maṭlūb al-muʾminīn, and Āghāz wa anjām of Naṣīr al-Dīn Ṭūsī*. London and New York: I. B. Tauris, 2010, pp. 1–22.

Badakhchani, S. J., ed. and trans. *Paradise of submission: A medieval treatise on Ismaili thought*. London: I. B. Tauris, 2005.

Badeen, Edward. *Sunnitische Theologie in osmanischer Zeit*. Würzburg: Ergon, 2008.

Baffioni, Carmela. "Bodily resurrection in the Iḫwān al-ṣafāʾ." In *Philosophy and arts in the Islamic world: Proceedings of the eighteenth congress of the Union Européenne des Arabisants et Islamisants held at the Katholieke Universiteit Leuven (September 3–September 9, 1996)*. Edited by Urbain Vermeulen and Daniel de Smet. Leuven: Peeters, 1998, pp. 201–8.

Bashier, Shahzad. *Sufi bodies: Religion and society in medieval Islam*. New York: Columbia University Press, 2011.

Bauer, Thomas. "Islamische Totenbücher." In *Studies in Arabic and Islam: Proceedings of the 19th Congress, Union Européenne des Arabisants et Islamisants, Halle 1998*. Edited by Stefan Leder, Hillary Kilpatrick, Bernadette Martel-Thoumian, and Hannelore Schönig. Sterling, VA: Peeters, 2002, pp. 421–36.

"The relevance of early Arabic poetry for Qurʾānic studies." In Neuwirth, Sinai, and Marx, eds. *The Quran in context*, pp. 699–732.

Beal, Timothy K. *Religion and its monsters*. New York: Routledge, 2002.

Beck, Edmund. "Eine christliche Parallele zu den Paradiesjungfrauen des Korans?" *Orientalia Christiana Periodica* 14 (1948), pp. 398–405.
"Les houris du Coran et Ephrem le Syrien," *MIDEO* 6 (1959–61), pp. 405–8.
Begley, Wayne E. "The myth of the Taj Mahal and a new theory of its symbolic meaning." *The Art Bulletin* 61,1 (1979), pp. 7–37.
Bell, Catherine. *Ritual theory, ritual practice*. New York and Oxford: Oxford University Press, 1992.
Bell, Richard. *A commentary on the Qur'ān*. Edited by Clifford E. Bosworth and M. E. M. Richardson. Manchester, UK: University of Manchester, 1991.
Introduction to the Qur'ān. Revised and enlarged by William Montgomery Watt. *Bell's introduction to the Qur'ān*. Edinburgh: Edinburgh University Press, 1970.
The origin of Islam in its Christian environment. London: Macmillan and Co., 1926.
Bellamy, James A. "*Fa-ummuhū hāwiyah:* A note on sūrah 101:9." *JAOS* 112 (1992), pp. 485–7.
"Some proposed emendations to the text of the Koran." *JAOS* 113,4 (1993), pp. 562–73.
Benjamins, H. S. "Paradisiacal life: The story of paradise in the early Church." In *Paradise interpreted: Representations of biblical paradise in Judaism and Christianity*. Edited by Gerard P. Luttikhuizen. Leiden: Brill, 1999, pp. 153–67.
Berkey, Jonathan. *Popular preaching and religious authority in the medieval Islamic Near East*. Seattle: University of Washington Press, 2001.
Berthels, E. "Die paradiesischen Jungfraun (Ḥūrīs) im Islam." *Islamica* 1 (1925), pp. 263–88.
Birkeland, Harris. *The Lord guideth: Studies on primitive Islam*. Oslo: I kommisjon hos H. Aschehoug (W. Nygaard), 1956.
Bisaha, Nancy. *Creating East and West: Renaissance humanists and Ottoman Turks*. Philadelphia: University of Pennsylvania Press, 2006.
Blair, Sheila, and Bloom, Jonathan M., eds. *Images of paradise in Islamic art*. Hanover, NH: Hood Museum of Art, 1991.
Bloom, Jonathan M. "Paradise as a garden, the garden as paradise." In Dévényi and Fodor, eds. *Proceedings* [Part 1], pp. 37–53.
Bobzin, Hartmut. *Der Koran: Eine Einführung*. Munich: C. H. Beck, 1999.
Bockmuehl, Markus. "Locating paradise." In *Paradise in antiquity: Jewish and Christian views*. Edited by Markus Bockmuehl and Guy G. Stroumsa. Cambridge: Cambridge University Press, 2010, pp. 192–209.
Bonner, Michael David. *Aristocratic violence and holy war: Studies in the Jihad and the Arab-Byzantine frontier*. New Haven, CT: American Oriental Society, 1996.
Bouhdiba, Abdelwahab. *Sexuality in Islam*. Translated by Alan Sheridan. London and Boston: Routledge and Kegan Paul, 1985.
Bouyges, Maurice. *Essai de chronologie des œuvres de al-Ghazali (Algazel)*. Edited and updated by Michel Allard. Beirut: Imprimerie catholique, 1959.
Böwering, Gerhard. *The mystical vision of existence in classical Islam: The Qur'ānic hermeneutics of the Ṣūfī Sahl al-Tustarī (d. 283/896)*. Berlin and New York: de Gruyter, 1980.

Boyce, Mary. *Textual sources for the study of Zoroastrianism*. Chicago: University of Chicago Press, 1984.
Braun, Oscar. "Beiträge zur Geschichte der Eschatologie in den syrischen Kirchen." *Zeitschrift für katholische Theologie* 16 (1892), pp. 273–312.
Bravmann, M. M. *The Spiritual background of early Islam: Studies in ancient Arab concepts*. Leiden: Brill, 1972.
Brisch, Klaus. "Observations on the iconography of the mosaics in the Great Mosque at Damascus." In *Contexts and contents of visual arts in the Islamic world: Papers from a colloquium in memory of Richard Ettinghausen*. Edited by Priscilla Soucek and Carol Bier. University Park: Published for the College Art Association of America by the Pennsylvania State University Press, 1988, pp. 13–20.
Brock, Sebastian. *The luminous eye: The spiritual world vision of Saint Ephrem*. First publ. 1982. Rev. ed. Kalamazoo, MI: Cistercian Publications, 1992.
Brown, Jonathan. "Even if it's not true it's true: Using unreliable ḥadīth in Sunni Islam." *Islamic Law and Society* 18 (2011), pp. 1–52.
Misquoting Muhammad: The challenge and choices of interpreting the Prophet's legacy. London: Oneworld, 2014.
The canonization of al-Bukhārī and Muslim: The formation and function of the Sunnī ḥadīth canon. Leiden: Brill, 2007.
Brown, Norman O. "The apocalypse of Islam." *Social Text* 3,8 (1983–4), pp. 155–71. Republ. in *The Qur'an: Style and content*. Edited by Andrew Rippin. Aldershot, UK: Ashgate, 2001, pp. 355–80.
Brown, Peter. "Late antiquity." In *A history of private life*. Vol. 1: *From pagan Rome to Byzantium*. Edited by Philippe Ariès and George Duby. Cambridge, MA: Belknapp Press of Harvard University Press, 1987–91, pp. 235–312.
Buck, Christopher. "Sapiential theosis: A new reading of Ephrem the Syrian's *Hymns on paradise*." *Journal of the Assyrian Academic Society* 9,2 (1995), pp. 80–125.
Buckley, Ronald P. "The Muḥtasib." *Arabica* 39 (1992), pp. 59–117.
The Night Journey and Ascension in Islam: The reception of religious narrative in Sunnī, Shīʿī and Western culture. London and New York: I. B. Tauris, 2013.
Burge, Stephen R. *Angels in Islam: Jalāl al-Dīn al-Suyūṭī's* al-Ḥabā'ik fī akhbār al-malā'ik. London and New York: Routledge, 2012.
Busse, Heribert. "Die Kanzel des Propheten im Paradiesgarten." *Welt des Islams* 28 (1988), pp. 99–111.
Campo, Juan Eduardo. "Authority, ritual and spatial order in Islam: The pilgrimage to Mecca." *Journal of Ritual Studies* 5 (1991), pp. 65–91.
Canova, Giovanni. "Animals in Islamic paradise and hell." In Dévényi and Fodor, eds., *Proceedings* [Part 1], pp. 55–81.
Carlyle, Thomas. "The hero as prophet. Mahomet: Islam." In *On heroes, hero-worship, and the heroic in history*. Edited by Archibald MacMechan. Boston: Ginn and Company, 1901, pp. 48–88.
Carra de Vaux, Bernard. "Fragments d'eschatologie musulmane." In *Compte rendu du troisième congrès scientifique international des catholiques tenu à Bruxelles du 3 au 8 septembre 1894*. Bruxelles: Société Belge de Librairie, 1895, Vol. 2, pp. 5–34.
Casanova, Paul. *Mohammed et la fin du monde. Étude critique sur l'Islam primitif*. Paris: P. Gauthier, 1911–24.

Casewit, Yousef. "The forgotten mystic: Ibn Barrajān (d. 536/1141) and the Andalusian *muʿtabirūn*." PhD diss., Yale University, 2014.
Casey, John. *After lives: A guide to heaven, hell, and purgatory*. Oxford: Oxford University Press, 2009.
Castillo Castillo, Concepción. *Kitāb Šaŷarat al-Yaqīn. See Daqāʾiq al-akhbār.*
Cerulli, Enrico. *Il "Libro della scala" e la question delle fonti arabo-spagnole della Divina Commedia*. Vatican: Bibliotheca Apostolica, 1949.
Nuove ricerche sul Libro della Scala e la conoscenza dell'Islam in Occidente. Vatican: Bibliotheca Apostolica Vaticana, 1972.
Chebel, Malek. *L'imaginaire arabo-musulman*. Paris: Presses Universitaires de France, 1993.
Chittick, William. "Death and the world of imagination: Ibn al-ʿArabī's eschatology." *MW* 78 (1988), pp. 51–82.
"Eschatology in Islamic thought." In *In search of the lost heart: Explorations in Islamic thought*. Edited by Mohammed Rustom, Atif Khalil, and Kazuyo Murata. Albany, NY: SUNY Press, 2012, pp. 233–57.
Imaginal worlds: Ibn al-ʿArabī and the problem of religious diversity. Albany, NY: SUNY Press, 1994.
"Muslim eschatology." In *The Oxford Handbook of Eschatology*. Edited by Jerry A. Walls. Oxford: Oxford University Press, 2008, pp. 132–50.
"The myth of Adam's Fall in Aḥmad Samʿānī's *Rawḥ al-arwāḥ*." In *The heritage of Sufism*. Vol. 1: *Classical Persian Sufism from its origins to Rumi (700–1300)*. Edited by Leonard Lewisohn. Oxford: Oneworld, 1999, pp. 337–59.
The self-disclosure of God: Principles of Ibn al-ʿArabī's cosmology. Albany, NY: SUNY Press, 1998.
The Sufi path of love: The spiritual teachings of Rumi. Albany, NY: SUNY Press, 1983.
Chodkiewicz, Michel. *Le sceau des saints: Prophétie et sainteté dans la doctrine d'Ibn Arabî*. [Paris]: Gallimard, 1986.
"The Vision of God according to Ibn ʿArabī." In *Sufism: Love and Wisdom*. Edited by J. L. Michon and R. Gaetani. Bloomington, IN: World Wisdom, 2006, pp. 33–48.
Christensen, Arthur. *Recherches sur les Rubāʿiyāt de ʿOmar Ḫayyām*. Heidelberg: Carl Winter's Universitätsbuchhandlung, 1905.
Christie, Niall. "Paradise and hell in the *Kitāb al-jihād* of ʿAbī b. Ṭāhir al-Sulamī (d. 500/1106)." In Günther and Lawson, eds. *Roads to paradise*, forthcoming.
Ciulianu, Ioan P. "The body reexamined." In *Religious reflections on the human body*. Edited by Jane Marie Law. Bloomington: Indiana University Press, 1995, pp. 1–18.
Cobb, Paul. "Virtual sacrality: Making Muslim Syria sacred before the Crusades." *Medieval Encounters* 8,1 (2002), pp. 35–55.
Coffey, Heather M. "Contesting the eschaton in medieval Iberia: The polemical intersection of Beatus of Liébana's Commentary on the Apocalypse and the Prophet's *Miʿrājnāma*." In Gruber and Colby, eds. *The Prophet's ascension*, pp. 97–137.
Colby, Frederick S. "Constructing an Islamic ascension narrative: The interplay of official and popular culture in Pseuo-Ibn ʿAbbās." PhD diss., Duke University, 2002.

"Fire in the upper heavens: Locating hell in Middle Period narratives of Muḥammad's Ascension." In Lange, ed. *Locating hell*, pp. 124-43.

Narrating Muḥammad's Night Journey: Tracing the development of the Ibn ʿAbbās Ascension discourse. Albany, NY: SUNY Press, 2008.

Coleridge, Samuel T. *Biographia Literaria: Vol. 1*. Edited by James Engell and W. Jackson Bate. Princeton, NJ: Princeton University Press, 1983.

Collins, John J. "The afterlife in apocalyptic literature." In *Judaism in late antiquity*. Edited by Jacob Neusner, Alan J. Avery-Peck, and Bruce Chilton. Leiden and New York: Brill, 1995–2001, Vol. 3, pp. 119–40.

Cook, David. *Studies in Muslim apocalyptic*. Princeton, NJ: Darwin Press, 2002.

Coppens, Pieter. "Seeing God in this world and the otherworld: Crossing boundaries in Sufi commentaries on the Qurʾān." PhD diss., Utrecht University, 2015.

Corbin, Henry. *En Islam iranien: Aspects spirituels et philosophiques*. Vol. 4: *L'école d'Ispahan, l'école shaykhie, le douzième Imâm*. Paris: Gallimard, 1972.

Spiritual body and celestial earth: From Mazdean Iran to Shīʿite Iran. Translated by Nancy Pearson. London: Tauris, 1990.

Costa, José. *L'au-delà et la résurrection dans la littérature rabbinique ancienne*. Paris and Louvain: Peeters, 2004.

Crone, Patricia. "Abū Saʿīd al-Ḥaḍrī and the punishment of unbelievers." *JSAI* 31 (2006), pp. 92–106.

"How did the Quranic pagans make a living?" *BSOAS* 68,3 (2005), pp. 387–99.

The nativist prophets of early Islamic Iran: Rural revolt and local Zoroastrianism. New York: Cambridge University Press, 2012.

"The Quranic *mushrikūn* and the resurrection (Part I)." *BSOAS* 75,3 (2012), pp. 445–72.

Custers, Martin. *Al-Ibāḍiyya: A bibliography*. 3 vols. Maastricht: Maastricht University Press, 2006.

Czachesz, István. "Why body matters in the afterlife: Mind reading and body imagery in synoptic tradition and the Apocalypse of Peter." In *The human body in death and resurrection*. Edited by Tobias Nicklas, Friedrich V. Reiterer, and Joseph Verheyden. Berlin and New York: de Gruyter, 2009, pp. 391–411.

Czapkiewicz, Andrzej. *The views of the medieval Arab philologists on language and its origin in the light of as-Suyûtî's "al-Muzhir."* Cracow: Nakład. Uniw. Jagiellońskiego, 1988.

Dafni, Amots, Levy, Shay, and Lev, Efraim. "The ethnobotany of Christ's Thorn Jujube (Ziziphus spina-christi) in Israel." *Journal of Ethnobiology and Ethnomedicine* 1,8 (2005) (http://www.ethnobiomed.com/content/1/1/8) (accessed 23 January 2012).

Daftary, Farhad. *Ismaʿilis in medieval Muslim societies*. London and New York: I. B. Tauris, 2005.

The Assassin legends: Myths of the Ismaʿilis. London: I. B. Tauris, 1994.

The Ismāʿīlīs: Their history and doctrines. Cambridge and New York: Cambridge University Press, 1990.

Daiber, Hans. *The Islamic concept of belief in the 4th/10th century: Abū l-Laith al-Samarqandī's commentary on Abū Ḥanīfa (d. 150/767)* al-Fiqh al-absaṭ. Tokyo: Institute for the Study of Languages and Cultures of Asia and Africa, 1995.

Daley, Brian E. "'At the Hour of Our Death': Mary's Dormition and Christian dying in late Patristic and early Byzantine literature." *Dumbarton Oaks Papers* 55 (2001), pp. 71–89.

The hope of the early Church: A handbook of Patristic eschatology. Cambridge: Cambridge University Press, 1991.

Dallal, Ahmad. "The origins and objectives of Islamic revivalist thought, 1750–1850." *JAOS* 113,3 (1993), pp. 341–59.

Dalley, Stephanie. "Gilgamesh in the Arabian Nights." *JRAS*, Third Series 1,1 (1991), pp. 1–17.

Daniel, Norman. *Islam and the West: The making of an image*. Edinburgh: Edinburgh University Press, 1960. Rev. ed. Oxford: Oxford University Press, 1993.

Dayeh, Islam. "*Al-ḥawāmīm*: Intertextuality and coherence in Meccan surahs." In Neuwirth, Sinai, and Marx, eds. *The Quran in context*, pp. 461–98.

Davidson, Herbert A. *Alfarabi, Avicenna, and Averroes on intellect: Their cosmologies, theories of the active intellect, and theories of human intellect*. New York: Oxford University Press, 1992.

de Certeau, Michel. *L'invention du quotidien*. Vol. 1: *Arts de faire*. Translated by Steven Rendall. *The practice of everyday life*. Berkeley: University of California Press, 1984.

de Prémare, Alfred-Louis. "Wahb b. Munabbih, une figure singulière du premier Islam." *Annales: Histoire, Sciences Sociales* 60 (2005), pp. 531–49.

de Smet, Daniel. "Isma'ili-Shi'i visions of hell: From the 'spiritual' torment of the Fatimids to the Ṭayyibī Rock of Sijjīn." In Lange, ed., *Locating hell*, pp. 241–67.

"Religiöse Anwendung philosophischer Ideen." In *Philosophie in der islamischen Welt*. Vol. 1: *8.-10. Jahrhundert*. Edited by Ulrich Rudolph (with Renate Würsch). Basel: Schwabe Verlag, 2012, pp. 518–39.

Dejugnat, Yann. "Voyage au centre du monde: Logiques narratives et cohérence du projet dans la *Rihla* d'Ibn Jubayr." In *Géographes et voyageurs au Moyen Age*. Edited by Henri Bresc and Emmanuelle Tixier du Mesnil. Nanterre: Presses Universitaires de Paris Ouest, 2010, pp. 13–206.

"La méditerranée come frontière dans le récit de voyage (*riḥla*) d'Ibn Ǧubayr: Modalités et enjeux d'une perception." In *Mélanges de la Casa de Velázquez, nouvelle série* 38,2 (2008), pp. 149–70.

Denkha, Ataa. *L'imaginaire du paradis et de l'au-delà dans le christianisme et dans l'islam*. Paris: L'Harmattan, 2014.

Dévényi, Kinga, and Fodor, Alexander, eds. *Proceedings of the colloquium on Paradise and Hell in Islam, Keszthely, 7–14 July 2002*. In *The Arabist*, 28–29 (2008), pp. 1–195 [Part 1]; 30 (2012), pp. 1–98 [Part 2].

Diem, Werner, and Schöller, Marco. *The living and the dead: Studies in Arabic epitaphs*. 3 vols. Wiesbaden: Harrassowitz, 2004.

Donaldson, Dwight M. *The Shī'ite religion: A history of Islam in Persia and Irak*. London: Luzac and Co., 1933.

Donner, Fred. *Muhammad and the believers: At the origins of Islam*. Cambridge, MA: Harvard University Press, 2010.

Dreher, Josef. *Maṭāli' al-nūr al-sanī al-munabbi' 'an ṭahārat nasab al-nabī al-'arabī. Le traité de 'Abdī Effendī al-Busnawī*. Cairo: IFAO, 2013.

Duerr, Hans Peter. *Traumzeit: Über die Grenze zwischen Wildnis und Zivilisation*. First publ. 1978. Translated by F. Goodman. *Dreamtime: Connecting the boundary between wilderness and civilization*. Oxford: Basil Blackwell, 1985.

Dye, Guillaume. "Le Coran et son contexte: Remarques sur un ouvrage recent." *Oriens Christianus* 95 (2011), pp. 247–70.

Ebstein, Michael. "Ḏū l-Nūn and early Islamic mysticism." *Arabica* 61 (2014), pp. 559–612.

Mysticism and philosophy in al-Andalus: Ibn Masarra, Ibn al-ʿArabī, and the Ismāʿīlī tradition. Leiden and Boston: Brill, 2014.

Eichler, Paul Arno. *Die Dschinn, Teufel und Engel im Koran*. Leipzig: Klein, 1928.

Eilers, W. "Iranisches Lehngut im arabischen Lexicon: Über einige Berufsnamen und Titel." *Indo-Iranian Journal* 5,3 (1962), pp. 203–32.

Eklund, Ragnar. *Life between death and resurrection according to Islam*. Uppsala: Almqvist & Wiksells, 1941.

El Masri, Ghassan. "*Min al-baʿd ilá l-āḫira:* Poetic time and Qurʾanic eschatology." In *Les origines du Coran, le Coran des origines*. Edited by François Deroche, Christian Julien Robin and Michel Zink. Paris: Académie des Inscriptions et Belles-Lettres, 2015, pp. 129–49.

Elad, Amikam. *Medieval Jerusalem and Islamic worship: Holy places, ceremonies, pilgrimage*. Leiden: E. J. Brill, 1995.

Eliade, Mircea. "Les Américains en Océanie et le nudisme eschatologique." *La nouvelle revue française* 8 (1960), pp. 58–74.

El-Rouayheb, Khaled. *Before homosexuality in the Arab-Islamic world, 1500–1800*. Chicago: University of Chicago Press, 2005.

El-Saleh, Soubhi. *La vie future selon le Coran*. Paris: J. Vrin, 1971.

Encyclopaedia Islamica. Edited by Wilferd Madelung and Farhad Daftary. Abridged translation of *Dāʾirat al-maʿārif-i buzurg-i Islāmī*. Edited by Kāẓim Mūsavī Bujnurdī. Leiden: Brill, 2008–. Online publication.

Encyclopédie, ou dictionnaire raisonné des sciences, des arts et des métiers. Edited by Denis Diderot and Jean le Rond d'Alembert. 28 vols. Paris: Le Breton, 1751–72.

Ende, Werner. "Steine des Anstoßes: Das Mausoleum der Ahl al-bayt in Medina." In *Differenz und Dynamik im Islam: Festschrift für Heinz Halm zum 70. Geburtstag*. Edited by Hinrich Biesterfeldt and Verena Klemm. Würzburg: Ergon, 2012, pp. 181–200.

Ettinghausen, Richard, Grabar, Oleg, and Jenkins-Madina, Marilyn. *Islamic art and architecture, 650–1250*. New Haven, CT, and London: Yale University Press, 2001.

Ewald, Heinrich. *Grammatica critica linguae arabicae*. Leipzig: sumtibus librariae Hahnianae, 1831–3.

Fahd, Toufic. "La naissance du monde selon l'Islam." In *Sources Orientales*. Vol. 1: *La naissance du monde*. Paris: Éditions du Seuil, [1959], pp. 237–77.

ed. *Le Shîʿisme imâmite: colloque de Strasbourg (6–9 mai, 1968)*. Paris: Presses Universitaires de France, 1970.

Fakhry, Majid. *Al-Fārābī: Founder of Islamic Neoplatonism*. Oxford: Oneworld, 2002.

Farhad, Massumeh (with Serpil Bağcı). *Falnama: The Book of Omens*. London: Thames and Hudson, 2009.

Farrin, Raymond. *Structure and Qur'anic interpretation: A study of symmetry and coherence in Islam's holy text*. Asland, OR: White Cloud Press, 2014.
Fierro, Maribel. *'Abd al-Rahman III: The first Cordoban caliph*. Oxford: Oneworld, 2005.
"En tomo a la decoración con mosaicos de las mezquitas omeyas." In *Homenaje al Prof. Jacinto Bosch Vilá*. Granada: Universidad de Granada, 1991, Vol. 1, pp. 131–44.
"Madīnat al-Zahrā', el Paraíso y los Fatimíes." *Al-Qanṭara* 25,2 (2004), pp. 299–327.
Filiu, Jean-Pierre. *L'Apocalypse dans l'Islam*. Paris: Fayard, 2008.
Fischer, Wolfdietrich. *Farb- und Formgebung in der Sprache der altarabischen Dichtung. Untersuchungen zur Wortbedeutung und zur Wortbildung*. Wiesbaden: Harrassowitz, 1965.
Flügel, Gustav. *Die arabischen, persischen, türkischen Handschriften der k.u.k. Hofbibliothek zu Wien*. 3 vols. Vienna: K. K. Hof- und Staatsdruckerei, 1865–7.
Frank, Richard. "The divine attributes according to the teaching of Abū l-Hudhayl al-ʿAllāf." *Le Muséon* 82 (1969), pp. 451–506.
"The neoplatonism of Jahm ibn Ṣafwān." *Le Muséon* 78 (1965), pp. 395–424.
Franke, Patrick. "Propheteneltern-Problem." (http://de.wikipedia.org/wiki/Propheteneltern-Problem) (accessed 21 June 2014).
Freitag, Rainer. *Seelenwanderung in der islamischen Häresie*. Berlin: Schwarz, 1985.
Fudge, Bruce. *Qur'ānic hermeneutics: Al-Tabrīsī and the craft of commentary*. Abingdon, UK, and New York: Routledge, 2011.
"Underworlds and otherworlds in *The Thousand and One Nights*." *Middle Eastern Literatures* 15,3 (2012), pp. 257–72.
Gacek, Adam. *Arabic manuscripts: A vademecum for readers*. Leiden: Brill, 2009.
Gardet, Louis. *Dieu et la destinée de l'homme*. Paris: J. Vrin, 1967.
Gauvain, Richard. "Ritual rewards: A consideration of three recent approaches to Sunni purity laws." *Islamic Law and Society* 12,3 (2005), pp. 333–93.
Geiger, Abraham. *Was hat Mohammed aus dem Judenthume aufgenommen?* Bonn: F. Baaden, 1833.
Geoffroy, Éric. *Le soufisme en Égypte et en Syrie sous les derniers Mamelouks et les premiers Ottomans: Orientations spirituelles et enjeux culturels*. Damascus: Institut Français d'Études Arabes, 1995.
Giladi, Avner. *Children of Islam: Concepts of childhood and medieval Muslim society*. Basingstoke, UK: Macmillan, 1992.
Gilliot, Claude. "A schoolmaster, storyteller, exegete and warrior at work in Khurāsān: Al-Ḍaḥḥāk b. Muzāhim al-Hilālī (d. 106/724)." In *Aims, methods and contexts of Qur'ānic exegesis (2nd/8th-9th/15th centuries)*. Edited by Karen Bauer. Oxford: Oxford University Press, 2013, pp. 311–92.
"La vision de Dieu dans l'au-delà: Exégèse, tradition et théologie en Islam." In *Pensée grecque et sagesse d'Orient. Hommage à Michel Tardieu*. Edited by by M. A. Amir-Moezzi, J.-D. Dubois, Ch. Jullien, and F. Jullien. Turnhout: Brepols 2009, pp. 237–70.
"L'embarras d'un exégète face à un palimpseste: Māturīdī et la sourate de l'Abondance (al-Kawthar, sourate 108), avec une note savante sur le commentatire d'Ibn al-Naqīb (m. 698/1298)." In *Words, texts and concepts cruising the Mediterranean Sea: Studies on the sources, contents and influences of Islamic*

civilization and Arabic philosophy and science; dedicated to Gerhard Endress on his sixty-fifth birthday. Edited by Rüdiger Arnzen and Jörn Thielmann. Leuven and Paris: Peeters, 2004, pp. 33–69.

"Muqātil, grand exégète, traditionniste et théologien maudit." *Journal Asiatique* 279,1–2 (1991), pp. 39–92.

Ginzberg, Louis. *The legends of the Jews*. 7 vols. Philadelphia: Jewish Publication Society of America, 1909–38.

Gleave, Robert. *Scripturalist Islam: The history and doctrines of the Akhbārī Shīʿī school*. Leiden and Boston: Brill, 2007.

Goitein, S. D. "Beholding God on Friday." *Islamic Culture* 34,3 (1960), pp. 163–8.

Goldziher, Ignaz. *Muhammedanische Studien*. First publ. 1889–90. Translated by C. R. Barber and S. M. Stern. *Muslim studies*. 2 vols. Albany, NY: SUNY Press, 1971.

Die Richtungen der koranischen Koranauslegung. Leiden: Brill, 1920.

Nyelvtudomány történetérl az araboknál. Translated and edited by Kinga Dévényi and Tamás Iványi. *On the history of grammar among the Arabs*. Amsterdam and Philadelphia: J. Benjamins, 1994.

Vorlesungen über den Islam. Heidelberg: C. Winter, 1910. Translated by Andras and Ruth Hamori. *Introduction to Islamic theology and law*. Princeton, NJ: Princeton University Press, 1981.

"Zur Geschichte der hanbalitischen Bewegungen." *ZDMG* 62 (1908), pp. 1–28.

Graham, William A. *Beyond the written word: Oral aspects of scripture in the history of religion*. Cambridge: Cambridge University Press, 1987.

Divine word and prophetic word in early Islam: A reconsideration of the sources, with special reference to the Divine Saying or Ḥadîth Qudsî. The Hague: Mouton, 1977.

"Islam in the mirror of ritual." In *Islam's understanding of itself*. Edited by Richard G. Hovannisian and Speros Vryonis. Malibu, CA: Undena Publications, 1983, pp. 53–71.

"*Qurʾān* as spoken word: An Islamic contribution to the understanding of scripture." In *Approaches to Islam in Religious Studies*. Edited by Richard C. Martin. Tuscon: University of Arizona Press, 1985, pp. 23–40.

Gramlich, Richard. *Alte Vorbilder des Sufitums*. Wiesbaden: Harrassowitz, 1995.

Weltverzicht: Grundlagen und Weisen islamischer Askese. Wiesbaden: Harrassowitz Verlag, 1997.

Graves, Margaret, and Junod, Benoît, eds. *Architecture in Islamic arts: Treasures of the Agha Khan Museum*. Geneva: Agha Khan Trust for Culture, 2011.

Greenwood, Tim. "Correspondence between ʿUmar II and Leo III." In *CMR*, s.v. Online publication (2010).

Griffel, Frank. *Apostasie und Toleranz im Islam: Die Entwicklung zu al-Ġazālīs Urteil gegen die Philosophie und die Reaktionen der Philosophen*. Leiden and Boston: Brill, 2000.

Griffith, Sidney H. "St. Ephraem the Syrian, the Quran, and the grapevines of paradise: An essay in comparative eschatology." In Günther and Lawson, eds. *Roads to paradise*, forthcoming.

Grimme, Hubert. *Mohammed*. 2 vols. (Vol 1: *Das Leben*. Vol. 2: *Einleitung in den Koran. System der koranischen Theologie*.) Münster: Aschendorff, 1892–5.

Gruber, Christiane J. "Signs of the Hour: Eschatological imagery in Islamic book arts." *Ars Orientalis* 44 (2014), pp. 40–60.

The Ilkhanid Book. *See* Īlkhānid *Miʿrājnāma*.

Gruber, Christiane J., and Colby, Frederick S., eds. *The Prophet's ascension: Cross-cultural encounters with the Islamic Miʿrāj tale*. Bloomington: Indiana University Press, 2009.

Gruendler, Beatrice. "'That you be brough near': Union beyond the grave in the Arabic literary tradition." In *Love after death: Concepts of posthumous love in medieval and early modern Europe*. Edited by Bernhard Jussen and Rami Targoff. Berlin: de Gruyter, 2015, pp. 71–95.

Günther, Sebastian. "'God disdains not to strike a simile (Q 2:26)': The poetics of Islamic eschatology; Narrative, personification, and colors in Muslim discourse." In Günther and Lawons, eds. *Roads to paradise*, forthcoming.

"Fictional narration and imagination within an authorative framework: Toward a new understanding of Ḥadīth." In *Story-telling in the framework of non-fictional Arabic literature*. Edited by Stefan Leder. Wiesbaden: Harrassowitz, 1998, pp. 433–71.

"'Gepriesen sei der, der seinen Diener bei Nacht reisen ließ' (Koran 17:1): Paradiesvorstellungen und Himmelsreisen im Islam — Grundfesten des Glaubens und literarische Topoi." In *Eranos 2009 und 2010: Jenseitsreisen*. Edited by Erich Hornung and Andreas Schweizer. Basel: Schwabe Verlag, 2011, pp. 15–56.

Günther, Sebastian, and Lawson, Todd, eds. *Roads to paradise: Eschatology and concepts of the hereafter in Islam*. Leiden: Brill, forthcoming.

Gutas, Dimitri. "Avicenna's Eastern ('Oriental') philosophy: Nature, scope, transmission." *Arabic Sciences and Philosophy* 10 (2000), pp. 159–80.

Hämeen-Anttila, Jaakko. "Paradise and nature in the Quran and in pre-Islamic poetry." In Günther and Lawson, eds. *Roads to paradise*, forthcoming.

Hajnal, István. "The events of paradise: Facts and eschatological doctrine in medieval Ismaʿili history." In Dévényi and Fodor, eds. *Proceedings* [Part 1], pp. 83–104.

Halevi, Leor E. *Muhammad's grave: Death, ritual and society in the early Islamic world*. New York: Columbia University Press, 2007.

Halm, Heinz. *Das Reich des Mahdi: Der Aufstieg der Fatimiden (875–973)*. Munich: Beck, 1991.

"Die Sieben und die Zwölf: Die ismāʿilitische Kosmogonie und das Mazdak-Fragment des Šahrastānī." In *XVIII. Deutscher Orientalistentag vom 1. bis 5. Oktober 1972 in Lübeck*. Edited by Wolfgang Voigt. Wiesbaden: Franz Steiner, 1974, pp. 170–7.

Die Kalifen von Kairo: Die Fatimiden in Ägypten (973–1074). Munich: Beck, 2003.

Die Schia. Darmstadt: Wissenschaftliche Buchgesellschaft, 1988.

Kosmologie und Heilslehre der frühen Ismāʿīlīya. Wiesbaden: Steiner, 1978.

Hamilton, Robert William. *The structural history of the Aqsa mosque: A record of archeological gleanings from the repairs of 1938–1942*. London: Oxford University Press, 1949.

Hamza, Feras. "To hell and back: A study of the concepts of hell and intercession in early Islam." PhD diss., Oxford University, 2002.

Hanaway, William L. "Paradise on earth: The terrestrial garden in Persian literature." In *The Islamic garden*. Edited by Elisabeth B. MacDougall and Richard Ettinghausen. Washington, DC: Dumbarton Oaks, 1976, pp. 41–67.

Hasan-Rokem, Galit. "Erotic Eden: A rabbinic nostalgia for paradise." In *Paradise in antiquity: Jewish and Christian views*. Edited by Markus Bockmuehl and Guy G. Stroumsa. Cambridge: Cambridge University Press, 2010, pp. 156–65.

Hawting, Gerald. "The case of Ja'd b. Dirham and the punishment of 'heretics' in the early caliphate." In Lange and Fierro, eds. *Public violence*, pp. 27–41.

Heck, Paul. "Religious renewal in Syria: The case of Muḥammad al-Ḥabash." *Journal of Islam and Muslim-Christian Religions* 15,4 (2004), pp. 185–207.

Heinen, Anton. *Islamic cosmology: A study of as-Suyūṭī's* al-Hay'a as-sanīya fī l-hay'a as-sunnīya. Beirut: F. Steiner Verlag, 1982.

Heinrichs, Wolfhart. "*Takhyīl*: Make-believe and image creation in Arabic literary theory." In Takhyīl: *The imaginary in classical Arabic poetics*. Edited by Geert Jan van Gelder and Marlé Hammond. [Cambridge]: Gibb Memorial Trust, 2008, pp. 1–14.

Henning, Agnes. *Die Turmgräber von Palmyra: Eine lokale Bauform im kaiserzeitlichen Syrien als Ausdruck kultureller Identität*. Rahden: Verlag Marie Leidor, 2013.

Henninger, Joseph. *Spuren christlicher Glaubenswahrheiten im Koran*. Schöneck and Beckenried: s.n., 1951.

Hillenbrand, Robert. "The Seljuq monuments of Turkmenistan." In *The Seljuqs: Politics, society and culture*. Edited by Christian Lange and Songul Mecit. Edinburgh: Edinburgh University Press, 2011, pp. 277–308.

Himmelfarb, Martha. *Ascent to heaven in Jewish and Christian apocalypses*. New York: Oxford University Press, 1993.

Tours of hell: An apocalyptic form in Jewish and Christian literature. Philadelphia: University of Philadelphia Press, 1983.

Hirschkind, Charles. *The ethical soundscape: Cassette sermons and Islamic counterpublics*. New York: Columbia University Press, 2006.

Hobbes, Thomas. *Leviathan*. First publ. 1651. New York: Touchstone, 1997.

Hodgson, Marshal G. S. *The order of the Assassins: The struggle of the early Nizârî Ismâ'îlîs against the Islamic world*. 'S-Gravenhage: Mouton, 1955.

Hoover, Jon. "Against Islamic universalism? 'Alī al-Ḥarbī's 1990 attempt to prove that Ibn Taymiyya and Ibn Qayyim al-Jawziyya affirm the eternity of Hell-Fire." In *Islamic theology, philosophy and law: Debating Ibn Taymiyya and Ibn Qayyim al-Jawziyya*. Edited by Birgit Krawietz and Georges Tamer. Berlin and New York: de Gruyter, 2013, pp. 377–99.

"Islamic universalism: Ibn Qayyim al-Jawziyya's Salafī deliberations on the duration of hell-fire." *MW* 99 (2009), pp. 181–201.

"Withholding judgment on Islamic universalism: Ibn al-Wazīr (d. 840/1436) on the duration and purpose of hell-fire." In Lange, ed. *Locating hell*, pp. 208–37.

Horovitz, Josef. "Bulūqjā." *ZDMG* 55 (1901), pp. 519–25.

"Das koranische Paradies." In *Scripta Universitatis atque Bibliothecae Hierosolymitanarum* 6 (1923), pp. 1–16. Reprinted in *Der Koran*. Edited by Rudi Paret. Darmstadt: Wissenschaftliche Buchgesellschaft, 1975, pp. 53–75.

Koranische Untersuchungen. Berlin: de Gruyter, 1926.

"Muhammeds Himmelsfahrt." *Der Islam* 9 (1919), pp. 159–83.

Housley, Norman. "The crusades and Islam." *Medieval Encounters* 13 (2007), pp. 189–208.

Hoyland, Robert G. *Seeing Islam as others saw it: A survey and evaluation of Christian, Jewish and Zoroastrian writings on early Islam*. Princeton, NJ: Darwin, 1997.

Hughes, Aaron W. "*Miʿrāj* and the language of legitimation in the medieval Islamic and Jewish philosophical traditions: A case study of Avicenna and Abraham ibn Ezra." In Gruber and Colby, eds. *The Prophet's ascension*, pp. 172–91.

Huitema, Taede. *De voorspraak (shafāʿa) in de Islam*. Leiden: Brill, 1936.

Hutter, Manfred. "The impurity of the corpse (*nasā*) and the future body (*tan ī pasēn*): Death and afterlife in Zoroastrianism." *Deuterocanonical and Cognate Literature Yearbook* (2009), pp. 13–26.

Ibrahim, Lutpi. "The concept of *iḥbāṭ* and *takfīr* according to al-Zamakhsharī and al-Bayḍāwī." *Welt des Orients* 11 (1980), pp. 117–21.

Iser, Wolfgang. *Das Fiktive und das Imaginäre: Perspektiven literarischer Anthropologie*. Frankfurt am Main: Suhrkamp, 1991.

Isutzu, Toshihiko. *The concept of belief in Islamic theology*. Tokyo: The Keio Institute of Cultural and Linguistic Studies, 1965.

Jacob, Georg. *Altarabisches Beduinenleben*. 2nd rev. ed. Berlin: Mayer & Müller, 1897.

Jaffer, Tariq. "Bodies, souls and resurrection in Avicenna's *al-Risāla al-aḍḥawīya fī amr al-maʿād*." In *Before and after Avicenna: Proceedings of the first conference of the Avicenna study group*. Edited by David C. Reisman. Leiden and Boston: Brill, 2003, pp. 163–74.

Jambet, Christian. *La grande résurrection d'Alamūt: Les formes de la liberté dans le shīʿisme ismaélien*. Lagrasse: Verdier, 1990.

Mort et résurrection en Islam: L'au-delà selon Mullâ Sadrâ. [Paris]: Albin Michel, 2008.

Jeffery, Arthur. *The foreign vocabulary of the Quran*. Baroda: Oriental Institute, 1938.

Materials for the history of the text of the Quran: The old codices. Leiden: E. J. Brill, 1937.

Jomier, Jacques. "Le nom divin 'al-Raḥmān' dans le Coran." In *Mélanges Louis Massignon*. 3 vols. Damascus: Institut Français d'Études Arabes en Damas, 1957, Vol. 2, pp. 361–81.

Jones, Alan. "Introduction." In idem, trans. *The Qurʾān*. [Cambridge]: Gibb Memorial Trust, 2007, pp. 1–22.

"Paradise and hell in the Qurʾan." In Dévényi and Fodor, eds., *Proceedings* [Part 1], pp. 105–22.

Jones, Linda G. *The power of oratory in the medieval Muslim world*. New York: Cambridge University Press, 2012.

Jung, C. G. "On synchronicity [1951]." In *Man and time: Papers from the Eranos Yearbooks*. Translated by Ralph Manheim and R. F. C. Hull. London: Routledge and Kegan Paul, 1958, pp. 201–11.

Juynboll, G. H. A. *Muslim tradition: Studies in chronology, provenance and authorship of early* ḥadīth. Cambridge: Cambridge University Press, 1983.

"Some *isnād*-analytical methods illustrated on the basis of several woman-demeaning sayings from *ḥadīth* literature." *Al-Qanṭara* 10 (1989), pp. 343–83.

"Review of R. G. Khoury, *K. al-Zuhd*." *Bibliotheca Orientalis* 36 (1979), pp. 243–4.

Kaḥḥāla, ʿUmar Riḍā. *Muʿjam al-muʾallifīn: Tarājim muṣannifī al-kutub al-ʿarabiyya*. 15 vols. Damascus: Maṭbaʿat al-Taraqqī, 1957–61.

Muʿjam qabāʾil al-ʿarab al-qadīma wa-l-ḥadītha. 3 vols. Damascus: Al-Maṭbaʿa al-Hāshimiyya, 1949.

Kalisch, Sven. "Anmerkungen zu Jenseitsvorstellungen im Islam." In *Glaubensgewissheit und Gewalt: Eschatologische Erkundungen in Islam und Christentum*. Edited by Jürgen Werbick, Sven Kalisch, and Klaus von Stosch. Paderborn, München, Wien, and Zürich: Ferdinand Schöningh, 2011, pp. 87–104.

Kalmar, Ivan. *Imagined Islam and the notion of sublime power*. London and New York: Routledge, 2013.

Kaplony, Andreas. *The Ḥaram of Jerusalem: Temple, Friday mosque, area of spiritual power*. Stuttgart: Franz Steiner Verlag, 2002.

Karamustafa, Ahmet T. *God's unruly friends: Dervish groups in the Islamic later middle period, 1250–1550*. Salt Lake City: University of Utah Press, 1994.

Sufism: The formative period. Edinburgh: Edinburgh University Press, 2007.

Katz, Jonathan G. "Dreams and their interpretation in Sufi thought." In *Dreams and visions in Islamic societies*. Edited by Özgen Felek and Alexander D. Knysh. Albany, NY: SUNY Press, 2012, pp. 181–97.

Katz, Marion Holmes. *Body of text: The emergence of the Sunnī law of ritual purity*. Albany, NY: SUNY Press, 2002.

"The ḥajj and the study of Islamic ritual." *SI* 98–9 (2004), pp. 95–129.

Kaya, Veysel. "İzmirli Ismail Hakkı cehennemin sonluluğu hakkında risalesi." *Uludağ Üniversitesi İlâhiyat Fakültesi Dergisi* 18,1 (2009), pp. 529–57.

Kennedy, Philip F. "Muslim sources of Dante?" In *The Arab influence in medieval Europe*. Edited by Dionisius A. Agius and Richard Hitchcock. Reading, UK: Ithaca Press, 1993, pp. 62–82.

Kermani, Navid. *Gott ist schön: Das ästhetische Erleben des Koran*. Munich: Beck, 2011, 4th ed.

Khalek, Nancy A. *Damascus after the Muslim conquest: Text and image in early Islam*. New York: Oxford University Press, 2011.

Khalidi, Tarif. *The Muslim Jesus: Sayings and stories in Islamic culture*. Cambridge, MA: Harvard University Press, 2001.

Khalil, Mohammad Hassan. "Is hell truly everlasting? An introduction to medieval Islamic universalism." In Lange, ed. *Locating hell*, pp. 165-74.

Islam and the fate of others: The salvation question. Oxford: Oxford University Press, 2012.

Khoury, Georges. "Importance et authenticité des textes de *Ḥilyat al-Awliyā' wa-Ṭabaqat al-Aṣfiyā'* d'Abū Nuʿaym Al-Iṣbahānī (336–430/948–1038)." *SI* 46 (1977), pp. 73–113.

Kiltz, David. "The relationship between Arabic *Allāh* and Syriac *Allāhā*." *Der Islam* 88,1 (2011), pp. 33–50.

Kinberg, Leah. "Interaction between this world and the afterworld in early Islamic tradition." *Oriens* 29–30 (1986), pp. 285–308.

Kister, Meir Jacob. "Adam: A study of some legends in *tafsīr* and *ḥadīth* literature." *IOS* 13 (1993), pp. 113–74.

"Maqām Ibrāhīm: A stone with an inscription." *Le Muséon* 84 (1971), pp. 477–94.

"Sanctity joint and divided: On holy places in the Islamic tradition." *JSAI* 20 (1996), pp. 16–65.

"Some reports concerning al-Ṭā'if." *JSAI* 1 (1979), pp. 1–18. Reprinted in *Studies in Jāhiliyya and early Islam*. London: Variorum, 1980, nr. XI.

"'You shall only set put for three mosques': A study of an early tradition." *Le Muséon* 82 (1969), pp. 173–96.

Klein, Ernest David. *A comprehensive etymological dictionary of the Hebrew language for readers of English*. Jerusalem: Carta, 1987.

Klein, Yaron. "Between public and private: An examination of *ḥisba* literature." *Harvard Middle Eastern and Islamic Review* 7 (2006), pp. 41–62.

Knysh, Alexander. *Islamic mysticism: A short history*. Leiden: Brill, 2000.

Kohlberg, Etan. "Aspects of Akhbari thought in the seventeenth and eighteenth century." In *Eighteenth-century renewal and reform in Islam*. Edited by N. Levtzion and J. O. Voll. Syracuse, NY: Syracuse University Press, 1987, pp. 133–55.

"From Imāmiyya to Ithnā-ʿAshariyya." *BSOAS* 39,3 (1976), pp. 521–34.

"Some Imāmī Shīʿī views on the *ṣaḥāba*." *JSAI* 5 (1984), pp. 143–75. Reprinted in *Belief and law in Imāmī Shīʿism*. Aldershot, UK: Variorum, 1991, ch. IX.

"The position of the *walad zinā* in Imāmī Shīʿism." *BSOAS* 48 (1985), pp. 237–66. Reprinted in *Belief and law in Imāmī Shīʿism*. Aldershot, UK: Variorum, 1991, ch. XI.

Kraemer, Joel. "Apostates, rebels and brigands." *IOS* 10 (1980), pp. 35–73.

Kremers, Dieter. "Islamische Einflüsse auf Dantes «Göttliche Komödie»." In *Orientalisches Mittelalter* (Neues Handbuch der Literaturwissenschaft, Bd. 5). Edited by Wolfhart Heinrichs. Wiesbaden: Aula-Verlag, 1990, pp. 202–15.

Kropp, Manfred. "Koranische Texte als Sprechakte am Beispiel der Sure 85." In *Vom Koran zum Islam*. Edited by Markus Groß und Karl-Heinz Ohlig. Berlin: Hans Schiler Verlag, 2009, pp. 483–91.

Kugle, Scott A. "Heaven's witness: The uses and abuses of Muḥammad Ghawth's mystical ascension." *JIS* 14,1 (2003), pp. 1–36.

Kutubi, E. S. *Mulla Sadra and eschatology: Evolution of being*. London: Routledge, 2014.

Lammens, H. "La cité arabe de Ṭāʾif à la veille de l'Hegire." *Mélanges de l'Université Saint-Joseph* 8,4 (1922), pp. 115–327.

Lamoreaux, John C. "Abū Qurra." In *CMR*, s.v. Online publication (2010).

Lane, Edward William. *An Arabic-English lexicon*. 8 vols. First published 1863. Reprinted Beirut: Librairie du Liban, 1968.

Landolt, Hermann. "'Being-towards-resurrection:' Mullā Ṣadrā's critique of Suhraward's eschatology." In Günther and Lawson, eds. *Roads to paradise*, forthcoming.

"Le soufisme à travers l'oeuvre de ʿAzîz-eNasafî: Étude du *Ketâb-e Tanzîl*." *Annuaire de l'Ecole Pratique des Hautes Etudes, Section sciences religieuses* 103 (1996), pp. 227–9.

Lang, Bernhard. *Himmel und Hölle: Jenseitsglaube von der Antike bis heute*. Munich: Beck, 2009, 2nd ed.

Lange, Christian. "A Sufi's paradise and hell: Azīz-i Nasafī's (fl. mid-7th/13th c.) epistle on the otherworld." In *No tapping around philology: Festschrift Wheeler Thackston*. Edited by Alireza Korangy and Dan Sheffield. Wiesbaden: Harrassowitz, 2014, pp. 193–214.

"Contemporary Salafi literature on paradise and hell: The case of ʿUmar Sulaymān al-Ashqar (d. 2012)." In *Claiming tradition: Modern re-readings of the classical Islamic heritage*. Edited by Elisabeth Kendall and Ahmad Khan. Edinburgh: Edinburgh University Press, forthcoming.

"Ibn Ḥazm on sins and salvation." In *Ibn Ḥazm of Cordoba: The life and works of a controversial thinker*. Edited by Camilla Adang, Maribel Fierro, and Sabine Schmidtke. Leiden: Brill, 2013, pp. 429–53.

"Introducing hell in Islamic Studies." In idem, ed. *Locating hell*, pp. 1-28.

"Islamische Höllenvorstellungen: Genese – Struktur – Funktion." In *Eranos 2009 und 2010: Jenseitsreisen*. Edited by Erich Hornung and Andreas Schweizer. Basel: Schwabe Verlag, 2011, pp. 153–93.

Justice, punishment, and the medieval Muslim imagination. Cambridge: Cambridge University Press, 2008.

ed. *Locating hell in Islamic traditions*. Leiden: Brill, 2015.

"'On that day when faces will be black' (Q3:106): Toward a semiology of the human face in the Arabo-Islamic tradition." *JAOS* 127,4 (2007), pp. 429–46.

"Revisiting hell's angels in the Quran." In idem, ed. *Locating hell*, pp. 75-99.

"Sins, expiation and non-rationality in Ḥanafī and Shāfiʿī *fiqh*." In *Islamic law in theory: Studies on jurisprudence in honor of Bernard Weiss*. Edited by Kevin Reinhart and Robert Gleave. Leiden and Boston: Brill, 2014, pp. 143–75.

"Sitting by the ruler's throne: Al-Ghazālī on justice and mercy in this world and the next." in *Narrar y suscitar: Violencia, compasión y crueldad en la literatura árabo-islámica*. Edited by Delfina Serrano. Madrid: CSIC, 2011, pp. 131–48.

"The 'eight gates of paradise'-tradition in Islam: A genealogical and structural study." In Günther and Lawson, eds. *Roads to paradise*, forthcoming.

"Where on earth is hell? State punishment and eschatology in the Islamic Middle Period." In Lange and Fierro, eds. *Public violence*, pp. 156–78.

Lange, Christian, and Fierro, Maribel, eds. *Public violence in Islamic societies: Power, discipline and the construction of the public sphere, 7th–19th centuries*. Edinburgh: Edinburgh University Press, 2009.

Langermann, Y. Tzvi. "Ibn al-Qayyim's *Kitāb al-Rūḥ*: Some literary aspects." In *Islamic theology, philosophy and law*. Edited by Birgit Krawietz and Georges Tamer. Berlin: de Gruyter, 2013, pp. 125–45.

Laoust, Henri. *Essai sur les doctrines sociales et politiques de Taḳī d-dīn Aḥmad b. Taimīya, canoniste ḥanbalite, né à Harrān en 661/1262, mort à Damas en 728/1328*. Cairo: Institut Français d'Archéologie Orientale, 1939.

"Ibn Kaṯīr, historien." *Arabica* 2,1 (1955), pp. 42–88.

La profession de foi d'Ibn Baṭṭa. Damascus: s.n., 1958.

Latour, Bruno. "'Thou shall not freeze-frame'—or how not to misunderstand the science and religion debate." In *Science, religion, and the human experience*. Edited by James D. Proctor. Oxford and New York: Oxford University Press, 2005, pp. 27–48.

Lawson, Todd. "Akhbārī Shīʿī approaches to tafsīr." In *Approaches to the Qurʾan*. Edited by Gerald R. Hawting and Abdul-Kader A. Shareef. New York and London: Routledge, 1993, pp. 173–210.

"The music of apocalypse: Paradise in the Quran." In Günther and Lawson, eds. *Roads to paradise*, forthcoming.

"Shaykh Aḥmad al-Aḥsāʾī and the World of Images." In *Shīʿi trends and dynamics in modern times*. Edited by Denis Herman and Sabrina Mervin. Beirut: Ergon Verlag Würzburg, 2010, pp. 19–31.

Lazarus-Yafeh, Hava. *Studies in al-Ghazzālī*. Jerusalem: Magnes Press, 1975.

Le Goff, Jacques. "Introduction." In *The medieval imagination*. Translated by Arthur Goldhammer. Chicago and London: University of Chicago Press, 1988, pp. 1–17.

"The repudiation of pleasure." In *The medieval imagination*. Translated by Arthur Goldhammer. Chicago and London: University of Chicago Press, 1988, pp. 93–103.

Le Strange, Guy. "Description of the Noble Sanctuary at Jerusalem in 1470 A.D. by Kamāl (or Shams) al-Dīn as Suyūṭī." *JRAS*, New Series 19,2 (1887), pp. 247–305.

Palestine under the Muslims: A description of Syria and the Holy Land from A.D. 650 to 1500. [London]: Published for the Committee of the Palestine Exploration Fund by Alexander P. Watt, 1890.

Leaman, Oliver. *Islamic aesthetics: An introduction*. Edinburgh: Edinburgh University Press, 2004.

Leder, Stefan. "Charismatic scripturalism: The Ḥanbalī Maqdisīs of Damascus." *Der Islam* 74,2 (1997), pp. 297–304.

Leiser, Gary. "Ḥanbalism in Egypt before the Mamluks." *SI* 54 (1981), pp. 155–82.

Leisten, Thomas. *Architektur für Tote: Bestattung in architektonischen Kontexten in den Kernländern der islamischen Welt zwischen dem 3./9. und 6./12. Jahrhundert*. Berlin: D. Reimer, 1998.

"Between orthodoxy and exegesis: Some aspects of attitudes in the Shariʿa toward funerary architecture." *Muqarnas* 7 (1990), pp. 12–22.

Leszynzsky, Rudolf. *Mohammedanische Traditionen über das jüngste Gericht: Eine vergleichende Studie zur jüdisch-christlichen und mohammedanischen Eschatologie*. Kirchhain: Max Schmersow, 1909.

Lewis, Bernard. "An Ismaili interpretation of the fall of Adam." *BSOAS* 9,3 (1938), pp. 691–704.

Librande, Leonard. "Ibn Abī l-Dunyā': Certainty and morality." *SI* 100–1001 (2005), pp. 5–42.

Livne-Kafri, Ofer. "Jerusalem: The navel of the earth in Muslim tradition." *Der Islam* 84,1 (2008), pp. 46–72.

Lohlker, Rüdiger, and Nowak, Andrea. "Das islamische Paradies als Zeichen: Zwischen Märtyrerkult und Garten." *Wiener Zeitschrift für die Kunde des Morgenlandes* 99 (2009), pp. 199–225.

Lory, Pierre. *Les commentaires ésotériques du Coran d'après ʿAbd ar-Razzâq al-Qâshânî*. Paris: Les Deux Océans, 1980.

"Le *miʿrāǧ* d'Abū Yazīd Basṭāmī." In Amir-Moezzi, ed. *Le voyage initiatique*, pp. 223–37.

"Les lieux saints du Hedjaz et de Palestine." In *Lieux d'Islam: cultes et culture d'Afrique à Java*. Edited by Mohammad Ali Amir-Moezzi. Paris: Éditions Autrement, 1996, pp. 24–45.

Loucel, Henri. "L'origine du language d'après les grammairiens arabes: IV." *Arabica* 11 (1964), pp. 151–87.

Lucini Baquerizo, Mercedes. "Aproximación a la literature escatológica musulmana." *Qurṭuba: estudios andalucíes* 2 (1997), pp. 107–21.

Lüling, Günter. *A challenge to Islam for reformation: The rediscovery and reliable reconstruction of a pre-Islamic Christian hymnal hidden in the Koran under earliest Islamic reinterpretations*. First publ. 1974, Erlangen 1993, 2nd ed. Engl. tr. Delhi: Motilal Barnasidass Publishers, 2003.

Lumpe, Adolf, and Bietenhard, Hans. "Himmel." In *Reallexikon für Antike und Christentum: Sachwörterbuch zur Auseinandersetzung des Christentums mit der antiken Welt*. Edited by Franz Joseph Dölger et al. Stuttgart: Hiersemann, 1950–2014, Vol. 15, pp. 173–212.

Luxenberg, Christoph. *Die syro-aramäische Lesart des Koran: Ein Beitrag zur Entschlüsselung des Koran*. 3rd rev. ed. Berlin: Schiler, 2007. Translated as *The Syro-Aramaic reading of the Koran: A contribution to the decoding of the language of the Koran*. Berlin: Schiler, 2007.

MacDannell, Colleen, and Lang, Bernard. *Heaven: A history*. New Haven, CT, and London: Yale University Press, 1988.

MacDonald, John. "Islamic eschatology I-VI." *IS* 3 (1964), pp. 285–308, 485–519; 4 (1965), pp. 55–102, 137–79; 5 (1966), pp. 129–97, 331–83.

Madelung, Wilferd. "Apocalyptic prophecies in Ḥimṣ in the Umayyad Age." *Journal of Semitic Studies* 31 (1986), pp. 141–85.

"Imamism and Muʿtazilite Theology." In Fahd, ed. *Le Shîʿisme imâmite*, pp. 13–30.

"The Spread of Māturīdism and the Turks." In *Actas do IV Congresso dos Estudos Árabes e Islâmicos, Coimbra-Lisboa 1968*. Leiden: Brill, 1971, pp. 109–68.

Madigan, Daniel. "Themes and topics." In *The Cambridge Companion to the Qurʾān*. Edited by Jane Dammen McAuliffe. Cambridge and New York: Cambridge University Press, 2006, pp. 80–95.

Maḥmūd, Ibrāhīm. *Jughrāfiyyat al-maladhdhāt: al-jins fī l-janna*. Beirut: Riyāḍ al-Rayyis li-l-Kutub wa-l-Nashr, 1998.

Mainusch, H., and Warning, R. "Imagination." In *Historisches Wörterbuch der Philosophie*. Edited by Joachim Ritter und Karlfried Gründer. Darmstadt: Wissenschaftliche Buchgesellschaft, 1971–2007, Vol. 4, pp. 217a–219b.

Makdisi, George. "L'Islam hanbalisant." *REI* 42 (1974), pp. 211–44.

Marcotte, Roxanne D. "Suhrawardī's realm of the imaginal." *Ishraq* 2 (2011), pp. 68–79.

Marmura, Michael. "Paradise in Islamic philosophy." In Günther and Lawson (eds). *Roads to paradise*, forthcoming.

Marquet, Yves. "Imāmat, résurrection et hiérarchie selon les Ikhwān al-ṣafāʾ." *REI* 30 (1962), pp. 49–142.

La philosophie des Iḫwān al-Ṣafāʾ. Algiers: Études et documents, 1973.

Martin, Aubert. *La vie future selon l'Islam*. Liège: Faculté de Philosophie et Lettres ('Les civilisations Orientales' no. 36), [1992?].

Massad, Joseph A. *Desiring Arabs*. Chicago: Chicago University Press, 2007.

Massignon, Louis. *Essai sur les origines du lexique technique de la mystique musulmane*. First publ. 1922. Rev. and enlarged ed. Paris: J. Vrin, 1954.

"Les 'sept dormants'. Apocalypse de l'Islam." *Analecta Bollandiana* 68 (1950), pp. 245–60.

Opera minora. 3 vols. Paris: Presses Universitaires de France, 1969.

Recueil de textes inédits concernant l'histoire de la mystique en pays d'Islam. Paris: Geunthner, 1929.

Masud, Muhammad Khalid. "Sufi understanding of *hajj* rituals." In *El Sufismo y las normas del Islam*. Edited by Alfonso Carmona. Murcia: Editora Regional de Murcia, 2006, pp. 271–90.

McDermott, Martin J. *The theology of al-Shaikh al-Mufīd, d. 413/1022*. Beirut: Dar al-Machreq, 1978.

Mehren, A. F. "Muhammedansk Eschatologi eller Islams Laere om Doden og Menneskets Tilstand efter denne." *For Romantik og Historie* 13 (1874), pp. 641–72.

Meier, Fritz. *Abū Saʿīd-i Abūl-Khayr (357–440/1067–1049): Wirklichkeit und Legende*. Leiden: Brill, 1976.

Bahāʾ-i Walad. Grundzüge seines Lebens und seiner Mystik. Leiden: E. J. Brill, 1989.

Bemerkungen zur Mohammedverehrung. Edited by Bernd Radtke and Gudrun Schubert. 2 vols. Leiden: Brill, 2002.

Das Problem der Natur im esoterischen Monismus des Islams. Zürich: Rhein-Verlag, 1947.

"Die Schriften des ʿAzīz-i Nasafī." *Wiener Zeitschrift für die Kunde des Morgenlandes* 52 (1953), pp. 125–82. Reprinted in *Bausteine: Ausgewählte Aufsätze zur Islamwissenschaft. Band I*. Edited by Erika Glassen and Gudrun Schubert. Stuttgart: Steiner, 1992, pp. 178–235.

"The ultimate origin and the hereafter in Islam." In *Islam and its cultural divergence: Studies in honor of Gustav E. von Grunebaum*. Edited by Ghirdari L. Tikku. Urbana: University of Illinois Press, [1971], pp. 96–112.

Meisami, Julie Scott. "Palaces and paradises: Palace descriptions in medieval Persian poetry." In *Islamic art and literature*. Edited by Oleg Grabar and Cynthia Robinson. Princeton, NJ: Markus Wiener, 2001, pp. 21–54.

"The palace-complex as emblem: Some Samarran qaṣīdas." In *A medieval Islamic city reconsidered: An interdisciplinary approach to Samarra*. Edited by Chase F. Robinson. Oxford: Oxford University Press, 2001, pp. 69–78.

Meisami, Sayeh. *Mulla Sadra*. Oxford: Oneworld, 2013.

Melchert, Christopher. "Aḥmad b. Ḥanbal's *Book of Renunciation*." *Der Islam* 85 (2011), pp. 345–59.

"Exaggerated fear in the early Islamic renunciant tradition." *JRAS*, Third Series 21 (2011), pp. 283–300.

"Ibn al-Mubārak's *K. al-jihād* and early renunciant literature." In *Violence in Islamic thought*. Vol. 1: *From the Qurʾān to the Mongols*. Edited by Robert Gleave and István Kristó-Nagy. Edinburgh: Edinburgh University Press, forthcoming.

"Locating hell in early renunciant literature." In Lange, ed. *Locating hell*, pp. 103–23.

"The *Musnad* of Aḥmad ibn Ḥanbal: How it was composed and what distinguishes it from the Six Books." *Der Islam* 82 (2005), pp. 32–51.

Mensia, Mongia Arfa. "L'acte expiatoire en Islam: 'al Kaffāra.'" In *Rituals and ethics: Patterns of repentance; Judaism, Christianity, Islam*. Edited by Adriana Destro and Mauro Pesce. Paris and Louvain: Peeters, 2004, pp. 125–39.

Meyer, Jonas. *Die Hölle im Islam*. PhD diss., Basel University, 1901.

Meyerhof, Max, and Schacht, Joseph. *The theologus autodidactus of Ibn al-Nafīs*. Oxford: Clarendon Press, 1968.

Michot, Jean R. "A Mamluk theologian's commentary on Avicenna's *Risāla aḍḥawiyya*. Being a translation of a part of the *Darʾ al-taʿāruḍ* of Ibn Taymiyya with introduction, annotation, and appendices. Part I." *JIS* 14,2 (2003), pp. 149–203.

La destinée de l'homme selon Avicenne: Le retour a Dieu (maʿād) *et l'imagination*. Louvain: Peeters, 1986.

Milstein, Rachel. "*Kitāb Shawq-nāma* – An illustrated tour of holy Arabia." *JSAI* 25 (2001), pp. 275–345.

"Paradise as a parable." In Dévényi and Fodor, eds., *Proceedings* [Part 1], pp. 147–55.

Milstein, Rachel, Rührdanz, Karin, and Schmitz, Barbara. *Stories of the prophets: Illustrated manuscripts of the* Qiṣas al-anbiyāʾ. Costa Mesa, CA: Mazda Publishers, 1999.

Minov, Sergey. "Regarder la montagne sacrée: représentations du Paradis dans la tradition chrétienne syrienne." In *Mondes clos: Cultures et jardins*. Edited by Daniel Barbu, Philippe Borgeaud, Mélanie Lozat, and Youri Volokhine. Gollion: Infolio, [2013], pp. 241–69, 367–74.

Miquel, André. *La géographie humaine du monde musulmane jusq'au milieu du IIe siécle: Géographie et géographie humaine dans la littérature arabe (des origines á 1050)*. Paris and The Hague: Mouton, 1967.

Mitha, Farouk. *Al Ghazālī and the Ismailis: A debate on reason and authority in medieval Islam* (Ismaili Heritage Series, 5). London and New York: I. B. Tauris, 2001.

Mittermayer, Amira. *Dreams that matter: Egyptian landscapes of the imagination*. Berkeley: University of California Press, 2011.

Modarressi Tabataba'i, Hosein. *Tradition and survival: A bibliographical survey of early Shīʿite literature*. Oxford: Oneworld, 2003-.

Monferrer Sala, Juan Pedro. "A propósito de Wādī Yahannam." *Al-Andalus Maghreb* 5 (1997), pp. 149–62.

Kitâb waṣf al-firdaws (La descripción del paraíso): Introducción, traducción y estudio. Granada: Al-Mudun, 1997.

Moosa, Ebrahim. *Al-Ghazālī and the poetics of imagination*. First published 2005. Oxford and New York: Oxford University Press, 2006.

Morony, Michael G. *Iraq after the Muslim conquest*. Princeton, NJ: Princeton University Press, 1984.

Morris, James W. *The wisdom of the throne: An introduction to the philosophy of Mulla Sadra*. Princeton, NJ: Princeton University Press, 1981.

"Spiritual ascension: Ibn ʿArabî and the Miʿrâj." *JAOS* 107 (1987), pp. 629–52; 108 (1988), pp. 63–77.

Motzki, Harald. "The Prophet and the debtors: A Ḥadīth analysis under scrutiny." In *Analysing Muslim traditions: Studies in legal, exegetical and* maghāzī *ḥadīth*. Edited by Harald Motzki, with Nicolette Boekhoff van der Voort and Sean W. Anthony. Leiden: Brill, 2009, pp. 125–205.

"Review of G. A. H. Juynboll, *Encyclopedia of canonical ḥadīth*." *JSAI* 36 (2009), pp. 539–49.

Murata, Sachiko, and Chittick, William C. *The vision of Islam*. New York: Paragon House, 1997.

Nabielek, Rainer. "Weintrauben statt Jungfrauen als paradiesische Freude." *DAVO Nachrichten* 17 (2003), pp. 37a–45b.

Nafi, Basheer M. "A teacher of Ibn ʿAbd al-Wahhāb: Muḥammad Ḥayāt al-Sindī and the revival of *aṣḥāb al-ḥadīth*'s methodology." *Islamic Law and Society* 13,2 (2006), pp. 208–41.

Nagel, Tilman. *Geschichte der islamischen Theologie: Von Mohammed bis zur Gegenwart*. Munich: Beck, 1994.

Medinensische Einschübe in mekkanischen Suren. Göttingen: Vandenhoeck und Ruprecht, 1995.

Nakamura, Kojiro. "Imām Ghazālī's cosmology reconsidered with special reference to the concept of 'Jabarūt.'" *SI* 80 (1994), pp. 29–46.

Nasr, Seyyed Hossein. "Le shīʿisme et le soufisme." In Fahd, ed. *Le Shīʿisme imâmite*, pp. 215–33.

Nebes, Norbert. "The martyrs of Najrān and the end of Ḥimyar: On the political history of South Arabia in the early sixth century." In Neuwirth, Sinai, and Marx, eds. *The Quran in context*, pp. 27–59.

Neuwirth, Angelika. *Der Koran als Text der Spätantike: Ein europäischer Zugang*. Berlin: Verlag der Weltreligionen, 2010.

Der Koran. Vol. 1: *Frühmekkanische Suren; Handkommentar mit Übersetzung* [= *Handkommentar*]. Berlin: Verlag der Weltreligionen, 2011.

"Qurʾanic readings of the psalms." In Neuwirth, Sinai, and Marx, eds. *The Quran in context*, pp. 733–78.

"Reclaiming paradise lost." In *Orientalia Christiana: Festschrift für Hubert Kaufhold zum 70. Geburtstag*. Edited by Peter Bruns and Heinz Otto Luthe. Wiesbaden: Harrassowitz, 2013, pp. 333–54.

Studien zur Komposition der mekkanischen Suren. Berlin and New York: de Gruyter, 1981.

"Zeit und Ewigkeit in den Psalmen und im Koran." In *Zeit und Ewigkeit als Raum göttlichen Handelns: Religionsgeschichtliche, theologische und philosophische Perspektiven*. Edited by Reinhard G. Kratz and Hermann Spieckermann. Berlin and New York: de Gruyter, 2009, pp. 319–42.

Neuwirth, Angelika, Sinai, Nicolai, and Marx, Michael, eds. *The Quran in context: Historical and literary investigations into the Qurʾānic milieu*. Leiden: Brill, 2010

Newby, Gordon D. "The development of Qurʾan commentary in early Islam in its relationship to Judaeo-Christian traditions of scriptural commentary." *Journal of the American Academy of Religion* 47,4 (1980), pp. 685–97.

Nicholson, Richard A. "An early Arabic version of the miʿrāj of Abū Yazīd al-Bisṭāmī." *Islamica* 2,3 (1926), pp. 403–8.

Nilsson, Martin P. *Geschichte der griechischen Religion*. 2 vols. First publ. 1941. Munich: Beck, 1967–74, 3rd ed.

Nöldeke, Arnold. *Das Heiligtum al-Husains zu Kerbalâ*. Berlin: Mayer & Müller, 1909.

Nöldeke, Theodor. *Geschichte des Qorāns*. Vol. 1: *Über den Ursprung des Qorāns*. 2nd ed. prepared by Friedrich Schwally. Leipzig: T. Dieter, 1909.

Nünlist, Tobias. *Himmelfahrt und Heiligkeit im Islam: Eine Studie unter besonderer Berücksichtigung von Ibn Sinās* Miʿrāğ-nāmeh. Bern and New York: P. Lang, 2002.

Nwyia, Paul. *Exégèse Coranique et langage mystique: Nouvel essai sur le lexique technique des mystiques musulmans*. Beirut: Dar el-Machreq, 1970.

Nwyia, Paul, ed. *Trois oeuvres inédites de mystiques musulmanes: Šaqīq al-Balkhī, Ibn ʿAṭāʾ, Niffarī*. Beirut: Dar al-Machreq, 1976.

Obermann, Julian. "Islamic origins: A study in background and formation." In *The Arab heritage*. Edited by Nabih Amin Faris. Princeton, NJ: Princeton University Press, 1944, pp. 58–120.

Ohlander, Eric. "Ibn Kathīr." In *Essays in Arabic literary biography, 1350–1850*. Edited by Joe Lowry and Devin Stewart. Wiesbaden: Harrassowitz, 2009, pp. 147–59.

O'Meara, Simon. "Muslim visuality and the visibility of paradise and this world." In Günther and Lawson, eds. *Roads to paradise*, forthcoming.

Space and Muslim urban life: At the limits of the labyrinth of Fes. London and New York: Routledge, 2007.

Ormsby, Eric. "The faith of Pharaoh: A disputed question in Islamic theology." *SI* 98–9 (2004), pp. 5–28.

O'Shaughnessy, Thomas J. *Eschatological themes in the Qur'ān*. [Manila]: Cardinal Bea Institute, Loyola School of Theology, Ateneo de Manila University, 1986.

Muhammad's thoughts on death: A thematic study of the Qur'anic data. Leiden: E. J. Brill, 1969.

"The seven names for hell in the Qur'ān." *BSOAS* 24,3 (1961), pp. 444–69.

Ott, Claudia. "Das Paradies in den Erzählungen aus Tausendundeiner Nacht." In *1001 Nacht: Wege ins Paradies*. Edited by Andrea Müller and Hartmut Roder. Mainz: von Zabern, 2006, pp. 11–18.

"Paradise, Alexander, and the *Arabian nights*." In Günther and Lawson, eds. *Roads to paradise*, forthcoming.

Pagani, Samuela. "Ibn ʿArabī and political hell." In Lange, ed. *Locating hell*, pp. 175–207.

"Un paradiso in terra: Il ḥammām e la economia della salvezza." In *Hammam: Le terme nel Islam*. Edited by Rosita d'Amora and Samuela Pagani. Florence: Leo S. Olschki Editore, 2010, pp. 133–58.

"Vane speranze, false minacce: L'islam e la durata dell'inferno." In *Inferni temporanei: Visioni dell'aldilà dall'estremo Oriente all'estremo Occidente*. Edited by Maria Chiara Migliore and Samuela Pagani. Rome: Carocci editore, 2011, pp. 179–222.

Palmer, Edward Henry. *Oriental mysticism: A treatise on sufistic and unitarian theosophy of the Persians*. First published London: Bell and Daldy, 1867. London: Luzac, 1938.

Paret, Rudi. *Der Koran: Kommentar und Konkordanz*. 2 vols. Stuttgart: W. Kohlhammer, 1977, 2nd ed.

Frühislamische Liebesgeschichten: Ein Beitrag zur vergleichenden Literaturgeschichte. Basel: P. Haupt, 1927.

Pautz, Otto. *Muhammeds Lehre von der Offenbarung*. Leipzig: J. C. Hinrichs'sche Buchhandlung, 1898.

Pedersen, J. "The Islamic preacher: Wāʿiẓ, mudhakkir, qāṣṣ." In *Ignace Goldziher memorial volume*. Edited by Samuel Löwinger and Joseph Somogyi. 2 vols. Budapest: s.n., 1948–58, Vol. 1, pp. 226–51.

Pennachietti, F. A. "Il racconto di Giomgiomé di Faridoddin Attàr e le sue fonti cristiane." *Orientalia Christiana Periodica* 62 (1996), pp. 89–112.

Pérès, Henri. *La poésie andalouse en arabe classique au XIe siècle: Ses aspects généraux, ses principaux thèmes et sa valeur documentaire*. Paris: Adrien-Maisonneuve, 1953.

Peters, Rudolph. *Crime and punishment in Islamic law: Theory and practice from the sixteenth to the twenty-first century*. Cambridge and New York: Cambridge University Press, 2005.

Phillips, Jonathan P. *Holy warriors: A modern history of the Crusades*. London: Vintage, 2010.
Philonenko, Marc. "Une expression qoumranienne dans le Coran." In *Atti del Terzo Congresso di Studi Arabi e Islamici, Ravello 1–6 settembre 1966*. Naples: Istituto universitario orientale, 1967, pp. 553–6.
Picken, Gavin. "*Tazkiyat al-nafs:* the Qurʾānic paradigm." *JQS* 7,2 (2005), pp. 101–27.
Pinder-Wilson, R. "The Persian garden: Bagh and chahar bagh." In *The Islamic garden*. Edited by Elisabeth B. MacDougall and Richard Ettinghausen. Washington, DC: Dumbarton Oaks, 1976, pp. 69–85.
Pisani, Emmanuel. "Hors de l'Islam point de salut? Juifs, chrétiens et hétérodoxes dans l'eschatologie d'al-Ghazālī." *MIDEO* 30 (2014), 139–84.
Pococke, Edward. *Notae miscellaneae philologico-biblicae*. Edited by Christian Reineccius. Leipzig: Sumptibus Haeredum Lanckisianorum, 1705.
Pomerantz, Maurice A. "Muʿtazilī theory in practice: The repentance (*tawba*) of government officials in the 4th/10th century." In *A common rationality: Muʿtazilism in Islam and Judaism*. Edited by Camilla Adang, Sabine Schmidtke, and David Sklare. Würzburg: Ergon, 2007, pp. 463–93.
Poonawala, Ismail K. "Al-Sijistānī and his *K. al-Maqālīd*." In *Essays on Islamic civilization presented to Niyazi Berkes*. Edited by Donald P. Little. Leiden: Brill, 1976, pp. 274–83.
"Ismāʿīlī taʾwīl of the Qurʾān." In *Approaches to the history of the interpretation of the Qurʾān*. Edited by Anrew Rippin. Oxford: Clarendon Press, 1988, pp. 199–222.
Preckel, Claudia. "Screening Ṣiddīq Ḥasan Khān's library: The use of Ḥanbalī literature in 19th-century Bhopal." In *Islamic theology, philosophy and law: Debating Ibn Taymiyya and Ibn Qayyim al-Jawziyya*. Edited by Birgit Krawietz and Georges Tamer. Berlin: de Gruyter, 2013, pp. 162–219.
Pregill, Michael. "ʿIsrāʾīliyyāt, myth, and pseudepigraphy: Wahb b. Munabbih and the early Islamic version of the fall of Adam and Eve." *JSAI* 34 (2008), pp. 215–84.
Rabin, Chaim. ""Islam and the Qumran Sect." First publ. 1957. Reprinted in *The Qur'an: Style and Contents*. Edited by Andrew Rippin. Aldershot, UK: Ashgate Variorum, 2001, pp. 1–20.
Radscheit, Matthias. "Der Höllenbaum." In *Der Koran und sein religiöses und kulturelles Umfeld*. Edited by Tilman Nagel (with Elisabeth Müller-Luckner). Munich: R. Oldenbourg Verlag, 2010, pp. 97–133.
Rahman, Fazlur. "Dreams, imagination, and *ʿālam al-mithāl*." *IS* 3,2 (1964), pp. 167–80.
Major themes of the Qurʾān. Minneapolis, MN: Bibliotheca Islamica, 1980.
The philosophy of Mullā Ṣadrā (Ṣadr al-Dīn al-Shīrāzī). Albany, NY: SUNY Press, 1975.
Raphael, Simcha Paul. *Jewish views of the afterlife*. First publ. 1994. 2nd ed. Lanham, MD: Rowman and Littlefield Publishers, 2009.
Raven, Wim. "A Kitāb al-ʿAẓama: On cosmology, hell and paradise." In *Miscellanea Arabica et Islamica: Dissertationes in Academia Ultratrajectina prolatae* (Orientalia Lovaniensia Analecta, 53). Edited by Fred de Jong. Leuven: Peeters, 1993, pp. 135–42.
"Hell in popular Muslim imagination: The anonymous *Kitāb al-ʿAẓama*." In Lange, ed. *Locating hell*, pp. 144–62.

Reat, N. R. "The tree symbol in Islam." *Studies in Comparative Religion* 9 (1975), pp. 164–82.

Rebstock, Ulrich. "Das 'Grabesleben': Eine islamische Konstruktion zwischen Himmel und Hölle." In *Islamstudien ohne Ende: Festschrift für Werner Ende zum 65. Geburtstag*. Edited by Rainer Brunner. Würzburg: Ergon, 2002, pp. 371–82.

Reeves, Minou. *Muhammad in Europe: A thousand years of Western myth-making*. New York: New York University Press, 2003.

Reinert, Benedikt. *Die Lehre vom* tawakkul *in der klassischen Sufik*. Berlin: de Gruyter, 1968.

Reinhart, Kevin. "Impurity/no danger." *History of Religions* 30,1 (1990), pp. 1–24.

"Ritual action and practical action: The incomprehensibility of Muslim devotional action." In *Islamic law in theory: Studies on jurisprudence in honor of Bernard Weiss*. Edited by Kevin Reinhart and Robert Gleave. Leiden: Brill, 2014, pp. 55–103.

"The here and the hereafter in Islamic religious thought." In *Images of paradise in Islamic art*. Edited by Sheila S. Blair and Jonathan M. Bloom. Hanover, NH: Hood Museum of Art, 1991, pp. 15–21.

"What to do with ritual texts: Islamic *fiqh* texts and the study of Islamic ritual." In *Surveying Islamic Studies: Innovations, transformations, continuities*. Edited by Léon Buskens. Amsterdam: Amsterdam University Press, forthcoming.

Reland, Adriaan. *De religione Mohammedica libri duo*. First publ. 1705. Utrecht: Gulielmi Broedelet, 1717, 2nd ed.

Rescher, Otto. "Studien über den Inhalt von 1001 Nacht." *Der Islam* 9 (1919), pp. 1–94.

Reuschel, Wolfgang. *Aspekt und Tempus in der Sprache des Korans*. Frankfurt: Peter Lang, 1996.

Reynolds, Gabriel Said. "Introduction." In idem, ed. *The Qurʾān in its historical context*. London and New York: Routledge, 2008, pp. 1–25.

"Le problème de la chronologie du Coran." *Arabica* 58 (2011), pp. 477–502.

The Qurʾān and its biblical subtext. London and New York: Routledge, 2010.

Ri, Andreas Su-Min. *Commentaire de la* Caverne des trésors: *Étude sur l'histoire du texte et de ses sources*. Louvain: Peeters, 2000.

Ridgeon, Lloyd. *ʿAzīz Nasafī*. Richmond, UK: Curzon Press, 1998.

Ritter, Helmut. *Das Meer der Seele: Mensch, Welt und Gott in den Geschichten des Farīduddīn ʿAttār*. Leiden: E. J. Brill, 1955.

"Die Aussprüche des Bāyezīd Bisṭāmī: Eine vorläufige Skizze." In *Westöstliche Abhandlungen: Rudolf Tschudi zum siebzigsten Geburtstag überreicht von Freunden und Schülern*. Edited by Fritz Meier. Wiesbaden: Harrassowitz, 1954, pp. 231–43.

"Studien zur Geschichte der islamischen Frömmigkeit: I. Ḥasan al-Baṣrī." *Der Islam* 21 (1933), pp. 1–83.

Rizvi, Sajjad. *Mullā Ṣadrā and metaphysics: Modulation of being*. London and New York: Routledge, 2009.

Rippin, Andrew. "The commerce of eschatology." In *The Qurʾan as text*. Edited by Stefan Wild. Leiden: E. J. Brill, 1996, pp. 125–35.

Robin, Christian Julien. "Nagrān vers l'époque du massacre: notes sur l'histoire politique, économique et institutionelle et sur l'introduction du christianisme (avec un réexamen du *Martyre d'Azqīr*)." In *Juifs et chrétiens en Arabie aux Ve et VIe siècles. Regards croisés sur les sources*. Edited by Joëlle Beaucamp, Françoise Briquel-Chatonnet, and Christian Julien Robin. Paris: Association des amis du Centre d'histoire et civilisation de Byzance, 2010, pp. 39–106.

Robson, James. "Is the Moslem hell eternal?" *MW* 28 (1938), pp. 386–96.

Roggema, Barbara. "Letter of ʿUmar b. ʿAbd al-ʿAzīz." In *CMR*, s.v. ["Title uncertain"]. Online publication (2010).

Rosenthal, Franz. *A history of Muslim historiography*. Leiden: E. J. Brill, 1952.

"Nineteen." *Analecta Biblica* 12 (1959), pp. 304–18.

"Reflections on love in paradise." In *Love and death in the ancient Near East: Essays in honor of Marvin H. Pope*. Edited by John H. Marks and Robert M. Good. Guilford: Four Quarters Publishing, 1987, pp. 247–54.

"Sweeter than hope": Complaint and hope in medieval Islam. Leiden: E. J. Brill, 1983.

Rowson, Everett. *A Muslim philosopher on the soul and its fate*. New Haven, CT: American Oriental Society, 1988.

"Reveal or conceal: Public humiliation and banishment as punishments in early Islamic times." In Lange and Fierro, eds. *Public violence*, pp. 119–29.

Rubin, Uri. "Apes, pigs, and the Islamic identity." *IOS* 17 (1997), pp. 89–112.

Between Bible and Qurʾān: The children of Israel in the Islamic self-image. Princeton, NJ: Darwin Press, 1999.

"The Kaʿba: Aspects of its ritual function." *JSAI* 8 (1986), pp. 97–131.

Rudolph, Ulrich. "Abū Naṣr al-Farābī." In *Philosophie in der islamischen Welt. Vol. 1: 8.-10. Jahrhundert*. Edited by Ulrich Rudolph (with Renate Würsch). Basel: Schwabe Verlag, 2012, pp. 365–457.

Al-Māturīdī und die sunnitische Theologie in Samarkand. New York: E. J. Brill, 1997.

Ruggles, D. Fairchild. *Gardens, landscapes, and vision in the palaces of Islamic Spain*. University Park: Pennsylvania State University Press, 2000.

Rüling, J. B. *Beiträge zur Eschatologie des Islam*. Leipzig: Harrassowitz, 1895.

Rustom, Mohammed. "Psychology, eschatology and imagination in Mullā Ṣadrā Shīrāzī's commentary on the ḥadīth of awakening." *Islamic Science* 5,1 (2007), pp. 9–22.

"Review of S. Rivzi, *Mullā Ṣadrā and metaphysics: Modulation of being*." *JIS* 22,3 (2011), pp. 409–12.

The triumph of mercy: Philosophy and scripture in Mullā Ṣadrā. Albany, NY: SUNY Press, 2012.

Rustomji, Nerina. *The Garden and the Fire: Heaven and hell in Islamic culture*. New York: Columbia University Press, 2009.

Ryad, Amr. "Eschatology between reason and revelation: Death and resurrection in modern Islamic theology." In Günther and Lawson, eds. *Roads to paradise*, forthcoming.

Saeedullah. *The life and works of Muḥammad Ṣiddīq Ḥasan Khan, Nawab of Bhopal, 1248–1307/1832–1890*. Lahore: Sh. Muhammad Ashraf, 1973.

Safi, Omid. *The politics of knowledge in premodern Islam: Negotiating ideology and religious inquiry*. Chapel Hill: University of North Carolina Press, 2006.

Sale, George. "Preliminary discourse." In *The Korân*. London and New York: Frederick Warne and Co. Ltd., n.d., pp. 1–208.

Saleh, Walid A. "Paradise in an Islamic *ʿajāʾib* work: *The delight of onlookers and the signs for investigators* of Marʿī b. Yūsuf al-Karmī (d. 1033/1624)." In Günther and Lawson, eds. *Roads to paradise*, forthcoming.

The formation of the classical tafsīr *tradition: The Qurʾān commentary of al-Thaʿlabī (d. 427/1035).* Boston: Brill, 2004.

Sanderson, Gordon. *A guide to the buildings and gardens, Delhi Fort.* Delhi: Manager of Publications, 1937.

Sands, Kristin Zahra. *Sufi commentaries on the Qurʾan in classical Islam.* London and New York: Routledge, 2005.

Sauvaget, Jean. *La mosquée omeyyade de Médine: Étude sur les origines architecturales de la mosquée et de la basilique.* Paris: Vanoest, 1947.

Savage-Smith, Emilie. "In medieval Islamic cosmography, where is paradise?" In *The cosmography of paradise: The other world from ancient Mesopotamia to early modern Europe.* Edited by Alessandro Scafi. London: Warburg Institute, forthcoming.

Schimmel, Annemarie. *Die Träume des Kalifen: Träume und ihre Deutung in der islamischen Kultur.* Munich: C. H. Beck, 1998.

"'I take of the dress of the body': Eros in Sufi literature and life." In *Religion and the body.* Edited by Sarah Coakley. Cambridge: Cambridge University Press, 2000, pp. 262–88.

"The celestial garden in Islam." in *The Islamic garden.* Edited by Elizabeth B. MacDougall and Richard Ettinghausen. Washington, DC: Dumbarton Oaks, 1976, pp. 11–39.

The triumphal sun: A study of the works of Jalāloddīn Rumi. London: Fine Books, 1978.

Schmidtke, Sabine. *A Muʿtazilite creed of al-Zamakhsharī (d. 538/1144).* Stuttgart: Franz Steiner Verlag, 1997.

"The doctrine of transmigration of the soul according to Suhrawardī (killed 587/1191) and his followers." *Studia Iranica* 28 (1999), pp. 237–54.

The theology of al-ʿAllāma al-Ḥillī (d. 726/1325). Berlin: K. Schwarz, 1991.

Theologie, Philosophie und Mystik im zwölferschiitischen Islam des 9./15. Jahrhunderts: Die Gedankenwelten des Ibn Abī Ǧumhūr al-Aḥsāʾī (um 838/1434-nach 905/1501). Boston: Brill, 2000.

Schöck, Cornelia. *Adam im Islam: Ein Beitrag zur Ideengeschichte der Sunna.* Berlin: K. Schwarz, 1993.

Schrieke, Bertram. "Die Himmelsreise Mohammeds." *Der Islam* 6 (1916), pp. 1–30.

Séd, N. "Les hymnes sur le paradis de Saint Ephrem et les traditions juives." *Le Muséon* 81 (1968), pp. 455–501.

Segal, Alan S. *Life after death: A history of the afterlife in the religions of the West.* New York: Doubleday, 2004.

Séguy, Marie-Rose. *The miraculous journey of Mahomet: Mirâj Nâmeh Bibliothèque Nationale, Paris (Manuscrit Supplément Turk 190).* New York: Georges Braziller, 1977.

Seidensticker, Tilman. "Der rūḥ der Toten." In *Kaškūl: Festschrift zum 25. Jahrestag der Wiederbegründung des Instituts für Orientalistik an der Justus-Liebig-Universität Giessen.* Edited by Ewald Wagner and Klaus Röhrborn. Wiesbaden: Harrassowitz, 1989, pp. 141–56.

Sells, Michael. *Approaching the Qurʾān: The early revelations.* Ashland, OR: White Cloud Press, 1999.

Early Islamic mysticism: Sufi, Qur'an, Mi'raj, poetic and theological writings. New York: Paulist Press, 1996.
Shalem, Avinoam. "Bi'r al-waraqa, legend and truth: A note on medieval sacred geography." *Palestine Exploration Quarterly* 127 (1995), pp. 50–61.
Shoemaker, Stephen J. "Muḥammad and the Qur'ān." In *The Oxford handbook of Late Antiquity*. Edited by Scott Fitzgerald Johnson. Oxford: Oxford University Press, 2012, pp. 1078–1108.
The death of a prophet: The end of Muḥammad's life and the beginnings of Islam. Philadelphia: University of Philadelphia Press, 2012.
Shoshan, Boaz. "High culture and popular culture in medieval Islam." *SI* 73 (1991), pp. 67–107.
Popular culture in medieval Cairo. Cambridge: Cambridge University Press, 1993.
Silverstein, Adam. "On the original meaning of the Qur'ānic term *al-shayṭān al-rajīm*." *JAOS* 133,1 (2013), pp. 21–33.
Sinai, Nicolai. *Der Koran: Die heilige Schrift*. Freiburg, Basel, and Vienna: Herder, 2012.
"Kommentar." In idem, trans. *Shihāb al-Dīn al-Suhrawardī: Philosophie der Erleuchtung*. Berlin: Verlag der Weltreligionen, 2011, pp. 223–432.
Fortschreibung und Auslegung: Studien zur frühen Koraninterpretation. Wiesbaden: Harrassowitz, 2009.
"The Qur'an as process." In Neuwirth, Sinai, and Marx, eds. *The Quran in context*, pp. 407–39.
Sirriyeh, Elizabeth. *Sufi visionary of Ottoman Damascus: ʿAbd al-Ghanī al-Nābulusī, 1641–1731*. London: Routledge, 2005.
Smith, Edmund W. *Akbar's tomb, Sikandarah, near Agra*. Allahabad: F. Luker, 1909.
Smith, Jane Idleman. "Concourse between the living and the dead in Islamic eschatological literature." *History of Religions* 19,3 (1980), pp. 224–36.
"Introduction." In eadem, trans. *The Precious Pearl*. Missoula, MT: Scholars Press, 1979, pp. 1–12.
"Old French travel accounts of Muslim beliefs concerning the afterlife." In *Christian-Muslim encounters*. Edited by Yvonne Yazbeck Haddad and Wadi Z. Haddad. Gainesville: University Press of Florida, 1995, pp. 221–41.
Smith, Jane Idleman, and Haddad, Yvonne Yazbeck. *The Islamic understanding of death and resurrection*. First published 1981. Oxford: Oxford University Press, 2002.
Smith, Jonathan Z. "The devil in Mr. Jones." In *Imagining religion: From Babylon to Jonestown*. Chicago: University of Chicago Press, 1982, pp. 102–20.
Smith, Margaret. *Al-Ghazālī, the mystic: A study of the life and personality of Abū Ḥāmid al-Ghazālī, together with an account of his mystical teaching and an estimate of his place in the history of Islamic mysticism*. London: Luzac and Co., 1944.
"The Forerunner of al-Ghazālī." *JRAS*, New Series 68,1 (1936), pp. 65–78.
Snouck Hurgronje, Christiaan. "Der Mahdi." *Revue Coloniale Internationale* 1 (1886), pp. 25–59.
Sourdel, Dominique. "L'Imamisme vu par le cheikh al-Mufīd." *REI* 40 (1972), pp. 217–96.
Stanner, W. E. H. "The Dreaming (1953)." In *The dreaming and other essays*. Melbourne: Black Inc. Agenda, [2009?], pp. 57–72.

Stehly, Ralph. "Un problème de théologie musulmane: La définition des fautes graves (*kabāʾir*)." *REI* 45 (1977), pp. 165–81.

Stieglecker, Hermann. *Die Glaubenslehren des Islam.* Munich, Paderborn, and Vienna: Ferdinand Schöningh, 1962.

Stolz, Fritz. "Paradiese und Gegenwelten." *Zeitschrift für Religionswissenschaft* 1,1 (1993), pp. 5–24.

Stowasser, Barbara Freyer. *The day begins at sunset: Perceptions of time in the Islamic world.* London and New York: I. B. Tauris, 2014.

Strack, H. L., and Stemberger, Günter. Einleitung in Talmud und Midrasch. First published in 1982. Translated and edited by Markus Bockmuehl. *Introduction to the Talmud and Midrash.* 2nd printing. Minneapolis, MN: Fortress Press, 1996.

Strohmaier, Gotthard. "Die angeblichen und die wirklichen orientalischen Quellen der 'Divina Comedia.'" In *Von Demokrit bis Dante.* Hildesheim, Zurich, and New York: Georg Olms Verlag, 1996, pp. 471–86.

Stroumsa, Sarah. "'True felicity': Paradise in the thought of Avicenna and Maimonides." *Medieval Encounters* 4,1 (1998), pp. 51–77.

Stytkevych, Jaroslav. *Muḥammad and the golden bough: Reconstructing Arabian myth.* Bloomington: Indiana University Press, 1996.

Sublet, Jacqueline. "Nommer l'animal." In Mohammed Hocine Benkheira, Catherine Mayeur-Jaouen, and Jacqueline Sublet, *L'animal en islam.* Pairs: Les Indes savantes, 2005, pp. 45–76.

Sviri, Sara. "Between fear and hope: On the coincidence of opposites in Islamic mysticism." *JSAI* 9 (1987), pp. 316–49.

Szombathy, Zoltán. "Come hell or high water: Afterlife as a poetic convention in mediaeval Arabic literature." In Dévényi and Fodor, eds., *Proceedings* [Part 1], pp. 163–78.

Tamer, Georges. *Zeit und Gott: Hellenistische Zeitvorstellungen in der altarabischen Dichtung und im Koran.* Berlin and New York: de Gruyter, 2008.

ter Haar, J. G. J. *Follower and heir of the Prophet: Shaykh Aḥmad Sirhindī (1564–1624) as mystic.* Leiden: Het oosters instituut, 1992.

Tesei, Tommaso. "The *barzakh* and the intermediate state of the dead in the Quran." In Lange, ed. *Locating hell*, pp. 31-55.

"Some cosmological notions from late antiquity in Q 18:60–65: The Qurʾān in light of its cultural context." *JAOS* 135,1 (2015), pp. 19–32.

"The Prophecy of Ḏū-l-Qarnayn (Q 18:83–102) and the origins of the Qurʾānic corpus." In *Miscellanea arabica 2013-14.* Edited by A. Arioli. Rome: Aracne Editrice, 2014, pp. 273-90.

Thomas, David. "Ḥumayd ibn Saʿīd ibn Bakhtiyār." In *CMR*, s.v. Online publication (2010).

Thomassen, Einar. "Islamic hell." *Numen* 56 (2009), pp. 401–16.

Tillier, Mathieu. "The *qāḍī* before the Judge: The social use of eschatology in Muslim courts." In *The divine courtroom in comparative perspective.* Edited by Ari Mermelstein and Shalom E. Holtz. Leiden and Boston: Brill, 2014, pp. 260–75.

Toelle, Heidi. *Le Coran revisité: Le feu, l'eau, l'air et la terre.* Damascus: Institut français d'études arabes, 1999.

Tolan, John. *Petrus Alfonsi and his medieval readers.* Gainesville: University Press of Florida Press, 1998.

Saracens: Islam in the Medieval European Imagination. New York: Columbia University Press, 2002.

"Sermons [of Jacques de Vitry]." In *CMR*, s.v. Online publication (2014).

Tora-Niehoff, Isabel. *Al-Ḥīra: Eine arabische Kulturmetropole im spätantiken Kontext.* Leiden: Brill, 2014.

Tottoli, Roberto. *Biblical prophets in the Qurʾān and Muslim literature.* London: Routledge, 2002.

"Muslim eschatological literature and Western studies." *Der Islam*, 83 (2008), pp. 452–77.

"Muslim eschatology and the Ascension of the Prophet Muḥammad: Describing paradise in *miʿrāj* traditions and literature." In Günther and Lawson, eds. *Roads to paradise*, forthcoming.

"The Qurʾan, Qurʾanic exegesis and Muslim traditions: The case of *zamharīr* (Q. 76:13)." *JQS* 10,1 (2009), pp. 142–52.

"The story of Jesus and the skull in Arabic literature: The emergence and growth of a religious tradition." *JSAI* 28 (2003), pp. 225–59.

"Tours of hell and punishment of sinners in *miʿrāj* narratives: Use and meaning of eschatology in Muḥammad's Ascension." In Gruber and Colby, eds. *The Prophet's ascension*, pp. 11–26.

Turner, Bryan. *Weber and Islam: A critical study.* London and Boston: Routledge and Kegan Paul, 1998, 2nd ed.

Tweed, Thomas A. *Crossing and dwelling: A theory of religion.* Cambridge, MA: Harvard University Press, 2006.

Tye, Michael. "Imagery." In *Routledge encyclopedia of philosophy.* Edited by Edward Craig et al. Routledge: London and New York, 1998, Vol. 4, pp. 703b–705b.

Ulbert, Thilo. *Die Basilika des heiligen Kreuzes in Resafe-Sergiopolis.* Mainz: Zabern, 1986.

Vadet, Jean-Claude. "L''acculturation' des sudarabiques de Fusṭāṭ au lendemain de la conquête arabe." *Bulletin d'Etudes Orientales* 22 (1969), pp. 7–14.

Vajda, Georges. "Le problème de la vision de Dieu (*ruʾya*) d'après quelques auteurs šīʿites duodécimains." In Fahd, ed. *Le Shîʿisme imâmite*, pp. 31–54.

Vakily, Abdollah. "Some notes on Shaykh Aḥmad Sirhindī and the problem of the mystical significance of paradise." In *Reason and inspiration in Islam: Theology, philosophy and mysticism in Muslim thought.* Edited by Todd Lawson. London: I. B. Tauris, 2005, pp. 407–17.

van Amersfoort, J., and W. J. van Asselt. *Liever Turks dan Paaps? De visies van Johannes Coccejus, Gisbertus Voetius en Adrianus Relandus op de islam.* Zoetermeer: Uitgeverij Boekencentrum, 1997.

van Bladel, Kevin. "Heavenly cords and Prophetic authority in the Quran and its late antique context." *BSOAS* 70,2 (2007), pp. 223–46.

"The *Alexander Legend* in the Qurʾān 18:83–102." In *The Qurʾān in its historical context.* Edited by Gabriel Said Reynolds. London and New York: Routledge, 2008, pp. 175–203.

van Ess, Josef. "ʿAbd al-Malik and the Dome of the Rock: An analysis of some texts." In *Bayt al-Maqdis: ʿAbd al-Malik's Jerusalem.* Edited by Julian Raby and Jeremy Johns. Oxford: Oxford University Press, 1992, Vol. 1, pp. 89–103.

"Das begrenzte Paradies." In *Mélanges d'Islamologie. Volume dédié à la mémoire de Armand Abel.* Edited by P. Salmon. Leiden: Brill, 1974, pp. 108–27.

Das K. al-Nakṯ *des Naẓẓām und seine Rezeption im Kitāb al-Futyā des Ǧāḥiẓ*. Göttingen: Vandenhoeck and Ruprecht, 1972.
Der Eine und das Andere: Beobachtungen an islamischen häresiographischen Texten. 2 vols. Berlin and New York: de Gruyter, 2011.
Der Fehltritt des Gelehrten: Die "Pest von Emmaus" und ihre theologischen Nachspiele. Heidelberg: Winter, 2001.
"Schönheit und Macht: Verborgene Ansichten des islamischen Gottesbildes." In *Eranos 2005 und 2006: Schönheit und Mass*. Edited by Erich Hornung and Andreas Schweizer. Basel: Schwabe Verlag, 2007, pp. 15–42.
The flowering of Muslim theology. Cambridge, MA: Harvard University Press, 2006.
The youthful god: Anthropomorphism in early Islam. The University Lecture in Religion at Arizona State University. [Tempe]: Arizona State University, 1989.
Theologie und Gesellschaft im 2. und 3. Jahrhundert Hidschra: Eine Geschichte des religiösen Denkens im frühen Islam. Berlin and New York: de Gruyter, 1991–7.
"Zum Geleit." In Günther and Lawson, eds. *Roads to paradise*, forthcoming.
van Ess, Josef (with Hans Küng). *Christentum und Weltreligionen: Islam*. Munich and Zurich: Piper, 1994.
van Gelder, Geert Jan, and Hammond, Marlé, eds. Takhyīl: *The imaginary in classical Arabic poetics*. [Cambridge]: Gibb Memorial Trust, 2008.
van Leeuwen, Richard. "Literature and religious controversy: The vision of hell in Jamīl Ṣidqī al-Zahāwī's *Thawra fī al-jaḥīm*." In Lange, ed. *Locating hell*, pp. 337-51.
van Lit, Eric. "Eschatology and the world of image in Suhrawardī and his commentators." PhD diss., Utrecht University, 2014.
van Lit, Eric, and Lange, Christian. "Al-Shahrazūrī's epistle on the 'World of Image' (*ʿālam al-mithāl*)," forthcoming.
van Reeth, Jan M. "Le vignoble du Paradis et le chemin qui y mène: La thèse de C. Luxenberg et les sources du Coran." *Arabica* 53,4 (2006), pp. 511–24.
Vasalou, Sophia. *Moral agents and their deserts: The character of Muʿtazilite ethics*. Princeton, NJ: Princeton University Press, 2008.
Velji, Jamel A. "Fashioning empires at the edges of time: Apocalyptic and the rise of the medieval Ismāʿīlīs." PhD diss., University of California at Santa Barbara, 2011.
Voll, John O. "Hadith scholars and tariqahs: An ulama group in the 18th century Haramayn and their impact in the Islamic world." *Journal of Asian and African Studies* 15,3–4 (1980), pp. 264–73.
Volz, Paul. *Jüdische Eschatologie von Daniel bis Akiba*. Tübingen and Leipzig: Mohr, 1903.
von Grunebaum, Gustav E. "Ausbreitungs- und Anpassungsfähigkeit." In *Studien zum Kulturbild und Selbstverständnis des Islams*. Zurich and Stuttgart: Artemis, 1969, pp. 11–22.
"Observations on the Muslim concept of evil." *SI* 31 (1970), pp. 117–34.
"The sacred character of Islamic cities." *Mélanges Taha Husain*. Edited by ʿAbd al-Raḥmān Badawī. Cairo: Dār al-Maʿārif, 1962, pp. 25–37.
von Hees, Syrinx. "The astonishing: A critique and re-reading of *ʿağāʾib* literature." *Middle Eastern Literatures* 8 (2005), pp. 101–20.

Voorhoeve, P. *Handlist of Arabic manuscripts in the library of the University of Leiden and other collections in the Netherlands*. Leiden: Bibliotheca Universitatis, 1957.
Vrolijk, Arnoud, and van Leeuwen, Richard. *Arabic Studies in the Netherlands: A short history in portraits, 1580–1950*. Leiden: Brill, 2014.
Vuckovic, Brooke Olson. *Heavenly journeys, earthly concerns*. New York: Routledge, 2005.
Waines, David. *The odyssey of Ibn Battuta: Uncommon tales of a medieval adventurer*. London and New York: I. B. Tauris, 2010.
Walbridge, John. *The science of mystic lights: Quṭb al-Dīn al-Shīrāzī and the illuminationist tradition in Islamic philosophy*. Cambridge, MA: Harvard University Press, 1992.
Walker, Paul E. "Abū Tammām and his Kitāb al-Shajara: A new Ismaili treatise from tenth-century Khurasan." *JAOS* 114 (1994), pp. 343–52.
"Introduction." In *The wellsprings of wisdom: A study of Abū Yaʿqūb al-Sijistānī's Kitāb al-Yanābīʿ including a complete English translation with commentary and notes on the Arabic text*. Salt Lake City: University of Utah Press, 1994, pp. 1–20.
"The doctrine of metempsychosis in Islam." In *Islamic studies presented to Charles J. Adams*. Edited by Wael Hallaq and Donald Little. Leiden: Brill, 1991, pp. 219–38.
Wansbrough, John. *Qurʾanic studies: Sources and methods of scriptural interpretation*. Oxford: Oxford University Press, 1977.
Warner, Marina. *Fantastic metamorphoses, other worlds: Ways of telling the self*. Oxford and New York: Oxford University Press, 2002.
Watt, William Montgomery, trans. *Islamic creeds: A selection*. Edinburgh: Edinburgh University Press, 1994.
Watt, William Montgomery. *Muhammad at Medina*. Oxford: Clarendon Press, 1956.
"The authenticity of the works attributed to al-Ghazālī." *JRAS*, New Series 84,1–2 (1952), pp. 24–45.
Weipert, Reinhart. "Die erhaltenen Werke des Ibn Abī d-Dunyā. Fortsetzung und Schluss." *Arabica* 56 (2009), pp. 450–65.
Weipert, Reinhart, and Stefan Weninger. "Die erhaltenen Werke des Ibn Abī d-Dunyā. Eine vorläufige Bestandsaufnahme." *ZDMG* 146 (1996), pp. 416–55.
Wellhausen, Julius. *Reste arabischen Heidentums*. Berlin: Georg Reimer, 1887.
Wendell, Charles. "The denizens of paradise." *Humaniora Islamica* 2 (1974), pp. 29–59.
Wensinck, Arent Jan. "On the relation between Ghazālī's cosmology and his mysticism." *Mededeelingen der koninklijke akademie van weteschappen, afdeeling letterkunde* 75, Serie A 6. Amsterdam: Noord-Hollandsche Uitgevers-Maatschappij, 1933, pp. 183–207.
The Muslim creed: Its genesis and historical development. Cambridge: The University Press, 1932.
Wheeler, Brannon. *Mecca and Eden: Ritual, relics, and territory in Islam*. Chicago: Chicago University Press, 2006.
Wild, Stefan. "Lost in philology? The virgins of paradise and the Luxenberg hypothesis." In Neuwirth, Sinai, and Marx, eds. *The Quran in context*, pp. 625–48.

Wilk, Florian. "Jesajanische Prophetie im Spiegel exegetischer Tradition. Zu Hintergrund und Sinngehalts des Schriftzitats in 1 Kor 2,9." In *Die Septuaginta – Entstehung, Sprache, Geschichte*. Edited by Siegfried Kreuzer, Martin Meiser, and Marcus Sigismund. Tübingen: Mohr Siebeck, 2012, pp. 480–504.

Winter, Michael. "Islamic attitudes toward the human body." In *Religious reflections on the human body*. Edited by Jane Marie Law. Bloomington: Indiana University Press, 1995, pp. 36–45.

Society and religion in early Ottoman Egypt: Studies in the writings of ʿAbd al-Wahhab al-Shaʿrani. New Brunswick, NJ: Transaction Books, 1982.

Winter, Timothy J. "Introduction." In idem, trans. *The remembrance of death and the afterlife: Book XL of the Revival of the religious sciences*. Cambridge: Islamic Texts Society, 1989, pp. xiii–xxx.

Witkam, Jan Just. "The battle of images: Mekka vs. Medina in the iconography of the manuscripts of al-Jazūlī's *Dalāʾil al-khayrāt*." In *Theoretical approaches to the transmission and edition of Oriental manuscripts: Proceedings of a symposium held in Istanbul March 28–30, 2001*. Edited by Judith Pfeiffer and Manfred Kropp. Beirut: Ergon Verlag Würzburg, 2007, pp. 67–82.

Witztum, Joseph Benzion. "The Syriac milieu of the Qurʾān: The recasting of biblical narratives." PhD diss., Princeton University, 2011.

Wolf, Kenneth Baxter. "Muhammad as antichrist in ninth-century Córdoba." In *Christians, Muslims, and Jews in Medieval and early modern Spain*. Edited by Mark D. Meyerson and Edward D. English. South Bend, IN: Notre Dame Press, 1999, pp. 3–19.

Wolfensohn, Israel. "Ka'b al-Aḥbār und seine Stellung im ḥadīṯ und in der islamischen Legendenliteratur." PhD diss., Johann Wolfgang Goethe-Universität Frankfurt, 1933.

Wolff, Moritz. *Muhammedanische Eschatologie*. Leipzig: Brockhaus, 1872. Reprint Hildesheim: G. Olms, 2004.

"Bemerkungen zu der Schrift Aḥwāl al-ḳiyâme." *ZDMG* 52 (1898), pp. 418–24.

Wright, J. Edward. *The early history of heaven*. New York: Oxford University Press, 2000.

Würtz, Thomas. "The orthodox conception of the hereafter: Saʿd al-Dīn al-Taftāzānī's (d. 793/1390) examination of some Muʿtazilite and philosophical objections." In Günther and Lawson, eds. *Roads to paradise*, forthcoming.

Yazigi, Maya. "Ḥadīth al-ʿashara or the political uses of a tradition." *SI* 86 (1997), pp. 159–67.

Yıldız, Osman. *Aḥvāl-i ḳiyāmet: Giriş, inceleme, metin, dizinler*. Istanbul: Şûle Yayınlarĭ, 2002.

Zakeri, Mohsen. *Persian wisdom in Arabic garb: ʿAlī B. ʿUbayda Al-Rayḥānī (D. 219/834) and his* Jawāhir Al-Kilam wa-Farāʾid al-Ḥikam. 2 vols. Leiden and Boston: Brill, 2007.

Zamitt, Martin R. *A comparative lexical study of Qurʾānic Arabic*. Leiden: Brill, 2002.

Index of Names

Index of Terms